The Golden Age of American
Anthropology

The
GOLDEN AGE
of AMERICAN
ANTHROPOLOGY

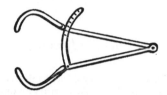

Selected and edited

with introduction and notes by

MARGARET MEAD

and

RUTH L. BUNZEL

GEORGE BRAZILLER

NEW YORK 1960

Acknowledgments

The editors and publishers have made every effort to determine and credit the holders of copyright of the selections in this book. Any errors or omissions may be rectified in future volumes. For permission to use these selections, the editors and publisher make grateful acknowledgment to the following authors and publishers who reserve all rights to the matter printed:

From THE DISCOVERY AND CONQUEST OF MEXICO by Bernal Díaz del Castillo. Copyright 1956 by Farrar, Straus and Cudahy. By permission of the publishers, Farrar, Straus and Cudahy.

From GENERAL HISTORY OF THE THINGS OF NEW SPAIN (Florentine Codex) by Bernardino de Sahagún, translated by Arthur J. O. Anderson and Charles E. Dibble. By permission of the University of Utah Press.

From THE CHEYENNE INDIANS by George Bird Grinnell. Copyright 1923 by Yale University Press. By Permission of Yale University Press.

From MEMOIRS OF THE AMERICAN MUSEUM OF NATURAL HISTORY, and ANTHROPOLOGICAL PAPERS, AMERICAN MUSEUM OF NATURAL HISTORY. By permission of The American Museum of Natural History.

From AN INTRODUCTION TO THE STUDY OF SOUTHWESTERN ARCHAE-OLOGY by A. V. Kidder. By permission of the R. S. Peabody Foundation, Phillips Academy, Andover, Mass.

From THE CROW INDIANS by Robert H. Lowie. (Farrar and Rinehart, 1935; re-issued 1956 by Rinehart.) By permission of Holt, Rinehart and Winston, Inc.

From THE MIND OF PRIMITIVE MAN by Franz Boas. Copyright 1911 and 1938 by the Macmillan Company. By permission of The Macmillan Company.

From RACE, LANGUAGE AND CULTURE by Franz Boas. Copyright 1940 by The Macmillan Company. By permission of The Macmillan Company.

Editor's Note

WE HAVE SELECTED AS THE GOLDEN AGE OF AMERICAN ANTHROPOLOGY THE PERIOD THAT began in 1880, when the Bureau of American Ethnology was just getting under way, and ended in 1920, before the post-World War I reorganization of university departments of anthropology. In the 1920's, a new generation began to undertake new kinds of research, some of it far afield in the South Seas and in Africa. We have confined our choices of individual anthropologists to those who were already productive before 1920, although some of the selections we have made were published later, especially the papers in Part Six, which foreshadows new theoretical developments. The preparation of this volume has been facilitated by the many colleagues who generously responded to our request for advice and suggestions.

Limitations of space, generous though they are, necessitated heartbreaking omissions, as we struggled over which Sun Dance, which prophet, which ritual sacrifice or vision quest was to be included and which left out. The choice among those whose names stand as respected ancestral figures in some branch of anthropology was equally hard, as we tried—and failed—to find selections which would convey the contribution of a man like Albert Gallatin, statesman and diplomat, who has also been called the "father of American ethnology."

It was necessary to find selections written in non-technical language, which were sufficiently condensed to convey to the reader whole pieces of material or a whole point of view, and which at the same time gave the full tone of a scholar's work. As the work of the classical period received its impetus from research done on North American Indians, we have omitted those anthropologists whose work was done in other parts of the world and was not yet reflected in theory. The roster of names of those who have not been included is too long to recite. But it has been heartening to make a collection in which Alfred Kroeber, A. V. Kidder, and Leslie Spier provide the living links that anthropologists best understand to the works of their great contemporaries.

Contents

PART IV. PRESERVING THE REMNANTS OF INDIAN CULTURES: THE ROLE OF THE PRIVATE MUSEUMS

PART V. BUILDING A SCIENCE OF MAN IN AMERICA: THE CLASSICAL PERIOD IN AMERICAN ANTHROPOLOGY, 1900-1920

PART VI. NEW HORIZONS

Introduction

by Margaret Mead

SCIENCE KNOWS NO NATIONAL BOUNDARIES AND, HOWEVER VIVID SUDDEN steps forward may be, is steadily cumulative. The task of selecting for a golden age of American anthropology might therefore seem to be an impossible one, for the very phrasing is national and suggests a time in the past to which later and lesser ages should look back with nostalgia. But the attempt to place this one of the human sciences in the same category with literature, history, and philosophy can be an occasion for delineating some of the peculiarities of anthropology as, in some respects, a science, and in others, a humanity.

Anthropology deals with human beings living in different societies, with the products of these societies—houses and parliamentary systems, temples and religious beliefs, pottery borders and art styles, poems and languages— and with the processes—physical, mental, and social—through which these products are created. While anthropologists seek for ways of describing man that will apply to all cultures at all times in history, anthropology remains closely bound to the living detail of the way special men have lived at given times and places. However abstract the statement that is made about the diverse versions of the Sun Dance, the abstraction is never wholly separated from the description of a real Sun Dance among the Oglalla Sioux as Walker observed it or from Spier's analysis of its distribution. The precious concrete reference is never lost. Real Indians hunt real buffalo, or stare at the sun until they fall unconscious, or fast in the lonely wilderness seeking a guardian spirit for life. So anthropological theory has thrived upon accounts of the lives of particular primitive peoples studied at a given period by a given group of explorers, traders or missionaries, and, later still, professional anthropologists. American anthropology has been built on detailed studies of the living behavior, the buried remnants of earlier periods, the vanishing complicated languages, and the remembered customs of the American Indians. The huge edifices of Yucatan and Mexico, the unforeseeable combinations of bravery, savagery, and spirituality of the simpler tribes of the East Coast, the fantastic unexpectedness of the way a Kwakiutl artist slices up the image of a killer whale have all been part of the thinking of American anthropologists. Had there been no American Indians, anthropology ultimately would have been taught and perhaps elaborated in the United States on the basis of German,

1

British, and French models that were developed as Europeans struggled to produce order from the accounts brought back by those few travelers who sought colonial enterprise in faraway lands. But American anthropology would not have been the same.

The actual presence of the Indians appealed deeply to the characteristically American interest in phenomena, to the Amercan preference for the empirical and the inductive. Furthermore, American Indians also had been immigrants to the great empty continents of the New World where, like later European immigrants, they began a life without historical precedents. In the imagination of those who came from Europe, these earlier dwellers became a different kind of ancestor. Having broken away from the kinship of blood and the continuity of a long tradition which had contributed so much to the European sense of identity, Americans were able to develop a new kind of identity. And in the Americas, men of another race, who thousands of years ago had separated from the Old World cultural stream —before the wheel, the alphabet, or the working of metals had reached them in Asia—were able to contribute to this new identity because they had hunted in the same hills, had grown maize in the same soil as the newcomers. It has, indeed, been said of Americans that they have substituted space for time. Where Europeans derive both a sense of continuity and a sense of contrast from the steady contemplation of a historical tradition that reaches back to Greece and Rome, Americans—a great proportion of whose ancestors were simple and unlettered men with very little share in the Great Tradition—have had to build a new identity based not on their own past on this continent but on their growing sense of what men of all races and all creeds, whose immediate ancestors were peasants or savages, princes or statesmen, might "bring forth upon this continent."

So a golden age of American anthropology falls naturally into the period when the young science could still draw on the living memories of Indians and often on their still living practices and could use these to illumine the records of the early travelers. Very possibly, also, the virtual destruction of the American Indians, which began in the 16th century, added to the sense of ethical conviction with which the young science of anthropology proclaimed the psychic unity of mankind, the essential dignity and comparability of each culture. In their thinking about culture anthropologists included equally peoples who lived in houses made of earth or stone, skin or bricks, snow or marble, those who were literate and those who knew nothing of writing, those whose gods were local representatives of the power that lay in the universe and those who served a deity who was worshiped by millions within a single canon of belief and practice.

During the period when systematic anthropological field work began, individual American Indians became the responsible collaborators of those who attempted to understand their disappearing culture. Later individual American Indians made occasional pilgrimages to our great museums where their sacred pipes and sacred medicine bundles had been preserved through the efforts of those who found the old ways valuable. At the same time a few of their young men pushed on to become proficient in the new culture, but others—the majority—sank into apathy, fenced within bits of land which were inadequate to support their ancient ways of life and out of which they were only too likely to be maneuvered on the morrow. As Wissler said:

As we look back upon the long and tortuous career of man in the New World, comprehend his crude equipment as he first set foot upon the land, and pass in review his later achievements, we cannot but regret that the end came so suddenly.

For Europeans, the American Indian has been the romantic symbol of the settling of the American continent. For Americans, the struggle with the Indians remains the epic of conquest, the human symbol of the strangeness, the distances, the dangers, and the unpredictability of the New World. The struggle was shaped by the primary emphasis on land. Land, not labor, was the key to the expansion of Europeans in America north of Mexico.

During the early days of exploration, conquest, and colonization, when adventurers, trappers, missionaries, and soldiers all participated in the struggle, there emerged diverse images of the Indians—as noble savages, or as treacherous, cruel varmints, or as children of nature specially related to the natural world, untamable and heroic, or cowardly and cruel. The anthropologists who succeeded this early group had a two-fold image of the Indians, for they saw them both as the carriers of priceless vanishing records of human potentialities and as the victims of a historical process which seemed all the more wasteful because they themselves experienced so intensely the complexity and the intricacy of the Indian cultures. Humanitarians lament the spectacle of the reservation Indian, riddled with tuberculosis, eking out a miserable existence on grudging federal rations, debauched or apathetic, withdrawing further from—rather than becoming more adjusted to—white civilization. This spectacle was far more vivid to anthropologists than to casual humanitarians who were concerned with Indian rights and had a sentimental view of Indian ceremonial. For anthropologists realized just how dependent Indian cultures had been on the balance between men and land, weapons and quarry, sun and rain and corn, and they recognized that in the meeting of two cultural systems so contrasting in technology and point of view, the Indian cultures had no chance of survival. American anthropologists, when they took sides, were on the side of the Indians and did not become involved in efforts to reduce Indians to orderly conformity. Nor did they specialize in teaching government officials how to achieve this aim as, in varying degrees, European anthropologists did in the case of other native peoples governed by the

English, the Germans, the French, and the Dutch. Nevertheless, they recognized the essential hopelessness of the situation. Given the tools and the ideas that existed in the first half of the 20th century, the Indians were doomed even though they might live on as physical types, stripped of all the complex beauty of their aboriginal cultures. Appreciation of these cultures has continued to grow, but despite the greater sophistication of attempts at transformation in the second quarter of the century, the sense of doom has only deepened. American anthropologists, their conscience quickened by the sight of the irremediable plight of the Indians, have directed their attention to questions of racial equality and the problems of other racial and ethnic minorities in the United States and have attempted to combat racist theories around the world by documenting the extent to which man is what his culture makes him. Study of the Indians contributed to the moral fervor and hopefulness that went into the delineation of man as a culture-building animal, belonging to one species with common poten- tialities waiting only for the appropriate historical situation to blossom. But the Indians themselves have not been the beneficiaries. Only more recently have anthropologists thrown themselves into the arduous and unrewarding task of trying to rescue these peoples who have lived for several generations in a situation of cultural disintegration while still cling- ing to the last shreds of their cultural identity.

The men of the golden age of American anthropology treated with de- tachment the Indians whom they studied and around whom they built up a great body of ethnographic fact and basic cultural theory. In doing so they established a tradition of objectivity which later could coexist with a new style of anthropology with disciplined subjective identification and commitment to immediate human ends, as was foreshadowed in Ruth Benedict's *Patterns of Culture.*

There is another sense in which anthropology must, perhaps more than other sciences, be seen as part of the particular national period to which it belongs. The most abstract developments in science are, of course, de- pendent on the climate of opinion of the age; discoveries can be made too early or too late for optimum contribution. Medical knowledge languishes in a society where individual human beings are not valued. The principles of mechanics find little expression in labor-saving machinery where human slaves are cheap and plentiful. Even more deeply affected are those dis- ciplines the subject matter of which is human behavior. In the distinctively American climate of opinion in which anthropology in this country de- veloped, an important part was played by an emphasis on the unique and admirable qualities of the United States. In its beginnings, evaluation of the place of the Indians in human history and in the divine scheme was compromised by the exigencies of colonization, the problem of slavery, and the vigorous assertiveness of the polemicists who defended the emerg- ing American culture; at the same time there was a curious indifference to the findings of African and Oceanic explorers and to the flurry of discussion which they set off in Europe. Most of the early scholars were Old Americans and, despite some wider sophistication, what is most striking about this period is its provincialism.

When American anthropology began to emerge as a science, new evidence appeared of a distinctively American climate of opinion. The men of the classic period—from 1880 to 1920—were about evenly divided between old Americans, who were typically self-conscious about a particular name and lineage, and new Americans, immigrants who came to this country after some period of experience of a European culture and for whom the attainment of an American identity was a self-conscious and urgent aim, which was finally focused by World War I. Franz Boas settled here as a scholar who had finished his university work and had completed his first field investigations. Robert Lowie left Vienna as a child, but the memory tied him closely to German scholarship all his life. Edward Sapir was born in Germany and reared in the United States; for a long period he was a Canadian citizen. Alexander Goldenweiser spent his school days in Russia and enlivened his seminars with tales of waiters in Russian railway stations bearing trays laden with delectable foods.

Anthropology, a new science, welcomed the stranger. As a science which accepted the psychic unity of mankind, anthropology was kinder to women, to those who came from distant disciplines, to members of minority groups in general (with American Indians assuming a special position as both the victims of injustice and the carriers of a precious and vanishing knowledge), to the "over-mature," the idiosyncratic, and the capriciously gifted or experienced, to refugees from political or religious oppression. Elsie Clews Parsons, a woman of wealth who pioneered in new investigations on the effect of culture on women, could be herself and drop the pseudonym of John Main under which, as a sociologist, she had written about ceremonial chastity. La Flesche, the Omaha Indian, recorded not only the ceremonies of his own people but those of the Osage as well. Jochelson and Bogoras, in Czarist Russia, were recruited to work during their political exile among the Siberian tribes.

This professional tradition of liberality has not been complete or unblemished. There were universities where anthropology was still treated as an appropriate occupation for wealthy amateurs, where penniless graduate students were advised to marry money or get out of anthropology. There were anthropologists who objected to Boas' custom of bringing to lunch his secretaries, budding anthropologists who could take shorthand. The large number of Jewish names in the roster of distinguished anthropologists was sometimes inveighed against by the less successful members of the profession. Women have been made more welcome than in other professions, but not unequivocally. Racist doctrines of a refined and limited sort have occasionally cropped up, and equally unjustified romantic attempts to obliterate race or to deny the reality of constitutional differences have marred the later scene. But on the whole the tradition established in the first quarter of this century—that anthropologists treat human beings as human beings, members of one species, inheritors of cultures of different adequacy and complexity but of equal dignity—has stood. In troubled times when advocacy of racial equality has been tarred as evidence of communism, the professional status of the anthropologist has been almost as clear as that of the priest or doctor, in whom friendship and association with members of other races has not been politically suspect.

During the post-Civil War period, the same assertive patriotism which earlier had led Jefferson to defend the Indian in the course of defending all American men and animals against Buffon's accusation of ecological inferiority found expression both in the growth of national institutions like the Bureau of American Ethnology and the Smithsonian Institution and in a rising claim for the uniqueness of American culture. This assertiveness vis-à-vis Europe and the blaze of activity during the settling of the West merged imperceptibly into the isolationism of the early 20th century. In anthropology this isolationism took the form of insistence on the independent development of the high civilizations of the Americas. In their publications it is true that the advocates of total independence remained cautious and reasonable. Both Tozzer and Boas recognized the possibility of occasional, intermittent contacts between the Old World and the New, via Greenland or across the Pacific, in addition to the accepted theory that very primitive peoples had migrated slowly across the Bering Strait. Nevertheless the idea of a separately developing modern American culture was extended to the American Indian high civilizations and added fuel to the fires of controversy kindled by the theories of Graebner in Germany, who postulated the existence of old cultural horizons which included such isolated areas as Tasmania and Tierra del Fuego, and the alternative theories of the romantic English school of Perry and Eliot Smith, who believed that a single originating civilization in Egypt had been carried around the world by the "Children of the Sun." Young men were frowned upon for suggesting origins outside the Americas for a style of art or architecture; violent arguments raged over the question of whether a single design represented a macaw or an elephant. The strength of this isolationist feeling can only be measured today. In 1949, at the International Congress of Americanists held in New York, similar suggestions about small intermittent contacts with the high civilizations of Asia roused hardly a flicker of controversy. By this time isolationism was in eclipse in public life and in anthropology.

The concentration of American anthropologists on Indians whom Europeans had never seen and knew about only through extremely romantic fiction had one important consequence. American anthropology developed in a way that had very little effect in Europe either on specifically anthropological thought or on areas of social science concerned more widely with the understanding of human behavior. Once the significance of culture was fully realized, a generation of American anthropologists, half of them European-born and well versed in European languages, settled down under the leadership of Franz Boas to detailed empirical research. Their intention was to rescue the past and document the differences between one culture and another—between the Blackfoot and the Crow, the Zuñi and the Hopi, the Kwakiutl and the Tlingit. Seen through the words of its old men and women, each tribe was explored as a whole until the central pattern emerged, and the store of material and immaterial practices was analyzed to show what had been borrowed and what had been lent and how the pattern of creative readaptation of cultural materials had in each case been accomplished. Though Boas had been trained as a physicist, he was free of the wearying direct modeling on the physical sciences that has bedeviled so many men in their attempts to be "scientific." The work of a generation was dominated by his insistence that only by unflagging industry could the data be collected from which it might be possible to begin to draw conclusions.

In their choice of problems he and his students remained in lively awareness of the grand schemes and blanket solutions that were being proposed in Europe. In his seminars before World War I, it was a commonplace for Boas to give the first reference in German, the second in some other language, and only the third in English. The American group struggled with the ideas of Ratzel, Tylor, Graebner, Crawley, Van Gennep, Durkheim, Freud, and Lévy-Bruhl. But they did so in the context of the most minute ethnographic discussions in which the counters might be the shapes of Eskimo needlecases or the differences in the proportions of painted oblongs on parfleches. The materials which anthropologists collected as they sat patiently taking down word by word the broken memories of old men, foreshadowed in their meticulousness the attention that is given today to exactly who said what, when, and to whom. Steeped in field work they could use the details from the cultures of other peoples, and fragments of African, Asian, and Oceanic behavior crowd American discussions of anthropological theory. But this was a one-way process. Boas might write indefatigably about the mind of primitive man; Freud and Piaget continued to draw on the armchair fantasies of Wundt and Lévy-Bruhl.

In 1897, the Jesup Expedition set out from the American Museum of Natural History to examine evidence of similarities among the peoples of Siberia and the Northwest Coast and to throw light on the origins of the American Indian. A year later, in 1898, the Torres Strait Expedition set out from Cambridge University to examine, with the help of psychologists, relationships and contrasts in the cultures and behavior of a group of New Guinea peoples. Once the anthropologists were in the field, English and American anthropology began to develop along parallel lines. But a genuine convergence was established only in the late 1920's, when Rad-cliffe-Brown and Malinowski came to this country. Armchair theorizing lingered on even longer in France. In Sweden, Nordenskiold provided a center of training for future Americanists. The early industry of the Ger-mans in their great colonial empire was cut short by the loss of their colonies in World War I, when a lone field anthropologist working on the Sepik River in New Guinea became the object of an Australian expedi-tionary force. There were ardent Americanists among later German field workers in South America, but they had little contact with North American anthropology.

Thus the footnotes of America's golden age writers are studded with references to European works, but they themselves had less impact abroad. Only Morgan, writing at an earlier period on problems of "communism" and concerned with the development of a broad, comparative evolutionary scheme, caught the imagination of Engels. In this way Morgan's work became incorporated in the views which radical and liberal Europeans held about man. His proposed scheme of early promiscuity, matriliny, and finally patriliny (later elaborated by Marxist theory into the property-oriented type of marriage of contemporary European cultures) still haunts the pages of much psychoanalytic theorizing and, by a historical accident, became an article of faith in the Soviet Union.

In the central concept of culture as it was developed by Boas and his students, human beings were viewed as dependent neither on instinct nor on genetically transmitted specific capabilities but on learned ways of life that accumulated slowly through endless borrowing, readaptation, and innovation. In their thinking, American anthropologists drew on field studies of the Indian and also on the work of such students as Tylor, in England, and Ratzel, in Germany. But the concept of culture penetrated only very gradually into the thought of European students of behavior. Even today the French find a certain difficulty in translating the *s* in "pat-terns of culture," for in their view there is only one contemporary pattern of high civilization. In fact, at the time that the groundwork was being laid, American thought itself was not much affected. In 1922, when Golden-weiser published the first American textbook of American anthropology, in which he included a description of five primitive cultures, and entitled the book *Early Civilization,* there were cries of outraged fury because he placed the ways of savage peoples in the same context with our own. Other disciplines retained their outmoded representations of "primitive man," sometimes picturing "him" as prelogical and incapable of logical thought, sometimes describing how "he" belonged to a horde dominated by an old man, or worshiped fertility mother-goddesses, or lived in a group which held all property in common in a state of paradisical primitive communism. Only belatedly have students of human behavior become willing to see the ways of life of each people as variations on universal cultural themes, in which our progressive control over nature has provided the means for different levels of energy use but has not necessarily resulted in greater complexity in art or religion, grammar or human relations.

Yet it is just here, in a recognition of the uniqueness and wholeness of each culture, that anthropology meets the traditional preoccupations of the humanities. The arts of primitive peoples, while interesting theoretically and sometimes aesthetically arresting, do not produce the consciously created masterpieces of the great civilizations. Among preliterate peoples, composers and poets work within traditional styles and contribute anonymously to their uniqueness. It is rather primitive cultures as whole aesthetic compositions that compare dramatically with the more individualized work of great artists, poets, and musicians in the Great Tradition. American anthropologists in the classic period treated the specific culture of each Indian tribe in its uniqueness and also showed how, in certain respects, all of them could be seen as versions of North American Indian culture, or American Indian culture, or, at the widest extension, as primitive versions of human culture. In so doing they laid the basis for a new relationship of anthropology to the humanities.

There has been another consequence of the approach to each given tribe as a whole, in which physical type, language, the remains of earlier periods buried in the ground, and the living culture are all treated together. The other human sciences from economics to biology, working within the parochial framework of our Euro-American tradition, have taken for granted many aspects of man's life. Consumption has been discussed without details of fur and lace, carrots and caviar, family income without history, sex habits without language, color recognition as if it depended only on biology, heredity as if it were a matter of gene pools alone and not also of the rules of mating. Some aspects of living—usually many aspects of living—have been regarded as so much a part of the milieu that it has seemed neither necessary nor relevant to spell them out. The position of the anthropologist has been quite different. Because the physique of a people threw light on their history, because without a written language their past culture had to be inferred from bits of pots and bones, because the language had to be learned in all its strangeness, because the reader of a monograph could not immediately identify the referents of words like *pemmican* or *tapir, sago* or *sennit,* the anthropologist had to present the complete human texture of historical man with a given physique in a given environment.

This has been the peculiar contribution of American anthropology. In other countries the study of the measurements of the human skeleton had been separated from the study of growth; both had been divorced from the study of human institutions; and this in turn had not been related to the study of the structure of languages. For a time it seemed that something similar might take place in the United States. In the 1920's, students of

Boas, Kroeber and Tozzer felt that their teachers had been able to master the new knowledge of the relations between man's physique, heredity, speech, customs, and past as it emerged because they had grown up with the new science. But would we ourselves be able to do so? Would not anthropology, like other sciences, fragment into separate specialties whose practitioners could not communicate with one another? So far this fear has not been realized. The vast panorama which Boas sketched out in 1932 in his discussion of the aims of anthropological research is still the heritage of American anthropology.

In planning this volume we have placed our classical period, 1880-1920, within a wider context. Part One of the book, *Exploring the New World,* is devoted to the explorers and conquistadors, the wonders and horrors of the first encounters, the great civilization of the Aztecs laid in ruins, and the strangeness of the simpler Indians to the North.

In Part Two, *Trying to Cope with the Indians,* are accounts by those who had to deal with the Indians as traders or missionaries, statesmen or soldiers, and who struggled with problems of culture difference and the meaning of race. Throughout this period problems of conscience and practicality accompany the vivid descriptions written by men who were oriented to action.

Part Three, *Gaining Understanding of the Indians: Research by the Federal Government,* takes up the task of rescuing records. The contribution of this period was a hospitable series of great olive-green volumes in which an infinite wealth of strange detail found publication. In the 1920's, young and impecunious anthropologists still could write to the Bureau and receive a set of these enormous, impressive volumes which provided a substantial fund of scholarship for their scantily furnished rooms.

In Part Four, *Preserving the Remnants of Indian Culture: The Role of the Private Museums,* we show how the organization of voluntary effort shaped the future development of American anthropology. So, as the relics of the Indians were collected in the American Museum of Natural History, the tradition was established by which anthropology—complete with tipis, stone age axes, carved ivory figures, and porcupine quill embroidery—became part of natural history rather than a separate part of man's history from which his kinship with other living creatures of the earth had been carefully shorn. We did not group primitive art with the art of the Great Tradition, primitive tools with the history of technology, primitive musical instruments with the history of music. Instead, the records of evolutionary changes in human culture, accomplished by the new mechanism of the transmission of learned and cumulated behavior, were displayed together with the evidences of biological evolution in the rest of the living world from which man had emerged. The tipi and the earth lodge, the mound and the fort were presented not as crude forms of the "houses" of Greek and Roman and Renaissance men, but as comparable and incomparable with the ant hill, the beaver dam, the oriole nest. Man was shown to be a part of nature, although a dramatically special and unique part. The models which showed the development of his brain, his divergence into different physical stocks, the increasing cunning of his opposable thumbs could be seen side by side with his first attempts at tool making and picture writing and the ritual objects which represented his relationship to an expanding cosmos. Man in nature and man transcending nature—with his precious new skills of teaching and learning that made it possible for any new generation to stand on the shoulders of the last—were kept together.

Part Five, *Building a Science of Man in America,* includes the writers who laid the groundwork of anthropological theory. Because they worked inductively and empirically, always relating their analyses to their voluminous materials, the magnitude of their achievement has not always been recognized. In their work, the development of theory paralleled the systematic collection of materials captured from the memories of the Indian peoples. The museum collections and the field sketches and diagrams helped to preserve the sense of the visual quality of these cultures that had by now almost disappeared. The earlier ethnographers had looked and collected, often without understanding a word and without any systematic frame of reference. Under Boas' leadership, the anthropologists of the classical period listened, analyzed, organized, and compared. Their theory grew from the material and with it. Without the earlier travelers' accounts and the gleaming surface of the porcupine quills, or the soft sole of a worn moccasin, or the spread-out contents of medicine bundles that were kept in the museums, the great volumes of words that poured in torrents from the pens of the first generation of scientific ethnographers—their descriptions sprinkled with phonetic renderings of unintelligible Indian words—would have been even less accessible to the next generation of students, those who, with the anthropologist's traditional delight in kinship models, described themselves as the generation of grandchildren.

But the groundwork of American anthropology was laid down in these carefully and lovingly recorded words—the precise words used by Indian informants and the steadily growing, abstract cross-cultural vocabulary of the anthropologist. New generations have added to these words, and because a living science looks to the future as well as to the past, we have added, in Part Six, *New Horizons,* a brief glimpse at more recent years. Unlike art or music, in which the great culminating periods hold no further possibilities for straight line development, it is the nature of science, once the lines are laid down, to develop continuously with ever-increasing acceleration. For anthropology particularly, we must hope that with better communication among the great nations of the world and with traditional and preliterate peoples entering the scientific tradition, we may profit by the culturally unique, but not culturally limited, insights of the many cultures of the world.

AMERICAN MUSEUM OF NATURAL HISTORY
NEW YORK, NEW YORK
May 10, 1960

PART I

EXPLORING
THE
NEW WORLD

Introduction

by Ruth L. Bunzel

THE DISCOVERY OF AMERICA BROUGHT EUROPEANS FACE TO FACE WITH
the Savage. Not the organized Negro kingdoms of West Africa versed in
the arts and knowing in the ways of trade, who sold slaves and ivory
secured by means which the white traders had no need to know and whose
cruel secret societies were kept well hidden from prying eyes. Not even
the nomadic horsemen of the Asiatic steppes whose culture was familiar
to the learned from ancient writings and whose way of life was not too
different from that of the Old Testament. No, the natives whom the Europeans first encountered in the Indies were, indeed, naked savages who covered their bodies with paint instead of clothes, who lived in flimsy huts,
slept in hammocks, ate strange foods and practiced weird and gruesome
rites; who spoke no language known to civilized man and with whom communication was impossible until they had been taken captive and instructed.

So strange were they that it is not surprising that Europeans wondered
whether they were members of the human race or some different and
lower species. This question was promptly settled by the Church, which
decreed that they were indeed human and might receive the Sacraments.
But the theory that, though belonging to the genus *Hominidae,* they were
nevertheless of a different species, lingered on into the 19th century. (See
Bachman on the unity of the human race, p. 85.)

As Bourne points out, Columbus, an Italian in the employ of Spain,
was the first American anthropologist. Perhaps because Spain had but
recently emerged from centuries of conflict with the Moors and had not
yet expelled her Moorish minority and Spaniards were therefore sensitive
to cultural differences and were aware of their importance, or perhaps
because wherever they went they were accompanied by friars or monks
full of the missionary zeal of a Church flushed with recent victory, who
yet valued scholarship and learning; perhaps because they understood out
of their Moorish experience that one had to understand people in order
effectively to control them—whatever the cause, wherever the Spaniards
went they made systematic and faithful records of the cultures of the
conquered people, often employing converted natives as informants or
scribes (Sahagún's literate informants and Ixtilxochitl in Mexico, Gar-
cilaso de la Vega in Peru).

14

Cortés' letters to Charles V describing the conquest of Mexico day by day contain a wealth of concrete detail on native customs and possess a literary elegance that contemporary anthropologists might well envy. These Spanish chronicles are the first anthropological documents to come out of the New World. Their veracity has never been questioned (the sites of the temples described by Bernal Dìaz can be identified; the gold statues and gold plates from the walls of the Inca palaces did indeed reach Spain as part of the Crown's share of the treasure), and they have an inimitable flavor of fresh wonder and sophisticated appreciation punctuated with revulsion at some of the horrors they witnessed.

More famous even than Cortés' letters is Bernal Díaz del Castillo's *True Story of the Conquest of New Spain.* Bernal Díaz was born in that impoverished western frontier of Spain which gave so many of her sons to the Conquest. He was a "gentleman," the son of a modest official. He is often described as a "blunt soldier" but he was obviously a man of discrimination, of no insignificant learning and of considerable if not overwhelming piety. He left Spain in 1514, being then about twenty-two years of age. He went first to Cuba in the company of Pedro Arias de Avila. The Conquistadores had already fallen out among themselves; Bernal left Cuba, and after three years of doing "nothing of note" joined Cortés in 1517. After several abortive attempts to land on the mainland of Mexico the company finally effected a landing at Cempoala, where Cortés burned his ships to prevent any of his company from mutinying and seizing them. They then began the march inland. Bernal Díaz fought bravely and loyally through the battles and the dreadful siege of Mexico. He lived more than eighty-four years and died in Santiago de Guatemala. His *History* was written when he was an old man, having "gained nothing of value to leave to my children and descendants but this my true story, and they will presently find out what a wonderful story it is."

Bernal Díaz first sounds that note of sadness that is to recur so often in later accounts, as he stands looking across the gardens of Iztapalapa, with their water gate opening on the lake: "I say again that I stood looking at it and thought that never in the world would there be discovered other lands such as these, for at that time there was no Peru, nor any thought of it. Of all these wonders that I then beheld today all is overthrown and lost, nothing left standing."

The first settlers in New England and Virginia left no such shining records of the aborigines they encountered. The small bands of Indians along the Atlantic coast retreated to the forest at the approach of the ships and emerged only to raid and kill—or so the settlers thought. And indeed they had cause to fear. One Virginia settlement was wiped out in the early days by an Indian war party, and deaths from ambush and on lonely farms were not uncommon. The English settlers brought along no learned friars to conduct research, only hard-working elders who toiled like everyone else to keep the struggling settlements alive. It is not until the 18th century that there is any evidence of interest in the Indians on the part of the British colonists.

The French did very much better along these lines. The country of their first explorations was just as bleak, just as sparsely populated, the Indians no less warlike. Perhaps because they came in the first instance not to possess the land but to trade, they were able to establish friendly relations with the northern tribes. They brought beads and steel knives and cloth and muskets but above all brandy, which they exchanged for the skins of animals. This trade suited the Indians; the trading posts established along the St. Lawrence and the Great Lakes and, later, along the great rivers of the interior, became centers of social life for Indians within a radius of hundreds of miles, where men from different tribes could meet peaceably and where tribal hostilities were temporarily laid aside. Not that the French settlements were without their tragedies. As late as 1659 the settlement of Lachine on the St. Lawrence was wiped out by an Iroquois war party. However, it was not *their* Indians who massacred the settlers; they were the victims of the unremitting warfare between the Hurons and the Iroquois. The massacre at Natchez was of a different order; it was a planned revolt, more like the Pueblo Rebellion of 1680.

Jacques Cartier was the first white man (if we except possible visits from the Vikings) to sail up the St. Lawrence, but it was Champlain who built New France. Samuel de Champlain was born in 1567 in the town of Brouage, the son of a sea captain with the salt of the sea in his veins. A devout Catholic and ardent Royalist, he fought for Henry IV in the religious wars, but when peace was declared the sea claimed him. After a voyage to Mexico and Peru he suggested that a canal through the Isthmus of Panama would shorten the trip to the East Indies by 1,500 leagues.

In 1602 Champlain joined an expedition to establish a fur monopoly in Canada and so was launched on his life work, the exploration of Canada and the search for the Northwest Passage. Champlain formed friendly relationships with the Indians—Montagnais and Huron. He established colonies at Port Royal (Annapolis) and Quebec; but profits of the fur trade interested him only to the extent that they financed exploration, his first and last love, although he was not averse to fighting, either. He joined a war party of the Huron attacking the Iroquois at Ticonderoga, using firearms against them, thus calling down on the heads of the French the wrath of the implacable Iroquois. The Jesuit missions along the routes of travel across Canada and eventually down the Mississippi did much to strengthen the position of France in the New World. The lines of the future struggle were already being drawn: the English colonists with their

Iroquois allies in contest against the French and the Huron for the rich plains and mighty rivers of the interior. This phase of the conflict was settled in Europe some 130 years later by the defeat of France in the Seven Years' War.

Although Champlain was a French nobleman he got along well with the violent northern tribes. He grieved for their souls and hoped they would accept the blessings of Christianity. He was a good observer and his journals are full of vivid detail. Like all observers of Indians, early or late, who looked at Indians as people, he noted their indulgence of children, but far from being charmed by this trait he was shocked, as any well-bred Frenchman would be, to see children strike their parents.

France held the Lower Mississippi Valley territory until Jefferson put an end to the power of France in America with the Louisiana Purchase. The expedition which explored the new territories to report on conditions for settlement and if possible to find a passage to the Western sea, was actually planned before the Purchase was even thought about. It is too well known to need any introduction. Lewis and Clark were soldiers and explorers, not ethnologists; they did not penetrate below the surface of Indian life, although they made many shrewd observations about the character of the Indians and their style of life. Their journals contained much valuable information on houses and costumes and especially on the use of horses. They were especially impressed by the horsemanship of the Shoshone and devoted much space to descriptions of their horse gear and management of horses—a fact of some interest since it is now known that the Shoshone were the tribe through whom horses were distributed to the Northern Plains.

EDWARD GAYLORD BOURNE

(1860-1908)

Columbus, Ramon Pane and the Beginnings of American Anthropology, 1493-1496

ABOUT THREE WEEKS HENCE ON MAY TWENTIETH WILL BE CELEBRATED the four hundredth anniversary of the death of Columbus. Apparently little notice will be taken of this anniversary in the United States. To the American people at large the event of supreme interest in the career of the Admiral is, of course, the discovery of the New World, and the quadri-centenary of that was celebrated with an elaboration which naturally precludes any considerable expenditure of effort and enthusiasm within the same generation in commemoration of the death of the discoverer. Yet this anniversary should not pass unnoticed, least of all by a learned society devoted to the study of American antiquities, for Christopher Columbus not only revealed the field of our studies to the world but actually in person set on foot the first systematic study of American primitive custom, religion and folklore ever undertaken. He is in a sense therefore the founder of American Anthropology. This phase of the varied activities of the discoverer has received in our day little or no attention. To all appearances it is not even mentioned in Justin Winsor's six-hundred page biography. Such neglect is owing in part to the discredit that has been cast upon the life of Columbus by his son Ferdinand in consequence of which its contents have not been studied with due critical appreciation.

In Ferdinand's biography of his father, commonly referred to under the first word of the Italian title as the *Historie,* are imbedded not a few fragments of Columbus' own letters and other documents not commonly reproduced in the selections from his writings. To two such documents as

From Bourne, "Columbus, Ramon Pane and the beginnings of American Anthropology." Worcester: *Proceedings of the American Antiquarian Society,* Vol. XVII, April (1906), pp. 310-313.

presenting the evidence of Columbus' interest and efforts in the field of American Anthropology I invite your attention this morning.

The first contains the discoverer's own brief summary of what he was able to learn of the beliefs of the natives of Española during the period of his second voyage, 1493—96, and the record of his commissioning the Friar Ramon Pane who had learned the language of the islanders, "to collect all their ceremonies and antiquities." The second is Ramon's report of his observations and inquiries and is not only the first treatise ever written in the field of American Antiquities, but to this day remains our most authentic record of the religion and folk-lore of the long since extinct Tainos, the aboriginal inhabitants of Hayti. . . .

The observations of Columbus first referred to were recorded in his narrative of his second voyage which we possess only in the abridgments of Las Casas and Ferdinand Columbus. Both of these authors in condensing the original, incorporated passages in the exact words of the Admiral, and it is from such a passage in Ferdinand's abridgment that we derive the Admiral's account of the religion of primitive Hayti. Ferdinand writes: "Our people also learned many other things which seem to me worthy to be related in this our history. Beginning then with religion I will record here the very words of the Admiral who wrote as follows:"

"I was able to discover neither idolatry nor any other sect among them, although all their kings, who are many, not only in Española but also in all the other islands and on the main land[1] each have a house apart from the village, in which there is nothing except some wooden images carved in relief which are called *cemis*,[2] nor is there anything done in such a house for any other object or service except for these *cemis*, by means of a kind of ceremony and prayer which they go to make in it as we go to churches. In this house they have a finely wrought table, round like a wooden dish in which is some powder which is placed by them on the heads of these *cemis* in performing a certain ceremony; then with a cane that has two branches which they place in their nostrils they snuff up this dust. The words that they say none of our people understand. With this powder they lose consciousness and become like drunken men.

They give a name to this figure, and I believe it is that of a father, grandfather or of both, since they have more than one such, and some more than ten, all in memory, as I have said, of some one of their ancestors. I have heard them praise one more than another, and have seen them show it more devotion and do more reverence to one than another as we do in processions where there is need.

Both the Caciques and the peoples boast to each other of having the best *cemis*. When they go to these *cemis* of theirs and enter the house where he is they are on their guard with respect to the Christians and do not suffer them to

---

[1] i.e. Cuba, which Columbus believed to be the main land.

[2] Ulloa in his Italian gives this word in various forms e. g. *cemi, cimi, cimini* and *cimiche*. The correct form is *cemi* with the accent on the last syllable. Las Casas says, "Estas—llamaban *cemi*, la ultima silaba luenga y aguda." Docs. Inéditos para la Historia de España, LXVI, 436.

enter it. On the contrary, if they suspect they are coming, they take the *cemi* or the *cemis* away and hide them in the woods for fear they may be taken from them; and what is more laughable they have the custom of stealing each other's *cemis*. It happened once, when they suspected us, that the Christians entered the said house with them and of a sudden the *cemi* gave a loud cry and spoke in their language from which it was discovered that it was artfully constructed because being hollow, they had fitted to the lower part a trumpet or tube which extended to a dark part of the house covered with leaves and branches where there was a person who spoke what the Cacique wanted him to say so far as it could be done with a tube. Whereupon our men having suspected what might be the case, kicked the *cemi* over and found the facts as I have just described. When the Cacique saw that it was discovered by our men he besought them urgently not to say anything to the Indians, his subjects, nor to others because by this deceit he kept them in obedience.

This then we can say, there is some semblance of idolatry, at least among those who do not know the secret and the deception of their Caciques because they believe that the one who speaks is the *cemi*. In general all the people are deceived and the Cacique alone is the one who is conscious of and promotes their false belief by means of which he draws from his people all those tributes as seems good to him. Likewise most of the Caciques have three stones to which they and their peoples pay great reverence. One they say helps the corn and the vegetables that are planted; another the child-bearing of women without pain; and the third helps by means of water (i. e. rain) and the sun when they have need of it. I sent three of these stones to your Highness by Antonio de Torres[3] and another set of three I have to bring with me.

When these Indians die they have the funerals in different ways. The way the Caciques are buried, is as follows. They open the Cacique and dry him by the fire in order that he may be preserved whole, (or, entirely). Of others they take only the head. Others are buried in a cave and they place above their head a gourd of water and some bread. Others they burn in the house where they die and when they see them on the point of death they do not let them finish their life but strangle them. This is done to the Caciques. Others they drive out of the house; and others they put into a *hamaca,* which is their bed of netting, and put water and bread at their head and leave them alone without returning to see them any more. Some again that are seriously ill they take to the Cacique and he tells them whether they ought to be strangled or not and they do what he commands.

I have taken pains to learn what they believe and if they know where they go after death; especially from Caunabo, who is the chief king in Española, a man of years, of great knowledge and very keen mind; and he and others replied that they go to a certain valley which every principal Cacique believes is situated in his own country, affirming that there they find their father and all their ancestors; and that they eat and have women and give themselves to pleasures and recreation as is more fully contained in the following account in which I ordered one Friar Roman (Ramon) who knew their language to collect all their ceremonies and their antiquities although so much of it is fable that one cannot extract anything fruitful from it beyond the fact that each one of them has a certain natural regard for the future and believes in the immortality of our souls."[4]

[3] Antonio de Torres set forth on the return voyage here referred to February 2, 1494.

[4] *Historie.* Ed. 1571, Alfonso Ulloa, Venice; folios 125–126.

BERNAL DÍAZ DEL CASTILLO

(c. 1498-1560)

Cortés and Montezuma

THE APPROACH TO THE CITY OF MEXICO

THUS, WE ARRIVED NEAR IZTAPALAPA, TO BEHOLD THE SPLENDOUR OF THE other Caciques who came out to meet us, who were the Lord of the town named Cuitlahuac, and the Lord of Culuacan, both of them near relations of Montezuma. And then when we entered the city of Iztapalapa, the appearance of the palaces in which they lodged us! How spacious and well built they were, of beautiful stone work and cedar wood, and the wood of other sweet scented trees, with great rooms and courts, wonderful to behold, covered with awnings of cotton cloth.

When we had looked well at all of this, we went to the orchard and garden, which was such a wonderful thing to see and walk in, that I was never tired of looking at the diversity of the trees, and noting the scent which each one had, and the paths full of roses and flowers, and the many fruit trees and native roses, and the pond of fresh water. There was another thing to observe, that great canoes were able to pass into the garden from the lake through an opening that had been made so that there was no need for their occupants to land. And all was cemented and very splendid with many kinds of stone [monuments] with pictures on them, which gave much to think about. Then the birds of many kinds and breeds which came into the pond. I say again that I stood looking at it and thought that never in the world would there be discovered other lands such as these, for at that time there was no Peru, nor any thought of it. Of all these wonders that I then beheld to-day all is overthrown and lost, nothing left standing.

Let us go on, and I will relate that the Caciques of that town and of Coyoacan brought us a present of gold, worth more than two thousand pesos.

From Bernal Díaz del Castillo, *The Discovery and Conquest of Mexico*, translated with an introduction and notes by A. P. Maudslay (London: George Routledge & Sons, Ltd., 1928), pp. 270-273, 298-305.

Early next day we left Iztapalapa with a large escort of those great Caciques whom I have already mentioned. We proceeded along the Causeway which is here eight paces in width and runs so straight to the City of Mexico that it does not seem to me to turn either much or little, but, broad as it is, it was so crowded with people that there was hardly room for them all, some of them going to and others returning from Mexico, besides those who had come out to see us, so that we were hardly able to pass by the crowds of them that came; and the towers and cues were full of people as well as the canoes from all parts of the lake. It was not to be wondered at, for they had never before seen horses or men such as we are.

Gazing on such wonderful sights, we did not know what to say, or whether what appeared before us was real, for on one side, on the land, there were great cities, and in the lake ever so many more, and the lake itself was crowded with canoes, and in the Causeway were many bridges at intervals, and in front of us stood the great City of Mexico, and we— we did not even number four hundred soldiers! and we well remembered the words and warnings given us by the people of Huexotzingo and Tlaxcala, and the many other warnings that had been given that we should beware of entering Mexico, where they would kill us, as soon as they had us inside.

Let the curious readers consider whether there is not much to ponder over in this that I am writing. What men have there been in the world who have shown such daring? But let us get on, and march along the Causeway. When we arrived where another small causeway branches off [leading to Coyoacan, which is another city] where there were some buildings like towers, which are their oratories, many more chieftains and Caciques approached clad in very rich mantles, the brilliant liveries of one chieftain differing from those of another, and the causeways were crowded with them. The Great Montezuma had sent these great Caciques in advance to receive us, and when they came before Cortés they bade us welcome in their language, and as a sign of peace, they touched their hands against the ground, and kissed the ground with the hand.

There we halted for a good while, and Cacamatzin, the Lord of Texcoco, and the Lord of Iztapalapa and the Lord of Tacuba and the Lord of Coyoacan went on in advance to meet the Great Montezuma, who was approaching in a rich litter accompanied by other great Lords and Caciques, who owned vassals. When we arrived near to Mexico, where there were some other small towers, the Great Montezuma got down from his litter, and those great Caciques supported him with their arms beneath a marvellously rich canopy of green coloured feathers with much gold and silver embroidery and with pearls and chalchihuites suspended from a sort of bordering, which was wonderful to look at. The Great Montezuma was richly attired according to his usage, and he was shod with sandals, the soles were of gold and the upper part adorned with precious stones. The four Chieftains who supported his arms were also richly clothed according to their usage, in garments which were apparently held ready for them on the road to enable them to accompany their prince, for they did not appear in such attire when they came to receive us. Besides these four Chieftains, there were four other great Caciques who supported the canopy over their heads, and many other Lords who walked before the Great Montezuma, sweeping the ground where he would tread and spreading cloths on it, so that he should not tread on the earth. Not one of these chieftains dared even to think of looking him in the face, but kept their eyes lowered with great reverence, except those four relations, his nephews, who supported him with their arms.

When Cortés was told that the Great Montezuma was approaching, and he saw him coming, he dismounted from his horse, and when he was near Montezuma, they simultaneously paid great reverence to one another. Montezuma bade him welcome and our Cortés replied through Doña Marina wishing him very good health. And it seems to me that Cortés, through Doña Marina, offered him his right hand, and Montezuma did not wish to take it, but he did give his hand to Cortés and then Cortés brought out a necklace which he had ready at hand, made of glass stones, which I have already said are called Margaritas, which have within them many patterns of diverse colours, these were strung on a cord of gold and with musk so that it should have a sweet scent, and he placed it round the neck of the Great Montezuma and when he had so placed it he was going to embrace him, and those great Princes who accompanied Montezuma held back Cortés by the arm so that he should not embrace him, for they considered it an indignity.

THE MARKETS AND TEMPLES OF TLALTELOLCO

Our Captain and all of those who had horses went to Tlaltelolco on horseback, and nearly all of us soldiers were fully equipped, and many Caciques whom Montezuma had sent for that purpose went in our company. When we arrived at the great market place, called Tlaltelolco, we were astounded at the number of people and the quantity of merchandise that it contained, and at the good order and control that was maintained, for we had never seen such a thing before. The chieftains who accompanied us acted as guides. Each kind of merchandise was kept by itself and had its fixed place marked out. Let us begin with the dealers in gold, silver, and precious stones, feathers, mantles, and embroidered goods. Then there were other wares consisting of Indian slaves both men and women; and I say that they bring as many of them to that great market for sale as the Portuguese bring negroes from Guinea; and they brought them along tied to long poles, with collars round their necks so that they could not escape,

and others they left free. Next there were other traders who sold great
pieces of cloth and cotton, and articles of twisted thread, and there were
cacahuateros who sold cacao. In this way one could see every sort of
merchandise that is to be found in the whole of New Spain. There were
those who sold cloths of hennequen and ropes and the sandals with which
they are shod, which are made from the same plant, and sweet cooked
roots, and other tubers which they get from this plant, all were kept in
one part of the market in the place assigned to them. In another part
there were skins of tigers and lions, of otters and jackals, deer and other
animals and badgers and mountain cats, some tanned and others untanned,
and other classes of merchandise.

Let us go on and speak of those who sold beans and sage and other
vegetables and herbs in another part, and to those who sold fowls, cocks
with wattles, rabbits, hares, deer, mallards, young dogs and other things
of that sort in their part of the market, and let us also mention the fruiterers,
and the women who sold cooked food, dough and tripe in their own part
of the market; then every sort of pottery made in a thousand different
forms from great water jars to little jugs, these also had a place to themselves; then those who sold honey and honey paste and other dainties
like nut paste, and those who sold lumber, boards, cradles, beams, blocks
and benches, each article by itself, and the vendors of *ocote*[1] firewood, and
other things of a similar nature. But why do I waste so many words in
recounting what they sell in that great market?—for I shall never finish if
I tell it all in detail. Paper, which in this country is called *amal,* and reeds
scented with *liquidambar,* and full of tobacco, and yellow ointments and
things of that sort are sold by themselves, and much cochineal is sold under
the arcades which are in that great market place, and there are many
vendors of herbs and other sorts of trades. There are also buildings where
three magistrates sit in judgment, and there are executive officers like
Alguacils who inspect the merchandise. I am forgetting those who sell
salt, and those who make the stone knives, and how they split them off
the stone itself; and the fisherwomen and others who sell some small
cakes made from a sort of ooze which they get out of the great lake, which
curdles, and from this they make a bread having a flavour something like
cheese. There are for sale axes of brass and copper and tin, and gourds
and gaily painted jars made of wood. I could wish that I had finished
telling of all the things which are sold there, but they are so numerous
and of such different quality and the great market place with its surrounding arcades was so crowded with people, that one would not have been
able to see and inquire about it all in two days.

Then we went to the great Cue, and when we were already approaching
its great courts, before leaving the market place itself, there were many

---

[1] Pitch-pine for torches.

more merchants, who, as I was told, brought gold for sale in grains, just as it is taken from the mines. The gold is placed in thin quills of the geese of the country, white quills, so that the gold can be seen through, and according to the length and thickness of the quills they arrange their accounts with one another, how much so many mantles or so many gourds full of cacao were worth, or how many slaves, or whatever other thing they were exchanging.

Before reaching the great Cue there is a great enclosure of courts, it seems to me larger than the plaza of Salamanca, with two walls of masonry surrounding it, and the court itself all paved with very smooth great white flagstones. And where there were not these stones it was cemented and burnished and all very clean, so that one could not find any dust or a straw in the whole place.

When we arrived near the Great Cue and before we had ascended a single step of it, the great Montezuma sent down from above, where he was making his sacrifices, six priests and two chieftains to accompany our Captain. On ascending the steps, which are one hundred and fourteen in number, they attempted to take him by the arms so as to help him to ascend, (thinking that he would get tired), as they were accustomed to assist their lord Montezuma, but Cortés would not allow them to come near him. When we got to the top of the great Cue, on a small plaza which has been made on the top where there was a space like a platform with some large stones placed on it, on which they put the poor Indians for sacrifice, there was a bulky image like a dragon and other evil figures and much blood shed that very day.

When we arrived there Montezuma came out of an oratory where his cursed idols were, at the summit of the great Cue, and two priests came with him, and after paying great reverence to Cortés and to all of us he said: "You must be tired, Señor Malinche, from ascending this our great Cue," and Cortés replied through our interpreters who were with us that he and his companions were never tired by anything. Then Montezuma took him by the hand and told him to look at his great city and all the other cities that were standing in the water, and the many other towns on the land round the lake, and that if he had not seen the great market place well, that from where they were they could see it better.

So we stood looking about us, for that huge and cursed temple stood so high that from it one could see over everything very well, and we saw the three causeways which led into Mexico, that is the causeway of Iztapalapa by which we had entered four days before, and that of Tacuba, and that of Tepeaquilla,[2] and we saw the fresh water that comes from Chapultepec which supplies the city, and we saw the bridges on the three causeways which were built at certain distances apart through which the

---

[2] Guadelupe.

water of the lake flowed in and out from one side to the other, and we beheld on that great lake a great multitude of canoes, some coming with supplies of food and others returning loaded with cargoes of merchandise; and we saw that from every house of that great city and of all the other cities that were built in the water it was impossible to pass from house to house, except by drawbridges which were made of wood or in canoes; and we saw in those cities Cues and oratories like towers and fortresses and all gleaming white, and it was a wonderful thing to behold; then the houses with flat roofs, and on the causeways other small towers and oratories which were like fortresses.

After having examined and considered all that we had seen we turned to look at the great market place and the crowds of people that were in it, some buying and others selling, so that the murmur and hum of their voices and words that they used could be heard more than a league off. Some of the soldiers among us who had been in many parts of the world, in Constantinople, and all over Italy, and in Rome, said that so large a market place and so full of people, and so well regulated and arranged, they had never beheld before.

Let us leave this, and return to our Captain, who said to Fray Bartolomé de Olmedo, who happened to be near by him: "It seems to me, Señor Padre, that it would be a good thing to throw out a feeler to Montezuma, as to whether he would allow us to build our church here"; and the Padre replied that it would be a good thing if it were successful, but it seemed to him that it was not quite a suitable time to speak about it, for Montezuma did not appear to be inclined to do such a thing.

Then our Cortés said to Montezuma: "Your Highness is indeed a very great prince and worthy of even greater things. We are rejoiced to see your cities, and as we are here in your temple, what I now beg as a favour is that you will show us your gods and Teules." Montezuma replied that he must first speak with his high priests, and when he had spoken to them he said that we might enter into a small tower and apartment, a sort of hall, where there were two altars, with very richly carved boardings on the top of the roof. On each altar were two figures, like giants with very tall bodies and very fat, and the first which stood on the right hand they said was the figure of Huichilobos their god of War; it had a very broad face and monstrous and terrible eyes, and the whole of his body was covered with precious stones, and gold and pearls, and with seed pearls stuck on with a paste that they make in this country out of a sort of root, and all the body and head was covered with it, and the body was girdled by great snakes made of gold and precious stones, and in one hand he held a bow and in the other some arrows. And another small idol that stood by him, they said was his page, and he held a short lance and a shield richly decorated with gold and stones. Huichilobos had round his neck some

Indians' faces and other things like hearts of Indians, the former made of gold and the latter of silver, with many precious blue stones.

There were some braziers with incense which they call copal, and in them they were burning the hearts of the three Indians whom they had sacrificed that day, and they had made the sacrifice with smoke and copal. All the walls of the oratory were so splashed and encrusted with blood that they were black, the floor was the same and the whole place stank vilely. Then we saw on the other side on the left hand there stood the other great image the same height as Huichilobos, and it had a face like a bear and eyes that shone, made of their mirrors which they call *Tezcat,* and the body plastered with precious stones like that of Huichilobos, for they say that the two are brothers; and this Tezcatepuca was the god of Hell and had charge of the souls of the Mexicans, and his body was girt with figures like little devils with snakes' tails. The walls were so clotted with blood and the soil so bathed with it that in the slaughter houses of Spain there is not such another stench.

They had offered to this Idol five hearts from the day's sacrifices. In the highest part of the Cue there was a recess of which the woodwork was very richly worked, and in it was another image half man and half lizard, with precious stones all over it, and half the body was covered with a mantle. They say that the body of this figure is full of the seeds that there are in the world, and they say that it is the god of seed time and harvest, but I do not remember its name, and everything was covered with blood, both walls and altar, and the stench was such that we could hardly wait the moment to get out of it.

They had an exceedingly large drum there, and when they beat it the sound of it was so dismal and like, so to say, an instrument of the infernal regions, that one could hear it a distance of two leagues, and they said that the skins it was covered with were those of great snakes. In that small place there were many diabolical things to be seen, bugles and trumpets and knives, and many hearts of Indians that they had burned in fumigating their idols, and everything was so clotted with blood, and there was so much of it, that I curse the whole of it, and as it stank like a slaughter house we hastened to clear out of such a bad stench and worse sight. Our Captain said to Montezuma through our interpreter, half laughing: "Señor Montezuma, I do not understand how such a great Prince and wise man as you are has not come to the conclusion, in your mind, that these idols of yours are not gods, but evil things that are called devils, and so that you may know it and all your priests may see it clearly, do me the favour to approve of my placing a cross here on the top of this tower, and that in one part of these oratories where your Huichilobos and Tezcatepuca stand we may divide off a space where we can set up an image of Our Lady (an image which Montezuma had already seen) and you will see by the fear in which these Idols hold it that they are deceiving you."

Montezuma replied half angrily (and the two priests who were with him showed great annoyance), and said: "Señor Malinche, if I had known that you would have said such defamatory things I would not have shown you my gods, we consider them to be very good, for they give us health and rains and good seed times and seasons and as many victories as we desire, and we are obliged to worship them and make sacrifices, and I pray you not to say another word to their dishonour."

When our Captain heard that and noted the angry looks he did not refer again to the subject, but said with a cheerful manner: "It is time for your Excellency and for us to return," and Montezuma replied that it was well, but that he had to pray and offer certain sacrifices on account of the great *tatacul*, that is to say sin, which he had committed in allowing us to ascend his great Cue, and being the cause of our being permitted to see his gods, and of our dishonouring them by speaking evil of them, so that before he left he must pray and worship.

Then Cortés said: "I ask your pardon if it be so," and then we went down the steps, and as they numbered one hundred and fourteen, and as some of our soldiers were suffering from tumours and abscesses, their legs were tired by the descent.

SAMUEL DE CHAMPLAIN

(1567-1635)

The Character and Customs of the Huron

THE COUNTRY OF THE NATION OF THE ATTIGOUANTANS[1] IS IN LATITUDE
44° 30′, and extends two hundred and thirty leagues in length westerly,
and ten in breadth. It contains eighteen villages, six of which are enclosed
and fortified by palisades of wood in triple rows, bound together, on the
top of which are galleries, which they provide with stones and water; the
former to hurl upon their enemies and the latter to extinguish the fire
which their enemies may set to the palisades. The country is pleasant,
most of it cleared up. It has the shape of Brittany, and is similarly situated,
being almost surrounded by the *Mer Douce*. They assume that these
eighteen villages are inhabited by two thousand warriors, not including
the common mass, which amounts to perhaps thirty thousand souls.

Their cabins are in the shape of tunnels or arbors, and are covered
with the bark of trees. They are from twenty-five to thiry fathoms long,
more or less, and six wide, having a passage-way through the middle from
ten to twelve feet wide, which extends from one end to the other. On the
two sides there is a kind of bench, four feet high, where they sleep in
summer, in order to avoid the annoyance of the fleas, of which there were
great numbers. In winter they sleep on the ground. . . .

All these people have a very[2] jovial disposition, although there are many
of them who have a sad and gloomy look. Their bodies are well proportioned. Some of the men and women are well formed, strong, and robust.
There is a moderate number of pleasing and pretty girls, in respect to
figure, color, and expression, all being in harmony. Their blood is but
little deteriorated, except when they are old. There are among these tribes
powerful women of extraordinary height. These have almost the entire

[1] One of the divisions of the Huron Federation.
[2] Fr. *assez, i.e.,* somewhat.

From Champlain, *Voyages of Samuel de Champlain, 1604-1618,* edited by W. L.
Grant (New York: Charles Scribner's Sons, 1907), pp. 317-323; 327-330.

care of the house and work; namely, they till the land, plant the Indian corn, lay up a store of wood for the winter, beat the hemp and spin it, making from the thread fishing-nets and other useful things. The women harvest the corn, house it, prepare it for eating, and attend to household matters. Moreover they are expected to attend their husbands from place to place in the fields, filling the office of pack-mule in carrying the baggage, and to do a thousand other things. All the men do is to hunt for deer and other animals, fish, make their cabins, and go to war. Having done these things, they then go to other tribes with which they are acquainted to traffic and make exchanges. On their return, they give themselves up to festivities and dances, which they give to each other, and when these are over they go to sleep, which they like to do best of all things.

They have some sort of marriage, which is as follows: when a girl has reached the age of eleven, twelve, thirteen, fourteen, or fifteen years she has suitors, more or less according to her attractions, who woo her for some time. After this, the consent of their fathers and mothers is asked, to whose will the girls often do not submit, although the most discreet and considerate do so. The lover or suitor presents to the girl some necklaces, chains, and bracelets of porcelain. If the girl finds the suitor agreeable, she receives the present. Then the lover comes and remains with her three or four nights, without saying anything to her during the time. They receive thus the fruit of their affections. Whence it happens very often that, after from eight to fifteen days, if they cannot agree, she quits her suitor, who forfeits his necklaces and other presents that he has made, having received in return only a meagre satisfaction. Being thus disappointed in his hopes, the man seeks another woman, and the girl another suitor, if it seems to them desirable. Thus they continue to do until a favorable union is formed. It sometimes happens that a girl thus passes her entire youth, having more than twenty mates, which twenty are not alone in the enjoyment of the creature, mated though they are; for when night comes the young women run from one cabin to another, as do also the young men on their part, going where it seems good to them, but always without any violence, referring the whole matter to the pleasure of the woman. Their mates will do likewise to their women-neighbors, no jealousy arising among them on that account, nor do they incur any reproach or insult, such being the custom of the country.

Now the time when they do not leave their mates is when they have children. The preceding mate returns to her, renews the affection and and friendship which he had borne her in the past, asserting that it is greater than that of any other one, and that the child she has is his and of his begetting. The next says the same to her. In fine, the victory is with the stronger, who takes the woman for his wife. Thus it depends upon the choice of the woman to take and accept him who shall please her best, having meantime in her searching and loves gained much porcelain and, besides, the choice of a husband. The woman remains with him without leaving him; or if she do leave him, for he is on trial, it must be for some good reason other than impotence. But while with this husband, she does not cease to give herself free rein, yet remains always at home, keeping up a good appearance. Thus the children which they have together, born from such a woman, cannot be sure of their legitimacy. Accordingly, in view of this uncertainty, it is their custom that the children never succeed to the property and honors of their fathers, there being doubt, as above indicated, as to their paternity. They make, however, the children of their sisters, from whom they are known to have issued, their successors and heirs.

The following is the way they nourish and bring up their children: they place them during the day on a little wooden board, wrapping them up in furs or skins. To this board they bind them, placing them in an erect position, and leaving a little opening for the child to do its necessities. If it is a girl, they put a leaf of Indian corn between the thighs, which presses against its privates. The extremity of the leaf is carried outside in a turned position, so that the water of the child runs off on it without inconvenience. They put also under the children the down of certain reeds that we call hare's-foot, on which they rest very softly. They also clean them with the same down. As an ornament for the child, they adorn the board with beads, which they also put on its neck, however small it may be. At night they put it to bed, entirely naked, between the father and mother. It may be regarded as a great miracle that God should thus preserve it so that no harm befalls it, as might be expected, from suffocation, while the father and mother are in deep sleep, but that rarely happens. The children have great freedom among these tribes. The fathers and mothers indulge them too much, and never punish them. Accordingly they are so bad and of so vicious a nature, that they often strike their mothers and others. The most vicious, when they have acquired the strength and power, strike their fathers. They do this whenever the father or mother does anything that does not please them. This is a sort of curse that God inflicts upon them.

In respect to laws, I have not been able to find out that they have any, or anything that approaches them, inasmuch as there is not among them any correction, punishment, or censure of evil-doers, except in the way of vengeance when they return evil for evil, not by rule but by passion, which produces among them conflicts and differences, which occur very frequently.

Moreover, they do not recognize any divinity, or worship any God and believe in anything whatever, but live like brute beasts. They have, however, some respect for the devil, or something so called, which is a matter of uncertainty, since the word which they use thus has various significations and comprises in itself various things. It is accordingly difficult to determine whether they mean the devil or something else, but what especially leads to the belief that what they mean is the devil is this: whenever they see a man doing something extraordinary, or who is more capable than usual, or is a valiant warrior, or furthermore who is in a rage as if out of his reason and senses, they call him *oqui,* or, as we should say, a great knowing spirit, or a great devil. However this may be, they have certain persons, who are the *oqui,* or, as the Algonquins and Montagnais call them, *manitous;* and persons of this kind are the medicine-men, who heal the sick, bind up the wounded, and predict future events, who in fine practice all abuses and illusions of the devil to deceive and delude them. These *oquis* or conjurers persuade their patients and the sick to make, or have made banquets and ceremonies that they may be the sooner healed, their object being to participate in them finally themselves and get the principal benefit therefrom. Under the pretence of a more speedy cure, they likewise cause them to observe various other ceremonies, which I shall hereafter speak of in the proper place. These are the people in whom they put especial confidence, but it is rare that they are possessed of the devil and tormented like other savages living more remote than themselves.

This gives additional reason and ground to believe that their conversion to the knowledge of God would be more easy, if their country were inhabited by persons who would take the trouble and pains to instruct them. But it is not enough to send to them friars, unless there are those to support and assist them. For although these people have the desire to-day to know what God is, to-morrow this disposition will change when they are obliged to lay aside and bring under their foul ways, their dissolute manners, and their savage indulgences. So that there is need of people and families to keep them in the way of duty, to constrain them through mildness to do better, and to move them by good example to mend their lives. Father Joseph and myself have many times conferred with them in regard to our belief, laws, and customs. They listen attentively in their assemblies, sometimes saying to us:

You say things that pass our knowledge, and which we cannot understand by words, being beyond our comprehension; but if you would do us a service come and dwell in this country, bringing your wives and children, and when they are here we shall see how you serve the God you worship, and how you live with your wives and children, how you cultivate and plant the soil, how you obey your laws, how you take care of animals, and how you manufacture all that we see proceeding from your inventive skill. When we see all this, we shall learn more in a year than in twenty by simply hearing you discourse; and if we cannot then understand, you shall take our children, who shall be as your own. And thus being convinced that our life is a miserable one in comparison with yours, it is easy to believe that we shall adopt yours, abandoning our own.

The following is their mode of government: the older and leading men assemble in a council, in which they settle upon and propose all that is necessary for the affairs of the village. This is done by a plurality of voices, or in accordance with the advice of some one among them whose judgment they consider superior: such a one is requested by the company to give his opinion on the propositions that have been made, and this opinion is minutely obeyed. They have no particular chiefs with absolute command, but they show honor to the older and more courageous men, whom they name captains, as a mark of honor and respect, of which there are several in a village. But, although they confer more honor upon one than upon others, yet he is not on that account to bear sway, nor esteem himself higher than his companions, unless he does so from vanity. They make no use of punishments nor arbitrary command, but accomplish everything by the entreaties of the seniors, and by means of addresses and remonstrances. Thus and not otherwise do they bring everything to pass.

They all deliberate in common, and whenever any member of the assembly offers to do anything for the welfare of the village, or to go anywhere for the service of the community, he is requested to present himself, and if he is judged capable of carrying out what he proposes, they exhort him, by fair and favorable words, to do his duty. They declare him to be an energetic man, fit for undertakings, and assure him that he will win honor in accomplishing them. In a word, they encourage him by flatteries, in order that this favorable disposition of his for the welfare of his fellow-citizens may continue and increase. Then, according to his pleasure, he refuses the responsibility, which few do, or accepts, since thereby he is held in high esteem.

When they engage in wars or go to the country of their enemies, two or three of the older or valiant captains make a beginning in the matter, and proceed to the adjoining villages to communicate their purpose, and make presents to the people of these villages, in order to induce them to accompany them to the wars in question. In so far they act as generals of armies. They designate the place where they desire to go, dispose of the prisoners who are captured, and have the direction of other matters of especial importance, of which they get the honor, if they are successful; but, if not, the disgrace of failure in the war falls upon them. These captains alone are looked upon and considered as chiefs of the tribes.

They have, moreover, general assemblies, with representatives from remote regions. These representatives come every year, one from each province, and meet in a town designated as the rendezvous of the assembly. Here are celebrated great banquets and dances, for three weeks or a month, according as they may determine. Here they renew their friendship, resolve upon and decree what they think best for the preservation of their country against their enemies, and make each other handsome presents, after which they retire each to his own district.

In burying the dead, they take the body of the deceased, wrap it in furs, and cover it very carefully with the bark of trees. Then they place it in a cabin, of the length of the body, made of bark and erected upon four posts. Others they place in the ground, propping up the earth on all sides, that it may not fall on the body, which they cover with the bark of trees, putting earth on top. Over this trench they also make a little cabin. Now it is to be understood that the bodies remain in these places, thus inhumed, but for a period of eight or ten years, when the men of the village recommend the place where their ceremonies are to take place; or, to speak more precisely, they hold a general council, in which all the people of the country are present, for the purpose of designating the place where a festival is to be held. After this they return each to his own village, where they take all the bones of the deceased, strip them and make them quite clean. These they keep very carefully, although they smell like bodies recently interred. Then all the relatives and friends of the deceased take these bones, together with their necklaces, furs, axes, kettles, and other things highly valued, and carry them, with a quantity of edibles, to the place assigned. Here, when all have assembled, they put the edibles in a place designated by the men of the village, and engage in banquets and continual dancing. The festival continues for the space of ten days, during which time other tribes, from all quarters, come to witness it and the ceremonies. The latter are attended with great outlays.

Now, by means of these ceremonies, including dances, banquets, and assemblies, as above stated, they renew their friendship to one another, saying that the bones of their relatives and friends are to be all put together, thus indicating by a figure that, as their bones are gathered together, and united in one and the same place, so ought they also, during their life, to be united in one friendship and harmony, like relatives and friends, without separation. Having thus mingled together the bones of their mutual relatives and friends, they pronounce many discourses on the occasion. Then, after various grimaces or exhibitions, they make a great trench, ten fathoms square, in which they put the bones, together with the necklaces, chains of porcelain, axes, kettles, sword-blades, knives, and various other trifles, which, however, are of no slight account in their estimation. They cover the whole with earth, putting on top several great pieces of wood, and placing around many posts, on which they put a covering. This is their manner of proceeding with regard to the dead, and it is the most prominent ceremony they have. Some of them believe in the immortality of the soul, while others have only a presentiment of it, which, however, is not so very different; for they say that after their decease they will go to a place where they will sing like crows, a song, it must be confessed, quite different from that of angels.

MERIWETHER LEWIS

(1774-1809)

The Lewis and Clark Expedition

THE SHOSHONE: THEIR WEAPONS AND HORSE GEAR

ALTHOUGH OPPRESSED BY THE MINNETAREES, THE SHOSHONEES ARE STILL a very military people. Their cold and rugged country inures them to fatigue; their long abstinence makes them support the dangers of mountain warfare, and worn down, as we saw them, by want of sustenance, have a look of fierce and adventurous courage. The Shoshonee warrior always fights on horseback; he possesses a few bad guns, which are reserved exclusively for war, but his common arms are the bow and arrow, a shield, a lance, and a weapon called by the Chippeways, by whom it was formerly used, the poggamoggon. The bow is made of cedar or pine, covered on the outer side with sinews and glue. It is about two and a half feet long, and does not differ in shape from those used by the Sioux, Mandans, and Minnetarees. Sometimes, however, the bow is made of a single piece of the horn of an elk, covered on the back like those of wood with sinews and glue, and occasionally ornamented by a strand wrought of porcupine quills and sinews, which is wrapped round the horn near its two ends. The bows made of the horns of the bighorn are still more prized, and are formed by cementing with glue flat pieces of the horn together, covering the back with sinews and glue, and loading the whole with an unusual quantity of ornaments. The arrows resemble those of the other Indians, except in being more slender than any we have seen. They are contained, with the implements for striking fire, in a narrow quiver formed of different kinds of skin, though that of the otter seems to be preferred. It is just long enough to protect the arrows from the weather, and is worn on the back by means of a strap passing over the right shoulder and under the left arm.

From Lewis, *History of the Expedition of Captains Lewis and Clark 1804-5-6,* 2 vols. (Chicago: A. C. McClurg & Company, 1902), Vol. I, pp. 451-455; Vol. II, pp. 130-146. Reprinted from the edition of 1814 with an Introduction and Index by James K. Hosmer.

The shield is a circular piece of buffaloe hide about two feet four or five inches in diameter, ornamented with feathers, and a fringe round it of dressed leather, and adorned or deformed with paintings of strange figures. The buffaloe hide is perfectly proof against any arrow, but in the minds of the Shoshonees, its power to protect them is chiefly derived from the virtues which are communicated to it by the old men and jugglers. To make a shield is indeed one of their most important ceremonies. It begins by a feast, to which all the warriors, old men, and jugglers are invited. After the repast a hole is dug in the ground about eighteen inches in depth, and of the same diameter as the intended shield; into this hole red-hot stones are thrown and water poured over them, till they emit a very strong, hot steam. The buffaloe skin, which must be the entire hide of a male two years old, and never suffered to dry since it was taken from the animal, is now laid across the hole, with a fleshy side to the ground, and stretched in every direction by as many as can take hold of it. As the skin becomes heated, the hair separates and is taken off by the hand, till at last the skin is contracted into the compass designed for the shield. It is then taken off and placed on a hide prepared into parchment, and then pounded during the rest of the festival by the bare heels of those who are invited to it. This operation sometimes continues for several days, after which it is delivered to the proprietor, and declared by the old men and jugglers to be a security against arrows, and, provided the feast has been satisfactory, against even the bullets of their enemies. Such is the delusion that many of the Indians implicitly believe that this ceremony has given to the shield supernatural powers, and that they have no longer to fear any weapons of their enemies.

The paggamoggon is an instrument consisting of a handle twenty-two inches long, made of wood, covered with dressed leather about the size of a whip-handle; at one end is a thong of two inches in length, which is tied to a round stone weighing two pounds and held in a cover of leather; at the other end is a loop of the same material, which is passed round the wrist so as to secure the hold of the instrument, with which they strike a very severe blow.

Besides these, they have a kind of armour something like a coat of mail, which is formed by a great many folds of dressed antelope skins, united by means of a mixture of glue and sand. With this they cover their own bodies and those of their horses, and find it impervious to the arrow.

The caparison of their horses is a halter and a saddle; the first is either a rope of six or seven strands of buffaloe hair platted or twisted together, about the size of a man's finger, and of great strength; or merely a thong of raw hide, made pliant by pounding and rubbing, though the first kind is much preferred. The halter is very long, and is never taken from the neck of the horse when in constant use. One end of it is first tied round the neck in a knot, and then brought down to the under jaw, round which it is formed into a simple noose, passing through the mouth; it is then drawn up on the right side and held by the rider in his left hand, while the rest trails after him to some distance. At other times the knot is formed at a little distance from one of the ends, so as to let that end serve as a bridle, while the other trails on the ground. With these cords dangling alongside of them the horse is put to his full speed without fear of falling, and when he is turned to graze the noose is merely taken from his mouth. The saddle is formed, like the pack-saddles used by the French and Spaniards, of two flat thin boards which fit the sides of the horse, and are kept together by two cross pieces, one before and the other behind, which rise to a considerable height, ending sometimes in a flat point extending outwards, and always making the saddle deep and narrow. Under this a piece of buffaloe skin, with the hair on, is placed so as to prevent the rubbing of the boards, and when they mount they throw a piece of skin or robe over the saddle, which has no permanent cover. When stirrups are used, they consist of wood covered with leather; but stirrups and saddles are conveniences reserved for old men and women. The young warriors rarely use anything except a small leather pad stuffed with hair, and secured by a girth made of a leathern thong. In this way they ride with great expertness, and they have a particular dexterity in catching the horse when he is running at large. If he will not immediately submit when they wish to take him, they make a noose in the rope, and although the horse may be at a distance, or even running, rarely fail to fix it on his neck; and such is the docility of the animal that, however unruly he may seem, he surrenders as soon as he feels the rope on him. This cord is so useful in this way that it is never dispensed with, even when they use the Spanish bridle, which they prefer, and always procure when they have it in their power. The horse becomes almost an object of attachment; a favourite is frequently painted and his ears cut into various shapes; the mane and tail, which are never drawn nor trimmed, are decorated with feathers of birds, and sometimes a warrior suspends at the breast of his horse the finest ornaments he possesses.

Thus armed and mounted the Shoshonee is a formidable enemy, even with the feeble weapons which he is still obliged to use. When they attack at full speed they bend forward and cover their bodies with the shield, while with the right hand they shoot under the horse's neck.

The only articles of metal which the Shoshonees possess are a few bad knives, some brass kettles, some bracelets or arm-bands of iron and brass, a few buttons worn as ornaments in their hair, one or two spears about a foot in length, and some heads for arrows made of iron and brass. All these they had obtained in trading with the Crow or Rocky mountain Indians, who live on the Yellowstone. The few bridle-bits and stirrups they procured from the Spanish colonies.

The instrument which supplies the place of a knife among them is a piece of flint with no regular form, and the sharp part of it not more than one or two inches long; the edge of this is renewed, and the flint itself is formed into heads for arrows by means of the point of a deer or elk horn, an instrument which they use with great art and ingenuity. There are no axes or hatchets, all the wood being cut with flint or elk-horn, the latter of which is always used as a wedge in splitting wood. Their utensils consist, besides the brass kettles, of pots in the form of a jar, made either of earth, or of a stone found in the hills between Madison and Jefferson rivers, which, though soft and white in its natural state, becomes very hard and black after exposure to the fire. The horns of the buffaloe and the bighorn supply them with spoons.

The fire is always kindled by means of a blunt arrow and a piece of well-seasoned wood of a soft spongy kind, such as the willow or cotton-wood.

THE CHINNOOK: THEIR HOUSES

The houses in this neighbourhood are all large wooden buildings, varying in length from twenty to sixty feet and from fourteen to twenty in width. They are constructed in the following manner: Two posts of split timber or more, agreeably to the number of partitions, are sunk in the ground, above which they rise to the height of fourteen or eighteen feet. They are hollowed at the top, so as to receive the ends of a round beam or pole stretching from one to the other, and forming the upper point of the roof for the whole extent of the building. On each side of this range is placed another, which forms the eaves of the house, and is about five feet high; but as the building is often sunk to the depth of four or five feet, the eaves come very near the surface of the earth. Smaller pieces of timber are now extended by pairs, in the form of rafters, from the lower to the upper beam, where they are attached at both ends with cords of cedar bark. On these rafters two or three ranges of small poles are placed horizontally, and secured in the same way with strings of cedar bark. The sides are now made with a range of wide boards sunk a small distance into the ground, with the upper ends projecting above the poles at the eaves, to which they are secured by a beam passing outside, parallel with the eave-poles, and tied by cords of cedar bark passing through holes made in the boards at certain distances. The gable ends and partitions are formed in the same way, being fastened by beams on the outside parallel to the rafters. The roof is then covered with a double range of thin boards, except an aperture of two or three feet in the centre for the smoke to pass through. The entrance is by a small hole cut out of the boards, and just large enough to admit the body. The very largest houses only are divided by partitions, for though three or four families reside in the same room, there is quite space enough for all of them. In the centre of each room is a space six or eight feet square sunk to the depth of twelve inches below the rest of the floor, and inclosed by four pieces of square timber. Here they make the fire, for which purpose pine bark is generally preferred. Around this fireplace mats are spread, and serve as seats during the day and very frequently as beds at night; there is, however, a more permanent bed made, by fixing, in two or sometimes three sides of the room, posts reaching from the roof down to the ground, and at the distance of four feet from the wall. From these posts to the wall itself one or two ranges of boards are placed so as to form shelves, on which they either sleep or where they stow away their various articles of merchandise. The uncured fish is hung in the smoke of their fires, as is also the flesh of the elk when they are fortunate enough to procure any, which is but rarely.

THE CANOES OF THE NORTHWESTERN TRIBES

In a country where so much of the intercourse between different tribes is carried on by water, the ingenuity of the people would naturally direct itself to the improvement of canoes, which would gradually become, from a mere safe conveyance, to an elegant ornament. We have accordingly seen, on the Columbia, canoes of many forms, beginning with the simple boats near the mountains, to those more highly decorated, because more useful, nearer the mouth of the Columbia. Below the grand cataract there are four forms of canoes: the first and smallest is about fifteen feet long, and calculated for one or two persons; it is, indeed, by no means remarkable in its structure, and is chiefly employed by the Cathlamahs and Wahkiacums among the marshy islands. The second is from twenty to thirty-five feet long, about two and a half or three feet in the beam and two feet in the hold. It is chiefly remarkable in having the bowsprit, which rises to some height above the bow, formed by tapering gradually from the sides into a sharp point. Canoes of this shape are common to all the nations below the grand rapids.

But the canoes most used by the Columbia Indians, from the Chilluckittequaws inclusive to the ocean, are about thirty or thirty-five feet long. The bow, which looks more like the stern of our boats, is higher than the other end, and is ornamented with a sort of comb, an inch in thickness, cut out of the same log which forms the canoe, and extending nine or eleven inches from the bowsprit to the bottom of the boat. The stern is nearly rounded off, and gradually ascends to a point. This canoe is very light and convenient, for though it will contain ten or twelve persons, it may be carried with great ease by four.

The fourth and largest species of canoe we did not meet till we reached tide-water, near the grand rapids below, in which place they are found among all the nations, especially the Killamucks and others residing on the seacoast. They are upwards of fifty feet long, and will carry from eight to ten thousand pounds weight, or from twenty to thirty persons. Like all the canoes we have mentioned, they are cut out of a single trunk of a tree, which is generally white cedar, though the fir is sometimes used. The sides are secured by cross-bars, or round sticks, two or three inches in thickness, which are inserted through holes made just below the gunwhale, and made fast with cords. The upper edge of the gunwhale itself is about five-eighths of an inch thick and four or five in breadth, and folds outwards so as to form a kind of rim which prevents the water from beating into the boat. The bow and stern are about the same height, and each provided with a comb reaching to the bottom of the boat. At each end, also, are pedestals formed of the same solid piece, on which are placed strange grotesque figures of men or animals, rising sometimes to the height of five feet, and composed of small pieces of wood, firmly united with great ingenuity by inlaying and mortising, without a spike of any kind. The paddle is usually from four feet and a half to five feet in length, the handle being thick for one-third of its length, when it widens, and is hollowed and thinned on each side of the centre, which forms a sort of rib. When they embark, one Indian sits in the stern and steers with a paddle, the others kneel in pairs in the bottom of the canoe, and sitting on their heels paddle over the gunwhale next to them. In this way they ride with perfect safety the highest waves, and venture without the least concern in seas where other boats or seamen could not live an instant.

THE COLUMBIA RIVER TRIBES

The Killamucks, Clatsops, Chinnooks, and Cathlamahs, the four neighbouring nations with whom we have had most intercourse, preserve a general resemblance in person, dress, and manners. They are commonly of a diminutive stature, badly shaped, and their appearance by no means prepossessing. They have broad, thick, flat feet, thick ankles, and crooked legs, the last of which deformities is to be ascribed, in part, to the universal practice of squatting, or sitting on the calves of their legs and heels, and also to the tight bandages of beads and strings worn round the ankles by the women, which prevent the circulation of the blood, and render the legs, of the females particularly, ill-shaped and swollen. The complexion is the usual copper-coloured brown of the North American tribes, though the complexion is rather lighter than that of the Indians of the Missouri and the frontier of the United States; the mouth is wide and the lips thick; the nose of a moderate size, fleshy, wide at the extremities, with large nostrils, and generally low between the eyes, though there are rare instances of high acqueline noses; the eyes are generally black, though we occasionally see them of a dark yellowish brown, with a black pupil. But the most distinguishing part of their physiognomy is the peculiar flatness and width of their forehead, a peculiarity which they owe to one of those customs by which nature is sacrificed to fantastic ideas of beauty. The custom, indeed, of flattening the head by artificial pressure during infancy prevails among all the nations we have seen west of the Rocky mountains. To the east of that barrier the fashion is so perfectly unknown that there the western Indians, with the exception of the Alliatan or Snake nation, are designated by the common name of Flatheads. The singular usage, which nature could scarcely seem to suggest to remote nations, might perhaps incline us to believe in the common and not very ancient origin of all the western nations. Such an opinion might well accommodate itself with the fact that while on the lower parts of the Columbia both sexes are universally flatheads, the custom diminishes in receding eastward from the common centre of the infection, till among the remoter tribes near the mountains nature recovers her rights, and the wasted folly is confined to a few females. Such opinions, however, are corrected or weakened by considering that the flattening of the head is not, in fact, peculiar to that part of the continent, since it was among the first objects which struck the attention of Columbus.

But wherever it may have begun, the practice is now universal among these nations. Soon after the birth of her child, the mother, anxious to procure for her infant the recommendation of a broad forehead, places it in the compressing machine, where it is kept for ten or twelve months, though the females remain longer than the boys. The operation is so gradual that it is not attended with pain, but the impression is deep and permanent. The heads of the children, when they are released from the bandage, are not more than two inches thick about the upper edge of the forehead, and still thinner above; nor with all its efforts can nature ever restore its shape, the heads of grown persons being often in a straight line from the nose to the top of the forehead. . . .

The robe of the women is like that worn by the men, except that it does not reach below the waist. Those most esteemed are made of strips of sea-otter skin, which being twisted are interwoven with silk-grass or the bark of the white cedar, in such a manner that the fur appears equally on both sides so as to form a soft and warm covering. The skin of the raccoon or beaver are also employed in the same way, though on other occasions these skins are simply dressed in the hair, and worn without further preparation. The garment which covers the body from the waist as low as the knee before and the thigh behind, is the tissue already described, and is made either of the bruised bark of white cedar, the twisted cords of silk-grass, or of flags and rushes. Neither leggings nor moccasins are ever used, the mildness of the climate not requiring them as a security from the weather, and their being so much in the water rendering them an incumbrance. The only covering for the head is a hat made of bear-grass and the bark of cedar, interwoven in a conic form, with a knob of the same shape at the top. It has no brim, but is held on the head by a string passing under the chin, and tied to a small rim inside of the hat. The colours are generally black and white only, and these are made into squares, triangles, and sometimes rude figures of canoes and seamen harpooning whales. This is all the usual dress of females; but if the weather be unusually severe, they add a vest formed of skins like the robe, tied behind, without any shoulder-straps to keep it up. As this vest covers the body from the armpits to the waist, it conceals the breasts, but on all other occasions they are suffered to remain loose and exposed, and present, in old women especially, a most disgusting appearance.

The Clatsops and other nations at the mouth of the Columbia have visited us with great freedom, and we have endeavoured to cultivate their intimacy, as well for the purpose of acquiring information as to leave behind us impressions favourable to our country. In their intercourse with us they are very loquacious and inquisitive. Having acquired much of their language, we are enabled with the assistance of gestures to hold conversations with great ease. We find them inquisitive and loquacious, with understandings by no means deficient in acuteness, and with very retentive memories; and though fond of feasts, and generally cheerful, they are never gay. Everything they see excites their attention and inquiries, but having been accustomed to see the whites, nothing appeared to give them more astonishment than the air-gun. To all our inquiries they answer with great intelligence, and the conversation rarely slackens, since there is a constant discussion of the events and trade and politics in the little but active circle of Killamucks, Clatsops, Cathlamahs, Wahkiacums, and Chinnooks. Among themselves, the conversation generally turns on the subjects of trade or smoking or eating or connexion with females, before whom this last is spoken of with a familiarity which would be in the highest degree indecent if custom had not rendered it inoffensive.

COMMENTS ON THE POSITION OF WOMEN AND OLD PEOPLE

The treatment of women is often considered as the standard by which the moral qualities of the savages are to be estimated. Our own observation, however, induced us to think that the importance of the female in savage life has no necessary relation to the virtues of the men, but is regulated wholly by their capacity to be useful. The Indians whose treatment of the females is mildest, and who pay most deference to their opinions, are by no means the most distinguished for their virtues; nor is this deference attended by any increase of attachment, since they are equally willing with the most brutal husband to prostitute their wives to strangers. On the other hand, the tribes among whom the women are very much debased possess the loftiest sense of honour, the greatest liberality, and all the good qualities of which their situation demands the exercise. Where the women can aid in procuring subsistence for the tribe they are treated with more equality, and their importance is proportioned to the share which they take in that labour; while in countries where subsistence is chiefly procured by the exertions of the men, the women are considered and treated as burdens. Thus, among the Clatsops and Chinnooks, who live upon fish and roots, which the women are equally expert with the men in procuring, the former have a rank and influence very rarely found among Indians. The females are permitted to speak freely before the men, to whom indeed they sometimes address themselves in a tone of authority. On many subjects their judgments and opinions are respected, and in matters of trade their advice is generally asked and pursued. The labours of the family, too, are shared almost equally. The men collect wood and make fires, assist in cleansing the fish, make the houses, canoes, and wooden utensils; and whenever strangers are to be entertained, or a great feast prepared, the meats are cooked and served up by the men. The peculiar province of the female is to collect roots and to manufacture the various articles which are formed of rushes, flags, cedar-bark, and bear-grass; but the management of the canoes, and many of the occupations which elsewhere devolves wholly on the female, are here common to both sexes.

The observation with regard to the importance of females applies with equal force to the treatment of old men. Among tribes who subsist by hunting, the labours of the chase, and the wandering existence to which that occupation condemns them, necessarily throws the burden of procuring provisions on the active young men. As soon, therefore, as a man is unable to pursue the chase he begins to withdraw something from the precarious supplies of the tribe. Still, however, his counsels may compensate his want of activity; but in the next stage of infirmity, when he can no longer travel from camp to camp, as the tribe roams about for subsistence, he is then found to be a heavy burden. In this situation they are abandoned among the Sioux, Assiniboins, and the hunting tribes on the Missouri. As they are setting out for some new excursion, where the old man is unable to follow, his children or nearest relations place before him a piece of meat and some water, and telling him that he has lived long enough, that it is now time for him to go home to his relations, who could take better care of him than his friends on earth, leave him, without remorse, to perish when his little supply is exhausted. The same custom is said to prevail among the Minnetarees, Ahnahawas, and Ricaras, when they are attended by old men on their hunting excursions. Yet, in their villages, we saw no want of kindness to old men. On the contrary, probably because in villages the means of more abundant subsistence renders such cruelty unnecessary, the old people appeared to be treated with attention, and some of their feasts, particularly the buffaloe dances, were intended chiefly as a contribution for the old and infirm.

PART II

TRYING TO COPE WITH THE INDIANS

Introduction

by Ruth L. Bunzel

SETTLING INTO THE NEW COUNTRY MEANT COMING TO TERMS IN ONE way or another with its former inhabitants. Missionaries and traders, hunters and business men, government officials and naturalists, and just ordinary men concerned about the fate of the Indian peoples and cultures had to cope in one way or another with the problem of sharing this continent with these people, so strange, so apparently unassimilable. In this great land, so sparsely populated, surely there was room for everyone. The Indian had only to learn how to make better use of the land and its resources.

In contrast to the explorers, who simply observed, these later comers were all *doing* something to the Indians—baptizing them or teaching them or trading with them or moving them around from one part of the country to another, negotiating treaties or preventing the signing of treaties. Many of the doers also left records of their experiences, formal reports of their activities such as the *Jesuit Relations,* advice (unsolicited) to government officials (Adair), and the first systematic ethnographies written by dedicated amateurs like Morgan and Grinnell.

BERNARDINO DE SAHAGÚN

(1499?-1590)

*Fray Bernardino de Sahagún first arrived in Mexico in 1529, eight years
after the conquest and destruction of the ancient Aztec capital. Little is
known of his early life except that he left the University of Salamanca to
join the Franciscan Order. He was sent to New Spain in 1529 and remained
there until his death in the Franciscan Convent in Mexico City in 1590.*

*On arriving in Mexico he immediately learned Nahuatl, the language of
the people among whom he was to spend his life.*

The work that occupied him fully until 1578 was his monumental General History of the Things of New Spain. *During most of these years he
taught in the Convent of Tlatelulco where he could command the assistance
of young bilingual students. He had with him in the pueblo of Tepeopulco,
during the period of intensive work, some ten or twelve Indians well versed
in ancient lore, who had lived under the Aztec empire before the conquest. The old men dictated texts in Nahuatl which he wrote out and had
interpreted by his young Spanish-speaking informants, former students of
the Convent. Although he had mastered the Nahuatl language, he nevertheless used interpreters. He also had his old men write out portions of
the text in Nahuatl hieroglyphs and had these interpreted.*

*After many trials and obstructions, orders given and rescinded, the
twelve books of the* History *were completed and a copy of the manuscript
was sent to Spain. In the end Sahagún's subvention was withdrawn and
his copyists taken away, as being "inconsistent with the Franciscan ideal
of poverty," and Sahagún, then over seventy years old, had to make the
final copy, the eighth, in his own hand.*

*The cause of Sahagún's troubles was Book IX, "The History of the
Conquest," told in Nahuatl by old men who had lived through it and embodying their version of events and their feelings about them. Sahagún was
ordered to "correct" this chapter which, being under Orders, he did. The
final copy of this book was accordingly written in three columns: the
original Nahuatl version, the "corrected" version in Nahuatl, and the
Spanish translation of the "corrected" version. The original version still
exists, but in Nahuatl only. Thus the pious monk fulfilled his vows of
obedience and yet maintained his integrity as a scientist.*

*The history of this great work after it was sent to Spain is even more
extraordinary than its previous history. As of today, nearly four hundred
years after it was finished, no complete version of Sahagún's work has
ever been published in any language. Only one copy of the original manuscript is known to exist, the one in the Laurentian Library in Florence
(The Florentine Codex). A microfilm copy is in the School of American
Research in New Mexico. The Nahuatl and English edition, a joint production by Arthur A. O. Anderson of the School of American Research
and Charles E. Dibble of the Univesrity of Utah will be, when finished, the
first complete translation.*

*(The most important work of the other great anthropologist of that era,
Bartolomé de las Casas, "The Apostle of the Indians," who pleaded the
cause of the Indians in the court of Spain and who believed in the psychic
unity of man and the evolution of culture, shared a similar fate. His
Historia Apologética de los Indios, in which he developed these ideas, has
never been translated into English, and the Spanish edition is almost
inaccessible and is but little read.)*

*Sahagún was undoubtedly one of the great anthropologists of all times.
His method of procedure—using native texts dictated or written out by
Nahuatl-speaking informants—was to be rediscovered three hundred years
after his death.*

*We would like to know more about what manner of man Sahagún was.
He had a disciplined mind; he was able to bring order into the exuberance
of Aztec ceremonialism and was able to make the complexities of the
calendar comprehensible. Of himself he says nothing in his writings; we
can only infer his patience, humility and integrity from the events of his
life and from his work and from the devotion of his students to him. In
1590, after 60 years of living and studying among the Aztecs, he died and
was buried in the Franciscan Convent in Mexico City.—R.L.B.*

Aztec Beliefs and Practices

THE FEAST OF TEZCATLIPOCA

THIS FEAST WAS THE MOST IMPORTANT OF ALL THE FEASTS. IT WAS LIKE
Easter, and fell near Easter Sunday—a few days after. This youth, reared
as hath been said, was very comely, and chosen from many. He had long
hair—down to the waist.

From Sahagún, *General History of the Things of New Spain* (Florentine Codex),
translated from the Aztec into English by Arthur J. O. Anderson and Charles E.
Dibble (Santa Fe, N. M.: School of American Research and the University of Utah,
1955). Selections from Pt. III, bk. II; Pt. VIII, bk. VII; Pt. V, bk. IV; Pt. VIII, bk.
VIII.

When, on this feast, they slew the young man who had been reared for [the rôle], they at once produced another, who was to die after one year. He walked everywhere in the town finely arrayed with flowers in his hand, and with people who accompanied him. He greeted with good grace those whom he met. All knew that this one was the likeness of Tezcatlipoca, and they bowed before him and worshiped him whenever they met him.

Twenty days before this feast came, they gave this young man four comely young women reared for [the part], with whom for all the twenty days, he had carnal relations. And they changed his array when they gave him these young women: [they] clipped his hair like a war captain and gave him more finery [even] braver [than what he had had].

Five days before he was to die, they celebrated feasts for him and banquets, in cool and pleasant places. Many of the leading men accompanied him. On the arrival of the day he was to die, they took him to a pyramid or sanctuary which they called Tlacochcalco; and, before he arrived there, at a place which they called Tlapitzauayan, the women withdrew and left him. Arrived at the place where they were to kill him, he ascended the steps himself; on each of them he shattered one of the flutes which he had played as he walked, all during the year. When he had reached the summit [of the pyramid], they threw him upon the sacrificial stone; they tore out his heart; they brought down the body, carrying it in their hands; below, they cut the head off and ran through it [the crosspiece of the skull rack] which is called *tzompantli*. Many other ceremonies were enacted in this feast, which are set forth at length in their account.

CEREMONY FOR MAKING THE NEW FIRE

When [came] the time of the binding of our years, always they gradually neared and approached [the year] Two Reed. This is to say: they then reached and ended [a period of] fifty-two years. For at that time [these years] were piled up, added one to another, and brought together; wherefore the thirteen-year [cycles] had four times made a circle, as hath been made known. Hence was it said that then were tied and bound our years, and that once again the years were newly laid hold of. When it was evident that the years lay ready to burst into life, everyone took hold of them, so that once more would start forth—once again—another [period of] fifty-two years. Then [the two cycles] might proceed to reach one hundred and four years. It was called "One Old Age" when twice they had made the round, when twice the times of binding the years had come together.

Behold what was done when the years were bound—when was reached the time when they were to draw the new fire, when now its count was accomplished. First they put out fires everywhere in the country round. And the statues, hewn in either wood or stone, kept in each man's home and regarded as gods, were all cast into the water. Also [were] these [cast away]—the pestles and the [three] hearth stones [upon which the cooking pots rested]; and everywhere there was much sweeping—there was sweeping very clean. Rubbish was thrown out; none lay in any of the houses.

And when they drew the new fire, they drew it there at Uixachtlan, at midnight, when the night divided in half. They drew it upon the breast of a captive, and it was a well-born one on whose breast [the priest] bored the fire drill. And when a little [fire] fell, when it took flame, then speedily [the priest] slashed open the breast of the captive, seized his heart, and quickly cast it there into the fire. Thus he revived and fed the fire. And the body of [the captive] all came to an end in the flames. And those who drew fire were exclusively the priests, the fire priests, the devout. Of the fire priest of Copulco, who was experienced, it was his office to draw, to drill, the new fire.

At nightfall, from here in Mexico, they departed. All the fire priests were arranged in order, arrayed in and wearing the garb of the gods. Each one represented and was the likeness of perhaps Quetzalcoatl, or Tlaloc, etc., or whichever one he went representing. Very deliberatly, very stately, they proceeded, went spread out, and slowly moved. It was said: "They walk like gods." Thus, in deep night, they arrived there at Uixachtlan.

And the one who was the fire priest of Copulco, who drew new fire, then began there. With his hands he proceeded to bore continuously his fire drill; he went about making trials with his drill, the firemaker.

And when it came to pass that night fell, all were frightened and filled with dread. Thus was it said: it was claimed that if fire could not be drawn, then [the sun] would be destroyed forever; all would be ended; there would evermore be night. Nevermore would the sun come forth. Night would prevail forever, and the demons of darkness would descend, to eat men.

Hence everyone ascended the terraces; all went upon the housetops. None remained in their houses, on the ground below. And women with child put on masks of maguey leaves and took up their maguey-leaf masks. [They] placed [the women] in granaries, for they were looked upon with fear. It was said and claimed that if, truly, the new fire were not drawn, these also would eat men; [for] they would be changed into fierce beasts.

And the small children they likewise masked with maguey leaves. In truth, none [of them] could sleep, or close, shut, or [even] half-close their eyes. From time to time their mothers and fathers were [there with them]; they kept waking them, punching and nudging them, calling out to them. They woke, cuffed, and nudged them. Because if they were to sleep—it was thought—they would turn into mice; they would become mice.

Hence was heed paid only one thing; there was unwavering attention and expectation as all remained facing, with neck craned, the summit of Uixachtecatl. Everyone was apprehensive, waiting until, in time, the new fire might be drawn—until, in good time, [a flame] would burst forth and shine out. And when a little came forth, when it took fire, lit, and blazed, then it flared and burst into flames, and was visible everywhere. It was seen from afar.

Then all the people quickly cut their ears, and spattered the blood repeatedly toward the fire. Although [a child] still lay in the cradle, they also cut his ears, took his blood, and spattered it [toward] the fire. Thus, it was said, everyone performed a penance.

Then [the priests] slashed open [the captive's] breast. In his breast [cavity] the new fire was drawn. They opened the breast of the captive with a flint knife called *ixquauac*. Etc.

And then everyone—the priests and fire priests—took the fire from there. [Having come] from all directions, the fire priests of Mexico had been sent there, charged with the task, as well as those who had come from distant [places] everywhere—messengers and runners. For these were all only chosen ones, strong warriors, valiant men, picked as best; the fleet, the swift, who could run like the wind. Because through them they could quickly have fire come to their cities.

First, the fire brand was prepared and adorned. It was called *tlepilli*. And this the fire priests brought. Before [doing] anything else, they took it up, direct, to the top of the temple [pyramid], where was kept the image of Uitzilopochtli, and placed it in the fire holder. Then they scattered and strewed white incense [over it]. And then they came down, and, also before [doing] anything further, they brought and took it direct to the priests' house, the place named Mexico. Later, this was dispersed, and fires were started everywhere in each priests' house and each tribal temple; whereupon it went everywhere to each of the young men's houses. At that time all of the common folk came to the flame, hurled themselves at it, and blistered themselves as fire was taken. When thus the fire had been quickly distributed everywhere among them, each one laid a fire, and was quieted in his heart.

Then, at this time, all renewed their household goods, the men's array, and the women's array, the mats—the mats of large, fat reeds,—and the seats. All was new which was spread about, as well as the hearth stones and the pestles. Also at this time [the men] were newly dressed and wrapped in capes. A woman—[such as she] dressed newly in their new skirts and shifts.

Thus it was said that truly the year newly started. There was much happiness and rejoicing. And they said: "For thus it is ended; thus sickness and famine have left us." Then incense was offered; [quail] were decapitated, and incense was offered. They grasped this incense ladle, and raised it in dedication to the four directions in the courtyard. Then they cast it into the hearth. Thus was incense offered.

Thereupon amaranth seed cakes overspread with honey were eaten.

Then all were bidden to fast, and [it was ordered] that no one should drink
from the time that it was completely light until it came to be considered
midday. And when noon came, then captives and ceremonially bathed
ones died. Then all rejoiced and there was feasting. Then once again fires
were newly laid and placed.

THE MEANING OF THE DAYS

Here beginneth the count of each day. Just as each week was reckoned,
so each of the thirteen-day periods went taking its place until one year
had passed. Once more at its start began the count of each day.

The first day count was named One Crocodile. It was the very beginning
and precise starting point of all the day counts, whereby began, continued,
and came to an end the year [of 260 days].

It became as the leader of this group of thirteen days which belonged
with it: Two [Wind], Three House, Four Lizard, Five Serpent, Six Death,
Seven Deer, Eight Rabbit, Nine Water, Ten Dog, Eleven Monkey, Twelve
Grass, and Thirteen Reed.

These various days,[1] as it was said, all were good. He who was then
born a nobleman, it was stated, would be a lord, a ruler; he would prosper;
he would be rich and wealthy. And if a commoner were then born, he
would be a brave warrior—a valiant chief, esteemed, honored, and great.
He would always eat. And if a woman were then born, she would also
prosper and be rich. She would have drink and food available. She would
have food for others to eat; she would invite others to feast. She would
be respectful. She would be visited by others; she would await them with
drink and food, with which to revive and refresh the spirits and bodies of
those who lived in misery on earth, who, as they slept so they awoke—
the destitute old men and women, and orphans; the foresaken; and all
would be realized and come to pass that was undertaken; nothing would
fail; of her fatigue and effort, nothing would be in vain. Successful would
be her dealings around the market place, in the place of business; it was as
if it would sprinkle, shower, and rain her wares upon her.

And furthermore they said that even though favorable was the day
sign on which he had been born, if he did not strictly perform his penances, if he took not good thought, if he did not accept the reprimands
and punishment meted out to him, the punishment with which he was
punished and the correction with which he was corrected, the exhorta-
tions of the old men and the old women; if he became bad and perverse
and followed not the way of righteousness, succeeded in nothing, and en-

---

[1] The 260-day count is still used for magic and divination by the Highland Maya
of Guatemala and Chiapas. R. Bunzel: *Chichicastenango*. Publ. American Ethnological Society, 1951.—R.L.B.

tirely by his own acts brought himself to ruin, despised himself, brought harm to himself, failed, lost through his own neglect, gave up, and endangered that which might be his good fortune,— his reward, and his lot: then he tarnished, polluted, and ruined with debauchery his birthright. . . .

And of anyone who had gained merit and reward being then born, his fathers and mothers said: "Upon a good day sign hath he been born and created and come forth on earth; he hath arrived upon the earth on [the day sign] One Crocodile. Let him be bathed."

Whereupon they gave him a name. They called him Cipac. Or else, they gave him the name of another one of his grandparents. Etc.

And, on the other hand, if it were the wish [of the parents], perchance they passed over the days; perchance they settled upon still another day for him to be bathed. For One Crocodile bore with it all favorable day signs.

THE EDUCATION OF A PRINCE

And here is described the rearing of the sons of those who were lords, and of all the princes, who were the sons of lords and noblemen.

Their mothers and fathers nourished and raised them, or nursemaids raised them while they were still small children.

And when they could run, when they were perhaps six years old, thereupon [the boys] went [forth] to play. Their pages—perhaps two, or three —accompanied them that they might amuse them. [The child's] father or mother charged these [pages] that [the boy] not behave ill, that he not taint himself with vice, as he went along the streets.

And also they took great care that he should converse fittingly with others—that his conversation should be proper; that he should respect and show reverence to others—[when] perchance he somewhere might chance to meet a judge, or a leading militia officer, or a seasoned warrior, or someone of lesser rank; or a revered old man, or a respected old woman; or someone who was poor. He should greet him and bow humbly. He said: "Come hither, my beloved grandfather; let me bow before thee." And the old one who had been greeted then said: "O my beloved grandson, O precious stone, O precious feather, thou has shown me favor. May it go well with thee."

And when the young boy thus saluted others, they praised him highly for it. They rejoiced greatly over it; they were joyful because of it. They said: "How will this beloved child be, if he shall live? He will in sooth be a nobleman. Mayhap his reward will be something [great]."

And when he was already maybe ten, twelve, or thirteen years old, they placed him in the priests' house; they delivered him into the hands of the fire priests and [other] priests, that he might be reared there, corrected, and instructed; that he might live an upright life. They constrained him to do the penances, setting fir branches [on the city altars] at night, or there where they went to place the fir branches on mountain tops—there where sacrifices were made at midnight. Or else he entered the song house; they left him in the hands of the masters of the youths. They charged him with the sweeping, or with dancing and song—with all which was concerned with the performance of penances.

And when he was already fifteen years old, then he took up arms; or, reaching twenty years of age, then he went forth to war. First [his parents] summoned those who were seasoned warriors. They gave them to eat and to drink, and they gave gifts to all the seasoned warriors. They gave them large, cotton capes, or carmine colored breech clouts, or capes painted with designs. And then they besought the seasoned warriors; in just the same way as hath been told above, so they entreated them.

And then they took him to the wars. The seasoned warriors went taking great care of him, lest somewhere he might be lost. And they taught him well how to guard himself with a shield; how one fought; how a spear was fended off with a shield. And when a battle was joined, when already there was fighting and perhaps already captives were being taken, they taught him well and made him see how he might take a captive. Perhaps then he took a captive with the aid of others, or he [alone] could take one. For truly it was well seen to that many men become brave warriors.

And when captives were being taken, then at once couriers, of marriageable age, quickly went forth, called victory messengers, who speedily went to inform Moctezuma.

And when the victory messengers had come to arrive, then they quickly entered into the presence of Moctezuma and said to him: "O our lord, O my youth, pay thy debt and thy service [to the god]; for the omen of evil, Uitzilopochtli, hath shown favor and been gracious. For they have pierced the rampart of men dexterous in arms of the city against which they have gone. . . .

And there in battle was when captives were taken. When it had come to pass that they went against and conquered the city, then the captives were counted, there, in wooden cages: how many had been taken by Tenochtitlan, how many had been taken by Tlatilulco, and by the people of the swamp lands and the people of the dry lands everywhere. The captives were examined [to determine] how many groups of four hundred were formed.

Those who counted were the generals and the commanding generals. And then they sent messengers here to Mexico. Those who were sent as messengers were seasoned warriors, who informed Moctezuma of the great veracity of the four-hundred count. They brought word of how many groups of four hundred had been made captive.

And then they declared to him how many of the noblemen had won their reward for having made captives; that haply a number [of them] had had their hair shorn as seasoned warriors, or that some [had been made] leaders of the youths. When Moctezuma heard this, he rejoiced exceedingly, because his noblemen had taken captives. . . .

And if war should be proclaimed against Atlixco, or Uexotzinco, and if there once again they took captives, they won much glory thereby; Moctezuma accorded them great honor for it. For his noblemen had taken captives, and had gained repute, and had reached the station of nobility— the estate of the eagle and the ocelot warriors. From there they came to rule, to govern cities; and at that time they seated them with [the nobility], and they might eat with Moctezuma.

PRAYER TO TEZCATLIPOCA BEFORE GOING TO WAR

Our most loving and merciful Lord, our protector and defender, invisible and impalpable god through whose will and wisdom we rule and govern and beneath whose reign we live! Lord of Battles, it is certain and assured that our enemies begin to prepare and order themselves for a great war. The God of War opens his mouth with hunger to devour the blood of the many who will die in this war, because there is need to delight the heart of the Sun and the God of the Earth who is called Tlatecutli, because they wish to give food and drink to the Gods of Heaven and Earth, to regale them with the flesh and blood of the men who are destined to die in this war. Already the Gods of Heaven and Earth have seen which will be the ones to conquer and which will be conquered; which are those who will kill and which are those who will be killed; whose blood will be drunk and whose flesh will be eaten. This is not revealed to the noble mothers and fathers of those who are to die; likewise it is not revealed to their wives and relatives, to the mothers who cared for them when they were children, who gave them the milk with which they grew, and their fathers who endured much labor in seeking the things necessary to eat and drink, to wear upon their bodies and their feet, in order to bring them to the condition in which they now are. Indeed, they do not know the fate of the sons whom they reared with so much labor—whether they will be taken captives or be slain upon the field of battle.

Grant, furthermore, our Lord, that those noble ones who die in the course of war may be received peacefully and joyously by the Sun and the Earth, who are the father and mother of all, and the heart of love. For assuredly you do not deceive us in what you do—in loving whose who die in war, for indeed it is for that that you sent them into this world, in order that with their flesh and blood they may give to eat to the Sun and the Earth.

Do not be enraged anew, Lord, at these in the pursuance of war; for in the place where these shall die many have already died, honorable and noble lords and captains and valiant men. Because the nobility and honor of the noble and honorable ones in the exercise of war has already been

revealed and made manifest. Grant, therefore, Lord, that all may understand the worth and value of each one, that he may be cherished and
valued like a precious jewel and a rich plume.

Most merciful God, Lord of Battles, Emperor of the World, whose name
is Tezcatlipoca, invisible and impalpable one, we beseech you that whomsoever you may permit to be killed in this war may be received in the house
of the Sun, that he may be received with love and honor in Heaven, and
may be given his rightful place and rank among the valiant and famous
heroes who have died in battle—with Sr. Quitziquatzin, Sr. Maciehcatzin,
Tlacavepatzin, Yxtlicenhavac, and all the other valiant and famous men
who have died in war before these, who even now are giving delight and
joy to our Lord the Sun, with whom they rejoice and are rich in eternal
joy and wealth, which will be without end. Now perpetually they drink the
sweetness of the sweetest flowers and those most delicious to taste. This is
the pleasure of the valiant and honorable heroes who die in war. And so
they are drunk with joy; they have no cares, nor do they care to keep count
of the days and the nights or of the years and the seasons, for their joy
and happiness is without end and flowers which they sip will never wither
nor will their sweetness depart. Longing for this, the men of good counte-
nance strive to die honorably.

Finally, that which we beseech your Majesty, for you are our most
merciful Lord, our invincible Emperor, that you will grant that those who
shall die in this war be received with hearts of mercy and love by our
Father the Sun, our Mother the Earth, for you alone live and reign and
are our most merciful God. And we pray not only for the leaders, the
chiefs and nobles, but also for all the common soldiers whose hearts
are afflicted, and who call upon your presence asking that you do not hold
at naught their lives, for they face the enemy without fear and with the
desire of death. Grant them, therefore, some small portion of what they
desire, which is some repose and rest in this life, or, if they are not to
prosper in this world, let them be marked as the servants and officials of
the Sun, to give meat and drink to the Gods of Heaven and Earth.

And as for those who are charged with the government of the republic,
or to be *Tlacatecatl* or *tlacochicalatl,* give them such virtue that they may
be fathers and mothers of warriors, and those who go about in the fields
and the forests, who climb the peaks and descend into the ravines, and
those who hold in their hands the right of judgment over criminals and
enemies, and also those who distribute your dignities, the offices and arms
of war, the shields and other arms and insignia, who bestow the right to
wear helmets and plumes in the hair, the jewels for the ears and lip, the
bracelets and belts of gold, the collars and anklets, and who decree the
new pattern of the robes and mantles which each may wear. They are the
ones who give permission to wear precious jewels—jades and turquoises—
and to wear rich plumes and embroideries, and collars and jewels of gold—

all things that are rare and precious and which are given from your wealth and which you bestow as a mark of favor upon those who perform feats of valor and heroism in war. We pray also that you may grant the favor of your largesse to more lowly soldiers; grant them some covering for their bodies and good lodging in this world, make them valiant and intrepid, remove all cowardice from their hearts so that not only may they greet death with joyousness—for that is what they desire and hold sweet and good—but that they may fear neither swords nor arrows, but rather hold them as something sweet and gentle, as flowers and sweet confections, that they may not be frightened or startled by the cries and shouts of their enemies. Deal thus with them as with your friends.

And, in accordance with your greatness, Lord of Battles, upon whose desire victory depends, who will aid whom you wish and forsake whom you wish, and need take counsel with no one, we beseech your Majesty: may you disregard and confound our enemies, so that they may rush into our arms and without injuring us fall into our hands and the hands of our warriors and fighters, who endure poverty and labor. O our Lord, regard your realm, for you are God and all-powerful, you ordain all things and understand and dispose all things; you ordain whether this your republic will be rich and prosperous and exalted and honored and famed among nations for the exercise of arms and valor in war; and whether or not those shall live and prosper who now bear arms in the service of the Sun. And if in the time ahead you may deem it best that they die in war, may they go to the house of the Sun among the famous and valiant youths who live there and who have died in battle.

> (*Translated here for the first time by Ruth L. Bunzel
> from the Spanish text in Edward King, Viscount
> Kingsborough,* Antiquities of Mexico, London,
> Aglio, 1830-1848, 9 vols.)

The Jesuit Relations

PAUL LE JEUNE
(1592-1664)

JACQUES MARQUETTE
(1637-1675)

MATURIN LE PETIT
(1693-1739)

The first Jesuits arrived in the New World with Champlain in 1632, and the care of souls in New France became their responsibility. Their missions along the St. Lawrence, the Great Lakes and the Mississippi became centers for exploration and trade. The missions at Michillimackinac (on the strait between Lake Huron and Lake Michigan in Huron country) and Kaskaskia (on the Mississippi at the mouth of the Kaskaskia River in Illinois country) were the most famous. From these outposts explorers and voyageurs *struck out into the dark wilderness; to them they returned months or years later, weary, often ill, their numbers reduced, to enjoy once more such rude comforts as the frontier offered, the companionship of their own people and the solace of religion.*

The labors of the Jesuits among the tribes to which they were sent are best told in their own words. Each year the head of the Jesuit Order in New France received from each of the missions under his jurisdiction a report of the year's activities, and such information concerning the native people as had been gathered by the industrious fathers. These were gathered together into the Relation *for that year and forwarded to the mother house in Paris, together with sundry other documents relating to Jesuit activities in New France—special reports, letters from members of the Society visiting various missions, etc. In Paris the* Relations *were promptly published by a French printer. The seventy-three volumes, covering the years 1601-1791, comprise the basic sources for the history of that period and the ethnography of the area, which included such key tribes as the Iroquois, the Montagnais, the Huron, the Ottawa, the Ojibwa, and, in the later period, the Illinois, the Arkansas, and the Natchez.*

Le Jeune was the head of Jesuit missions at Quebec during the early years of exploration. His Relations *are compilations from reports from*

58

outlying stations, and include his own researches. They contain the fullest and earliest accounts of the Northern tribes. In his own investigations Le Jeune, like Sahagún, used Indian converts to interpret and explain Indian life, while he himself wrestled with the complexities of the Algonkian language. In his accounts the native people are not "savages" or "Indians" but Montagnais, Huron, or Iroquois, each tribe having its characteristic way of life. Out of this multipilicity the concept of culture was beginning to emerge.

French settlement of the interior of the American continent did not strike inland over mountain trails as in New England but followed the great inland waterways. Jacques Marquette's name is linked with the exploration and settlement of the Mississippi as Champlain's is with the St. Lawrence. Marquette came to America as a missionary in 1666. In the nine years before his untimely death he left enduring marks upon the New World. He founded the Jesuit Mission at Sault Ste. Marie on Lake Superior, then the uttermost wilderness, built the chapel and mission at Michillimackinac, the center of the fur trade for two centuries, and from there embarked on his greatest enterprise, the exploration with Louis Joliet of the great river which visiting Indians from the west had described. Leaving Michillimackinac in the spring of 1673, they went up Lake Michigan and Green Bay, ascended the Fox River through Winnebago country to the portage that took them to the Wisconsin, down the Wisconsin to the Mississippi. They descended the Mississippi by canoe to the mouth of the Arkansas, a journey of over 2,000 miles, before returning to their base. Wherever Marquette went he made friends with the Indians, whose cultures he described with a sympathy rare among the Jesuit missionaries. While visiting the Illinois he had a chance to see the "Calumet Dance," portions of which he describes. This beautiful ceremony, widely distributed among the Indians of the Southern Plains, to which many early travelers allude, was never fully described until the 20th century when Alice Fletcher witnessed its performance by the Pawnee. (See p. 239.)

At the request of the Kaskaskia Indians Marquette returned the following year to found a mission among them. After conducting an Easter service at the new shrine, Marquette, ill with dysentery, attempted to return to Michillimackinac, but died on the shore of Lake Michigan near the river that bears his name. The Mission at Kaskaskia remained the great center of Indian trade and communication on the Mississippi for two hundred years.

Le Petit was the head of the Jesuit Mission at New Orleans at the time of the Natchez revolt. The Natchez, before their destruction a proud and warlike tribe and a great power in the Lower Mississippi Valley, goaded

by the arrogance of the French commander rose one night and massacred French missionaries, traders, and settlers. Le Petit's account to his Superior of this tragic event begins with a systematic description of the religion, political organization and social structure of the Natchez tribe which he regarded as necessary background for an understanding of the situation.
—R.L.B.

PAUL LE JEUNE

(1592-1664)

Notes on the Northern Tribes

RELIGION OF THE ALGONQUAIN INDIANS

THEY BELIEVE THAT THERE ARE CERTAIN GENII OF LIGHT, OR GENII OF THE air, which they call *Khichikouai* from the word *Khichikou,* which means "light" or "the air." The Genii, or *Khichikouai,* are acquainted with future events, they see very far ahead; this is why the Savages consult them, not all [the savages] but certain jugglers, who know better than the others how to impose upon and amuse these people. I have chanced to be present when they consulted these fine Oracles, and here is what I have observed.

Towards nightfall, two or three young men erected a tent in the middle of our Cabin; they stuck six poles deep into the ground in the form of a circle, and to hold them in place they fastened to the tops of these poles a large ring, which completely encircled them; this done, they enclosed this Edifice with Castelognes, leaving the top of the tent open; it is all that a tall man can do to reach to the top of this round tower, capable of holding 5 or 6 men standing upright. This house made, the fires of the cabin are entirely extinguished, and the brands thrown outside, lest the flame frighten away the Genii or *Khichikouai,* who are to enter this tent; a young juggler slipped in from below, turning back, for this purpose, the covering which enveloped it, then replaced it when he had entered, for they must be very careful that there be no opening in this fine palace except from above. The juggler, having entered, began to moan softly, as if complaining; he shook the tent at first without violence; then becoming animated little by little, he commenced to whistle, in a hollow tone, and as if it came from afar; then to talk as if in a bottle; to cry like the owls of these countries, which it seems to me have stronger voices than those of France; then to howl

From *The Jesuit Relations and Allied Documents 1610-1791,* edited by R. G. Thwaites (Cleveland: The Burrows Brothers Company, 1897), "Le Jeune's *Relation of 1634,*" Vol. 6, pp. 163-173; 21-23.

and sing, constantly varying the tones; ending by these syllables, *ho ho, hi hi, gui gui, nioué,* and other similar sounds, disguising his voice so that it seemed to me I heard those puppets which showmen exhibit in France. Sometimes he spoke Montagnais, sometimes Algonquain, retaining always the Algonquain intonation, which, like the Provençal, is vivacious. At first, as I have said, he shook this edifice gently; but, as he continued to become more animated, he fell into so violent an ecstasy, that I thought he would break everything to pieces, shaking his house with so much force and violence, that I was astonished at a man having so much strength; for, after he had once begun to shake it, he did not stop until the consultation was over, which lasted about three hours. Whenever he would change his voice, the Savages would at first cry out, *moa, moa,* "listen, listen;" then, as an invitation to these Genii, they said to them, *Pitoukhecou, Pitoukhecou,* "enter, enter." At other times, as if they were replying to the howls of the juggler, they drew this aspiration from the depths of their chests, *ho, ho.* I was seated like the others, looking on at this wonderful mystery, forbidden to speak; but as I had not vowed obedience to them, I did not fail to intrude a little word into the proceedings. Sometimes I begged them to have pity on this poor juggler, who was killing himself in this tent; at other times I told them they should cry louder, for the Genii had gone to sleep.

Some of these Barbarians imagined that this juggler was not inside, that he had been carried away, without knowing where or how. Others said that his body was lying on the ground, and that his soul was up above the tent, where it spoke at first, calling these Genii, and throwing from time to time sparks of fire. Now to return to our consultation. The Savages having heard a certain voice that the juggler counterfeited, uttered a cry of joy, saying that one of these Genii had entered; then addressing themselves to him, they cried out, *Tepouachi, tepouachi,* "call, call;" that is, "call thy companions." Thereupon the juggler, pretending to be one of the Genii and changing his tone and his voice, called them. In the meantime our sorcerer, who was present, took his drum, and began to sing with the juggler who was in the tent, and the others answered. Some of the young men were made to dance, among others the Apostate, who did not wish to hear of it, but the sorcerer made him obey.

At last, after a thousand cries and howls, after a thousand songs, after having danced and thoroughly shaken this fine edifice, the Savages believing that the Genii or *Kichikouai* had entered, the sorcerer consulted them. He asked them about his health, (for he is sick), and about that of his wife, who was also sick. These Genii, or rather the juggler who counterfeited them, answered that, as to his wife, she was already dead, that it was all over with her. I could have said as much myself, for one needed not to be a prophet or a sorcerer to guess that, inasmuch as the poor creature was already struck with death; in regard to the sorcerer, they said that he would see the Spring. Now, knowing his disease,—which was a pain in the loins, or rather an infirmity resulting from his licentiousness and excesses, for he is vile to the last degree,—I said to him, seeing that he was otherwise healthy, and that he drank and ate very heartily, that he would not only see the spring but also the Summer, if some other accident did not overtake him, and I was not mistaken.

After these interrogations, these fine oracles were asked if there would soon be snow, if there would be much of it, if there would be Elks or Moose, and where they could be found. They answered, or rather the juggler, always disguising his voice, that they saw a little snow and some moose far away, without indicating the place, having the prudence not to commit themselves.

So this is what took place in this consultation, after which I wished to get hold of the juggler; but, as it was night, he made his exit from the tent and from our little cabin so swiftly, that he was outside almost before I was aware of it. He and all the other Savages, who had come from the other Cabins to these beautiful mysteries, having departed, I asked the Apostate if he was so simple as to believe that the Genii entered and spoke in this tent. He began to swear his belief, which he had lost and denied, that it was not the juggler who spoke, but these *Khichikouai* or Genii of the air, and my host said to me, "Enter thou thyself into the tent, and thou wilt see that thy body will remain below, and thy soul will mount on high." I did want to go in; but, as I was the only one of my party, I foresaw that they might commit some outrage upon me, and, as there were no witnesses there, they would boast that I had recognized and admired the truth of their mysteries.

Now I had a great desire to know the nature of these Genii; the Apostate knew nothing about them. The sorcerer, seeing that I was discovering his mines, and that I disapproved of his nonsense, did not wish to explain anything to me, so that I was compelled to make use of my wits. I allowed a few weeks to pass; then, springing this subject upon him, I spoke as if I admired his doctrine, saying to him that it was wrong to refuse me, since to all the questions which he asked me in regard to our belief, I answered him frankly and without showing any reluctance. At last he allowed himself to be won over by this flattery, and revealed to me the secrets of the school. Here is the fable which he recounted to me touching the nature and the character of these Genii.

Two Savages having consulted these Genii at the same time, but in two different tents, one of them, a very wicked man who had treacherously killed three men with his hatchet, was put to death by the Genii, who, crossing over into the tent of the other Savage to take his life, as well as that of his companion, were themselves surprised; for this juggler defended himself so well that he killed one of these *Khichikouai* or Genii; and thus it was found out how they were made, for this One remained in the place where he was killed. Then I asked him what was his form.

"He was as large as the fist," he replied; "his body was of stone, and rather long." I judged that he was cone-shaped, large at one end, and gradually becoming smaller towards the other. They believe that in this stone body there is flesh and blood, for the hatchet with which this Spirit was killed was bloody. I inquired if they had feet and wings, and was told they had not. "Then how," said I, "can they enter or fly into these tents, if they have neither feet nor wings?" The sorcerer began to laugh, saying in explanation, "In truth, this black robe has no sense." This is the way they pay me back when I offer some objections to something which they cannot answer.

As they made a great deal of the fire which this juggler threw out of his tent, I told them that our Frenchmen could throw it better than he could; for he only made a few sparks fly from some rotten wood which he carried with him, as I am inclined to think, and if I had had some resin I could have made the flames rise for them. They insisted that he entered this house without fire; but I had happened to see some one give him a red-hot coal which he asked to light his pipe.

So that is their belief touching the foundations of things good. What astonishes me is their ingratitude; for, although they believe that the Messou has restored the world, that Nipinoukhé and Pipounoukhe bring the seasons, that their Khichikouai teach them where to find Elks or Moose, and render them a thousand other good offices,—yet up to the present I have not been able to learn that they render them the slightest honor. I have only observed that, in their feasts, they occasionally throw a few spoonfuls of grease into the fire, pronouncing these words: *Papeouekou, Papeouekou;* "Make us find something to eat, make us find something to eat." I believe this prayer is addressed to these Genii, to whom they present this grease as the best thing they have in the world.

ON THE LANGUAGE OF THE MONTAGNAIS SAVAGES

I wrote last year that their language was very rich and very poor, full of abundance and full of scarcity, the latter appearing in a thousand different ways. All words for piety, devotion, virtue; all terms which are used to express the things of the other life; the language of Theologians, Philosophers, Mathematicians, and Physicians, in a word, of all learned men; all words which refer to the regulation and government of a city, Province, or Empire; all that concerns justice, reward and punishment; the names of an infinite number of arts which are in our Europe; of an infinite number of flowers, trees, and fruits; of an infinite number of animals, of thousands and thousands of contrivances, of a thousand beauties and riches, all these things are never found either in the thoughts or upon the lips of the Savages. As they have no true religion nor knowledge of the virtues, neither public authority nor government, neither Kingdom nor

Republic, nor sciences, nor any of those things of which I have just spoken, consequently all the expressions, terms, words, and names which refer to that world of wealth and grandeur must necessarily be absent from their vocabulary; hence the great scarcity. Let us now turn the tables and show that this language is fairly gorged with richness.

First, I find an infinite number of proper nouns among them, which I cannot explain in our french, except by circumlocutions.

Second, they have some Verbs which I call absolute, to which neither the Greeks, nor Latins, nor we ourselves, nor any language of Europe with which I am familiar, have anything similar. For example, the verb *Nimitison* means absolutely, "I eat," without saying what; for, if you determine the thing you eat, you have to use another Verb.

Third, they have different Verbs to signify an action toward an animate or toward an inanimate object; and yet they join with animate things a number of things that have no souls, as tobacco, apples, etc. Let us give some examples: "I see a man," *Niouapaman iriniou;* "I see a stone," *niouabatē*; but in Greek, in Latin, and in French the same Verb is used to express, "I see a man, a stone, or anything else." "I strike a dog," *ni noutinau attimou;* "I strike wood," *ninoutinen misticou.* This is not all; for, if the action terminates on several animate objects, another Verb has to be used,—"I see some men," *niouapamaoueth irinioueth, ninoutinaoueth attimoueth,* and so on with all the others.

In the fourth place, they have Verbs suitable to express an action which terminates on the person reciprocal, and others still which terminate on the things that belong to him; and we cannot use these Verbs, referring to other persons not reciprocal, without speaking improperly. I will explain myself. The Verb *nitaouin* means, "I make use of something;" *nitaouin agouniscouehon,* "I am using a hat;" but when I come to say, "I am using his hat," that is, the hat of the man of whom I speak, we must change the verb. . . .

JACQUES MARQUETTE

(1637-1675)

The Character and Customs of the Illinois

WHEN ONE SPEAKS THE WORD "ILINOIS," IT IS AS IF ONE SAID IN THEIR language, "the men,"—As if the other Savages were looked upon by them merely as animals. It must also be admitted that they have an air of humanity which we have not observed in the other nations that we have seen upon our route. The shortness Of my stay among Them did not allow me to secure all the Information that I would have desired; among all Their customs, the following is what I have observed.

They are divided into many villages, some of which are quite distant from that of which we speak, which is called peouarea.[1] This causes some difference in their language, which, on the whole, resembles allegonquin, so that we easily understood each other. They are of a gentle and tractable disposition; we Experienced this in the reception which they gave us. They have several wives, of whom they are Extremely jealous; they watch them very closely, and Cut off Their noses or ears when they misbehave. I saw several women who bore the marks of their misconduct. Their Bodies are shapely; they are active and very skillful with bows and arrows. They also use guns, which they buy from our savage allies who Trade with our french. They use them especially to inspire, through their noise and smoke, terror in their Enemies; the latter do not use guns, and have never seen any, since they live too Far toward the West. They are warlike, and make themselves dreaded by the Distant tribes to the south and west, whither they go to procure Slaves; these they barter, selling them at a high price to other Nations, in exchange for other Wares. Those very Distant Savages against whom they war have no Knowledge of Europeans; neither do they know anything of iron, or of Copper, and they have only stone

[1] Peoria.—R.L.B.

From *The Jesuit Relations and Allied Documents 1610-1791*, edited by R. G. Thwaites (Cleveland: The Burrows Brothers Company, 1897), "F. Marquette's First Voyage," Vol. 59, pp. 125-135.

Knives. When the Ilinois depart to go to war, the whole village must be notified by a loud Shout, which is uttered at the doors of their Cabins, the night and The Morning before their departure. The Captains are distinguished from the warriors by wearing red Scarfs. These are made, with considerable Skill, from the Hair of bears and wild cattle. They paint their faces with red ocher, great quantities of which are found at a distance of some days' journey from the village. They live by hunting, game being plentiful in that country, and on indian corn, of which they always have a good crop; consequently, they have never suffered from famine. They also sow beans and melons, which are Excellent, especially those that have red seeds. Their Squashes are not of the best; they dry them in the sun, to eat them during The winter and the spring. Their Cabins are very large, and are Roofed and floored with mats made of Rushes. They make all Their utensils of wood, and Their Ladles out of the heads of cattle, whose Skulls they know so well how to prepare that they use these ladles with ease for eating their sagamité.

They are liberal in cases of illness, and Think that the effect of the medicines administered to them is in proportion to the presents given to the physician. Their garments consist only of skins; the women are always clad very modestly and very becomingly, while the men do not take the trouble to Cover themselves. I know not through what superstition some Ilinois, as well as some Nadouess[2] while still young, assume the garb of women, and retain it throughout their lives. There is some mystery in this, For they never marry and glory in demeaning themselves to do everything that the women do. They go to war, however, but can use only clubs, and not bows and arrows, which are the weapons proper to men. They are present at all the juggleries, and at the solemn dances in honor of the Calumet; at these they sing, but must not dance. They are summoned to the Councils, and nothing can be decided without their advice. Finally, through their profession of leading an Extraordinary life, they pass for Manitous,—That is to say, for Spirits,—or persons of Consequence.

There remains no more, except to speak of the Calumet. There is nothing more mysterious or more respected among them. Less honor is paid to the Crowns and scepters of Kings than the Savages bestow upon this. It seems to be the God of peace and of war, the Arbiter of life and of death. It has but to be carried upon one's person, and displayed, to enable one to walk safely through the midst of Enemies—who, in the hottest of the Fight, lay down Their arms when it is shown. For That reason, the Ilinois gave me one, to serve as a safeguard among all the Nations through whom I had to pass during my voyage. There is a Calumet for peace, and one for war, which are distinguished solely by the Color of the feathers with which they are adorned; Red is a sign of war. They also use it to

[2] The Sioux.—R.L.B.

put an end to Their disputes, to strengthen Their alliances, and to speak to Strangers. It is fashioned from a red stone, polished like marble, and bored in such a manner that one end serves as a receptacle for the tobacco, while the other fits into the stem; this is a stick two feet long, as thick as an ordinary cane, and bored through the middle. It is ornamented with the heads and necks of various birds, whose plumage is very beautiful. To these they also add large feathers,—red, green, and other colors,—wherewith the whole is adorned. They have a great regard for it, because they look upon it as the calumet of the Sun; and, in fact, they offer it to the latter to smoke when they wish to obtain a calm, or rain, or fine weather. They scruple to bathe themselves at the beginning of Summer, or to eat fresh fruit, until after they have performed the dance, which they do as follows:

The Calumet dance,[3] which is very famous among these peoples, is performed solely for important reasons; sometimes to strengthen peace, or to unite themselves for some great war; at other times, for public rejoicing. Sometimes they thus do honor to a Nation who are invited to be present; sometimes it is danced at the reception of some important personage, as if they wished to give him the diversion of a Ball or a Comedy. In Winter, the ceremony takes place in a Cabin; in Summer, in the open fields. When the spot is selected, it is completely surrounded by trees, so that all may sit in the shade afforded by their leaves, in order to be protected from the heat of the Sun. A large mat of rushes, painted in various colors, is spread in the middle of the place, and serves as a carpet upon which to place with honor the God of the person who gives the Dance; for each has his own god, which they call their Manitou. This is a serpent, a bird, or other similar thing, of which they have dreamed while sleeping, and in which they place all their confidence for the success of their war, their fishing, and their hunting. Near this Manitou, and at its right, is placed the Calumet in honor of which the feast is given; and all around it a sort of trophy is made, and the weapons used by the warriors of those Nations are spread, namely: clubs, war-hatchets, bows, quivers, and arrows.

Everything being thus arranged, and the hour of the Dance drawing near, those who have been appointed to sing take the most honorable place under the branches; these are the men and women who are gifted with the best voices, and who sing together in perfect harmony. Afterward, all come to take their seats in a circle under the branches; but each one, on arriving, must salute the Manitou. This he does by inhaling the smoke, and blowing it from his mouth upon the Manitou, as if he were offering to it incense. Every one, at the outset, takes the Calumet in a respectful manner, and, supporting it with both hands, causes it to dance

[3] The Pipe Ceremonial of the Southern Plains described at length in A. C. Fletcher: *The Hako: A Pawnee Ceremony*. See page 239.—R.L.B.

in cadence, keeping good time with the air of the songs. He makes it execute many differing figures; sometimes he shows it to the whole assembly, turning himself from one side to the other. After that, he who is to begin the Dance appears in the middle of the assembly, and at once continues this. Sometimes he offers it to the sun, as if he wished the latter to smoke it; sometimes he inclines it toward the earth; again, he makes it spread its wings, as if about to fly; at other times, he puts it near the mouths of those present, that they may smoke. The whole is done in cadence; and this is, as it were, the first Scene of the Ballet.

MATURIN LE PETIT

(1693-1739)

Concerning the Natchez

THEIR TEMPLES

THIS NATION OF SAVAGES INHABITS ONE OF THE MOST BEAUTIFUL AND fertile countries in the World, and is the only one on this continent which appears to have any regular worship. Their Religion in certain points is very similar to that of the ancient Romans. They have a Temple filled with Idols, which are different figures of men and of animals, and for which they have the most profound veneration. Their Temple in shape resembles an earthen oven, a hundred feet in circumference. They enter it by a little door about four feet high, and not more than three in breadth. No window is to be seen there. The arched roof of the edifice is covered with three rows of mats, placed one upon the other, to prevent the rain from injuring the masonry. Above on the outside are three figures of eagles made of wood, and painted red, yellow, and white. Before the door is a kind of shed with folding-doors, where the Guardian of the Temple is lodged; all around it runs a circle of palisades, on which are seen exposed the skulls of all the heads which their Warriors had brought back from the battles in which they had been engaged with the enemies of their Nation.

In the interior of the Temple are some shelves arranged at a certain distance from each other, on which are placed cane baskets of an oval shape, and in these are enclosed the bones of their ancient Chiefs, while by their side are those of their victims who had caused themselves to be strangled, to follow their masters into the other world. Another separate shelf supports many flat baskets very gorgeously painted, in which they preserve their Idols. These are figures of men and women made of stone or baked clay, the heads and the tails of extraordinary serpents, some

From *The Jesuit Relations and Allied Documents 1610-1791*, edited by R. G. Thwaites (Cleveland: The Burrows Brothers Company, 1897), "Le Petit's Letter to Davaugour," Vol. 68, pp. 123-135.

stuffed owls, some pieces of crystal, and some jaw-bones of large fish. In the year 1699, they had there a bottle and the foot of a glass, which they guarded as very precious.

In this Temple they take care to keep up a perpetual fire, and they are very particular to prevent it ever blazing; they do not use anything for it but dry wood of the walnut or oak. The old men are obliged to carry, each one in his turn, a large log of wood into the enclosure of the palisade. The number of the Guardians of the Temple is fixed, and they serve by the quarter. He who is on duty is placed like a sentinel under the shed, from whence he examines whether the fire is not in danger of going out. He feeds it with two or three large logs, which do not burn except at the extremity, and which they never place one on the other, for fear of their getting into a blaze.

Of the women, the sisters of the great Chief alone have liberty to enter within the Temple. The entrance is forbidden to all the others, as well as to the common people, even when they carry something there to feast to the memory of their relatives, whose bones repose in the Temple. They give the dishes to the Guardian, who carries them to the side of the basket in which are the bones of the dead; this ceremony lasts only during one moon. The dishes are afterward placed on the palisades which surround the Temple, and are abandoned to the fallow-deer.

THEIR GREAT CHIEFS

The Sun is the principal object of veneration to these people, as they cannot conceive of anything which can be above this heavenly body, nothing else appears to them more worthy of their homage. It is for the same reason that the great Chief of this Nation, who knows nothing on the earth more dignified than himself, takes the title of brother of the Sun, and the credulity of the people maintains him in the despotic authority which he claims. To enable them better to converse together, they raise a mound of artificial soil, on which they build his cabin, which is of the same construction as the Temple. The door fronts the East, and every morning the great Chief honors by his presence the rising of his elder brother, and salutes him with many howlings as soon as he appears above the horizon. Then he gives orders that they shall light his calumet; he makes him an offering of the first three puffs which he draws; afterward raising his hand above his head, and turning from the East to the West, he shows him the direction which he must take in his course. . . .

When the great Chief dies, they demolish his cabin, and then raise a new mound, on which they build the cabin of him who is to replace him in this dignity, for he never lodges in that of his predecessor. The old men prescribe the Laws for the rest of the people, and one of their principles is to have a sovereign respect for the great Chief, as being the brother of the Sun and the master of the Temple. They believe in the immortality of the soul, and when they leave this world they go, they say, to live in another, there to be recompensed or punished. The rewards to which they look forward, consist principally in feasting, and their chastisement in the privation of every pleasure. Thus they think that those who have been the faithful observers of their laws will be conducted into a region of pleasures, where all kinds of exquisite viands will be furnished them in abundance that their delightful and tranquil days will flow on in the midst of festivals, dances, and women; in short, they will revel in all imaginable pleasures. On the contrary, the violators of their laws will be cast upon lands unfruitful and entirely covered with water, where they will not have any kind of corn, but will be exposed entirely naked to the sharp bites of the mosquitoes, that all Nations will make war upon them, that they will never eat meat, and have no nourishment but the flesh of crocodiles, spoiled fish, and shell-fish.

These people blindly obey the least wish of their great Chief. They look upon him as absolute master, not only of their property but also of their lives, and not one of them would dare to refuse him his head, if he should demand it; for whatever labors he commands them to execute, they are forbidden to exact any wages. The French, who are often in need of hunters or of rowers for their long voyages, never apply to any one but the great Chief. He furnishes all the men they wish, and receives payment, without giving any part to those unfortunate individuals, who are not permitted even to complain. One of the principal articles of their Religion, and particularly for the servants of the great Chief, is that of honoring his funeral rites by dying with him, that they may go to serve him in the other world. In their blindness they willingly submit to this law, in the foolish belief that in the train of their Chief they will go to enjoy the greatest happiness.

To give an idea of this bloody ceremony, it is necessary to know that as soon as an heir presumptive has been born to the great Chief, each family that has an infant at the breast is obliged to pay him homage. From all these infants they choose a certain number whom they destine for the service of the young Prince, and as soon as they are of a competent age, they furnish them with employments suited to their talents. Some pass their lives in hunting, or in fishing, to furnish supplies for the table; others are employed in agriculture, while others serve to fill up his retinue. If he happen to die, all these servants sacrifice themselves with joy to follow their dear master. They first put on all their finery, and repair to the place opposite to the Temple, where all the people are assembled. After having danced and sung a sufficiently long time, they pass around their neck a cord of buffalo hair with a running knot, and immediately the Ministers appointed for executions of this kind, come forward to strangle them, recommending them to go to rejoin their master, and render to him in the other world services even more honorable than those which had occupied them in this.

The principal servants of the great Chief having been strangled in this way, they strip the flesh off their bones, particularly those of their arms and thighs, and leave them to dry for two months, in a kind of tomb, after which they take them out to be shut up in the baskets which are placed in the Temple by the side of the bones of their master. As for the other servants, their relatives carry them home with them, and bury them with their arms and clothes.

The same ceremony is observed in like manner on the death of the brothers and sisters of the great Chief. The women are always strangled to follow the latter, except when they have infants at the breast, in which case they continue to live, for the purpose of nourishing them. And we often see many who endeavor to find nurses, or who themselves strangle their infants, so that they shall not lose the right of sacrificing themselves in the public place, according to the ordinary ceremonies, and as the law prescribes.

This Government is hereditary; it is not, however, the son of the reigning Chief who succeeds his father, but the son of his sister, or the first Princess of the blood. This policy is founded on the knowledge they have of the licentiousness of their women. They are not sure, they say, that the children of the chief's wife may be of the blood Royal, whereas the son of the sister of the great Chief must be, as least on the side of the mother.

The Princesses of the blood never espouse any but men of obscure family, and they have but one husband, but they have the right of dismissing him whenever it pleases them, and of choosing another among those of the Nation, provided he has not made any other alliance among them. If the husband has been guilty of infidelity, the Princess may have his head cut off in an instant; but she is not herself subject to the same law, for she may have as many Lovers as she pleases, without the husband having any power to complain. In the presence of his wife he acts with the most profound respect, never eats with her, and salutes her with howls, as is done by her servants. The only satisfaction he has is, that he is freed from the necessity of laboring, and has entire authority over those who serve the Princess.

THOMAS JEFFERSON

(1743-1826)

Jefferson, child of the Enlightenment, was naturally concerned with man, and with all varieties of man. As a scientist, he recognized the unity of the human race; as a philosopher and a humanist, he believed in the psychic unity of man; as a historian, he took a long view of the history of human culture. In his writings, especially in his controversy with the naturalist, Buffon, appears for the first time the idea that the savages of today are not to be compared to the men of contemporary France and England but to their ancestors, the roving tribes of Gaul, the barbarians at the gates of Rome. He also understood at that early date that each culture was to be understood and explained in terms of itself.

Jefferson occupied himself also with the practical side of Indian affairs. Monticello was still frontier country; there were Indians practically at his doorstep. He carried on voluminous correspondence with Indian leaders, advised them on tribal constitutions, legal codes; he was concerned with their education for a new way of life. His farsightedness is apparent in his letter of instruction to Captain Lewis before the latter set out on his famous expedition:

. . . The commerce which may be carried on with the people inhabiting the line you will pursue renders a knowledge of those people important. You will, therefore, endeavour to make yourself acquainted as far as a diligent pursuit of your journey shall admit, with the names of the nations and their numbers;

The extent and limits of their possessions;

Their relations with other tribes or nations;

Their language, traditions, monuments;

Their ordinary occupations in agriculture, fishing, hunting, war, arts, and the implements for these;

Their food, clothing, and domestic accommodations;

The diseases prevalent among them, and the remedies they use;

Moral and physical circumstances which distinguish them from the tribes we know;

Peculiarities in their laws, customs, and dispositions;

And articles of commerce they may need or furnish, and to what extent.

And, considering the interest which every nation has in extending and strengthening the authority of reason and justice among the people around them, it will be useful to acquire what knowledge you can of the state of moral-

ity, religion, and information among them; as it may better enable those who may endeavour to civilize and instruct them to adapt their measures to the existing notions and practices of those on whom they are to operate.

. . . In all your intercourse with the natives, treat them in the most friendly and conciliatory manner which their own conduct will admit; allay all jealousies as to the object of your journey; satisfy them of its innocence; make them acquainted with the position, extent, character, peaceable and commercial dispositions of the United States; of our wish to be neighbourly, friendly, and useful to them, and of our dispositions to a commercial intercourse with them; confer with them on the points most convenient as mutual emporiums, and the articles of most desirable interchange for them and us. If a few of their influential chiefs, within practicable distance, wish to visit us, arrange such a visit with them, and furnish them with authority to call on our officers on their entering the United States, to have them conveyed to this place at the public expense. If any of them should wish to have some of their young people brought up with us, and taught such arts as may be useful to them, we will receive, instruct, and take care of them. Such a mission, whether of influential chiefs, or of young people, would give some security to your own party. Carry with you some matter of the kine-pox; inform those of them with whom you may be of its efficacy as a preservative from the small-pox, and instruct and encourage them in the use of it. This may be especially done where you winter. . . .

—R.L.B.

On the Character and Capacities of the North American Indians

HITHERTO I HAVE CONSIDERED THIS HYPOTHESIS[1] AS APPLIED TO BRUTE animals only, and not in its extension to the man of America, whether aboriginal or transplanted. It is the opinion of Mons. de Buffon that the former furnishes no exception to it: "Although the savage of the new world is about the same height as man in our world, this does not suffice for him to constitute an exception to the general fact that all living nature has become smaller on that continent. The savage is feeble, and has small organs of generation; he has neither hair nor beard, and no ardor whatever for his female; although swifter than the European because he is better accustomed to running, he is, on the other hand, less strong in body; he is also less sensitive, and yet more timid and cowardly; he has no vivacity, no activity of mind; the activity of his body is less an exercise, a voluntary motion, than a necessary action

[1] Buffon's hypothesis "that domestic animals are subject to degeneration from the climate of America."—R.L.B.

From Jefferson, *Notes on the State of Virginia* (London: J. Stockdale, 1787). Edited by Wm. Peden with an introduction and notes. Published for the Institute of Early American History and Culture (Chapel Hill: University of North Carolina Press, 1955), Vol. 2, pp. 58-65.

caused by want; relieve him of hunger and thirst, and you deprive him
of the active principle of all his movements; he will rest stupidly upon
his legs or lying down entire days. There is no need for seeking further
the cause of the isolated mode of life of these savages and their repugnance for society: the most precious spark of the fire of nature has been
refused to them; they lack ardor for their females, and consequently
have no love for their fellow men: not knowing this strongest and most
tender of all affections, their other feelings are also cold and languid;
they love their parents and children but little; the most intimate of all
ties, the family connection, binds them therefore but loosely together;
between family and family there is no tie at all; hence they have no
communion, no commonwealth, no state of society. Physical love con-
stitues their only morality; their heart is icy, their society cold, and their
rule harsh. They look upon their wives only as servants for all work,
or as beasts of burden, which they load without consideration with the
burden of their hunting, and which they compel without mercy, without gratitude, to perform tasks which are often beyond their strength.
They have only few children, and they take little care of them. Everywhere the original defect appears: they are indifferent because they
have little sexual capacity, and this indifference to the other sex is the
fundamental defect which weakens their nature, prevents its development, and—destroying the very germs of life—uproots society at the
same time. Man is here no exception to the general rule. Nature, by
refusing him the power of love, has treated him worse and lowered him
deeper than any animal." An afflicting picture indeed, which, for the
honor of human nature, I am glad to believe has no original. Of the
Indian of South America I know nothing; for I would not honor with
the appelation of knowledge, what I derive from the fables published of
them. These I believe to be just as true as the fables of Æsop. This
belief is founded on what I have seen of man, white, red, and black,
and what has been written of him by authors, enlightened themselves,
and writing amidst an enlightened people. The Indian of North America being more within our reach, I can speak of him somewhat from
my own knowledge, but more from the information of others better
acquainted with him, and on whose truth and judgment I can rely.
From these sources I am able to say, in contradiction to this representation, that he is neither more defective in ardor, nor more impotent with his female, than the white reduced to the same diet and
exercise: that he is brave, when an enterprize depends on bravery;
education with him making the point of honor consist in the destruction
of an enemy by stratagem, and in the preservation of his own person
free from injury; or perhaps this is nature; while it is education which
teaches us to honor force more than finesse; that he will defend himself against an host of enemies, always chusing to be killed, rather than

to surrender, though it be to the whites, who he knows will treat him well: that in other situations also he meets death with more deliberation, and endures tortures with a firmness unknown almost to religious enthusiasm with us: that he is affectionate to his children, careful of them, and indulgent in the extreme: that his affections comprehend his other connections, weakening, as with us, from circle to circle, as they recede from the center: that his friendships are strong and faithful to the uttermost extremity: that his sensibility is keen, even the warriors weeping most bitterly on the loss of their children, though in general they endeavour to appear superior to human events: that his vivacity and activity of mind is equal to ours in the same situation; hence his eagerness for hunting, and for games of chance. The women are submitted to unjust drudgery. This I believe is the case with every barbarous people. With such, force is law. The stronger sex therefore imposes on the weaker. It is civilization alone which replaces women in the enjoyment of their natural equality. That first teaches us to subdue the selfish passions, and to respect those rights in others which we value in ourselves. Were we in equal barbarism, our females would be equal drudges. The man with them is less strong than with us, but their woman stronger than ours; and both for the same obvious reason; because our man and their woman is habituated to labour, and formed by it. With both races the sex which is indulged with ease is least athletic. An Indian man is small in the hand and wrist for the same reason for which a sailor is large and strong in the arms and shoulders, and a porter in the legs and thighs.—They raise fewer children than we do. The causes of this are to be found, not in a difference of nature, but of circumstance. The women very frequently attending the men in their parties of war and of hunting, child-bearing becomes extremely inconvenient to them. It is said, therefore, that they have learnt the practice of procuring abortion by the use of some vegetable; and that it even extends to prevent conception for a considerable time after. During these parties they are exposed to numerous hazards, to excessive exertions, to the greatest extremities of hunger. Even at their homes the nation depends for food, through a certain part of every year, on the gleanings of the forest: that is, they experience a famine once in every year. With all animals, if the female be badly fed, or not fed at all, her young perish: and if both male and female be reduced to like want, generation becomes less active, less productive. To the obstacles then of want and hazard, which nature has opposed to the multiplication of wild animals, for the purpose of restraining their numbers within certain bounds, those of labour and of voluntary abortion are added with the Indian. No wonder then if they multiply less than we do. Where food is regularly supplied, a single farm will shew more of cattle, than a whole country of forests can of buffaloes. The same Indian women, when married to white traders, who feed them and their children plentifully and regularly, who exempt them from excessive drudgery, who keep them stationary and unexposed to accident, produce and raise as many children as the white women. Instances are known, under these circumstances, of their rearing a dozen children. An inhuman practice once prevailed in this country of making slaves of the Indians. (This practice commenced with the Spaniards with the first discovery of America). It is a fact well known with us, that the Indian women so enslaved produced and raised as numerous families as either the whites or blacks among whom they lived.—It has been said, that Indians have less hair than the whites, except on the head. But this is a fact of which fair proof can scarcely be had. With them it is disgraceful to be hairy on the body. They say it likens them to hogs. They therefore pluck the hair as fast as it appears. But the traders who marry their women, and prevail on them to discontinue this practice, say, that nature is the same with them as with the whites. Nor, if the fact be true, is the consequence necessary which has been drawn from it. Negroes have notoriously less hair than the whites; yet they are more ardent. But if cold and moisture be the agents of nature for diminishing the races of animals, how comes she all at once to suspend their operation as to the physical man of the new world, whom the Count acknowledges to be "about the same size as the man of our hemisphere," and to let loose their influence on his moral faculties? How has this "combination of the elements and other physical causes, so contrary to the enlargement of animal nature in this new world, these obstacles to the development and formation of great germs," been arrested and suspended, so as to permit the human body to acquire its just dimensions, and by what inconceivable process has their action been directed on his mind alone? To judge of the truth of this, to form a just estimate of their genius and mental powers, more facts are wanting, and great allowance to be made for those circumstances of their situation which call for a display of particular talents only. This done, we shall probably find that they are formed in mind as well as in body, on the same module with the "Homo sapiens Europæus." The principles of their society forbidding all compulsion, they are to be led to duty and to enterprize by personal influence and persuasion. Hence eloquence in council, bravery and address in war, become the foundations of all consequence with them. To these acquirements all their faculties are directed. Of their bravery and address in war we have multiplied proofs, because we have been the subjects on which they were exercised. Of their eminence in oratory we have fewer examples, because it is displayed chiefly in their own councils. Some, however, we have of very superior lustre. I may challenge the whole orations of Demosthenes and Cicero, and of any more eminent orator, if Europe has furnished more eminent, to produce a single passage, superior to the speech of Logan, a Mingo chief, to Lord Dunmore, when governor of this state. And, as a testimony of their talents in this line, I beg leave to introduce it, first stating the incidents necessary for understanding it. In the spring of the year 1774, a robbery was committed by some Indians on certain land-adventurers on the river Ohio. The whites in that quarter, according to their custom, undertook to punish this outrage in a summary way. Captain Michael Cresap, and a certain Daniel Great-house, leading on these parties, surprized, at different times, travelling and hunting parties of the Indians, having their women and children with them, and murdered many. Among these were unfortunately the family of Logan, a chief celebrated in peace and war, and long distinguished as the friend of the whites. This unworthy return provoked his vengeance. He accordingly signalized himself in the war which ensued. In the autumn of the same year a decisive battle was fought at the mouth of the Great Kanhaway, between the collected forces of the Shawanese, Mingoes, and Delawares, and a detachment of the Virginia militia. The Indians were defeated, and sued for peace. Logan however disdained to be seen among the suppliants. But, lest the sincerity of a treaty should be distrusted, from which so distinguished a chief absented himself, he sent by a messenger the following speech to be delivered to Lord Dunmore.

"I appeal to any white man to say, if ever he entered Logan's cabin hungry, and he gave him not meat; if ever he came cold and naked, and he clothed him not. During the course of the last long and bloody war, Logan remained idle in his cabin, an advocate for peace. Such was my love for the whites, that my countrymen pointed as they passed, and said, 'Logan is the friend of white men.' I had even thought to have lived with you, but for the injuries of one man. Col. Cresap, the last spring, in cold blood, and unprovoked, murdered all the relations of Logan, not sparing even my women and children. There runs not a drop of my blood in the veins of any living creature. This called on me for revenge. I have sought it: I have killed many: I have fully glutted my vengeance. For my country, I rejoice at the beams of peace. But do not harbour a thought that mine is the joy of fear. Logan never felt fear. He will not turn on his heel to save his life. Who is there to mourn for Logan?—Not one."

Before we condemn the Indians of this continent as wanting genius, we must consider that letters have not yet been introduced among them. Were we to compare them in their present state with the Europeans North of the Alps, when the Roman arms and arts first crossed those mountains, the comparison would be unequal, because, at that time, those parts of Europe were swarming with numbers; because numbers produce emulation, and multiply the chances of improvement, and one improvement begets another. Yet I may safely ask, How many good poets, how many able mathematicians, how many great inventors in arts or sciences, had Europe North of the Alps then produced? And it was sixteen centuries after this before a Newton could be formed. I do not mean to deny, that there are varieties in the race of man, distinguished by their powers both of body and mind. I believe there are, as I see to be the case in the races of other animals. I only mean to suggest a doubt, whether the bulk and faculties of animals depend on the side of the Atlantic on which their food happens to grow, or which furnishes the elements of which they are compounded? Whether nature has enlisted herself as a Cis or Trans-Atlantic partisan? I am induced to suspect, there has been more eloquence than sound reasoning displayed in support of this theory; that it is one of those cases where the judgment has been seduced by a glowing pen: and whilst I render every tribute of honor and esteem to the celebrated Zoologist, who has added, and is still adding, so many precious things to the treasures of science, I must doubt whether in this instance he has not cherished error also, by lending her for a moment his vivid imagination and bewitching language.

So far the Count de Buffon has carried this new theory of the tendency of nature to belittle her productions on this side of the Atlantic. Its application to the race of whites, transplanted from Europe, remained for the Abbé Raynal. "One must be astonished (he says) that America has not yet produced one good poet, one able mathematician, one man of genius in a single art or a single science." "America has not yet produced one good poet." When we shall have existed as a people as long as the Greeks did before they produced a Homer, the Romans a Virgil, the French a Racine and Voltaire, the English a Shakespeare and Milton, should this reproach be still true, we will enquire from what unfriendly causes it has proceeded, that the other countries of Europe and quarters of the earth shall not have inscribed any name in the roll of poets. But neither has America produced "one able mathematician, one man of genius in a single art or a single science." In war we have produced a Washington, whose memory will be adored while liberty shall have votaries, whose name will triumph over time, and will in future ages assume its just station among the most celebrated worthies of the world, when that wretched philosophy shall be forgotten which would have arranged him among the degeneracies of nature. In physics we have produced a Franklin, than whom no one of the present age has made more important discoveries, nor has enriched philosophy with more, or more ingenious solutions of the phænomena of nature. We have supposed Mr. Rittenhouse second to no astronomer living: that in genius he must be the first, because he is self-taught. As an artist he has exhibited as great a proof of mechanical genius as the world has ever produced. He has not indeed made a world; but he has by imitation approached nearer its Maker than any man who has lived from the creation to this day. As in philosophy and war, so in government, in oratory, in painting, in the plastic art, we might shew that America, though but a child of yesterday, has already given hopeful proofs of genius, as well of the nobler kinds, which arouse the best feelings of man, which call him into action, which substantiate his freedom, and conduct him to happiness, as of the subordinate, which serve to amuse him only. We therefore suppose, that this reproach is as unjust as it is unkind; and that, of the geniuses which adorn the present age, America contributes its full share. For comparing it with those countries, where genius is most culti- vated, where are the most excellent models for art, and scaffoldings for the attainment of science, as France and England for instance, we calcu- late thus. The United States contain three millions of inhabitants; France twenty millions; and the British islands ten. We produce a Washington, a Franklin, a Rittenhouse. France then should have half a dozen in each of these lines, and Great-Britain half that number, equally eminent. It may be true, that France has: we are but just becoming acquainted with her, and our acquaintance so far gives us high ideas of the genius of her inhabitants. It would be injuring too many of them to name particularly a Voltaire, a Buffon, the constellation of Encyclopedists, the Abbé Raynal himself, &c. &c. We therefore have reason to believe she can produce her full quota of genius. The present war having so long cut off all communi- cation with Great-Britain, we are not able to make a fair estimate of the state of science in that country. The spirit in which she wages war is the only sample before our eyes, and that does not seem the legitimate off- spring either of science or of civilization. The sun of her glory is fast descending to the horizon. Her philosophy has crossed the Channel, her freedom the Atlantic, and herself seems passing to that awful dissolution, whose issue is not given human foresight to scan.

Men of Good Will

JOHN BACHMAN   JOHN G. E. HECKEWELDER
(1790-1879)   (1783-1823)
MANASSEH CUTLER
(1742-1823)

Some of the major contributions to American anthropology in the early 19th century came from the pens of ministers of God for whom "the increase and diffusion of knowledge" about their fellowmen was a moral issue. The three men of good will represented here were pastors of three different faiths and were all concerned in different ways with the science of man.

John Bachman was a naturalist, Professor of Natural History at the College of Charleston, South Carolina, and a pastor of the Lutheran Church. He was no dilettante in natural history, but one of the leading naturalists of his day. A friend of Audubon, he collaborated with him on his great work in ornithology. The controversy over the unity of the human race was at its height with Morton, Nott, and Gliddon, the most prominent physical anthropologists of the day, declaring for plurality. A naturally modest man, averse to controversy, and living in a slave-holding state, Bachman nevertheless felt that here was a moral issue which he could not evade. His little book on the unity of the human race grew out of a paper read before the Literary Club of Charleston. Speaking of himself in the third person, Bachman states his purpose as follows:

Asked to speak on a subject of natural history, he felt himself constrained by a sense of duty to investigate those branches of science that appeared to militate against the truth of Christianity and selected the Unity of the Human Race as a subject to be discussed at the meeting which in turn took place at his house.

Several of the advocates of a plurality in the races expressed a desire that the public should have an opportunity of becoming acquainted with the observations and reasons of an opponent for whom they honestly differed.

. . . In discussing a subject the most difficult in the whole range of sciences, he has often felt himself obliged to differ from the views of other naturalists. . . . He need not add that he has been studious that no difference of views should be expressed in personal or offensive language.

82

. . . *In his attempt at defending the long-established doctrine of the unity of the human race he has neither sought fame or controversy; to the former he believes he is now indifferent and the latter is adverse to his behavior, his profession and the admonition of declining life. If in this publication he shall give offense, he will regret it; if errors have escaped him he is ready to correct them; and if he has been enabled to add any to the store of human knowledge or any argument in defense of truth, he will feel that his labors have been amply rewarded.*

John Gottlieb Ernestus Heckewelder was one of those missionaries with a warm and enduring devotion to his flock. He was born in England; but his parents, who probably came to England as refugees, emigrated when John was a child and joined the Moravian colony in Quebec. Heckewelder first met his beloved Delaware Indians when he went with Christian Post, another missionary, to search out a suitable place in Ohio to settle a band of Christian Indians. The project was interrupted by the outbreak of Pontiac's War in 1763 which threw the whole of the western frontier into turmoil. He returned some years later as a missionary to the Delawares. He remained with them through the troubled years that followed, accompanying them in their various moves that split the tribe into widely-separated fragments. He went with the group that sought refuge in Canada after the American Revolution, helping them to get settled in their new home. He formed many warm personal friendships with individual Indians; when he writes of them he is talking about known and identified individuals rather than some generalized "Indian" or even "Delaware."

The victory of the British in the French and Indian War, with their more aggressive policy toward the Indians and their intention of fully occupying the newly-acquired areas, was disastrous for the Indians. The crushing of Pontiac's rebellion demonstrated once again the futility of military resistance. Popé, who organized the Pueblo Rebellion of 1680, and Pontiac employed active methods supported by belief in divine sanction for their movements. The new revivalism that swept the Indian tribes on the western frontier promised that victory was to be achieved through spiritual regeneration

The "Delaware Prophet"—his name has been lost to us—was the first of a whole series of Indian Messiahs who preached that the white man would disappear from the continent when the ancient virtues—plus a few extra ones such as peaceableness, borrowed from Christian dogma—were restored. Heckewelder has left us an account of this early prophet, and his curious revelation.

Manasseh Cutler was a servant of the Lord of the kind, it seems, that only the 18th century produced. He rivaled Jefferson in the scope and depth of his interests. He studied theology and was pastor of the Congregational Church at Hamilton, Massachusetts. He studied and practiced law. Finding him-

self in a community without a doctor, he studied medicine so that he could minister to his flock. He lobbied in Congress for a land grant to found a colony in Ohio, then the wild frontier, helped draft the laws under which the old Northwest Territory was governed, and served two terms in the House of Representatives. Natural science was his avocation; he published the first systematic classification and description of the flora of New England. In 1788 he drove a sulky to Ohio where he remained for nearly a year to establish the settlement at Marietta. During this time he explored the mounds in the vicinity of Marietta. In one of those flashes of brilliance that approach genius, he hit upon a method of using tree rings to establish the dates. He also surmised that it was Mexico rather than Palestine or India that might contain the key to their mystery.

"Of his scientific and political pursuits, though in themselves highly interesting and beneficial to the community, congenial to his taste, and introductory to intercourse and correspondence with men of celebrity on both sides of the Atlantic, he observed during his last sickness that he reviewed them with but little comparative satisfaction, as interfering in some measure with the more imperious claims of that holy office, to which all other claims should be subordinated by those who are invested with it. He regarded the employment of an ambassador of Christ as the most important and honorable on earth."[1]—R.L.B.

[1] From an obituary notice of Dr. Cutler, published in the *Salem Observer* and reprinted in William P. and Julia R. Cutler: *Life Journals and Correspondence of Rev. Mannaseh Cutler LL.D.*

JOHN BACHMAN

(1790-1897)

The Doctrine of the Unity of the Human Race Examined on the Principles of Pure Science

THE OPPONENTS OF THE UNITY OF THE HUMAN RACE CANNOT, THEREFORE, fail to perceive that the position they have assumed is surrounded with infinite difficulty; that in order to establish their views they must overturn all the principles which science has adopted for the designation of species; and that in departing from our ancient landmarks which have hitherto enabled us to decide with accuracy on the character of species, they would not only demolish the simple and beautiful temple reared by the labour of Linnæus, Cuvier and their coadjutors, but would scatter the very materials to the winds, and leave us with no other guides than those of uncertain conjecture. The new and obscure path in which they have invited us to tread, is opposed to our views of science. A vast majority of naturalists disclaim them as leaders, and will leave them to pursue their journey alone, whilst we are content to follow the safe and long-trodden paths.

The important fact must not be overlooked that our opponents are the assailants in this controversy. When Voltaire first promulgated his crude and most unscientific notions on this subject, and attempted to show that not only the African, but the Albino also, were distinct species of men, his object confessedly was not so much to establish a truth in science as to invalidate the testimony and throw contempt on the christian Scriptures. It is but recently that the advocates of the theory of a plurality have denied the long received doctrine of the unity of the human race, as inconsistent with those principles which are received as the established laws

From Bachman, *The Doctrine of the Unity of the Human Race Examined on the Principles of Pure Science* (Charleston: C. G. Canning, 1850), pp. 146-151.

85

of science. The onus probandi therefore rests with them. They have not been able to prove the truth of their position. We have no hesitation in saying that they are incapable of proving it. Until they shall have succeeded in this, the faith of men will remain unchanged.

We will now, in the conclusion of this chapter, sum up the evidence which we have produced in various parts of this Essay, or which are self-evident, and require no further proof in favour of the unity of the species.

1. There is but one true species in the genus homo.

In this he does not form an exception to the general law of nature. There are many of our genera which contain but a single species in the genus. Among American quadrupeds the musk ox, (*Ovibos moschutos,*) the beaver, (*Castor fiber,*) and the glutton or wolverine, (*Gulo luscus,*) and among birds, the wild turkey, (*Meleagris gallipavo,*) are familiar examples. The oscillated turkey, which was formerly regarded as a second species, has recently been discovered not to be a true turkey;—in addition to its different conformation, it makes its nest on trees, and lays only two eggs, possessing in this and other particulars the habits of the pigeon.

2. We have shown that all the varieties evidence a complete and minute correspondence in the number of the teeth and in the 208 additional bones contained in the body.

3. That in the peculiarity in the shedding of the teeth, so different from all other animals, they all correspond.

That they are perfectly alike in the following particulars:

4. In all possessing the same erect stature.

5. In the articulation of the head with the spinal column.

6. In the possession of two hands.

7. In the absence of the intermaxillary bone.

8. In the teeth of equal length.

9. In a smooth skin of the body, and the head covered with hair.

10. In the number and arrangement of the muscles in every part of the body, the digestive and all the other organs.

11. In the organs of speech and the power of singing.

12. They all possess mental faculties, conscience, and entertain the hope of immortality. It is scarcely necessary to add that in these two last characteristics man is placed at such an immeasurable distance above the brute creation as to destroy every vestige of affinity to the monkey or any other genus or species.

13. They are all omnivorus and are capable of living on all kinds of food.

14. They are capable of inhabiting all climates.

15. They all possess a slower growth than any other animal, and are later in arriving at puberty.

16. A peculiarity in the physical constitution of the female, differing from all the other mammalians.

17. All the races have the same period of gestation, on an average produce the same number of young, and are subject to similar diseases.

If an objection is advanced against the rules by which we have been governed, and we are told that we have been blending specific and generic characters, we answer that in all the genera a species is selected and described as a type of the genus: hence there being but one species in the genus we have, in accordance with the rules by which naturalists are governed, selected the species as a type.

18. We have shown that man, as a domestic animal, is subject to the same changes which are effected in all domesticated animals; hence as species are taken in a different acceptation, in wild and domestic animals, our examinations of the varieties in men must be subjected to the same rules of examination. That these changes in men are constantly taking place, is evident, from the fact that great variations have occurred in several of the branches which we admit to be Caucasians, whilst wild animals with few exceptions have not undergone the slightest change. We have shown that from the many intermediate grades of form and color, in a being more subject to varieties than in any known species of animals, we can find no specific character so permanent as to warrant us in separating the varieties into distinct species. We insist on the right of applying the rules of classification to man as a domestic species. If our opponents urge the right of comparing him with wild animals, then they must first prove that men, like wild species are not subject to produce varieties. This is an experiment on which we think they will not venture. The human species cannot, therefore, be compared with wild animals that with few exceptions present a perfect uniformity. Place before you a hundred specimens of any wild species of quadruped or bird, with the few exceptions above alluded to, and there is scarcely a variation among any of the specimens. The descriptions of Aristotle are as applicable now as they were in his day. On the other hand, look at the countenances even of our neighbours and the members of our own families, gathered together around the social circle, and you see the most striking differences in the color of the eyes, the hair, and the complexion, in size, in form, in length of nose, shape of the head, volume of the brain, etc. These peculiarities are so striking that we can every where recognize those whom we have previously seen. On the other hand, the countenances of the individuals even in domestic animals can seldom be distinguished from each other. The eccentric poet, Hogg, or as he was proud to call himself the Ettric Shepherd, was able, as he stated, and no doubt correctly, to distinguish the individuals of the flock which he daily carried to the hills; but this talent even in distinguishing the countenances of domesticated animals, is possessed by few others; on the contrary the very child learns to distinguish individuals of the human race by their countenances; no two individuals even in the same family, can be found possessing the same set of features.

Man must, therefore, be compared and examined by the same rules that govern us in an examination of domesticated animals. Let us compare him with any of these species. Take those about whose origin no difficulty exists; the horse for instance, the only true species in the genus, for naturalists have now classed all the others under the asses and zebras; or take the hog, whose origin is admitted by all naturalists; first examine the characteristics of Sus scrofus, then all the races which have sprung from it; apply the same rule first to the species and then to the varieties of men, and by these fair and legitimate rules of science, we are willing to enter into a comparison, and abide by the decision. The most eminent naturalists of all past ages, have with a unanimity almost unsurpassed, already decided the question, and those who are now entering into the field, about whose qualifications, as judges, the world as yet knows nothing, and is therefore, unprepared to pronounce an opinion, are bound to give some satisfactory reasons for their dissent.

19. That the varieties in men are not greater than are known to exist among domestic animals.

20. That all the varieties of men produce with each other a fertile offspring which is perpetuated, by which new races have been formed; and that this is not the case with any two species of animals.

21. That the insects which are found on the surface, and the vermes within the body, as far as they have been examined, are the same in all the varieties of men, and that where peculiar parasites infest men in particular countries they are equally found in all the races.

Until our opponents have proved that these propositions are not in accordance with the laws of science, or in violation of truth, we must regard their new theory as founded in error.

JOHN G. E. HECKEWELDER

(1783-1823)

Indian Preachers and Prophets

THERE WAS A TIME WHEN THE PREACHERS AND PROPHETS OF THE INDIANS, by properly exerting the unbounded influence which the popular super- stitions gave them, might have excited among those nations such a spirit of general resistance against the encroachments of the Europeans, as would have enabled them, at least, to make a noble stand against their invaders, and perhaps to recover the undisturbed possession of their country. Instead of following the obvious course which reason and nature pointed out; in- stead of uniting as one nation in defence of their natural rights, they gave ear to the artful insinuations of their enemies, who too well understood the art of sowing unnatural divisions among them. It was not until Canada, after repeated struggles, was finally conquered from the French by the united arms of Great Britain and her colonies, that they began to be sensible of their desperate situation—this whole northern continent being now in the possession of one great and powerful nation, against whom it was vain to attempt resistance. Yet it was at this moment that their proph- ets, impelled by ambitious motives, began to endeavour by their eloquence to bring them back to independent feelings, and create among them a genuine national spirit; but it was too late. The only rational resource that remained for them to prevent their total annihilation was to adopt the religion and manners of their conquerors, and abandon savage life for the comforts of civilised society; but of this but a few of them were sensible; in vain Missionaries were sent among them, who, through the greatest hardships and dangers exerted themselves to soften their misfortunes by the consolations of the Christian faith, and to point out to them the way of salvation in this world and the next; the banner of Christ was compara-

From Heckewelder, "An Account of the History, Manners and Customs of the Indian Nations Who Once Inhabited Pennsylvania and the Neighboring States," *Transactions of the Historical and Literary Committee of the American Philosophical Society* (Philadelphia: Abraham Small, 1819), pp. 290-297.

tively followed but by small numbers, and these were persecuted by their friends, or, at least, those who ought to have been such, as well as by their enemies. Among the obstacles which the Missionaries encountered, the strong opposition which was made to them by the prophets of the Indian nations was by no means the least.

I have known several of these preachers and prophets during my residence in the Indian country, and have had sufficient opportunities to observe the means which they took to operate on the minds of their hearers. I shall content myself with taking notice here of a few of the most remarkable among them.

In the year 1762, there was a famous preacher of the Delaware nation, who resided at *Cayahaga,* near Lake Erie, and travelled about the country, among the Indians, endeavouring to persuade them that he had been appointed by the great Spirit to instruct them in those things that were agreeable to him and to point out to them the offences by which they had drawn his displeasure on themselves, and the means by which they might recover his favour for the future. He had drawn, as he pretended, by the direction of the great Spirit, a kind of map on a piece of deer skin, somewhat dressed like parchment, which he called "the great Book or Writing." This, he said, he had been ordered to shew to the Indians, that they might see the situation in which the Mannitto had originally placed them, the misery which they had brought upon themselves by neglecting their duty, and the only way that was now left them to regain what they had lost. This map he held before him while preaching, frequently pointing to particular marks and spots upon it, and giving explanations as he went along.

The size of this map was about fifteen inches square, or, perhaps, something more. An inside square was formed by lines drawn within it, of about eight inches each way, two of those lines, however, were not closed by about half an inch at the corners. Across these inside lines, others of about an inch in length were drawn with sundry other lines and marks, all which was intended to represent a strong inaccessible barrier, to prevent those without from entering the space within, otherwise than at the place appointed for that purpose. When the map was held as he directed, the corners which were not closed lay at the left hand side, directly opposite to each other, the one being at the south-east by south, and the nearest at the north-east by north. In explaining or describing the particular points on this map, with his fingers always pointing to the place he was describing, he called the space within the inside lines "the heavenly regions," or the place destined by the great Spirit for the habitation of the Indians in future life; the space left open at the south-east corner, he called the "avenue," which had been intended for the Indians to enter into this heaven, but which was now in the possession of the white people, wherefore the great Spirit had since caused another "avenue" to be made on the opposite side, at which, however, it was both difficult and dangerous for them to enter, there being many impediments in their way, besides a large ditch leading to a gulf below, over which they had to leap; but the evil spirit kept at this very spot a continual watch for Indians, and whoever he laid hold of, never could get away from him again, but was carried to his regions, where there was nothing but extreme poverty; where the ground was parched up by the heat for want of rain, no fruit came to perfection, the game was almost starved for want of pasture, and where the evil spirit, at his pleasure, transformed men into horses and dogs, to be ridden by him and follow him in his hunts and wherever he went.

The space on the outside of this interior square, was intended to represent the country given to the Indians to hunt, fish, and dwell in while in this world; the east side of it was called the ocean or "great salt water Lake." Then the preacher drawing the attention of his hearers particularly to the south-east avenue, would say to them: "Look here! See what we have lost by neglect and disobedience; by being remiss in the expression of our gratitude to the great Spirit, for what he has bestowed upon us; by neglecting to make to him sufficient sacrifices; by looking upon a people of a different colour from our own, who had come across a great lake, as if they were a part of ourselves; by suffering them to sit down by our side, and looking at them with indifference, while they were not only taking our country from us, but this (pointing to the spot), this, our own avenue, leading into those beautiful regions which were destined for us. Such is the sad condition to which we are reduced. What is now to be done, and what remedy is to be applied? I will tell you, my friends! Hear what the great Spirit has ordered me to tell you! You are to make sacrifices, in the manner that I shall direct; to put off entirely from yourselves the customs which you have adopted since the white people came among us; you are to return to that former happy state, in which we lived in peace and plenty, before these strangers came to disturb us, and above all, you must abstain from drinking their deadly *beson,* which they have forced upon us, for the sake of increasing their gains and diminishing our numbers. Then will the great Spirit give success to our arms; then he will give us strength to conquer our enemies, to drive them from hence, and recover the passage to the heavenly regions which they have taken from us."

Such was in general the substance of his discourses. After having dilated more or less on the various topics which I have mentioned, he commonly concluded in this manner: "And now, my friends, in order that what I have told you may remain firmly impressed on your minds, and to refresh your memories from time to time, I advise you to preserve, in every family, at least, such a book or writing as this, which I will finish off for you, provided you bring me the price, which is only one buck-skin or two doeskins a piece."[1] The price was of course bought,[2] and the book purchased. In some of those maps, the figure of a deer or turkey, or both, was placed in the heavenly regions, and also in the dreary region of the evil spirit; the former, however, appeared fat and plump, while the latter seemed to have nothing but skin and bones.

I was also well acquainted with another noted preacher, named *Wangomend,* who was of the Monsey tribe. He began to preach in the year 1766, much in the same manner as the one I have just mentioned. When Mr. Zeisberger first came to *Goschgoschink* town on the Allegheny river, this Indian prophet became one of his hearers, but finding that the Missionary's doctrine did not agree with his own, he became his enemy. This man also pretended that his call as a preacher was not of his own choice, but that he had been moved to it by the great and good Spirit, in order to teach his countrymen, who were on the way to perdition, how they could become reconciled to their God. He would make his followers believe that he had once been taken so near to heaven, that he could distinctly hear the crowing of the cocks, and that at another time he had been borne by unseen hands to where he had been permitted to take a peep into the heavens, of which there were three, one for the Indians, one for the negroes, and another for the white people. That of the Indians he observed to be the happiest of the three, and that of the whites the unhappiest; for they were under chastisement for their ill treatment of the Indians, and for possessing themselves of the land which God had given to them. They were also punished for making beasts of the negroes, by selling them as the Indians do their horses and dogs, and beating them unmercifully, although God had created them as well as the rest of mankind.

The novelty of these visions procured him hearers for a time; he found, however, at last, that the Indians became indifferent to his doctrines, particularly as he frequently warned them not to drink the *poison* brought to them by the white people, of which his congregation were very fond. Then he bethought himself of a more popular and interesting subject, and began to preach against witchcraft and those who dealt in the black art. Here he had all the passions and prejudices of the poor Indians on his side, and he did not fail to meet with the general approbation, when he declared to them that wizards were getting the upper hand, and would destroy the nation, if they were not checked in their career. He travelled in 1775, to *Goschachking,* at the forks of the Muskingum, to lay this business before the great council of the Delawares, and take their opinion upon it. The first report which the Missionaries on the Muskingum heard on this subject, was that the chiefs had at first united in having every conjurer and witch in the nation brought to an account and punished with death, that, however, on a more mature consideration, they had thought

[1] Of the value of one dollar.
[2] For *"bought"* read *"brought."*

proper in the first place to ascertain the number and names not only of those who were known, but even of those who were suspected of dealing in sorcery, and Wangomend was appointed to cause the enumeration to be made. He accordingly hastily set off for his home; and on his arrival immediately entered on the duties of his mission; when behold! it was discovered that the number of offenders was much greater than had been at first imagined, and he found himself in danger of having his own name inserted in the black list. His zeal, in consequence, became considerably cooled, and by the time when he returned the chiefs were no longer disposed to meddle with this dangerous subject, justly fearing that it could not but terminate in the ruin of their nation. Wangomend, therefore, returned to his former mode of preaching, recommending to his hearers to purge themselves from sin by taking certain prescribed medicines, and making frequent sacrifices to the great Spirit.

The last whom I shall take notice of is the Prophet-warrior *Tecumseh*, lately so celebrated among us, and who lost his life in the last war at the battle of the Thames, on the 30th of September, 1813, at the age, it is said, of 43 years. The details of his military life have been made sufficiently known through the medium of journals and newspapers, and his famous speech to the British general Proctor delivered at Amhertsburg, a short time before the battle which decided his fate, is in every body's hands. But his character as a prophet and the means that he took to raise himself to power and fame are not so well nor so particularly understood, although it is, in general, admitted that he was admirably skilled in the art of governing Indians through the medium of their passions. The sketch which I am going to draw will sufficiently prove how well this opinion is founded.

From the best information that I was able to obtain of this man, he was by nation a Shawanese, and began his career as a preacher much in the manner that others had done before him. He endeavoured to impress upon the minds of his Indian hearers, that they were a distinct people from the whites, that they had been created and placed on this soil for peculiar purposes, and that it had been ordered by the supreme being that they should live unconnected with people of a different colour from their own. He painted in vivid colours, the misery that they had brought upon themselves by permitting the whites to reside among them, and urged them to unite and expel those lawless intruders from their country. But he soon discovered that these once popular topics no longer produced any effect on the minds of the dispirited Indians, and that it was impossible to persuade them to resort to strong measures, to oppose the progress of the whites, much less to endeavour to drive them beyond the great lake. He had long observed that whenever he touched on the subject of witchcraft, his discourses were always acceptable to his hearers, whose belief in those supernatural powers, instead of diminishing, seemed constantly to gain ground. He knew that his predecessor, Wangomend, had failed in his endeavour to gain influence and power by availing himself of these popular opinions. But his ill success did not deter him from making the same attempts. He did not, however, like him, seek the assistance of the national councils, but boldly determined to try what his talents and courage could do without any other aid. There is a saying among the Indians, "That God ordained man to live until all his teeth are worn out, his eyesight dim and his hair grey." Of this he artfully availed himself to persuade those ignorant people, that the early deaths which constantly took place could not be attributed to any natural cause, since it was the will of God that every man should live to an advanced old age. When he found that he had thus obtained a fast hold on the minds of his hearers, by raising their fears of the powers of witchcraft to the highest pitch, he thought it was time to work on their hopes, and after gradually feeling the pulses of those he had to deal with, after successively throwing out a great number of hints and insinuations, the effects of which he had carefully observed, he at last did what no preacher before him had ventured to do, by declaring that the great Mannitto had endowed him with supernatural powers, to foretel future events, and to discover present secrets, and that he could point out with certainty, not only those, whether men or women, who were in the full possession of the art of witchcraft, but those who had even a tincture of it, however small. His bold assertions met with implicit belief, and he obtained by that means such an unlimited command over a credulous multitude, that at last, he had only to speak the word, or even to nod, and the pile was quickly prepared by willing executioners to put to death whomsoever he thought proper to devote. Here was a wide field opened for the gratification of the worst passions. Whoever thought himself injured, denounced his enemy as a wizard; the least real or pretended cause of resentment, nay, even a paltry bribe, would bring the most innocent man to the pile or tomahawk, and no one availed himself more of this frantic delusion of the populace, than the great prophet himself. Having his spies out in every direction, he well knew who were his friends and who his enemies, and wo (*sic*) to all who were reported to him or even suspected by him to be of the latter class! The tyrant had only to will their deaths, and his commands no one durst contradict, but all were ready to execute.

Among the number of his victims was the venerable Wyandot Chief Sha-te-ya-ron-yah, called by the whites *Leather-lips*. He was one of those who in August, 1795, signed the treaty of Greenville on behalf of the Huron tribe. His only crime was honesty, and the honourable character which he had acquired. In a fit of jealousy Tecumseh ordered him to be put to death, and his commands were but too readily obeyed.

MANASSEH CUTLER

(1742-1823)

A Frontier Mission

CHARGE BY REV. DR. CUTLER, AT THE ORDINATION OF
REV. MR. STORY, PASTOR OF THE CHURCH AT
MARIETTA, OHIO, GIVEN AT HAMILTON, MASS.,
AUGUST 15, 1798.

YOU ARE NOW, SIR, BY THE LAYING ON OF HANDS, AND SOLEMN PRAYER
to God, set apart to the work of the Gospel Ministry. To your special care
and charge are committed the Church and Christian Society at Marietta,
by whose express desire you are ordained their pastor. In the name of
the great Head of the church, we most solemnly charge you to be a faithful
minister of the gospel. . . .

You have the honor, Sir, to be the first regularly ordained and settled
minister of the Congregational denomination in that extensive country
westward of the Alleghany Mountains. We who are convinced that this
denomination is most conformable to the Sacred Scriptures, and, from
long experience, think it most consistent with the rights of conscience and
religious liberty, most congenial with our National Government, and most
friendly to those numerous municipal advantages which well-formed
Christian societies endeavor to promote, feel much satisfaction in seeing
it transplanted into that growing country. You, Sir, are going to a country
favorable to a high degree of population, capable of supporting, and probably will one day contain inhabitants as numerous as those of the Atlantic
States. You are entering on an active scene, and the noblest motives to
exertion will continually present themselves to your view. To behold a
country which was lately, very lately, a howling wilderness, the gloomy
abode of numerous savage tribes, the haunts and lurking-places of the

From Cutler, *Life, Journals and Correspondence of Rev. Manasseh Cutler, LL.D.*,
by his grandchildren, William Parker Cutler and Julia Perkins Cutler, 2 vols.
(Cincinnati: Robert Clarke & Co., 1888), Vol. 2, pp. 10-17.

cruel invaders of our defenseless frontiers, regardless of age and sex, sport-
ing with the agonies of captives while expiring under their infernal tortures—a people ignorant of the true God and devoted to their heathen rites
and barbarous superstitions; to see this country so rapidly changing into
cultured fields, inhabited by civil and well-regulated societies, peaceably
enjoying the fruits of their enterprise, industry, culture, and commerce; to
hear the voice of plenty, urbanity, and social enjoyment; above all, to see
it illumined by the pure and benevolent religion of the gospel, enjoyed in
all its regular ministrations and divine ordinances. To behold scenes and
events like these, My Brother, are not merely pleasing contemplations, they
are animating motives to zeal and activity in your ministerial labors. It
would have afforded great additional happiness to have seen the savage
tribes converted to the Christian faith, but it gives much satisfaction, and
may prepare the way for the introduction of the gospel among them, that
a peace, wise and just in its principles, and which promises a permanent
duration, has been concluded with them. Government having fairly and
honorably purchased of them their right to the soil, they are quietly re-
treating to distant parts of the wilderness. I can not forbear reminding you,
my dear sir, that on the very ground where you are statedly to dispense
the gospel you behold those ancient ruins, those extended walls and elevated mounds, which were erected many years ago. These works must have
required for years the labors of thousands, and are certain indications that
vast numbers of the natives once inhabited this place. When these antiquities are minutely examined, they induce a belief that part of them, at
least, are the monuments of ancient superstition. Their temples and their
idols were probably placed on the elevated square mounds, where the
ceremonies of their gloomy, heathenish devotions were performed. On
these mounds, in all probability, numerous *human sacrifices* have been
offered. May we adore that *Providence* which is now planting on this
memorable spot the evangelical religion of Jesus. Here may it be permanently established, and may its benign influence be extended throughout
every part of the American world. Here may you, sir, be long continued
a faithful and successful minister. In contemplating the magnitude and
importance of the work to which you are this day solemnly consecrated,
well may you ask: *Who is sufficient for these things?* Trust not in your own
strength, but in Him whose grace is sufficient for you. Feel the influence,
not merely of those local considerations which your particular situation
so naturally suggests, but of those great truths and momentous concerns
which the gospel will continually present to your view. You are now about
to take your leave, probably a final leave of your nearest connections. May
the painful hour of parting with them be cheered by the reflection that you
are going on a great and useful, an honorable and glorious errand, a work
which holy angels would with pleasure perform. Those benevolent spirits
who sang praises to God in the highest, because there was on earth, peace

and good will toward men, would cheerfully be employed in turning men
from the error of their ways, and saving souls from death.

Go, then, my Friend, and the God of peace be with you.

A NOTE ON THE ANTIQUITY OF THE OHIO MOUNDS AS SHOWN BY THE COUNT OF TREE RINGS[1]

Vestiges of ancient works, of which the present natives retain no tradition, are found in various parts of the western territory. Of those that
have yet been discovered, the works at Marietta are of the greatest magnitude. Their situation is on an elevated plain. They consist of walls and
mounds of earth, in direct lines, and in square and in circular forms. The
largest square contains 40 acres. On each side are three openings, at
equal distances, resembling twelve gateways. The smallest square contains 20 acres, with a gateway in the center of each side. At the angles
of the squares are openings similar to those at the sides. The walls, which
were made of earth, were not thrown up from ditches, but raised by bringing the earth from some distant place, or taking it up uniformly from the
surface of the plain. They were probably made of equal height and breadth,
but the waste of time had rendered them lower and broader in some parts
than in others. By an accurate measurement they were found to be from
4 to 8 feet in height, and from 25 to 26 feet, at the base, in breadth. Two
parallel walls, running from an angle of the largest square toward the
Muskingum River, which seemed to have been designed for a covered
way, were 175 feet distant from each other, and measured on the inner
side, in the most elevated part, 24 feet in height, and 42 feet broad at the
base. Within and contiguous to the squares, are many elevated mounds,
of a conic form and of different magnitudes. The most remarkable of the
mounds within the walls are three, of an oblong square form, in the
great square. The largest of these is 188 feet in length, 100 feet in width,
and 9 feet in height, level on the summit, and nearly perpendicular at the
sides. At the center of each of the sides the earth is projected, forming
gradual ascents to the summit, extremely regular, and about 6 feet in
width. Near the smallest square is a mound raised in the form of a sugar-
loaf, of a magnitude that strikes the beholder with astonishment. Its base
is a regular circle, 115 feet in diameter, and is 30 feet in altitude. It is
surrounded by a ditch, at the distance of 33 feet from its base, 15 feet
wide, and 4 feet deep, forming a bank 4 feet in height, leaving an opening
or gateway, toward the square, about 20 feet wide. Besides these, there are
other works, but the limits of this note will not admit of a description.

At the commencement of the settlement (at Marietta) the whole of these
works were covered by a prodigious growth of trees. When I arrived, the

[1] The following note is appended to Dr. Cutler's charge at the ordination of Rev.
Daniel Story.—R.L.B.

ground was in part cleared, but many large trees remained on the walls and mounds. The only possible data for forming any probable conjecture respecting the antiquity of the works, I conceived, must be derived from the growth upon them. By the concentric circles, each of which contains the annual growth, the ages of the trees might be ascertained. For this purpose a number of the trees were felled, and in the presence of Governor St. Clair and many other gentlemen, the number of circles were carefully counted. The trees of the greatest size were hollow. In the largest of those which were sound, there were from three to four hundred circles. One tree, somewhat decayed at the center, was found to contain at least four hundred and sixty-three circles. Its age was undoubtedly more than 463 years. Other trees, in a growing state, were from their appearance much older. There were, likewise, the strongest marks of a previous growth as large as the present. Decaying stumps could be traced at the surface of the ground, on different parts of the works, which measured from 6 to 8 feet in diameter. In one of the angles of a square, a decayed stump measured 8 feet in diameter at the surface of the ground; and though the body of the tree was so moldered as scarcely to be perceived above the surface of the earth, we were able to trace the decayed wood, under the leaves and rubbish, nearly an hundred feet. A thrifty beach, containing 136 circles, appeared to have first vegetated within the space occupied by an ancient predecessor of a different kind of wood.

Admitting the age of the present growth to be 450 years, and that it had been preceded by one of equal size and age, which as probably as otherwise was not the first, the works have been deserted more than 900 years. If they were occupied one hundred years, they were erected more than a thousand years ago.

It is highly probable the exterior walls were erected for defense. An opening being made at the summit of the great conic mound, there were found the bones of an adult in an horizontal position covered with a flat stone. Beneath this skeleton were thin stones placed vertically at small and different distances, but no bones were discovered. That this venerable monument might not be defaced, the opening was closed without further search. The cells formed by the thin stones might have contained, like the charnel houses in Mexico, the skulls of the sacrifices; or the mound may be a general depository for the dead, collected in the manner described by Lafitau and other travelers among the Indian tribes.

The large mounds in the great square, it can hardly be doubted, were appropriated to religious purposes. On them they erected their temples, placed their idols, and offered their sacrifices; for it is difficult to conceive of any other purpose for which they could have been designed. Comparing their form and situation with the places of worship in Mexico and other parts of the country, when first discovered, we find as great a similarity as there was in the places of worship among those different tribes. Their temples were generally erected and their idols placed on natural or artificial elevations, with gradual ascents. If the Mexican tribes, agreeably to their historic paintings and traditions, came from the northward, and some of them in their migrations went far to the eastward, it is not improbable that either some of those tribes, or others similar to them in their customs and manners, and who practiced the same religious rites, were the constructors of those works. The present natives bear a general resemblance, in their complexion, form, and size to the ancient Mexicans. Though their rites and ceremonies differ, they profess the general principles of the Mexican religion; believing in the Great Spirit, good and evil genii, and a state of existence after death. They have no temples, nor images, but some faint notions of religious oblations are to be found among them. When it is considered how long it must have been since these works were erected, how generally the practice of offering human sacrifices anciently prevailed among all the tribes from Louisiana to the western ocean; that men, women, and children were sacrificed in their smaller as well as most populous towns; that in the dominions of Montezuma, only, as historians say, twenty thousand were yearly sacrificed, and in some years fifty thousand, will it not strengthen the probability that human sacrifices were among the religious rites of the ancient possessors of this ground?

Speculation on the Origin of
the American Indian

CALEB ATWATER
(1778-1867)

JAMES ADAIR
(d. 1783)

The question of whether the Indians were an autochthonous race or had migrated from elsewhere arose early and persisted long in American anthropological literature. For Jefferson the problem was one of scientific interest, but for many men of the 18th century it became a problem of faith. Where did the Indians fit in God's scheme of Creation? What explanation for their presence could be found in the Bible? The two most frequent explanations were that they were the descendants of Japheth, the third son of Noah, separated from the Semites after the Deluge, or that they were descendants of the ten lost tribes of Israel. The latter view received new support in the 19th century from Mormons among whom it became an article of faith.

Atwater and Adair approached the problem of Indian origins from two different points of view—archaeology and comparative ethnology respectively—and reached the same conclusion, namely, that the Indians had come from Asia, specifically the Near East, thus demonstrating to their satisfaction the reliability of the Bible as a source of world history.

Caleb Atwater was born in Massachusetts and graduated from Williams College. He moved on to Ohio while that state was still the frontier. He served as postmaster, member of the State Legislature of Ohio, State Archaeologist, and finally as Commissioner of Indian Affairs under Jackson. As State Archaeologist, he made the first scientific survey of American archaeology, visiting and mapping the mounds of Ohio and neighboring states. His survey, illustrated with beautiful engraved plans of the mounds, was published by the Antiquarian Society in the first volume of its Transactions. *The early settlers in Ohio could not believe that the rude Indians who then inhabited the area could have been the builders of anything so elaborate as the Ohio mounds.*

The search for origins took Atwater on a literary world tour of mounds. He based his final historical conclusions on superficial formal similarities

100

without regard to time relationships. A century later Elliot Smith used the same kind of thinking in his reconstruction of global history.

James Adair characterized himself simply as "a trader with the Indians and resident in their country for forty years." His History was a compendium of diverse matters. The first part deals with his argument, on the basis of a comparison of details such as the use of horns on masks, for the Hebraic origin of the Indians. This is followed by a detailed history of the Cherokee nation since earliest white contact; a Cherokee and Chickasaw ethnography, with comparisons of Indian values with those of whites (to the disparagement of the latter); and suggestions for the management of Indian affairs. Included also is a description of the southern territories, with suggestions for their development. Adair's ethnographic writings had an unexpectedly wide circulation when they were plagiarized by Jonathan Carver in his enormously popular book of travels. Adair characterized his own book in this manner:

> The production of one who hath been chiefly engaged in an Indian life ever since the year 1735 . . . The work was carried on with great disadvantages, separated by his situation from libraries, compelled to conceal his papers from the natural jealousy of the natives, and the secrecy of Indians concerning their own affairs and prying disposition into those of others . . .
>
> I sat down to draw the Indians on the spot and had many years' standing before me and lived with them as a friend and brother. My intentions were pure when I wrote—truth hath been my standard. With inexpressible concern I read the several imperfect and fabulous accounts of the Indians. Fiction and conjecture have no place in the following pages. The public may depend on the fidelity of the author and that his descriptions are genuine although not so polished and romantic as other Indian histories and accounts they may have seen.
>
> My grand objects were to give the literati proper and good materials for tracing the origin of the American Indians, and to incite the higher powers zealously to promote the best interests of the British Colonies and the mother country.—R.L.B.

CALEB ATWATER

(1778-1867)

Conjectures, respecting the Origin and History of the Authors of the Ancient Works in Ohio, &c.

THE READER, AFTER HAVING BECOME ACQUAINTED WITH MANY OF OUR ancient works, naturally inquires, Who were their authors? Whence did they emigrate? At what time did they arrive? How long did they continue to inhabit this country? To what place did they emigrate? and, Where shall we look for their descendants?

These questions have often been asked, within the last thirty years, and as often answered, but not satisfactorily, especially to those who, on all occasions, require proofs amounting to mathematical certainty.

If we look into the Bible, the most authentick, the most ancient history of man, we shall there learn, that mankind, soon after the deluge, undertook to raise a tower high as heaven, which should serve to keep them together, as a place of worship, and stand to future ages as a monument of their industry, their religious zeal, their enterprize, their knowledge of the arts. Unacquainted, as they undoubtedly were, with the use of letters, in what better way could their names have been handed down to their posterity with renown? But in this attempt they were disappointed, and themselves dispersed through the wide world. Did they forget to raise afterwards, similar monuments and places of worship? They did not; and, to use the words of an inspired penman, "high places," of various altitudes and dimensions, were raised "on every high hill, and under every green tree," throughout the land of Palestine, and all the east.

Some of these "high places" belonged to single families, some to a

From Atwater, "Description of the Antiquities Discovered in the State of Ohio and Other Western States," Worcester: *Archeologica Americana—Transactions of the American Antiquarian Society*, Vol. I, 1820, pp. 220-232.

mighty chieftain, a petty tribe, a city, or a whole nation. Some were places of worship for the individual, the tribe, the village, the town, the city, or the nation, to which they respectively belonged.

At those "high places," belonging to great nations, great national affairs were transacted. Here they crowned and deposed their kings; here they concluded peace and declared war. Here the nation assembled at stated seasons, to perform the solemn worship of their deities. Here they celebrated anniversaries of great national events, and buried the illustrious dead.

The Jews, on many great occasions, assembled at Gilgal. The name of the place, signifies "a heap." Here was a pile of stones, which were brought from the bed of the river Jordan, and piled up on the spot where they encamped for the first night after they crossed that river, on their entrance into "the promised land." Let the reader examine similar piles of stones on the waters of the Licking, near Newark, in the counties of Perry, Pickaway and Ross, and then ask himself, Whether those who raised our monuments, were not originally from Asia? Shiloh, where the Jews frequently assembled to transact great national affairs, and perform acts of devotion, was situated upon a high hill. When this place was deserted, the loftier hill of Zion was selected in its stead. Upon Sinai's awful summit the law of God was promulgated. Moses was commanded to ascend a mountain to die. Solomon's temple was situated upon a high hill by Divine appointment. Samaria, a place celebrated for the worship of idols, was built upon the high hill of Shemer, by Omri, king of Israel, who was there buried. How many hundreds of mounds in this country are situated on the highest hills, surrounded by the most fertile soils? Traverse the counties of Licking, Franklin, Pickaway and Ross; examine the loftiest mounds, and compare them with those described as being in Palestine. Through the wide world, such places seem to have been preferred by the men of ancient times who erected them. . . .

It is interesting to the philosopher, to observe the progressive improvements made by man in the several useful arts. Without letters, in the first rude stages of society, the tree is marked with a view to indicate what is already done, or is intended to be done. Though our Indians had lived along our Atlantick border for ages, yet they had advanced no farther in indicating projected designs, or in recording past events. The abundance of wild game, and the paucity of their numbers, will satisfactorily account for their ignorance in this, and almost every other respect. Coming here at an early age of the world, necessity had not civilized them. At that period, in almost all parts of the globe then inhabited, a small mound of earth served as a sepulchre and an altar, whereon the officiating priest could be seen by the surrounding worshippers.

For many ages we have reason to believe there were none but such altars. From Wales, they may be traced to Russia, quite across that empire, to our continent; across it from the mouth of the Columbia on the Pacifick ocean, to Black River, on the east end of lake Ontario. Thence turning in a southwestern direction, we find them extending quite to the southern parts of Mexico and Peru.

In the Russian empire, mounds are numerous, and were every where seen by the learned Adam Clarke, LL. D. in his tour from St. Petersburg to the Crimea, in the year 1800. [After describing the mounds of Russia Mr. Clarke says:]

"If there exists any thing of former times, which may afford monuments of antediluvian manners, it is this mode of burial.—They seem to mark the progress of population in the first ages, after the dispersion, rising wherever the posterity of Noah came. Whether under the form of a mound in Scandinavia and Russia, a barrow in England, a *cairn* in Ireland, Scotland, and Wales, or those heaps, which the modern Greeks and Turks call *Tepe;* lastly, in the more artificial shape of a pyramid in Egypt; they had universally the same origin. They present the simplest and sublimest monuments, which any generation could raise over the bodies of their progenitors; calculated for almost endless duration, and speaking a language more impressive than the most studied epitaph upon Parian marble. When beheld in a distant evening's horizon, skirted by the rays of the setting sun, and touching, as it were, the clouds which hang over them, imagination pictures the spirits of heroes of remoter periods descending to irradiate the warriour's grave. Some of them rose in such regular forms, with so simple and yet so artificial a shape, in a plain, otherwise so perfectly level and flat, that no doubt whatever could be entertained respecting them. Others, still more ancient, have at last sunk into the earth, and left a hollow place, which still marks their pristine situation. Again, others, by the passage of the plough upon their surfaces, have been considerably diminished."[1]

How exactly does this description of Clarke's apply to our mounds in the west? Who ever described with more accuracy, that species of mounds of earth in Ohio, which were used as cemeteries? Unless we knew to the contrary, who of us in Ohio, would ever suspect, that Dr. Clarke was not describing with fidelity, our western mounds? In one conjecture, however, he is mistaken; that is, in supposing those to be the most ancient, which were but just begun. I have seen them in all stages, from the time that a circular fosse, with a hole in its centre, was made, until these mounds were brought to a perfect point at the summit.

In Scioto county, a few miles from Portsmouth, is a circular fosse, with a hole in the centre of the area which it encloses. The owner makes use of this work as a barn yard.

There is a work of a similar form between two walls, belonging to the

[1] Clarke's *Travels*, Vol. I, p. 138.

works at Newark; and I have seen several on the Kenhawa river, not far from Point Pleasant, and others, left in the same unfinished state, in a great number of places. It would seem that where a ditch was to enclose a tumulus, this ditch was first dug, then a hole made in the centre, which was covered over with wood, earth, stones, or brick, then a large funeral pile constructed, and the corpse of some distinguished personage placed on it and burnt. An examination of the works already described, will amply justify these conjectures.

I have a brick, now before me, over which lay, when found, wood ashes, charcoal, and human bones, burnt in a large and hot fire. And from what was found at Circleville, in the mound already described, it would seem that females were sometimes burnt with the males. I need not say, that this custom was derived from Asia, as it is well known to all my readers, that this is the only country to look to for the origin of such a custom.—The Greeks and Romans practised burning their illustrious dead. It was practised by several other nations, but they all derived it from Asia.

In the same volume of travels,[2] Dr. Clarke says, "The Cossacks at Ekaterinedara, dug into some of these mounds for the purpose of making cellars, and found several ancient vases." Such vases are discovered in ours. Several have been found in our mounds, which resemble one found in Scotland, and described by Pennant. Another, somewhat resembling a small keg in its construction, and a tea kettle in the use to which it was put, appears to be made of a composition of clay and shells.

Dr. Clarke informs us, that the bones of horses, as well as human bones, were found in some mounds in Russia. The teeth of bears, otters and beavers, are found in ours, lying beside the bones of human beings; but no bones of horses have been found to my knowledge.

Thus we learn from the most authentick sources, that these ancient works existing in Europe, Asia, and America, are as similar in their construction, in the materials with which they were raised, and in the articles found in them, as it is possible for them to be. Let those who are constantly seeking for some argument, with which to overthrow the history of man by Moses, consider this fact. Such persons have more than once asserted, that there were different stocks or races of men; but this similarity of works almost all over the world, indicates that all men sprung from one common origin. I have always considered this fact, as strengthening the Mosaic account of man, and that the scriptures throw a strong and steady light on the path of the Antiquarian.

[2] Clarke's *Travels,* Vol. I, p. 236.

JAMES ADAIR

(d. 1783)

The Cheerake Nation

THEIR OPINION OF OUR METHODS OF WAR

THEY ARE EXCEEDINGLY POINTED AGAINST OUR METHODS OF WAR, AND conferring of titles. By the surprising conduct of a Georgia governor, both the Muskohge and Cheerake, who attended our army in the war before the last, against St. Augustine, have entertained, and will continue to have the meanest opinion of the Carolina martial disposition, till by some notable brave actions, it wears off. The Indians concluded that there was treachery in our letting prisoners of distinction return to the fort to put the rest on their guard, and in our shutting up the batteries for four or five days successively, not having our cannon dismounted, nor annoying the enemy, but having flags of truce frequently passing and repassing. They said, that it was plain to their eyes, we only managed a sham fight with the Spaniards—and they became very uneasy, and held many conferences about our friendly intercourse with the garrison; concluding that we had decoyed them down to be slaughtered, or delivered to the Spaniard to purchase a firm peace for ourselves—and they no sooner reached their own countries than they reported the whole affair in black colours, that we allured them to a far-distant place, where we gave them only a small quantity of bad food; and that they were obliged to drink saltish water, which, instead of allaying, inflamed their thirst, while we were carousing with various liquors, and shaking hands with the Spaniard, and sending the white beloved speech to one another, by beat of drum, although we had the assurance to affirm that we held fast the bloody tomohawk. The minutest circumstance was so strongly represented, that both nations were on the very point of commencing war against us. But the "Raven" of

From Adair, *History of the American Indians, Particularly Those Nations Adjoining to the Mississippi, East and West Florida, Georgia, South and North Carolina and Virginia* (London: printed for Edward and Charles Dilly in the Poultry, 1775), pp. 399-402, 421, 427-431.

Euwase, a leading head warrior of the Cheerake, was confined in Augusta garrison, till he sent up runners to stop a war, that his speeches and messages had nearly fomented—his life was threatened on failure, and he had large promises given, if he complied and succeeded.

THEIR GAMES

The Indians are much addicted to gaming, and will often stake every thing they possess. Ball-playing is their chief and most favourite game: and is such severe exercise, as to shew it was originally calculated for a hardy and expert race of people, like themselves, and the ancient Spartans. The ball is made of a piece of scraped deer-skin, moistened, and stuffed hard with deer's hair, and strongly sewed with deer's sinews.—The ball-sticks are about two feet long, the lower end somewhat resembling the palm of a hand, and which are worked with deer-skin thongs. Between these, they catch the ball, and throw it a great distance, when not prevented by some of the opposite party, who fly to intercept them. The goal is about five hundred yards in length: at each end of it, they fix two long bending poles into the ground, three yards apart below, but slanting a considerable way outwards. The party that happens to throw the ball over these, counts one; but, if it be thrown underneath, it is cast back, and played for as usual. The gamesters are equal in number on each side; and, at the beginning of every course of the ball, they throw it up high in the center of the ground, and in a direct line between the two goals. When the crowd of players prevents the one who catched the ball, from throwing it off with a long direction, he commonly sends it the right course, by an artful sharp twirl. They are so exceedingly expert in this manly exercise, that, between the goals, the ball is mostly flying the different ways, by the force of the playing sticks, without falling to the ground, for they are not allowed to catch it with their hands. It is surprising to see how swiftly they fly, when closely chased by a nimble footed pursuer; when they are intercepted by one of the opposite party, his fear of being cut by the ball sticks, commonly gives them an opportunity of throwing it perhaps a hundred yards; but the antagonist sometimes runs up behind, and by a sudden stroke dashes down the ball. It is a very unusual thing to see them act spitefully in any sort of game, not even in this severe and tempting exercise.

By education, precept, and custom, as well as strong example, they have learned to shew an external acquiescence in every thing that befalls them, either as to life or death. By this means, they reckon it a scandal to the character of a steady warrior to let his temper be ruffled by any accidents,—their virtue they say, should prevent it. Their conduct is equal to their belief of the power of those principles: previous to this sharp exercise of ball playing, notwithstanding the irreligion of the Choktah in other respects, they will supplicate *Yo He Wah,* to bless them with success. To move the deity to enable them to conquer the party they are to play against, they mortify themselves in a surprising manner; and, except a small intermission, their female relations dance out of doors all the preceeding night, chanting religious notes with their shrill voices, to move *Yo He Wah* to be favourable to their kindred party on the morrow. The men fast and wake from sunset, till the ball play is over the next day, which is about one or two o'clock in the afternoon. During the whole night, they are to forbear sleeping under the penalty of reproaches and shame; which would sit very sharp upon them, if their party chanced to lose the game, as it would be ascribed to that unmanly and vicious conduct. They turn out to the ball ground, in a long row, painted white, whooping as if Pluto's prisoners were all broke loose: when that enthusiastic emotion is over, the leader of the company begins a religious invocation, by saying *yah,* short, then *yo,* long, which the rest of the train repeat with a short accent, and on a low key like the leader: and thus they proceed with such acclamations and invocations, as have been already noticed, on other occasions. Each party are desirous to gain the twentieth ball, which they esteem a favourite divine gift. As it is in the time of laying by the corn, in the very heat of summer, they use this severe exercise, a stranger would wonder to see them hold it so long at full speed, and under the scorching sun, hungry also, and faint with the excessive use of such sharp physic as the button snake root, the want of natural rest, and of every kind of nourishment. But their constancy, which they gain by custom, and their love of virtue, as the sure means of success, enable them to perform all their exercises, without failing in the least, be they ever so severe in the pursuit.

The warriors have another favourite game, called *Chungke;* which, with propriety of language, may be called "Running hard labour." They have near their state house, a square piece of ground well cleaned, and fine sand is carefully strewed over it, when requisite, to promote a swifter motion to what they throw along the surface. Only one, or two on a side, play at this ancient game. They have a stone about two fingers broad at the edge, and two spans round: each party has a pole of about eight feet long, smooth, and tapering at each end, the points flat. They set off a-breast of each other at six yards from the end of the play ground; then one of them hurls the stone on its edge, in as direct a line as he can, a considerable distance toward the middle of the other end of the square: when they have ran a few yards, each darts his pole anointed with bear's oil, with a proper force, as near as he can guess in proportion to the motion of the stone that the end may lie close to the stone—when this is the case the person counts two of the game, and, in proportion to the nearest of the poles to the mark, one is counted unless by measuring, both are found to be at an equal distance from the stone. In this manner, the players will keep running most part of the day, at half speed, under the violent heat of the sun, staking their silver ornaments, their nose, finger, and ear rings; their breast, arm, and wrist plates, and even all their wearing apparel, except that which barely covers their middle. All the American Indians are much addicted to this game, which to us appears to be a task of stupid drudgery: it seems however to be of early origin, when their fore-fathers used diversions as simple as their manners. The hurling stones they use at present, were time immemorial rubbed smooth on the rocks, and with prodigious labour; they are kept with the strictest religious care, from one generation to another, and are exempted from being buried with the dead. They belong to the town where they are used, and are carefully preserved.

THEIR GOVERNMENT

Every town has a large edifice which with propriety may be called the mountain house, in comparison of those already described. But the only difference between it, and the winter house or stove, is in its dimensions, and application. It is usually built on the top of a hill; and, in that separate and imperial state house, the old beloved men and head warriors meet on material business, or to divert themselves, and feast and dance with the rest of the people. They furnish the inside with genteel couches, either to sit or lie on, about seven feet wide, and a little more in length, with a descent towards the wall, to secure them from falling off when asleep. Every one takes his seat, according to his reputed merit; a worthless coxcomb dare not be guilty of the least intrusion—should he attempt it, he is ordered to his proper place, before the multitude, with the vilest disgrace, and bears their stinging laughter. This may not be an unprofitable lesson to some of our young red coated men, who never traversed the rough bloody fields of Flanders; they would be more respected if they were more modest, and displayed superior virtues to those whom they affect to despise.

This leads me to speak of the Indian method of government.—In general, it consists in a foederal union of the whole society for mutual safety. As the law of nature appoints no frail mortal to be a king, or ruler, over his brethren; and humanity forbids the taking away of pleasure, the life or property of any who obey the good laws of their country, they consider that the transgressor ought to have his evil deeds retaliated upon himself in an equal manner. The Indians, therefore, have no such titles or persons, as emperors, or kings; nor an appellative for such, in any of their dialects. Their highest title, either in military or civil life, signifies only a *Chieftain:* they have no words to express despotic power, arbitrary kings, oppressed, or obedient subjects; neither can they form any other ideas of the former, than of "bad war chieftains of a numerous family, who inslaved the rest." The power of their chiefs, is an empty sound. They can only persuade or dissuade the people, either by the force of good-nature and clear reasoning, or colouring things, so as to suit their prevailing passions. It is reputed merit alone, that gives them any titles of distinction above the meanest of the people. If we connect with this their opinion of a theocracy, it does not promise well to the reputed establishment of extensive and puissant Indian American empires. When any national affair is in debate, you may hear every father of a family speaking in his house on the subject, with rapid, bold language, and the utmost freedom that a people can use. Their voices, to a man, have due weight in every public affair, as it concerns their welfare alike. Every town is independent of another. Their own friendly compact continues the union. An obstinate war leader will sometimes commit acts of hostility, or make peace for his own town, contrary to the good liking of the rest of the nation. But a few individuals are very cautious of commencing war on small occasions, without the general consent of the head men: for should it prove unsuccessful, the greater part would be apt to punish them as enemies, because they abused their power, which they had only to do good to the society. They are very deliberate in their councils, and never give an immediate answer to any message sent them by strangers, but suffer some nights first to elapse. They reason in a very orderly manner, with much coolness and good-natured language, though they may differ widely in their opinions. Through respect to the silent audience, the speaker always addresses them in a standing posture. In this manner they proceed, till each of the head men hath given his opinion on the point in debate. Then they sit down together, and determine upon the affair. Not the least passionate expression is to be heard among them, and they behave with the greatest civility to each other. In all their stated orations they have a beautiful modest way of expressing their dislike of ill things. They only say, "it is not good, goodly, or commendable." And their whole behaviour, on public occasions, is highly worthy of imitation by some of our British senators and lawyers.

Most of their regulations are derived from the plain law of nature. Nature's school contemns all quibbles of art, and teaches them the plain easy rule, "do to others, as you would be done by," when they are able, without greater damage to themselves, than benefit to their creditor, they discharge their honest debts. But, though no disputes pass between them on such occasions, yet if there be some heart-burnings on particular affairs, as soon as they are publicly known, their red Archimagus, and his old beloved men, convene and decide, in a very amicable manner, when both parties become quite easy. They have no compulsive power to force the debtor to pay; yet the creditor can distrain his goods or chattels, and justly satisfy himself without the least interruption—and, by one of his relations, he sends back in a very civil manner, the overplus to the owner. These instances indeed seldom happen, for as they know each other's temper, they are very cautious of irritating, as the consequences might one day prove fatal—they never scold each other when sober—they conceal their enmity be it ever so violent, and will converse together with smooth kind language, and an obliging easy behaviour, while envy is preying on their heart. In general, they are very punctual in paying what they owe among themselves, but they are grown quite careless in discharging what they owe to the traders, since the commencement of our destructive plan of general licences. "An old debt," is a proverbial expression with them, of "nothing."

There are many petty crimes which their young people are guilty of,— to which our laws annex severe punishment, but their's only an ironical way of jesting. They commend the criminal before a large audience, for practising the virtue, opposite to the crime, that he is known to be guilty of. If it is for theft, they praise his honest principles; and they commend a warrior for having behaved valiantly against the enemy, when he acted cowardly; they introduce the minutest circumstances of the affair, with severe sarcasms which wound deeply.

Formerly, the Indian law obliged every town to work together in one body, in sowing or planting their crops; though their fields are divided by proper marks, and their harvest is gathered separately. The Cheerake and Muskohge still observe that old custom, which is very necessary for such idle people, in their element. The delinquent is assessed more or less, according to his neglect, by proper officers appointed to collect those assessments, which they strictly fulfil, without the least interruption, or exemption of any able person. They are likewise bound to assist in raising public edifices. They have not the least trace of any other old compulsive law among them; and they did not stand in need of any other in their state. As they were neither able nor desirous to obtain any thing more than a bare support of life, they could not credit their neighbours beyond a morsel of food, and that they liberally gave, whenever they called. Most of them observe that hospitable custom to this day. Their throwing away all their old provisions, as impure food, whenever the new harvest was sanctified, helped greatly to promote a spirit of hospitality. Their wants, and daily exercise in search of needful things, kept them honest. Their ignorance of the gay part of life, helped in a great measure to preserve their virtue. In their former state of simplicity, the plain law of nature was enough; but, as they are degenerating very fast from their ancient simplicity, they, without doubt, must have new laws to terrify them from committing new crimes, according to the usage of other nations, who multiply their laws, in proportion to the exigencies of time.

Dedicated Amateurs

GEORGE CATLIN
(1796-1872)

LEWIS HENRY MORGAN
(1818-1881)

GEORGE BIRD GRINNELL
(1849-1948)

In the present age of professionalism it is only in the field of sports that the word amateur has retained its original meaning and its good repute— someone who engages in an activity out of interest rather than for profit or advantage.

Although Catlin, Morgan and Grinnell are amateurs in this old-fashioned sense, there is nothing the least bit amateurish about their work. They were the most serious and dedicated anthropologists of their time; each one made a unique contribution to the science. But they did not hold academic positions. Grinnell was connected briefly with the Peabody Museum of Yale University as a zoologist; Morgan was offered a professorship at Rochester but declined it. But for all of them ethnological research was the first order of business and their studies carried on with dedicated zeal over the years were labors of love—love of truth and justice and love of the land and its native people.

In the popular imagination the image of "the Indian" was taking shape, complete with war bonnet, lance and tipi, and mounted on a swift horse. An image full of contradictions—the "good" Indian, possessing to the highest degree all the martial virtues, and the "bad" Indian, cruel and treacherous. By their side was the frontiersman: the white nomad, the trader, trapper, hunter, soldier, explorer, the man without a home or kinfolk, wandering from camp to camp among the tribes. George Catlin was a frontiersman of a special kind—a part-time frontiersman, but like many men of the frontier, a man with a mission. His mission was to record in paint and so "rescue from oblivion the looks and customs of the vanishing races of native man in America."

Catlin practiced law briefly but it was not to his taste and he soon gave it up for art. He was a successful portrait painter. DeWitt Clinton and Dolly Madison were among his subjects. His summers he spent among the Indians; in the winter he returned to Washington or other cities to earn enough by portrait painting to finance another summer in the field. Although his paintings were his chief concern, he kept a journal with voluminous notes explaining his pictures and describing the events they depicted. His journals contain large amounts of ethnographic material dealing with all aspects of Indian life, especially from the Mandan of the upper Missouri. His description of a "Mandan Initiation Ceremony," unfortunately too long for inclusion here, contains one of the few eye-witness accounts of the Sun Dance ritual in all its gory detail. His collection of 600 Indian portraits and scenes eventually found a home in the National Museum.

Lewis H. Morgan grew up in the vicinity of Aurora, New York, surrounded by Seneca Indians. Back in his native town from college, and reading for the law, he joined a secret society of young men called "The Gordian Knot." The society was patterned after the Iroquois Confederacy, with chiefs and sachems; its members wore Indian garb and held their secret "councils" around campfires in the forest. Morgan, with the help of the famous Seneca chief, Ely S. Parker, made a thorough study of the social organization of the Iroquois Confederacy; the club was rechristened "The Grand Order of the Iroquois", and took as its purpose the study and preservation of Indian lore, the education of Indians and assistance to them in accepting the conditions of civilized life.

Sent by the "Grand Order" to Washington, Morgan was instrumental in defeating the ratification of a treaty which would have deprived the Seneca of their land. In recognition of his services to them, he was adopted into the Seneca tribe and given the name of Tayadawahkugh, "One Lying Across," that is, one who served as a bond between Indians and whites.

Throughout his life, Morgan maintained his interest in Indian welfare. A devout Christian himself, he had many friends among the missionaries working in the western territories for whose efforts in educating and Christianizing the Indians he had the highest respect.

Morgan's early researches, in collaboration with Parker, culminated in The League of the Ho-dé-no-sau-nee or Iroquois *which John Wesley Powell characterized as "the first scientific account of an Indian tribe."*

Grinnell was by profession a naturalist, but by predilection an explorer and pioneer. It was to collect vertebrate fossils for the Peabody Museum of Yale University that he first went West. He joined Custer's expedition into the Black Hills, and the Ludlow expedition to the Yellowstone. For thirty-five years he edited Forest and Stream, *a journal devoted to wild life and the problems of conservation. He knew and loved the prairie when the buffalo ran, before it had been torn up by plows and railroads. He loved the people of the prairie, too. And of all the tribes he knew, it was the Cheyenne he loved best.*

He first met the Cheyenne, he writes, in 1890, and for the next forty years no summer passed that he did not visit them. After forty years of living with them as friend and brother, he was ready to write of the things he had learned sitting around their campfires. Of all the books written about Indians, none comes closer to their everyday life than Grinnell's classic monograph on the Cheyenne. Reading it, one can smell the buffalo grass and the wood fires, feel the heavy morning dew on the prairie.

—R.L.B.

GEORGE CATLIN

(1796-1872)

A Mandan Village on the Upper Missouri

I SAID THAT I WAS HERE IN THE MIDST OF A STRANGE PEOPLE, WHICH IS literally true; and I find myself surrounded by subjects and scenes worthy the pens of Irving or Cooper—of the pencils of Raphael or Hogarth; rich in legends and romances, which would require no aid of the imagination for a book or a picture.

The Mandans (or See-pohs-kah-nu-mah-kah-kee, "people of the pheasants," as they call themselves), are perhaps one of the most ancient tribes of Indians in our country. Their origin, like that of all the other tribes is from necessity, involved in mystery and obscurity. Their traditions and peculiarities I shall casually recite in this or future epistles; which when understood, will at once, I think, denominate them a peculiar and distinct race. They take great pride in relating their traditions, with regard to their origin; contending that they were the *first* people created on earth. Their existence in these regions has not been from a very ancient period; and, from what I could learn of their traditions, they have, at a former period, been a very numerous and powerful nation; but by the continual wars which have existed between them and their neighbours, they have been reduced to their present numbers.

This tribe is at present located on the west bank of the Missouri, about 1800 miles above St. Louis, and 200 below the Mouth of Yellow Stone river. They have two villages only, which are about two miles distant from each other; and number in all (as near as I can learn), about 2000 souls. Their present villages are beautifully located, and judiciously also, for defence against the assaults of their enemies. The site of the lower (or prin-

From Catlin, *Letters and Notes on the Manners, Customs, and Conditions of the North American Indians* (London: published for the Author by Tilt and Bogue, 1842), 2 vols., 3rd edition, vol. I, pp. 80-91.

cipal) town, in particular (PLATE 45), is one of the most beautiful and pleasing that can be seen in the world, and even more beautiful than imagination could ever create. In the very midst of an extensive valley (embraced within a thousand graceful swells and parapets or mounds of interminable green, changing to blue, as they vanish in distance) is built the city, or principal town of the Mandans. On an extensive plain (which is covered with a green turf, as well as the hills and dales, as far as the eye can possibly range, without tree or bush to be seen) are to be seen rising from the ground, and towards the heavens, domes—(not "of gold," but) of dirt—and the thousand spears (not "spires") and scalp-poles, &c. &c., of the semi-subterraneous village of the hospitable and gentlemanly Mandans.

These people formerly (and within the recollection of many of their oldest men) lived fifteen or twenty miles farther down the river, in ten contiguous villages; the marks or ruins of which are yet plainly to be seen. At that period, it is evident, as well from the number of lodges which their villages contained, as from their traditions, that their numbers were much greater than at the present day.

There are other, and very interesting, traditions and historical facts relative to a still prior location and condition of these people, of which I shall speak more fully on a future occasion. From these, when they are promulged, I think there may be a pretty fair deduction drawn, that they formerly occupied the lower part of the Missouri and even the Ohio and Muskingum, and have gradually made their way up the Missouri to where they now are.

There are many remains on the river below this place (and, in fact, to be seen nearly as low down as St. Louis), which shew clearly the peculiar construction of Mandan lodges, and consequently carry a strong proof of the above position. While descending the river, however, which I shall commence in a few weeks, in a canoe, this will be a subject of interest; and I shall give it close examination.

The ground on which the Mandan village is at present built, was admirably selected for defence; being on a bank forty or fifty feet above the bed of the river. The greater part of this bank is nearly perpendicular, and of solid rock. The river, suddenly changing its course to a right-angle, protects two sides of the village, which is built upon this promontory or angle; they have therefore but one side to protect, which is effectually done by a strong piquet, and a ditch inside of it, of three or four feet in depth. The piquet is composed of timbers of a foot or more in diameter, and eighteen feet high, set firmly in the ground at sufficient distances from each other to admit of guns and other missiles to be fired between them. The ditch (unlike that of civilized modes of fortification) is inside of the piquet, in which their warriors screen their bodies from the view and weapons of their enemies, whilst they are reloading and discharging their weapons through the piquets.

The Mandans are undoubtedly secure in their villages, from the attacks of any Indian nation, and have nothing to fear, except when they meet their enemy on the prairie. Their village has a most novel appearance to the eye of a stranger; their lodges are closely grouped together, leaving but just room enough for walking and riding between them; and appear from without, to be built entirely of dirt; but one is surprised when he enters them, to see the neatness, comfort, and spacious dimensions of these earth-covered dwellings. They all have a circular form, and are from forty to sixty feet in diameter. Their foundations are prepared by digging some two feet in the ground, and forming the floor of earth, by levelling the requisite size for the lodge. These floors or foundations are all perfectly circular, and varying in size in proportion to the number of inmates, or of the quality or standing of the families which are to occupy them. The superstructure is then produced, by arranging, inside of this circular excavation, firmly fixed in the ground and resting against the bank, a barrier or wall of timbers, some eight or nine inches in diameter, of equal height (about six feet) placed on end, and resting against each other, supported by a formidable embankment of earth raised against them outside; then, resting upon the tops of these timbers or piles, are others of equal size and equal in numbers, of twenty or twenty-five feet in length, resting firmly against each other, and sending their upper or smaller ends towards the centre and top of the lodge; rising at an angle of forty-five degrees to the apex or sky-light, which is about three or four feet in diameter, answering as a chimney and a sky-light at the same time. The roof of the lodge being thus formed, is supported by beams passing around the inner part of the lodge about the middle of these poles or timbers, and themselves upheld by four or five large posts passing down to the floor of the lodge. On the top of, and over the poles forming the roof, is placed a complete mat of willow-boughs, of half a foot or more in thickness, which protects the timbers from the dampness of the earth, with which the lodge is covered from bottom to top, to the depth of two or three feet; and then with a hard or tough clay, which is impervious to water, and which with long use becomes quite hard, and a lounging place for the whole family in pleasant weather—for sage—for wooing lovers—for dogs and all; an airing place—a look-out—a place for gossip and mirth—a seat for the solitary gaze and meditations of the stern warrior, who sits and contemplates the peaceful mirth and happiness that is breathed beneath him, fruits of his hard-fought battles, on fields of desperate combat with bristling Red Men.

The floors of these dwellings are of earth, but so hardened by use, and swept so clean, and tracked by bare and mocassined feet, that they have almost a polish, and would scarcely soil the whitest linen. In the centre, and immediately under the sky-light (PLATE 46) is the fire-place—a hole

G. Catlin.

Tossvill & C.º sc.

Plate 45, Plate 46

of four or five feet in diameter, of a circular form, sunk a foot or more below the surface, and curbed around with stone. Over the fire-place, and suspended from the apex of diverging props or poles, is generally seen the pot or kettle, filled with buffalo meat; and around it are the family, reclining in all the most picturesque attitudes and groups, resting on their buffalo-robes and beautiful mats of rushes. These cabins are so spacious, that they hold from twenty to forty persons—a family and all their connexions. They all sleep on bedsteads similar in form to ours, but generally not quite so high; made of round poles rudely lashed together with thongs. A buffalo skin, fresh stripped from the animal, is stretched across the bottom poles, and about two feet from the floor; which, when it dries, becomes much contracted, and forms a perfect sacking-bottom. The fur side of this skin is placed uppermost, on which they lie with great comfort, with a buffalo-robe folded up for a pillow, and others drawn over them instead of blankets. These beds, as far as I have seen them (and I have visited almost every lodge in the village), are uniformly screened with a covering of buffalo or elk skins, oftentimes beautifully dressed and placed over the upright poles or frame, like a suit of curtains; leaving a hole in front, sufficiently spacious for the occupant to pass in and out, to and from his or her bed. Some of these coverings or curtains are exceedingly beautiful, being cut tastefully into fringe, and handsomely ornamented with porcupine's quills and picture writings or hieroglyphics.

From the great number of inmates in these lodges, they are necessarily very spacious, and the number of beds considerable. It is no uncommon thing to see these lodges fifty feet in diameter inside (which is an immense room), with a row of these curtained beds extending quite around their sides, being some ten or twelve of them, placed four or five feet apart, and the space between them occupied by a large post, fixed quite firm in the ground, and six or seven feet high, with large wooden pegs or bolts in it, on which are hung and grouped, with a wild and startling taste, the arms and armour of the respective proprietor; consisting of his whitened shield, embossed and emblazoned with the figure of his protecting *medicine* (or mystery), his bow and quiver, his war-club or battle-axe, his dart or javelin—his tobacco pouch and pipe—his medicine bag—and his eagle—ermine or raven headdress; and over all, and on the top of the post (as if placed by some conjuror or Indian magician, to guard and protect the spell of wildness that reigns in this strange place), stands forth and in full relief the head and horns of a buffalo, which is, by a village regulation, owned and possessed by every man in the nation, and hung at the head of his bed, which he uses as a mask when called upon by the chiefs, to join in the buffalo-dance, of which I shall say more in a future epistle.

This arrangement of beds, of arms, &c., combining the most vivid display and arrangement of colours, of furs, of trinkets—of barbed and glistening points and steel—of mysteries and hocus pocus, together with the sombre and smoked colour of the roof and sides of the lodge; and the wild, and rude and red—the graceful (though uncivil) conversational, garrulous, storytelling and happy, though ignorant and untutored groups, that are smoking their pipes—wooing their sweethearts, and embracing their little ones about their peaceful and endeared fire-sides; together with their pots and kettles, spoons, and other culinary articles of their own manufacture, around them; present altogether, one of the most picturesque scenes to the eye of a stranger, that can be possibly seen; and far more wild and vivid than could ever be imagined.

Reader, I said these people were garrulous, story-telling and happy; this is true, and literally so; and it belongs to me to establish the fact, and correct the error which seems to have gone forth to the world on this subject.

As I have before observed, there is no subject that I know of, within the scope and reach of human wisdom, on which the civilized world in this enlightened age are more incorrectly informed, than upon that of the true manners and customs, and moral condition, rights and abuses, of the North American Indians; and that, as I have also before remarked, chiefly on account of the difficulty of our cultivating a fair and honourable acquaintance with them, and doing them the justice, and ourselves the credit, of a fair and impartial investigation of their true character. The present age of refinement and research has brought every thing else that I know of (and a vast deal more than the most enthusiastic mind ever dreamed of) within the scope and fair estimation of refined intellect and of science; while the wild and timid savage, with his interesting customs and modes has vanished, or his character has become changed, at the approach of the enlightened and intellectual world; who follow him like a phantom for awhile, and in ignorance of his true character at last turn back to the common business and social transactions of life.

Owing to the above difficulties, which have stood in the way, the world have (*sic*) fallen into many egregious errors with regard to the true modes and meaning of the savage, which I am striving to set forth and correct in the course of these epistles. And amongst them all, there is none more common, nor more entirely erroneous, nor more easily refuted, than the current one, that "the Indian is a sour, morose, reserved and taciturn man." I have heard this opinion advanced a thousand times and I believed it; but such certainly, is not uniformly nor generally the case.

I have observed in all my travels amongst the Indian tribes, and more particularly amongst these unassuming people, that they are a far more talkative and conversational race than can easily be seen in the civilized world. This assertion, like many others I shall occasionally make, will somewhat startle the folks at the East, yet it is true. No one can look into the wigwams of these people, or into any little momentary group of them, without being at once struck with the conviction that small-talk, gossip, garrulity, and story-telling, are the leading passions with them, who have little else to do in the world, but to while away their lives in the innocent and endless amusement of the exercise of those talents with which Nature has liberally endowed them, for their mirth and enjoyment.

One has but to walk or ride about this little town and its environs for a few hours in a pleasant day, and overlook the numerous games and gambols, where their notes and yelps of exultation are unceasingly vibrating in the atmosphere; or peep into their wigwams (and watch the glistening fun that's beaming from the noses, cheeks, and chins, of the crouching, cross-legged, and prostrate groups around the fire; where the pipe is passed, and jokes and anecdote, and laughter are excessive) to become convinced that it is natural to laugh and be merry. Indeed it would be strange if a race of people like these, who have little else to do or relish in life, should be curtailed in that source of pleasure and amusement; and it would be also strange, if a life-time of indulgence and practice in so innocent and productive a mode of amusement, free from the cares and anxieties of business or professions, should not advance them in their modes, and enable them to draw far greater pleasure from such sources, than we in the civilized and business world can possibly feel. If the uncultivated condition of their minds curtails the number of their enjoyments; yet they are free from, and independent of, a thousand cares and jealousies, which arise from mercenary motives in the civilized world; and are yet far a-head of us (in my opinion) in the real and uninterrupted enjoyment of their simple natural faculties.

They live in a country and in communities, where it is not customary to look forward into the future with concern, for they live without incurring the expenses of life, which are absolutely necessary and unavoidable in the enlightened world; and of course their inclinations and faculties are solely directed to the enjoyment of the present day, without the sober reflections on the past or apprehensions of the future.

With minds thus unexpanded and uninfluenced by the thousand passions and ambitions of civilized life, it is easy and natural to concentrate their thoughts and their conversation upon the little and trifling occurrences of their lives. They are fond of fun and good cheer, and can laugh easily and heartily at a slight joke, of which their peculiar modes of life furnish them an inexhaustible fund, and enable them to cheer their little circle about the wigwam fire-side with endless laughter and garrulity.

It may be thought, that I am taking a great deal of pains to establish this fact, and I am dwelling longer upon it than I otherwise should, inasmuch as I am opposing an error that seems to have become current through the world; and which, if it be once corrected, removes a material difficulty, which has always stood in the way of a fair and just estimation of the Indian character. For the purpose of placing the Indian in a proper light before the world, as I hope to do in many respects, it is of importance to me—it is but justice to the savage—and justice to my readers also, that such points should be cleared up as I proceed; and for the world who enquire for correct and just information, they must take my words for the truth, or else come to this country and look for themselves, into these grotesque circles of never-ending laughter and fun, instead of going to Washington City to gaze on the poor embarrassed Indian who is called there by his "Great Father," to contend with the sophistry of the learned and acquisitive world, in bartering away his lands with the graves and the hunting grounds of his ancestors. There is not the proper place to study the Indian character; yet it is the place where the sycophant and the scribbler go to gaze and frown upon him—to learn his character, and write his history! and because he does not speak, and quaffs the delicious beverage which he receives from white mens' hands, "he's a speechless brute and a drunkard." An Indian is a beggar in Washington City, and a white man is almost equally so in the Mandan village. An Indian in Washington is mute, is dumb and embarrassed; and so is a white man (and for the very same reasons) in this place—he has nobody to talk to.

A wild Indian, to reach the civilized world, must needs travel some thousands of miles in vehicles of conveyance, to which he is unaccustomed—through latitudes and longitudes which are new to him—living on food that he is unused to—stared and gazed at by the thousands and tens of thousands whom he cannot talk to—his heart grieving and his body sickening at the exhibition of white men's wealth and luxuries, which are enjoyed on the land, and over the bones of his ancestors. And at the end of his journey he stands (like a caged animal) to be scanned—to be criticised—to be pitied—and heralded to the world as a mute—as a brute, and a beggar.

A white man, to reach this village, must travel by steam-boat—by canoes —on horseback and on foot; swim rivers—wade quagmires—fight mosquitoes—patch his moccasins, and patch them again and again, and his breeches; live on meat alone—sleep on the ground the whole way, and think and dream of his friends he has left behind; and when he gets here, half-starved, and half-naked, and more than half sick, he finds himself a beggar for a place to sleep, and for something to eat; a mute amongst thousands who flock about him, to look and to criticise, and to laugh at him for his jaded appearance, and to speak of him as they do of all white men (without distinction) as liars. These people are in the habit of seeing no white men in their country but Traders, and know of no other; deeming us all alike, and receiving us all under the presumption that we come to trade or barter; applying to us all, indiscriminately, the epithet of "liars" or Traders.

The reader will therefore see, that we mutually suffer in each other's estimation from the unfortunate ignorance, which distance has chained us in; and (as I can vouch, and the Indian also, who has visited the civilized world) that the historians who would record justly and correctly the character and customs of a people, must go and live among them.

I have this morning, perched myself upon the top of one of the earth-covered lodges, which I have before described, and having the whole village beneath and about me (PLATE 47), with its sachems—its warriors—its dogs —and its horses in motion—its medicines (or mysteries) and scalp-poles waving over my head—its piquets—its green fields and prairies, and river in full view, with the din and bustle of the thrilling panorama that is about me. I shall be able, I hope, to give some sketches more to the life than I could have done from any effort of recollection.

I said that the lodges or wigwams were covered with earth—were of forty or sixty feet in diameter, and so closely grouped that there was but just room enough to walk and ride between them,—that they had a door by which to enter them, and a hole in the top for the admission of light, and for the smoke to escape,—that the inmates were at times grouped upon their tops in conversations and other amusements, &c.; and yet you know not exactly how they look, nor what is the precise appearance of the strange world that is about me. There is really a newness and rudeness in every thing that is to be seen. There are several hundred houses or dwellings about me, and they are purely unique—they are all covered with dirt—the people are all red, and yet distinct from all other red folks I have seen. The horses are wild—every dog is a wolf—the whole moving mass are strangers to me: the living, in everything, carry an air of intractable wildness about them, and the dead are not buried, but dried upon scaffolds.

The groups of lodges around me present a very curious and pleasing appearance, resembling in shape (more nearly than anything else I can compare them to) so many potash-kettles inverted. On the tops of these are to be seen groups standing and reclining, whose wild and picturesque appearance it would be difficult to describe. Stern warriors, like statues, standing in dignified groups, wrapped in their painted robes, with their heads decked and plumed with quills of the war-eagle; extending their long arms to the east or the west, the scenes of their battles, which they are re-counting over to each other. In another direction, the wooing lover, soften-ing the heart of his fair Taih-nah-tai-a with the notes of his simple lute. On other lodges, and beyond these, groups are engaged in games of the "moc-casin," or the "platter." Some are to be seen manufacturing robes and dresses, and others, fatigued with amusements or occupations, have stretched their limbs to enjoy the luxury of sleep, whilst basking in the sun. With all this wild and varied medley of living beings are mixed their dogs, which seem to be so near an Indian's heart, as almost to constitute a material link of his existence.

In the centre of the village is an open space, or public area, of 150 feet in diameter, and circular in form, which is used for all public games and

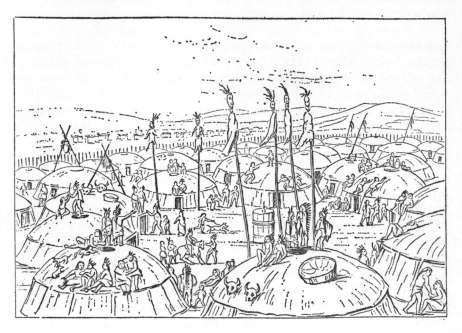

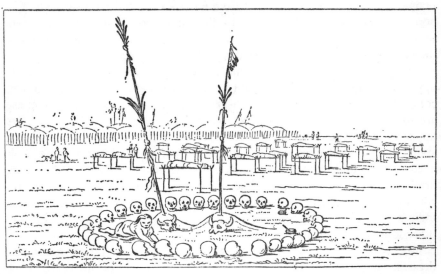

Plate 47, Plate 48

festivals, shews and exhibitions; and also for their "annual religious ceremonies," which are soon to take place, and of which I shall hereafter give
some account. The lodges around this open space front in, with their doors
towards the centre; and in the middle of this circle stands an object of great
religious veneration, as I am told, on account of the importance it has in
the conduction of those annual religious rites.

This object is in form of a large hogshead, some eight or ten feet high,
made of planks and hoops, containing within it some of their choicest
medicines or mysteries, and religiously preserved unhacked or scratched, as
a symbol of the "Big Canoe," as they call it.

One of the lodges fronting on this circular area, and facing this strange
object of their superstition, is called the "Medicine Lodge," or council
house. It is in this sacred building that these wonderful ceremonies, in
commemoration of the flood, take place. I am told by the Traders that
the cruelties of these scenes are frightful and abhorrent in the extreme; and
that this huge wigwam, which is now closed, has been built exclusively for
this grand celebration. I am every day reminded of the near approach of
the season for this strange affair, and as I have not yet seen any thing of it,
I cannot describe it; I know it only from the relations of the Traders who
have witnessed parts of it; and their descriptions are of so extraordinary a
character, that I would not be willing to describe until I can see for myself,
—which will, in all probability, be in a few days.

In ranging the eye over the village from where I am writing, there is
presented to the view the strangest mixture and medley of unintelligible
trash (independant of the living beings that are in motion), that can possibly be imagined. On the roofs of the lodges, besides the groups of living,
are buffaloes' skulls, skin canoes, pots and pottery; sleds and sledges—and
suspended on poles, erected some twenty feet above the doors of their wigwams, are displayed in a pleasant day, the scalps of warriors, preserved as
trophies; and thus proudly exposed as evidence of their warlike deeds. In
other parts are raised on poles the warriors' pure and whitened shields and
quivers, with medicine-bags attached; and here and there a sacrifice of red
cloth, or other costly stuff, offered up to the Great Spirit, over the door of
some benignant chief, in humble gratitude for the blessings which he is
enjoying. Such is a part of the strange medley that is before and around
me; and amidst them and the blue streams of smoke that are rising from
the tops of these hundred "coal-pits," can be seen in distance, the green
and boundless, treeless, bushless prairie; and on it, and contiguous to the
piquet which encloses the village, a hundred scaffolds, on which their
"dead live," as they term it.

These people never bury the dead, but place the bodies on slight scaffolds
just above the reach of human hands, and out of the way of wolves and
dogs; and they are there left to moulder and decay. This cemetery, or place
of deposite for the dead, is just back of the village, on a level prairie

(PLATE 48); and with all its appearances, history, forms, ceremonies, &c. is one of the strangest and most interesting objects to be described in the vicinity of this peculiar race.

Whenever a person dies in the Mandan village, and the customary honours and condolence are paid to his remains, and the body dressed in its best attire, painted, oiled, feasted, and supplied with bow and quiver, shield, pipe and tobacco—knife, flint and steel, and provisions enough to last him a few days on the journey which he is to perform; a fresh buffalo's skin, just taken from the animal's back, is wrapped around the body, and tightly bound and wound with thongs of raw hide from head to foot. Then other robes are soaked in water, till they are quite soft and elastic, which are also bandaged around the body in the same manner, and tied fast with thongs, which are wound with great care and exactness, so as to exclude the action of the air from all parts of the body.

There is then a separate scaffold erected for it, constructed of four upright posts, a little higher than human hands can reach; and on the tops of these are small poles passing around from one post to the others; across which a number of willow-rods just strong enough to support the body, which is laid upon them on its back, with its feet carefully presented towards the rising sun.

There are a great number of these bodies resting exactly in a similar way; excepting in some instances where a chief, or medicine-man, may be seen with a few yards of scarlet or blue cloth spread over his remains, as a mark of public respect and esteem. Some hundreds of these bodies may be seen reposing in this manner in this curious place, which the Indians call, "the village of the dead;" and the traveller, who visits this country to study and learn, will not only be struck with the novel appearance of the scene; but if he will give attention to the respect and devotions that are paid to this sacred place, he will draw many a moral deduction that will last him through life: he will learn, at least, that filial, conjugal, and paternal affection are not necessarily the results of civilization; but that the Great Spirit has given them to man in his native state; and that the spices and improvements of the enlightened world have never refined upon them.

There is not a day in the year in which one may not see in this place evidences of this fact, that will wring tears from his eyes, and kindle in his bosom a spark of respect and sympathy for the poor Indian, if he never felt it before. Fathers, mothers, wives, and children, may be seen lying under these scaffolds, prostrated upon the ground, with their faces in the dirt, howling forth incessantly the most piteous and heart-broken cries and lamentations for the misfortunes of their kindred; tearing their hair—cutting their flesh with their knives, and doing other penance to appease the spirits of the dead, whose misfortunes they attribute to some sin or omission of their own, for which they sometimes inflict the most excruciating self-torture.

When the scaffolds on which the bodies rest, decay and fall to the ground, the nearest relations having buried the rest of the bones, take the skulls, which are perfectly bleached and purified, and place them in circles of an hundred or more on the prairie—placed at equal distances apart (some eight or nine inches from each other), with the faces all looking to the centre; where they are religiously protected and preserved in their precise positions from year to year, as objects of religious and affectionate veneration (PLATE 48).

There are several of these "Golgothas" or circles of twenty or thirty feet in diameter, and in the centre of each ring or circle is a little mound of three feet high, on which uniformly rest two buffalo skulls (a male and female); and in the centre of the little mound is erected a "medicine pole," about twenty feet high, supporting many curious articles of mystery and superstition, which they suppose have the power of guarding and protecting this sacred arrangement. Here then, to this strange place do these people again resort, to evince their further affections for the dead—not in groans and lamentations however, for several years have cured the anguish; but fond affections and endearments are here renewed, and conversations are here held and cherished with the dead.

Each one of these skulls is placed upon a bunch of wild sage, which has been pulled and placed under it. The wife knows (by some mark or resemblance) the skull of her husband or her child, which lies in this group; and there seldom passes a day that she does not visit it, with a dish of the best cooked food that her wigwam affords, which she sets before the skull at night, and returns for the dish in the morning. As soon as it is discovered that the sage on which the skull rests is beginning to decay, the woman cuts a fresh bunch, and places the skull carefully upon it, removing that which was under it.

Independent of the above-named duties, which draw the women to this spot, they visit it from inclination, and linger upon it to hold converse and company with the dead. There is scarcely an hour in a pleasant day, but more or less of these women may be seen sitting or laying (*sic*) by the skull of their child or husband—talking to it in the most pleasant and endearing language that they can use (as they were wont to do in former days) and seemingly getting an answer back. It is not unfrequently the case, that the woman brings her needle-work with her, spending the greater part of the day, sitting by the side of the skull of her child, chatting incessantly with it, while she is embroidering or garnishing a pair of moccasins; and perhaps, overcome with fatigue, falls asleep, with her arms encircled around it, forgetting herself for hours; after which she gathers up her things and returns to the village.

There is something exceedingly interesting and impressive in these scenes, which are so strikingly dissimilar, and yet within a few rods of each other; the one is the place where they pour forth the frantic anguish of their souls—and afterwards pay their visits to the other, to jest and gossip with the dead.

The great variety of shapes and characters exhibited in these groups of crania, render them a very interesting study for the craniologist and phrenologist; but I apprehend that it would be a matter of great difficulty (if not of impossibility) to procure them at this time, for the use and benefit of the scientific world.

LEWIS HENRY MORGAN

(1818-1881)

League of the Iroquois

PREFACE

TO ENCOURAGE A KINDER FEELING TOWARDS THE INDIAN, FOUNDED UPON a truer knowledge of his civil and domestic institutions, and of his capabilities for future elevation, is the motive in which this work originated.

The present Iroquois, the descendants of that gifted race which formerly held under their jurisdiction the fairest portions of our Republic, now dwell within our limits as dependent nations, subject to the tutelage and supervision of the people who displaced their fathers. Their numbers, the circumstances of their past history and present condition, and more especially the relation in which they stand to the people of the State, suggest many important questions concerning their future destiny.

Born to an unpropitious fate, the inheritors of many wrongs, they have been unable, of themselves, to escape from the complicated difficulties which accelerate their decline. To aggravate these adverse influences, the public estimation of the Indian, resting, as it does, upon an imperfect knowledge of his character, and tinctured, as it ever has been, with the coloring of prejudice, is universally unjust.

The time has come in which it is befitting to cast away all ancient antipathies, all inherited opinions; and having taken a nearer view of their social life, condition and wants, to study anew our duty concerning them. Notwithstanding the embarrassments which have obstructed their progress, the obscurity in which they have lived, and the prevailing indifference to their welfare, they have gradually overcome many of the evils inherent in their social system, and raised themselves to a considerable degree of prosperity. Their present condition, when considered in connection with the ordeal through which they have passed, testifies to the presence of an element in their character which must eventually lead to important results. It brings before us the question of their ultimate reclamation, cer-

From Morgan, *League of the Ho-de-no-sau-nee or Iroquois,* edited by H. M. Lloyd (New York: Dodd Mead and Company, 1902), Vol. I, pp. ix-xi, 99-107, 114-115, 327, 321-322, 324-325, 331-335.

tainly a more interesting subject, in itself, than any other connected with the Indian. Can the residue of the Iroquois be reclaimed, and finally raised to the position of citizens of the State? To secure this end, at once so just and so beneficent, our own people have an important part to perform.

As this work does not profess to be based upon authorities, a question may arise in the mind of the reader, whence its materials were derived, or what reliance is to be placed upon its statements. The credibility of a witness is known to depend chiefly upon his means of knowledge. For this reason, it may not be inappropriate to state, that circumstances in early life, not necessary to be related, brought the author in frequent intercourse with the descendants of the Iroquois, and led to his adoption as a Seneca. This gave him favorable opportunities for studying minutely into their social organization, and the structure and principles of the ancient League. Copious notes were made from time to time, when leisure enabled him to prosecute his researches among them, until these had accumulated beyond the bounds of the present volume. As the materials increased in quantity and variety, the interest awakened in the subject finally induced the idea of its arrangement for publication.

THE COUNCILS OF THE IROQUOIS

In an oligarchy, where the administrative power is vested in the members of the Ruling Body jointly, a Council of the Oligarchs becomes the instrumentality through which the will of this body is ascertained and enforced. For this reason the Councils of the Iroquois are important subjects of investigation. By them were exercised all the legislative and executive authority incident to the League, and necessary for its security against outward attack and internal dissensions. When the sachems were not assembled around the general council-fire, the government itself had no visible existence. Upon no point, therefore, can an examination be better directed, to ascertain the degree of power vested in the Ruling Body, and the manner in which their domestic administration and political relations were conducted. When the sachems were scattered, like the people, over a large territory, they exercised a local and individual authority in the matters of every-day life, or in national council jointly adjusted the affairs of their respective nations. Those higher and more important concernments, which involved the interests of the League, were reserved to the sachems in general council. In this council resided the animating principle, by which their political machinery was moved. It was, in effect, the government.

The oligarchical form of government is not without its advantages, although indicative of a low state of civilization. A comparison of views, by the agency of a council, would at any time be favorable to the development of talent. It was especially the case among the Iroquois, in consequence of the greater diversity of interests, and the more extended reach of affairs incident to several nations in close alliance. Events of greater magnitude would spring up in the midst of a flourishing confederacy, than in a nation of inconsiderable importance; and it is demonstrated by the political history of all governments, that men develop intellect in exact proportion to the magnitude of the events with which they become identified. For these reasons, the League was favorable to the production of men higher in capacity than would arise among nations whose institutions and systems of government were inferior.

The extremely liberal character of their oligarchy is manifested by the *modus procedendi* of these councils. It is obvious that the sachems were not set over the people as arbitrary rulers, to legislate as their own will might dictate, irrespective of the popular voice; on the contrary, there is reason to believe that a public sentiment sprang up on questions of general interest, which no council felt at liberty to disregard. By deferring all action upon such questions until a council brought together the sachems of the League, attended by a concourse of inferior chiefs and warriors, an opportunity was given to the people to judge for themselves, and to take such measures as were necessary to give expression and force to their opinions. If the band of warriors became interested in the passing question, they held a council apart, and having given it a full consideration, appointed an orator to communicate their views to the sachems, their *Patres Conscripti*. In like manner would the chiefs, and even the women proceed, if they entertained opinions which they wished to urge upon the consideration of the council. From the publicity with which the affairs of the League were conducted, and the indirect participation in their adjustment thus allowed the people, a favorable indication is afforded of the democratic spirit of the government.

Oratory, from the constitutional organization of the council, was necessarily brought into high repute. Questions involving the safety of the race, and the preservation of the League, were frequently before it. In those warlike periods, when the Confederacy was moving onward amid incessant conflicts with contiguous nations, or, perchance, resisting sudden tides of migratory population, there was no dearth of those exciting causes, of those emergencies of peril, which rouse the spirit of the people, and summon into activity their highest energies. Whenever events converged to such a crisis, the council was the first resort; and there, under the pressure of dangers, and in the glow of patriotism, the eloquence of the Iroquois flowed as pure and spontaneous as the fountains of their thousand streamlets.

The Indian has a quick and enthusiastic appreciation of eloquence. Highly impulsive in his nature, and with passions untaught of restraint, he is strongly susceptible of its influence. By the cultivation and exercise of this capacity, was opened the pathway to distinction; and the chief or warrior gifted with its magical power could elevate himself as rapidly, as he who gained renown upon the war-path. With the Iroquois, as with the Romans, the two professions, oratory and arms, could establish men in the highest degree of personal consideration. To the ambitious Roman in the majestic days of the Republic, and to the proud Indian in his sylvan house, the two pursuits equally commended themselves; and in one or the other alone, could either expect success.

It is a singular fact, resulting from the structure of Indian institutions, that nearly every transaction, whether social or political, originated or terminated in a council. This universal and favorite mode of doing business became interwoven with all the affairs of public and private life. In council, public transactions of every name and character were planned, scrutinized and adopted. The succession of their rulers, their athletic games, dances, and religious festivals, and their social intercourse, were all alike identified with councils. It may be said that the life of the Iroquois was either spent in the chase, on the war-path, or at the council-fire. They formed the three leading objects of his existence; and it would be difficult to determine for which he possessed the strongest predilection. Regarding them in this light, and it is believed they are not over-estimated, a narrative of these councils would furnish an accurate and copious history of the Iroquois, both political and social. The absence of these records, now irreparable, has greatly abridged the fulness, and diminished the accuracy of our aboriginal history.

The councils of the League were of three distinct kinds; and they may be distinguished under the heads of civil, mourning and religious. Their civil councils, *Ho-de-os'-seh,* were such as convened to transact business with foreign nations, and to regulate the internal administration of the Confederacy. The mourning councils, *Hen-nun-do-nuh'-seh,* were those summoned to "raise up" sachems to fill such vacancies as had been occasioned by death or deposition, and also to ratify the investiture of such chiefs as the nations had raised up in reward of public services. Their religious councils, *Gä-e-wé-yo-do Ho-de-os-heń-dä-ko,* were, as the name imports, devoted to religious observances.

No event of any importance ever transpired without passing under the cognizance of one or another of these species of councils; for all affairs seem to have converged towards them by a natural and inevitable tendency. An exposition of the mode of summoning each, of their respective powers and jurisdictions, and of the manner of transacting business, may serve to unfold the workings of their political system, their social relations, and the range of their intellectual capacities.

The name *Ho-de-os'-seh,* by which the Iroquois designated a civil council, signifies "advising together." It was bestowed upon any council of sachems, which convened to take charge of the public relations of the League, or to provide for its internal administration. Each nation had

power, under established regulations, to convene such a council, and prescribe the time and place of convocation.

If the envoy of a foreign people desired to submit a proposition to the
sachems of the League, and applied to the Senecas for that purpose, the
sachems of that nation would first determine whether the question was of
sufficient importance to authorize a council. If they arrived at an affirmative
conclusion, they immediately sent out runners to the Cayugas, the nation
nearest in position, with a belt of wampum. This belt announced that, on a
certain day thereafter, at such a place, and for such and such purposes,
mentioning them, a council of the League would assemble. The Cayugas
then notified the Onondagas, they the Oneidas, and these the Mohawks.
Each nation, within its own confines, spread the information far and wide;
and thus, in a space of time astonishingly brief, intelligence of the council
was heralded from one extremity of their country to the other. It produced
a stir among the people in proporiton to the magnitude and importance
of the business to be transacted. If the subject was calculated to arouse
a deep feeling of interest, one common impulse from the Hudson to the
Niagara, and from the St. Lawrence to the Susquehanna, drew them towards
the council-fire. Sachems, chiefs and warriors, women, and even children,
deserted their hunting grounds and woodland seclusions, and taking the
trail, literally flocked to the place of council. When the day arrived, a
multitude had gathered together, from the most remote and toilsome
distances, but yet animated by an unyielding spirit of hardihood and
endurance.

Their mode of opening a council, and proceeding with the business
before it, was extremely simple, yet dilatory, when contrasted with the
modes of civilized life. Questions were usually reduced to single propositions, calling for an affirmative or negative response, and were thus either
adopted or rejected. When the sachems were assembled in the midst of
their people, and all were in readiness to proceed, the envoy was introduced
before them. One of the sachems, by previous appointment, then arose, and
having thanked the Great Spirit for his continued beneficence in permitting
them to meet together, he informed the envoy that the council was prepared
to hear him upon the business for which it had convened. The council
being thus opened, the representative proceeded to unfold the objects
of his mission. He submitted his propositions in regular form, and sustained them by such arguments as the case required. The sachems listened
with earnest and respectful attention to the end of his address, that they
might clearly understand the questions to be decided and answered. After
the envoy had concluded his speech, he withdrew from the council, as was
customary, to await at a distance the result of its deliberations. It then
became the duty of the sachems to agree upon an answer; in doing which,
as would be expected, they passed through the ordinary routine of speeches,
consultations, and animated discussions. Such was the usual course of

proceeding in the Iroquois council. Variations might be introduced by circumstances.

At this place another peculiar institution of the *Ho-dè-no-sau-nee* is presented. All the sachems of the League, in whom originally was vested the entire civil power, were required to be of "one mind," to give efficacy to their legislation. Unanimity was a fundamental law. The idea of majorities and minorities was entirely unknown to our Indian predecessors.

To hasten their deliberations to a conclusion, and ascertain the result, they adopted an expedient which dispensed entirely with the necessity of casting votes. The founders of the Confederacy, seeking to obviate as far as possible altercation in council, and to facilitate their progress to unanimity, divided the sachems of each nation into classes, usually of two and three each. . . . No sachem was permitted to express an opinion in council, until he had agreed with the other sachem or sachems of his class, upon the opinion to be expressed, and had received an appointment to act as speaker for the class. Thus the eight Seneca sachems, being in four classes, could have but four opinions; the ten Cayuga sachems but four. In this manner each class was brought to unanimity within itself. A cross-consultation was then held between the four sachems who represented the four classes; and when they had agreed, they appointed one of their number to express their resulting opinion, which was the answer of their nation. The several nations having, by this ingenious method, become of "one mind" separately, it only remained to compare their several opinions, to arrive at the final sentiment of all the sachems of the League. This was effected by a conference between the individual representatives of the several nations; and when they had arrived at unanimity, the answer of the League was determined.

The sovereignty of the nations, by this mode of giving assent, was not only preserved, but made subservient to the effort itself to secure unanimity. If any sachem was obdurate or unreasonable, influences were brought to bear upon him which he could not well resist; and it was seldom that inconvenience resulted from their inflexible adherence to the rule. When, however, all efforts to produce unanimity failed of success, the whole matter was laid aside. Farther action became at once impossible. A result, either favorable or adverse, having, in this way, been reached, it was communicated to the envoy by a speaker selected for the purpose. This orator was always chosen from the nation with whom the council originated, and it was usual with him to review the whole subject presented to the council in a formal speech, and at the same time to announce the conclusions to which the sachems of the Confederacy had arrived. This concluding speech terminated the business of the council, and the Indian diplomatist took his departure.

The laws explained at different stages of the ceremonial, were repeated from strings of wampum, into which they "had been talked" at the time of their enactment. In the Indian method of expressing the idea, the string, or the belt can tell, by means of an interpreter, the exact law or transaction of which it was made, at the time, the sole evidence. It operates upon the principle of association, and thus seeks to give fidelity to the memory. These strings and belts were the only visible records of the Iroquois; and were of no use except by the aid of those special personages who could draw forth the secret records locked up in their remembrance.

It is worthy of note, that but little importance was attached to a promise or assurance of a foreign power, unless belts or strings were given to preserve it in recollection. Verbal propositions, or those not confirmed by wampum, were not considered worthy of special preservation.[1] As the laws and usages of the Confederacy were intrusted to the guardianship of such strings, one of the Onondaga sachems, *Ho-no-we-nǎ'-to,* was constituted "Keeper of the Wampum," and was required to be versed in its interpretation.

TREATIES

To the faith of treaties the Iroquois adhered with unwavering fidelity. Having endured the severest trials of political disaster, this faith furnishes one of the proudest monuments of their national integrity. They held fast to the "covenant chain" with the British until they were themselves deserted, and their entire country became the forfeit of their fidelity. In their numerous transactions with the several provinces formed out of their ancient territories, no serious cause of complaint was found against them for the nonfulfilment of treaty stipulations, although they were shorn of their possessions by treaty after treaty, and oftentimes made the victims of deception and fraud. In their intercourse with Indian nations, they frequently entered into treaties, sometimes of amity and alliance, sometimes of protection only, and in some instances for special purposes. All of these national compacts were "talked into" strings of wampum, to use the Indian expression, after which these were delivered into the custody of *Ho-no-we-nǎ'-to,* the Onondaga sachem, who was made hereditary keeper of the Wampum, at the institution of the League; and from him and his successors, was to be sought their interpretation from generation to generation. Hence the expression—"This belt preserves my words," so frequently met with at the close of Indian speeches, on the presentation of a belt. Indian nations, after treating, always exchanged belts, which were not only the ratification, but the memorandum of the compact.

THE CRIMINAL CODE

Crimes and offences were so unfrequent under their social system, that the Iroquois can scarcely be said to have had a criminal code. Yet there

[1] "It is obvious to all who are the least acquainted with Indian affairs, that they regard no message or invitation, be it of what consequence it will, unless attended or confirmed by strings or belts of wampum, which they look upon as we our letters, or rather bonds." Letter of Sir W. Johnson, 1753. Doc. Hist. N. Y., vol. ii, p. 624.

were certain misdemeanors which fell under the judicial cognizance of the sachems, and were punished by them in proportion to their magnitude. Witchcraft was punishable with death. Any person could take the life of a witch when discovered in the act. If this was not done, a council was called, and the witch arraigned before it, in the presence of the accuser. A full confession, with a promise of amendment, secured a discharge. But if the accusation was denied, witnesses were called and examined concerning the circumstances of the case; and if they established the charge to the satisfaction of the council, which they rarely failed to do, condemnation followed, with a sentence of death. The witch was then delivered over to such executioners as volunteered for the purpose, and by them was led away to punishment. After the decision of the council, the relatives of the witch gave him up to his doom without a murmur.

Adultery was punished by whipping; but the punishment was inflicted upon the woman alone, who was supposed to be the only offender. A council passed upon the question, and if the charge was sustained, they ordered her to be publicly whipped by persons appointed for the purpose. This was the ancient custom, when such transgressions were exceedingly rare.

The greatest of all human crimes, murder, was punished with death; but the act was open to condonation. Unless the family were appeased, the murderer, as with the ancient Greeks, was given up to their private vengeance. They could take his life whenever they found him, even after the lapse of years, without being held accountable. A present of white wampum, sent on the part of the murderer to the family of his victim, when accepted, forever obliterated and wiped out the memory of the transaction. Immediately on the commission of a murder, the affair was taken up by the tribes to which the parties belonged, and strenuous efforts were made to effect a reconciliation, lest private retaliation should lead to disastrous consequences. . . . As all quarrels were generally reconciled by the relatives of the parties, long-cherished animosities, and consequently homicides, were unfrequent in ancient times. The present of white wampum was not in the nature of a compensation for the life of the deceased, but of a regretful confession of the crime, with a petition for forgiveness. It was a peace-offering, the acceptance of which was pressed by mutual friends, and under such influences that a reconciliation was usually effected, except, perhaps, in aggravated cases of premeditated murder.

Theft, the most despicable of human crimes, was scarcely known among them. In the days of their primitive simplicity, a mercenary thought had not entered the Indian mind. After the commencement of their intercourse with the whites, the distribution of presents and of ardent spirits among them, and the creation of new kinds of property by the pursuits of trade, so far corrupted the habits of the Indian, that in some instances the vagrant and intemperate were led to the commission of this offence. But in justice to them it must be acknowledged, that no people ever possessed a higher sense of honor and self-respect in this particular, or looked down with greater disdain upon this shameful practice, than did the Iroquois. To this day, among their descendants, this offence is almost unknown. No locks, or bolts, or private repositories were ever necessary for the protection of property among themselves. The lash of public indignation, the severest punishment known to the red man, was the only penalty attached to this dereliction from the path of integrity.

THE TREATMENT OF CAPTIVES

The Iroquois never exchanged prisoners with Indian nations, nor ever sought to reclaim their own people from captivity among them. Adoption or the torture were the alternative chances of the captive. A distinguished war-chief would sometimes be released by them from admiration of his military achievements, and be restored to his people, with presents and other marks of favor. No pledges were exacted in these occasional instances of magnanimity, but the person thus discharged esteemed himself bound in honor never again to take the war-path against his generous enemy. If adopted, the allegiance and the affections of the captive were transferred to his adopted nation. When the Indian went forth to war, he emphatically took his life in his hand, knowing that if he should be taken it was forfeited by the laws of war; and if saved by adoption, his country, at least, was lost forever. From the foundation of the Confederacy, the custom of adoption has prevailed among the Iroquois, who carried this principle farther than other Indian nations. It was not confined to captives alone, but was extended to fragments of dismembered tribes, and even to the admission of independent nations into the League. It was a leading feature of their policy to subdue adjacent nations by conquest, and having absorbed them by naturalization, to mould them into one common family with themselves. Some fragments of tribes were adopted and distributed among the nations at large; some were received into the League as independent members, as the Tuscaroras, while others were taken under its shelter, like the Mohekunnucks, and assigned a territory within their own. The fruit of this system of policy was their gradual elevation to a universal supremacy; a supremacy which was spreading so rapidly at the epoch of their discovery, as to threaten the subjugation of all the nations east of the Mississippi.

A regular ceremony of adoption was performed in each case, to complete the naturalization. With captives, this ceremony was the gantlet, after which new names were assigned to them; and at the next religious festival, their names, together with the tribe and family into which they were respectively adopted, were publicly announced. Upon the return of a war-party with captives, if they had lost any of their own number in the expedition, the families to which these belonged were first allowed an opportunity to supply from the captives the places made vacant in their households. Any family could then adopt out of the residue any who chanced to attract their favorable notice, or whom they wished to save. At the time appointed, which was usually three or four days after the return of the band, the women and children of the village arranged themselves in two parallel rows just without the place, each one having a whip with which to lash the captives as they passed between the lines. The male captives, who alone were required to undergo this test of their powers of endurance, were brought out, and each one was shown in turn the house in which he was to take refuge, and which was to be his future home, if he passed successfully through the ordeal. They were then taken to the head of this long avenue of whips, and were compelled, one after another, to run through it for their lives, and for the entertainment of the surrounding throng, exposed at every step, undefended, and with naked backs, to the merciless inflictions of the whip. Those who fell from exhaustion were immediately despatched as unworthy to be saved; but those who emerged in safety from this test of their physical energies, were from that moment treated with the utmost affection and kindness. The effects of this contrast in behavior upon the mind of the captive must have been singular enough. . . . To the red man compassion has seldom been ascribed, but yet these scenes in the forest oftentimes revealed the most generous traits of character. Admiration for the chivalric bearing of a captive, the recollection of a past favor, or a sudden impulse of compassion, were sufficient to decide the question of adoption. When the perils of the gantlet, which was an enviable lot compared with the fate of the rejected, were over, he ceased to be an enemy, and became an Iroquois. Not only so, but he was received into the family by which he was adopted with all the cordiality of affection, and into all the relations of the one whose place he was henceforth to fill. By these means all recollections of his distant kindred were gradually effaced, bound as he was by gratitude to those who had restored a life which was forfeited by the usages of war. If a captive, after adoption, became discontented, which is said to have been seldom the case, he was sometimes restored, with presents, to his nation, that they might know he had lost nothing by his captivity among them.

The rejected captives were then led away to the torture, and to death. It is not necessary to describe this horrible practice of our primitive inhabitants. It is sufficient to say that it was a test of courage. When the Indian went out upon the warpath, he prepared his mind for this very contingency, resolving to show the enemy, if captured, that his courage was equal to any trial, and above the power of death itself. The exhibitions of heroism and fortitude by the red man under the sufferings of martyrdom, almost surpass belief. They considered the character of their nation in their keeping, and the glory of the race as involved and illustrated in the manner of their death.

GEORGE BIRD GRINNELL

(1849-1948)

The Cheyenne Indians

CHEYENNE CHILDHOOD

THE INFANT'S EDUCATION BEGAN AT AN EARLY AGE, ITS MOTHER TEACHING it first to keep quiet, in order that it should not disturb the older people in the lodge. Crying babies were hushed, or, if they did not cease their noise, were taken out of the lodge and off into the brush, where their screams would not disturb anyone. If older people were talking, and a tiny child entered the lodge and began to talk to its mother, she held up her finger warningly, and it ceased to talk, or else whispered its wants to her. Thus the first lesson that the child learned was one of self-control—self-effacement in the presence of its elders. It remembered this all through life.

This lesson learned, it was not taught much more until old enough, if a boy, to have given him a bow and arrows, or if a girl, to have a doll, made of deerskin, which she took about with her everywhere. Perhaps her mother or aunt made for her a tiny board or cradle for the doll, and on this she commonly carried it about on her back, after the precise fashion in which the women carried their babies. She treated her doll as all children do theirs, dressing and undressing it, singing lullabies to it, lacing it on its board, and, as time passed, making for it various required articles of feminine clothing. Often as a doll she had one of the tiny puppies so common in Indian camps, taking it when its eyes were scarcely open, and keeping it until the dog had grown too active and too much disposed to wander to be longer companionable.

As soon as she was old enough to walk for considerable distances, the little girl followed her mother everywhere, trotting along behind her, or at her side, when she went for water or for wood. In all things she imitated

From Grinnell, *The Cheyenne Indians* (New Haven: Yale University Press, 1923), 2 vols., pp. 108-123, 129-131, 353-356.

her parent. Even when only three or four years of age, she might be seen marching proudly along, bowed forward under the apparent weight of a back-load of slender twigs, which she carried in exact imitation of her mother, who staggered under a heavy burden of stout sticks.

Boys learned to ride almost as soon as they learned to walk. From earliest babyhood infants were familiar with horses and their motions, and children two or three years of age often rode in front of or behind their mothers, clinging to them or to the horses' manes. They thus gained confidence, learned balance, and became riders, just as they learned to walk—by practice. They did not fear a horse, nor dread a fall, for they began to ride old gentle pack-ponies, which never made unexpected motions; and by the time they were five or six years of age, the boys were riding young colts bareback. Soon after this they began to go into the hills to herd the ponies. They early became expert in the use of the rope for catching horses.

Little girls, too, learned to ride at an early age, and while they did not have the practice that boys had, they became good horsewomen, and in case of need could ride hard and far.

In summer little girls as well as little boys spent much time in the water, and all were good swimmers. The courage of such children in the water is shown by an incident in the lives of three old women who in 1912 were still alive on the Tongue River Indian Reservation. When ten or twelve years of age, these children had been sent down to the stream to get some water. Their mothers were at work fleshing buffalo-hides and had so many to work on that the hides were beginning to get dry. The little girls were sent to get water to keep the hides damp until their mothers could flesh them. They went to the stream, and one of them proposed that before carrying up the water they should take a swim. They took off their clothes and ran out onto a fallen tree that projected over the water; and, when about to dive in, one of them noticed a hole in the bank deep under the water, and proposed that they should see where it led to. They swam under the water into the hole. It was dark and nothing could be seen; but the little girls felt something large and soft pass by them, going out of the hole as they were going in. They went on a few feet and saw a little light and, raising their heads, found themselves in a beaver's house. A little frightened by the creature that they had met in the water, which was of course a beaver, they did not like to go back and, seeing the opening at the top of the house through which light filtered, they readily broke a hole through the roof and crept out onto the bottom. Here they found themselves in the midst of a thick growth of wild roses and had a very difficult time, and were much scratched up in getting out of the bushes. This must have taken place perhaps between 1850 and 1860, and the women were Buffalo Wallow Woman, Omaha Woman, and the wife of Big Head, who was sister to White Bull.

Little companies of small boys and girls often went off camping. The little girls packed the dogs, and moved a little way from the camp and there put up their little lodges—made and sewed for them by their mothers —arranging them in a circle just as did the old people in the big camp. In all that they did they imitated their elders. The little boys who accompanied them were the men of the mimic camp.

In the children's play camps the little girls used tiny lodge-poles—often the tall weed-stalks that are used for windbreaks about the lodge—and the boys sometimes acted as horses and dragged the lodge-poles, or hauled travois with the little babies on them. To the sticks they rode as horses, as well as on the dogs, they sometimes fixed travois.

When the lodges were put up the boys used to stand in line, and the older girls asked them to choose their mothers. Each boy selected the girl who should be his mother, and they played together. The girls played in this way until they were pretty well grown, fourteen or fifteen years of age; but the boys gave it up when they were younger, for they strove to be men early, and usually soon after they had reached their twelfth year they began to try to hunt buffalo, killing calves as soon as they could ride well and were strong enough to bend the bow. . . .

The children did not stay out all night, but during the day they pretended that it was night, and went to bed. During the day they moved the camp often; even every hour or two.

These children imitated the regular family life, pretending to be man and wife, and the tiny babies—who were their brothers and sisters— served them for children. Little boys courted little girls; a boy sent to the girl's lodge sticks to represent horses, and if his offer was accepted received with her other sticks and gifts in return. Babies able to sit up were taken out into these camps, but not those that were too young. Sometimes a baby might get hungry and cry, and its little sister who was caring for it was obliged to carry it home to her mother, so that the baby might nurse.

Soon after the little boy was able to run about easily, a small bow and some arrows were made for him by his father, uncle, or elder brother, and he was encouraged to use them. When he went out of the lodge to play, his mother said to him, "Now, be careful; do nothing bad; do not strike anyone; do not shoot anyone with your arrow." He was likely to remember these oft-repeated injunctions.

After that, much of his time was spent in practice with the bow. He strove constantly to shoot more accurately at a mark, to send the shaft farther and farther, and to drop his arrow nearer and nearer to a given spot. As he grew more accustomed to the use of the bow, he hunted sparrows and other small birds among the sagebrush and in the thickets along the streams, with other little fellows of his own age; and as his strength and skill increased, began to make excursions on the prairie for rabbits, grouse, and even turkeys. Little boys eight or ten years of age killed numbers of small birds with their arrows, and sometimes even killed them on the wing.

Though he keenly enjoyed the pursuit, the Cheyenne boy did not hunt merely for pleasure. To him it was serious work. He was encouraged to hunt by his parents and relatives, and was told that he must try hard to be a good hunter, so that hereafter he might be able to furnish food for the lodge, and might help to support his mother and sisters. When successful, he was praised; and if he brought in a little bird, it was cooked and eaten as a matter of course, quite as seriously as any other food was treated. The first large bird, or the first rabbit, killed by the boy, he exhibited to the family with no little pride, in which all shared. . . .

A boy had usually reached his twelfth, thirteenth, or fourteenth year when he first went out to hunt buffalo. Before this he had been instructed in the theory of buffalo running, and had been told how and where to ride, and where to hit the buffalo if he was to be successful. If on his first chase a boy killed a calf, his father was greatly pleased, and, if a well-to-do man, he might present a good horse to some poor man, and in addition might give a feast and invite poor people to come and eat with him. Perhaps he might be still more generous, and at the end of the feast give to his guests presents of robes or blankets. As soon as the boy reached home and his success was known, the father called out from his lodge something like this: "My son has killed a little calf, and I give the best horse that I have to Blue Hawk." If he gave a feast, he explained again, saying: "My little boy has killed a calf. He is going to be a good man and a good hunter. We have had good luck." The man to whom the horse had been presented rode about the camp to show it to the people, and as he rode he sang a song, mentioning the name of the donor, and telling why the horse had been given to him.

Bird Bear, whose boy name was Crow Bed, told me that as a child his father talked to him but little, while his grandfather gave him much advice. This was natural enough, since at that age the father was still engaged in war and hunting, which occupied most of his time, while the older man had passed the period of active life.

Crow Bed was quite young when he went on his first buffalo chase, but he had a good horse, and was soon among the buffalo and close up along-side of a little calf. He was excited and shot a good many arrows into it, but he kept shooting until the animal fell. After he had killed the calf he felt glad and proud. He dismounted and butchered the calf, and with much labor put it on his horse and took the whole animal home, not cutting the meat from the bones and leaving the skeleton on the ground, as a man would have done. When he reached his lodge, his people laughed at him a little for bringing it all home, but his father praised him and said that he had done well. "After a little while," he said, "you will get to killing larger ones, and pretty soon you will kill big buffalo."

His father then shouted out, calling a certain man named White Thunder to come to the lodge and see what his son had done; that he had brought meat into the camp. After White Thunder had come to the lodge, his father presented to White Thunder the horse the boy had ridden and the pack of meat that he had brought in. The incident was discussed all through the village, so that everyone knew of Crow Bed's success.

A year or two later, when a party was made up to go to war against the Snakes, his grandfather advised Crow Bed to go with it. Before they started out the old man said to him: "Now, when the party is about to make a charge on the enemy, do not be afraid. Do as the others do. When you fight, try to kill. When you meet the enemy, if you are brave and kill and count a coup, it will make a man of you, and the people will look on you as a man. Do not fear anything. It is not a disgrace to be killed in a fight."

When Crow Bed started, his father gave away the best horse that he had, because his son was starting on his first war-path. He cried out, asking any poor person in the village who needed a horse to come and see his son starting to war for the first time. He did the same thing when Crow Bed returned from the war-path, although on this first war journey the party had traveled for many days without finding enemies, and returned to the village without accomplishing anything. . . .

Older men gave much advice to their grandsons, sons, and nephews, and tried constantly to warn them against mistakes and to make life easier for them. A well-brought-up man was likely to advise his grown son that occasionally, when he killed a good fat buffalo, he should seek out some old man who possessed spiritual power and offer him the meat, in order to secure his friendliness and the benefit of his prayers. If the old man accepted the present the carcass was pulled around on its belly until the head faced the east. The old man slit the animal down its back, took out the right kidney, and handed it to the young man, who pointed it toward the east, south, west, and north, then up to the sky, and down to the ground, and placed it on a buffalo-chip. The old man was likely to say to the young man: "May you live to be as old as I am, and always have good luck in your hunting. May you and your family live long and always have abundance." As the old man went back to camp with the meat he called aloud the name of the young man, so that all might know he had given him a buffalo. This was an ancient custom.

The training of the little girls was looked after even more carefully than that of the boys. Their mothers, aunts, and grandmothers constantly gave them good advice. They recommended them especially to stay at home, not to run about the camp, and this was so frequently impressed on them that it became a matter of course for them to remain near the lodge, or to go away from it only in company. Both mothers and fathers talked to their daughters, and quite as much to their sons, but in a different way. The mother said: "Daughter, when you grow up to be a young woman, if you see anyone whom you like, you must not be foolish and run off with him. You must marry decently. If you do so, you will become a good woman, and will be a help to your brothers and to your cousins." They warned girls not to be foolish, and the advice was repeated over and over again.

As a girl grew larger she was sent for water, and when still older she took a rope and went for wood, carrying it on her back. The old women early began to teach the girls how to cut moccasins, and how to apply quills and to make beadwork. As they grew older they learned how to cook, and to dress hides, but girls were not put regularly to dressing hides until they were old enough to marry.

Boys and girls alike had each some special friend of their own sex to whom they were devotedly attached, and each pair of friends talked over the advice received from parents.

Children seldom or never quarreled or fought among themselves, and though, as they grew older, continually engaging in contests of strength, such as wrestling and kicking matches, and games somewhat like football, they rarely lost their temper. . . . The Cheyenne boys are naturally good-natured and pleasant, and the importance of living on good terms with their fellows having been drilled into them from earliest childhood, they accepted defeat and success with equal cheerfulness. Among a group of white children there would be much more bickering.

Usually, but by no means always, the Cheyenne boy learned to kill buffalo before he made his first journey to war. Sometimes—as in the case of Bald Faced Bull,—the little fellow's ambition for glory, and ignorance of what war meant, led him to join a war-party at a very tender age. Little boys who did this received much consideration from the older members of the party, and were carefully looked after. They were taken in charge by some older man, and were kept apart from the younger members, who would be likely to tease and embarrass them, and in all ways the journey was made easy for them. Yet when the moment came to fight, they were given every opportunity to distinguish themselves, which meant to fight and to be killed. Because on the occasion referred to Bald Faced Bull was riding a very fast horse, he was chosen as one of ten to charge the camp of the enemy, the most dangerous work in the fight. While such little boys did not often accomplish any great feat, yet sometimes they did so, and returned to the village covered with glory, to the unspeakable delight and pride of their families, and to be objects of respect and admiration to their less ambitious and energetic playfellows. Even when they did nothing especially noteworthy, they were undergoing a training, were learning to know themselves, and to be steady under all conditions, and were hardening themselves to the toils which were to be their most important occupation for the next twenty-five years.

If on such a journey the boy performed any especially creditable act

—if by some chance he killed an enemy, or counted a coup—some one of his near relations, his mother or aunt or an uncle, gave away a horse on the return of the party, and presented him with a new name. If the mother gave the horse, she selected a name that her brother had borne; if the aunt, she chose her brother's name; if the uncle, his brother's name. The name was always a good name—that of some brave man. The name before being given was discussed in the home and chosen with deliberation. If the name given was that of a living man, that man took another name, perhaps that of his father or of an uncle. . . .

The passage of a girl from childhood to young womanhood was considered as hardly less important to the tribe than to her own family. She was now to become the mother of children and thus to contribute her part toward adding to the number of the tribe and so to its power and importance.

When a young girl reached the age of puberty and had her first menstrual period, she, of course, told her mother, who in turn informed the father. Such an important family event was not kept secret. It was the custom among well-to-do people for the father of the girl publicly to announce from the lodge door what had happened and as an evidence of his satisfaction to give away a horse.

The girl unbraided her hair and bathed, and afterward older women painted her whole body with red. Then, with a robe about her naked body, she sat near the fire, a coal was drawn from it and put before her, and sweet grass, juniper needles, and white sage was sprinkled on it. The girl bent forward over the coal and held her robe about it, so that the smoke rising from the incense was confined and passed about her and over her whole body. Then she and her grandmother left the home lodge, and went into another small one near by, where she remained for four days.

If there was no medicine, no sacred bundle, and no shield in her father's lodge, the girl might remain there; but if she did so, everything that possessed a sacred character—even the feathers that a man wore tied in his head—must be taken out.

At the end of the four days, her grandmother, taking a coal from the fire, and sprinkling on it sweet grass, juniper needles, and white sage, caused the girl, wrapped in a robe or sheet, to stand over the smoke, with feet on either side of the coal, purifying herself. This was always done by young unmarried women.

For four days a woman in this condition might not eat boiled meat. Her meat must be roasted over coals. If the camp moved she might not ride a horse, but was obliged to ride a mare.

Young men might not eat from the dish nor drink from the pot used by her; one who did so would expect to be wounded in his next fight. She might not touch a shield or any other war implement, nor any sacred bundle or object. A married woman during this time did not sleep at home, but went out and slept in one of the menstrual lodges. Men believed that if they lay beside their wives at this time they were likely to be wounded in their next battle. Women in this condition were careful to avoid entering a lodge where there was a medicine bundle or bag. For four days women did not walk about much. They spent almost all their time in the small lodge.

The owner of a shield was required to use special care to avoid menstruating women. He might not go into a lodge where one was nor even into a lodge where one had been, until a ceremony of purification had been performed. If the woman thoughtlessly visited the lodge of a neighbor, no shield owner might enter it until sweet grass and juniper leaves had been burned in the lodge, the pins removed and the lodge covering thrown back, as if the lodge were about to be taken down. When this had been done, the covering might be thrown forward again, and pinned together. The lodge having been thus purified, the shield owner might enter it.

The Cheyenne young women and young girls always wore the protective rope, and most of them still do so. This is a small rope or line which passes about the waist, is knotted in front, passes down and backward between the thighs, and each branch is wound around the thigh down nearly to the knee. The wearing of this rope is somewhat confining, yet those who wear it can walk freely. It is worn always at night and during the day when women go abroad.

It is a complete protection to the woman wearing it and is assumed by girls as soon as the period of puberty is reached. All men, young and old, respect this rope, and anyone violating it would certainly be killed by the male relations of the girl. I have heard of one case where a middle-aged man attempted to disregard this protection. The girl and her mother were the only two of the family left, all their male relatives having died. Not long after the attempt was made, the mother and daughter, arming themselves with heavy stones, waylaid the man, took him by surprise, gave him a frightful pounding, and left him for dead. He recovered after a long siege, during which he received sympathy from no one.

THE TREATMENT OF MURDERERS

While certain customs and rules prevailed, there was no form of law as we understand it. There was no such thing as a legal death penalty. If a man killed a tribe fellow, he was often obliged to flee, at least for a time, for he was likely to be killed by some near relative of the dead man. If he saved himself by flight, the council considered the case, and the chief called in the relatives of the dead man and from them learned how much it would take to satisfy them for their loss. The relatives of the slayer were then called together and the penalty stated to them. When they had paid over this fine to the dead man's relatives, the slayer might return to the camp. Whether the matter was thus settled or not, the man who had done the killing was ostracized by his fellows, temporarily expelled from camp, and lost all standing in the tribe, which he never recovered. He was obliged for a time to camp away from the main tribe, and often he went away from their camp and spent a year or more with some other tribe. A common refuge for Cheyennes was the Arapaho camp, where no guilt attached to them and they were regarded as being as good as anyone else. Lapse of time might cause partial forgetfulness of the event by the people at large, but this forgetfulness never extended to the relatives of the man who had been killed. Their anger flamed hot long after all others in the camp had measurably forgotten the deed and in a sense had condoned it. Nevertheless, the slayer of a tribesman, or indeed of anyone belonging in the camp, even though he might be a member of another tribe, remained all his life a marked man.

The slayer of his fellow might not eat in the same lodge with other people, nor from their dishes, nor might he drink out of their cups. He had a special dish, a cup of his own, and if by any chance he drank from a cup not his own, the cup was often thrown away; if not, it was purified. No one would smoke with him. He might not receive the pipe as it was passed from hand to hand, but carried his own pipe and tobacco. If unmarried, he probably never took a wife, for no woman would consent to live with him. . . .

It was said that his pipe did not taste or smell as it should, that he was not a fit person to smoke with. The word *ok kliwŭs,* meaning "one who has killed another," carried the idea of decay, putrefaction, rotting.

If people were talking and the murderer came up to join in the conversation, someone might tell him to be silent, that he should not speak. It was supposed that such a man suffered an inward decay, and would ultimately die and blow away. He was supposed to smell bad, either from this decay or from the bad dreams and thoughts that he must suffer. It was believed by some that from time to time he would vomit portions of his own dead and decaying flesh. A part of this old belief was that a man who had done this could never get close to the buffalo, because the buffalo would smell this dead or decaying flesh and would run away.

An outlaw appears actually to have lost his membership in the tribe, and the fact that he was not allowed to camp with it seems to have been a real expulsion. The man was "thrown away." True, after the gravity of the offense had been partly forgotten with the lapse of time, he might come back to the tribe, but could never recover his old standing. Not only was the man himself hopelessly disgraced, but his whole family lost caste. A young man or woman wishing to marry a daughter or a son of an outlaw was felt to have more or less disgraced his own family. It made no difference how prominent the man might have been nor how good his family, the commission of the act of bloodshed cast a stigma over his family and his relations shared in the disgrace. . . .

It was not solely the killing of a blood member of the Cheyenne tribe that was regarded as so heinous an offense; the same feeling existed if the man killed had been adopted into the tribe. There were many men in the camp, by birth Sioux, Arapaho, Ponca, or others, who had married Cheyenne women and had Cheyenne children, and who were regarded as Cheyennes. If one of these was killed, the murderer became an outlaw.

The fact that they were outlaws justified the chiefs of the Cheyennes in not allowing Porcupine Bear and his party to count the first coup in the fight with the Kiowas and Comanches in 1838. At the time they were regarded as not being members of the tribe, and the coup was no more to be allowed to them as Cheyennes, than it would have been allowed to the member of any foreign tribe as a Cheyenne.

The Disappearance of the Buffalo

IT WAS, INDEED, A GLORIOUS COUNTRY WHICH THE BLACKFEET HAD WRESTED from their southern enemies. Here nature has reared great mountains and spread out broad prairies. Along the western border of this region, the Rocky Mountains lift their snow-clad peaks above the clouds. Here and there, from north to south, and from east to west, lie minor ranges, black with pine forests if seen near at hand, or in the distance mere gray silhouettes against a sky of blue. Between these mountain ranges lies everywhere the great prairie; a monotonous waste to the stranger's eye, but not without its charm. It is brown and bare; for, except during a few short weeks in spring, the sparse bunch-grass is sear and yellow, and the silver gray of the wormwood lends an added dreariness to the landscape. Yet this seemingly desert waste has a beauty of its own. At intervals it is marked with green winding river valleys, and everywhere it is gashed with deep ravines, their sides painted in strange colors of red and gray and brown, and their perpendicular walls crowned with fantastic columns and figures of stone or clay, carved out by the winds and the rains of ages. Here and there, rising out of the plain, are curious sharp ridges, or square-topped buttes with vertical sides, sometimes bare, and sometimes dotted with pines,—short, sturdy trees, whose gnarled trunks and thick, knotted branches have been twisted and wrung into curious forms by the winds which blow unceasingly, hour after hour, day after day, and month after month, over mountain range and prairie, through gorge and coulée.

From Grinnell, *Blackfoot Lodge Tales, The Story of a Prairie People* (New York: Charles Scribner's Sons, 1903), pp. 178-180.

These prairies now seem bare of life, but it was not always so. Not very long ago, they were trodden by multitudinous herds of buffalo and antelope; then, along the wooded river valleys and on the pine-clad slopes of the mountains, elk, deer, and wild sheep fed in great numbers. They are all gone now. The winter's wind still whistles over Montana prairies, but nature's shaggy-headed wild cattle no longer feel its biting blasts. Where once the scorching breath of summer stirred only the short stems of the buffalo-grass, it now billows the fields of the white man's grain. Half-hidden by the scanty herbage, a few bleached skeletons alone remain to tell us of the buffalo; and the broad, deep trails, over which the dark herds passed by thousands, are now grass-grown and fast disappearing under the effacing hand of time. The buffalo have disappeared, and the fate of the buffalo has almost overtaken the Blackfeet.

As known to the whites, the Blackfeet were true prairie Indians, seldom venturing into the mountains, except when they crossed them to war with the Kutenais, the Flatheads, or the Snakes. They subsisted almost wholly on the flesh of the buffalo. They were hardy, untiring, brave, ferocious. Swift to move, whether on foot or horseback, they made long journeys to war, and with telling force struck their enemies. They had conquered and driven out from the territory which they occupied the tribes who once inhabited it, and maintained a desultory and successful warfare against all invaders, fighting with the Crees on the north, the Assinaboines on the east, the Crows on the south, and the Snakes, Kalispels, and Kutenais on the southwest and west. In those days the Blackfeet were rich and powerful. The buffalo fed and clothed them, and they needed nothing beyond what nature supplied. This was their time of success and happiness.

Crowded into a little corner of the great territory which they once dominated, and holding this corner by an uncertain tenure, a few Blackfeet still exist, the pitiful remnant of a once mighty people. Huddled together about their agencies, they are facing the problem before them, striving, helplessly but bravely, to accommodate themselves to the new order of things; trying in the face of adverse surroundings to wrench themselves loose from their accustomed ways of life; to give up inherited habits and form new ones; to break away from all that is natural to them, from all that they have been taught—to reverse their whole mode of existence. They are striving to earn their living, as the white man earns his, by toil. The struggle is hard and slow, and in carrying it on they are wasting away and growing fewer in numbers. But though unused to labor, ignorant of agriculture, unacquainted with tools or seeds or soils, knowing nothing of the ways of life in permanent houses or of the laws of health, scantily fed, often utterly discouraged by failure, they are still making a noble fight for existence.

Only within a few years—since the buffalo disappeared—has this change been going on; so recently has it come that the old order and the new meet face to face. In the trees along the river valleys, still quietly resting on their aërial sepulchres, sleep the forms of the ancient hunter-warrior who conquered and held this broad land; while, not far away, Blackfoot farmers now rudely cultivate their little crops, and gather scanty harvests from narrow fields.

It is the meeting of the past and the present, of savagery and civilization. The issue cannot be doubtful. Old methods must pass away. The Blackfeet will become civilized, but at a terrible cost. To me there is an interest, profound and pathetic, in watching the progress of the struggle.

PART III

GAINING UNDERSTANDING OF THE INDIANS

Introduction

by Ruth L. Bunzel

GEORGE WASHINGTON IN HIS FAREWELL ADDRESS OF 1796 RECOMMENDED the establishment in the City of Washington of a national research institute of learning. A plan for such an institute was drawn up by Joel Barlow but the project languished during the early struggles of the young republic. However, in 1835 it received aid from an unexpected source.

James Smithson—illegitimate son of Sir Hugh Smithson and Elizabeth Macie, graduate of Oxford and Fellow of the Royal Society with a brilliant record in chemistry and mineralogy—died and willed his fortune to the United States Government for the establishment in Washington of an institution to bear his name, for the "increase and diffusion of knowledge among men." After several years of debate in Congress over the legality of accepting a bequest from a private source it was finally accepted, largely through the efforts of John Quincy Adams, and in 1838 Richard Rush was sent to England to claim the estate. In September of that year the clipper *Mediator* delivered to the Mint in Philadelphia for conversion into U.S. currency £104,960 in gold sovereigns. A residuary legacy brought the Smithsonian endowment up to $650,000.

After further debates in Congress and much bickering over the investment of funds and jurisdiction over the new institution, a plan was finally adopted and the first Board of Regents of the Smithsonian Institution, consisting of three members of the Senate, three members of the House of Representatives, four "inhabitants of four different States" and two representatives from the National Institute, met and elected Joseph Henry, Professor of Natural Philosophy in the College of New Jersey (Princeton University) as the first Secretary and Director. His program of organization described the proposed activities as follows:

> *To increase knowledge* it is proposed (1) to stimulate men of talent to make original researches by offering suitable rewards for memoirs containing new truths; (2) to appropriate annually a portion of the income for particular researches under the direction of suitable persons.
>
> *To diffuse knowledge* it is proposed (1) to publish a series of periodical reports on the progress of different branches of knowledge; and (2) to publish occasionally separate treatises on subjects of general interest.

152

The second half of the 19th century was the period of the opening of the West and the epic struggle for the control of the great Plains. The solitary trapper gliding down the great rivers in a canoe, who accommodated himself so well to the life of the wilderness that he frequently abandoned his native culture entirely, had already given way to packs of greedy hunters driving down the buffalo at all seasons of the year, stampeding the herds with firearms, slaughtering without restraint and leaving stinking carcasses rotting on the prairie; and the hunter in turn was having to give way to the homesteader.

As the Indian tribes were pushed back against the mountains the conscience of the nation was alternately troubled by their plight and revolted by the savage ferocity of their bursts of resistance, and always puzzled by the apparent inability of the Indians to settle down on their nice reservations and become civilized. An understanding of the ways of Indian life was sorely needed, and it was this research that the newly formed Smithsonian Institution took on as one of its major commitments. It must be said to the everlasting credit of those who labored in this field that they pursued their tasks with humanity and dedication to the cause of justice.

Among the "suitable persons" whose researches the Smithsonian sponsored was Lewis Henry Morgan, who was embarking on his world-wide study of kinship systems. The Institution undertook to distribute his *Circular in Reference to the Degrees of Relationship among Different Nations,* a questionnaire on kinship terminologies, to consular offices throughout the world. The replies to this questionnaire, plus the seventy or more systems recorded by Morgan himself on three trips to the Indian tribes west of the Mississippi, provided the material for Morgan's monumental study, *Systems of Consanguinity and Affinity in the Human Family,* the first systematic application of the comparative method in ethnology, which was published in 1871 as Volume XVII of the *Smithsonian Contributions to Knowledge.*

Another "suitable person" enlisted to direct particular researches was Major John Wesley Powell, explorer and geologist, veteran of the Civil War (in which he lost his right arm), educator who inaugurated the summer field-work school by taking a group of students into the Rocky Mountains, and a man of exceptional energy and imagination. In 1867 Powell led a party down the Colorado River from its source through the Grand Canyon to the sea, one of the most remarkable trips of exploration in North America. Three members of the expedition who deserted, frightened by the canyons and rapids, were ambushed and killed by Shewits Indians. Powell continued but lost most of his scientific notes. To rectify this he organized a more extended and better-provisioned expedition which yielded large amounts of ethnographic as well as geographic data, and which eventually grew into the Geographical and Geological Survey of the Rocky Mountain Region.

Joseph Henry, whose interests were largely geographic and meteorological, died in 1878. His successor, Spencer Baird, had held the post of Director of the National Museum and had done much to build up the archaeological and ethnological collections. The various geographical surveys were combined under the United States Geological Survey, and the ethnological work was transferred to the Smithsonian Institution under the newly organized Bureau of American Ethnology with Powell as its first director.

Powell organized the first systematic research in American linguistics and ethnology. The first area of concentration was the Southwest, recently brought under United States control through the Gadsden Purchase, and the field of Powell's own explorations. For these researches he gathered together distinguished scholars and talented young students from different fields and from many places. During these early years of the Bureau, James and Matilda Stevenson worked in Zuñi, Hopi and other pueblos and built up the collections of pueblo pottery and other artifacts in the National Museum; Frank Hamilton Cushing lived in Zuñi, penetrating more deeply than any ethnologist before him into the inner life of an Indian tribe; J. Walter Fewkes, working alternately in archaeology and ethnology, attempted to reconstruct Hopi history; Cosmo Mindelieff, an architect, spent a summer studying and sketching pueblo architecture. They were joined a little later by Hough and Holmes. Their concerted efforts constituted the first experiment in area research.

Although the Southwest had first claim on the attention of the Bureau, other areas were not neglected, notably the Plains. Cyrus Thomas who first gained recognition as an entomologist with the Geographical and Geological Survey, joined the Bureau in 1882, and devoted the rest of his life to anthropology. His definitive study of the Ohio Mounds, which had so excited the imagination of early 19th-century archaeologists and theologians, laid speculation to rest and conclusively demonstrated the mounds to be the work of Indians, in all probability ancestors of the Southern Creek. Thomas then turned his attention to another intriguing mystery, the deciphering of Maya hieroglyphs, and here, too, he made notable contributions.

On the Plains, using for the first time dictated texts for linguistic analysis, Riggs and James Owen Dorsey worked on Sioux linguistics and ethnology, Garrick Mallery collected pictographs and picture writing. James Mooney labored among the Cherokee of North Carolina, but after the Sioux outbreak of 1890 and the disaster of Wounded Knee, he was dispatched to the Plains to study the background of Indian unrest. His monumental work on the Ghost Dance Religion, combining field observations, documents, and comparative material from a wide variety of Indian and

European sources, defined the recurrent patterns of Messianic cults and provided a model for their interpretation.

Pursuing the aim of "diffusing knowledge among men," the Bureau early opened the pages of its Reports to the work of outside scholars. Among the great monographs published by the Bureau were Boas' *Central Eskimo* and *Tsimshian Mythology,* Matthews' *Mountain Chant,* Russell's *Pima Indians,* Fletcher and La Flesche's *Omaha Tribe* and their separate publications on the Pawnee and Osage, and many others too numerous to name.

Powell himself was no ethnographer. His ethnological writings were cast in the framework of the crude unilinear evolutionism that dominated anthropological theory in the closing years of the 19th century—"From Barbarism to Savagery," etc. His great contribution to knowledge was his *Classification of American Indian Languages* published in the *Eighth Annual Report* of the Bureau, which brought order into the study of American languages. Although later linguists (Sapir, Radin and others) have grouped Powell's seventy-eight stocks into a small number of stocks of a higher order, this classification added to but did not supersede Powell's original discriminations. However, Powell's greatest skills lay neither in ethnology nor in linguistics, but in administration. As the architect of the Bureau he possessed the most valuable quality of an administrator of research—the ability to recognize talent before it bore fruit, the confidence to tolerate originality and the tact to achieve cooperation without imposing a methodological strait jacket.

Powell died in 1902 and was succeeded by William H. Holmes who had long been associated with the Bureau. Holmes, apparently, had little taste for administration and retired after a few years to accept a post in the National Museum. During his administration, the great *Handbook of American Indian Languages,* begun under Powell, was completed and published as Bulletin 30. Its distinguished editor, Frederick Webb Hodge, followed Holmes as director of the Bureau.

After 1910 the Bureau declined as a force in American anthropology. It still continued to sponsor and publish researches of limited scope, but there were no more great co-operative projects. As the giants of the early days, the men of many parts, died or retired, their places were filled, insofar as they were filled, by specialists in American Indian ethnology. The fire was gone, and above all the dedication to the cause of the Indian people. Scientists did not get involved in causes, they eschewed "value judgments." There was no widespread concern, appropriations fell off, and the focus shifted to other centers.

Government-Sponsored Research

HENRY ROWE SCHOOLCRAFT
(1793-1864)

LEWIS HENRY MORGAN
(1818-1881)

Henry Schoolcraft's father was a glass manufacturer, and it was in connection with a projected book on glass that Schoolcraft went to Missouri in 1817 to investigate the lead mines of that area. There he first encountered the unconquered Indians of the Plains, and after this encounter he abandoned glassmaking. Two trips as geologist of exploring expeditions through the vast forest areas of the headwaters of the Mississippi qualified him as an ethnologist. (Anthropologists of the 19th century always started out as something else, geologists or entomologists or soldiers stranded in the wilderness at the close of frontier wars.) He remained in the Northwest, was appointed Indian agent and married a quarter-breed Chippewa girl.

Schoolcraft was an avid collector of Indian lore. His output was enormous and he was active in promoting ethnological studies. His commitment to Indian research did not, however, prevent him from negotiating a treaty whereby the Chippewa surrendered to the whites the greater portion of their lands bordering the Great Lakes, cutting the tribe in two.

Schoolcraft saw the value of recording songs and tales; it is perhaps his most characteristic contribution. And in his pages we meet again the recurrent theme of Indian life wherever white civilization encroaches: the Messianic prophet and preacher urging a return to goodness.

It was business—mines again and railroads to reach the mines—that brought Lewis Morgan into the North Woods and started him on the research on kinship which culminated in his Systems of Consanguinity and Affinity in the Human Family. *Morgan's scientific life falls into three periods, each occupied with a different problem and each culminating in a major work.*

The first period closed with the publication of his valuable monograph on the Iroquois.

The second period was devoted to the collection and analysis of kinship terminologies. *It closed with the publication of* Ancient Society, *in which the varieties of kinship terminologies were interpreted in terms of an evolutionary scheme of cultural development, from promiscuity through matriliny and patriliny to the North European bilateral family, each system with its appropriate system of kinship nomenclature. Although Morgan's evolutionary scheme never had acceptance among anthropologists (Lowie in his article on social organization [page 486] discusses the arguments against it) probably no work of American anthropology has been more widely read outside America or has had more influence. Published at the time when evolutionism was the dominant mode of thought, it caught the attention of Friedrich Engels who incorporated much of its argument in his* History of the Family, *thus translating it into the realm of dogma for a large part of the world.*

The final years of Morgan's life, less well known than the earlier periods, were devoted to a study of aboriginal houses in relation to social structure. His last major work, Houses and House Life of the American Aborigines *(1881), was the first systematic attempt at a functional analysis of cultural data.*

Morgan has fared rather badly at the hands of later anthropologists in the general reaction against the simple, ethnocentric evolutionary scheme which ranged our primitive contemporaries along a straight path leading from our civilization—taken as the highest expression of the human spirit—back to the dim point in the past when man emerged from his animal ancestry. Now that the heat of that particular controversy has all but died down, it is possible to take another look at Morgan and properly evaluate his very real contributions to ethnography, method and theory, and his role in establishing and promoting scientific anthropology in America.—R.L.B.

HENRY ROWE SCHOOLCRAFT

(1793-1864)

Nursery and Cradle Songs of the Forest

THE TICKENAGUN, OR INDIAN CRADLE, IS AN OBJECT OF GREAT PRIDE WITH an Indian mother. She gets the finest kind of broad cloth she possibly can to make an outer swathing band for it, and spares no pains in ornamenting it with beads and ribbons, worked in various figures. In the lodges of those who can afford it, there is no article more showy and pretty than the full bound cradle. The frame of the cradle itself is a curiosity. It consists of three pieces. The vertebral board, which supports the back, the hoop or foot-board, which extends tapering up each side, and the arch or bow, which springs from each side, and protects the face and head. These are tied together with deer's sinews or pegged. The whole structure is very light, and is carved with a knife by the men, out of the linden or maple tree.

Moss constitutes the bed of the infant, and is also put between the child's feet to keep them apart and adjust the shape of them, according to custom. A one-point blanket of the trade, is the general and immediate wrapper of the infant, within the hoop, and the ornamented swathing band is wound around the whole, and gives it no little resemblance to the case of a small mummy. As the bow passes directly above the face and eyes, trinkets are often hung upon this, to amuse it, and the child gets its first ideas of ornament from these. The hands are generally bound down with the body, and only let out occasionally, the head and neck being the only part which is actually free. So bound and laced, hooped and bowed, the little fabric, with its inmate, is capable of being swung on its mother's back, and carried through the thickest forest without injury. Should it even fall no injury can happen. The bow protects the only exposed part of the frame. And when she stops to rest, or enters the lodge, it can be set aside like any other household article, or hung up by the cradle strap on a peg. Nothing,

From Schoolcraft, "Nursery and cradle songs of the forest," and "Mythology, superstitions and religion of the Algonquins," in *The American Indians, Their History, Condition and Prospects from Original Notes and Manuscripts* (new and revised edition, Buffalo: George H. Derby & Company, 1851), pp. 390-393, 397-398, 206-211.

indeed, could be better adapted to the exigencies of the forest life. And in such tiny fabrics, so cramped and bound, and bedecked and trinketed, their famous Pontiacs and King Philips, and other prime warriors, were once carried, notwithstanding the skill they afterwards acquired in wielding the lance and war club.

The Indian child, in truth, takes its first lesson in the *art of endurance,* in the cradle. When it cries it need not be unbound to nurse it. If the mother be young, she must put it to sleep herself. If she have younger sisters or daughters they share this care with her. If the lodge be roomy and high, as lodges sometimes are, the cradle is suspended to the top poles to be swung. If not, or the weather be fine, it is tied to the limb of a tree, with small cords made from the inner bark of the linden, and a vibratory motion given to it from head to foot by the mother or some attendant. The motion thus communicated, is that of the pendulum or common swing, and may be supposed to be the easiest and most agreeable possible to the child. It is from this motion that the leading idea of the cradle song is taken.

I have often seen the red mother, or perhaps a sister of the child, leisurely swinging a pretty ornamented cradle to and fro in this way, in order to put the child to sleep, or simply to amuse it. The following specimens of these wild-wood chaunts, or wigwam lullabys, are taken from my notes upon this subject, during many years of familiar intercourse with the aboriginals. If they are neither numerous nor attractive, placed side by side with the rich nursery stores of more refined life, it is yet a pleasant fact to have found such things even existing at all amongst a people supposed to possess so few of the amenities of life, and to have so little versatility of character.

Meagre as these specimens seem, they yet involve no small degree of philological diligence, as nothing can be more delicate than the inflexions of these pretty chaunts, and the Indian woman, like her white sister, gives a delicacy of intonation to the roughest words of her language. The term wa·wa often introduced denotes a *wave* of the air, or the circle described by the motion of an object through it, as we say, swing, swing, a term never applied to a wave of water. The latter is called tegoo, or if it be crowned with foam, beta.

In introducing the subjoined specimens of these simple see saws of the lodge and forest chaunts, the writer felt, that they were almost too frail of structure to be trusted, without a gentle hand, amidst his rougher materials. He is permitted to say, in regard to them, that they have been exhibited to Mrs. Elizabeth Oakes Smith, herself a refined enthusiast of the woods, and that the versions from the original given, are from her chaste and truthful pen.

In the following arch little song, the reader has only to imagine a playful girl trying to put a restless child to sleep, who pokes its little head, with black hair and keen eyes over the side of the cradle, and the girl sings, imitating its own piping tones.

Ah wa nain?   (Who is this?)
Ah wa nain?   (Who is this?)
Wa yau was sa—(Giving light—meaning the light of the eye)
Ko pwasod.   (On the top of my lodge.)
           Who is this? who is this? eye-light bringing
           To the roof of the lodge?

And then she assumes the tone of the little screech owl, and answers—

Kob kob kob   (It is I—the little owl)
Nim be e zhau   (Coming,)
Kob kob kob   (It is I—the little owl)
Nim be e zhau   (Coming,)
Kit che—kit che.   (Down! down!)
     It is I, it is I, hither swinging,   (wa wa)
     Dodge, dodge, baby dodge;

And she springs towards it and down goes the little head. This is repeated with the utmost merriment upon both sides.

           Who is this, who is this eye-light bringing
           To the roof of my lodge?
           It is I, it is I, hither swinging,
           Dodge, dodge, baby dodge.

Here is another, slower and monotonous, but indicating the utmost maternal content:

           Swinging, swinging, lul la by,
               Sleep, little daughter sleep,
           'Tis your mother watching by,
               Swinging, swinging she will keep,
           Little daughter lul la by.

           'Tis your mother loves you dearest,
               Sleep, sleep, daughter sleep,
           Swinging, swinging, ever nearest,
               Baby, baby, do not weep;
           Little daughter, lul la by.

           Swinging, swinging, lul la by,
               Sleep, sleep, little one,
           And thy mother will be nigh—
               Swing, swing, not alone—
           Little daughter, lul la by.

This of course is exceedingly simple, but be it remembered these chaunts are always so in the most refined life. The ideas are the same, that of tenderness and protective care only, the ideas being few, the language is in accordance. To my mind it has been a matter of extreme interest to observe how almost identical are the expressions of affection in all states of society, as though these primitive elements admit of no progress, but are perfect in themselves. The e-we-yea of the Indian woman is entirely analogous to the lul la by of our language, and will be seen to be exceedingly pretty in itself.

The original words of this, with their literal import, are also added, to preserve the identity:

(a.)

Wa wa—wa wa—wa we yea, (Swinging, twice, lullaby.)
Nebaun—nebaun—nebaun, (Sleep thou, thrice.)
Nedaunis-ais, e we yea, (Little daughter, lullaby.)
Wa wa—wa wa—wa wa, (Swinging, thrice.)
Nedaunis-ais, e we yea, (Little daughter lullaby.)

(b.)

Keguh, ke gun ah wain e ma, (Your mother cares for you.)
Nebaun—nebaun—nebaun, e we yea, (Sleep, thrice, lullaby.)
Kago, saigizze-kain, nedaunis-ais, (Do not fear, my little daughter.)
Nebaun—nebaun—nebaun, (Sleep, thrice.)
Kago, saigizze-kain, wa wa, e we yea, (third line repeated.)

(c.)

Wa wa—wa wa—wa we yea, (Swinging, twice, lullaby.)
Kaween neezheka kediausee, (Not alone art thou.)
Ke kan nau wai, ne me go, suhween, (Your mother is caring for you.)
Nebaun—nebaun—nedaunis-ais, (Sleep, sleep, my little daughter.)
Wa wa—wa wa—wa we yea, (Swinging, &c. lullaby.)
Nebaun—nebaun—nebaun, (Sleep! sleep! sleep.[1])

A still farther view of Indian manners and opinions is hid under this simple chant. Opinion among the forest race, makes the whole animated creation cognizant and intelligent of their customs.

[1] These translations are entirely literal—the verbs to "sleep" and to "fear," requiring the imperative mood, second person, present tense, throughout. In rendering the term "wa-wa" in the participial form some doubt may exist, but this has been terminated by the idea of the *existing* motion, which is clearly implied, although the word is not marked by the usual form of the participle in *ing*. The phrase lul-la-by, is the only one in our language, which conveys the evident meaning of the choral term e-we-yea. The substantive verb is wanting, in the first line of b. and the third of c. in the two forms of the verb, to care, or take care of a person; but it is present in the phrase "kediausee" in the second line of c. These facts are stated, not that they are of the slightest interest to the common reader, but that they may be examined by philologists, or persons curious in the Indian grammar.

A young married woman is supposed to go out from the lodge, and busy herself in breaking up dry limbs, and preparing wood, as if to lay in a store for a future and approaching emergency.

A raven, perched on a neighbouring tree, espies her, at her work, and begins to sing; assuming the expected infant to be *a boy*.

> In dosh ke zhig o mun
> In dosh ke zhig o mun
> In dosh ke zhig o mun

My eyes! my eyes! my eyes! Alluding to the boy (and future man) killing animals as well as men, whose eyes will be left, as the singer antici- pates, to be picked out by ravenous birds. So early are the first notions of war implanted.

A woodpecker, sitting near, and hearing this song, replies; assuming the sex of the infant to be *a female*.

> Ne mos sa mug ga
> Ne mos sa mug ga
> Ne mos sa mug ga.

My worms! my worms! my worms! Alluding to the custom of the fe- male's breaking up dry and dozy wood, out of which, it could pick its favourite food, being the mösa or wood-worm.

Want of space induces the writer to defer, to a future number, the re- mainder of his collection of these cradle and nursery chants. They con- stitute in his view, rude as they are, and destitute of metrical attractions, a chapter in the history of the human heart, in the savage phasis, which deserves to be carefully recorded. It has fallen to his lot, to observe more perhaps, in this department of Indian life, than ordinary, and he would not acquit himself of his duty to the race, were he to omit these small links out of their domestic and social chain. The tie which binds the mother to the child, in Indian life, is a very strong one, and it is conceived to admit of illustration in this manner. It is not alone in the war-path and the council, that the Red Man is to be studied. To appreciate his whole charac- ter, in its true light, he must be followed into his lodge, and viewed in his seasons of social leisure and retirement. If there be any thing warm and abiding in the heart or memory of the man, when thus at ease, surrounded by his family, it must come out here; and hence, indeed, the true value of his lodge lore, of every kind.

It is out of the things mental as well as physiological, that pertain to maternity, that philosophy must, in the end, construct the true ethnological chain, that binds the human race, in one comprehensive system of unity.

Indian Prophets

IT IS KNOWN THAT THE INDIAN TRIBES OF THIS CONTINENT LIVE IN A STATE of mental bondage to a class of men, who officiate as their priests and sooth-sayers. These men found their claims to supernatural power on early fast-ings, dreams, ascetic manners and habits, and often on some real or feigned fit of insanity. Most of them affect a knowledge of charms and incantations. They are provided with a sack of mystic implements, the contents of which are exhibited in the course of their ceremonies, such as the hollow bones of some of the larger anseres, small carved representations of animals, cowrie and other sea-shells, &c. Some of these men acquire a character for much sanctity, and turn their influence to political purposes, either per-sonally or through some popular warrior, as was instanced in the success of the sachems Buchanjahela, Little Turtle and Tecumthè.

We have recently had an opportunity of conversing with one of this class of sacred person, who has within late years embraced Christianity; and have made some notes of the interview, which we will advert to for the purpose of exhibiting his testimony, as to the true character of this class of impostors. Chusco, the person referred to, is an Ottawa Indian who has long exercised the priestly office, so to say, to his brethren on the northern frontiers. He is now a man turned of seventy. He is of small stature, somewhat bent forward, and supports the infirmities of age by walking with a staff. His sight is impaired, but his memory ac-curate, enabling him to narrate with particularity events which transpired more than half a century ago. He was present at the great convocation of northern Indians at Greenville, which followed Gen. Wayne's victories in the west—an event to which most of these tribes look back, as an era in their history. He afterwards returned to his native country in the upper lakes, and fixed his residence at Michilimackinac, where in late years, his wife became a convert to the Christian faith, and united herself to the mission church on that island. A few years after, the old prophet, who despised this mode of faith, and thought but little of his wife's sagacity in uniting herself to a congregation of believers, felt his own mind arrested by the same truths, and finally also embraced them, and was propounded for admission, and afterwards kept on trial before the session. It was about this time, or soon after he had been received as an applicant for membership, that the writer visited his lodge, and entered into a full examination of his sentiments and opinions, contrasting them freely with what they had formerly been. We requested him to narrate to us the facts of his conversion to the principles of Chris-

tianity, indicating the progress of truth on his mind, which he did in substance, through an interpreter, as follows:

"In the early part of my life I lived very wickedly, following the
META, the JEESUKAN, and the WABENO, the three great superstitious
observances of my people. I did not know that these societies were made
up of errors until my wife, whose heart had been turned by the missionaries, informed me of it. I had no pleasure in listening to her on this
subject, and often turned away, declaring that I was well satisfied with
the religion of my forefathers. She took every occasion of talking to
me on the subject. She told me that the Indian societies were bad, and
that all who adhered to them were no better than open servants of the
Evil Spirit. She had, in particular, *four* long talks with me on the subject, and explained to me who God was, and what sin was, as it is written
in God's book. I believed before, that there was One Great Spirit
who was the Master of life, who had made men and beasts. But she
explained to me the true character of this Great Spirit, the sinfulness of
the heart, and the necessity of having it changed from evil to good by
praying through Jesus Christ. By degrees I came to understand it. She
told me that the Ghost of God or Holy Spirit only could make the
heart better, and that the souls of all who died, without having felt this
power, would be burned in the fires. The missionaries had directed her
to speak to me and put words in her mouth; and she said so much that,
at length, I did not feel satisfied with my old way of life. Amongst other
things she spoke against drinking, which I was very fond of.

"I did not relish these conversations, but I could not forget them.
When I reflected upon them, my heart was not as fixed as it used to be.
I began to see that the Indian Societies were bad, for I knew from my
own experience, that it was not a good Spirit that I had relied upon. I
determined that I would not undertake to *jeesukà* or to look into futurity
any longer for the Indians, nor practice the *Meta's* art. After a while I
began to see more fully that the Indian ceremonies were all bad, and I
determined to quit them altogether, and give heed to what was declared in
God's book.

"The first time that I felt I was to be condemned as a sinner, and that I
was in danger of being punished for sin by God, is clearly in my mind.
I was then on the Island of Bois Blanc, making sugar with my wife. I
was in a conflict of mind, and hardly knew what I was about. I walked
around the kettles, and did not know what I walked for. I felt sometimes like a person wishing to cry, but I thought it would be unmanly
to cry. For the space of two weeks, I felt in this alarmed and unhappy
mood. It seemed to me sometimes as if I must die. My heart and my
bones felt as if they would burst and fall asunder. My wife asked me if I
was sick, and said I looked pale. I was in an agony of body and mind,
especially during *one* week. It seemed, during this time, as if an evil spirit

haunted me. When I went out to gather sap, I felt conscious that this spirit went with me and dogged me. It appeared to animate my own shadow.

"My strength was failing under this conflict. One night, after I had been busy all day, my mind was in great distress. This shadowy influence seemed to me to persuade me to go to sleep. I was tired, and I wished rest, but I could not sleep. I began to pray. I knelt down and prayed to God. I continued to pray at intervals through the night; I asked to know the truth. I then laid down and went to sleep. This sleep brought me rest and peace. In the morning my wife awoke me, telling me it was late. When I awoke I felt placid and easy in mind. My distress had left me. I asked my wife what day it was. She told me it was the Sabbath (in the Indian, prayer-day). I replied, 'how I wish I could go to the church at the mission! Formerly I used to avoid it, and shunned those who wished to speak to me of praying to God, but now my heart longs to go there.' This feeling did not leave me.

"After three days I went to the mission. The gladness of my heart continued the same as I had felt it the first morning at the camp. My first feeling when I landed, was pity for my drunken brethren, and I prayed that they might also be brought to find the true God. I spoke to the missionary, who at subsequent interviews explained to me the truth, the rite of baptism, and other principles. He wished, however, to try me by my life, and I wished it also. It was the following autumn, that I was received into the church. . . ."

The autumn succeeding his conversion, he went over to the spot on the island where he had planted potatoes. The Indian method is, not to visit their small plantations from the time that their corn or potatoes are *hilled*. He was pleased to find that the crop in this instance promised to yield abundantly, and his wife immediately commenced the process of raising them. "Stop!" exclaimed the grateful old man, "dare you dig these potatoes until we have thanked the Lord for them?" They then both knelt in prayer, and afterwards gathered the crop.

This individual appeared to form a tangible point in the intellectual chain between Paganism and Christianity, which it is felt important to examine. We felt desirous of drawing from him such particulars respecting his former practice in necromancy and the prophetic art, as might lead to correct philosophical conclusions. He had been the great juggler of his tribe. He was now accepted as a Christian. What were his own conceptions of the power and arts he had practised? How did these things appear to his mind, after a lapse of several years, during which his opinions and feelings had undergone changes, in many respects so striking? We found not the slightest avoiding of this topic on his part. He attributed all his ability in deceptive arts to the agency of the Evil Spirit; and he spoke of it with the same settled tone that he had manifested in reciting other points in his personal experience. He believed that he had followed a spirit whose object it was to deceive the Indians and make them miserable. He believed that this spirit had left him and that he was now following, in the affections of his heart, the spirit of Truth.

Numerous symbols of the classes of the animate creation are relied on by the Indian *metays* and *wabenos,* to exhibit their affected power of working miracles and to scrutinize the scenes of futurity. The objects which this man had appealed to as personal spirits in the arcanum of his lodge, were the tortoise, the swan, the woodpecker and the crow. He had dreamed of these at his initial fast in his youth, during the period set apart for this purpose, and he believed that a satanic influence was exerted, by presenting to his mind one or more of these solemnly appropriated objects at the moment of his invoking them. This is the theory drawn from his replies. We solicited him to detail the *modus operandi,* after entering the juggler's lodge. This lodge resembles an acute pyramid with the apex open. It is formed of poles, covered with tightdrawn skins. His replies were perfectly ingenuous, evincing nothing of the natural taciturnity and shyness of the Indian mind. The great object with the operator is to agitate this lodge, and cause it to move and shake without uprooting it from its basis, in such a manner as to induce the spectators to believe that the *power of action is superhuman.* After this manifestation of spiritual *presence,* the priest within is prepared to give oracular responses. The only articles within were a drum and rattle. In reply to our inquiry as to the mode of procedure, he stated that his first essay, after entering the lodge, was to strike the drum and commence his incantations. At this time his personal manitos assumed their agency, and received, it is to be inferred, *a satanic energy.* Not that he affects that there was any visible form assumed. But he felt their spirit-like presence. He represents the agitation of the lodge to be due to currents of air, having the irregular and gyratory power of a whilrwind. He does not pretend that his responses were guided by truth, but on the contrary affirms that they were given under the influence of the evil spirit.

We interrogated him as to the use of physical and mechanical means in effecting cures, in the capacity of a meta, or a medicine man. He referred to various medicines, some of which he thinks were antibilious or otherwise sanatory. He used two bones in the exhibition of his physical skill, one of which was *white* and the other *green.* His arcanum also embraced two small stone images. He affected to look *into* and *through* the flesh, and to draw from the body fluids, as bile and blood. He applied his mouth in suction. He characterized both the *meta* or medicine dances and the *wabeno* dances by a term which may be translated *deviltry.* Yet he discriminated between these two popular institutions by adding that the *meta* included the use of medicines, good and bad. The *wabeno,* on the contrary, consisted wholly in a wild exhibition of mere braggadocio and trick. It is not, according to him, an ancient institution. It originated, he said, with a Pottawattomie, who was sick and lunatic a month. When this man recovered he pretended that he had ascended to heaven, and had brought thence divine arts, to aid his countrymen.

LEWIS HENRY MORGAN

(1818-1881)

General Observations Upon Systems of Relationships

AS FAR BACK AS THE YEAR 1846, WHILE COLLECTING MATERIALS ILLUS-
trative of the institutions of the Iroquois, I found among them, in daily
use, a system of relationship for the designation and classification of
kindred, both unique and extraordinary in its character, and wholly unlike
any with which we are familiar. In the year 1851 I published a brief
account of this singular system, which I then supposed to be of their own
invention, and regarded as remarkable chiefly for its novelty. Afterwards,
in 1857, I had occasion to reëxamine the subject, when the idea of its
possible prevalence among other Indian nations suggested itself, together
with its uses, in that event, for ethnological purposes. In the following
summer, while on the south shore of Lake Superior, I ascertained the
system of the Ojibwa Indians; and, although prepared in some measure
for the result, it was with some degree of surprise that I found among
them the same elaborate and complicated system which then existed among
the Iroquois. Every term of relationship was radically different from the
corresponding term in the Iroquois; but the classification of kindred
was the same. It was manifest that the two systems were identical in
their fundamental characteristics. It seemed probable, also, that both were
derived from a common source, since it was not supposable that two peoples, speaking dialects of stock-languages as widely separated as the
Algonkin and Iroquois, could simultaneously have invented the same
system, or derived it by borrowing one from the other.

From this fact of identity several inferences at once suggested themselves. As its prevalence among the Seneca-Iroquois rendered probable

From Morgan, "Systems of Consanguinity and Affinity of the Human Family,"
Smithsonian Contributions to Knowledge 218, Vol. XVIII (Washington: Government
Printing Office, 1871), pp. 490-495, 500-507.

its like prevalence among other nations speaking dialects of the Iroquois stock-language, so its existence and use among the Ojibwas rendered equally probable its existence and use among the remaining nations speaking dialects of the Algonkin speech. If investigation should establish the affirmative of these propositions it would give to the system a wide distribution. In the second place, its prevalence among these nations would render probable its like prevalence among the residue of the American aborigines. If, then, it should be found to be universal among them, it would follow that the system was coeval, in point of time, with the commencement of their dispersion over the American continent; and also that, as a system transmitted with the blood, it might contain the necessary evidence to establish their unity of origin. And in the third place, if the Indian family came, in fact, from Asia, it would seem that they must have brought the system with them from that continent, and have left it behind them among the people from whom they separated; further than this, that its perpetuation, upon this continent would render probable its like perpetuation upon the Asiatic, where it might still be found; and, finally, that it might possibly furnish some evidence upon the question of the Asiatic origin of the Indian family.

This series of presumptions and inferences was very naturally suggested by the discovery of the same system of consanguinity and affinity in nations speaking dialects of two stock-languages. It was not an extravagant series of speculations upon the given basis, as will be more fully understood when the Seneca and Ojibwa systems are examined and compared. On this simple and obvious line of thought I determined to follow up the subject until it was ascertained whether the system was universal among the American aborigines; and, should it become reasonably probable that such was the fact, then to pursue the inquiry upon the Eastern Continent, and among the islands of the Pacific.

The work was commenced by preparing a schedule of questions describing the persons in the lineal, and the principal persons embraced in the first five collateral lines, which, when answered, would give their relationship to *Ego,* and thus spread out in detail the system of consanguinity and affinity of any nation with fullness and particularity. This schedule, with an explanatory letter, was sent in the form of a printed circular to the several Indian missions in the United States, to the commanders of the several military posts in the Indian country, and to the government Indian agents. It was expected to procure the information by correspondence as the principal instrumentality. From the complicated nature of the subject the results, as might, perhaps, have been foreseen, were inconsiderable. This first disappointment was rather a fortunate occurrence than otherwise, since it forced me either to abandon the investigation, or to prosecute it, so far as the Indian nations were concerned, by personal inquiry. . . . By this means all the nations, with but a few exceptions, between the Atlantic and the Rocky Mountains, and between the Arctic Sea and the Gulf of Mexico, were reached directly, and their systems of relationship procured. Some of the schedules, however, were obtained by correspondence, from other parties.

Having ascertained as early as the year 1859 that the system prevailed in the five principal Indian stock-languages east of the mountains, as well as in several of the dialects of each, its universal diffusion throughout the Indian family had become extremely probable. This brought me to the second stage of the investigation, namely to find whether it prevailed in other parts of the world. To determine that question would require an extensive foreign correspondence, which a private individual could not hope to maintain successfully. To make the attempt effectual would require the intervention of the national government, or the co-operation of some literary or scientific institution. It is one of the happy features of American society that any citizen may ask the assistance of his government, or of any literary or scientific institution in the country, with entire freedom; and with the further consciousness that his wishes will be cheerfully acceded to if deserving of encouragement. This removed what might other-wise have been a serious obstacle. In this spirit I applied to Prof. Joseph Henry, Secretary of the Smithsonian Institution, for the use of the name of the latter in foreign countries in the conduct of the correspondence; and further desired him to procure a letter from the Secretary of State of the United States to our diplomatic and consular representatives abroad, commending the subject to their favorable attention. With both of these requests Prof. Henry complied in the most cordial manner. From January, 1860, until the close of the investigation, the larger part of the corre-spondence was conducted under the official name of the Institution, or under cover by the Secretary of State. By these means an unusual degree of attention was secured to the work in foreign countries, the credit of which is due to the influence of the Smithsonian Institution, and to the official circular of the late General Cass, then Secretary of State. In addition to these arrangements I had previously solicited and obtained the co-opera-tion of the secretaries of the several American missionary boards, which enabled me to reach, under equally favorable conditions, a large number of American missionaries in Asia and Africa, and among the islands of the Pacific.

From the distinguished American missionary, Dr. Henry W. Scudder, of Arcot, India, who happened to be in this country in 1859, I had obtained some evidence of the existence of the American Indian system of relation-ship among the Tamilian people of South-India. This discovery opened still wider the range of the proposed investigation. It became necessary to find the limits within which the systems of the Aryan and Semitic families prevailed, in order to ascertain the line of demarcation between their forms and that of the eastern Asiatics. The circumscription of one was necessary to the circumscription of the other. In addition to this it seemed imperative to include the entire human family within the scope of the research, and to work out this comprehensive plan as fully as might be possible. The nearer this ultimate point was approximated the more instructive would be the final results. It was evident that the full significance of identity of systems in India and America would be lost unless the knowledge was made definite concerning the relations of the Indo-American system of relationship to those of the western nations of Europe and Asia, and also to those of the nations of Africa and Polynesia. This seeming necessity greatly increased the magnitude of the undertaking, and at the same time encumbered the subject with a mass of subordinate materials.

In the further prosecution of the enterprise the same schedule and circular were sent to the principal missions of the several American boards, with a request that the former might be filled out, according to its design, with the system of relationship of the people among whom they were respectively established; and that such explanations might be given as would be necessary to its interpretation. This class of men possess peculiar qualifications for linguistic and ethnological researches; and, more than this, they reside among the nations whose systems of consanguinity were relatively of the most importance for the purpose in hand. The tables will show how admirably they performed the task.

They were also sent to the diplomatic and consular representatives of the United States in foreign countries, through whom another, and much larger, portion of the human family was reached. By their instrumentality, chiefly, the system of the Aryan family was procured. A serious difficulty, however, was met in this direction, in a difference of language, which the official agents of the government were unable, in many cases, to surmount. In Europe and Asia the number of schedules obtained through them, in a completely executed form, was even larger than would reasonably have been expected; while in Africa, in South America, and in Mexico and Central America the failure was nearly complete.

To supply these deficiencies an attempt was made to reach the English missions in the Eastern Archipelago and in Polynesia; and also Spanish America through the Roman Catholic bishops and clergy of those countries; but the efforts proved unsuccessful.

The foregoing are the principal, but not the exclusive, sources from which the materials contained in the tables were derived.

A large number of schedules, when returned, were found to be imperfectly filled out. Misapprehension of the nature and object of the investigation was the principal cause. The most usual form of mistake was the translation of the questions into the native language, which simply reproduced the questions and left them unanswered. A person unacquainted with the details of his own system of relationship might be misled by the form of each question which describes a person, and not at once perceive that the true answer should give the relationship sustained by this person to *Ego*. As our own system is descriptive essentially, a correct answer to most of the questions would describe a person very much in the form of the question itself, if the system of the nation was descriptive. But, on the contrary, if it was classificatory, such answers would not only be incorrect in fact, but would fail to show the true system. The utmost care was taken to guard against this misapprehension, but, notwithstanding, the system of several important nations, thus imperfectly procured, was useless from the difficulty, not to say impossibility, of repeating the attempt in remote parts of the earth, where it required two years, and sometimes three, for a schedule to be received and returned. In some cases, where the correspondent was even as accessible as India, it required that length of time, and the exchange of several letters, to correct and perfect the details of a single schedule. Every system of relationship is intrinsically difficult until it has been carefully studied. The classificatory form is complicated in addition to being difficult, and totally unlike our own. It is easy, therefore, to perceive that when a person was requested to work out, in detail, the system of a foreign people he would find it necessary, in the first instance, to master his own, and after that to meet and overcome the difficulties of another, and, perhaps, radically different form. With these considerations in mind it is a much greater cause for surprise that so many schedules were completely executed than that a considerable number should have failed to be so.

The schedule is necessarily self-corrective as to a portion of the persons described, since the position of *Ego* and his or her correlative person is reversed in different questions. It was also made self-confirmatory in other ways, so that a careful examination would determine the question of its correctness or non-correctness in essential particulars. This was especially true with respect to the classificatory system. Notwithstanding all the efforts made to insure correctness, it is not supposable that the tables are free from errors; on the contrary, it is very probable that a critical examination will bring to light a large number. I believe, however, that they will be found to be substantially correct.

In considering the elements of a system of consanguinity the existence of marriage between single pairs must be assumed. Marriage forms the basis of relationships. In the progress of the inquiry it may become necessary to consider a system with this basis fluctuating, and, perhaps, altogether wanting. The alternative assumption of each may be essential to include all the elements of the subject in its practical relations. The natural and necessary connection of consanguinei with each other would be the same in both cases; but with this difference, that in the former the lines of descent from parent to child would be known, while in the latter they would, to a greater or less extent, be incapable of ascertainment. These considerations might affect the form of the system of consanguinity.

The family relationships are as ancient as the *family*. They exist in virtue of the law of derivation, which is expressed by the perpetuation of the species through the marriage relation. A system of consanguinity, which is founded upon a community of blood, is but the formal expression and recognition of these relationships. Around every person there is a circle or group of kindred of which such person is the centre, the *Ego,* from whom the degree of the relationship is reckoned, and to whom the relationship itself returns. Above him are his father and his mother and their ascendants, below him are his children and their descendants; while upon either side are his brothers and sisters and their descendants, and the brothers and sisters of his father and of his mother and their descendants, as well as a much greater number of collateral relatives descended from common ancestors still more remote. To him they are nearer in degree than other individuals of the nation at large. A formal arrangement of the more immediate blood kindred into lines of descent, with the adoption of some method to distinguish one relative from another, and to express the value of the relationship, would be one of the earliest acts of human intelligence.

Should the inquiry be made how far nature suggests a uniform method or plan for the discrimination of the several relationships, and for the arrangement of kindred into distinct lines of descent, the answer would be difficult, unless it was first assumed that marriage between single pairs had always existed, thus rendering definite the lines of parentage. With this point established, or assumed, a natural system, numerical in its character, will be found underlying any form which man may contrive; and which, resting upon an ordinance of nature, is both universal and unchangeable. All of the descendants of an original pair, through intermediate pairs, stand to each other in fixed degrees of proximity, the nearness or remoteness of which is a mere matter of computation. If we ascend from ancestor to ancestor in the lineal line, and again descend through the several collateral lines until the widening circle of kindred circumscribes millions of the living and the dead, all of these individuals, in virtue of their descent from common ancestors, are bound to the "*Ego*" by the chain of consanguinity.

The blood relationships, to which specific terms have been assigned, under the system of the Aryan family, are few in number. They are grandfather and grandmother, father and mother, brother and sister, son and daughter, grandson and granddaughter, uncle and aunt, nephew and niece, and cousin. Those more remote in degree are described either by an augmentation or by a combination of these terms. After these are the affineal or marriage relationships, which are husband and wife, father-in-law and mother-in-law, son-in-law and daughter-in-law, brother-in-law and sister-in-law, step-father and step-mother, step-son and step-daughter, and step-brother and step-sister; together with such of the husbands and wives of blood relatives as receive the corresponding designation by courtesy. These terms are barely sufficient to indicate specifically the nearest relationships, leaving much the largest number to be described by a combination of terms.

So familiar are these ancient household words, and the relationships which they indicate, that a classification of kindred by means of them, according to their degrees of nearness, would seem to be not only a simple undertaking, but, when completed, to contain nothing of interest beyond its adaptation to answer a necessary want. But, since these specific terms are entirely inadequate to designate a person's kindred, they contain in themselves only the minor part of the system. An arrangement into lines, with descriptive phrases to designate such relatives as fall without the specific terms, becomes necessary to its completion. In the mode of arrangement and of description diversities may exist. Every system of consanguinity must be able to ascend and descend in the lineal line through several degrees from any given person, and to specify the relationship of each to *Ego;* and also from the lineal, to enter the several collateral lines and follow and describe the collateral relatives through several generations. When spread out in detail and examined, every scheme of consanguinity and affinity will be found to rest upon definite ideas, and to be framed, so far as it contains any plan, with reference to particular ends. In fine, a system of relationship, originating in necessity, is a domestic institution, which serves to organize a family by the bond of consanguinity. As such it possesses a degree of vitality and a power of self-perpetuation commensurate with its nearness to the primary wants of man.

In a general sense, as has elsewhere been stated, there are but two radically distinct forms of consanguinity among the nations represented in the tables. One of these is descriptive and the other classificatory. The first, which is that of the Aryan, Semitic, and Uralian families, rejecting the classification of kindred, except so far as it is in accordance with the numerical system, describes collateral consanguinei, for the most part, by an augmentation or combination of the primary terms of relationship. These terms, which are those for husband and wife, father and mother, brother and sister, and son and daughter, to which must be added, in such languages as possess them, grandfather and grandmother, and grandson and granddaughter, are thus restricted to the primary sense in which they are here employed. All other terms are secondary. Each relationship is thus made independent and distinct from every other. But the second, which is that of the Turanian, American Indian, and Malayan families, rejecting descriptive phrases in every instance, and reducing consanguinei to great classes by a series of apparently arbitrary generalizations, applies the same terms to all the members of the same class. It thus confounds relationships, which, under the descriptive system, are distinct, and enlarges the signification both of the primary and secondary terms beyond their seemingly appropriate sense.

Although a limited number of generalizations have been developed in the system of the first-named families, which are followed by the introduction of additional special terms to express in the concrete the relationships thus specialized, yet the system is properly characterized as descriptive, and was such originally. It will be seen in the sequel that the partial classification of kindred which it now contains is in harmony with the principles of the descriptive form, and arises from it legitimately to the extent to which it is carried; and that it is founded upon conceptions entirely dissimilar from those which govern in the classificatory form. These generalizations, in some cases, are imperfect when logically considered; but they were designed to realize in the concrete the precise relationships which the descriptive phrases suggest by implication. In the Erse, for example, there are no terms for uncle or aunt, nephew or niece, or cousin; but they were described as *father's brother, mother's brother, brother's son,* and so on. These forms of the Celtic are, therefore, purely descriptive. In most of the Aryan languages terms for these relationships exist. My father's brothers and my mother's brothers, in English, arc generalized into one class, and the term *uncle* is employed to express the relationship. The relationships to *Ego* of the two classes of persons are equal in their degree of nearness, but not the same in kind; wherefore, the Roman method is preferable, which employed *patruus* to express the former, and *avunculus* to indicate the latter. The phrase "father's brother" describes a person, but it likewise implies a bond of connection which *patruus* expresses in the concrete. In like manner, my father's brother's son, my father's sister's son, my mother's brother's son, and my mother's sister's son are placed upon an equality by a similar generalization, and the relationship is expressed by the term *cousin.* They stand to me in the same degree of nearness, but they are related to me in four different ways. The use of these terms, however, does not invade the principles of the descriptive system, but attempts to realize the implied relationships in a simpler manner. On the other hand, in the system of the last-named families, while corresponding terms exist, their application to particular persons is founded upon very different generalizations, and they are used in an apparently arbitrary manner. In Seneca-Iroquois, for example, my father's brother is my father. Under the system he stands to me in that relationship and no other. I address him by the same term, *Hä-nih',* which I apply to my own father. My mother's brother, on the contrary, is my uncle, *Hoc-no'seh,* to whom, of the two, this relationship is restricted. Again, with myself a male, my brother's son is my son, *Ha-ah'-wuk,* the same as my own son; while my sister's son is my nephew, *Ha-yă'-wan-da;* but with myself a female, these relationships are reversed. My brother's son is then my nephew; while my sister's son is my son. Advancing to the second collateral line, my father's brother's son and my mother's sister's son are my brothers, and they severally stand to me in the same relationship as my own brother; but my father's sister's son and by mother's brother's son are my cousins. The same relationships are recognized under the two forms, but the generalizations upon which they rest are different.

In the system of relationship to the Aryan, Semitic, and Uralian families, the collateral lines are maintained distinct and perpetually divergent from the lineal, which results, theoretically as well as practically, in a dispersion of the blood. The value of the relationships of collateral consanguinei is depreciated and finally lost under the burdensomeness of the descriptive method. This divergence is one of the characteristics of the descriptive system. On the contrary, in that of the Turanian, American Indian, and Malayan families, the several collateral lines, near and remote, are finally brought into, and merged in the lineal line, thus theoretically, if not practically, preventing a dispersion of the blood. The relationships of collaterals by this means is both appreciated and preserved. This mergence is, in like manner, one of the characteristics of the classificatory system.

How these two forms of consanguinity, so diverse in their fundamental conceptions and so dissimilar in their structure, came into existence it may be wholly impossible to explain. The first question to be considered relates to the nature of these forms and their ethnic distribution, after the ascertainment of which their probable origin may be made a subject of investigation. While the existence of two radically distinct forms appears to separate the human family, so far as it is represented in the tables, into two great divisions, the Indo-European and the Indo-American, the same testimony seems to draw closer together the several families of which these divisions are composed, without forbidding the supposition that a common point of departure between the two may yet be discovered. If the evidence deposited in these systems of relationship tends, in reality, to consolidate the families named into two great divisions, it is a tendency in the direction of unity of origin of no inconsiderable importance.

After the several forms of consanguinity and affinity, which now prevail in the different families of mankind, have been presented and discussed, the important question will present itself, how far these forms become changed with the progressive changes of society. The uses of systems of relationship to establish the genetic connection of nations will depend, first, upon the structure of the system, and, secondly, upon the stability of its radical forms. In form and feature they must be found able, when once established, to perpetuate themselves through indefinite periods of time. The question of their use must turn upon that of the stability of their radical features. Development and modification, to a very considerable extent, are revealed in the tables in which the comparison of forms is made upon an extended scale; but it will be observed, on further examination, that these changes are further developments of the fundamental conceptions which lie, respectively, at the foundation of the two original systems.

There is one powerful motive which might, under certain circumstances, tend to the overthrow of the classificatory form and the substitution of the descriptive, but it would arise after the attainment of civilization. This is the inheritance of estates. It may be premised that the bond of kindred, among uncivilized nations, is a strong influence for the mutual protection of related persons. Among nomadic stocks, especially, the respectability of the individual was measured, in no small degree, by the number of his kinsmen. The wider the circle of kindred the greater the assurance of safety, since they were the natural guardians of his rights and the avengers of his wrongs. Whether designedly or otherwise, the Turanian form of consanguinity organized the family upon the largest scale of numbers. On the other hand, a gradual change from a nomadic to a civilized condition would prove the severest test to which a system of consanguinity could be subjected. The protection of the law, or of the State, would become substituted for that of kinsmen; but with more effective power the rights of property might influence the system of relationship. This last consideration, which would not arise until after a people had emerged from barbarism, would be adequate beyond any other known cause to effect a radical change in a pre-existing system, if this recognized relationships which would defeat natural justice in the inheritance of property. In Tamilian society, where my brother's son and my cousin's son are both my sons, a useful purpose may have been subserved by drawing closer, in this manner, the kindred bond; but in a civilized sense it would be manifestly unjust to place either of these collateral sons upon an equality with my own son for the inheritance of my estate. Hence the growth of property and the settlement of its distribution might be expected to lead to a more precise discrimination of the several degrees of consanguinity if they were confounded by the previous system.

Where the original system, anterior to civilization, was descriptive, the tendency to modification, under the influence of refinement, would be in the direction of a more rigorous separation of the several lines of descent, and of a more systematic description of the persons or relationships in each. It would not necessarily lead to the abandonment of old terms nor to the invention of new. This latter belongs, usually, to the formative period of a language. When that is passed, compound terms are resorted to if the descriptive phrases are felt to be inconvenient. Wherever these compounds are found it will be known at once that they are modern in the language. The old terms are not necessarily radical, but they have become so worn down by long-continued use as to render the identification of their component parts impossible. While the growth of nomenclatures of relationship tends to show the direction in which existing systems have been modified, it seems to be incapable of throwing any light upon the question whether a classificatory form ever becomes changed into a descriptive, or the reverse. It is more difficult, where the primitive system was classificatory, to ascertain the probable direction of the change. The uncivilized nations have remained substantially stationary in their condition through all the centuries of their existence, a circumstance eminently favorable to the permanency of their domestic institutions. It is not supposable, however, that they have resisted all modifications of their system of consanguinity. The opulence of the nomenclature of relationships, which is characteristic of the greater portion of the nations whose form is classificatory, may tend to show that, if it changed materially, it would be in the direction of a greater complexity of classification. It is extremely difficult to arrive at any general conclusions upon this question with reference to either form. But it may be affirmed that if an original system changes materially, after it has been adopted into use, it is certain to be done in harmony with the ideas and conceptions which it embodies, of which the changes will be further and logical developments.

It should not be inferred that forms of consanguinity and affinity are either adopted, modified, or laid aside at pleasure. The tables entirely dispel such a supposition. When a system has once come into practical use, with its nomenclature adopted, and its method of description or of classification settled, it would, from the nature of the case, be very slow to change. Each person, as has elsewhere been observed, is the centre around whom a group of consanguinei is arranged. It is my father, my mother, my brother, my son, my uncle, my cousin, with each and every human being; and, therefore, each one is compelled to understand, as well as to use, the prevailing system. It is an actual necessity to all alike, since each relationship is personal to *Ego*. A change of any of these relationships, or a subversion of any of the terms invented to express them, would be extremely difficult if not impossible; and it would be scarcely less difficult to enlarge or contract the established use of the terms themselves. The possibility of this permanence is increased by the circumstance that these systems exist by usage rather than legal enactment, and therefore the motive to change must be as universal as the usage. Their use and preservation are intrusted to every person who speaks the common language, and their channel of transmission is the blood. Hence it is that, in addition to the natural stability of domestic institutions, there are special reasons which contribute to their permanence, by means of which it is rendered not improbable that they might survive changes of social condition sufficiently radical to overthrow the primary ideas in which they originated.

The United States National Museum

OTIS T. MASON
(1838-1908)

WILLIAM H. HOLMES
(1846-1933)

When Otis T. Mason, whose early training had been in classical studies, joined the Smithsonian Institution in 1872 as collaborator in ethnology, he entertained a dream of a national museum where the growing ethnological collections could be properly housed and displayed. The dream became an actuality in 1881. Soon after, Mason gave up all other work to become the Smithsonian's curator of ethnology.

To him fell the task of identifying, cataloguing and arranging the specimens. An expert in classification, he set up a typology for each category of objects, supplementing his catalogue with descriptive papers on such subjects as throwing sticks, cradles, women's knives, etc. He arranged the exhibits by types in series designed to show the history of inventions, thus introducing the evolutionary point of view into museum arrangement.

Although he recognized the role of a museum in making vivid the life of peoples and arranged one exhibit as an ethnic unit, his real interest was taxonomy, and his most important published contributions, such as his great monograph on Aboriginal American Basketry, *deal with classification and description. Textiles particularly delighted him; their construction challenged him. He did not go into the field; he learned from things rather than from people. He was, in short, the model museum man.*

Similarly William H. Holmes was essentially a museum man, concerned with things rather than with people. His only field work was as geologist for an archaeological expedition. Although he was Chief of the Bureau of Ethnology for a number of years, he was not happy in an administrative role (Lowie reports that he was "stiff" and "forbidding"), and he resigned after a few years to go back to museum work.

Holmes' early training and great love was art. It was a fellow-student in his art classes who first introduced him to the director of the Smithsonian Institution and his first work there was drawing illustrations for a publication on shells. His early training stood him in good stead; his sensitivity to form and to the problems of design made him one of the very few great writers in the field of primitive art. He recognized the influence of motor habits, material, and technique on the development of form, thereby anticipating Boas' more developed handling of these ideas.—R.L.B.

OTIS T. MASON

(1838-1908)

The Carrying of Children

NEXT TO GETTING ABOUT AND CARRYING THINGS COMES THE ACTIVITY OF carrying persons, or passenger traffic, and this commences with the transportation of helpless children.

Invention has had in this art an opportunity of elaboration along the lines of geographic conditions in obedience to the commands of ethnic peculiarities, but the most primitive method resorts to no machinery whatever. (Fig. 186.)

The traffic of the world in the present day is always numbered in millions, whether of persons, of miles, of tons of freight carried or coal consumed, or of dollars invested. It began with naked mothers carrying naked children, without the expenditure of one dollar. To study this art from its simple to its complex forms one must commence with tropical peoples who have never been elsewhere. Here the infant is transported upon the person of the mother, both of them clinging one to the other by a semiautomatic habit or instinct. In this paper little attention will be paid to the bed and wrappings of infants. That subject has already been discussed.[1]

African mothers, on the testimony of the U. S. National Museum, have never invented a single device for their tiny passengers, who are usually gathered into the folds of the sash or shawl or mantle. Doubtless this garment is worn frequently to give the child a resting place, and netting tied about the neck furnishes support to the nestling; but it is practically true

---

[1] E. Pokrowski, Trans. Soc. Friends of Nat. Sci., Moscow; Mason, "Cradles of the American Aborigines," Rep. Smithsonian Inst. (U. S. Nat. Mus.), 1887, pp. 164-212; J. H. Porter, "Notes on the Artificial Deformation of Children among Savage and Civilized Peoples," ibid., pp. 213-235; H. Ploss, "Das Kind in Brauch und Sitte der Völker," Leipzig, 1884, 2 vols.

From Mason, "Primitive Travel and Transportation," *Report of the U. S. National Museum in the Annual Report of the Board of Regents of the Smithsonian Institution for 1894* (Washington: Government Printing Office, 1896), pp. 490-495, 500-507.

that the spirit of invention in Africa has not been awakened by the necessity of carrying infants.

Schurtz figures a Masakara negro woman in the interior of Africa, grinding grain on the metate, with a muller, at the same time bearing an infant in the folds of the shawl upon her back.[2] And the union of the manufacturer with the carrier is one of the commonest occurrences there.

Ratzel gives an interesting picture, after Falkenstein, of a Loango mother, barefooted, wearing a head handkerchief, hoeing in the field, and carrying a sleeping infant on her back, securely held in place by a cloth or shawl, tied around her body under the arms and above the breasts, and reaching to her ankles.[3]

Holub, in his illustrated catalogue of the South African Exposition in Prague, pictures a Bechuana woman engaged in the

Fig. 186. WOMAN OF BRITTANY CARRYING CHILD. *From sketch by W. E. Chandler*

same double exercise, and illustrated books and journals describing the west coast of Africa show the usual position of the African babe riding astride the mother's hips and enfolded in the loose garment. (Fig. 187.) In many places the attachment to her body is reduced to a mere string.

The Zulu mother carries her babe in a shawl, or wide sash, which passes around her body above her breasts, close under her arms, and reaching quite down to her hips.[4] The child sits in the shawl as in a swing, which passes about the loins above the center of gravity.

The Hottentot women generally wear the krass—a square piece of the skin of a wild beast, generally a wildcat, tied on with the hairy side outward—around their shoulders, which, like those of the men, cover their backs and sometimes reach down to their hams. Between two krasses they fasten a suckling child, if they have one, with the head just peeping over their shoulders. The under krass prevents their bodies being hurt by the children at their back.[5]

Ratzel figures Abyssinian women in the double function of carrying children and carrying freight. In the former, the tiny passenger rests in the folds of the dress on the back. In the latter, the load is borne on the back and sustained by ropes, knapsackwise[6]

2 "Katechismus der Völkerkunde," Leipzig, 1893, p. 180.
3 "Völkerkunde," Leipzig, 1887, I, p. 155.
4 Ratzel, "Völkerkunde," Leipzig, 1887, I, p. 150.
5 Kolben, "Voyage to the Cape of Good Hope," IV, p. 14.
6 "Völkerkunde," III, p. 229.

Fig. 187. AFRICAN METHOD OF
CARRYING CHILD.
*From a photograph in the
U. S. National Museum*

In European countries for the most part, the child has been consigned to a wheel carriage of some kind. The simplest form of this is the Baschkir Kumé, which is merely one form of California cradle (fig. 188), with wheels on the hindmost cross bar, and a hood of birch bark instead of reed mat.[7]

A forked stick is the frame of the cradle and hounds of the axle. On this rests an oblong cylinder of birch bark, ovoid in horizontal outline, and having a lattice bottom. The hood is of birch bark, and not unlike that of a common wagon.

A differentiation has also taken place among cradle frames, one form dropping the suspension strings, by means of which it became now a bed to be swung, now a vehicle to be carried, assumes the rockers or wheels and is no longer lifted from the ground; the other remains in the condition wherein it may be now a swinging bed, now a carrying frame.

The carrying of children on the person has been affected in European countries by this differentiation. Wherever the old-time carrying frame and swing becomes a rocking cradle or a wagon, the process of carrying the child reverts to the most primitive type, chiefly on one arm, after the manner of the African mother.

The commonest sight and often a painful sight in the poorer settlements of any modern city is that of a girl, often quite young, lugging an infant on the left arm, distorting her body hopelessly.

Likewise may be seen among the folk in sport or in serious humor and in the pastimes of children survivals of past practices in the carriage of infants. In art, as has been previously stated, the drudgeries of life are glorified. If the caryatid and atlas are the æstheticising and apotheosis of burden bearing on head and back, the many renditions of the Madonna exalt in art and religion the transportation of the human infant on the left arm.[8]

Hercules was cradled in his father's shield: Dionysius in a winnowing fan, which has the same shape. The Greeks do not seem to have carried

[7] Cf. Pokrowski, Rev. d'Ethnog., 1889, fig. 27, p. 34, with Rep. Smithsonian Inst. (U. S. Nat. Mus.), 1887, p. 180, fig. 12.
[8] Cf. "Woman's Share in Primitive Culture," New York, 1894, p. 186, fig. 50. Woman of India carrying burden and child.

children in cradles, but the Romans had gotten so far, although the figures resemble the Sioux shoe shaped device without the wooden support.[9]

The Semite mother who carries her child about her neck puts it astride one shoulder, shifting it to the other as occasion demands (fig. 189). No device or invention is used, but a semiautomatic habit, a kind of instinct for clinging to each other, keeps the young passenger in position. This should be compared with the position of the child among other peoples. . . .

In the Indo-Pacific area there is little change, only local modifications in the primitive method of having as little machinery as possible involved in the transportation of the infant. Of course none of these peoples have ever so much as thought of differentiating the carriage device from the sleeping device. . . .

The child's bed and carriage in one piece exists in Russia, in all the countries under her sway, and in the lands along the southern border of these. It

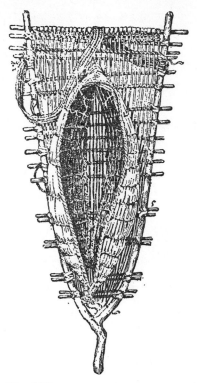

Fig. 188. CRADLE OF RUSHES, WITH HANDLE, USED BY KLAMATH INDIANS OF CALIFORNIA.

had a wide development in America. This combination carriage and bed exists in two forms— that in which the whole body of the child is bandaged, legs and all, and that in which the body is swaddled and the legs are partly free. These two have relation to climate and pedagogic notions and superstitions; but they have profound relations also to the nomadic and hunting life of the people.

Pokrowski traces the rigid cradle wherein the child is laid upon its back and strapped therein so as often to produce deformation among the Georgians, Nogaïs, Sartes, Kirghiz, Kalmuck, Yakut, Buriat, Ostiak, and Samoyed.[10] He says that it is the most ancient and widely spread. In central Russia it is formed of four planks about a finger and a half high, in shape of a box, 1 meter long and 80 centimeters wide, on which is fixed a cloth bottom, and from the corners are ropes which unite in a ring above for suspension. In fact, it is a wooden hammock that has lost its carrying function. But Pokrowski affirms that these cradles often preserve the

[9] Smith, Dictionary of Greek and Roman Antiquities, s. v., *Cunae.*
[10] Mém. Soc. d. Amis. d. Sc. Nat., 1886. See also Rev. d'Anthrop., 1885, p. 364; 1887, p. 238.

ancient form that they may be carried about as well as hung up in the house. They are both carriage and swinging cradle in one. The cords from the two borders of the cradle cross over the woman's breast as in the bandolier[11] (fig. 192).

Fig. 189. WOMAN OF PAL-
ESTINE CARRYING CHILD.
*From a sketch in the
Christian Herald*

The American aboriginal cradle is influenced by climate. It can not exist in extremes of heat or cold. In one case the child would be smothered, in the other it would be frozen.

Again, whatever may be the material, whether birch bark, rawhide, a flat board, a dugout, a frame of rods, the infant's head is never placed in contact with it. There is always between the head and this hard frame or board a pillow of fur, hair, shredded bark, down, or some other substance. It is idle, therefore, to collect cradles in order to study intentional and undesigned head flattening unless we secure also the pillow. One cradle, from the Yumas, has two little pads about 4 inches apart to catch the head of the infant; another has a regular pillow, and so on.

Finally, all the U. S. National Museum cradles are made to stand up or to hang up. A great many persons who are familiar with the subject have been questioned, and it seems to be true that Indian cradles are very seldom laid flat on the ground. In that case the head is perfectly free, and after the child is a few weeks old, excepting during sleep, the head does not touch the pillow at all.

As explained elsewhere, the exigencies of climate prevent the Eskimo from carrying their children in open frames. But the Lamut and Tungus devices just named exist in a climate as cold as any endured by the Eskimo. It is necessary to seek the explanation of the absence of any device among the Eskimo in the difference of the culture grade. The Asiatics are herdsmen and hang the children to the saddlebow. The Eskimo have generally no good wood for frames and no good reason to separate the infant from the mother. When the child is young it rides in the mother's hood, between her fur coat and her skin. To prevent the young passenger from getting lost Boas intimates that a strap is worn about the mother's waist. The costume of this unique people over many hundreds of miles of coast east and west is uniform in this regard.[12]

When children are about a month old they are put into a jacket made

11 Rev. d'Ethnog., Paris, 1889, p. 10.
12 Sixth Ann. Rep. Bureau of Ethnology, p. 556.

from the skin of a deer fawn having a cap of the same material, their legs remaining bare, as they are always carried in their mother's hood. In some places, where large boots are in use, they are said to be carried in these.[13]

The hood of the jacket is much the larger in that of the women, for the purpose of holding a child. The back of the jacket also bulges out in the middle to give the child a footing, and a strap or girdle below this, secured round the waist by two large wooden buttons in front, prevents the infant from sliding down.[14]

Fig. 192. WOMAN OF LITTLE RUSSIA
CARRYING CHILD.
From a figure in the Revue d'Ethnographie

The mode of treating infants is one of the national customs of a people that changes most slowly says Richardson.[15]

Peary says that the woman of North Greenland, like the man, wore the ahtee and netcheh, made respectively of bird skin and sealskin. They differed in pattern from those of the man only in the back, where

[13] Ibid., p. 556.
[14] Ibid., p. 557.
[15] Richardson, "Arctic Searching Expedition," New York, 1852, p. 218.

an extra width is sewed in, which forms a pouch extending the entire length of the back of the wearer and fitting tight around the hips. In this pouch or hood the baby is carried; its little body, covered only by a shirt reaching to the waist, made of the skin of a young blue fox, is placed against the bare back of the mother, and the head, covered by a tight-fitting skull-cap made of seal skin, is allowed to rest against the mother's shoulder. In this way the Eskimo child is carried constantly, whether awake or asleep, and without clothing except the shirt and cap, until it can walk, which is usually at the age of 2 years; then it is clothed in skin and allowed to toddle about. If it is the youngest member of the family, after it has learned to walk, it still takes its place in the mother's hood whenever it is sleepy or tired, just as American mothers pick up their little toddlers and rock them.[16]

When the Eskimo babe is large enough to escape from the hood and walk it has still to be carried a great deal. Of this sort, both father and mother take the youngster by one arm and one leg, give it a toss, and in a twinkling the youthful rider is sitting pickaback astride the parent's neck. The author has seen both men and women carrying young children after this fashion.

Women carry their young astride their backs. The child is held in place by a strap passing under its thighs and around over the mother's breasts.[17]

When a child is born in Ungava, on the authority of Lucien Turner, the mother wraps it in the softest skin she is able to procure and during its infancy it is carried in the ample hood attached to her coat.

The carrying devices for infants among the American Indians, as distinguished from the Eskimos, may now be examined. . . .

Mackenzie somewhere intimates that the Chippewayan mothers make their upper garments full in the shoulders. When traveling they carry their infants upon their backs next the skin and convenient to giving them nourishment. This is a transition habit between Eskimo and Indian and not prevalent among the Athapascans.

"The Kutchin women," says Richardson, "do not carry their infants in their hoods or boots after the Eskimo fashion, nor do they stuff them into a bag with moss, as the Chippewayan and Crees do, but they place them in a seat of birch bark, with back and sides like those of an armchair, and a pommel in front resembling the peak of a Spanish saddle. This hangs at the woman's back, suspended by a strap which passes over her shoulders, and the infant is seated in it, with back to hers, and its legs, well cased in warm boots, hanging down on each side

---

[16] J. Peary, "My Arctic Journal," New York and Philadelphia, 1893, p. 43.

[17] John W. Kelly, "Ethnographical Memoranda Concerning the Arctic Eskimos of Alaska and Siberia," Bureau of Education, Circular of Information No. 2, 1890, p. 18.

of the pommel. The child's feet are bandaged to prevent their growing, small feet being thought handsome; and the consequence is that short, unshapely feet are characteristic of the people."[18]

The Lower Yukon trough-shaped cradle of birch bark (example No. 32986, in the U. S. National Museum, fig. 199) is made of three pieces, the bottom, the top or hood, and the awning piece. The two parts constituting the body of the cradle overlap an inch and a half and are sewed together with a single basting of pine root, with stitches half an inch apart. Around the body just under the margin, and continuously around the border of the hood and awning, lies a rod of osier. A strip of birch bark laid on the upper side of the awning serves as a stiffener and is sewed down by an ingenious basting with stitches an inch or more long which pass down through two thicknesses of birch bark, around the osier twig just below the margin, and up again through the two thicknesses of birch bark by another opening to form the next stich. The hood is formed by puckering the birch bark after the manner of a grocer's bag. The bordering osier is neatly seized to the edge of the hood and awning by a coil of split spruce root. Rows of beads of many colors adorn the awning piece. In a country intolerable by reason of the mosquitoes it is not strange that provisions for sustaining some sort of netting should be devised.

Immediately after birth, without being washed, the northeastern Tinneh infant is laid naked on a layer of moss in a bag made of leather and lined with hare skins. If it be in summer, the latter is dispensed with. This bag is then securely laced, restraining the limbs in natural positions, and leaving the child freedom to move the head only. In this phase of its existence it resembles strongly an Egyptian mummy. Cradles are never used, but this machine, called a "moss bag," is an excellent adjunct to the rearing of children up to a certain age, and has become almost, if not universally, adopted in the families of the Hudson Bay Company's employees. . . .[19]

The Southern Canadian cradle is a board with two flaps of cloth which lace together up the center. The child is laid on its back on the board, packed with soft moss, and laced firmly down with its arms to its side and only its head at liberty. The cradle is strung on the back of the mother when traveling, or reared against a tree when resting in camp, the child being only occasionally released from bondage for a few moments. The little prisoners are remarkably good. No squalling disturbs an Indian camp.[20]

Catlin figures a Cree woman carrying a child on her right arm, and holding the buffalo robe around the child with the left hand.[21] The

[18] Richardson, "Arctic Searching Expedition," New York, 1852, p. 227.
[19] Bernard R. Ross, Rep. Smithsonian Inst., 1866, p. 305.
[20] Fitzwilliams, "The Northwest Passage by Land," p. 85.
[21] Catlin, "North American Indians," I, p. 33.

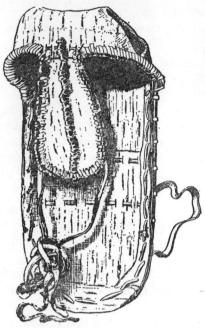

Fig. 199. ATHAPASCAN CRADLE OF
BIRCH BARK.
Collected by E. W. Nelson

Kickapoos, of the same stock, carry the small child on the back in the shawl (fig. 200).

Mr. Lucien Turner reports that the Nascopi of Labrador and Ungava, who are much affected by their proximity to Eskimo, use no cradle board for children.

The principal factor in the Chippewa infant's house, according to Kohl, is a flat board. For this purpose poplar wood is selected; in the first place because it is light, and secondly, because it does not crack or splinter. On this board a small frame of thin, peeled sapling is fastened, much after the shape of the child's body, and stands up from the board like the sides of a violin from the sounding board. It is fastened on with bast, because the Indians never use nails, screws, or glue. The cavity is filled with very soft substances for the reception of the child. They prepare for this purpose a mixture composed of very fine, dry moss, rotted cedar wood, and a species of tender wool found in the seed vessels of a species of reed. This wool was recommended as a most useful ingredient in the stuffing, for it sucks up all moisture as greedily as a sponge, and hence there is no need to inspect the baby continually. In this bed the little beings nestle up to the armpits—so far they are wrapped up tightly with bandages and coverings, but the head and arms are free. At a convenient distance above the head is a stiff circle of wood, also fastened to the cradle with bast. It serves as a protection to the head, and if the cradle happens to fall over it rests on this arch. In fact, they may roll an Indian tikinagan over as much as you please, but the child can not be injured. The squaws at times display extraordinary luxury in the gaily embroidered coverlid which they throw over the whole cradle.[22]

The Iroquois cradle, example No. 18806, has the backboard carved in imitation of peacocks and is painted in bright colors. It is square at the top and the awning frame is mortised at the ends, which allows them to slide over the awning bar held down and guyed by stays on the opposite sides; has a movable foot rest at the bottom and thongs along the sides for lashing the baby in. Length, 29¼ inches; width, top,

[22] J. G. Kohl, "Wanderings round Lake Superior," 1860, pp. 6-7.

10½ inches, bottom, 8⅛ inches; foot rest, height, 3½ inches; width, 6 inches. The St. Regis Iroquois, in the north of New York and near Canada, have for many years bought their cradle boards from the whites or made them of material bought from a white man.

Example No. 8894 is like the last, with gaudily painted and carved backboard, and awning frame carved. Length, 31 inches; width, top 11 inches, bottom 7¾ inches; height of awning frame, 12¼ inches; width of top 9¼, bottom 12 inches.

Morgan says that the Iroquois baby frame, "ga-ose-ha," is an Indian invention. It appears to have been designed rather as a convenience to the Indian mother for the transportation of her infant than, as has generally been supposed, to secure an erect figure. The frame is about 2 feet in length by about 14 inches in width, with a carved footboard at the small end and a hoop or bow at the head, arching over at right angles. After being inclosed in a blanket, the infant is lashed upon the frame with belts of beadwork, which firmly secure and cover its person, with the exception of the face. A separate article for covering the face is then drawn over the bow, and the child is wholly protected. When in use, the burden strap attached to the frame is placed around the forehead of the

Fig. 200. KICKAPOO (ALGONQUIAN) WOMAN CARRYING CHILD.
After Hoppe

mother, and the "ga-ose-ha" upon her back. This frame is often elaborately carved, and its ornaments are of the choicest description. When cultivating the maize, or engaged in any outdoor occupation, the mother hangs the "ga-ose-ha" upon a limb of the nearest tree and left to swing in the breeze. The patience and quiet of the Indian child in this close confinement are quite remarkable. It will hang thus suspended for hours without uttering a complaint.[23]

Among the relics of the Catlin collection are two old cradles. Of one the following description will suffice: Backboard square at the top; carved

---

[23] Lewis H. Morgan, "League of the Iroquois," 1851, pp. 390-391, with illustration.

and painted; awning frame bent and painted; covering cloth decorated with beads and tacked around the edge of the side board, brought up and laced in the middle like a shoe; length, 28¾ inches; width, 13 inches.

The description of the second example (fig. 203) is as follows: Backboard carved on front above; back brace with large, rounded ends extending outward; footrest low, curved around at the bottom; cradle covered over with quill work in red, white, and black patterns—lozenges, women, horses, etc.; decorated with iron bells; opening across the cradle covered in the middle with embroidered quilt; length, 31½ inches; width, 10¾ inches; head frame, 9½ inches; height, 13¾ inches.[24]

Fig. 203. ALGONQUIAN CRADLE, DECO-
RATED WITH QUILL WORK.
Collected by George Catlin

[24] Rep. Smithsonian Inst. (U. S. Nat. Mus.), 1887, p. 202.

WILLIAM H. HOLMES

(1846-1933)

Form and Ornament in Ceramic Art

SUGGESTIONS OF NATURAL FEATURES OF OBJECTS

THE FIRST ARTICLES USED BY MEN IN THEIR SIMPLE ARTS HAVE IN MANY cases possessed features suggestive of decoration. Shells of mollusks are exquisitely embellished with ribs, spines, nodes, and colors. The same is true to a somewhat limited extent of the shells of the turtle and the armadillo and of the hard cases of fruits.

These decorative features, though not essential to the utensil, are nevertheless inseparable parts of it, and are cast or unconsciously copied by a very primitive people when similar articles are artificially produced in plastic material. In this way a utensil may acquire ornamental characters long before the workman has learned to take pleasure in such details or has conceived an idea beyond that of simple utility. This may be called unconscious embellishment. In this fortuitous fashion a ribbed variety of fruit shell would give rise to a ribbed vessel in clay; one covered with spines would suggest a noded vessel, etc. When taste came to be exercised upon such objects these features would be retained and copied for the pleasure they afforded.

Passing by the many simple elements of decoration that by this unconscious process could be derived from such sources, let me give a single example by which it will be seen that not only elementary forms but even so highly constituted an ornament as the scroll may have been brought thus naturally into the realm of decorative art. The sea-shell has always been intimately associated with the arts that utilize clay and abounds in suggestions of embellishment. The *Busycon* was almost universally employed as a vessel by the tribes of the Atlantic drainage

From Holmes, "Origin and development of form and ornament," *Fourth Annual Report, Bureau of American Ethnology* (Washington: Government Printing Office, 1886), pp. 454-465.

191

of North America. Usually it was trimmed down and excavated until only about three-fourths of the outer wall of the shell remained. At one end was the long spike-like base which served as a handle, and at the other the flat conical apex, with its very pronounced spiral line or ridge expanding from the center to the circumference, as seen in Fig. 475 *a*. This vessel was often copied in clay, as many good examples now in our museums testify. The notable feature is that the shell has been copied literally, the spiral appearing in its proper place. A specimen is illustrated in Fig. 475 *b* which, although simple and highly conventionalized, still retains the spiral figure.

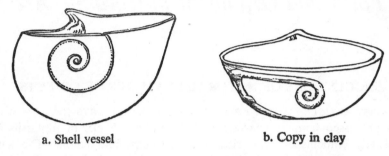

a. Shell vessel   b. Copy in clay

Fig. 475. SCROLL DERIVED FROM THE SPIRE OF A CONCH SHELL.

In another example we have four of the noded apexes placed about the rim of the vessel, as shown in Fig. 476 *a*, the conception being that of four conch shells united in one vessel, the bases being turned inward and the apexes outward. Now it is only necessary to suppose the addition of the spiral lines, always associated with the nodes, to have the result shown in *b*, and by a still higher degree of convention we have the classic scroll ornament given in *c*. Of course, no such result as this could come about adventitiously, as successful combination calls for the exercise of judgment and taste; but the initiatory steps could be taken— the motive could enter art—without the conscious supervision of the human agent.

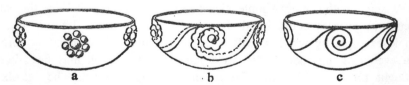

a   ·b   c

Fig. 476. POSSIBLE DERIVATION OF THE CURRENT SCROLL.

Constructional features.—Features of vessels resulting from construction are infinitely varied and often highly suggestive of decoration. Constructional peculiarities of the clay utensils themselves are especially worthy of notice, and on account of their actual presence in the art itself are more likely to be utilized or copied for ceramic ornament than those of other materials. The coil, so universally employed in construction, has had a decided influence upon the ceramic decoration of certain peoples, as I have shown in a paper on ancient Pueblo art. From it we have not only a great variety of surface ornamentation produced by simple treatment of the coil in place, but probably many forms suggested by the use of the coil in vessel building, as, for instance, the spiral formed in beginning the base of a coiled vessel, Fig. 478 *a,* from which the double scroll *b,* as a separate feature, could readily be derived, and finally the chain of scrolls so often seen in border and zone

a. Coiled filet of clay   b. Double coil

Fig. 478. SCROLL DERIVED FROM A COIL OF CLAY.

decoration. This familiarity with the use of fillets or ropes of clay would also lead to a great variety of applied ornament, examples of which, from Pueblo art, are given in Fig. 479. The sinuous forms assumed by a rope of clay so employed would readily suggest to the Indian the form of the serpent and the means of representing it, and might thus lead to the introduction of this much revered creature into art.

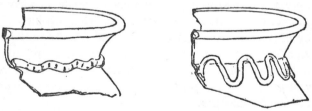

Fig. 479. ORNAMENTAL USE OF FILLETS.

Of the various classes of utensils associated closely with the ceramic art, there are none so characteristically marked by constructional features as nets and wicker baskets. The twisting, interlacing, knotting, and stitching of filaments give relieved figures that by contact in manufacture impress themselves upon the plastic clay. Such impressions come in time to be regarded as pleasing features, and when free-hand methods of reproducing are finally acquired they and their derivatives become essentials of decoration. At a later stage these characters of basketry influence ceramic decoration in a somewhat different way. By the use of variously-colored fillets the woven surface displays figures in color corresponding to those in relief and varying with every new combination. Many striking patterns are thus produced, and the potter who has learned to decorate his wares by the stylus or brush reproduces these patterns by free-hand methods. We find pottery in all countries ornamented with patterns, painted, incised, stamped, and relieved, certainly derived from this source. So well is this fact known that I need hardly go into details.

In the higher stages of art the constructional characters of architecture give rise to many notions of decoration which afterwards descend to other arts, taking greatly divergent forms. Aboriginal architecture in some parts of America had reached a development capable of wielding a strong influence. This is not true, however, of any part of the United States.

SUGGESTIONS OF ACCIDENTS

Besides the suggestions of surface features impressed in manufacture or intentionally copied as indicated above, we have also those of accidental imprints of implements or of the fingers in manufacture. From this source there are necessarily many suggestions of ornament, at first of indented figures, but later, after long employment, extending to the other modes of representation.

IDEOGRAPHIC AND PICTORIAL SUBJECTS

Non-ideographic forms of ornament may originate in ideographic features, mnemonic, demonstrative, or symbolic. Such significant figures are borrowed by decorators from other branches of art. As time goes on they lose their significance and are subsequently treated as purely decorative elements. Subjects wholly pictorial in character, when such come to be made, may also be used as simple decoration, and by long processes of convention become geometric.

The exact amount of significance still attached to significant figures after adoption into decoration cannot be determined except in cases of actual identification by living peoples, and even when the signification is known by the more learned individuals the decorator may be wholly without knowledge of it.

MODIFICATION OF ORNAMENT

There are comparatively few elementary ideas prominently and generally employed in primitive decorative art. New ideas are acquired, as already shown, all along the pathway of progress. None of these ideas retain a uniform expression, however, as they are subject to modification by environment just as are the forms of living organisms. A brief classification of the causes of modification is given in the following synopsis:

$$\text{Modification of ornament} \dots \dots \begin{cases} \text{Through material.} \\ \text{Through form.} \\ \text{Through methods of realization.} \end{cases}$$

Through material.—It is evident at a glance that *material* must have a strong influence upon the forms assumed by the various decorative motives, however derived. Thus stone, clay, wood, bone, and copper, although they readily borrow from nature and from each other, necessarily show different decorative results. Stone is massive and takes form slowly and by peculiar processes. Clay is more versatile and decoration may be scratched, incised, painted, or modeled in relief with equal facility, while wood and metal engender details having characters peculiar to themselves, producing different results from the same motives or elements. Much of the diversity displayed by the art products of different countries and climates is due to this cause.

Peoples dwelling in arctic climates are limited, by their materials, to particular modes of expression. Bone and ivory as shaped for use in the arts of subsistence afford facilities for the employment of a very restricted class of linear decoration, such chiefly as could be scratched with a hard point upon small irregular, often cylindrical, implements. Skins and other animal tissues are not favorable to the development of ornament, and the textile arts—the greatest agents of convention—do not readily find suitable materials in which to work.

Decorative art carried to a high stage under arctic environment would be more likely to achieve unconventional and realistic forms than if developed in more highly favored countries. The accurate geometric and linear patterns would hardly arise.

Through form.—Forms of decorated objects exercise a strong influence upon the decorative designs employed. It would be more difficult to tattoo the human face or body with straight lines or rectilinear patterns than with curved ones. An ornament applied originally to a vessel of a given form would accommodate itself to that form pretty much as costume becomes adjusted to the individual. When it came to be required for another form of vessel, very decided changes might be necessary.

With the ancient Pueblo peoples rectilinear forms of meander patterns were very much in favor and many earthen vessels are found in which bands of beautiful angular geometric figures occupy the peripheral zone, Fig. 480 *a,* but when the artist takes up a mug having a row of hemispherical nodes about the body, *b,* he finds it very difficult to apply

Fig. 480. VARIATIONS IN A MOTIVE THROUGH THE
INFLUENCE OF FORM.

his favorite forms and is almost compelled to run spiral curves about the
nodes in order to secure a neat adjustment.

Through methods of realization.—It will readily be seen that the forms
assumed by a motive depend greatly upon the character of the mechanical
devices employed. In the potter's art devices for holding and turning the
vessel under manipulation produce peculiar results.

In applying a given idea to clay much depends upon the method of
executing it. It will take widely differing forms when executed by incising,
by modeling, by painting, and by stamping.

Intimately associated with methods of execution are peculiarities of
construction, the two agencies working together in the processes of modification and development of ornament.

I have previously shown how our favorite ornament, the scroll, in its
disconnected form may have originated in the copying of natural forms
or through the manipulation of coils of clay. I present here an example of its possible origin through the modification of forms derived
from constructional features of basketry. An ornament known as the
guilloche is found in many countries. The combination of lines resembles
that of twisted or platted fillets of wood, cane, or rushes, as may be
seen at a glance, Fig. 481 *a.* An incised ornament of this character,
possibly derived from basketry by copying the twisted fillets or their
impressions in the clay, is very common on the pottery of the mounds
of the Mississippi Valley, and its variants form a most interesting study.
In applying this to a vessel the careless artist does not properly connect
the ends of the lines which pass beneath the intersecting fillets, and the
parts become disconnected, *b.* In many cases the ends are turned in
abruptly as seen in *c,* and only a slight further change is necessary to
lead to the result, *d,* the running scroll with well-developed links. All
of these steps may be observed in a single group of vessels.

It may be thought by some that the processes of development indicated above are insufficient and unsatisfactory. There are those who,
seeing these forms already endowed with symbolism, begin at what I

conceive to be the wrong end of the process. They derive the form of symbol directly from the thing symbolized. Thus the current scroll is, with many races, found to be a symbol of water, and its origin is attributed to a literal rendition of the sweep and curl of the waves. It is more probable that the scroll became the symbol of the sea long after its development through agencies similar to those described above, and that the association resulted from the observation of incidental resemblances. This same figure, in use by the Indians of the interior of the continent, is regarded as symbolic of the whirlwind, and it is probable that any symbol-using people will find in the features and phenomena of their environment, whatever it may be, sufficient resemblance to any of their decorative devices to lead to a symbolic association.

Fig. 481. THEORETICAL DEVELOPMENT OF THE CURRENT SCROLL.

One secret of modification is found in the use of a radical in more than one art, owing to differences in constructional characters. For example, the tendency of nearly all woven fabrics is to encourage, even to compel, the use of straight lines in the decorative designs applied. Thus the attempt to employ curved lines would lead to stepped or broken lines. The curvilinear scroll coming from some other art would be forced by the constructional character of the fabric into square forms, and the rectilinear meander or fret would result, as shown in Fig. 482, *a* being the plain form, painted, engraved, or in relief, and *b* the same idea developed in a woven fabric. Stone or brick-work would lead to like results, but the modification could as readily move in the other direction. If an ornament originating in the constructional character of a woven fabric, or remodeled by it, and hence rectilinear, should be desired for a smooth structureless or featureless surface, the difficulties of drawing the angular forms would lead to the delineation of curved forms, and we would have exactly the reverse of the order shown in Fig. 482. The two forms given in

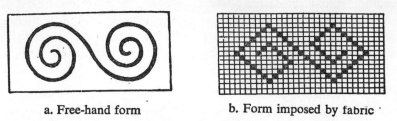

a. Free-hand form   b. Form imposed by fabric

Fig. 482. FORMS OF THE SAME MOTIVE EXPRESSED IN DIFFERENT ARTS.

Fig. 484 actually occur in one and the same design painted upon an ancient Pueblo vase. The curved form is apparently the result of careless or hurried work, the original angular form having come from a textile source.

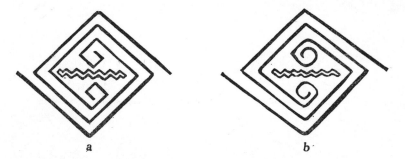

a   b

Fig. 484. VARIATIONS RESULTING FROM CHANGE OF METHOD.

Many excellent examples illustrative of this tendency to modification are found in Pueblo art. Much of the ornament applied to pottery is derived from the sister art, basketry. In the latter art the forms of decorative figures are geometric and symmetrical to the highest degree, as I have frequently pointed out. The rays of a radiating ornament, worked with the texture of a shallow basket, spring from the center and take uniform directions toward the margin, as shown in Fig. 485. But when a similar idea derived from basketry (as it could have no other origin) is executed in color upon an earthen vessel, we observe a tendency to depart from symmetry as well as from consistency. I call attention here to the *arrangement* of the *parts* merely, not to the motives employed, as I happen to have no examples of identical figures from the two arts.

It will be seen by reference to the design given in Fig. 486, taken

Fig. 485. GEOMETRIC FORM OF TEXTILE ORNAMENT.

from the upper surface of an ancient vase, that although the spirit of the decoration is wonderfully well preserved the idea of the origin of all the rays in the center of the vessel is not kept in view, and that by carelessness in the drawing two of the rays are crowded out and terminate against the side of a neighboring ray. In copying and recopying by free hand methods many curious modifications take place in these designs, as, for example, the unconformity which occurs in one place in the example given may occur at a number of places, and there will be a series of independent sections, a small number only of the bands of devices remaining true rays.

Fig. 486. LOSS OF GEOMETRIC ACCURACY IN PAINTING.

A characteristic painted design from the interior of an ancient bowl is shown in Fig. 487, in which merely a suggestion of the radiation is preserved, although the figure is still decorative and tasteful. This process of modification goes on without end, and as the true geometric textile forms recede from view innovation robs the design of all traces of its original character, producing much that is incongruous and unsatisfactory.

Fig. 487. DESIGN PAINTED UPON
POTTERY.

The growth of decorative devices from the elementary to the highly constituted and elegant is owing to a tendency of the human mind to elaborate because it is pleasant to do so or because pleasure is taken in the result, but there is still a directing and shaping agency to be accounted for.

I have already shown that such figures as the scroll and the guilloche are not *necessarily* developed by processes of selection and combination of simple elements, as many have thought, since they may have come into art at a very early stage almost full-fledged; but there is nothing in these facts to throw light upon the processes by which ornament followed particular lines of development throughout endless elaboration. In treating of this point, Prof. C. F. Hartt[1] maintained that the development of ornamental designs took particular and uniform directions owing to the structure of the eye, certain forms being chosen and perpetuated because of the pleasure afforded by movements of the eye in following them. In connection with this hypothesis, for it is nothing more, Mr. Hartt advanced the additional idea, that in unison with the general course of nature decorative forms began with simple elements and developed by systematic methods to complex forms. Take for example the series of designs shown in Fig. 488. The meander *a* made up of simple parts would, according to Mr. Hartt, by further elaboration under the supervision of the muscles of the eye, develop into *b*. This, in time, into *c,* and so on until the elegant anthemium was achieved. The series shown in Fig. 489 would develop in a similar way, or otherwise would be produced by modification in free-hand copying of the rectilinear series. The processes here suggested, although to all appearances reasonable enough, should not be passed over without careful scrutiny.

Taking the first series, we observe that the ornaments are projected in straight continuous lines or zones, which are filled with more or less complex parts, rectilinear and geometrically accurate. Still higher forms are marvelously intricate and graceful, yet not less geometric and symmetrical.

Let us turn to the primitive artisan, and observe him at work with rude brush and stylus upon the rounded and irregular forms of his utensils and weapons, or upon skins, bark, and rock surfaces. Is it

[1] Hartt: Popular Science Monthly, Vol. VI, p. 266.

probable that with his free hand directed by the eye alone he will be able to achieve these rhythmic geometric forms. It seems to me that the whole tendency is in the opposite direction. I venture to surmise that if there had been no other resources than those named above the typical rectilinear fret would never have been known, at least to the

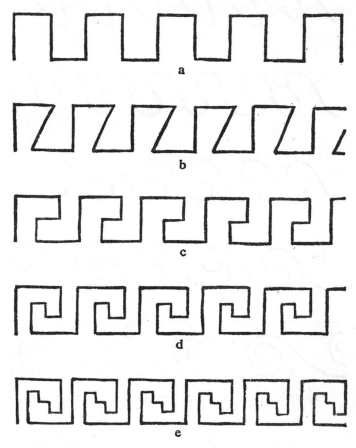

Fig. 488. THEORETICAL DEVELOPMENT OF FRET WORK.

primitive world; for, notwithstanding the contrary statement by Professor Hartt, the fret is in its more highly developed forms extremely difficult to follow with the eye and to delineate with the hand. Until arts, geometric in their construction, arose to create and to combine mechanically the necessary elements and motives, and lead the way by a long series of object-lessons to ideas of geometric combination, our typical border ornament would not be possible. Such arts are the textile arts and architecture. These brought into existence forms and ideas not met with in nature and not primarily thought of by man, and combined them in defiance of human conceptions of grace. Geometric ornament is the offspring of technique.

Fig. 489. THEORETICAL DEVELOPMENT OF SCROLL WORK.

The Bureau of American Ethnology: Areal Research in the Southwest

FRANK HAMILTON CUSHING
(1857-1900)

MATILDA COXE STEVENSON
(c. 1850-1915)

J. WALTER FEWKES
(1850-1930)

WASHINGTON MATTHEWS
(1843-1905)

The last outposts of aboriginal life in the United States were the tribes of the Southwestern desert.

The active resistance of the village Indians was broken after the Pueblo Rebellion of 1680. This was the best organized of the efforts of Indian resistance, and the only one that was, for a time at least, successful. The rebellion was organized by Popé, a Jemez Indian, who sent to all the pueblo villages counting strings of the kind still used by the Zuñi Indians to count the days of ceremonies. On the appointed night the Indians rose and massacred more than 2,000 missionaries and settlers. Two priests, warned by friendly Indians, escaped; the other surviving colonists fled south along the Rio Grande. Popé occupied the Spanish city of Santa Fé, and from there attempted to organize the villages into a confederation. A strong punitive expedition was sent out from Mexico to reconquer the area. In the wars that followed some villages were destroyed, others abandoned.

When peace was restored in 1692 the population had declined and it continued to decline for the next 200 years, but the tribal distribution was substantially as it is today. Resistance did not cease, it merely took a new form—withdrawal and secrecy and a stubborn unfriendliness, more pronounced along the Rio Grande where contact with whites was closest, and slightly more relaxed among the Hopi and Zuñi in the more inaccessible areas of the western desert. In the pueblo of San Ildefonso, for instance, although the natives were ostensibly converted to Catholicism, attended church and celebrated the Church festivals, the old religious rituals centering on ceremonies for weather control were practiced in secret. The two large circular kivas in the center of the village, ostensibly the center for

203

native cults, were used only for the most public ceremonies. The really secret ceremonies which held the heart of the rituals were performed in small ceremonial rooms hidden in the blocks of houses, and the masked dances were held in secret places in the mountains with sentries posted along all trails to turn back curious travelers. Even in the western pueblos, secrecy was intensified as whites moved in in greater numbers.

The Navaho had a somewhat different fate. A semi-nomadic people depending but slightly on agriculture, they had an old pattern of raiding the village Indians. This was intensified after the Spanish Conquest when the villages had horses and sheep. As game became scarcer, raids became more frequent. When the Southwest passed into the hands of the United States, Kit Carson was given orders to take whatever measures were necessary to suppress the raids. A large number of Navahos were trapped in the Canyon de los Muertos and in western New Mexico and massacred. Their stock was slaughtered and their fields destroyed. After this disaster, the Navahos were persuaded to surrender and turn in their arms. Those who answered the call to surrender were disarmed and marched across the desert to Fort Sumner where they were held in prison encampments for four years. During their confinement thousands died of sicknesses of the body and of the soul. The remnant that survived was given a few sheep with which to start a new life.

When the Bureau of American Ethnology was organized in 1879, the western pueblos were the first area chosen for study. Powell had visited Zuñi on one of his trips of exploration in 1870 and the "marvelous savage and barbaric culture" which he saw there haunted his imagination. At that time, Colonel James Stevenson was collecting pueblo artifacts. On his staff was a young man, Frank Hamilton Cushing, whom Powell persuaded to take on the Zuñi investigation.

Cushing had spent most of his childhood in western New York State. A frail child, he had no formal schooling and was entirely self-taught. Cut off by ill health from the companionship of his age mates, he learned the secrets of the forest and delighted in the companionship of wild creatures. He collected arrowheads and other Indian artifacts, became interested in geology and scoured the area for specimens. These activities brought him into contact with a number of well-known scholars who became fascinated by the strange and eager boy. His interest in technology led to his first regular job, with the Philadelphia Centennial Exposition.

Cushing visited Zuñi with Powell in 1879 and then decided that the only way one could penetrate the lives of these hostile and secretive people would be to live among them, learn their language, participate in their activities, and gradually gain access to their secrets. The following year he joined the Bureau and settled at Zuñi, where he remained for five years, leaving only once to take a group of Zuñi friends to Washington.

During these five years he led a completely Indian life, speaking nothing but Zuñi and participating fully in tribal activities. He was initiated into one of their secret medicine fraternities, and later into the Bow Priesthood (War Chief Society), one of the highest offices in the tribe. He was a man of great perceptiveness and insight, and was in a position to learn the most esoteric lore of the tribe.

Cushing's sudden departure from Zuñi is something of a mystery. He never went back, and he never completed the study of Zuñi mythology, the first part of which was published in the Thirteenth Annual Report of the Bureau of American Ethnology. *He never organized for publication the vast body of material he collected during his residence at Zuñi. The collection of masks which he made and which are now in the Brooklyn Museum was never catalogued. Occasionally bits of Cushing's manuscripts turn up, showing with what meticulous care he recorded texts of prayers and other data. But all this irreplaceable wealth of material was lost to anthropology. A series of articles which he wrote for* The Millstone, *a grain trade journal, is the only description of the ordinary life of the Zuñi people, which he was so well equipped to know and understand.*

After leaving Zuñi, Cushing spent two years in archaeological investigations of the ruins of the Gila River for the Hemenway Southwestern Archaeological Expedition, the first systematic excavation in the Southwest. He was looking for the key to Zuñi mysteries in the region where Zuñi tradition placed their original home, and he discovered the culture which later came to be known as Hohokam.

Cushing left the Southwest in 1888 because of ill health. He had begun work among the Seminoles of Florida when his career was cut short by an untimely death.

Cushing was followed in Zuñi by Matilda Coxe Stevenson, the widow of James Stevenson, who had accompanied her husband on his earlier collecting expeditions. In the beginning, as part of a husband-wife team she had paid especial attention to the activities of women and children, and was, indeed, the first American ethnologist to consider children worthy of notice. After Colonel Stevenson's death she incorporated his voluminous notes, mostly dealing with ceremonial matters, with her own further observations in a comprehensive study of the Zuñi tribe. Less perceptive than Cushing, less able to enter native life and let information come to her, she was nevertheless an active and industrious field worker and collected a large body of detailed information. She lived in Zuñi during the troubled period following the building of the railroad and the opening of the country to white trade and settlement. She deplored the changes that this made in native life and character, but unfortunately her observations are undated and despite her great knowledge it is difficult to organize her reports into a coherent picture of native life. After com-

pleting her Zuñi studies, she spent several years in the eastern pueblos and published some rather startling but inconclusive papers about their ceremonial life.

Colonel and Mrs. Stevenson had visited the Hopi pueblos in the early days, but it was J. Walter Fewkes who made the history and ethnology of the Hopi a life work. He first came to the Southwest as a member of the Hemenway Expedition. He was by training a zoologist, with a Ph.D. in Zoology from Harvard, several years of graduate study in Europe and years of museum work at Cambridge. But once he entered the field of Southwestern studies he never left it. He was an indefatigable field worker and a prolific writer. He joined the Bureau of American Ethnology in 1895, and remained there until 1930, becoming Chief in 1918. He divided his time between ethnology and archaeology, and his aim was to work out the relations between the contemporary villages and the many ruins scattered around the Hopi country. To this end he collected clan legends and origin myths, accepting them as history, trying to identify the places mentioned in them. This attempt at historic reconstruction was doomed to failure; the writing of the history of the Hopi area had to await the establishment of time sequences. As an ethnographer, Fewkes was interested almost exclusively in ritual. He published many detailed descriptions of Hopi rituals, but left no key to their significance.

Like so many of the great anthropologists of his day, Washington Matthews came into anthropology through a lucky accident. He had been an army surgeon during the Civil War, and at the close of the war he reentered the army and was assigned to various frontier army posts along the upper Missouri. Here he first came in contact with Indians, and began a study of their language. His Hidatsa grammar came to the notice of Powell who, with his gift for collecting talent, suggested that Matthews be transferred to Fort Wingate, in the heart of the Navaho country. He remained there from 1880 to 1884, and was reassigned for a second period of four years after several years of service in the Army Medical Museum in Washington.

While at Fort Wingate, Matthews devoted all his spare time to the study of Navaho language and culture. His early studies, published in reports of the Bureau, dealt with such externals of Navaho life as weaving and silverwork, but gradually he penetrated more deeply into Navaho life and produced his poetic translations of the great Navaho chants. Matthews wrote poetry himself, and if his poetry is not especially distinguished, his concern with the beauty of language enabled him to do justice to a great poetic tradition. He contributed admirably in many fields—physical anthropology and anthropometry, linguistics, technology and folklore—but it is his beautiful translations of Navaho poetry that set him apart.—R.L.B.

FRANK HAMILTON CUSHING

(1857-1900)

The Preparation of the Cornfield

EARLY IN THE MONTH OF THE "LESSER SANDSTORMS" THE SAME ZUÑI, WE
will say, who preëmpted, a year since, a distant arroyo-field, goes forth, hoe
and axe in hand, to resume the work of clearing, etc. Within the sand
embankment he now selects that portion which the arroyo enters from
above, and cutting many forked cedar branches, drives them firmly into
the dry stream-bed, in a line crossing its course, and extending a considerable distance beyond either bank. Against this row of stakes he places
boughs, clods, rocks, sticks, and earth, so as to form a strong barrier or
dry-dam; open, however, at either end. Some rods below this on either
side of the streamcourse, he constructs, less carefully, other and longer
barriers. Still farther down, he seeks in the "tracks" of some former torrent,
a ball of clay, which, having been detached from its native bank, far above,
has been rolled and washed, down and down, ever growing rounder and
smaller and tougher, until in these lower plains it lies embedded in and
baked by the burning sands. This he carefully takes up, breathing reverently
from it, and places it on one side of the stream-bed, where it is desirable
to have the rain-freshets overflow. He buries it, with a brief supplication,
in the soil, and then proceeds to heap over it a solid bank of earth which
he extends obliquely across, and to some distance beyond the arroyo. Returning, he continues the embankment past the clay ball either in line of,
or at whatever angle with the completed portion seems to his practiced
eye most suited to the topography.

To those not acquainted with savage ways of thought, this proceeding
will gain interest from explanation. The national game of the Zuñi is
ti'-kwa-we, or, the race of the kicked stick. Two little cylindrical sticks
of hard wood are cut, each the length of the middle finger. These, dis-

From Cushing, "Zuñi breadstuff," *Indian Notes and Monographs,* Vol. VIII, Part
III (New York: Museum of the American Indian, Heye Foundation, 1920), pp. 157-
166. Reprinted from *The Millstone* (Minneapolis: 1887-1888).

tinguished one from the other by bands of red paint, are laid across the toes of either leader and kicked in the direction the race is to be run. At full speed of the runners these sticks are dexterously shoveled up on the toes, and kicked on and on. The party which gets its stick over the goal first is counted the winning side. This race is usually run by no fewer than twelve men, six opposed to an equal number. The distance ordinarily accomplished without rest or even abatement, is twenty-five miles. Now, the time taken in running this race is marvelously short, never exceeding three hours; yet, were you to ask one of the runners to undertake the race without his stick, he would flatly tell you he could not possibly do it. So imbued with this idea are the Zuñis that frequently, when coming in from distant fields, and wishing to make haste, they cut a stick, and kick it on ahead of them, running to catch up with it, and so on. The interesting feature about all this is, that the Indian in this, as in most things else, confounds the cause with the effect, thinks the stick helps him, instead of himself being the sole motive power of the stick. The lump of clay before mentioned is supposed to be the *ti'-kwa* of the water gods, fashioned by their invisible hands and pushed along by their resistless feet, not hindering, but adding to the force and speed of the waters. The field-maker fancies that the waters, when they run down this trail again, will be as anxious to catch up with their *ti'-kwa* as he would be. So he takes this way of tempting the otherwise tameless (*he* thinks) torrents out of their course. Yet, to make doubly sure, he has thrown a dam across their proper pathway. On the outskirts of the field thus planned, little inclosures of soil, like earthen bins, are thrown up wherever the ground slopes how littlesoever from a central point, these inclosures being either irregularly square or in conformity to the lines of the slope (pl. II).

My hope has been in so minutely describing these beginnings of a Zuñi farm to give a most precious hint to any reader of *The Millstone* interested in agriculture, or who may possess a field some portions of which are barren because too dry. We may smile at the superstitious observances of the Indian agriculturist, but when we come to learn what he accomplishes, we shall admire and I hope find occasion to imitate his hereditary ingenuity. The country of the Zuñis is so desert and dry, that times out of number within even the fickle memory of tradition, the possession of water for drinking and cooking purposes alone has been counted a blessing. Yet, by his system of earth banking, the Zuñi Indian, and a few of his western brothers and pupils, the Moquis, have heretofore been the only human beings who could, without irrigation from living streams, raise to maturity a crop of corn within its parched limits.

The use of the principal barriers and embankments may be inferred from the terms of the invocation with which the field is consecrated after the completion of all the earthworks. The owner then applies to whatever corn-priest is keeper of the sacred "medicine" of his clan or order. This

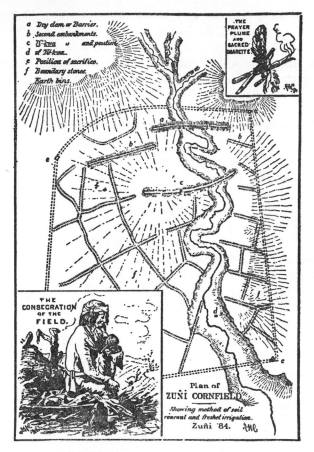

a *Dry dam or Barrier.*
b *Second embankments.*
c *U̅-kwa " and position*
d *of Tá̅-kwa.*
e *Position of sacrifice.*
f *Boundary stones.*
Earth bins.

THE PRAYER PLUME AND SACRED CIGARETTE

THE CONSECRATION OF THE FIELD.

Plan of
ZUÑI CORNFIELD
*Showing method of soil
renewal and freshet irrigation.*
Zuñi '84.

Plate II. PLAN OF A ZUÑI CORNFIELD.

priest cuts and decorates a little stick of red willow with plumes from the legs and hips of the eagle, turkey, and duck, and with the tail-feathers from the Maximilian's jay, night-hawk, yellow-finch, and ground-sparrow, fastening them on, one over the other, with cords of fine cotton. From the store of paint which native tradition claims was brought from the original birthplace of the nation (a kind of plumbago), he takes a tiny particle, leavening with it a quantity of black mineral powder. To a sufficient measure of rainwater he adds a drop of ocean water with which he moistens the pigment, and with a brush made by chewing the end of a yucca-leaf, applies the paint to the stick. With the same paint he also decorates a section of cane filled with wild tobacco supposed to have been planted by rain, hence sacred. These two objects, sanctified by his breath, he gives to the applicant. Taking them carefully in his left hand, the latter goes forth to his new field. Seeking a point in the middle of the arroyo below all his earthworks, he kneels, or sits down on his blanket, facing east. He then lights his cane cigarette and blows smoke toward the north, west, south, east, the upper and the lower regions. Then holding the smoking stump and the plumed stick near his breast, he says a prayer. From the substance of his prayer which, remarkably curious though it be, is too long for literal reproduction here, we learn the important facts relative to his intentions and his faith. We find he believes that: He has infused the consciousness of his prayer into the plumed stick; that with his sacred cigarette he has prepared a way 'like the trails of the winds and rains' [clouds] for the wafting of that prayer to the gods of all regions. That, having taken the cloud-inspiring down of the turkey, the strength-giving plume of the eagle, the water-loving feather of the duck, the path-finding tails of the birds who counsel and guide summer; having moreover severed and brought hither the flesh of the water-attracting tree, which he has dipped in the god-denizened ocean, beautified with the very cinders of creation, bound with strands from the dress of the sky-born goddess of cotton —he beseeches the god-priests of earth, sky, and cavern, the beloved gods whose dwelling places are in the great embracing waters of the world, not to withhold their mist-laden breaths, but to canopy the earth with cloud banners, and let fly their shafts little and mighty of rain, to send forth the fiery spirits of lightning, lift up the voice of thunder whose echoes shall step from mountain to mountain, bidding the mesas shake down streamlets. The streamlets shall yield torrents; the torrents, foam-capped, soil-laden, shall boil toward the shrine he is making, drop hither and thither the soil they are bearing, leap over his barricades unburdened and stronger, and in place of their lading, bear out toward the ocean as payment and faith-gift the smoke-cane and the prayer-plume. Thus thinking, thus believing, thus yearning, thus beseeching (in order that the seeds of earth shall not want food for their growing, that from their growth he may not lack food for his living, means for his fortune), he this day plants, standing in the trail of the waters, the smoke-cane and prayer-plume.

The effect of the network of barriers is what the Indian prayed for (attributes, furthermore, as much to his prayer as to his labors), namely, that with every shower, although the stream go dry three hours afterward, water has been carried to every portion of the field, has deposited a fine loam over it all, and moistened from one end to the other, the substratum. Not only this, but also, all rainfall on the actual space is retained and absorbed within the system of minor embankments.

At the stage of operations above last described, the field is again left for a year, that it may become thoroughly enriched. Meanwhile, during the same month (the first of spring) each planter repairs the banks in his old fields, and proceeds to adopt quite a different method for renewing or enriching the soil.

Along the western sides of his field, as well as of such spots throughout it as are worn out or barren, he thickly plants rows of sagebrush, leaving them standing from six inches to a foot above the surface. As the prevailing winds of the Zuñi plains hail from the southwest, and, as during the succeeding month (the "Crescent of the greater sand-storms"), these winds are laden many tens of feet high in the air with fine dust and sand, behind each row of the sagebrush a long, level, deep deposit of soil is drifted. With the coming of the first (and as a rule the only) rainstorm of springtime, the water, carried about by the embankments and retained lower down by the "earth bins," redistributes this "soil sown by the winds" and fixes it with moisture to the surface it has usurped.

Thus, with the aid of nature's hand, without plow or harrow, the Zuñi fits and fertilizes his lands, for the planting of Maytime, or the Nameless month.

MATILDA COXE STEVENSON

(c. 1850-1930)

Zuñi Origin Myth: The Origin of Corn

DAY AFTER DAY [THE A'SHIWI] WERE FOLLOWED BY THOSE WHO HAD failed to come to this world with them, for many, becoming tired had fallen back. Every time the A'shiwi heard a rumbling of the earth (earthquake) they knew that others were coming out. They would say: "My younger brother comes;" or, "Some of my people come." The exodus from the underworlds continued four years.[1] The last observed to come forth were two witches, a man and a wife, who were all-powerful for good or evil. Kŏw'wituma and Wats'usi, hearing a rumbling of the earth, looked to see who had arrived, and met the two witches, whose heads were covered with loose hoods of coarse fiber blowing in the breeze. Kŏw'wituma inquired of the witches: "Whither are you going?" They replied: "We wish to go with your people to the Middle place of the world." Kŏw'wituma said: "We do not want you with us." The witches, holding seeds in their closed hands under their arms, said: "If we do not go we will destroy the land. We have all seeds here." When the Divine Ones again told the witches they were not wanted, they declared that it would not be well if they were not allowed to go, saying: "We have all things precious for your people." The man, extending his closed hands over the seeds, said: "See, I wish to give this to the Kïa'kwemosi; and I wish him to give us two of his children, a son and a daughter. When we have the children the corn shall be his." "Why do you wish the children?" asked Kŏw'wituma. "We wish to kill the children that the rains may come."

The Divine Ones hastened to repeat what they had seen and heard to the Kïa'kwemosi, who replied: "It is well." When the witches appeared

[1] "Of old two days were as four years, and four days as eight years," reference being to time periods. Years throughout this paper will refer to indefinite time periods, unless it is otherwise explained.

From Stevenson, "The Zuñi Indians," *Twenty-third Annual Report, Bureau of American Ethnology* (Washington: Government Printing Office, 1905), pp. 29-32.

before the Kĭa'kwemosi and claimed two of his children, he said: "I have no infant children; I have a youth and a maiden; what do you wish to do with them?" "We wish to destroy them that there may be much rain. We have things of great value to you, but we must first have much rain." "It is well," said the Kĭa'kwemosi; and when the youth and maiden slept the two witches shot their medicine into their hearts by touching the children with their hands, causing their deaths. Their remains were buried in the earth, and the rains fell four days. On the fifth morning a rumbling noise was heard, and Kŏw'wituma saw the youth appearing from his grave. Again there were four days of heavy rains, and on the fifth morning after the resurrection of the youth a rumbling was heard, and Kŏw'wituma saw the girl coming from the earth. The same night the two witches planted all the seeds in the wet earth, and the following morning the corn was a foot high and the other things were of good size. By evening all was matured and the A'shiwi ate of the new food, but they were not pleased; everything was hot, like pepper. Then Kŏw'wituma and Wats'usi called the raven, who came and ate much of the corn and other things. Again the Divine Ones called the owl, who ate the heart of the grain, leaving the remainder on the cob, so that the corn became soft. The Divine Ones then called the coyote to come and eat the corn; he ate of everything in the field. The raven, owl, and coyote, by eating of the food, softened and sweetened it so that it became palatable to the A'shiwi. Since that time the fields have had to be watched, for the raven takes the corn in the day and the coyote robs the fields at night. At this time the Divine Ones instructed the A'shiwi in fire making and cooking.

While the earth was not muddy, it was so soft that the A'shiwi found difficulty in proceeding. Long years were consumed, and many villages were built, and then abandoned, as they pushed on their quest for the Middle of the world. Even when they tarried at the towns which they built they were driven therefrom by the corruption of their dead, and they desired even to escape from the effluvium of their own bodies, which was unbearable. "It was like burning sulphur; it was an odor that killed." Repeated divisions of the people occurred during the years consumed in their migrations, some going to the north, others to the south; thus the Zuñis account for many of the ruins north and south of their line of march.

Unseen and unknown, the Corn maidens came with the A'shiwi from the undermost world and remained with them until they had been four years at Shi'pololo kwi (Fog place), when they were discovered by the two witches sitting under a häm'pone (out-of-door covered place), a pavilion of pine boughs. The witches inquired: "Who are you?" The maidens replied: "We are the a'towae'washtokïi (Corn maidens)." "Where is your corn?" asked the witches. "We have none." "This is not right. If you are Corn maidens you should have corn;" and, handing a yellow ear of corn to one of the maidens, the witches said: "You are the Yellow Corn maiden and a'wankïo'wu (great or elder sister)." To another they handed a blue ear of corn, saying: "You are the younger sister, the Blue Corn maiden; you two will be the directors or leaders of the others." Handing a red ear of corn to the third one, they said: "You are a younger sister, the Red Corn maiden." And to the fourth they handed an ear of white corn, saying: "You are a younger sister, the White Corn maiden." And to the fifth they said, as they handed her an ear of multicolored corn: "You are the Every-colored Corn maiden and a younger sister." And to the sixth they handed a black ear of corn, saying: "You are the younger sister, the Black Corn maiden." And to the seventh they handed an ear of sweet corn, saying: "You are the younger sister, the Sweet Corn maiden." And to the eighth they said, as they handed her squash seeds: "You are the younger sister, the Squash maiden." And to the ninth they handed watermelon seeds saying: "You are the younger sister, the Watermelon maiden." And to the tenth they handed muskmelon seeds saying: "You are the younger sister, the Muskmelon maiden."[2]

After receiving the corn the elder sister said "I will dance with my corn, and so will my sisters," and she formed her sisters into two lines, facing the east that they might see the coming forth of the Sun Father. They danced all night under a bower walled with ho'mawe (cedar), whose roof was a'wehlwia'we (cumulus clouds) fringed with kïä'latsilo (spruce of the west). The witches observed the dance through the night, and in the morning continued their migrations with the A'shiwi, but said not a word to them of the Corn maidens, who remained at Shi'pololo kwi, where "they bathed in the dew (or mist), but did not drink of it."

[2] The A'shiwi say that the Mexicans brought beans, but that they always had watermelons and muskmelons. Although the Zuñis make this statement, it is declared by the representatives of the Department of Agriculture that neither the watermelon nor the muskmelon is indigenous to this country.

J. WALTER FEWKES

(1850-1930)

Hopi Snake Washing

NEW STUDIES OF HOPI SNAKE DANCES HAVE REVEALED THE FACT THAT no two of the five celebrations of this dance are identical in details. Some of these variations have already been pointed out[1] in an account of the dances at Oraibi and the pueblos of the Middle Mesa, and there are other differences which will be considered in an exhaustive account of the Hopi Snake Dance which I have in preparation.

One of the most significant variations in the component rites of the Snake Dance ceremonials, in different Hopi pueblos, is the absence of altars in the *kivas* of the Snake Societies of every pueblo except Walpi. This absence has necessarily modified secret rites, especially that weird ceremony, the washing of reptiles, which is celebrated at noon on the ninth day. As the details of Snake washing in a *kiva* where there is no altar have never been described, and as the Miconinovi variant is probably typical of these ceremonials in four pueblos, I have thought it well to put on record a few notes on this rite as observed in 1897.

The Snake washing at Walpi was first witnessed by me in 1891. Before that year no one except Indian members of the Snake Society had been allowed to remain in the *kiva* during this event. The late A. M. Stephen had an intimation of the existence of Snake washing rites, but repeated attempts to remain in the *kiva* to witness them had been met with a firm refusal. Some time before the Walpi Snake dance in 1891, Mr A. M. Stephen, Mr. T. V. Keam, and myself tried in various ways to induce the Snake Chief, Kopeli, to allow us to see the Snake washing. We found Kopeli willing to admit us, but some of the older and more conservative priests strongly objected. It was evident that only one white man could

---

[1] 16th Annual Report of the Bureau of American Ethnology.

From Fewkes, "Hopi Snake Washing," *American Anthropologist,* o.s. XI (Lancaster, 1898), pp. 313-319.

be admitted, and there were doubts, up to the opening of the ceremony, whether even that one would be allowed to remain throughout the whole event. The Indians at last decided that I should be permitted to witness the rite, and that the late J. G. Owens should serve as tyler at the *kiva* hatch, and see what he could from that place.

In 1893, the next performance, both Mr Stephen and myself witnessed the Snake washing at Walpi, and the notes made in these presentations were published in 1894 in the form of a memoir on the Walpi Snake Dance.[2]

In 1895, the author was the only white spectator of the Walpi Snake washing, and in 1897 he was accompanied by Professor G. Wharton James, with whom he also witnessed the ceremony at Micoñinovi, which is here described.[3]

The first event directly connected with the Snake washing at Micoñinovi was the entrance of a man with a bag full of sand, which he had gathered in the valley. This sand he spread on the floor south of the fireplace, covering a rectangular area, one side of which was bounded by the *kiva* wall. Seats were arranged on the other three sides for the men who were to participate in the rite.

It is customary at the Middle Mesa to keep the captured reptiles in the *kiva* in four large earthen amphoræ or canteens, similar to those in which women carry water from the springs to the pueblos. In preparation for the Snake washing, the reptiles were removed from these receptacles before the songs began. This removal took place very quietly, and while it was taking place several of the men walked about the room, while others prepared their paraphernalia for the public dance, which took place at sundown of the same day. The men in the *kiva* were naked,, as they generally are in ceremonial work, and their bodies were painted red with an iron oxide. All had a little feather, stained red, in their hair. Some of the more experienced priests smiled at the difficulty which the novices had in getting the reptiles to emerge from the mouth of the canteen. The occupants of the *kiva* did not hesitate to speak aloud, which is *taboo* at Walpi, and their faces had not the solemn look characteristic of East Mesa priests during similar rites.

The reptiles were driven out of the canteens by being prodded with a snake whip inserted through a hole in the side, and as soon as a snake protruded its head from the mouth of the vessel he was seized by the neck and transferred to a cloth bag. While the reptiles were being removed from the vessels a small boy, about ten years old, began to cry.[4] His father or

[2] Snake Ceremonials at Walpi. Jour. Amer. Eth. and Arch., vol. IV, pp. 81-87.

[3] This preliminary note will be supplemented by an account, with illustrations, which will be later published in a report of the Bureau of American Ethnology, under the auspices of which institution these studies were made.

[4] One of my informants said the lad was bitten by a snake.

some relative comforted the frightened lad, but there were a few harsh words of disapproval from other men present.

Finally, at about noon, after patient waiting on our part, the Snake priests took their seats around the sanded floor, sitting so closely together that their naked bodies touched each other, forming a human corral.

The Snake chief seated himself about the middle of the line of men on the longest side of the sanded area, and one or two older men, with rattles, took places at either side. The remainder of the Snake men sat around the sand closely crowded together, holding their snake whips, with which to beat time to the songs.

After all the priests were seated, except a few in charge of the bag of snakes and two or three lads who stood in the middle of the *kiva* back of the line of seated men, the Snake chief made symbols of sacred meal on a hillock of sand before him. Upon this hillock he then deposited a large earthen wash-bowl, such as is used in bathing the head, and then poured liquid into this bowl from the north, west, south, and east sides, following a sinistral ceremonial circuit. Pinches of sacred meal were then dropped into the liquid, first on the north side, then on the west, south, and east, adding two more, one for the above and another for the below. The chief then took from his mouth a fragment of chewed root and dropped it also into the bowl. All remained silent during these acts, and soon a lighted pipe was passed from one to another of the priests, beginning with the chief, who puffed great clouds of tobacco smoke into the liquid and to the cardinal points in the prescribed circuit.

Individual prayers followed the ceremonial smoke. These began with the Snake chief, and were taken up in turn by the other members of the society. The prayers were immediately followed by songs, accompanied by the rattles to secure rhythm and while these songs were sung the reptiles were washed. The Snake men held their snake whips erect, on a level with the shoulder, keeping time to the rhythm of the songs.

Soon after the priests began to sing I noticed that the men with the bag of reptiles handed the snakes to the chief and his neighbors, and that they plunged the reptiles into the bowl before them, later depositing the snakes on the sand covering the floor. While this transpired the singers kept on with their songs, and other snakes were handed to the chief, who plunged them into the liquid and placed them on the sand. The floor enclosed by the row of sitting priests was soon covered with a mass of writhing reptiles, the rapidly moving species darting from one end to the other of the sanded area, the rattlers, which move in a more deliberate way, extending themselves at length or coiling for defense. Several of the whip snakes, crawling between the legs of the seated priests, escaped to the floor of the *kiva,* but were dextrously picked up and returned to the enclosure. Three or four snakes climbed up the side of the *kiva* wall and wound their bodies into a small niche, from which their heads protruded as if spectators

218 J. WALTER FEWKES

of the curious ceremony. When the snakes huddled too closely together one of the priests separated them, using the end of his snake whip as a kind of pitchfork.

The songs closed with prayer and ceremonial smoke, and the priests returned to the preparation of their dance paraphernalia, leaving the reptiles on the floor, where they were herded by one or two of their number. Several white men came into the *kiva* after the washing to see this mass of reptiles on the sand, and Professor James obtained a good photograph of the snakes on the floor, a printed copy of which has been widely distributed. Subsequent rites with these snakes belong to another chapter in descriptions of the Snake Dance and do not now concern us.

It has been suggested that the liquid in which the reptiles are bathed is a stupefying compound into which they are introduced in order to render them more tractable when carried on the plaza a few hours after. I find no good evidence that such is the object of the washing, nor do I believe that any means are adopted to stupefy them.

The statement that the snakes are "washed repeatedly in various kinds of medicine water and are frequently handled or stroked with a downward squeezing movement of the hand" has not been verified by me. They are washed but once, and I have never seen them stroked, as the above quotation implies. No "course of treatment" is, so far as I know, adopted in the *kiva* by the Snake priests to render the rattlesnake innocuous. Some of the larger rattlesnakes have been held up for my examination, and I have been invited to take them in my own hands, which invitation was not accepted, and the Indian who held them may, in commenting on their size, have stroked the body, but no systematic treatment by stroking or squeezing has been observed.

The Snake washing is simply a purification rite, analogous to the head washing of the priests on the same day, rather than treatment to stupefy or otherwise render the snakes harmless in subsequent handling. The treatment of the reptiles, venomous or otherwise, during the Snake ceremonials and the way they are addressed at capture justifies the belief that they are regarded as kin or members of the same family or clan as the priests. The legends of the society distinctly state that the children of the Snake woman became reptiles, and this same ancestress is regarded as the parent of the Snake family, out of which the Snake society has grown. In totemism, which is the key-note of the Snake ceremony, we find the explanation of this fancied kinship, for both human and reptilian beings are supposed to have a common ancestress, with characters of each.

It is but natural, following this line of thought, that when the reptiles are brought into the pueblo to participate with their human kindred in the great family ceremony their heads, no less than those of the priests, should be bathed as a preparation for the dance in which they participate.

Early in the day the heads of novices are washed as a necessary preparation for the dance.

The portion of the Snake tradition which refers to the snake washing is as follows: "On the fifth evening of the ceremony and for three succeeding evenings low clouds trailed over Tokonabi, and Snake people from the underworld came from them and went into the kivas and ate only corn pollen for food, and on leaving were not seen again. Each of four evenings brought a new group of Snake people, and on the following morning they were found in the valleys metamorphosed into reptiles of all kinds."[5]

On the *ninth* morning the *Tcüamana* (Snake maidens) said: "We understand this. Let the younger brothers [the Snake Society] go out and bring them all in and *wash their heads,* and let them dance with you." Again, when the Snake maid gave birth to reptiles "their heads were washed, and they were dried in sand heaps on the floor, and their mothers sat beside them."

The Snake washing is one of many ceremonial acts by which the Hopi have perpetuated their ancient beliefs. Another way of preserving these beliefs is by means of the myth or legend, which is transmitted by word of mouth from one generation to another.

The Snake washing at Micoñinovi, and the same may probably be said of that at Oraibi, Cipaulovi, and Cuñopavi, is a tame affair as compared with that at Walpi, which has always seemed to me the most fearless episode of the Snake Dance. When the snakes are removed from the jars, at the last pueblo, the Snake men fearlessly plunge their hands into receptacles filled with reptiles, any one of which might strike them. This is done in a dimly lighted room, at a time when there is great excitement, with men yelling at the top of their voices. How the Snake men escape the poisonous fangs of the rattlesnakes is a wonder to me, and yet, although I have witnessed the Walpi Snake washing four times, I have never seen one of the men bitten. The snakes are carefully taken out of the receptacles at Micoñinovi before the rites begin. They are not thrown across the room on an altar, but are simply thrust into a bowl of liquid and placed on sand to dry.

The simplicity of the Snake washing at Micoñinovi as compared with that at Walpi is probably due to the absence of a snake altar and snake *tiponi* at the former pueblo. The fact that the rite is simpler in this and three other pueblos may indicate that the ancient rite was less complicated than that now observed at Walpi. On the other hand, it is possible that the simplicity of the Snake washing at the three pueblos of the Middle Mesa and Oraibi is due to the fact that the cult as there observed is an offshoot from a more complex form. A third possible explanation, that the simple celebrations are survivals, due to syncopation, of more complicated rites, has less to commend it, for it seems hardly probable that they once had snake altars and *tiponis* which in course of time were lost.

[5] Jour. Amer. Eth. and Arch., vol. ii, p. 116.

WASHINGTON MATTHEWS

(1843-1905)

The Night Chant: A Navaho Ceremony

IN ORDER TO GIVE A CLEAR UNDERSTANDING OF THE WORK OF THE LAST
night, it will be necessary to repeat some statements already made.

The medicine-lodge, as has been said, was built before the ceremony
began and we have noted that, at different times, other preparations were
made; that the ground in front of the lodge was cleared and levelled for
the dancers; that an enclosure of evergreen branches and saplings, which
we call the arbor or greenroom, was constructed about one hundred paces
east of the lodge; that the ground between the greenroom and the dancing-
place was cleared of brush, weeds, and other obstructions in order that
the dancers might pass easily back and forth in the dark, and that great
piles of dried wood were placed at the edges of the dance-ground, north
and south, to serve for fuel and as seats for the spectators. Four great fires
are kindled on each side of the dance-ground at nightfall, and other fires
may be made later in the same locality. The arrangements, when all is
ready for the ceremonies of the last night, may be best understood by
referring to figure 15.

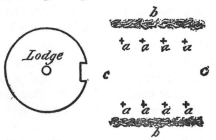

Fig. 15. DIAGRAM OF DANCING-GROUND.
a, fires; b, piles of wood; c, c, dancing ground.

From Matthews, "The Night Chant, a Navaho Ceremony," *Memoirs of the American Museum of Natural History,* Vol. VI (Publication of the Hyde Southwestern
Expedition), (New York: 1902), pp. 140-145.

The characters paint themselves in the medicine-lodge, simultaneously, facing the east. The right hand is the part first painted; then they whiten from above downward. While they paint, a song called Atsá'*lei* Ye*dad*iglés is sung without accompaniment of drum or rattle. The following is offered as an approximate, free translation of this song:

> Now the holy one paints his form,
> The Wind Boy, the holy one, paints his form,
> All over his body, he paints his form,
> With the dark cloud he paints his form,
> With the misty rain he paints his form,
> With the rainy bubbles he paints his form,
> To the ends of his toes he paints his form,
> To fingers and rattle he paints his form,
> To the plume on his head he paints his form.

After the painting is done, they dress, with assistance, while another song, which has not been recorded, is sung. The masks and rattles which were painted and decorated during the day, the wands of spruce which were prepared, and the fox-skins are carried out, after dark, and laid in a row in the north of the greenroom. When the characters are ready, in the lodge, they go out blanketed to the greenroom to assume their masks.

The public performance of the night begins with the ceremony of the Atsá'*lei* or First Dancers, and this is usually conducted in the manner to be now described.

The performers consist of four yébaka or ordinary male divinities and *H*astséyal*t*i, the Talking God or Yéb*i*tsai. Besides these, the chanter and the patient appear on the scene. The yébaka, like those who appear later in the dance of the naak*h*aí, are nearly naked, their bodies heavily coated with a mixture of white earth and water. Each wears moccasins, long blue stockings of Navaho make, a short kilt or loin-cloth of red baize, crimson silk, or some showy material, a silver-studded belt from which the skin of a kit-fox hangs at the back, numerous rich necklaces borrowed from friends for the occasion, and the blue, plumed mask of the yébaka with its attached collar of spruce twigs. Large plumes are attached to the stockings and small feathers to the wrists. Each carries, in his left hand, a wand of spruce twigs, attached for security to his mask, by means of a string of yucca fibres, and in his right hand a gourd rattle. The fifth character is *H*astséyal*t*i, who wears the peculiar mask of that god, with a collar of spruce. In one hand he carries a fawnskin bag. Unlike his four companions, he is comfortably clothed in some form of Navaho dress.

Each one of the four yébaka represents a different character. The first is a chief, genius, or god of corn; the second is a chief of the child-rain; the third is a chief of all kinds of plants, of vegetation, and the fourth is a chief of pollen. Such is the order of their precedence in the dance, and in this order they are mentioned in the songs. Besides being chiefs of these four things, they are spoken of as thunder-birds and as having the colors of the four cardinal points.

Hastséyalti masks and dresses himself completely in the lodge. Usually about 8 P.M. they all leave the lodge together. Hastséyalti whoops as they come out and then clears the dance-ground, motioning intruders away, while the four others precede him to the greenroom to don their masks. Before putting on their masks they chew spruce leaves, bitten off their wands, and spit juice and leaves into the masks in the belief that this act helps the masks to go on. They often have to stretch and pull their masks, finding difficulty in making them fit at first.

When they are all ready, they leave the green-room for the dance-ground in the following order: the chanter, Hastséyalti, the four Atsá'lei in the order of their precedence. When they start, the chanter, uttering the benediction, "Hozóles kóte sïtsówe," scatters pollen on the ground, toward the west along the way they are to follow. They move very quietly, in single file, softly shaking their rattles and singing in a low tone. Sometimes they stop on the way to readjust their masks. They enter softly and stealthily on to the dance-ground.

As they enter the ground a watcher at the door of the lodge cries, "Biké hatáli hakú," and the patient emerges from the lodge bearing meal in a sacred basket, and, on top of the meal, sometimes four kethawns. While the priest says a prayer over the meal, the four yébaka keep up a constant motion of the feet somewhat similar to that of the dance to be presently described. The following diagram (fig. 16) shows the position of the whole party at this time:

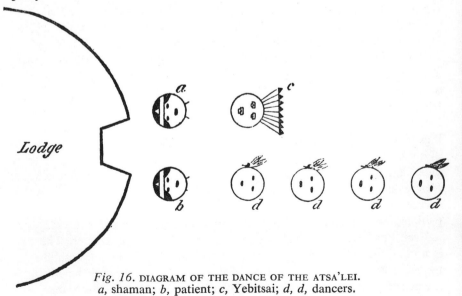

Fig. 16. DIAGRAM OF THE DANCE OF THE ATSA'LEI.
a, shaman; b, patient; c, Yebitsai; d, d, dancers.

After this prayer, the patient, prompted and assisted by the chanter (or the chanter, if the patient is a child), advances to each of the Atsá'lei in turn, and sprinkles meal on him thus: He picks up a large pinch between the thumb and two fingers, allows the substance to fall on the right hand of the subject, up the right arm, over the top of the forehead, and down the left arm; he drops what remains into the palm of the left hand. Immediately after, he may deposit a sacrificial cigarette in the left hand. Four cigarettes thus given form a set which is sometimes made and sacrificed on the fourth day, and sometimes, according to rules and theories not ascertained, on the last night. When reserved for the last night they are thus given to the Atsá'lei. In applying the meal the patient carries the basket on the left arm.

When the application is finished, patient and shaman resume their former position in the west, facing the east, and the priest prays a long prayer to each god, which the patient repeats after him, sentence by sentence, in the usual manner. The four prayers are alike in all respects, except in the mention of certain attributes of the gods. I have collected and translated one of these prayers and have given text, interlinear translation and free translation in "Navaho Legends." To make clearer the description of the rite, I here repeat the free translation of the prayer to the dark bird who is the chief of pollen. While the prayer is being said, the dancers keep up a constant motion, bending and straightening the left knee and swaying the head from side to side.

In Tse'gíhi,
In the house made of the dawn,
In the house made of the evening twilight,
In the house made of the dark cloud,
In the house made of the he-rain,
In the house made of the dark mist,
In the house made of the she-rain,
In the house made of pollen,
In the house made of grasshoppers,
Where the dark mist curtains the doorway,
The path to which is on the rainbow,
Where the zigzag lightning stands high on top,
Where the he-rain stands high on top,
Oh, male divinity!
With your moccasins of dark cloud, come to us.
With your leggings of dark cloud, come to us.
With your shirt of dark cloud, come to us.
With your head-dress of dark cloud, come to us.
With your mind enveloped in dark cloud, come to us.
With the dark thunder above you, come to us soaring.
With the shapen cloud at your feet, come to us soaring.
With the far darkness made of the dark cloud over your head, come to us
    soaring.

With the far darkness made of the he-rain over your head, come to us soaring.

With the far darkness made of the dark mist over your head, come to us soaring.

With the far darkness made of the she-rain over your head, come to us soaring.

With the zigzag lightning flung out on high over your head, come to us soaring.

With the rainbow hanging high over your head, come to us soaring.

With the far darkness made of the dark cloud on the ends of your wings, come to us soaring.

With the far darkness made of the he-rain on the ends of your wings, come to us soaring.

With the far darkness made of the dark mist on the ends of your wings, come to us soaring.

With the far darkness made of the she-rain on the ends of your wings, come to us soaring.

With the zigzag lightning flung out on high on the ends of your wings, come to us soaring.

With the rainbow hanging high on the ends of your wings, come to us soaring.

With the near darkness made of the dark cloud, of the he-rain, of the dark mist and of the she-rain, come to us.

With the darkness on the earth, come to us.

With these I wish the foam floating on the flowing water over the roots of the great corn.

I have made your sacrifice.

I have prepared a smoke for you.

My feet restore for me.

My limbs restore for me.

My body restore for me.

My mind restore for me.

My voice restore for me.

To-day, take out your spell for me.

To-day, take away your spell for me.

Away from me you have taken it.

Far off from me it is taken.

Far off you have done it.

Happily I recover.

Happily my interior becomes cool.

Happily my eyes regain their power.

Happily my head becomes cool.

Happily my limbs regain their power.

Happily I hear again.

Happily for me (the spell) is taken off.

Happily I walk (or, may I walk).

Impervious to pain, I walk.

Feeling light within, I walk.

With lively feelings, I walk.

Happily (or in beauty) abundant dark clouds I desire.

Happily abundant dark mists I desire.

Happily abundant passing showers I desire.

Happily an abundance of vegetation I desire.
Happily an abundance of pollen I desire.
Happily abundant dew I desire.
Happily may fair white corn, to the ends of the earth, come with you.
Happily may fair yellow corn, to the ends of the earth, come with you.
Happily may fair blue corn, to the ends of the earth, come with you.
Happily may fair corn of all kinds, to the ends of the earth, come with you.
Happily may fair plants of all kinds, to the ends of the earth, come with
    you.
Happily may fair goods of all kinds, to the ends of the earth, come with
    you.
Happily, may fair jewels of all kinds, to the ends of the earth, come with
    you.
With these before you, happily may they come with you.
With these behind you, happily may they come with you.
With these below you, happily may they come with you.
With these above you, happily may they come with you.
With these all around you, happily may they come with you.
Thus happily you accomplish your tasks.
Happily the old men will regard you.
Happily the old women will regard you.
Happily the young men will regard you.
Happily the young women will regard you.
Happily the boys will regard you.
Happily the girls will regard you.
Happily the children will regard you.
Happily the chiefs will regard you.
Happily, as they scatter in different directions, they will regard you.
Happily, as they approach their homes, they will regard you.
Happily may their roads home be on the trail of pollen (peace).
Happily may they all get back.
In beauty (happily) I walk.
With beauty before me, I walk.
With beauty behind me, I walk.
With beauty below me, I walk.
With beauty above me, I walk.
With beauty all around me, I walk.
It is finished (again) in beauty,
It is finished in beauty,
It is finished in beauty,
It is finished in beauty.

When these prayers are ended, the patient, followed by the chanter,
passes eastward, down the north side of the line and back again. As they
pass east, the former scatters meal up the right arm of each dancer from
hand to shoulder, and the latter scatters pollen in a similar manner. When
they return to the west, the patient lays down his basket and sits beside it
near the door of the lodge. The chanter sits to the left of the patient. Both
face east, looking at the dancers. All the spectators now become silent and
attentive, waiting for the sacred song.

*H*astséyal*t*i, who has been standing north of the line of dancers, facing south, rushes whooping to the east and holds up his bag as a signal to the four Atsá'*l*ei, who are now facing the west. Immediately the Atsá'*l*ei advance the left foot, bend bodies to the right, whoop, shake their rattles, dip them with a long sweep of the arm as if dipping water and bring them up close to their mouths. They almost touch the ground in doing this. *H*astséyal*t*i rushes to the west and repeats his acts, while the dancers face east and repeat their acts. They face west again, always turning sunwise.

After a brief pause in the west, *H*astséyal*t*i stamps twice, violently, with his right foot as a signal; whereat the Atsá'*l*ei begin a peculiar dancing step in which the right foot, held horizontally, is lifted from the ground. This may be considered marking time rather than dancing. Meanwhile, the right forearm moves up and down, in time with the corresponding foot, and shakes the rattle. The left arm hangs inactive. This step is taken four times in silence before the song begins and continues through the song. At certain parts of each stanza the singers face the east and at other parts they face the west again; thus there are eight changes of direction during the song. They poise themselves on the toes of the left foot before they turn and slowly shake their rattles at a distance, laterally, from their bodies, as they wheel around.

The song sung on this occasion, although it consists mostly of meaningless syllables, is, perhaps, the most important of the whole ceremony. The singers are drilled long and thoroughly in private before they are allowed to sing in public. It is said that, if a single syllable is omitted or misplaced, the ceremony terminates at once; all the preceding work of nine days is considered valueless and the participators and spectators may return, at once, to their homes.

Collaboration with Indian Anthropologists

ALICE CUNNINGHAM FLETCHER
(1838-1923)

FRANCIS LA FLESCHE
(1857-1932)

The relationship of these two scholars is one of those rare collaborations of scholarship, made more striking by the difference in age, sex and race. Alice Fletcher, a white woman from a New England family, and Francis La Flesche, an Omaha Indian, twenty years her junior, regarded each other as adopted mother and son.

Their formal collaboration extended over a quarter of a century and resulted in the production of the monumental volume, The Omaha Tribe *(27th Annual Report, Bureau of American Ethnology). Although this is the only publication that bears both names, their spiritual companionship extends far beyond the single volume.*

Alice Fletcher's first interest was in Indian music and she spent several years among the Omaha, recording their songs by notation. In those days there were no phonographs and no tape recorders. Because of her knowledge of the Omaha people she was sent in 1883 to supervise the distribution of reservation lands under the allotment system. She was sent later to the Winnebago and the Nez Percé on a similar mission, and on the basis of her experience formulated rules for use with other tribes. She also wrote a treatise on Indian education in response to a Senate resolution. She would, therefore, qualify as America's first applied anthropologist.

These good works absorbed her time for many years and took her away from her primary interest. A Thaw fellowship from the Peabody Museum of Harvard University enabled her to return to her Omaha studies. This time she had the help of Francis La Flesche.

In 1901 she heard that the "Pipe Ceremony," extinct among the Omaha and now only rarely performed elsewhere, was to be performed by the Pawnee. Through the good offices of La Flesche, she was able to make arrangements to see it, and brought back to Washington with her James Murie, one of the ceremonial leaders, with whom she recorded the com-

plete ceremony, including the music of the hundreds of songs. Marquette, in his travels, saw a part of the "dance performed in honor of the Calumet or tobacco pipe," and was much impressed by it. Later writers referred to the "Pipe Dance" of the tribes of the Southern Plains, but no description of it or suggestion of its significance was available. Fletcher's description of this beautiful ceremony, in which the most sacred possessions of the tribe, the feathered pipestems, are borne in procession to another tribe in celebration of the procreative forces of the universe, still stands as the only complete description of a major Indian ceremony. Other excellent descriptions, such as Matthews' Night Chant, do not contain the music of the songs.

Francis La Flesche grew up among the Omaha while the buffalo still ran, and remembered war parties though he had not participated in them. He was educated at a Presbyterian mission college. On a visit to Washington as a member of a delegation of Indians he met the Secretary of the Interior, who persuaded him to join the Bureau of Indian Affairs. Here he began his fruitful collaboration with Alice Fletcher. After the completion of the Omaha volume he was transferred to the Bureau of American Ethnology and worked on the Osage, a closely related tribe.

Fletcher and La Flesche have provided us with most of what we know of the aboriginal cultures of the Southern Plains with their complex social structure and elaborate ceremonialism, standing geographically and culturally midway between the pueblos and the tribes of the Mississippi. And so another link in North American culture history was forged.—R.L.B.

ALICE CUNNINGHAM FLETCHER

(1838-1923)

and

FRANCIS LA FLESCHE

(1857-1932)

The Omaha Tribe: Ceremonies for Children

INTRODUCTION OF THE OMAHA CHILD TO THE COSMOS

WHEN A CHILD WAS BORN IT WAS NOT REGARDED AS A MEMBER OF ITS gens or of the tribe but simply as a living being coming forth into the universe, whose advent must be ceremonially announced in order to assure it an accepted place among the already existing forms. This ceremonial announcement took the form of an expression of the Omaha belief in the oneness of the universe through the bond of a common life-power that pervaded all things in nature animate and inanimate.

This ceremony of introduction took place on the eighth day after birth. Unfortunately the full details of the ceremony have been lost through the death of the priests who had charge of it. The hereditary right to perform the ceremony belonged to the Washe'to^n subgens of the I^{n}shta'çu^{n}da gens.

On the appointed day the priest was sent for. When he arrived he took his place at the door of the tent in which the child lay and raising his right hand to the sky, palm outward, he intoned the following in a loud, ringing voice:

> Ho! Ye Sun, Moon, Stars, all ye that move in the heavens,
> I bid you hear me!

From Fletcher and La Flesche, "The Omaha Tribe," *Twenty-seventh Annual Report, Bureau of American Ethnology* (Washington: Government Printing Office, 1911).

229

Into your midst has come a new life.
    Consent ye, I implore!
Make its path smooth, that it may reach the brow of the first hill!

Ho! Ye Winds, Clouds, Rain, Mist, all ye that move in the air,
    I bid you hear me!
Into your midst has come a new life.
    Consent ye, I implore!
Make its path smooth, that it may reach the brow of the second hill!

Ho! Ye Hills, Valleys, Rivers, Lakes, Trees, Grasses, all ye of the earth,
    I bid you hear me!
Into your midst has come a new life.
    Consent ye, I implore!
Make its path smooth, that it may reach the brow of the third hill!
Ho! Ye Birds, great and small, that fly in the air,
Ho! Ye Animals, great and small, that dwell in the forest,
Ho! Ye insects that creep among the grasses and burrow in the ground—
    I bid you hear me!
Into your midst has come a new life.
    Consent ye, I implore!
Make its path smooth, that it may reach the brow of the fourth hill!

Ho! All ye of the heavens, all ye of the air, all ye of the earth:
    I bid you all to hear me!
Into your midst has come a new life.
    Consent ye, consent ye all, I implore!
Make its path smooth—then shall it travel beyond the four hills!

This ritual was a supplication to the powers of the heavens, the air, and the earth for the safety of the child from birth to old age. In it the life of the infant is pictured as about to travel a rugged road stretching over four hills, marking the stages of infancy, youth, manhood, and old age.

The ceremony which finds oral expression in this ritual voices in no uncertain manner the Omaha belief in man's relation to the visible powers of the heavens and in the interdependence of all forms of life. The appeal bears evidence of its antiquity, breathing of a time antedating established rites and ceremonies. It expresses the emotions of the human soul, touched with the love of offspring, alone with the might of nature, and companioned only by the living creatures whose friendliness must be sought if life is to be secure on its journey.

. . . Among the Omaha no further ceremony took place in reference to the child in its relation to the cosmos, to its gens, or to the tribe, until it was able to walk. When the period arrived at which the child could walk steadily by itself, the time was at hand when it must be introduced into the tribe. This was done ceremonially.

INTRODUCTION OF THE CHILD INTO THE TRIBE

CEREMONY OF TURNING THE CHILD

. . . All children, both boys and girls, passed through this ceremony, which is a survival of that class of ceremonies belonging to the lowest, or oldest, stratum of tribal rites; it is directly related to the cosmic forces— the wind, the earth, and the fire. Through this ceremony all the children who had reached the period when they could move about unaided, could direct their own steps, were symbolically "sent into the midst of the winds" —that element essential to life and health; their feet were set upon the stone—emblem of long life upon the earth and of the wisdom derived from age; while the "flames," typical of the life-giving power, were invoked to give their aid toward insuring the capacity for a long, fruitful, and successful life within the tribe. Through this ceremony the child passed out of that stage in its life wherein it was hardly distinguished from all other living forms into its place as distinctively a human being, a member of its birth gens, and through this to a recognized place in the tribe. As it went forth its baby name was thrown away, its feet were clad in new moccasins made after the manner of the tribe, and its *ni'kie* name was proclaimed to all nature and to the assembled people.

The significance of the new moccasins put on the child will appear more clearly by the light of the following custom, still observed in families in which all the old traditions of the tribe are conserved: When moccasins are made for a little baby, a small hole is cut in the sole of one. This is done in order that "if a messenger from the spirit world should come and say to the child, 'I have come for you,' the child could answer, 'I can not go on a journey—my moccasins are worn out!' " A similar custom obtains in the Oto tribe. A little hole is cut in the first pair of moccasins made for a child. When the relatives come to see the little one they examine the moccasins, and, seeing the hole, they say: "Why, he (or she) has worn out his moccasins; he has traveled over the earth!" This is an indirect prayer that the child may live long. The new (whole) moccasins put on the child at the close of the ceremony of introducing it into the tribe constitute an assurance that it is prepared for the journey of life and that the journey will be a long one.

The ceremony of Turning the Child took place in the springtime, after the first thunders had been heard. When the grass was well up and the birds were singing, "particularly the meadow lark," the tribal herald proclaimed that the time for these ceremonies had come. A tent was set up for the purpose, made sacred, and the keeper of these rites, who belonged to the Washe'to^n subgens of the I^{n}shta'çu^{n}da gens, made himself ready and entered the tent. Meanwhile the parents whose children had arrived at the proper age, that is, could walk steadily unassisted, took their little ones and proceeded to the Sacred Tent. The only requisite for the child was a pair of new moccasins, but large fees were given to the priest for his services.

Only parts of the ritual belonging to this ceremony have been obtained. Those whose prerogative it was to conduct the rites are all dead, and with them knowledge of much of the ceremony passed away. The preservation of the fragments here given came about thus: An old and trusted friend of Joseph La Flesche, a former principal chief of the tribe, was greatly interested when a boy, in the tribal rites. One of his near kinsmen was a priest of this rite. When the Sacred Tent was set up this boy more than once succeeded in secreting himself behind packs within and from his hiding place was able to observe what took place. Having a retentive memory and a quick ear for song, he was able to learn and remember the six songs here given. Subsequent inquiries have added somewhat to the knowledge secured from this informant, although, so far as the writers have been able to ascertain, no one seems ever to have obtained quite so close an inside view of the entire ceremony as this inquisitive boy. Of course no one who had passed through the ceremony could accurately remember it, as the child was generally only 3 or 4 years of age at the time it had a part in the rite.

The tent was always a large one, set facing the east, and open at the entrance, so that the bystanders, who kept at a respectful distance, could see something of what was going on within. As the ceremony was one of tribal interest, many flocked to the Sacred Tent to watch the proceedings. In the center was a fire. On the east of the fire was placed a stone. There was also a ball of grass, placed at the west of the fire-place near its edge. It was the mother who led the child to the tent. At the door she paused, and addressed the priest within, saying: "Venerable man! I desire my child to wear moccasins." Then she dropped the hand of the child, and the little one, carrying his new moccasins, entered the tent alone. He was met by the priest, who advanced to the door to receive the gifts brought by the mother as fees. Here she again addressed him, saying: "I desire my child to walk long upon the earth; I desire him to be content with the light of many days. We seek your protection; we hold to you for strength." The priest replied, addressing the child: "You shall reach the fourth hill sighing; you shall be bowed over; you shall have wrinkles; your staff shall bend under your weight. I speak to you that you may be strong." Laying his hand on the shoulder of the child, he added: "What you have brought me shall not be lost to you; you shall live long and enjoy many possessions; your eyes shall be satisfied with many good things." Then, moving with the child toward the fireplace in the center of the lodge, and speaking in the capacity of the Thunder, whose priest he was, he uttered these words:

"I am a powerful being; I breathe from my lips over you." Then he began to sing the Invocation addressed to the Winds: . . .

> Ye four, come hither and stand, near shall ye stand
> In four groups shall ye stand
> Here shall ye stand, in this place stand
>   (The Thunder rolls)

. . . At the close of this ritual song the priest faces the child to the east, lifting it by the shoulders; its feet are allowed to rest upon the stone. He then turns the child completely around, from left to right. If by any chance the child should struggle or move so as to turn from right to left the on-lookers set up a cry of alarm. It was considered very disastrous to turn ever so little in the wrong way, so the priest was most careful to prevent any accident. When the child had been turned, its feet rested on the stone as it faced the south. The priest then lifted it by the arms, turned it, and set its feet on the stone as it faced the west; then he again lifted the child, turned it, and set its feet on the stone as it faced the north. Lastly the child was lifted to its feet and placed on the stone as it again faced the east. During this action the following ritual song was sung: . . .

> Turned by the winds goes the one I send yonder;
> Yonder he goes who is whirled by the winds;
> Goes, where the four hills of life and the four winds are standing;
> There, in the midst of the winds do I send him,
> Into the midst of the winds, standing there.
>   (The Thunder rolls)

The winds invoked by the priest stand in four groups, and receive the child, which is whirled by them, and by them enabled "to face in every direction." This action symbolizes that the winds will come and strengthen him as hereafter he shall traverse the earth and meet the vicissitudes he must encounter as he passes over the four hills and completes the circuit of a long life. It was believed that this ceremony exercised a marked influence on the child, and enabled it to grow in strength and in the ability to practise self-control.

The priest now put the new moccasins on the feet of the child, as the following ritual song was sung. Toward its close the child was lifted, set on its feet, and made to take four steps typical of its entrance into a long life. . . .

> Here unto you has been spoken the truth;
> Because of this truth you shall stand.
> Here, declared is the truth.
> Here in this place has been shown you the truth.
> Therefore, arise! go forth in its strength!
>   (The Thunder rolls)

The *ni'kie* name of the child was now announced, after which the priest cried aloud: "Ye hills, ye grass, ye trees, ye creeping things both great and small, I bid you hear! This child has thrown away its baby name. Ho!" (a call to take notice).

The priest next instructed the child as to the tabu it must observe, and what would be the penalty for disobedience. If the child was a girl, she now passed out of the tent and rejoined her mother.

Up to this point the ceremony of introducing the child into the tribe was the same for male and female; but in the case of boys there was a supplemental rite which pertained to them as future warriors.

CONSECRATION OF THE BOY TO THUNDER

This ceremony was called We'bashna, meaning "to cut the hair." According to traditions, this specialized ceremony belonged to the period in the growth of the political development of the tribe when efforts were being made to hold the tribe more firmly together by checking the independence of the warriors and placing them under control—efforts that finally resulted in the placing of the rites of war in charge of the We'zhi^{n}shte gens.

In the ceremony of cutting the hair the priest in charge gathered a tuft from the crown of the boy's head, tied it, then cut it off and laid it away in a parfleche case, which was kept as a sacred repository, singing as he cut the lock a ritual song explanatory of the action. The severing of the lock was an act that implied the consecration of the life of the boy to Thunder, the symbol of the power that controlled the life and death of the warrior—for every man had to be a warrior in order to defend the home and the tribe. The ritual song which followed the cutting of the lock indicated the acceptance of the offering made; that is, the life of the warrior henceforth was under the control of the Thunder to prolong or to cut short at will.

The Washe'to^n subgens, which had charge of this rite of the consecration of the boy to the Thunder as the god of war, camped at the northern side of the entrance into the camp circle when the opening faced the east; while the We'zhi^{n}shte gens, which had charge of the rites pertaining to war, including the bestowal of honors, formed the southern side of the entrance. Thus the "door," through which all must pass who would enter the camp circle, was guarded on each side by gentes having charge of rites pertaining to Thunder, as the god of war, the power that could not only hold in check enemies from without, but which met each man child at his entrance into the tribe and controlled him even to the hour of his death.

In a community beginning to crystallize into organized social relations the sphere of the warrior would naturally rise above that of the mere fighter; and when the belief of the people concerning nature is taken into consideration it is not surprising that the movement toward social organization should tend to place the warriors—the men of power—in close relation to those natural manifestations of power seen in the fury of the storm and heard in the rolling of the thunder. Moreover, in the efforts toward political unification such rites as those which were connected with the Thunder would conduce to the welding of the people by the inculcation of a common dependence upon a powerful god and the sign of consecration to him would be put upon the head of every male member of the tribe.

The priest took the boy to the space west of the fire; there, facing the east, he cut a lock of hair from the crown of the boy's head, as he sang the following ritual song:

Tigoⁿha moⁿshia ta ha
Shabe tithe noⁿzhia ha
Tigoⁿha moⁿshia ta ha
Shabe tithe noⁿzhia shethu aha
Tigoⁿha moⁿshia ta ha
Shabe tithe noⁿzhia
Tigoⁿha moⁿshia ta ha
Shabe tithe noⁿzhia ha shethu aha
Tigoⁿha moⁿshia ta ha
Shabe tithe noⁿzhia ha

Grandfather! far above on high,
The hair like a shadow passes before you.
Grandfather! far above on high,
Dark like a shadow the hair sweeps before you into the midst of your realm.
Grandfather! there above, on high,
Dark like a shadow the hair passes before you.
Grandfather! dwelling afar on high,
Like a dark shadow the hair sweeps before you into the midst of your realm.
Grandfather! far above on high,
The hair like a shadow passes before you.

From this ritual song we learn that the lock laid away in the sacred case in care of the Thunder priest symbolically was sent to the Thunder god dwelling "far above on high," who was ceremonially addressed as "Grandfather"—the term of highest respect in the language. The hair of a person was popularly believed to have a vital connection with the life of the body, so that anyone becoming possessed of a lock of hair might work his will on the individual from whom it came. In ceremonial expressions of grief the throwing of locks of hair upon the dead was indicative of the vital loss sustained. In the light of customs that obtained among the people the hair, under certain conditions, might be said to typify life. Because of the belief in the continuity of life a part could stand for the whole, so in this rite by cutting off a lock of the boy's hair and giving it to the Thunder the life of the child was given into the keeping of the god. It is to be noted that later, when the hair was suffered to grow on the boy's head, a lock on the crown of the head was parted in a circle from the rest of the hair and kept constantly distinct and neatly braided. Upon this lock the war honors of the warrior were worn, and it was this lock that was cut from the head of a slain enemy and formed the central object in the triumph ceremonies, for the reason that it preeminently represented the life of the man who had been slain in battle.

In the next ritual song the Thunder god speaks and proclaims his acceptance of the consecration of the life through the lock of hair and also declares his control over the life of the warrior. . . .

In the closing song there is a return to the cosmic forces which were appealed to and represented in the ceremony of Turning the Child. . . .

At the conclusion of this tribal ceremony, when the child reached its home the father cut the hair of his son after the symbolic manner of his gens; the hair was thus worn until the second dentition. Then the hair was allowed to grow, and the scalp lock, the sign of the warrior to which reference has already been made was parted off and kept carefully braided, no matter how frowzy and tangled the rest of the hair might be.

FRANCIS LA FLESCHE

(1857-1932)

Rite of the Chiefs: Prayer for Painting the Body

VERILY, AT THAT TIME AND PLACE, IT HAS BEEN SAID, IN THIS HOUSE,
They (the people of the gentes) said: The little ones have nothing with
which to paint their faces.
And he (the Priest representing the Black Bear) replied: When the little
ones paint their faces,
They shall use for their paint the god that appears first in the day,
The god that strikes the sky with a red glow.
It is the color of that god the little ones shall put upon their faces.
When the little ones put upon their faces this color,
They shall always live to see old age as they travel the path of life.

Verily, at that time and place, it has been said, in this house,
The Black Bear that is without a blemish.
By that animal also
The little ones shall cause themselves to be identified by Wa-ķon'-da.
It was he who said: My body which is black in color
I have made to be as my charcoal.
When the little ones also make it to be as their charcoal,
They shall always be identified by Wa-ķon'-da as they travel the path of
life.
Behold the white spot on my throat.
Behold the god of day who sitteth in the heavens.
Close to this god (as its symbol) we shall place this spot.
When we place this spot close to the god of day as its symbol,
The little ones shall always live to see old age as they travel the path of
life.

From La Flesche, "The Osage Tribe," *Thirty-Sixth Annual Report, Bureau of American Ethnology* (Washington: Government Printing Office, 1921).

Verily, at that time and place, it has been said, in this house,
They spake to the great white swan,
Saying: O, grandfather,
The little ones have nothing of which to make their bodies.
Verily, at that time and place,
The swan spake, saying: You say the little ones have nothing of which to
    make their bodies.
The little ones shall make of me their bodies.
When the little ones make of me their bodies,
They shall always live to see old age.
Behold my feet that are dark in color.
I have made them to be as my charcoal.
When the little ones make of me their bodies,
When they make my feet to be as their charcoal,
They shall always be identified by Wa-ķon'-da as they travel the path of
    life.
Behold the tip of my beak, which is dark in color.
I have made it to be as my charcoal.
When the little ones make the tip of my beak to be as their charcoal,
They shall cause themselves to be identified by Wa-ķon'-da as they travel
    the path of life.

Behold also my wings.
The feathers of my wings the little ones shall use as plumes.
When they use the feathers of my wings as plumes,
The days of cloudless skies
Shall always be at their command as they travel the path of life.
The four great divisions of the days
They shall always be able to reach as they travel the path of life.

    At the close of the recitation the Xo'-ķa puts upon himself the sacred
symbols, following the order in which they were mentioned.

ALICE CUNNINGHAM FLETCHER

(1838-1923)

The Hako: A Pawnee Ceremony

THE CEREMONY OF THE HAKO IS A PRAYER FOR CHILDREN IN ORDER THAT the tribe may increase; and also that the people may have long life, enjoy plenty, and be happy and at peace . . .

In this ceremony we are to carry the sacred articles to one not of our kindred in order to bind him to us by a sacred and strong tie; we are to ask for him many good gifts, long life, health, children, and we should receive gifts from him in return. . . . Honor is conferred upon a man who leads a Hako party to a distant tribe and there makes a son, while to the Son help is given from all the powers represented by the sacred objects. Between the Father and the Son and their immediate families a relationship such as that which exists between kindred is established through this ceremony. It is a sacred relationship, for it is made by the supernatural powers that are with the Hako.—R.L.B.

SONGS AND CEREMONIES OF THE WAY

The Hako party was an impressive sight as it journeyed over the country. It could never be mistaken for an ordinary group of hunters, warriors, or travelers. At the head of the long procession, sufficiently in advance to be distinguished from the others, walked three men—the Ku'rahus [medicine man], holding before him the brown-eagle feathered stem, on his right the chief, grasping with both hands the wildcat skin and Mother Corn, and at his left the assistant Ku'rahus, bearing the white-eagle feathered stem. These three men wore buffalo robes with the hair outside. On their heads was the white downy feather of their office and their

From Fletcher, and James Murie, "The Hako, a Pawnee Ceremony," *Twenty-second Annual Report, Bureau of American Ethnology* (Washington, 1904), pp. 301-303, 345-350.

faces were anointed with the sacred ointment and red paint. They bore
the sacred objects forward steadily and silently, looking neither to the
right nor left, believing that they were under supernatural guidance. Behind them walked the doctors with their insignia, the eagle wings; then
the singers with the drum, and behind them the men and women of the
party with the ponies laden with gifts and needed supplies of food.

Over the wide prairie for miles and miles this order was preserved
day after day until the journey came to an end. If from some distant
vantage point a war party should descry the procession, the leader would
silently turn his men that they might not meet the Hako party, for the
feathered stems are mightier than the warrior; before them he must lay
down his weapon, forget his anger, and be at peace.

No object met on the journey to the Son presented its ordinary aspect
to the Hako party. Everything seen was regarded as a manifestation of the
supernatural powers under whose favor this ceremony was to take place;
hence the trees, the streams, the mountains, the buffalo were addressed
in song. This attitude toward nature is strikingly brought out in the two
songs, which are in sequence, sung at the crossing of a stream.

Throughout this ceremony water is treated as one of the lesser powers.
It is employed only for sacred purposes, and is never used in the ordinary
way. To profane water would bring punishment upon the whole party,
and consequently when a stream ran across a line of travel no person
could step into it as he commonly would do. A halt was called and the
Ku'rahus led in the singing of the song in which Kawas is asked to grant
the party permission to ford the stream. According to Pawnee rituals,
water at the creation was given to the woman, so Kawas, representing the
mother, could grant permission. The request is embodied in four stanzas.
In the first the water touches the feet; in the second the feet stand in the
water; in the third the feet move in the water; in the fourth the water covers
the feet.

After the stream was crossed the people halted on the bank to sing
the song to the wind, led by the Ku'rahus. It also is in four stanzas.
The wind is called upon to come and dry the water which the people
may not irreverently touch. In the first stanza the wind touches the people; in the second it lightly brushes their bodies; in the third it circles
about them; in the fourth it envelops them. Thus the wind, one of the
lesser powers, comes between the people and the penalty incurred by
profanely touching water.

In these ceremonies the people were constantly reminded that they
were in the presence of the unseen powers manifested to them in the
natural objects met upon the journey. To those initiated into the inner
meaning of the rite, the appeal at the crossing of the stream to Kawas
(the feminine element) and to the wind (typical of the breath of life)
was connected with the symbolism of running water, explained in the

seventh ritual as representing the giving of life from generation to generation.

Three more songs originally belonged to the journey, but we are told the buffalo are no longer seen; neither are the mountains or the mesas; so these songs are now sung in the lodge and only that the objects seen by past generations may be remembered.

SONG TO THE TREES AND STREAMS

I

Dark against the sky yonder distant line
Lies before us. Trees we see, long the line of trees,
Bending, swaying in the breeze.

II

Bright with flashing light yonder distant line
Runs before us, swiftly runs, swift the river runs,
Winding, flowing o'er the land.

III

Hark! Oh hark! A sound, yonder distant sound
Comes to greet us, singing comes, soft the river's song,
Rippling gently 'neath the trees.

SONG WHEN CROSSING THE STREAMS

I

Behold, upon the river's brink we stand!
River we must cross;
Oh Kawas, come! To thee we call. Oh come, and thy permission give
Into the stream to wade and forward go.

After the Hako party arrives at the village of the Son the ceremony itself is performed, which is a symbolic reenactment of the birth of a child. In this ceremony the central figure is a child, usually a little son or daughter of the Son—the man who receives the Hako party.

Upon this child are put the signs of the promises which Mother Corn and the powers of the Sacred Pipes bring—the promise of children, increase, long life, plenty. The signs and promises are put on this little child but they are not meant for that particular child, but for its generation, that children already born may live and grow in strength and in their turn increase so that the family and the tribe may extend.—R.L.B.

SEEKING THE CHILD

At the first sign of dawn the Ku'rahus and his assistants, with the principal men of the Hako party, started for the lodge of the Son, there to seek his child and perform certain rites symbolic of birth. It is to be noted that these rites took place at the same hour as the singing of the Dawn ritual, which celebrated the mysterious birth of day.

They sang the first song of the ritual as they started, but when they were nearing their destination they repeated the song they had sung when they were about to enter the village of the Son.

The repetition of songs sung in the earlier part of the ceremony had the effect of tying back the later acts to those which were preparatory in character, and tended to consolidate the entire ceremony. When this song was sung for the first time the Father was seeking the Son, to whom he was bringing promises of good; when it was sung the second time the Father was seeking the child of the Son, that on it the promises brought might be fulfilled.

Of this part of the ceremony not only every detail, with its special meaning, but the function of each article used had been prefigured.

I

Where is he, the Son?
Where his dwelling place that I seek?
Which can be his lodge, where he sits
Silent, waiting, waiting there for me?

II

Here is he, the Son,
Here his dwelling place that I seek;
This here is his lodge where he sits
Silent, waiting, waiting here for me.

SYMBOLIC INCEPTION

The warriors—the male element—were the first to enter the lodge, in warlike fashion, as if to capture and hold it securely. The child was first touched by the representative of Kawas, that it might be given endurance; then it was touched by the chief, that it might be wise. After the warriors had performed their part, the Ku'rahus entered singing the song which had been sung when the messenger representing the Son was received outside the village. At that time he looked upon one who was to lead him to the Son; now he is looking upon the child which represents the continuation of the life of the Son.

FIRST SONG

I

Now our eyes look on him who is here;
He is as the Son we have sought;
He brings us again tidings of the Son:
"Father, come to me, here I sit
Waiting here for thee."

The Ku'rahus first touched the child with the ear of corn (second song), singing the same song as when the ear of corn made its mysterious journey to the sky and received its authority to lead in the ceremony. The power granted at that time was for this ultimate purpose, to make the paths and open the way for the child to receive the gift of fruitfulness.

SECOND SONG

I

Tira'wa, harken! Mighty one
Above us in blue, silent sky!
We standing wait thy bidding here;
The Mother Corn standing waits,
Waits to serve thee here;
The Mother Corn stands waiting here.

II

Tira'wa, harken! Mighty one
Above us in blue, silent sky!
We flying seek thy dwelling there;
The Mother Corn flying goes
Up to seek thee there;
The Mother Corn goes flying up.

III

Tira'wa, harken! Mighty one
Above us in blue, silent sky!
We touch upon thy country fair;
The Mother Corn touches there
Upon the border land;
The Mother Corn is touching there.

IV

Tira'wa, harken! Mighty one
Above us in blue, silent sky!
The path we reach leads up to thee;
The Mother Corn enters there,
Upward takes her way;
The Mother Corn to thee ascends.

V

Tira'wa, harken! Mighty one
Above us in blue, silent sky!
Behold! We in thy dwelling stand;
The Mother Corn, standing there,
Leader now is made;
The Mother Corn is leader made.

VI

Tira'wa, harken! Mighty one
Above us in blue, silent sky!
The downward path we take again;
The Mother Corn, leading us,
Doth thy symbol bear;
The Mother Corn with power leads.

Then the Ku'rahus united the two feathered stems, the male and the
female (third song), and with them touched the child, following with the
gift of procreation the paths opened by the corn.

THIRD SONG

I

Here stand we while upon Tira'wa now we wait;
Here Kawas stands, her mate with her is standing here;
They both are standing, waiting, bringing gifts with them.

II

We flying are, as on Tira'wa now we wait;
Here Kawas flies, her mate with her is flying here;
They both are flying, flying with the gifts they bring.

III

We touching are, as on Tira'wa now we wait;
Now Kawas and her mate the child so gently touch;
Its forehead touch they, there they gently touch the child.

ACTION SYMBOLIZING LIFE

The child, surrounded by the creative forces, is urged to move, to arise as the first song is sung.

FIRST SONG

I am ready; come to me now, fearing nothing; come now to me here!
Little one, come, come to me here; fearing nothing, come!

Then it was made to take four steps, symbolic of life, of long life, during the singing of the second song.

In the symbolizing, within the lodge of the Son, of the gift of birth by the power of the Hako, brought thither by the Father, we get a glimpse of the means by which the tie between the two unrelated men, the Father and the Son, was supposed to be formed; namely, the life of the Son was perpetuated through the gift of fruitfulness to his child, supernaturally bestowed by the Hako; consequently the Father who brought the Hako became symbolically the father of the future progeny of the Son.

SECOND SONG

Stepping forward is my child, he forward steps, the four steps takes and
     enters into life;
Forward stepping, four steps taking, enters into life.

The child was taken upon the back of one of the party and led the way to the ceremonial lodge, followed by the Ku'rahus and all the rest singing the third song.

THIRD SONG

Here we go singing, looking on the child
Borne in his father's arms, he leading us;
Follow we singing, looking on the child.

FRANZ BOAS

(1858-1942)

Franz Boas—who was destined to dominate American anthropology for forty years and who shaped its future course—was born in Minden, Westphalia, of German-Jewish parents of liberal tradition, and educated at the Universities of Kiel, Bonn, and Heidelberg. He was trained in the natural sciences; his doctorate was in physics, his dissertation on the color of sea water. But even as a student he became interested in the study of man. In 1883 he joined an Arctic expedition as geographer to map the coast of Baffinland, but his interest then as always was in the way people organize their lives.

Throughout his life Boas looked back with nostalgia to his days among the Eskimo. This was his first contact with primitive people, and it was his sense of common humanity with them that changed him from a geographer to an anthropologist. His monograph on the Central Eskimo, published by the Bureau of American Ethnology in 1888, is still one of the ethnographic classics and a model of lucidity.

After his return from the Arctic in 1884 Boas settled in the United States and laid the foundations for a less provincial science of anthropology. For the Bureau of American Ethnology he conceived and carried forward the Handbook of American Indian Languages, *a collection of grammatical sketches of key languages of North America. He wrote a number of the sketches himself, and he supplied the* Handbook *with a masterly introduction outlining a conceptual scheme for the study of primitive languages.*

An excerpt from Boas' observations of the Central Eskimo is presented here. His contributions to anthropological theory and method will be dealt with in Part V of this volume.—R.L.B.

The Central Eskimo:
Domestic Occupations and Amusements

IT IS WINTER AND THE NATIVES ARE ESTABLISHED IN THEIR WARM SNOW houses. At this time of the year it is necessary to make use of the short daylight and twilight for hunting. Long before the day begins to dawn the Eskimo prepares for hunting. He rouses his housemate; his wife supplies the lamp with a new wick and fresh blubber and the dim light which has been kept burning during the night quickly brightens up and warms the hut. While the woman is busy preparing breakfast the man fits up his sledge for hunting. He takes the snow block which closes the entrance of the dwelling room during the night out of the doorway and passes through the low passages. Within the passage the dogs are sleeping, tired by the fatigues of the day before. Though their long, heavy hair protects them from the severe cold of the Arctic winter, they like to seek shelter from the piercing winds in the entrance of the hut.

The sledge is iced, the harnesses are taken out of the storeroom by the door, and the dogs are harnessed to the sledge. Breakfast is now ready and after having taken a hearty meal of seal soup and frozen and cooked seal meat the hunter lashes the spear that stands outside of the hut upon the sledge, hangs the harpoon line, some toggles, and his knife over the antlers, and starts for the hunting ground. Here he waits patiently for the blowing seal, sometimes until late in the evening.

Meanwhile the women, who stay at home, are engaged in their domestic occupations, mending boots and making new clothing, or they visit one another, taking some work with them, or pass their time with games or in playing with the children. While sitting at their sewing and at the same time watching their lamps and cooking the meat, they incessantly hum their favorite tunes. About noon they cook their dinner and usually prepare at the same time the meal for the returning hunters. As soon as the first sledge is heard approaching, the pots, which have been pushed back during the afternoon, are placed over the fire, and when the hungry men enter the hut their dinner is ready. While hunting they usually open the seals caught early in the morning, to take out a piece of the flesh or liver, which they eat raw, for lunch. The cut is then temporarily fastened until the final dressing of the animal at home.

In the western regions particularly the hunters frequently visit the depots

From Boas, "The Central Eskimo," *Sixth Annual Report, Bureau of American Ethnology* (Washington: Government Printing Office, 1888), pp. 561-566.

of venison made in the fall, and the return is always followed by a great feast.

After the hunters reach home they first unharness their dogs and unstring the traces, which are carefully arranged, coiled up, and put away in the storeroom. Then the sledge is unloaded and the spoils are dragged through the entrance into the hut. A religious custom commands the women to leave off working, and not until the seal is cut up are they allowed to resume their sewing and the preparing of skins. This custom is founded on the tradition that all kinds of sea animals have risen from the fingers of their supreme goddess, who must be propitiated after being offended by the murder of her offspring. The spear is stuck into the snow at the entrance of the house, the sledge is turned upside down, and the ice coating is removed from the runners. Then it is leaned against the wall of the house, and at last the hunter is ready to enter. He strips off his deerskin jacket and slips into his sealskin coat. The former is carefully cleaned of the adhering ice and snow with the snowbeater and put into the storeroom outside the house.

This done, the men are ready for their dinner, of which the women do not partake. In winter the staple food of the Eskimo is boiled seal and walrus meat, though in some parts of the western districts it is musk ox and venison, a rich and nourishing soup being obtained by cooking the meat. The natives are particularly fond of seal and walrus soup, which is made by mixing and boiling water, blood, and blubber with large pieces of meat.

The food is not always salted, but sometimes melted sea water ice, which contains a sufficient quantity of salt, is used for cooking. Liver is generally eaten raw and is considered a tidbit. I have seen the intestines eaten only when there was no meat.

Forks are used to take the meat out of the kettle and the soup is generally poured out into a large cup. Before the introduction of European manufactures these vessels and dishes generally consisted of whalebone. One of these has been described by Parry. It was circular in form, one piece of whalebone being bent into the proper shape for the sides and another flat piece of the same material sewed to it for a bottom, so closely as to make it perfectly watertight. A ladle or spoon is sometimes used in drinking it, but usually the cup is passed around, each taking a sip in turn. In the same way large pieces of meat are passed round, each taking as large a mouthful as possible and then cutting off the bit close to the lips. They all smack their lips in eating. The Eskimo drink a great deal of water, which is generally kept in vessels standing near the lamps. When the men have finished their meal the women take their share, and then all attack the frozen meat which is kept in the storerooms. The women are allowed to participate in this part of the meal. An enormous quantity of meat is devoured every night, and sometimes they only suspend eating when they go to bed, keeping a piece of meat within reach in case they awake.

After dinner the seals, which have been placed behind the lamps to thaw, are thrown upon the floor, cut up, and the spare meat and skins are taken into the storerooms. If a scarcity of food prevails in the village and a hunter has caught a few seals, every inhabitant of the settlement receives a piece of meat and blubber, which he takes to his hut, and the successful hunter invites all hands to a feast.

The dogs are fed every second day after dinner. For this purpose two men go to a place at a short distance from the hut, taking the frozen food with them, which they split with a hatchet or the point of the spear. While one is breaking the solid mass the other keeps the dogs off by means of the whip, but as soon as the food is ready they make a rush at it, and in less than half a minute have swallowed their meal. No dog of a strange team is allowed to steal anything, but is kept at a distance by the dogs themselves and by the whip. If the dogs are very hungry they are harnessed to the sledge in order to prevent an attack before the men are ready. They are unharnessed after the food is prepared, the weakest first, in order to give him the best chance of picking out some good pieces. Sometimes they are fed in the house; in such a case, the food being first prepared, they are led into the hut singly; thus each receives his share.

All the work being finished, boots and stockings are changed, as they must be dried and mended. The men visit one another and spend the night in talking, singing, gambling, and telling stories. The events of the day are talked over, success in hunting is compared, the hunting tools requiring mending are set in order, and the lines are dried and softened. Some busy themselves in cutting new ivory implements and seal lines or in carving. They never spend the nights quite alone, but meet for social entertainment. During these visits the host places a large lump of frozen meat and a knife on the side bench behind the lamp and every one is welcome to help himself to as much as he likes.

The first comers sit down on the ledge, while those entering later stand or squat in the passage. When any one addresses the whole assembly he always turns his face to the wall and avoids facing the listeners. Most of the men take off their outer jackets in the house and they sit chatting until very late. Even the young children do not go to bed early.

The women sit on the bed in front of their lamps, with their legs under them, working continually on their own clothing or on that of the men, drying the wet footgear and mittens, and softening the leather by chewing and rubbing. If a bitch has a litter of pups it is their business to look after them, to keep them warm, and to feed them regularly. Generally the pups are put into a small harness and are allowed to crawl about the side of the bed, where they are tied to the wall by a trace. Young children are always carried in their mothers' hoods, but when about a year and a half old they are allowed to play on the bed, and are only carried by their mothers when they get too mischievous. When the mother is engaged in any hard work they are carried by the young girls. They are weaned when about two years old, but women suckle them occasionally until they are three or four years of age. During this time they are frequently fed from their mothers' mouths. When about twelve years old they begin to help their parents, the girls sewing and preparing skins, the boys accompanying their fathers in hunting expeditions. The parents are very fond of their children and treat them kindly. They are never beaten and rarely scolded, and in turn they are very dutiful, obeying the wishes of their parents and taking care of them in their old age.

JOHN R. SWANTON

(1873-1958)

Swanton was one of Boas' first students at Columbia to receive a graduate degree in anthropology. He was among the first of the early scholars to choose that discipline as a primary field of study, and he became established as a professional anthropologist immediately on leaving Columbia. That year, 1900, he entered the Bureau of American Ethnology and remained with it until he retired in 1944.

Swanton's chief interest was the coastal tribes of British Columbia. In connection with the Jesup North Pacific Expedition he wrote his Ethnology of the Haida *and* Haida Texts and Myths. *Later he turned his attention to the Southeastern United States, a region little known and little understood but of crucial importance for comprehending the growth of culture in North America. Southeastern cultures had long since disappeared, but Swanton gathered together in his* Indian Tribes of the Lower Mississippi *(Bulletin of the Bureau of American Ethnology) all available material from early travelers, arranging it topically for comparison. It was one of those labors of scholarship for which everyone interested in American cultural history can be grateful.—R.L.B.*

Types of Haida and Tlingit Myths

IN RECORDING MORE THAN TWO HUNDRED AND FIFTY STORIES OF THE Haida and Tlingit of the north Pacific coast the writer has found that many of them have very similar plots, and it has seemed to him that abstracts of the more important of these might be of interest to those engaged in comparative work. The story of Raven is of course similar to the stories of other transformers and need not be included. The same is true of the story of the brothers who traveled about overcoming monsters. Here it is evidently Tlingit, the heroes in all cases ending their career in an

From Swanton, "Types of Haida and Tlingit Myths," *American Anthropologist,* n.s. Vol. VII (Lancaster, 1905), pp. 94-103.

attempt to cross the Stikine, and from the Tlingit it has been transmitted to the Haida without losing its Tlingit names and atmosphere. Several other tales, repeated from end to end of the Haida-Tlingit area, are also strongly localized in certain towns or camps, and hardly fall into the present scheme. Such are the story of the man who was carried off by the salmon people, the story of the woman who was turned into an owl, the story of the man who obtained strength to kill sea-lions, the story of the man who made killer-whales out of wood, and the story of the hunters who changed into supernatural beings by putting themselves into the fire. A few of the plots given are so general that they can hardly be considered peculiar to the northwest coast, but others probably do not occur outside of that area.

1. The Man Captured by the Supernatural Beings.—A man out hunting is taken into the house of some supernatural being, usually on account of something he has said or done to displease the latter, and often it tries to turn him into an animal, especially if it be a land otter or a killer-whale. On the other hand the hero may be given a crest or a name, and such a story is told by the Haida to explain the origin of secret society performances.

2. The Man who Married the Grizzly Bear.—This is related to the above. A man out hunting hears his dogs bark in front of a grizzly bear's den. When he comes to it the male bear throws him inside, but the female conceals him, marries him, and kills her previous husband. He has several children by her. By and by he returns to his own people, but his bear wife enjoins him to have nothing to do with his human wife or children. Every day after his return he spears seals and carries them up to his bear family, who are waiting at the head of an inlet. After a while, however, he disobeys her instructions, and they kill him. Then his children wage war on human beings, but are finally destroyed.

3. The Woman who Married the Supernatural Being.—A woman says something about an animal or object which angers the supernatural being connected with it, or else her father refuses for a long time to let her marry anyone. The offended being appears to the girl, and she marries it. Sometimes she goes off with it and lives among the animals for a long time, and sometimes her husband remains with her. In the former case she usually comes back to her father's people after a time, bringing food, and her father may recover her by killing the people she has been among.

4. The Kidnapped Wife.—A man's wife is washing a skin in the sea, when she is carried off by a killer-whale. Her husband follows, descends to the sea floor, and assists some being there who in turn directs him how to get his wife back. Then he goes behind the town where she is kept, causes the wedges of a slave coming out to chop wood to break, restores them, and so obtains the slave's assistance. When the slave carries water into the house, he spills it upon the fire, and while the house is filled with

steam the man runs in and carries off his wife. He is pursued, but reaches home safely.

5. The Supernatural Helper.—A man who has been unsuccessful in gambling, hunting, or getting property, goes off into the forest or out on the sea, obtains assistance from some supernatural being, and is afterward fortunate, or,

6. A man or a woman leaves food for some animal or treats it kindly, and is afterward given plenty of food in return, thereby becoming rich.

7. The Supernatural Child.—A girl or a girl and her mother lose all their relatives and are left alone in the town. After a while the girl gives birth to a child who has supernatural power, grows up rapidly, destroys the enemies who have killed his mother's people, and usually restores them to life.

8. The Magic Feather.—The popular form of type 7 is the following: While the people in a certain town are playing shinny on the beach, a feather or some similar object comes down from above, and those who seize it are carried up out of sight. In this way everybody disappears except one or two women. The younger of these swallows something and gives birth to a supernatural child who revenges and protects them.

9. The Boy who was Abandoned.—For some action, trifling or otherwise, a boy is abandoned by all his people, who leave him alone in the town. His youngest uncle's wife, however, being fond of him, conceals a little food for him and some fire enclosed in mussel-shells. Then the youth receives assistance in some supernatural way and stores a great quantity of food, while those who have abandoned him are starving. After a while slaves are sent over to see what has become of him. He feeds them, but warns them not to carry any of the food away. One of them, however, conceals a piece for his (or her) infant, and the night after they return gives it to the child. While eating this, the child cries out, often from being choked or from having dropped the food, and the chief or his wife makes an investigation, thereby discovering the truth. Then the people of that town return to the place where the boy was left. All of his uncles' daughters dress themselves up, hoping that he will choose one of them for his wife, but he selects the daughter of his youngest uncle, although she has not adorned herself and arrives last. He becomes a chief.

10. The Boy and His Grandmother who were Banished.—A boy and his grandmother were either abandoned or forced to live outside the town. In the former case the story sometimes proceeds like type 9. In the latter case the boy is assisted by some supernatural being and obtains a great deal of food, while the other people are starving. They are obliged to purchase food of him, and he becomes wealthy. Sometimes he becomes a great shaman and obtains his property in that way.

11. The Ill-disposed Mother-in-law.—A man is badly treated by his mother-in-law because he lies in bed continually instead of working. After

a while he goes to a lake behind the town and kills a water-monster living there by splitting a tree along the middle, spreading the halves apart, and tolling the monster up until its head comes between the two portions. He skins this creature and begins to catch all kinds of fish and sea animals. These he leaves on the beach where his mother-in-law can find them, and by letting her find them regularly, he induces her to think that she has become a great shaman. After a long time he reveals himself before all the people and kills his mother-in-law with shame. Sometimes a monster is killed in the way indicated merely that the hero may obtain its skin to wear when he performs great deeds, not with a view to personal revenge.

12. The Goose Wife.—A man finds two female geese, in human form, bathing in a lake while their skins hang on the limb of a tree near by. He seizes these skins and so compels one or both of them to marry him. When the goose tribe passes over, his wives get them to throw down food. By and by they leave him and rejoin their people. He follows them and remains with them for a while, afterward returning to his own place. On his way to find his wife he is sometimes made to encounter a man chopping, whose chips turn into salmon as they fall into the water.

13. The Land Otter Sister.—The sister of a certain man is carried away by the land otters and married among them. Once, when he is encamped by himself making a canoe, his sister brings him food. By and by she sends some of the land otters to launch his canoe for him, and afterward he goes to the land-otter town to finish it. While he is there his sister takes his smallest child on her lap and sings to it, making a little tail grow out of it. When the man objects, she sings another song and it goes back. Finally he returns to his town.

14. The Eagle People.—A man is set adrift in a box or on a plank by his uncle and lands among the eagles. He is found by two girls, marries them, and is given a suit of feathers by the eagle people in which he goes fishing. After some time he flies to his uncle's town, seizes his uncle by the head, and flies up from the ground with him. A person seizes his uncle's foot and is also carried up. He in turn is seized by another, and the process is continued until all the people of that town are hanging in a string. He drowns them in the ocean.

15. Beaver and Porcupine.—Beaver carries porcupine out to an island from which he can not get ashore. Finally he sings for a north wind, the sea freezes over, and he walks home. Afterward he takes beaver up to the top of a tall tree and beaver gets down with difficulty. The two parts of this story are sometimes told in reverse order.

16. The Rival Towns.—(This story is usually localized in the neighborhood of Metlakatla or on Nass river, but it is also told of Sitka.) War breaks out between two towns, and all of the people in one of them are destroyed except a woman and her daughter who escape into the forest. Then the mother calls out, "Who will marry my daughter?" and the

animals and birds present themselves successively. She asks each of these what it can do, and is dissatisfied with the replies she receives, so she rejects all. Finally she is answered by the son of a sky deity (given variously as sky, sun, or moon), whom she accepts; whereupon her son-in-law puts her into a tree, where she becomes the creaking of boughs or the echo, and carries his wife up to his father's house in the sky. There they have a number of children, whom their grandfather teaches how to fight when they are grown up. Usually there is one sister able to heal wounds. Finally their grandfather puts them inside of beautifully painted houses, or a fort, and lowers them down on their old town site. When the people of the town opposite hear the noises there, they say that they must be produced by ghosts; but seeing the houses next morning, they start across to gamble with the newcomers. During this game trouble breaks out, and the children of the sky are about to be overwhelmed. Their grandfather intervenes, however, and enables them to destroy all their foes.

17. The Doomed Canoemen.—Some men out hunting in a canoe are hailed by a supernatural being, who informs them that on their way home they will die successively, beginning with the man in the bow, and that when the man in the stern has reached home and related his story, he too will die. The death of a shaman or the destruction of a village is also sometimes foretold through him.

18. The Protracted Winter.—The people in a certain town so offend some supernatural being that snow falls and almost covers the houses. Finally a bird is seen sitting on the edge of the smoke-hole with a berry in its mouth. Suspecting something is wrong, the people, or those who have survived, climb out and go to another place, where they find that it is already midsummer and the berries are ripe. Similar stories relate how people were punished by a flood, by stormy weather which prevents them from getting food, and in one or two stories otherwise of type 17, by fire.

19. The Magic Flight.—A person is captured by some supernatural beings, as in stories of type 3. He or a friend of his obtains some objects from an old woman, and as they run away they throw these behind them and [they] turn into obstructions through which their pursuers find difficulty in forcing a way. Usually this story is told of a woman who offended the grizzly bears. After she has exhausted her magic gifts, she comes out on the shore of a lake or the shores of the sea, where she is taken into a canoe, marries another supernatural being, and after a time returns to her father's people, bringing food. Sometimes the adventures of her son are also related, and again a story of type 4 may be added.

20. The Grand Catch.—A fisherman who has been long unsuccessful at length pulls up an enormous "nest" full of fishes, or else an enormous fish surrounded by smaller ones. All the canoes are filled, and the poor fisherman becomes wealthy.

21. The Unfaithful Wife.—Desiring to marry another person, the wife of a certain man pretends that she is about to die and is placed in the grave-box. Afterward her lover liberates her and carries her home or to another part of the country. By and by her former husband suspects the truth, goes to the grave-box, and finds her body missing. Then he goes at night to the house where she and her new husband are living and kills them by running pointed sticks into their hearts. Next morning he dresses well and goes out to gamble.

22. The Rejected Lover.—A man is in love with a woman who does not care for him. She induces him to pull all the hair out of his body and then leaves him. Too much ashamed to return to town, the man wanders off to another place, or climbs into the sky country on a chain of arrows. By and by he meets a supernatural being who restores his hair and takes him to another town where he marries the daughter of the town chief. Then he returns to his father's town with his new wife and puts the woman who had rejected him to shame.

It is interesting to note how conventional expressions, or what might be called the "mythic formulæ," differ as used by Haida and Tlingit. Thus the Tlingit indicate that a town was large by saying " it was a long town," while the Haida equivalent is, "it was a town of five rows of houses." In Tlingit a girl is carried off by some supernatural being because she had said something to offend it; in Haida it is because (or after) her father has refused a great many suitors for her hand. In Tlingit a man kills his unkind uncle or aunt by wishing that what he or she eats will not satisfy, but in Haida he does it by feeding the person on nothing but grease. Although the myths of both peoples speak of traveling in canoes which are alive and have to be fed, in Tlingit these are always grizzly bears. Often it is said that the turnings in rivers were made by grizzly bears who began to turn round as soon as they were hungry. While four is nearly always the story or mystic number in Haida, two appears quite as often in Tlingit. After a child with supernatural powers is born, the Tinglit story-teller is content to say that it grew up rapidly and hunted continually, but the Haida must add that it cried for a bow and arrows and was not satisfied until it obtained some made out of copper. Among the Haida, too, a supernatural being is usually killed by cutting its body apart and throwing a whetstone between, on which the body grinds itself "to nothing." To express plenty the Tlingit say that one could not see the inside of the house for the multitude of things in it; a child that has eaten something against the wishes of its elders has the inside of its mouth scratched; a medicine animal often appears in the shape of a bear; and it is always said of a supernatural being addicted to the habit of doing away with his wives periodically that "his wives do not last long."

JAMES MOONEY

(1861-1921)

James Mooney was working in the editorial room of the Richmond (Indiana) Paladium *when Major Powell met him in 1885. Mooney had read everything available on the subject of the American Indian, and Powell, impressed by his knowledge, brought him into the Bureau of American Ethnology. Mooney remained with the Bureau for the rest of his life, working mainly among the Cherokee and the Kiowa.*

His best-known research was done in 1891, when he was sent by Powell to investigate the circumstances which had led to the trouble on the Sioux reservation and which culminated in the horrible massacre of the Sioux at Wounded Knee.

The year before, a revivalistic cult had started among the Paiute and swept over the Western Plains. It had all the familiar features of Indian Messianic cults: spiritual regeneration and a return to the good ways of the ancestors were to be followed by the disappearance of the whites, the return of the dead, and the restoration of the old life. During the waiting period, people were to dance in the hope of producing mystical states in which they could establish communication with the dead or with supernatural forces. The cult spread across the Plains; it reached the Sioux when they were already restive because of many disappointments, and in a moment of panic a shot was fired and the explosive situation flared up.

Mooney's investigation of the events leading up to this disaster and of the whole ghost-dance phenomenon remains one of the classic studies of the social and psychological factors in the rise of revivalistic cults.—R.L.B.

The Ghost-Dance Religion

THE WISE MEN TELL US THAT THE WORLD IS GROWING HAPPIER—THAT WE live longer than did our fathers, have more of comfort and less of toil, fewer wars and discords, and higher hopes and aspirations. So say the wise men; but deep in our own hearts we know they are wrong.

From Mooney, "The Ghost-Dance Religion and the Sioux Outbreak of 1890," *Fourteenth Annual Report, Bureau of American Ethnology,* Part 2 (Washington, 1896), pp. 657, 777-778, 780-783, 920-926, 824-828.

. . . What tribe or people has not had its golden age, before Pandora's box was loosed, when women were nymphs and dryads and men were gods and heroes? And when the race lies crushed and groaning beneath an alien yoke, how natural is the dream of a redeemer, an Arthur, who shall return from exile or awake from some long sleep to drive out the usurper and win back for his people what they have lost. The hope becomes a faith and the faith becomes the creed of priests and prophets, until the hero is a god and the dream a religion, looking to some great miracle of nature for its culmination and accomplishment. The doctrines of the Hindu avatar, the Hebrew Messiah, the Christian millennium, and the Hesûnanin of the Indian Ghost dance are essentially the same, and have their origin in a hope and longing common to all humanity.

THE DOCTRINE OF THE GHOST DANCE

You must not fight.   Do no harm to anyone.   Do right always.—*Woroka.*

The great underlying principle of the Ghost dance doctrine is that the time will come when the whole Indian race, living and dead, will be re-united upon a regenerated earth, to live a life of aboriginal happiness, forever free from death, disease, and misery. On this foundation each tribe has built a structure from its own mythology, and each apostle and believer has filled in the details according to his own mental capacity or ideas of happiness, with such additions as come to him from the trance. Some changes, also, have undoubtedly resulted from the transmission of the doctrine through the imperfect medium of the sign language. The differences of interpretation are precisely such as we find in Christianity, with its hundreds of sects and innumerable shades of individual opinion. The white race, being alien and secondary and hardly real, has no part in this scheme of aboriginal regeneration, and will be left behind with the other things of earth that have served their temporary purpose, or else will cease entirely to exist.

All this is to be brought about by an overruling spiritual power that needs no assistance from human creatures; and though certain medicine-men were disposed to anticipate the Indian millennium by preaching resistance to the further encroachments of the whites, such teachings form no part of the true doctrine, and it was only where chronic dissatisfaction was aggravated by recent grievances, as among the Sioux, that the movement assumed a hostile expression. On the contrary, all believers were exhorted to make themselves worthy of the predicted happiness by discarding all things warlike and practicing honesty, peace, and good will, not only among themselves, but also toward the whites, so long as they were together. Some apostles have even thought that all race distinctions are to be obliterated, and that the whites are to participate with the

Indians in the coming felicity; but it seems unquestionable that this is equally contrary to the doctrine as originally preached.

Different dates have been assigned at various times for the fulfillment of the prophecy. Whatever the year, it has generally been held, for very natural reasons, that the regeneration of the earth and the renewal of all life would occur in the early spring. In some cases July, and particularly the 4th of July, was the expected time. This, it may be noted, was about the season when the great annual ceremony of the sun dance formerly took place among the prairie tribes. The messiah himself has set several dates from time to time, as one prediction after another failed to materialize, and in his message to the Cheyenne and Arapaho, in August, 1891, he leaves the whole matter an open question. The date universally recognized among all the tribes immediately prior to the Sioux outbreak was the spring of 1891. As springtime came and passed, and summer grew and waned, and autumn faded again into winter without the realization of their hopes and longings, the doctrine gradually assumed its present form—that some time in the unknown future the Indian will be united with his friends who have gone before, to be forever supremely happy, and that this happiness may be anticipated in dreams, if not actually hastened in reality, by earnest and frequent attendance on the sacred dance.

On returning to the Cheyenne and Arapaho in Oklahoma, after my visit to Wovoka in January, 1892, I was at once sought by my friends of both tribes, anxious to hear the report of my journey and see the sacred things that I had brought back from the messiah. The Arapaho especially, who are of more spiritual nature than any of the other tribes, showed a deep interest and followed intently every detail of the narrative. As soon as the news of my return was spread abroad, men and women, in groups and singly, would come to me, and after grasping my hand would repeat a long and earnest prayer, sometimes aloud, sometimes with the lips silently moving, and frequently with tears rolling down the cheeks, and the whole body trembling violently from stress of emotion. Often before the prayer was ended the condition of the devotee bordered on the hysterical, very little less than in the Ghost dance itself. The substance of the prayer was usually an appeal to the messiah to hasten the coming of the promised happiness, with a petition that, as the speaker himself was unable to make the long journey, he might, by grasping the hand of one who had seen and talked with the messiah face to face, be enabled in his trance visions to catch a glimpse of the coming glory. During all this performance the bystanders awaiting their turn kept reverent silence. In a short time it became very embarrassing, but until the story had been told over and over again there was no way of escape without wounding their feelings. The same thing afterward happened among the northern Arapaho in Wyoming, one chief even holding out his hands toward me with short exclamations of *hŭ! hŭ! hŭ!* as is sometimes done by the devotees about a priest in the Ghost dance, in the hope, as he himself explained, that he might thus be enabled to go into a trance then and there. The hope, however, was not realized.

After this preliminary ordeal my visitors would ask to see the things which I had brought back from the messiah—the rabbit-skin robes, the piñon nuts, the gaming sticks, the sacred magpie feathers, and, above all, the sacred red paint. . . .

The Indians were at last fully satisfied that I was really desirous of learning the truth concerning their new religion. A few days after my visit to Left Hand, several of the delegates who had been sent out in the preceding August came down to see me, headed by Black Short Nose, a Cheyenne. After preliminary greetings, he stated that the Cheyenne and Arapaho were now convinced that I would tell the truth about their religion, and as they loved their religion and were anxious to have the whites know that it was all good and contained nothing bad or hostile they would now give me the message which the messiah himself had given to them, that I might take it back to show to Washington. He then took from a beaded pouch and gave to me a letter, which proved to be the message or statement of the doctrine delivered by Wovoka to the Cheyenne and Arapaho delegates, of whom Black Short Nose was one, on the occasion of their last visit to Nevada, in August, 1891, and written down on the spot, in broken English, by one of the Arapaho delegates, Casper Edson, a young man who had acquired some English education by several years' attendance at the government Indian school at Carlisle, Pennsylvania. On the reverse page of the paper was a duplicate in somewhat better English, written out by a daughter of Black Short Nose, a school girl, as dictated by her father on his return. These letters contained the message to be delivered to the two tribes, and as is expressly stated in the text were not intended to be seen by a white man. The daughter of Black Short Nose had attempted to erase this clause before her father brought the letter down to me, but the lines were still plainly visible. It is the genuine official statement of the Ghost-dance doctrine as given by the messiah himself to his disciples. It is reproduced here in duplicate and verbatim, just as received, with a translation for the benefit of those not accustomed to Carlisle English. In accordance with the request of the Indians, I brought the original to Washington, where it was read by the Indian Commissioner, Honorable T. J. Morgan, after which I had two copies made, giving one to the commissioner and retaining the other myself, returning the original to its owner, Black Short Nose.

The Messiah Letter (Arapaho version)

What you get home you make dance, and will give you the same. when you dance four days and in night one day, dance day time, five days and then fift, will wash five for every body. He likes you flok you give him good many things, he heart been satting feel good. After you get home, will give good cloud, and give you chance to make you feel good. and he give you good spirit. and he give you al a good paint.

You folks want you to come in three [months] here, any tribs from there. There will be good bit snow this year. Sometimes rain's, in fall, this year some rain, never give you any thing like that. grandfather said when he die never no cry. no hurt anybody. no fight, good behave always, it will give you satisfaction, this young man, he is a good Father and mother, dont tell no white man. Jueses was on ground, he just like cloud. Every body is alive again, I dont know when they will [be] here, may be this fall or in spring.

Every body never get sick, be young again,—(if young fellow no sick any more,) work for white men never trouble with him until you leave, when it shake the earth dont be afraid no harm any body.

You make dance for six weeks night, and put you foot [food?] in dance to eat for every body and wash in the water. that is all to tell, I am in to you. and you will received a good words from him some time, Dont tell lie.

The Messiah Letter (*Cheyenne version*)

When you get home you have to make dance. You must dance four nights and one day time. You will take bath in the morning before you go to yours homes, for every body, and give you all the same as this. Jackson Wilson likes you all, he is glad to get good many things. His heart satting fully of gladness, after you get home, I will give you a good cloud and give you chance to make you feel good. I give you a good spirit, and give you all good paint, I want you people to come here again, want them in three months any tribs of you from there. There will be a good deal snow this year. Some time rains, in fall this year some rain, never give you any thing like that, grandfather, said, when they were die never cry, no hurt any body, do any harm for it, not to fight. Be a good behave always. It will give a satisfaction in your life. This young man is a good father and mother. Do not tell the white people about this, Juses is on the ground, he just like cloud. Every body is a live again. I don't know when he will be here, may be will be this fall or in spring. When it happen it may be this. There will be no sickness and return to young again. Do not refuse to work for white man or do not make any trouble with them until you leave them. When the earth shakes do not be afraid it will not hurt you. I want you to make dance for six weeks. Eat and wash good clean yourselves [The rest of the letter had been erased].

The Messiah Letter (*free Rendering*)

When you get home you must make a dance to continue five days. Dance four successive nights, and the last night keep up the dance until the morning of the fifth day, when all must bathe in the river and then disperse to their homes. You must all do in the same way.

I, Jack Wilson, love you all, and my heart is full of gladness for the gifts you have brought me. When you get home I shall give you a good cloud [rain?] which will make you feel good. I give you a good spirit and give you all good paint. I want you to come again in three months, some from each tribe there [the Indian Territory].

There will be a good deal of snow this year and some rain. In the fall there will be such a rain as I have never given you before.

Grandfather [a universal title of reverence among Indians and here meaning the messiah] says, when your friends die you must not cry. You must not hurt anybody or do harm to anyone. You must not fight. Do right always. It will give you satisfaction in life. This young man has a good father and mother. [Possibly this refers to Casper Edson, the young Arapaho who wrote down this message of Wovoka for the delegation].

Do not tell the white people about this. Jesus is now upon the earth. He appears like a cloud. The dead are all alive again. I do not know when they will be here; maybe this fall or in the spring. When the time comes there will be no more sickness and everyone will be young again.

Do not refuse to work for the whites and do not make any trouble with them until you leave them. When the earth shakes [at the coming of the new world] do not be afraid. It will not hurt you.

I want you to dance every six weeks. Make a feast at the dance and have food that everybody may eat. Then bathe in the water. That is all. You will receive good words again from me some time. Do not tell lies.

The moral code inculcated is as pure and comprehensive in its simplicity as anything found in religious systems from the days of Gautama Buddha to the time of Jesus Christ. *"Do no harm to any one. Do right always."* Could anything be more simple, and yet more exact and exacting? It inculcates honesty—*"Do not tell lies."* It preaches good will—*"Do no harm to any one."* It forbids the extravagant mourning customs formerly common among the tribes—*"When your friends die, you must not cry,"* which is interpreted by the prairie tribes as forbidding the killing of horses, the burning of tipis and destruction of property, the cutting off of the hair and the gashing of the body with knives, all of which were formerly the sickening rule at every death until forbidden by the new doctrine. As an Arapaho said to me when his little boy died, "I shall not shoot any ponies, and my wife will not gash her arms. We used to do this when our friends died, because we thought we would never see them again, and it made us feel bad. But now we know we shall all be united again." If the Kiowa had held to the Ghost-dance doctrine instead of abandoning it as they had done, they would have been spared the loss of thousands of dollars in horses, tipis, wagons, and other property destroyed, with much of the mental suffering and all of the physical laceration that resulted in consequence of the recent fatal epidemic in the tribe, when for weeks and months the sound of wailing went up night and morning, and in every camp men and women could be seen daily, with dress disordered and hair cut close to the scalp, with blood hardened in clots upon the skin, or streaming from mutilated fingers and fresh gashes on face, and arms, and legs. It preaches peace with the whites and obedience to authority until the day of deliverance shall come. Above all, it forbids war—*"You must not fight."* It is hardly possible for us to realize the tremendous and radical change which this doctrine works in the whole spirit of savage life. The career of every Indian has been the warpath. His proudest title has been that of warrior. His conversation by day and his dreams by night have been of bloody deeds upon the enemies of his tribe. His highest boast was in the number of his scalp trophies, and his chief delight at home was in the war dance and the scalp dance. The thirst for blood and massacre seemed inborn in every man, woman, and child of every tribe. Now comes a prophet as a messenger from God to forbid not only war, but all that savors of war—the war dance, the scalp dance, and even the bloody torture of the sun dance—and his teaching is accepted and his words obeyed by four-fifths of all the warlike predatory tribes of the mountains and the great plains. Only those who have known the deadly hatred that once animated Ute, Cheyenne, and Pawnee, one toward another, and are able to contrast it with their present spirit of mutual brotherly love, can know what the Ghost-dance religion has accomplished in bringing the savage into civilization. It is such a revolution as comes but once in the life of a race.

The beliefs held among the various tribes in regard to the final catastrophe are as fairly probable as some held on the same subject by more orthodox authorities. As to the dance itself, with its scenes of intense excitement, spasmodic action, and physical exhaustion even to unconsciousness, such manifestations have always accompanied religious upheavals among primitive peoples, and are not entirely unknown among ourselves. In a country which produces magnetic healers, shakers, trance mediums, and the like, all these things may very easily be paralleled without going far from home.

In conclusion, we may say of the prophet and his doctrine what has been said of one of his apostles by a careful and competent investigator: "He has given these people a better religion than they ever had before, taught them precepts which, if faithfully carried out, will bring them into better accord with their white neighbors, and has prepared the way for their final Christianization."

THE CEREMONY

The dance commonly begins about the middle of the afternoon or later, after sundown. When it begins in the afternoon, there is always an intermission of an hour or two for supper. The announcement is made by the criers, old men who assume this office apparently by tacit understanding, who go about the camp shouting in a loud voice to the people to prepare for the dance. The preliminary painting and dressing is usually a work of about two hours. When all is ready, the leaders walk out to the dance place, and facing inward, join hands so as to form a small circle. Then, without moving from their places they sing the opening song, according to previous agreement, in a soft undertone. Having sung it through once they raise their voices to their full strength and repeat it, this time slowly circling around in the dance. The step is different from that of most other

Indian dances, but very simple, the dancers moving from right to left, following the course of the sun, advancing the left foot and following it with the right, hardly lifting the feet from the ground. For this reason it is called by the Shoshoni the "dragging dance." All the songs are adapted to the simple measure of the dance step. As the song rises and swells the people come singly and in groups from the several tipis, and one after another joins the circle until any number from fifty to five hundred men, women, and children are in the dance. When the circle is small, each song is repeated through a number of circuits. If large, it is repeated only through one circuit, measured by the return of the leaders to the starting point. Each song is started in the same manner, first in an undertone while the singers stand still in their places, and then with full voice as they begin to circle around. At intervals between the songs, more especially after the trances have begun, the dancers unclasp hands and sit down to smoke or talk for a few minutes. At such times the leaders sometimes deliver short addresses or sermons, or relate the recent trance experience of the dancer. In holding each other's hands the dancers usually intertwine the fingers instead of grasping the hand as with us. Only an Indian could keep the blanket in place as they do under such circumstances. Old people hobbling along with sticks, and little children hardly past the toddling period sometimes form a part of the circle, the more vigorous dancers accommodating the movement to their weakness. Frequently a woman will be seen to join the circle with an infant upon her back and dance with the others, but should she show the least sign of approaching excitement watchful friends lead her away that no harm may come to the child. Dogs are driven off from the neighborhood of the circle lest they should run against any of those who have fallen into a trance and thus awaken them. The dancers themselves are careful not to disturb the trance subjects while their souls are in the spirit world. Full Indian dress is worn, with buckskin, paint, and feathers, but among the Sioux the women discarded the belts ornamented with disks of German silver, because the metal had come from the white man. Among the southern tribes, on the contrary, hats were sometimes worn in the dance, although this was not considered in strict accordance with the doctrine.

No drum, rattle, or other musical instrument is used in the dance, excepting sometimes by an individual dancer in imitation of a trance vision. In this respect particularly the Ghost dance differs from every other Indian dance. Neither are any fires built within the circle, so far as known, with any tribe excepting the Walapai. The northern Cheyenne, however, built four fires in a peculiar fashion outside of the circle, as already described. With most tribes the dance was performed around a tree or pole planted in the center and variously decorated. In the southern plains, however, only the Kiowa seem ever to have followed this method, they sometimes dancing around a cedar tree. On breaking the circle at the end of the dance the performers shook their blankets or shawls in the air, with the idea of driving away all evil influences. On later instructions from the messiah all then went down to bathe in the stream, the men in one place and the women in another, before going to their tipis. The idea of washing away evil things, spiritual as well as earthly, by bathing in running water is too natural and universal to need comment.

The peculiar ceremonies of prayer and invocation, with the laying on of hands and the stroking of the face and body, have several times been described and need only be mentioned here. As trance visions became frequent the subjects strove to imitate what they had seen in the spirit world, especially where they had taken part with their departed friends in some of the old-time games. In this way gaming wheels, shinny sticks, hummers, and other toys or implements would be made and carried in future dances, accompanied with appropriate songs, until the dance sometimes took on the appearance of an exhibition of Indian curios on a small scale.

The most important feature of the Ghost dance, and the secret of the trances, is hypnotism. It has been hastily assumed that hypnotic knowledge and ability belong only to an overripe civilization, such as that of India and ancient Egypt, or to the most modern period of scientific investigation. The fact is, however, that practical knowledge, if not understanding, of such things belongs to people who live near to nature, and many of the stories told by reliable travelers of the strange performances of savage shamans can be explained only on this theory. Numerous references in the works of the early Jesuit missionaries, of the Puritan writers of New England and of English explorers farther to the south, would indicate that hypnotic ability no less than sleight-of-hand dexterity formed part of the medicine-man's equipment from the Saint Lawrence to the Gulf. Enough has been said in the chapters on Smohalla and the Shakers to show that hypnotism exists among the tribes of the Columbia, and the author has had frequent opportunity to observe and study it in the Ghost dance on the plains. It can not be said that the Indian priests understand the phenomenon, for they ascribe it to a supernatural cause, but they know how to produce the effect, as I have witnessed hundreds of times. In treating of the subject in connection with the Ghost dance the author must be understood as speaking from the point of view of an observer and not as a psychologic expert.

Immediately on coming among the Arapaho and Cheyenne in 1890, I heard numerous stories of wonderful things that occurred in the Ghost dance—how people died, went to heaven and came back again, and how they talked with dead friends and brought back messages from the other world. Quite a number who had thus "died" were mentioned and their adventures in the spirit land were related with great particularity of detail, but as most of the testimony came from white men, none of whom had seen the dance for themselves, I preserved the scientific attitude of skepticism. So far as could be ascertained, none of the intelligent people of the agency had thought the subject sufficiently worthy of serious consideration to learn whether the reports were true or false. On talking with the Indians I found them unanimous in their statements as to the visions, until I began to think there might be something in it.

The first clew to the explanation came from the statement of his own experience in the trance, given by Paul Boynton, a particularly bright Carlisle student, who acted as my interpreter. His brother had died some time before, and as Paul was anxious to see and talk with him, which the new doctrine taught was possible, he attended the next Ghost dance, and putting his hands upon the head of Sitting Bull, according to the regular formula, asked him to help him see his dead brother. Paul is of an inquiring disposition, and, besides his natural longing to meet his brother again, was actuated, as he himself said, by a desire to try "every Indian trick." He then told how Sitting Bull had hypnotized him with the eagle feather and the motion of his hands, until he fell unconscious and did really see his brother, but awoke just as he was about to speak to him, probably because one of the dancers had accidentally brushed against him as he lay on the ground. He embodied his experience in a song which was afterward sung in the dance. From his account it seemed almost certain that the secret was hypnotism. The explanation might have occurred to me sooner but for the fact that my previous Indian informants, after the manner of some other witnesses, had told only about their trance visions, forgetting to state how the visions were brought about.

This was in winter and the ground was covered deeply with snow, which stopped the dancing for several weeks. In the meantime I improved the opportunity by visiting the tipis every night to learn the songs and talk about the new religion. When the snow melted, the dances were renewed, and as by this time I had gained the confidence of the Indians I was invited to be present and thereafter on numerous occasions was able to watch the whole process by which the trances were produced. From the outside hardly anything can be seen of what goes on within the circle, but being a part of the circle myself I was able to see all that occurred inside, and by fixing attention on one subject at a time I was able to note all the stages of the phenomenon from the time the subject first attracted the notice of the medicine-man, through the staggering, the rigidity, the unconsciousness, and back again to wakefulness. On two occasions my partner in the dance, each time a woman, came under the influence and I was thus enabled to note the very first nervous tremor of her hand and mark it as it increased in violence until she broke away and staggered toward the medicine-man within the circle.

Young women are usually the first to be affected, then older women, and lastly men. Sometimes, however, a man proves as sensitive as the average woman. In particular I have seen one young Arapaho become rigid in the trance night after night. He was a Carlisle student, speaking good English and employed as clerk in a store. He afterward took part in the sun dance, dancing three days and nights without food, drink, or sleep. He is of a quiet, religious disposition, and if of white parentage would perhaps have become a minister, but being an Indian, the same tendency leads him into the Ghost dance and the sun dance. The fact that he could endure the terrible ordeal of the sun dance would go to show that his physical organization is not frail, as is frequently the case with hypnotic or trance subjects. So far as personal observation goes, the hypnotic subjects are usually as strong and healthy as the average of their tribe. It seems to be a question more of temperament than of bodily condition or physique. After having observed the Ghost dance among the southern tribes at intervals during a period of about four years, it is apparent that the hypnotic tendency is growing, although the original religious excitement is dying out. The trances are now more numerous among the same number of dancers. Some begin to tremble and stagger almost at the beginning of the dance, without any effort on the part of the medicine-man, while formerly it was usually late in the night before the trances began, although the medicine-men were constantly at work to produce such result. In many if not in most cases the medicine-men themselves have been in trances produced in the same fashion, and must thus be considered sensitives as well as those hypnotized by them.

Not every leader in the Ghost dance is able to bring about the hypnotic sleep, but anyone may try who feels so inspired. Excepting the seven chosen ones who start the songs there is no priesthood in the dance, the authority of such men as Sitting Bull and Black Coyote being due to the voluntary recognition of their superior ability or interest in the matter. Any man or woman who has been in a trance, and has thus derived inspiration from the other world, is at liberty to go within the circle and endeavor to bring others to the trance. Even when the result is unsatisfactory there is no interference with the performer, it being held that he is but the passive instrument of a higher power and therefore in no way responsible. A marked instance of this is the case of Cedar Tree, an Arapaho policeman, who took much interest in the dance, attending nearly every performance in his neighborhood, consecrating the ground and working within the circle to hypnotize the dancers. He was in an advanced stage of consumption, nervous and excitable to an extreme degree, and perhaps it was for this reason that those who came under his influence in the trance constantly complained that he led them on the "devil's road" instead of the "straight road;" that he made them see monstrous and horrible shapes, but never the friends whom they wished to see. On this account they all dreaded to see him at work within the circle, but no one commanded him to desist as it was held that he was controlled by a stronger power and was to be pitied rather than blamed for his ill success. A similar idea exists in Europe in connection with persons reputed to possess the evil eye. Cedar Tree himself deplored the result of his efforts and expressed the hope that by earnest prayer he might finally be able to overcome the evil influence.

We shall now describe the hypnotic process as used by the operators, with the various stages of the trance. The hypnotist, usually a man, stands within the ring, holding in his hand an eagle feather or a scarf or handker-chief, white, black, or of any other color. Sometimes he holds the feather in one hand and the scarf in the other. As the dancers circle around sing-ing the songs in time with the dance step the excitement increases until the more sensitive ones are visibly affected. In order to hasten the result certain songs are sung to quicker time, notably the Arapaho song begin-ning Nŭ′nanŭ′naatani′na Hu′hu. We shall assume that the subject is a woman. The first indication that she is becoming affected is a slight muscu-lar tremor, distinctly felt by her two partners who hold her hands on either side. The medicine-man is on the watch, and as soon as he notices the woman's condition he comes over and stands immediately in front of her, looking intently into her face and whirling the feather or the handkerchief, or both, rapidly in front of her eyes, moving slowly around with the dancers at the same time, but constantly facing the woman. All this time he keeps up a series of sharp exclamations, Hu! Hu! Hu! like the rapid breathing of an exhausted runner. From time to time he changes the motion of the feather or handkerchief from a whirling to a rapid up-and-down move-ment in front of her eyes. For a while the woman continues to move around with the circle of dancers, singing the song with the others, but usually before the circuit is completed she loses control of herself entirely, and, breaking away from the partners who have hold of her hands on either side, she staggers into the ring, while the circle at once closes up again behind her. She is now standing before the medicine-man, who gives his whole attention to her, whirling the feather swiftly in front of her eyes, waving his hands before her face as though fanning her, and drawing his hand slowly from the level of her eyes away to one side or upward into the air, while her gaze follows it with a fixed stare. All the time he keeps up the Hu! Hu! Hu! while the song and the dance go on around them with-out a pause. For a few minutes she continues to repeat the words of the song and keep time with the step, but in a staggering, drunken fashion. Then the words become unintelligible sounds, and her movements violently spasmodic, until at last she becomes rigid, with her eyes shut or fixed and staring, and stands thus uttering low pitiful moans. If this is in the day-time, the operator tries to stand with his back to the sun, so that the full sunlight shines in the woman's face. The subject may retain this fixed, immovable posture for an indefinite time, but at last falls heavily to the ground, unconscious and motionless. The dance and the song never stop, but as soon as the woman falls the medicine-man gives his attention to another subject among the dancers. The first one may lie unconscious for ten or twenty minutes or sometimes for hours, but no one goes near to disturb her, as her soul is now communing with the spirit world. At last consciousness gradually returns. A violent tremor seizes her body as in the beginning of the fit. A low moan comes from her lips, and she sits up and looks about her like one awaking from sleep. Her whole form trembles violently, but at last she rises to her feet and staggers away from the dancers, who open the circle to let her pass. All the phenomena of recovery, except rigidity, occur in direct reverse of those which precede unconsciousness.

Sometimes before falling the hypnotized subject runs wildly around the circle or out over the prairie, or goes through various crazy evolutions like those of a lunatic. On one occasion—but only once—I have seen the medicine-man point his finger almost in the face of the hypnotized subject, and then withdrawing his finger describe with it a large circle about the tipis. The subject followed the direction indicated, sometimes being hidden from view by the crowd, and finally returned, with his eyes still fixed and staring, to the place where the medicine-man was standing. There is frequently a good deal of humbug mixed with these performances, some evidently pretending to be hypnotized in order to attract notice or to bring about such a condition from force of imitation, but the greater portion is unquestionably genuine and beyond the control of the subjects. In many instances the hypnotized person spins around for minutes at a time like a dervish, or whirls the arms with apparently impossible speed, or assumes and retains until the final fall most uncomfortable positions which it would be impossible to keep for any length of time under normal conditions. Frequently a number of persons are within the ring at once, in all the various stages of trance. The proportion of women thus affected is about three times that of men.

THE SIOUX OUTBREAK OF 1890

. . . Before going into the history of this short but costly war it is appropriate to state briefly the causes of the outbreak. In the documentary appendix to this chapter these causes are fully set forth by competent authorities —civilian, military, missionary, and Indian. They may be summarized as (1) unrest of the conservative element under the decay of the old life, (2) repeated neglect of promises made by the government, and (3) hunger.

In that year, in pursuance of a policy inaugurated for bringing all the In spite of wars, removals, and diminished food supply since the advent of the white man, they still number nearly 26,000. In addition to these there are about 600 more residing in Canada. They formerly held the headwaters of the Mississippi, extending eastward almost to Lake Superior, but were driven into the prairie about two centuries ago by their enemies, the Ojibwa, after the latter had obtained firearms from the French. On coming out on the buffalo plains they became possessed of the horse, by means of which reinforcement to their own overpowering numbers the Sioux were soon enabled to assume the offensive, and in a short time had made themselves the undisputed masters of an immense territory extending, in a general way, from Minnesota to the Rocky mountains and from the Yellowstone to the Platte. A few small tribes were able to maintain their position within these limits, but only by keeping close to their strongly built permanent villages on the Missouri. Millions of buffalo to furnish unlimited food supply, thousands of horses, and hundreds of miles of free range made the Sioux, up to the year 1868, the richest and most prosperous, the proudest, and withal, perhaps, the wildest of all the tribes of the plains.

The Sioux are the largest and strongest tribe within the United States. plains tribes under the direct control of the government, a treaty was negotiated with the Sioux living west of the Missouri by which they renounced their claims to a great part of their territory and had "set apart for their absolute and undisturbed use and occupation"—so the treaty states—a reservation which embraced all of the present state of South Dakota west of Missouri river. At the same time agents were appointed and agencies established for them; annuities and rations, cows, physicians, farmers, teachers, and other good things were promised them, and they agreed to allow railroad routes to be surveyed and built and military posts to be established in their territory and neighborhood. At one stroke they were reduced from a free nation to dependent wards of the government. It was stipulated also that they should be allowed to hunt within their old range, outside the limits of the reservation, so long as the buffalo abounded —a proviso which, to the Indians, must have meant forever.

The reservation thus established was an immense one, and would have been ample for all the Sioux while being gradually educated toward civilization, could the buffalo have remained and the white man kept away. But the times were changing. The building of the railroads brought into the plains swarms of hunters and emigrants, who began to exterminate the buffalo at such a rate that in a few years the Sioux, with all the other hunting tribes of the plains, realized that their food supply was rapidly going. Then gold was discovered in the Black hills, within the reservation, and at once thousands of miners and other thousands of lawless desperadoes rushed into the country in defiance of the protests of the Indians and the pledges of the government, and the Sioux saw their last remaining hunting ground taken from them. The result was the Custer war and massacre, and a new agreement in 1876 by which the Sioux were shorn of one-third of their guaranteed reservation, including the Black hills, and this led to deep and widespread dissatisfaction throughout the tribe. The conservatives brooded over the past and planned opposition to further changes which they felt themselves unable to meet. The progressives felt that the white man's promises meant nothing.

On this point Commissioner Morgan says, in his statement of the causes of the outbreak:

Prior to the agreement of 1876 buffalo and deer were the main support of the Sioux. Food, tents, bedding were the direct outcome of hunting, and with furs and pelts as articles of barter or exchange it was easy for the Sioux to procure whatever constituted for them the necessaries, the comforts, or even the luxuries of life. Within eight years from the agreement of 1876 the buffalo had gone and the Sioux had left to them alkali land and government rations. It is hard to overestimate the magnitude of the calamity, as they viewed it, which happened to these people by the sudden disappearance of the buffalo and the large diminution in the numbers of deer and other wild animals. Suddenly, almost without warning, they were expected at once and without previous training to settle down to the pursuits of agriculture in a land largely unfitted for such use. The freedom of the chase was to be exchanged for the idleness of the camp. The boundless range was to be abandoned for the circumscribed reservation, and abundance of plenty to be supplanted by limited and decreasing government subsistence and supplies. Under these circumstances it is not in human nature not to be discontented and restless, even turbulent and violent. (*Comr., 28.*)

It took our own Aryan ancestors untold centuries to develop from savagery into civilization. Was it reasonable to expect that the Sioux could do the same in fourteen years?

The white population in the Black hills had rapidly increased, and it had become desirable to open communication between eastern and western Dakota. To accomplish this, it was proposed to cut out the heart of the Sioux reservation, and in 1882, only six years after the Black hills had been seized, the Sioux were called on to surrender more territory. A commission was sent out to treat with them, but the price offered—only about 8 cents per acre—was so absurdly small, and the methods used so palpably unjust, that friends of the Indians interposed and succeeded in defeating the measure in Congress. Another agreement was prepared, but experience had made the Indians suspicious, and it was not until a third commission went out, under the chairmanship of General Crook, known to the Indians as a brave soldier and an honorable man, that the Sioux consented to treat. The result, after much effort on the part of the commission and determined opposition by the conservatives, was another agreement, in 1889, by which the Sioux surrendered one-half (about 11,000,000 acres) of their remaining territory, and the great reservation was cut up into five smaller ones, the northern and southern reservations being separated by a strip 60 miles wide.

Then came a swift accumulation of miseries. Dakota is an arid country with thin soil and short seasons. Although well adapted to grazing it is not suited to agriculture, as is sufficiently proven by the fact that the white settlers in that and the adjoining state of Nebraska have several times been obliged to call for state or federal assistance on account of failure of crops. To wild Indians hardly in from the warpath the problem was much more serious. As General Miles points out in his official report, thousands of white settlers after years of successive failures had given up the struggle and left the country, but the Indians, confined to reservations, were unable to emigrate, and were also as a rule unable to find employment, as the whites might, by which they could earn a subsistence. The buffalo was gone. They must depend on their cattle, their crops, and the government rations issued in return for the lands they had surrendered. If these failed, they must starve. The highest official authorities concur in the statement that all of these did fail, and that the Indians were driven to outbreak by starvation.

In 1888 their cattle had been diminished by disease. In 1889 their crops were a failure, owing largely to the fact that the Indians had been called into the agency in the middle of the farming season and kept there to treat with the commission, going back afterward to find their fields trampled and torn up by stock during their absence. Then followed epidemics of measles, grippe, and whooping cough, in rapid succession and with terribly fatal results. Anyone who understands the Indian character needs not the testimony of witnesses to know the mental effect thus produced. Sullenness and gloom, amounting almost to despair, settled down on the Sioux, especially among the wilder portion. "The people said their children were all dying from the face of the earth, and they might as well be killed at once." Then came another entire failure of crops in 1890, and an unexpected reduction of rations, and the Indians were brought face to face with starvation. They had been expressly and repeatedly told by the commission that their rations would not be affected by their signing the treaty, but immediately on the consummation of the agreement Congress cut down their beef rations by 2,000,000 pounds at Rosebud, 1,000,000 at Pine Ridge, and in less proportion at other agencies. Earnest protest against this reduction was made by the commission which had negotiated the treaty, by Commissioner Morgan, and by General Miles, but still Congress failed to remedy the matter until the Sioux had actually been driven to rebellion. As Commissioner Morgan states, "It was not until January, 1891, *after the troubles,* that an appropriation of $100,000 was made by Congress for additional beef for the Sioux." The protest of the commission, a full year before the outbreak, as quoted by Commissioner Morgan, is strong and positive on this point.

Commissioner Morgan, while claiming that the Sioux had before been receiving more rations than they were justly entitled to according to their census number, and denying that the reduction was such as to cause even extreme suffering, yet states that the reduction was especially unwise at this juncture, as it was in direct violation of the promises made to the Indians, and would be used as an argument by those opposed to the treaty to show that the government cared nothing for the Indians after it had obtained their lands. It is quite possible that the former number of rations was greater than the actual number of persons, as it is always a difficult matter to count roving Indians, and the difficulties were greater when the old census was made. The census is taken at long intervals and the tendency is nearly always toward a decrease. Furthermore, it has usually been the policy with agents to hold their Indians quiet by keeping them as well fed as possible. On the other hand, it must be remembered that the issue is based on the weight of the cattle as delivered at the agency in the fall, and that months of exposure to a Dakota winter will reduce this weight by several hundred pounds to the animal. The official investigation by Captain Hurst at Cheyenne River agency shows conclusively that the essential food items of meat, flour, and coffee were far below the amount stipulated by the treaty.

In regard to the effect of this food deficiency Bishop Hare says: "The people were often hungry and, the physicians in many cases said, died, when taken sick, not so much from disease as for want of food." General Miles says: "The fact that they had not received sufficient food is admitted by the agents and the officers of the government who have had opportunities of knowing," and in another place he states that in spite of crop failures and other difficulties, after the sale of the reservation "instead of an increase, or even a reasonable supply for their support, they have been compelled to live on half and two-thirds rations and received nothing for the surrender of their lands." The testimony from every agency is all to the same effect.

There were other causes of dissatisfaction, some local and others general and chronic, which need not be detailed here. Prominent among them were the failure of Congress to make payment of the money due the Sioux for the lands recently ceded, or to have the new lines surveyed promptly so that the Indians might know what was still theirs and select their allotments accordingly; failure to reimburse the friendly Indians for horses confiscated fourteen years before; the tardy arrival of annuities, consisting largely of winter clothing, which according to the treaty were due by the 1st of August, but which seldom arrived until the middle of winter; the sweeping and frequent changes of agency employees from the agent down, preventing anything like a systematic working out of any consistent policy, and almost always operating against the good of the service, especially at Pine Ridge, where so brave and efficient a man as McGillycuddy was followed by such a one as Royer—and, finally, the Ghost dance.

The Ghost dance itself, in the form which it assumed among the Sioux, was only a symptom and expression of the real causes of dissatisfaction, and with such a man as McGillycuddy or McLaughlin in charge at Pine

Ridge there would have been no outbreak, in spite of broken promises and starvation, and the Indians could have been controlled until Congress had afforded relief. That it was not the cause of the outbreak is sufficiently proved by the fact that there was no serious trouble, excepting on the occasion of the attempt to arrest Sitting Bull, on any other of the Sioux reservations, and none at all among any of the other Ghost-dancing tribes from the Missouri to the Sierras, although the doctrine and the dance were held by nearly every tribe within that area and are still held by the more important. Among the Paiute, where the doctrine originated and the messiah has his home, there was never the slightest trouble. It is significant that Commissioner Morgan in his official statement of the causes of the outbreak places the "messiah craze" eleventh in a list of twelve, the twelfth being the alarm created by the appearance of troops. The Sioux outbreak of 1890 was due entirely to local grievances, recent or long standing. The remedy and preventive for similar trouble in the future is sufficiently indicated in the appended statements of competent authorities.

PART IV

PRESERVING
THE REMNANTS
OF INDIAN CULTURES:

The Role of the
Private Museums

Introduction

by Ruth L. Bunzel

THE INTELLECTUAL CLIMATE OF THE LAST HALF OF THE NINETEENTH century was dominated by the writings of Darwin and Huxley and by the unfolding of man's prehistoric past. The increased interest in natural science expressed itself in the foundation of the great private museums of natural history. The Peabody Museums of Yale and Harvard and the American Museum of Natural History in New York, were established within a short time of each other. They preceded by a few years the National Museum in Washington.

In 1866 George Foster Peabody, a native of Massachusetts who had grown rich in England, founded the Peabody Museum of Harvard University "to preserve the antiquities of America which were fast disappearing. . ." The archaeological and ethnological collections were to be housed in a separate wing of the University Museum, a natural history museum designed by Louis Agassiz in 1859. The collections included, besides extensive archaeological specimens, "a Sioux hunting shirt and other objects collected by Francis Parkman in 1846," collections made by Miss Alice Fletcher from the Omaha, Sioux and Nez Percé, including paraphernalia of the Sun Dance of the Oglala. At this time a museum was an institution which collected and housed material objects.

Twenty years later Peabody came to realize that a museum may have a function as a center of research and education and he endowed the first chair of American Archaeology and Ethnology at Harvard. Frederick Ward Putnam was appointed to the new chair, and he also became curator of the Museum. Instruction was given in the Museum, a tradition still observed at Harvard. A few years later Frank Russell and Roland B. Dixon joined the staff of the department, and Harvard and Peabody were well launched on a program of teaching and research. It is fortunate for anthropology that the directors of the great museums realized at an early date that there is a body of knowledge as well as material objects to be preserved, and recognized their responsibility for preserving it. Throughout its history the Peabody Museum has emphasized archaeology. It acquired extensive archaeological collections and in the early years of this century sent out annual expeditions to Mexico and Central America. The list of those who worked for the Museum in this field includes such distinguished scholars as Maudslay, Saville, Spinden, Morley, Tozzer, Lothrop, and Kidder.

The American Museum of Natural History followed a few years later, in 1868. It was first housed in the old Armory in Central Park while the South Wing of the present building was under construction. John David Wolfe, the first president, outlined the aims of the Museum in his first annual report: ". . . . recognizing the necessity of such a museum as a means of education and recreation . . . we have, if properly supported and aided with funds by our fellow citizens, a guarantee of a prosperous future in the formation of a Museum of Natural History that will be second to none and which, while affording amusement and instruction to the public will be the means of teaching our youth to appreciate the wonderful works of the Creator." In accordance with these aims Albert S. Bickmore, who was superintendent when the Museum moved into its new building in 1877, inaugurated the system of education in the natural sciences in conjunction with the city schools which has been maintained to the present day.

It was under the presidency of Morris K. Jesup (1881-1908) that anthropology came fully into its own. Jesup was a man of great vigor and also of much wealth which he disbursed lavishly. He was deeply committed to anthropology. In his report of 1884 appealing for funds he expressed the purpose of the Museum as follows: ". . . Perhaps some child of genius, whose susceptibilities and faculties once aroused and quickened will repay in the field of discovery and science, through the force of some new law in its manifold applications, all your expenditures a hundredfold. . . . Commercial values and purely scientific values meet often on common ground; but their essential life belongs to opposite poles. To some it appears necessary to vindicate the employment of large amounts of public money from the charge of extravagance. Their ideas of value appear to be limited to that which is exchangeable in the current coin of the market. But the highest results of character and life offer something which cannot be weighed in the balances of the merchant, be he ever so wise in his generation."

Jesup established the Department of Anthropology and brought Frederick Ward Putnam from Cambridge to head it. He extended the archaeological and ethnological sections, acquiring many famous private collections. He also gathered about him a remarkable group of men including Boas, Saville, Bandelier, Lumholtz, Harlan Smith, the Russian anthropologists Jochelson and Bogoras, and many more. The central endeavor of his administration was the organization of the Jesup North Pacific Expedition, a plan for the investigation of all aspects of aboriginal life in an area extending from Puget Sound to the Arctic coast of Alaska and including the adjacent parts of Asia. Jesup described the aims of the expedition in his report for 1892: ". . . the theory [is held] that America was originally peopled by migratory tribes from the Asiatic continent. . . . The opportunities for solving this problem are rapidly disappearing. I would be deeply gratified to learn that some friends of the Museum may feel disposed to contribute means for the prosecution of systematic investigations in the hope of securing data to demonstrate the truth or falsity of the claims set forth by various prominent men of science." The expedition got under way in 1897, and was the most extensive anthropological project undertaken in America up to that time.

Today we would call the Jesup Expedition a "project," since the various tribes studied were not visited in turn by the "expedition" but were studied individually by men who had little contact with one another; the separate studies followed no fixed plan. In addition to conventional ethnographic descriptions there were studies of social structure, of ceremonialism, of art; collections of myths and tales and texts relating to everyday life; a number of studies of racial types on both sides of Bering Strait; and the beginning of the archaeological investigation of this important area.

The Jesup Expedition yielded a vast amount of ethnographic data on an area previously but little known. Its findings still provide the only scientific data on certain tribes. The reports are a great mine of valuable information and not all of the precious metal has been extracted. The field work was completed in 1903, excepting that Boas never considered his own field work among the Kwakiutl finished. He returned to their territory as late as 1931 at the age of seventy-three while he was president of the American Association for the Advancement of Science.

The next area to be tackled in a concerted effort was the Northern Plains of North America, where the rapid collapse of Plains culture gave these researches a special urgency.

Although the emphasis at the Museum of Natural History has always been on ethnology, archaeology was never wholly neglected. John Alden Mason collected material from Mexico and Central America. Nels C. Nelson had a wide knowledge of the prehistoric civilizations of both the old and the new world. His outstanding original research was in the Southwest, where he established the first chronology based on sequences of pottery types, which was later incorporated into Kidder's more extensive scheme. Leslie Spier also made a notable contribution to archaeological method when he used a statistical analysis of pottery types for establishing chronological relationships.

ALFRED VINCENT KIDDER

(1885-   )

Alfred Vincent Kidder is an archaeologist who combines breadth of view with intense specialization in his own work. Kidder belongs, by association and loyalties, to Peabody and Harvard, although he had no official connection with Harvard after getting his degree, and spent only one year in the Peabody Museum as Curator of American Archaeology. His work in the Southwest was done for the Phillips Academy, Andover, and his work in Central America for the Carnegie Institution of Washington.

In 1915 he began excavation at Pecos, New Mexico, a pueblo in the Rio Grande area which had a long history and which had been abandoned only in the 19th century. He continued excavation at Pecos until 1929. These excavations resulted in the establishment of a stratigraphy with a ceiling, with a known date, and with lower levels tying it to other sites. At a conference he organized at Pecos in the late 20's attended by virtually all the archaeologists and ethnologists then working in the Southwest, a definitive chronology was set up and a new nomenclature for Southwestern cultures and periods was agreed on. Kidder was convinced through his Southwest experience that archaeology and ethnology had much to contribute to each other, which led in the 30's to his great design for interdisciplinary areal research in the Guatemala Highlands.

Kidder summarized the results of Southwestern archaeological research in his book, An Introduction to the Study of Southwestern Archaeology, *the first such synthesis for any American area. The final chapter of this book is here reproduced. Although written more than twenty-five years ago, even before the Pecos Conference, and although much work has been done in the Southwest since that time, it is still the standard introduction, and the new discoveries, such as the very early remains discovered in Bat Cave and other sites, merely fill in the outlines which Kidder has drawn. The one point where Kidder's interpretations have been superseded is in physical anthropology. Kidder clings to the old theory of a change in physical type in the pre-Pueblo horizon. Since Seltzer's work on Pueblo skulls, it is now generally accepted that they represent a continuous series.*

—R.L.B.

Southwestern Archaeology: Conclusions

THE DATA, SO FAR AS WE CAN SUMMARIZE THEM AT PRESENT, ARE NOW before us. It remains to combine them into some sort of coherent whole. This can best be done in the form of an historical reconstruction, but it must be remembered that such a reconstruction is merely a working hypothesis, designed to correlate our information, and to indicate more clearly the needs of future study. We must have no hesitation in abandoning our conclusions, partly or *in toto,* if contradictory evidence appears.

To begin with, it is safe enough to postulate the former presence in the Southwest of a more or less nomadic people, thinly scattered over the country, ignorant of agriculture and of pottery-making. Their life must have resembled closely that of the modern Digger tribes of the Plateau; that is to say, they dwelt in more or less makeshift houses, and subsisted principally on small game: rabbits, prairie dogs, and doves; and on such wild vegetable products as grass-seeds, berries, and roots. As to their language, it is less safe to speculate; but from the fact that peoples of Uto-Aztecan speech seem to have formed the basic population of the highlands from Montana far south into Mexico, it is quite likely that they belonged to that group. Whoever they were, there could not have been many of them, for the natural food resources of the Southwest were probably, even in those ancient times, not sufficient to support more than a very small population. Remains of these aborigines have not yet been discovered, nor will they be easy to distinguish from those of such modern nomads as the Apache and Paiute, unless they are found buried below the relics of later cultures.

These supposedly original Southwesterners eventually acquired the knowledge of corn-growing; they took up farming in a more or less haphazard way, but its practice did not at first react very strongly upon their way of life; for the Basket Makers, as we call the earliest agriculturists, apparently had no permanent houses, nor did they make pottery. As to the date of the introduction of corn we are still ignorant, but it is possible to make certain deductions.

Corn was originally brought under cultivation in the highlands of Mexico or Central America. This general locality is indicated by the identification of the probable wild ancestor of corn, a heavy-seeded grass which grows only in that region.[1] How long ago Mexican agriculture began

From Kidder, *An introduction to the study of Southwestern archaeology with a preliminary account of the excavations at Pecos,* Department of Archaeology, Phillips Academy, Andover, Mass. (New Haven: Yale University Press, 1924), pp. 118-124.

[1] J. W. Harshberger, "Maize: a botanical and economic study," *Contributions from the Botanical Laboratory of the Univ. of Pennsylvania,* Vol. I, No. 2 (1893).

is unknown; the remains indeed, of the first farmers, the Mexican Basket Makers so to speak, still await discovery. Corn, however, is a very highly specialized cereal, a fact which would seem to indicate great antiquity. Be that as it may, corn-growing was without any question the factor which made possible the development of all the higher American civilizations, and so the discovery of agriculture must have long antedated their rise. Now the Maya, apparently the oldest and certainly the most brilliant of these civilizations, was at its zenith during the sixth century of the Christian era; and its complex calendar system, which we must suppose to have taken several centuries to develop, had undoubtedly been perfected by the year 1 A.D.[2] It is, therefore, not rash to guess that the Maya began to differentiate themselves from the other archaic corn-growing peoples as long ago as 1000 B.C. Judging by the rate of progress made by nascent civilizations elsewhere in the world, it seems safe to allow at least two thousand years more for the period that elapsed between the time of the first cultivation of corn (say at about 3000 B.C.) and the beginnings of the Maya culture. During these two millenniums we must allow for the early, localized practice of agriculture in the highlands; and the subsequent very extensive diffusion of the primitive corn-growing, pottery-making complex known as the Archaic Mexican culture.[3]

All this somewhat speculative time-reckoning does not help us directly in our attempt to arrive at an approximate date for the introduction of farming in the Southwest, and the consequent springing up there of the Basket Maker culture; but it does give us a certain sense of perspective, and makes it seem quite possible that the Basket Makers as we know them lived as long ago as fifteen hundred or two thousand years before Christ. I believe, indeed, because of the simple and undifferentiated nature of Basket Maker corn, that the practice of corn-growing may have spread into the Southwest in the pre-Archaic period of Mexico, and that the influence of the developed Archaic is perhaps to be seen in the pottery and crude figurines of the post-Basket Makers.

There is still another set of considerations which bear on the question of chronology, namely, the problem of whether the entire development of the Pueblo civilization was an autochthonous one, or whether it consisted of a series of cultural leaps stimulated from without. If the second supposition be true, the post-Basket Maker stage might have grown up elsewhere and imposed itself directly on the antecedent Basket Maker, the pre-Pueblo on the post-Basket Maker, and the true Pueblo on the pre-Pueblo. Such a process would not necessarily have required a great stretch

[2] Since the above was written Spinden has announced in the press the discovery that the Maya calendar was in use as early as the seventh century before Christ.

[3] For a valuable discussion of the Archaic, see H. J. Spinden, "Ancient Civilizations of Mexico and Central America," *American Museum of Natural History, Handbook Series,* No. 3, second edition (New York, 1922).

of time, for the long developmental stages of each culture might have taken place in other areas.

When our knowledge of Southwestern archaeology was less full than it is today, transition stages between the main periods were not recognizable, and a theory of development by jumps or influxes seemed necessary to account for the observed facts. Now that transitions are beginning to be found, it is becoming increasingly evident that the Southwest owes to outside sources little more than the germs of its culture, and that its development from those germs has been a local and almost wholly an independent one. This being the case, the time required must have been long, and the postulated date of Basket Maker origin of 1500 to 2000 B.C. does not seem at all improbable.

At some early time, then, the Southwestern nomads took up the practice of corn-growing; but at first their agriculture sat lightly upon them; their crops were not of sufficient importance, nor had their methods of cultivation become intensive enough, to tie them very closely to their fields. Eventually, however, better care brought fuller harvests, and it became necessary to provide storage places for the garnered grain. Where caves were available they were used, holes being dug in the floors for caches. The population undoubtedly increased, and the leisure acquired from the possession of surplus food-stuffs, and the consequent partial release from the exacting requirements of the chase, allowed the people to work at, and to perfect, their arts, and to lavish time upon elaborate sandal weaves, fine basketry, and carefully made implements. But they were as yet ignorant of pottery.

Such were the Basket Makers. Their range is known to have covered southcentral and southeastern Utah and northeastern Arizona (fig. 22); but from the fact that the knowledge of agriculture and the seeds of corn reached them from the south, it is probable that tribes of similar culture occupied parts of New Mexico and southern Arizona, and stretched southward well into Mexico. It seems likely, however, that Basket Maker culture reached its highest and most characteristic development in the San Juan, for the cultures which appear to have developed from it, and which ultimately spread out and gave rise to the later Pueblo civilization, had their origin, as will be shown presently, in that country.

In the course of time the Basket Makers, becoming more and more dependent upon their crops, and correspondingly more sedentary in habit, either discovered for themselves, or (more probably) learned from tribes to the south, that vessels fashioned from clay, dried in the sun, and finally fired, were easier to make, and more suitable for holding water and for cooking, than the baskets that had hitherto served these purposes. At about the same period they began to enlarge their storage cists into dwellings, to wall them higher with slabs, and to provide them with pole-and-brush roofs. These two great advances mark the opening of the post-

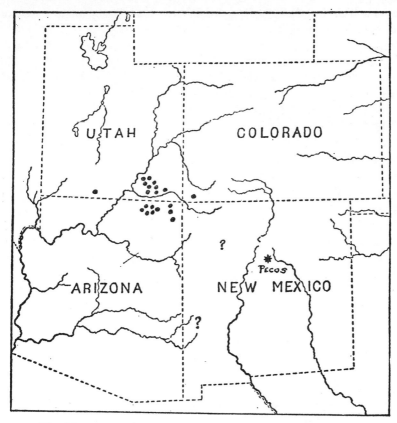

Fig. 22. DISTRIBUTION OF BASKET MAKER SITES AS KNOWN AT
THE PRESENT TIME.

Basket Maker period. That its culture was merely a developed phase of
the Basket Maker there can be little doubt, the headform of the people
remained the same, several old Basket-Maker arts, such as twined-woven
bag making, held on in degenerate form, and the territory occupied includes most of the known Basket Maker country. Post-Basket Maker remains occur throughout the whole San Juan drainage and also appear in
the northern parts of the Little Colorado watershed.

Guernsey has found indications that the pottery of certain post-Basket
Maker sites is much cruder than that of others, and Morris's Long-Hollow
settlements with their well-decorated black-on-white ware would seem to
represent a late phase of the culture little inferior to the pre-Pueblo.[4] Thus

---

[4] E. H. Morris, "Preliminary Account of the Antiquities of the Region between
the Mancos and La Plata Rivers in Southwestern Colorado," *Twenty-third Report
of the Bureau of American Ethnology* (Washington, 1919), pp. 155-206; and review
of same by Kidder and Guernsey in *American Anthropologist*, N. S. Vol. 22, No. 3
(1920), pp. 285-288.

we have a hint that the post-Basket Maker period was a long one, during which a steady evolution in all the arts went on.

There now comes one of the apparent breaks in continuity which formerly made it seem that Southwestern growth must have advanced in leaps stimulated from without the area. To be explicit: the pre-Pueblo, the next stage of which we have knowledge, shows a population with an entirely different headform. Furthermore, the houses began to be grouped into more or less compact communities.

It must be remembered that pre-Pueblo remains were known long before the discovery of the post-Basket Maker stage, and the gap between pre-Pueblo and Basket Maker was accordingly so very wide that it was hard to see any relationship between the two. With the post-Basket Maker culture now becoming understood, however, the break is being narrowed; we have the post-Basket Maker slab-walled house standing between the Basket Maker cist and the pre-Pueblo dwelling, and the crude and advanced styles of post-Basket Maker pottery to indicate a local growth in that art. The new and so far unexplained elements in the pre-Pueblo complex are the presence of the bow-and-arrow, the use of cotton, and particularly the practice of skull deformation.

The skulls of the Basket Makers and post-Basket Makers are dolichocephalic and undeformed; those of the pre-Pueblo are, as far as we know, always artificially flattened posteriorly. This flattening renders it difficult to tell what the natural form of the head might have been, and it is possible that the mere introduction of hard-bedded cradles (a not very radical cultural change) might have caused this effect, and that the pre-Pueblos were really as long-headed as their predecessors. My feeling is, however, that the pre-Pueblo were actually of a different physical type, naturally brachycephalic, and that their broad-headedness was merely accentuated by deformation.[5]

It seems, therefore, that we must recognize the arrival in the Southwest of a new race, which eventually became the preponderating one, to the submergence of the old dolichocephalic strain. But (and this point deserves emphasis) the new people, if such they were, introduced no new cultural elements except cotton and perhaps the bow-and-arrow. The really vital traits, agriculture, pottery, and semi-permanent houses, were already in the possession of the post-Basket Makers. The broad-heads, then, merely took over the old way of life and added certain improvements; but in general carried it on in a perfectly normal course of development.

The pre-Pueblo period saw some increase in the agricultural population of the Southwest and a considerable enlargement in the territory occupied. Pre-Pueblo sites are found throughout the entire San Juan country,

[5] For a discussion of the relation between skull deformation and headform see Hooton, Peabody Museum Papers, vol. VIII, no. 1, pp. 85-89.

as well as in parts of the Rio Grande, the Little Colorado, and the upper Gila (fig. 24). Wherever this culture penetrated it resulted in the introduction of more or less permanent settlements and in the manufacture of black-on-white and neck-coiled pottery. It is probable that as the houses became more solidly built, more drawn together, and more commonly

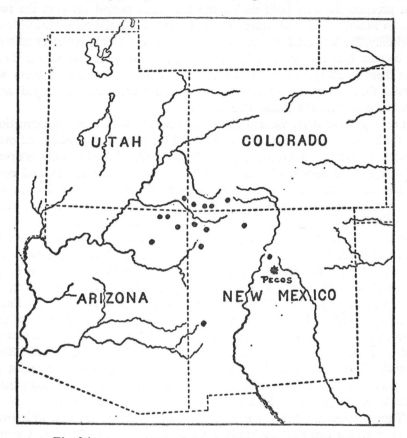

Fig. 24. DISTRIBUTION OF PRE-PUEBLO SITES AS KNOWN AT THE PRESENT TIME.

above ground, there was evolved a rudimentary type of kiva, a ceremonial survival of the subterranean and semi-subterranean dwellings of former days. Such rooms have been found in association with pre-Pueblo ruins in northeastern Arizona and southwestern Colorado,[6] both sites in the San Juan drainage. The San Juan, indeed, appears to have been the breeding ground and place of dissemination of all the traits typical of the pre-Pueblo culture, for it is there that the remains are most abundant and most

[6] A. V. Kidder and S. J. Guernsey, "Archaeological Explorations in Northeastern Arizona," *Bulletin 65, Bureau of American Ethnology* (Washington, 1919).
Morris, *op. cit.*, p. 186.

highly specialized; and as one goes out from the San Juan one seems to find the pre-Pueblo culture considerably less advanced.

At the present time we possess enough data as to pre-Pueblo ruins to enable us to characterize them fairly accurately. We also have abundant data as to the developed Pueblo culture. But the small pueblo-like ruins that presumably were built during the transition period between the two are, as Morris observes,[7] practically unknown. I use the term "transition" advisedly, for it is evident that there was no sharp break, either in culture or in race between pre-Pueblo and Pueblo. It is most important, then, that these small ruins be sought out and excavated, because in them we should find the germs of all the traits that were later developed and combined to form the classic Pueblo culture.

Lacking these data, we are forced to proceed with our reconstruction on the basis of very scanty information. All we know is that scattered over almost the entire Southwest are little ruins built of horizontally coursed masonry, or of adobe, with closely grouped rectangular rooms and containing corrugated and black-on-white pottery. All such sites I class together as belonging to the early Pueblo period, for wherever they are even cursorily investigated they prove to have antedated the larger pueblos. The limits of their enormous range (fig. 25) extend from southern Nevada east and north to Great Salt Lake in Utah, east again to Colorado, down the edge of the Rockies to the headwaters of the Rio Grande, east again around the southern end of the Rockies practically to the Texas border, thence southwest across New Mexico to the neighborhood of El Paso, along the southern border of New Mexico, south of the headwaters of the Gila and Salt, along the southern base of the Mogollons, thence across to the edge of the western Arizona desert and so northwest to southern Nevada. The only parts of the Southwest in which so far no remains of the small-house, black-on-white pottery people of the early Pueblo period have been found, are the Lower Gila and the Chihuahua basin.

Thus it appears that the early Pueblo culture spread far and wide over country which had not previously been occupied by pre-Pueblos. I speak of it with considerable confidence as a spreading, for it is virtually out of the question that so uniform a culture could have sprung up simultaneously and independently in several districts. We must, therefore, search for the point of origin, and all the information we now have points toward the San Juan drainage.

It may, of course, be due to the fact that the San Juan has been more thoroughly worked than other areas, but it is nevertheless very suggestive, that the most abundant and most highly developed exemplifications of the early cultures (the Basket Maker, post-Basket Maker, and pre-Pueblo) have been found in or near that country. And when we consider the early

[7] E. H. Morris, "Chronology of the San Juan area," *Proceedings of the National Academy of Sciences*, Vol. 7 (1921), pp. 18-22.

Pueblo remains we seem to see the same state of affairs. Early Pueblo ruins are very abundant in the San Juan, and they possess the traits most characteristic of Pueblo culture in greater perfection than do the early ruins in any other area. To be explicit: corrugated ware is at this period of marked excellence in the San Juan, and becomes progressively cruder as we proceed outward; the same is true, though perhaps to a less extent, in the case of black-on-white; the kiva also reaches an early high specialization in the San Juan, and becomes less common and less specialized the further away we get. As to other architectural traits we cannot yet speak, our data being still too scanty, but as will be shown in the consideration of a later period, the typical pueblo style of building also seems to have worked outward from the San Juan.

Somewhere, then, in the San Juan, probably in the northern tributaries, the pre-Puebloans had begun to build their houses of horizontally coursed masonry and to work their rooms into rectangular form. In so doing they were faced by the necessity of keeping certain round chambers, already used for ceremonies, separate from the house-clusters. These took on more and more the aspect of places apart, became specialized in construction and in function, and so finally developed into what we call kivas. At the same time the methods of pottery-making were improved; the neck coils of the pre-Pueblo water jars and cooking pots were found to be pleasing, and possibly also of practical value in increasing evaporation or the conduction of heat; they were accordingly extended to cover the entire bodies of the vessels. Black-on-white decoration became more varied. The above improvements in architecture and ceramics were taken over by neighboring groups, and having, so to speak, a head start over most of pre-Pueblo culture, did not encounter the resistance of competition by other localized improvements. They accordingly spread very easily. How rapidly they spread we have at present no means of knowing, but from the fact that great territorial expansion involved very little change, it would seem that the process must have been a relatively quick one.[8] At all events the early Pueblo culture ultimately diffused itself well beyond the former range of the pre-Pueblo, and became planted, as has been said, in territory not hitherto occupied by sedentary peoples. I think that this was not due to actual migration, but rather to a taking over of the culture by tribes who were already semi-agricultural, and therefore ready to embrace the manifest advantages of the new form of life. A certain increase in population, however, must have been brought about by the greater ease of existence and security of food-supply; and this increase would naturally have been most rapid at the original point of diffusion, and so would have caused more or less outward pressure therefrom.

[8] A parallel phenomenon is seen in the wide and uniform extension of the Archaic culture in middle America, see Spinden, *op. cit.,* Chap. I.

I have tentatively located the centre of diffusion in the San Juan, and believe that because of the early advantage thus gained by the inhabitants of the San Juan, they continued for a long time to be the leaders in the development of Southwestern culture. They seem to have evolved, late in this period, the "unit-type" dwelling, a compact and eminently practical home for a small farming community, and one which, as Prudden originally suggested, appears to have had a very important influence on the form of all later pueblo structures.

In assigning all small ruins containing true corrugated ware and more or less unspecialized black-on-white pottery to the early Pueblo period, I may of course be in error, it is wholly possible that some of the examples in the outlying regions may be peripheral survivals into much later times; but, as will be shown presently, the forces that tended to break up this early widespread population, and to concentrate it into more compact groups, would have been particularly unfavorable for the persistence of small isolated settlements along the borders.

The small sites show, as a general rule, little provision for defense against enemies. The villages are seldom large, nor do they often occupy protective sites. Gradually, however, we begin to see the working of the forces mentioned in the last paragraph which were ultimately to bring about the concentrations typical of the later prehistoric and the historic Pueblo periods. To what this integration may have been due cannot be stated definitely, but I am inclined to see in it the result of hostile pressure from without rather than the effect of climatic change. To begin with, many of the districts which were shortly to be abandoned are still among the most favorable as to water supply in the entire Southwest; secondly, many peripheral ruins (as in western Utah and eastern New Mexico) were seemingly deserted at an early time; lastly, the more recent villages are larger, and stronger, and occupy more easily defensible sites, than the older ones.

From the very beginning of agricultural life in the Southwest there must have been strife between the farmers and the hunting tribes. Even the Basket Makers probably had their difficulties with wilder neighbors. But, as has been said before, the Southwest is a land too poor in game to have supported a large non-agricultural population, and the first sedentary people presumably had few foes to trouble them. As the early Pueblos, however, increased in prosperity, and began to extend their sphere of influence outward from the point of origin, they presumably came in contact with the more powerful hunting tribes of the Great Plains, of the Rocky Mountains, and of the northern Plateau. Attacks by these hunters brought the latter rich stores of garnered corn, and they soon came to realize that by raiding the practically defenseless small towns they could supplement their food-supply and so maintain themselves in territory not hitherto open to them because of lack of game.

It is not necessary to postulate any great incursion of nomads. A few bands working in here and there and adopting a semi-parasitic existence might well have been sufficient to bring about the observed results. But when such a process was started, even in a small way, it must have had the most far-reaching consequences. The parasite ultimately destroys its host, and is then forced to seek new prey; and the nomad once blooded, so to speak, by the sack of frontier settlements, had to push farther in to gratify his new tastes. Ruined farmers, too, their crops destroyed or stolen, might themselves have turned hunter-raiders and so increased the inward pressure. Wars between village and village, or between stock and stock, may also have occurred, but as yet we have little evidence of such feuds.

There is reason to believe that the region north of the Colorado river was first given up, although some settlements evidently held out for a time along the Grand Canyon and in the Virgin valley. In the northern San Juan the "unit type" villages began to bunch together to form somewhat larger aggregations; the same thing appears to have gone on in the Mesa Verde country and south of the San Juan. In the Kayenta region there seems at first to have been less trouble. In the Rio Grande, the Little Colorado, and the upper Gila and Salt there was also little or no change from the easy, small-village life of earlier times.

Until this stage the danger from the postulated nomads seems to have come from the north, and the outlying Pueblos were pushed in, or destroyed. Now, however, wild tribes appear to have infiltrated from all sides. They spread out over the San Juan basin, and carried their incursions well to the south. The result was that the small towns of the San Juan had to be abandoned; but instead of giving up the struggle, their inhabitants gathered together in large communities, and these large communities became more or less isolated from each other. Thus their enemies seem to have forced the Pueblos into that very form of life which, by fostering communal effort, was to permit them to attain their highest cultural achievements.

I stress here, as before, the influence of the nomadic enemy; for this appears to me best to explain the observed facts of Pueblo history. The same facts, however, may also be, and indeed have been, explained in accordance with the theory of a progressive dessication of the Southwest.[9] ... Although the question is still an open one, the bulk of the evidence now available seems to me to indicate that as far back as the time of the Basket Makers the climate was much the same as it is today; and that

[9] E. L. Hewett, J. Henderson, W. W. Robbins, "The physiography of the Rio Grande Valley, New Mexico, in relation to Pueblo culture," *Bulletin 54, Bureau of American Ethnology* (Washington, 1913).
   E. Huntington, "The climatic Factor as illustrated in arid America," *Publications of the Carnegie Institution of Washington,* No. 192 (1914).

aridity, comparable to that of the present, has from the very beginning been one of the most vital factors in shaping Southwestern culture. I find it, therefore, hard to believe in a progressive drying up of the country during the period of its occupancy by man.

Whatever the cause may have been, whether aridity, the attacks of savage enemies, or a combination of the two; the Pueblos gave up great stretches of outlying territory, began to congregate into large communities, and entered that stage of their history which we may call the Great Period, or the Period of Specialization (see fig. 25).

In the San Juan it was indeed a Great Period, for it saw the building of the Chaco Canyon towns, the Mesa Verde cliff-houses and canyon-head fortresses, as well as the imposing cliff-dwellings of the Kayenta country. In the south, compact pueblos sprang up on the Rio Grande, on the Little Colorado, and even on the Upper Gila and Salt. Still further to the

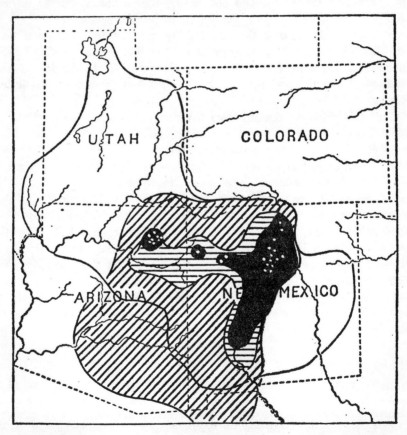

Fig. 25. DISTRIBUTION OF POPULATION DURING THE VARIOUS PERIODS OF PUEBLO HISTORY. EARLY PERIOD (UNSHADED). GREAT PERIOD (OBLIQUE SHADING). LATE PREHISTORIC PERIOD (HORIZONTAL SHADING). PERIOD OF THE CONQUEST (BLACK). PRESENT-DAY PUEBLO VILLAGES (WHITE DOTS).

south in northern Chihuahua, and to the southwest on the Lower Gila, there were coming into being the great adobe "casas grandes". The archaeology of the latter regions is too little understood to permit much speculation as to the origin and growth of their cultures; but though their peculiar architecture has no recognized prototype in the Southwest, their pottery is definitely puebloan in style. My feeling is that these two related and contemporaneous civilizations were rather rapidly achieved results of an amalgamation of Mexican Indians, forced northward, with Pueblos forced or strayed south. At all events it is probable that the Chihuahua-Gila cultures were just beginning to get under way at the time that the maximum development was taking place in the Chaco and on the Mesa Verde.

The underlying causes for the Great Period are not hard to discern. Pressure of one sort or another had forced the Pueblos to draw together into large aggregations, where community of interest stimulated community of effort. The difficulties confronting them were sufficient to spur them to their best endeavors, but not great enough to stunt their progress. Life was not too easy, nor yet too hard. They had reached that vital moment in their history when opportunity and necessity were evenly balanced. And, as before, the San Juan was the seat of the highest development; the achievements of its people in architecture, in the arts, and probably also in social and religious organization, were obviously of great importance in determining the development of the peoples to the south of them. This is most clearly seen in the spread of the massed-terraced style of building which during the Great Period began to come into vogue in the Rio Grande and the Little Colorado.

It was fortunate for the persistence of Pueblo culture that these tendencies did work southward, for the time of the San Juan was at hand. In spite of all they could do, the people of this region were finally forced to give up the struggle; but that they made a hard fight of it is witnessed by the strongly fortified nature of the latest dwellings, and the protective sites chosen for them, particularly in the frontier districts of the north.[10] But eventually Chaco Canyon was abandoned; then the Mesa Verde; lastly the Kayenta plateau; and from that time on the San Juan ceased to play any significant part in Pueblo history.[11]

As to the date of the desertion of the San Juan we have no information; but from the fact that pottery of Toltecan type has been found at Pueblo

[10] For example, the system of watchtowers evolved in the McElmo-Yellowjacket country. See S. G. Morley and A. V. Kidder, "The archaeology of McElmo Canyon, Colorado," *El Palacio,* Vol. IV, No. 4 (Santa Fe, 1917), p. 43.

[11] The occupation of the Gobernador-Largo district after the revolt of 1680, (see Kidder, *op. cit.*); and the possible use of Canyon de Chelly by the Hopi were merely temporary, see J. W. Fewkes, "Hopi ceremonial frames from Cañon de Chelly, Arizona," *American Anthropologist,* N. S., Vol. 8, No. 4 (1906), pp. 664-670.

Bonito, it would seem that these ruins must have been inhabited at some time between 800 and 1100 A.D. Their abandonment can hardly have been much later than 1100, for, as will be shown below, a considerable length of time must have elapsed between that event and the arrival of Europeans in 1540.

At the same time as the giving up of the San Juan, or shortly after, their inhabitants left the villages of the Upper Gila. At a somewhat later date the Lower Gila and Chihuahua basin settlements were abandoned. What caused this wholesale exodus of the Pueblos from their former homes we do not know. Many diverse factors doubtless operated; but from the fact that the process was merely a continuation of the concentration toward the geographical centre of the Southwest which began at the close of the early Pueblo period, it seems likely that the same cause, pressure by nomads, was again responsible. The result in deserted territory is obvious, but what the effect upon the actual size of Pueblo population may have been, is harder to gauge. There must have been a considerable shrinkage, but it is not likely that the entire population of the abandoned regions was wiped out. Although I am disinclined to allow any great degree of historical accuracy to the Hopi and Zuñi clan migration stories, they do seem to indicate that both communities received increments of population from the north and the south. The best argument for a movement of people from the peripherae toward the centre is provided by the marked increase in the number and size of pueblo ruins of relatively late date in and near that centre. During the early Pueblo period and even in the Great Period that had just closed, the Rio Grande and the Little Colorado were not very densely populated. The towns of those times (i.e., the black-on-white sites) were small when numerous, and few when they became larger; now, however, just as the northern and southern districts were being abandoned, villages became much more abundant and much greater in size. As examples of this we may name the great pueblos of the Rio Grande from Socorro to the headwaters of the Chama, and the many new towns that sprang up in the Zuñi country, along the Little Colorado, and about the Hopi mesas.

I think the connection between the two sets of phenomena, abandonment of the outlying districts and sudden increase in population in the central areas, cannot be mistaken. The puzzling thing about it is that the incoming people brought with them so little of their local cultures. No adobe "casas grandes" were built in the Little Colorado, no towns of the Mesa Verde or Chaco types were erected in the Rio Grande. The old styles of pottery became extinct, or were altered so rapidly and completely that the transitional stages have escaped identification. It would seem as if the transference of people must have been by small groups, rather than by whole communities, an infiltration rather than a migration. Each successive increment became amalgamated with the resident group that it joined, adopted the local culture, probably stimulated and strengthened it, possibly influenced it to a certain extent, but seldom, if ever, succeeded in changing it radically, or in turning its course of development sharply away from the channels in which it was already running.

As to the date of this era of redistribution we are as yet ignorant, but we must consider that it took place some centuries before 1540, because we have to allow time for the rise, development, and partial decline of the glazed pottery technique between the end of the Great Period and the coming of the Spaniards. It is reasonably certain that Glaze 1 of the Rio Grande series did not originate until after the abandonment of the Chaco ruins, for no Glaze 1 pottery, or its accompanying Biscuit wares, have ever been found at a Chaco site; nor has any Chaco black-on-white turned up in Glaze 1 Rio Grande settlements. As, however, the actual dating of many prehistoric ruins may be expected during the next few years, it is not necessary or even advisable at the present time to indulge in dating by guesswork.

When the redistribution had become well advanced, the entire Pueblo population was concentrated in the limits indicated on the map (see fig. 25). The shrinkage in territory held, and probably also to some extent in actual numerical strength, was not yet over, for many districts were abandoned between this time and the conquest. For example, a great number of large towns on the Chama and its tributaries, on the Pajarito plateau, and further south along the Rio Grande were certainly deserted before 1540. The same is true of many settlements in the Zuñi country, along the Little Colorado, and in the Hopi region. In this we seem to see merely a continuation of the pressure that had been felt ever since the early days of the true Pueblo period, rather than the working of new factors. The upshot of it was that in 1540 the entire population was gathered together in sixty or seventy towns, strung out along the Rio Grande from Socorro to Taos, and running westward in a narrow, interrupted line through Acoma and Zuñi to the Hopi villages. The still further shrinkage in the seventeenth and eighteenth centuries, the giving up of the Piro and Tano areas, and the concentration of many groups of other stocks into a smaller number of communities, are matters of documentary record. It should be noted that the extermination of the Piro was largely due to the persecution of the Apache.

To recapitulate, the Pueblo civilization owed its origin to stimuli from without, but once well on its feet it developed in its own peculiar way. It passed through an early phase of wide territorial expansion marked by great uniformity of culture. It then drew in upon itself and enjoyed a period of efflorescence characterized by strong specialization in its different branches. Finally it underwent great hardship, suffered a further diminution of territory, and in 1540 was waging a hard fight for mere existence.

Few races have gone as far toward civilization as did the Pueblos while still retaining the essential democracy of primitive life. Most other peoples, as they advanced from savagery, have first set up for themselves, and later fallen under the domination of, rulers temporal or religious; aristocracies or theocracies have sprung up, and the gap between the masses and the classes has become wider and wider. But among the Pueblos no such tendency ever made headway; there were neither very rich nor very poor, every family lived in the same sort of quarters, and ate the same sort of food, as every other family. Preëminence in social or religious life was to be gained solely by individual ability and was the reward of services rendered to the community.

In the 16th century the Pueblos had fallen upon hard times; they had been forced from many of their old ranges, were reduced in numbers, and had lost something of their former skill in material accomplishments. But their customs had not changed, and they still held out undismayed among their savage enemies. There can be little doubt that had they been allowed to work out their own salvation, they could eventually have overcome their difficulties, and might well have built up a civilization of a sort not yet attempted by any group of men. It is the tragedy of native American history that so much human effort has come to naught, and that so many hopeful experiments in life and in living were cut short by the devastating blight of the white man's arrival.

The sketch of Pueblo history which has just been presented is the merest outline. Great bodies of data have been lumped together, and no account has been taken of various complexities which are known to be present in some of the regions discussed. Many of the correlations made between one area and another are also unsatisfactorily vague, and some of them rest on the unreliable evidence of surface finds. Many corrections will have to be made, some of them, perhaps, fundamental. But whether or not our working hypothesis can stand the severe tests which we hope to apply to it in the future, it has shown how much still remains to be done. Nevertheless, we are far enough along in our studies to realize that the problems of any given district can be solved, and that accurate correlations between the different districts can eventually be made, so that in the end we shall surely be able to reconstruct with surprising fullness the history not only of the Pueblo culture in its perfected form, but also that of the early cultures from which it originated. The material is remarkably abundant, and, thanks to the dry climate of the Southwest, extraordinarily well preserved. I know of no other area in the Americas, with the possible exception of Peru, where all the steps in the development of a people from nomadic savagery to a comparatively high degree of civilization, can be traced so accurately and with such a wealth of detail.

When the long task is finished, we shall be able to tell a most interesting story, but the aim of our researches is, or should be, a much broader one than that. We must use our results for the solution of those general problems of anthropological science without a true understanding of which we can never hope to arrive at valid conclusions as to the history of mankind as a whole.

Anthropologists, particularly those who have concerned themselves with the various manifestations of human culture, have reasoned very loosely, have been prone to draw inferences from fragmentary data, to evolve theories which fit well with preconceived ideas. In no science is the need for empirical study more keenly felt. We have had much writing upon culture growth, trait transmission, divergent and convergent evolution, the tendencies of primitive art, the influence of environment on culture, and the like. But when one examines these writings closely, one finds all too often that they are based on data insufficient in quantity or even historically incorrect.

The Southwest alone cannot, of course, give us final answers to any of these broader problems, for the Southwest was only occupied for a relatively short time by a single small branch of the human race. But as to that time, and as to that people, we can learn a great deal; and we shall have, for this area at least, full data which are also historically correct. As chronology is the basis of history, information bearing on the age of Southwestern remains is diligently to be sought for, and we must be constantly on the lookout for new methods of obtaining it.

ALFRED M. TOZZER

(1877-1954)

Like the sacrificial pool of Chichen Itza, the field of Mayan scholarship swallows those who venture into it. Once a man enters its depths he rarely returns, but becomes more and more deeply involved in its complexities.

Alfred M. Tozzer was an exceptional Mayan scholar for, in spite of devoting the greater part of a long and active life to an intensive study of Mayan problems, he nevertheless was able to communicate with his fellow anthropologists. He was a Mayan scholar with a difference, because he was also an ethnologist. In fact he first entered the Mayan field by way of linguistics. On his first field trip to Yucatan he visited Chichen Itza when its cenote was being dredged; he was to return many years later to studies related to this event. He followed his linguistic research with three seasons of field work among the Lacandones, a contemporary Mayan people of the Chiapas jungles. He headed one archaeological expedition to Tikal and Nakum in 1910, and spent one year, cut short by political events, as Director of the International School of Archaeology in Mexico.

It is not as a field archaeologist that Tozzer made his greatest contribution, but as a teacher and a synthesizer. When the objects dredged out of the cenote of Chichen Itza came into the possession of the Peabody Museum of Harvard University, Tozzer planned a comprehensive publication on them that would cover the history, art, and industries of Chichen Itza, an endeavor that continued to occupy him until his death. As a by-product of this research he translated and edited the account of Mayan life by Diego de Landa, first Bishop of Yucatan, a document that ranks with those of Sahagún and Las Casas. Tozzer died before his monumental work on Chichen Itza was published.

Tozzer was one of the great teachers of anthropology. For a long time the emphasis at Harvard was on archaeology, and most of Tozzer's students became archaeologists. But some of his breadth of view, his interest in the relationship of archaeology to ethnology and linguistics and to early documentary sources, left its mark on his students.—R.L.B.

Chronological Aspects of American Archæology

FOR MANY DECADES THE STUDY OF AMERICAN ARCHÆOLOGY WAS IN A very nebulous state characterized, in many cases, by inaccurate observation, bold assumptions, and a general ignorance of the more scientific approach to the subject. These defects have, in great part, been remedied by a wider vision, a more careful training of investigators, more accurate observation, and a gradual tendency to place archæology among the more exact sciences.

American Archæology has also suffered a certain stigma for its failure to produce a literature as its hand-maiden with an accompanying chronology to give a certain vigor to its findings. It must be admitted that archæological data have an inert quality, a certain spinelessness when unaccompanied by a more or less definite chronological background. The psychologists may be able to tell us why we must have dates accompanying objects of antiquity to make them seem interesting and of value, whether these objects consist of furniture, a piece of pewter, or specimens coming from the graves of our early inhabitants. This paper is an attempt to give American Archæology an internal skeleton and thus to raise it to the status of a vertebrate.

It should be pointed out at once that the classification and nomenclature applied to European archæology cannot be used for the New World. This is not due to the scarcity of the data but to the fact that there are no metal ages in America. Iron was unknown as a metal before the advent of the white man[1] and the smelting of copper was not practised except in certain regions on the western coast of South America, Central America and parts of Mexico. Bronze, the resultant of a deliberate attempt at mixing copper and tin, was even less widely distributed.

There are two aspects of chronology the first of which is a relative one, self-contained, and dissociated with any larger aspect of time-relation. In northern New England and the maritime provinces of Canada as well as in other parts of the eastern United States, there are well-defined evidences of an earlier and a later pre-Columbian occupation, but there are at present no means of bringing these different cultures into the general background of history.

From Tozzer, "Chronological Aspects of American Archæology," *Proceedings of the Mass. Hist. Soc.,* Vol. LIX (Boston, 1926), pp. 283-292.

[1] The Eskimo made some use of meteoric iron.

The second variety of chronology and the one that has far more interest for us here has to do with definite epochs correlated with our own time-system, pre-historic passing over to the historic.

In the study of archæology as a whole there are four elements of control; geology, palæontology, stratigraphy, and the development of types from cruder to more developed forms. Geology and palæontology may be disregarded here as the question of primitive man in America, in the real sense of "first," does not concern us. No attempt will be made to prove or disprove the much-discussed question of the presence of man in the New World in geologically ancient times.

Stratification is of the utmost importance as showing successive occupation of the same site, each stratum indicating a more or less distinct culture allied with a time-element. In the Southwest, Dr. Kidder and Mr. Guernsey of the Peabody Museum have found four different levels of culture.[2] On the original floor of caves has been found the evidence of a people called "The Basket Makers" who were without pottery but were expert in the making of woven objects, textiles, baskets, and sandals. They were at the very horizon of agriculture with only one variety of corn. Above this there are data indicating two cultures differing slightly from each other with a first knowledge of pottery-making, this art developing rapidly. There are also included several varieties of corn indicating a more varied agricultural life. Finally there comes the top-most stratum, commonly called "Pueblo," with pottery and several of the other arts finely developed together with an abundant agriculture, developed under very adverse conditions. Until a few years ago, the Cliff-dwellers and other Pueblo peoples belonging to the last epoch, were the only early inhabitants recognized in this region. More intensive research has thus added three new elements in the archæology of the Southwest.

Stratification has also come to our assistance in Mexico.[3] Four and five meters below the present floor of the Valley of Mexico and in some cases under many feet of volcanic deposits there has come to light the so-called Archaic culture, characterized by crude clay figurines and several types of pottery. Most botanists interested in the question of the beginning of agriculture in America are now agreed that a grass, called *Teocentli,* found wild on the highlands of Mexico, is probably the progenitor of cultivated maize which the first American colonists found, on their advent, over the greater part of the New World. It is probable that

[2] Guernsey, S. J. and Kidder, A. V., Basket-maker caves in northeastern Arizona: *Papers of the Peabody Museum, Cambridge,* VIII. No. 2, 1921, and Kidder and Guernsey, Archaeological explorations in northeastern Arizona: *Bulletin 65, Bureau of American Ethnology,* Washington, 1919.

[3] Tozzer, A. M., The domain of the Aztecs and their relation to the prehistoric cultures of Mexico: *Holmes Anniversary Volume,* Washington, 1916. Spinden, H. J., Ancient civilizations of Mexico and Central America: *American Museum of Natural History,* (2d. ed.), New York, 1922.

the Archaic peoples were responsible for the artificial cultivation of this grass, the invention of agriculture, and also for the dissemination of this new industry over the arid portions of Mexico and Central America.[4] Figurines characteristic of the Archaic culture are found in many places as far south as Nicaragua and Costa Rica with modified types stretching into South America.

Returning to the Valley of Mexico, above the Archaic horizon is found the Toltec culture, the greatest of all Mexican civilizations, and over this and only for a few inches on the surface appear the evidences of the Aztecs. As will be shown later, the Aztec and Toltec periods can be definitely dated. Stratification also gives definite results on the succession of cultures in Peru, showing that of the Inca as a very late product.

The second chronological approach to the study of archæology is the investigation of the development of stylistic methods of decoration, mainly on pottery, of architecture, and of other products of man's activities. By an intensive study of the different ceramic wares of the Pueblo culture and after taking into account the various data available a definite sequence of pottery types and of decoration has been established from pre-Columbian down to modern times.[5]

When successive forms of the artistic impulse are found in connection with definite strata there is abundant proof of a time sequence as the basis of this development. When, as in the Maya area, various changes in architecture and in design go hand in hand with datable monuments, there is a solid foundation for history.

Another approach to this chronological study is the migration of objects far from their original place of manufacture, trade pieces, foreign to their present habitat but easily recognized as coming from afar. Red coral, for example, from the Mediterranean is found in graves of the early Iron Age in England. Dated Egyptian scarabs, found in Crete, were a great factor in establishing the entire chronology of the Aegean culture. The close association of objects in the same deposit prove that they are, in a sense, contemporaneous. This does not necessarily mean that they were made at the same time but that they were deposited at the same time. Heirloom pieces of carved jade, dating back several centuries, have been dredged from a great natural well in Yucatan. These are not later than the objects with which they are associated but, as a matter of fact, they are very much earlier than most of the associated remains. If sherds of a jar with a very special type of plaster cloisonné decoration are found in Pueblo Bonito in northern New Mexico and the home of this type of

---

[4] Spinden, H. J., The origin and spread of agriculture in America: *Proceedings of the 19th. International Congress of Americanists,* Washington, 1917.

[5] Kidder, A. V., An introduction to the study of Southwestern Archæology with a preliminary account of the excavations at Pecos; New Haven, 1924.

technique is in the Toltec culture in the Valley of Mexico, and, further-more, if this same pottery is found in a late period of a site in northern Yucatan, there is every reason to suppose that a contemporaneous feature can be assumed here. Movements in the other direction from the Maya region to the northward is shown by one of the finest of Maya jade orna-ments found at San Juan Teotihuacan. This probably originated in the southern part of the Maya area as it is carved in the best Old Empire style, travelling from Guatemala to northern Yucatan and thence to Mexico during the Toltec period of Yucatan. Gold figurines, definitely made in Colombia, Nicaragua, and Costa Rica and found in late Maya deposits, again help in the elucidation of a relative chronology. No metal objects of any kind have ever been found in the early Maya sites so that it seems quite clear that the knowledge of metallurgy came from the south at a comparatively late period.

These stray pieces also show the great importance of trade relations in early times, stretching in this case from Colombia in the south to northern New Mexico in the north, a distance of about thirty degrees of latitude or about three thousand miles.

The factors of stratification, stylistic development, and the association of objects from widely separated areas are all useful in establishing a relative chronology of a site or a series of sites but it is only by means of dated monuments correlated with Christian chronology that we arrive on satisfactory historical ground. The Maya area in southern Mexico and northern Central America presents evidence of an elaborate calendar as shown in the hieroglyphic inscriptions, the most remarkable achievement of the intellect in the New World. It is in these inscriptions that a litera-ture is provided American Archæology.

The material for the study of the hieroglyphic writing includes stone inscriptions carved on stelæ and altars set up in front of the various temples, on the door-lintels of buildings, a few painted inscriptions, three codices dating back to pre-Columbian times, and the so-called Books of Chilam Balam, manuscripts written in the Maya language but with Spanish characters. These are in many cases copies of original docu-ments reduced to writing after the advent of the Spaniards.[6]

There were two steps necessary in the elucidation of the Maya calendar as shown in the hieroglyphic inscriptions, the first of which was the determination of the calendar giving a relative chronology, the position of the different monuments in an inclusive series within the Maya area. This succession is definitely correlated with the stylistic development of stone

[6] Tozzer, A. M., The Chilam Balam Books and the possibility of their translation: *Proceedings of the 19th Interntional Congress of Americanists*, Washington, 1915. Also, Tozzer, A Maya Grammar: *Papers of the Peabody Museum*, Cambridge, IX. 182-192, 1921.

carving and of architecture. We are thus certain of the historical development of the Maya civilization.[7]

The second step was a correlation between the Maya and Christian chronology. In both these fields the late Charles P. Bowditch, long a member of this Society, played a very large part. From his pioneer work, so admirable and so necessary, advances have been made in this study by several others, among them being Mr. S. G. Morley of the Carnegie Institution, and Dr. H. J. Spinden of the Peabody Museum. The latter has shown conclusively that the Maya calendar began to function in 613 B.C.[8] The earliest dated inscription is on a small jade statuette of 96 B.C. The oldest Maya remains are found in the district of Petén in northern Guatemala. The great cities of this area flourished from about the beginning of the Christian Era until about 650 A.D. In the first half of the seventh century the southern cities seems to have been abandoned as no late dates appear there and a movement was made to the northward. Northern Yucatan was first populated about 450 A.D. and remained a center about two hundred years. The ancient chronicles in the Chilam Balam Books state that there was a period of abandonment of the northern part of this country from 630 to 960 A.D. when the sites in southern Yucatan were built. A great period of expansion in the north took place from 960 to about 1200 during which time a league of cities was formed. The most interesting period began about 1200 when foreigners entered the country. These were the Toltecs from Mexico under the leadership of Quetzalcoatl.

This figure was for a long time considered to have been purely mythological, dimly related to certain historical events, but, as is common in all culture-heroes, a vague and nebulous individual. Dr. Spinden has lately shown that Quetzalcoatl, far from being a myth, was a very real person—one of the great characters of history, "a warrior, a priest, an administrator, and a scientist." He served as leader of a force of Mexicans who put down a rebellion of the Mayas in 1191, subduing Chichen-Itza and making it a Toltec city. It was he who created much of the pomp and ceremony later used by the Aztec rulers and described with such vividness by the Spaniards.

The Toltecs brought with them a new religion and new art forms and the period from 1191 to 1450, when Mayapan fell and the Maya civiliza-

[7] Spinden, H. J., A Study of Maya Art: *Memoirs of the Peabody Museum,* VI. Cambridge, 1913.

[8] Bowditch, C. P., The numeration, Calendar systems and astronomical knowledge of the Mayas, Cambridge, 1910. Also by same author, On the age of the Maya ruins: *American Anthropologist,* (n. s.), III. 697-700. Morley, S. G., The inscriptions at Copan: *Carnegie Institution of Washington,* Washington, 1920, especially Appendix II. See also Morley's Bibliography in this volume. Spinden, H. J., The reduction of Mayan dates: *Papers of the Peabody Museum,* VI. No. 4, Cambridge, 1924, and other writings.

tion practically ceased to exist, was marked, especially at Chichen-Itza, by a very strong Mexican influence. This city has the longest *recorded* history of any in the New World, ancient or modern, of over eight hundred years.

The arrival of the Toltecs in Yucatan with definite dates on the Maya side enables us to supply them with a definite historical background, thus supplanting their mythological dates of origins and of migrations. The great empire of the Toltecs centering at San Juan Teotihuacan, thirty miles north of the present Mexico City, dates from about 1000 A.D. to 1200 A.D. Lesser sites in the Valley of Mexico continued to be occupied by these people until the coming of the Spaniards. The Toltecs had in their early days been strongly influenced by the early Maya culture in Guatemala which reached them from the south and west as shown by Maya details occurring at Monte Alban and Xochicalco. There was also a migration of Maya features northward along the coast of the Gulf of Mexico, reaching through the Totonacan area. The calendar of the Toltecs and later of the Aztecs undoubtedly was derived from that of the Mayas. The great expansion of the Toltec empire included practically all of the non-Maya peoples of central and southern Mexico, Guatemala, and as far south as Nicaragua and Costa Rica. Thus the Toltecs, receiving the seeds of culture and the calendar from the early and southern Mayas, later played a large part in shaping the destinies of the northern Mayas in the last period of their history.

The Aztecs who receive most of the credit in the popular mind for the achievements in cultural lines in Mexico were very late arrivals on the scene. They did not reach the shores of the lake on an island of which they were later to build their capital until 1325. They came as a wild hunting tribe from the north, remaining undisturbed until 1351 when they suffered defeat and enslavement at the hands of the Toltecs. Their period of expansion and preëminence did not begin until 1376 and even in 1519 under Montezuma they held only a fraction of the territory that was included in the Toltec empire in 1200. Every feature of their life was borrowed from the Toltecs and several of the Toltec cities in the Valley of Mexico never were completely subjugated by the Aztecs.

There are several dark spots in the picture I have tried to draw. We do not know what led the Mayas to abandon their great cities in the south and move northward. The exhaustion of cultivatable land may have been one of the reasons. We are also ignorant as to the events which led up to the fall of this civilization about 1450. Civil war, the injurious effects of the presence of foreigners, and, in all probability, epidemics of yellow fever were all possibly contributory.

The darkest spot, however, is our ignorance of the beginnings of the Maya peoples. It is certain that those responsible for this civilization were American natives and that their development is not due to any influence outside the New World. The impossibility that such a culture could grow up *in situ,* as it were, is always brought forward by those who think they see superficial similarities between the Mayas and certain Mongolian peoples. The calendar alone which no one has tried to prove originated outside of America shows the mental equipment of the Mayas, the presence of genius in their midst. A few naturally gifted individuals, a knowledge of agriculture, and a good environment are probably alone responsible for the beginnings of the Maya civilization.

It will be remembered that the Archaic peoples were probably at the horizon of agriculture and our next step must be to find a connection between them and the Mayas. There have never been found undisturbed contacts between these two peoples. This may be due to the comparatively small amount of actual excavation which has been undertaken in the older Maya sites. Archaic figurines appear in the Ulloa Valley in Honduras but they have been washed down from river-bank deposits and have seldom been found in their original positions. This is within the Maya area and there ought to be some possibility here of finding the two cultures, the Maya superimposed on the Archaic. Dr. S. K. Lothrop of the Heye Museum and Dr. Manuel Gamio have lately reported the presence of Archaic remains in Salvador and on the highlands of Guatemala and these discoveries may settle this question of contact which is pressing for an answer. There must, necessarily, have been long centuries of slow beginnings and small achievements by the early Maya before they burst upon the world about the beginning of the Christian Era with a highly developed civilization, characterized by great cities, an elaborate art and architecture, a highly organized theocracy, a remarkable astronomical knowledge, and a calendar system which was in actual operation for over 1900 years until it was destroyed by the Spaniards. Marginal corrections were applied to take care of the variation of the Maya year and of the true solar year, a means more accurate than our method of interpolating days. It should be pointed out that it was not until 1582 that the Julian day was invented, which corresponded to the Maya day count, 2000 years after the same principle had been adopted by the Mayas.

With the definite chronology thus established and its day-for-day correlation with the Mexican cultures, there is every reason to hope that with the study of the migrations of objects and stylistic contacts there will come a time when the sequences of cultures in our own Southwest and also those of the great civilizations of South America will be attached to the historical fabric.

Finally, as the result of modern research, a certain readjustment of values comes out clearly:—the small contribution made by the Aztecs to the ancient cultures of Mexico, the large part played by the Toltecs with their far-reaching empire, and the far greater primary impetus and development of a great civilization with astronomical knowledge and a calendar by the Mayas who handed all this on to the other peoples of Middle America.

If there are included in our history the present inhabitants of Yucatan and the Lacandones of Guatemala, also a Maya people, who still carry out many of the pre-Columbian religious practices, a definite historical background has been supplied to American Archæology, starting in the sixth century before Christ and extending in an unbroken series for over 2500 years.

FRANZ BOAS

(1858-1942)

One of the less well-known aspects of Boas' career was his work as a museum curator, yet it is one of the fields in which he was most successful both in the development of his theories and in the influence which he exerted on museum technique in America.

Boas first became involved in this aspect of museum work when he supervised the arrangement of ethnological collections for the Chicago Columbian Exposition in 1893—the collections which became the nucleus of the Field Museum. After this he came to the American Museum of Natural History, where his first task was the installation, in the now-famous Northwest Coast Hall, of the Bishop collection of materials gathered in British Columbia by J. W. Powell in 1882. He went on to arrange other North American Indian collections. These halls marked a departure in museum technique by grouping together—stressing ethnic rather than typological connections—all the materials from one tribe or one area to illustrate a way of life. The older principle of arrangement, followed by Mason at the National Museum, grouped together all objects of a given type, regardless of origin—all baskets, textiles, pottery, etc. Boas' arrangements provided a model for all subsequent collections at the Museum of Natural History and other ethnological museums throughout the country, and even influenced European museums (e.g. the new importance given to ethnic groupings in the recent rearrangement of the Musèe de l'homme *in Paris). Many refinements in techniques of display have been introduced since Boas' day—habitat groups, dramatic lighting and sound effects, the almost total elimination of cases so that the spectator goes into the collection instead of looking at it—but they have simply served to emphasize Boas' principles.*

Boas' approach to museum problems reflects some of his most strongly held convictions: his concern with man and man's way of living in the world, and, as a corollary of this preoccupation, his concern with culture wholes and the interrelationship of their parts—in this case all the objects used by any group of people. He grouped together baskets and canoes and ceremonial paraphernalia as material expressions of a unique style of life. The second theme he stressed in his grouping of halls was the

305

importance of geographical relationships and the point he frequently spelled out in his writing and teaching, that more can be learned about cultural processes by a study of variants within a continuous geographical area than by juxtaposing elements showing formal similarity but having no known genetic connection. Out of this heuristic device of grouping together geographically related cultures for purposes of comparison came the germs of the culture-area concept.

The fantastic style of Northwest Coast art, so different from the simplicity of Eskimo carving, was one of the things that first attracted Boas to the Northwest Coast cultures. What thought lay behind these grotesque distortions, these superimpositions of animal forms, this elaboration and proliferation of ornament over the whole decorative field? Boas wrote his first study of the art of the North Pacific Coast, in 1897. He rewrote it several times. The last and fullest treatment is contained in his book, Primitive Art *(1927). He did not change his ideas or his interpretations, but continued to incorporate new material out of his delight in the limitless ingenuity of the artists in decorating their spoon handles or bracelets or dance hats or house fronts.—R.L.B.*

The Decorative Art of the North Pacific Coast

IT HAS BEEN SHOWN THAT THE MOTIVES OF THE DECORATIVE ART OF MANY peoples developed largely from representations of animals. In course of time, forms that were originally realistic became more and more sketchy, and more and more distorted. Details, even large proportions, of the subject so represented were omitted, until finally the design attained a purely geometric character.

The decorative art of the Indians of the North Pacific Coast agrees with this oft-observed phenomenon in that its subjects are almost exclusively animals. It differs from other arts in that the process of conventionalizing has not led to the development of geometric designs, but that the parts of the animal body may still be recognized as such. The body of the animal, however, undergoes very fundamental changes in the arrangement and size of its parts. In the following paper I shall describe the characteristics of these changes, and discuss the mental attitude of the artist which led to their development.

From Franz Boas, "The Decorative Art of the Indians of the North Pacific Coast," *Bulletin of the American Museum of Natural History*, Volume 9, pages 123-176, 1897.—The tribes are the Tlingit, Haida, Tsimshian, Bella Coola, Kwakiutl, etc.

In treating this subject, we must bear in mind that almost all the plastic art of the Indians of the North Pacific Coast is decorative art. While some primitive people—for instance, the Eskimo—produce carvings which serve no practical ends, but are purely works of art, all the works of the Indian artists of the region which we are considering serve at the same time a useful end; that is to say, the form of the object is given, and the subject to be represented is more or less subordinate to the object on which it is shown. Only in the cases of single totemic figures is the artist free to mold his subject without regard to such considerations; but, owing to the large size of such figures, he is limited by the cylindrical form of the trunk of the tree from which he carves his figures. We may therefore say that the native artist is in almost all his works limited by the shape of the object on which he represents his subject.

The plastic arts of the Indians are carving and painting, in which latter we may include tattooing and weaving. Carving is done mostly in wood, but also in stone and horn. It is either in the round, bas-relief, or, although more rarely, in high relief. There is no art of pottery. . . .

Generally the object to be decorated has a certain given form to which the decoration must be subordinated, and the artist is confronted with the problem of how to adjust his subject to the form of the object to be decorated.

Before attempting an explanation of the method adopted by the artist in the solution of this problem, we must treat another aspect of our subject. We must premise that in consequence of the adaptation of the form to the decorative field, the native artist cannot attempt a realistic representation of his subject, but is often compelled to indicate only its main characteristics. In consequence of the distortion of the animal body, due to its adaptation to various surfaces, it would be all but impossible to recognize what animal is meant, if the artist did not emphasize what he considers the characteristic features of animals. These are so essential to his mind that he considers no representation adequate in which they are missing. In many cases they become the symbols of the animal. We find, therefore, that each animal is characterized by certain symbols, and great latitude is allowed in the treatment of all features other than symbols.

I will illustrate this feature of the art of the Indians of the North Pacific Coast by means of a number of characteristic examples.

Figure 6 is a figure from a totem pole, which represents the beaver. It will be noticed that the face is treated somewhat like a human face, particularly the region around eyes and nose. The position of the ears, however, indicates that the artist intended to represent an animal head, not a human head. While the human ear is represented, in its characteristic form, on a level with the eye, animal ears are indicated over the forehead; that is to say, approximately in the position in which they appear in a front view of the animal. Their characteristic shape may be seen in figure 6, and in many others. While the ears characterize the head as that of an animal, the two large incisors serve to identify the rodent *par excellence*—the beaver. The tail of the animal is turned up in front of its body. It is ornamented by cross-hatching, which is intended to represent the scales on the beaver's tail. In its fore paws it holds a stick. The large incisors, the tail with cross-hatching, and the stick, are symbols of the beaver, and each of these is a sufficient characteristic of the animal. . . .

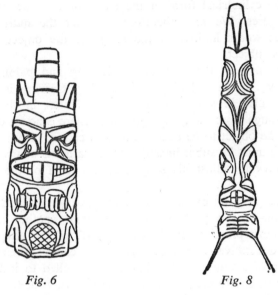

Fig. 6   Fig. 8

CARVINGS REPRESENTING THE BEAVER.

In figure 8, which is the handle of a spoon, we find only the first of the symbols of the beaver represented, namely, its incisors. Only the head and the forepaws of the animal are shown; and in its mouth are indicated an upper and a lower pair of incisors, all the other teeth being omitted. There is nothing except the teeth to indicate that the artist intended to represent the beaver.

Figure 9 is the front of a dancing head-dress, which is attached to a framework made of whalebone, and set on top with bristles of the sea-lion. To the back is attached a long train of ermine skins. The outer side of the carved front is set with abalone shells. The squatting figure which occupies the center of the front represents the beaver. The same symbols which were mentioned before will be recognized here. The face is human; but the ears, which rise over the eyebrows, indicate that an animal is meant. Two large pairs of incisors occupy the center of the open mouth. The tail is turned up in front of the body, and appears between the two hind legs, indicated by cross-hatching. The fore paws are raised to the height of the mouth, but they do not hold a stick. It will be noticed that on the chest of the beaver another head is represented, over which a number of small rings stretch towards the chin of the beaver. Two feet, which belong to this animal, extend from the corners of its mouth towards the haunches of the beaver. This animal represents the dragon-fly, which is symbolized by a large head and a slender segmented body. In many representations of the dragonfly there are two pairs of wings attached to the head. The face of this animal resembles also a human face; but the two ears, which rise over the eyebrows, indicate that an animal is meant. Combinations of two animals of this sort are found very frequently, a smaller figure of one animal being represented on the chest of a large carving. . . .

Fig. 9. HEADDRESS REPRESENTING A BEAVER. THE DRAGON-FLY IS SHOWN ON THE CHEST OF THE BEAVER. TRIBE, HAIDA.

Figures 18 and 19 are representations of the killer-whale. In the rattle (Fig. 18) the form of the whale will be easily recognized. Its tail is bent downward. The large head, one of the characteristic features of the whale, is much more pronounced in this than in the next figure. The eye appears on the front part of the rattle. Under the eye we see the large mouth, which is set with a number of curved spines. They

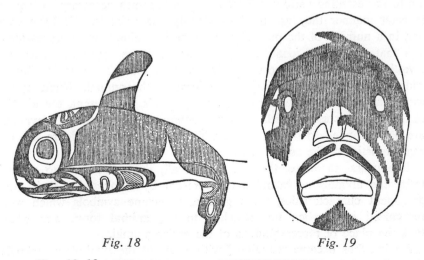

Fig. 18   *Fig. 19*

Figs. 18, 19. RATTLE AND MASK REPRESENTING THE KILLER-WHALE.

are intended to represent the teeth. Immediately behind the mouth, on the lower part of the carving, we find the flippers. The painted ornament, which has the form of a small face, in front of the huge dorsal fin, is intended to represent the blow-hole. . . .

Animals are characterized by their symbols, and the following series of symbols have been described in the preceding remarks:

1. Of the *beaver:* large incisors, scaly tail, and a stick held in the forepaws.

2. Of the *sculpin:* two spines rising over the mouth, and a continuous dorsal fin.

3. Of the *hawk:* large curved beak, the point of which is turned backward so that it touches the face.

4. Of the *eagle:* large curved beak, the point of which is turned downward.

5. Of the *killer-whale:* large head, large mouth set with teeth, blow-hole, and large dorsal fin.

6. Of the *shark:* an elongated rounded cone rising over the forehead, mouth with depressed corners, a series of curved lines on the cheeks, two circles and curved lines on the ornament rising over the forehead, round eyes, numerous sharp teeth, and heterocerc tail.

7. Of the *bear:* large paws, and large mouth set with teeth, with protruding tongue.

8. Of the *sea-monster:* bear's head, bear's paws with flippers attached, and gills and body of the killer-whale, with several dorsal fins.

9. Of the *dragon-fly:* large head, segmented, slender body, and wings.

So far I have considered the symbols only in connection with their use in representing various animals. It now becomes necessary to inquire in what manner they are used to identify the animals. We have seen that in a number of the preceding cases entire animals were represented, and that they were identified by means of these symbols. When we investigate this subject more closely, we find that the artist is allowed wide latitude in the selection of the form of the animal. Whatever the form may be, as long as the recognized symbols are present, the identity of the animal is established. We have mentioned before that the symbols arc often applied to human faces, while the body of the figure has the characteristics of the animal. . . .

It appears, therefore, that as, first of all, the artist tried to characterize the animals he intended to represent by emphasizing their most prominent characteristics, these gradually became symbols which were recognized even when not attached to the animal form, and which took the place of representations of the entire animal.

Having thus become acquainted with a few of the symbols of animals, we will next investigate in what manner the native artist adapted the animal form to the object he intended to decorate. First of all, we will direct our attention to a series of specimens which show that the native artist endeavors, whenever possible, to represent the whole animal on the object that he desires to decorate.

Figure 31 is a club used for killing seals and halibut before they are landed in the canoe. The carving represents the killer-whale. If the principal symbol of the killer-whale, its dorsal fin, were placed in an upright position on the club, the implement would assume an exceedingly awkward shape. On the other hand, the artist could not omit the dorsal fin, since it is the most important symbol of the animal. Therefore he has bent it downward along the side of the body, so that it covers the flippers. The tail of the whale would have interfered with the handle, and for this reason it has been turned forward over the back of the whale, so as to be in close contact with the body. . . .

Fig. 31. TLINGIT CLUB REPRESENTING THE KILLER-WHALE.

We have now to treat a series of peculiar phenomena which result from the endeavor on the part of the artist to adjust the animal that he desires to represent to the decorative field in such a manner as to preserve as far as possible the whole animal, and bring out its symbols most clearly.

Figure 39 is the top view of a wooden hat on which is carved the figure of a sculpin. The animal is shown in top view, as though it were lying with its lower side on the hat. The dancing hats of these Indians have the forms of truncated cones. To the top are attached a series of rings, mostly made of basketry, which indicate the social rank of the owner, each ring symbolizing a step in the social ladder. The top of the hat, therefore, does not belong to the decorative field, which is confined to the surface of the cone. The artist found it necessary, therefore, to open the back of the sculpin far enough to make room for the gap in the decorative field. He has done so by representing the animal as seen from the top, but split and distended in the middle, so that the top of the hat is located in the opening thus secured.

Figure 40 represents a dish in the shape of a seal. The whole dish is carved in the form of the animal; but the bottom, which corresponds to the belly, is flattened, and the back is hollowed out so as to form the bowl of the dish. In order to gain a wider rim the whole back has been distended so that the animal becomes inordinately wide as compared to its length. The flippers are carved in their proper positions

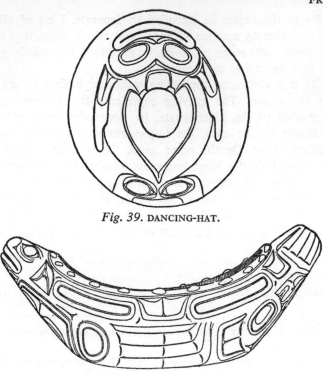

Fig. 39. DANCING-HAT.

Fig. 40. GREASE-DISH: SEAL.

at the sides of the dish. The hind flippers are turned back, and closely join the tail. A similar method of representation is used in decorating small boxes. The whole box is considered as representing an animal. The front of its body is painted or carved on the box front; its sides, on the sides of the box; the hind side of its body, on the back of the box. The bottom of the box is the animal's stomach; the top, or the open upper side, its back. These boxes, therefore, are decorated only on the sides, which are bent of a single piece of wood (Fig. 41). When we unbend the sides we find the decoration extended on a long band, which we may consider as consisting of two symmetrical halves. The center is occupied by the front view of the animal, the sides by a side view, and the ends by one-half of the hind view at each end of the board. An actual unbending of the sides of the box would not give a symmetrical form; but, since the ends are necessarily sewed at the corner, the hind view of the body will occupy one end.

In the decoration of silver bracelets a similar principle is followed, but the problem differs somewhat from that offered in the decoration of square boxes. While in the latter case the four edges make a natural division between the four views of the animal—front and right profile, back and left profile—there is no such sharp line of division in the round bracelet, and there would be great difficulty in joining the four aspects artistically, while two profiles offer no such difficulty. When the tail end of each profile is placed where the ends of the bracelet join, then there is only one point of junction; namely, in the median line of the head. This is the method of representation that the native artists have adopted (Fig. 42). The animal is cut in two from head to tail, so that the two halves cohere only at the tip of the nose and at the tip of the tail. The hand is put through this hole, and the animal now surrounds the wrist. In this position it is represented on the bracelet. The method adopted is therefore identical with the one applied in the hat (Fig. 39), except that the central opening is much larger, and that the animal has been represented on a cylindrical surface, not a conical one.

An examination of the head of the bear shown on the bracelet (Fig. 42), makes it clear that this idea has been carried out rigidly. It will be noticed that there is a deep depression between the eyes, extending down to the nose. This shows that the head itself must not be considered a front view, but as consisting of two profiles which adjoin at mouth and nose, while they are not in contact with each other on a level with the eyes and forehead. The peculiar ornament rising over the nose of the bear decorated with three rings, represents a hat with three rings, which designate the rank of the bearer. . . .

The transition from the bracelet to the painting or carving of animals on a flat surface is not a difficult one. The same principle is adhered to; and either the animals are represented as split in two so that the profiles

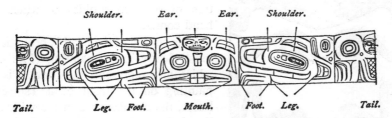

Fig. 41. CARVING ON THE SIDES OF A DISH, REPRESENTING A BEAVER. THE SIDES OF THE DISH ARE BENT OF A SINGLE PIECE OF WOOD, AND ARE SHOWN HERE FLATTENED OUT.

Fig. 42. DESIGN ON A BRACELET REPRESENTING A BEAR.

are joined in the middle, or a front view of the head is shown with two adjoining profiles of the body. In the cases considered heretofore the animal was cut through and through from the mouth to the tip of the tail. These points were allowed to cohere, and the animal was stretched over a ring, a cone, or the sides of a prism. If we imagine the bracelet opened, and flattened in the manner in which it is shown in figure 42, we have a section of the animal from mouth to tail, cohering only at the mouth, and the two halves spread over a flat surface. This is the natural development of the method here described when applied to the decoration of flat surfaces.

It is clear that on flat surfaces this method allows of modifications by changing the method of cutting. When the body of a long animal, such as that of a fish or of a standing quadruped, is cut in this manner, a design results which forms a long narrow strip. This mode of cutting is therefore mostly applied in the decoration of long bands. When the field that is to be decorated is more nearly square, this form is not favorable. In such cases a square design is obtained by cutting quadrupeds sitting on their haunches in the same manner as before, and unfolding the animal so that the two halves remain in contact at the nose and mouth, while the median line at the back is to the extreme right and to the extreme left.

Fig. 43. PAINTING REPRESENTING A BEAR. TRIBE, HAIDA.

Figure 43 (a Haida painting) shows a design which has been obtained in this manner. It represents a bear. The enormous breadth of mouth observed in these cases is brought about by the junction of the two profiles of which the head consists.

This cutting of the head is brought out most clearly in the painting (Fig. 44), which also represents the bear. It is the painting on the front of a Tsimshian horse, the circular hole in the middle of the design being the door of the house. The animal is cut from back to front, so that only the front part of the head coheres. The two halves of the lower jaw do not touch each other. The back is represented by the black outline on which the hair is indicated by fine lines. . . .

In the following figures we find a new cut applied. Figure 53 represents the shark. I explained, when discussing the symbols of the shark, that in the front view of the animal the symbols are shown to best advantage. For this reason side views of the face of the shark are avoided, and in representing the whole animal a cut is made from the back to the lower side, and the two sides are unfolded, leaving the head in front view.

The painting (Fig. 53) has been made in this manner, the two halves of the body being entirely separated from each other, and folded to the right and to the left. The heterocerc tail is cut in halves, and is shown at each end turned downward. The pectoral fins are shown unduly enlarged, in order to fill the vacant space under the head. . . .

In figure 62, which represents the design on a circular slate dish, we see a good case of the adaptation of a profile to the decorative field. The design represents a killer-whale with two dorsal fins. The animal is bent around the rim of a dish so that the

Fig. 44. PAINTING FROM A HOUSE-FRONT, REPRESENTING A BEAR.

head touches the tail. The two dorsal fins are laid flat along the back, while the large flipper occupies the center of the dish. . . .

I have described a number of sections applied in representing various animals. Heretofore we have had cases only in which the sections were rather simple. In many cases in which the adaptation of the animal form to the decorative field is more difficult, the sections and distortions are much more numerous and far-reaching than those described before. . . .

We can now sum up the results of our considerations. In the first part of this paper I described the symbols of a number of animals, and pointed out that in many cases there is a tendency to substitute the

Fig. 53. PAINTING REPRESENTING A SHARK. TRIBE, HAIDA.

symbol for the whole animal. The works of art which I describe in the second part of my paper may be said to illustrate a principle which is apparently diametrically opposed to the former. While the symbolism developed a tendency to suppress parts of the animal, we find in the efforts of the artist to adapt the form of the animal to the decorative field a far-reaching desire to preserve, so far as feasible, the whole animal; and, with the exception of a few profiles, we do not find a

Fig. 62. SLATE DISH WITH KILLER-WHALE
DESIGN. TRIBE, HAIDA.

single instance which can be interpreted as an endeavor to give a perspective and therefore realistic view of an animal. We have found a variety of methods applied which tend to bring the greatest possible part of the animal form into the decorative field. I conclude from this that it is the ideal of the native artist to show the whole animal, and that the idea of perspective representation is entirely foreign to his mind. His representations are combinations of symbols of the various parts of the body of the animal, arranged in such a way that if possible the whole animal is brought into view. The arrangement, however, is so that the natural relation of the parts is preserved, being changed only by means of sections and distortions, but so that the natural contiguity of the parts is preserved.

The success of the artist depends upon his cleverness in designing lines of dissection and methods of distortion. When he finds it impossible to represent the whole animal, he confines himself to rearranging its most characteristic parts, always of course including its symbols. There is a tendency to exaggerate the size of the symbols at the expense of other parts of the subject. I presume this is the line in which the two principles of the decorative art of the Indians of the North Pacific Coast of America merge into each other. The gradual emphasizing of the symbol at the expense of other parts of the body leads in many cases to their entire suppression, and to designs in which the animal is indicated only by its symbols.

The Jesup North Pacific Expedition

WALDEMAR BOGORAS
(Vladimir Germanovich Bogoraz)
(1865-1936)

WALDEMAR JOCHELSON
(1852-1937)

The aim of the Jesup Expedition was to explore the cultural connections between the Northwest Coast of North America and Northeastern Siberia. For the Siberian material the Museum enlisted the services of two involuntary residents of that area. Banished in their youth to Northeastern Siberia because of revolutionary activities, Waldemar Bogoras and Waldemar Jochelson had put in their years of exile studying the native people around them. Exile in Siberia did not in those days mean confinement; both men had traveled widely throughout Yakutsk province and apparently had no difficulty in arranging their employment by the Museum or in transmitting their manuscripts.

After the Revolution of 1917 Bogoras returned to Russia to the Institute of Ethnography in Leningrad. There he set up a museum of comparative religion (it was called the Museum of Atheism). Jochelson came to New York to finish work on his Yukaghir ethnology, publication of which had been interrupted by the War.

Exile, however distressing to the individual concerned and however deplorable from the ethical point of view, sometimes has its compensations for anthropologists. It is not likely that under other conditions Bogoras' great monograph on the Chukchee would have been written with quite its fullness of detail and we would have been without knowledge of one of the world's most distinctive cultures. (Just as later Malinowski's studies of the Trobriand Islands would not have been written as they were had he not been interned there for four years during World War I.)

The somberness of the Chukchee contrasts with the prevailing cheerfulness of the Eskimo. For the Chukchee the Arctic is not friendly; their world is peopled with several categories of hostile spirits who must constantly be appeased. The Chukchee of Siberia are the antithesis of the happy carefree savage. Anxiety is their normal state. Violence, mental breakdown and suicide are frequent among them.

Out of the Siberian researches a new concept of global cultural relationships emerged: that of a circum-polar culture which spanned two hemispheres and which, in spite of temperamental differences, had many consistent traits, both material and psychological.—R.L.B.

WALDEMAR BOGORAS

(1865-1936)

The Chukchee

SHAMANISM

SHAMANISM IS NOT RESTRICTED TO EITHER SEX. THE GIFT OF INSPIRATION is thought to be bestowed more frequently upon women, but it is reputed to be of a rather inferior kind, and the higher grades belong rather to men. The reason given for this is, that the bearing of children is generally adverse to shamanistic inspiration, so that a young woman with considerable shamanistic power may lose the greater part of it after the birth of her first child. She will recover it only after several years,—with the ending of the period of her maternity. It is also considered that all material objects in any way connected with the birth either of animals or of mankind may be detrimental to the shamanistic force, not only in women, but even in men who happen to come in contact with them. Thus, the grass which served for bedding to a woman in labor may be used to destroy the shamanistic power of any young man slowly "gathering inspiration." It need only be rubbed against the forehead of the young shaman during his sleep, and he will "come back" (to the usual life). A female shaman, by name Te′lpiñä, complained to me, in her description of "things seen by her," that her mother-in-law, seeing that she would be a great female shaman, gave her to drink of the amniotic fluid of a bitch. This injured her vitals, and the soul of the dog entered her own soul.

Since female shamanism is thought to be of an inferior order, it is considered to require a shorter period for "gathering inspiration," and to be attended with less pain, than male shamanism. Female shamans, however, may acquire a high degree of skill in almost any branch of shamanistic action, with the single exception of the ventriloquistic art, which is considered entirely beyond their reach.

From Bogoras, *The Chukchee*, The Jesup North Pacific Expedition, edited by Franz Boas, *Memoirs of the American Museum of Natural History*, Vol. VII (New York: 1904-1909), pp. 415-419, 424-425, 429-430, 507-508, 560-562.

The shamanistic call begins to manifest itself at an early age, in many cases during the critical period of transition from childhood to youth. It is also the period of rapid and intense growth; and it is well known that many persons of both sexes manifest during this time increased sensitiveness, and that the mind often becomes unbalanced. It is easy to understand that this critical period of human life, which is always full of unexpected changes and developments, is peculiarly adapted to the first implanting of shamanistic inspiration.

Nervous and highly excitable temperaments are most susceptible to the shamanistic call. The shamans among the Chukchee with whom I conversed were as a rule extremely excitable, almost hysterical, and not a few of them were half crazy. Their cunning in the use of deceit in their art closely resembled the cunning of a lunatic.

The Chukchee say that young persons destined to receive shamanistic inspiration may be recognized at a very early age, even in their teens, by the gaze, which, during a conversation, is not turned to the listener, but is fixed on something beyond him. In connection with this, they say that the eyes of a shaman have a look different from that of other people, and they explain it by the assertion that the eyes of the shaman are very bright, which, by the way, gives them the ability to see "spirits" even in the dark. It is certainly a fact that the expression of a shaman is peculiar,—a combination of cunning and shyness; and by this it is often possible to pick him out from among many others.

The Chukchee are well aware of the extreme nervousness of their shamans, and express it by the word nιñι′rkιlqin ("he is bashful"). By this word they mean to convey the idea that the shaman is highly sensitive even to the slightest change of the psychic atmosphere surrounding him during his exercises. For instance, the Chukchee shaman is diffident in acting before strangers, especially shortly after his initiation. A shaman of great power will refuse to show his skill when among strangers, and will yield only after much solicitation: even then, as a rule, he will not show all of his power. He is shy of strange people, of a house to which he is unaccustomed, of "alien" drums and charms which are hidden in their bags, and of "spirits" that hover around. The least doubt or sneer makes him break off the performance and retire.

The shamanistic "spirits" are likewise described as "fleeting" meaning that they want to flee before every unusual face or voice. When too many strange visitors come to the shaman, the "spirits" are shy of appearing, and, even when they do come, they are all the time anxious to slip away. Once when I induced a shaman to practise at my house, his "spirits" (of a ventriloquistic kind) for a long time refused to come. When at last they did come, they were heard walking around the house outside and knocking on its walls, as if still undecided whether to enter. When they entered, they kept near to the corners, carefully avoiding too close proximity to those present.

"Ke'let (spirits) belong to the wilderness," say the shamans, "just as much as any wild animal. This is the reason that they are so fleeting." Ke'let of the animal kind have this shyness to an extreme degree. When coming at the call of the shaman, they sniff and snort, and finally, after some short exercise on the drum, flee back to the freedom of the wilderness. All this, of course, is brought about by ventriloquism, as will be described later. Even the ke'let of diseases, especially those who cannot harm man much,—as, for instance, rheum or cold,—are described as very "fleeting." Thus, in one tale, the rheum, before mustering sufficient courage to enter a human habitation, makes several attempts, and each time goes back overcome by its shyness. When caught on the spot, it manifests the utmost fear, and in abject terms begs for freedom.

The Chukchee generally are highly susceptible to any physical or psychical impressions of a kind to which they are unused; as, for instance, to unfamiliar odors. This is especially the case in regard to diseases; and the saying, "The Chukchee people are 'soft to die,' " is frequently heard among them. Thus, though they are able to endure excessive hardships, they succumb quickly to any contagious disease brought from civilized countries. This sensitiveness is shared by other native tribes of northeastern Siberia, and even by the Russian creoles, who are just as susceptible to psychic influences of an unusual character; for instance, to warning received in dreams or from strange people, to threats on the part of shamans or high officials, etc. During the last epidemic of measles, a creole in Gishiga lived but one night after having been told by an official, who meant no harm, that in a dream he had seen him die. There have been several instances of suicide among the cossacks and Russianized natives as the result of reproof on the part of officials. In other cases, native guides of Lamut or Yukaghir origin, travelling with parties of Russian officials on exploring expeditions, have, on losing their way in the uninhabited country, run away from fear and despair, and every trace of them thereafter has been lost. Suicides are also frequent among the Chukchee.

It seems to me that Mr. Jochelson has in mind the same high degree of susceptibility when he calls attention to the fact that the young men of the Yukaghir were said in ancient times to be exceedingly bashful, so much so that they would die when a sudden affront was given them, even by their own relatives. The shamans possess this nervous sensitiveness in a still higher degree than other people. This finds expression in the proverb that shamans are even more "soft to die" than ordinary people.

While speaking of this subject, let me add, that the slightest lack of harmony between the acts of the shamans and the mysterious call of their "spirits" brings their life to an end. This is expressed by the Chukchee when they say that "spirits" are very bad-tempered, and punish with immediate death the slightest disobedience of the shaman, and that this is particularly so when the shaman is slow to carry out those orders which are intended to single him out from other people.

On the other hand, apart from the displeasure of his ke'let, a shaman is said to be "resistant to death" and especially "difficult to kill," even when vanquished by enemies. . . .

The shamanistic call manifests itself in various ways. Sometimes it is an inner voice, which bids the person enter into intercourse with the "spirits." If the person is dilatory in obeying, the calling "spirit" soon appears in some outward, visible shape, and communicates the call in a more explicit way. For instance, Aiñanwa't, whom I have mentioned before, says that at one time, after a severe illness, when his soul was ripe for inspiration, he saw several "spirits," but did not give much heed to the fulfilment of their orders. Then a "spirit" came to him. He was gaunt, and black of color, and said that he was the "spirit" of reindeer-scab. Aiñanwa't felt himself very much drawn toward that "spirit," and wanted him to stay and become his constant companion. The "spirit" hesitated at first, and then refused to stay. He said, however, "I may consent, if your desire for my company is strong enough,—if you wish me enough to take the drum, to handle it for three days and three nights, and to become a shaman." Aiñanwa't, in his turn, refused, and the "spirit" immediately vanished.

The shamanistic call is also manifested by various omens, such as meeting a certain animal, finding a stone or a shell of peculiar form, etc. Each of these omens has in itself nothing extraordinary, but derives its significance from its mystical recognizance in the mind of the person to whose notice it is brought. This process resembles the finding of amulets; and, indeed, the stone found, or the animal met, becomes the protector and the assistant "spirit" of the person in question.

Young people, as a rule, are exceedingly reluctant to obey the call, especially if it involves the adoption of some characteristic device in clothing or in the mode of life. They refuse to take the drum and to call the "spirits," leave the amulets in the field, from very fear,[1] etc.

The parents of young persons "doomed to inspiration" act differently, according to temperament and family conditions. Sometimes they protest against the call coming to their child, and try to induce it to reject the "spirits" and to keep to the ordinary life. This happens mostly in the case of only children, because of the danger pertaining to the shamanistic call, especially in the beginning. The protest of the parents is, however, of no avail, because the rejection of the "spirits" is much more dangerous even

[1] Compare also the story in Krasheninnikoff in which it is told that a Koryak found an important amulet on the bank of the river, but left it there from sheer fright. He became very ill, and his illness was ascribed to the anger of the amulet. After a considerable lapse of time he came back to look for the amulet, and at last carried it away with him.

than the acceptance of their call. A young man thwarted in his call to inspiration will either sicken and shortly die, or else the "spirits" will induce him to renounce his home and go far away, where he may follow his vocation without hindrance.

On the other hand, it is entirely permissible to abandon shamanistic performances at a more mature age, after several years of practice; and the anger of the "spirits" is not incurred by it. I met several persons who asserted that formerly they had been great shamans, but that now they had given up most of their exercises. As reason for this, they gave illness, age, or simply a decrease of their shamanistic power, which in the course of time manifested itself. One said that because of illness he felt as if his arms and legs were frozen, and that thereafter they did not thaw, so that he was unable to "shake himself" well upon the drum. Another said that he and his "spirits" became tired of each other. Most of the cases, probably, were simply the result of recovery from the nervous condition which had made the persons in question fit subjects for the inspiration. While the shaman is in possession of the inspiration, he must practise, and cannot hide his power. Otherwise it will manifest itself in the form of bloody sweat or in a fit of violent madness similar to epilepsy.

There are parents who wish their child to answer the call. This happens especially in families rich in children, with large herds, and with several tents of their own. Such a family is not inclined to feel anxious about a possible loss of one of its members. On the contrary, they are desirous of having a shaman of their own,—made to order, so to speak,—a special solicitor before the "spirits," and a caretaker in all extraordinary casualties of life.

A shaman by the name of Tei'ñet, in the country near the Wolverene River, told me that, when the call came to him and he did not want to obey, his father gave him the drum and induced him to begin the exercise. After that, he continued to feel "bashful" for several years. On days of ceremonials he even fled from the camp and hid himself, lest his relatives should find him out and bring him back to camp, to show to the assembled people his newly acquired and growing skill.

For men, the preparatory stage of shamanistic inspiration is in most cases very painful, and extends over a long time. The call comes in an abrupt and obscure manner, leaving the young novice in much uncertainty regarding it. He feels "bashful" and frightened; he doubts his own disposition and strength, as has been the case with all seers, from Moses down. Half unconsciously and half against his own will, his whole soul undergoes a strange and painful transformation. This period may last months, and sometimes even years. The young novice, the "newly inspired" loses all interest in the ordinary affairs of life. He ceases to work, eats but little and without relishing the food, ceases to talk to people, and does not even answer their questions. The greater part of his time he spends in sleep. . . .

The single means used by the Chukchee shamans, novice or experienced, for communication with "spirits," is the beating of the drum and singing. As said before, the usual family drum is employed with a drumstick of whalebone, while a wooden drum-stick is used chiefly in ceremonials. Some drums have two whalebone drum-sticks, of which the extra one is supposed to be intended for the use of "spirits," when they approach and want to "shake themselves;" that is, to beat the drum.

The beating of the drum, notwithstanding its seeming simplicity, requires some skill, and the novice must spend considerable time before he can acquire the desired degree of perfection. This has reference especially to the power of endurance of the performer. The same may be said of the singing. The manifestations continue for several hours, during all which time the shaman exercises the most violent activity without scarcely a pause. After the performance he must not show any signs of fatigue, because he is supposed to be sustained by the "spirits;" and, moreover, the greater part of the exercise is asserted to be the work of the "spirits" themselves, either while entering his body, or while outside his body. The degree of endurance required for all this, and the ability to pass quickly from the highest excitement to a state of normal quietude, can, of course, be acquired only by long practice. Indeed, all the shamans I conversed with said that they had to spend a year, or even two years, before sufficient strength of hand, and freedom of voice, were given to them by the "spirits." Some asserted that during all this preparatory time they kept closely to the inner room, taking up the drum several times a day, and beating it as long as their strength would allow.

The only other means of training for inspiration, of which I am aware, is abstention from all fat and rich foods, as well as great moderation in eating. The same strictness is observed ever afterwards in the preparation for each individual performance, in which the shaman tries to abstain wholly from food.

Various tricks performed by the Chukchee shamans, including ventriloquism, have to be learned in the preparatory stage. However, I could obtain no detailed information on this point, since the shamans, of course, asserted that the tricks were done by "spirits," and denied having any hand whatever in proceedings of such a character.

In some cases, evidently, the old men have taught the younger generation, who are said to have received their power from them. The transfer is final, and cannot be revoked. The man who gives a part of his power to another man loses correspondingly, and can hardly recover the loss afterwards. To transfer his power, the older shaman must blow on the eyes or into the mouth of the recipient, or he may stab himself with a knife, with the blade of which, still reeking with his "source of life," he will immedi-

ately pierce the body of the recipient. These methods are also supposed
to be used by shamans in the treatment of their patients.

Most of the shamans I knew claimed to have had no teachers, but to
have acquired their art by their own individual efforts. I am not aware of
a single instance of the transfer of shamanistic power in the whole domain
of Chukchee folk-lore. Among the Eskimo, I met women who had learned
their shamanistic performances from their husbands, and children who
had been taught by their parents. In one family on St. Lawrence Island,
the shamanistic power has been retained for a succession of generations,
evidently having been transferred from father to son. . . .

There can be no doubt, of course, that shamans, during their performances, employ deceit in various forms, and that they themselves are
fully cognizant of the fact. "There are many liars in our calling," Scratching-Woman said to me. "One will lift up the skins of the sleeping-room
with his right toe, and then assure you that it was done by 'spirits'; another
will talk into the bosom of his shirt or through his sleeve, making the voice
issue from a quite unusual place."

Of course, he was ready to swear that he never made use of any of
these wrong practices. "Look at my face," he continued; "he who tells
lies, his tongue stutters. He whose speech, however, flows offhand from
his lips, certainly must speak the truth." This was a rather doubtful argument, but I refrained from making any such suggestion.

Some of the people even are aware of the deceit of the shamans. Several
men, when talking of shamanistic feats, said that, though the tricks performed were very wonderful, they were by no means real, but were produced only through illusion on the part of the observers. Others went even
further. Thus, the trader Kuva'r at Indian Point, of whom I have spoken
several times, assured me that even the most renowned shamans are only
clever deceivers. "When I witness their best trick," he asserted, "even
then with proper attention, I can discover the fraud. He [the shaman] will
pretend to cut with a knife the abdomen of the patient; but I can follow
the direction of the knife, and see that it glances off without hurting the
skin and that the blood comes from the mouth of the operator."

This scepticism, perhaps, is the result of intercourse with civilized
people. With some of the shamans, fraud is not restricted to jugglery. We
caught Scratching-Woman in the very act of stealing our washing from
the line. The woman who, during our stay at Indian Point, was caught
thieving, was also a shaman.

However, in giving directions and answers to persons seeking advice,
Chukchee shamans often display much wisdom and circumspection, especially when they have to deal with matters out of the reach of their
knowledge and understanding. This is the case when the inquirer is of a
different stage of culture; for instance, with Russian officials or merchants,
who sometimes do not despise the help of the native "spirits." Thus the

assistant of the chief official of Anadyr asked Scratching-Woman, during a shamanistic séance, whether his Second Interior Loan bond, with prizes, would draw a lucky number in the yearly lottery. It was no little trouble to explain to the shaman what was meant by "an Interior Loan bond;" but, when he understood it, he immediately answered that he saw that the foundations of the wealth of the questioner, which were in his own country, were going to increase. To a cossack who wanted to know whether the yearly mail steamer would bring him a furlough, the shaman answered, "The big boat brings change and joy to all people in this country." I could cite other answers not less worthy of the oracle of Delphi. To my own questions of this kind, the shamans usually answered that my country was too far away, and the feet of their ke'let too small, to go there. Furthermore, the ke'let are too shy of the manners of the unknown dwellers in those distant localities. I saw similar circumspection displayed also in regard to the native questions. A shaman of the interior refused to give advice about the maritime pursuits of the people of the coast, explaining that his "spirits" were good only for walking upon the land, and that they were afraid of the sea.

LOVE INCANTATIONS

I. If I want to have this woman, I take out her heart and liver, then I go towards the Evening "direction," and hang her organs on both sides of the Evening. Then I say, "Here is the heart and the liver of that woman. Make them entangled in a seal-net! Let her be without her intestines! let her pine away with desire for me!—This man is not your husband. This is a seal's carcass drifted to the seashore, rotting upon the pebbles. Every wind blows upon it, and its bones are bared. And you are not a woman; you are a young reindeer-doe. The smell of the carrion comes to you, and you flee away, and come into my possession."

Told by Ke'ɛulin (man) in the village of Če'čin, 1900.

II. "Then you are this woman! You have so much of my husband's love that he begins to lose all liking for me. But you are not a human being! I make you into carrion lying on the pebbly shore,—old carrion inflated with rottenness. I make my husband into a big bear. The bear comes from a distant land. He is very hungry; he has been starving for a long time. He sees the carrion; seeing it, he eats of it. After a while he vomits it out. I make you into the stuff vomited. My husband sees you, and says, 'I do not want it!' My husband takes to despising you."

At the same time I make this body of mine into a young beaver that has just shed his hair. I make smooth every hair of mine. My husband will leave his former liking, and turn again to me, because she is repugnant to look upon. (She spits, and with the saliva smears her whole body from head to foot. Indeed, the husband begins to be drawn towards her.)

"I, who was till now neglected, I turn myself back towards him; I make myself into a deadly pain for him. Let him be attracted by the smell from here, and have a desire for me. If I reject him, let him be still more insistent!" And really the husband leaves off his former passion.

Told by Äqä′ññä (woman) in the village of Če′čin, 1901.

VOLUNTARY DEATH

Voluntary death is still of frequent occurrence among the Chukchee. It is inflicted by a friend or relative, upon the expressed wish of the person who desires to die. Though I had no occasion to witness a case of voluntary death, I know of about twenty cases which happened among the Chukchee during the time of my travels. One summer, while I was at Mariinsky Post, a large skin boat from the Telqä′p tundra arrived for trading-purposes. One of the new-comers, after a visit to the Russian barracks, felt a sudden pain in his stomach. During the night the pain became acute, the sufferer asked to be killed, and his fellow-travellers complied with his request.

From what has been related, it will be seen that the voluntary death of old men is not prompted by any lack of good feeling towards the old men, but rather by the hard conditions of their life, which make existence almost unendurable for any one unable to take full care of himself. Accordingly, not only old people, but also those afflicted by some illness, often prefer death to continued suffering; and their number is even greater than that of old people who die a voluntary death.

The position of an infirm man among the Chukchee is very hard indeed, be he young or old. On the western Kolyma tundra I met a man less than thirty years of age, A′nɪqai by name, who three years before was stricken with palsy, and, though partly recovered, had become feeble-minded. I saw him in February. It was cold and windy. The Chukchee of the western Kolyma tundra have no winter houses, and wander about throughout the year with their usual travelling-tent and sleeping-room. Thus did also the family of A′nɪqai. We visited them at a newly chosen camping-place. The women had just begun to unload the pack-sledges. The tent could be pitched only late in the evening. A′nɪqai lay on the snow, looking very much like a heap of old clothes. His wife put a clothing-bag under his head; but, the bag being short and round, his head almost immediately fell to the ground again. His cap also had fallen off, and the wind began to fill his hair with fine dry snow. The cold was so severe that even the Chukchee could keep warm only by continual exercise. A′nɪqai lay there quite motionless. I caught his look. Though dull and feeble, it was full of helpless pain, and had something of that of a dying animal.

Another tragic figure of my acquaintance was a woman of forty, who suffered from lung trouble, and whom I saw on the Dry Anui River when

I had to spend a couple of days in her camp. She had been very active in her youth, a good "shaker of the tent," as the Chukchee say. Even at that time she tried to prove that she was still good for something. She continued the hard toil of the Chukchee housewife, which knows almost no interruption; but her work was not so successful as before. Her tent was full of filth, the sleeping-room was damp and cold, and she herself was black with grease and soot. She would move about in the smoke from the fire, which was fed with the damp fuel of the tundra, rattling the kettles and pans. Then a fit of violent coughing would seize her; and her figure would emerge from the smoke, and she would stand on the snow, stamping her feet, and clutching her chest with her hands. When the fit was over, she would curse her fate and sufferings, and even her own life; and her face, black with soot, became still blacker with anger.

The most peculiar cause for voluntary death is the wrath, the lack of patience, of the Chukchee, which was mentioned by Lotteri as early as 1765. Unable to fight against suffering of any kind, physical or mental, the Chukchee prefers to see it destroyed, together with his own life. Thus Aiñanwa't told me how some years ago his neighbor in camp, Little-Spoon by name, requested that he be killed. "He and his wife often quarrelled because they had very bad sons. From quarrelling with his wife came his desire to be killed. One day his elder son and his mother picked a quarrel with him. Then he asked to be killed."

Other Chukchee of my acquaintance added the following explanation: "Among our people, when a father is very angry with his lazy and bad son, he says, 'I do not want to see him any more. Let me go away.' Then he asks to be killed, and charges the very son who offended him with the execution of his request. 'Let him give me the mortal blow, let him suffer from the memory of it.' "

Deep sorrow on account of the loss of some near friend must also be mentioned as a reason for voluntary death. I have spoken before of a husband who wanted to follow his dead wife.

Last among the motives of voluntary death, *tædium vitæ* should be mentioned. I have related the case of a man named Ka'tık, who, when speaking with me, declared that he did not desire to live any longer. He gave as his reason that fortune did not like him, though his herd and family were prospering. I did not pay much attention to his words, but a few months afterwards I heard that he had really had himself strangled.

Another case of the same character refers to a widow of forty, who lived with her son and two nephews, being an owner of a considerable herd. She felt that life held no pleasures for her. She was in fear that her herd might decrease, and that she would feel ashamed to live. She died by strangulation. The case was related to me by Aiñanwa't.

It must be borne in mind that all these psychical motives lead as often to suicide as to voluntary death. The difference is, that the younger people, especially those not yet fully grown, when desiring to die, destroy their life with their own hands, while those who are older more frequently ask to be killed. I know some cases of boys and girls who were not yet twenty, and who killed themselves from spite, shame, or sorrow. Not one of them could have induced his house-mates to be his "assistant" in dying. For the older people, such assistance is considered more becoming than death by their own hands.

An additional source for this inclination for voluntary death is the idea that death by violence is preferable to death by disease or old age. Even the term which is used for "voluntary death" has some connection with this idea. It is called vêrê'tırgın ("single fight"). A man who feels a desire to die a voluntary death sometimes even says, "Let us have a single fight," or "Since like a wild reindeer I became for thee" and this is understood as a request to be killed. Another expression is used chiefly in folk-tales: "Since I became for thee like thy quarry," or, more directly, "Like thy quarry treat me." These formulas are used by warriors when they are vanquished by an adversary and do not want to outlive their defeat. The meaning is, "Give me a mortal stroke, since I have become for you as a game-animal." The same formula is sometimes used in real life by those desiring voluntary death. The Chukchee explained the motive to me, saying, "We do not want to die through ke'let. We want to die a violent death, to die fighting, as if we were fighting with the Russians." The Russians were singled out probably for my own benefit. Death by disease, as has been explained before, is ascribed to the wiles of the ke'let. The tendency to desire voluntary death is more or less hereditary in some Chukchee families, not so much as a duty, as rather a fate which passes from father to son. In a detailed description of a case of voluntary death, which I noted down from the words of natives, it is said, "Since his father died this way, he wanted to imitate him." The father was stabbed with a knife; but, when death did not come immediately, he requested that he be strangled with a rope, which was done accordingly. The son also was stabbed, but the stroke was not mortal. So he went still further in imitating his father, and also requested that he might die by strangulation, which was immediately executed.

Aiñanwa't, whose name has been mentioned several times, told me that his father and elder brother died this way, and that he himself felt an inclination to end his life in the same manner, though it is by no means obligatory for a son to follow the example of his father. One of his brothers died a natural death, and so did not continue the tradition.

That voluntary death is considered praiseworthy, may be seen also from the fact, that, in the descriptions of the other world, those who have died this way are given one of the best dwelling-places. They dwell on the red blaze of the aurora borealis, and pass their time playing ball with a walrus-skull.

WALDEMAR JOCHELSON

(1852-1937)

Yukaghir Picture Writing and Loveletters

PICTOGRAPHIC WRITING IS STILL IN USE AMONG THE YUKAGHIR OF THE
Yassachnaya and Korkodon Rivers. Like the American Ojibway, they trace
with the point of a knife figures and lines on the inner surface of birchbark.
Drawings are also made by puncturing. Formerly this was done with a bone
awl.

We find two kinds of pictographic writing—realistic and conventionalized.

The realistic form of graphic art is used in birchbark letters in which
one person or a group of people communicate to other persons his or their
exploits or experiences. This form of writing, of course, can be called
realistic only so long as the writer is able to trace figures of men, animals
and objects. When a hunter is leaving his temporary camp or seasonal
habitation he leaves on a tree a birchbark letter to inform passing tribesmen where he has gone and what has happened.

Fig. 138 shows the Korkodon River (1) and its tributary, the Rassokha
(5). The rivers are indicated each by a pair of equidistant wavy lines. The
line in the middle of the river shows the route of the writer. The lines
across the Korkodon River just above the mouth of the Rassokha indicate the place where the river was dammed for fishing. Farther to the
right is a representation of a grave (2) with a double cross showing that
there a man died and was buried. Still farther to the right, three conical
tents (3) are shown. At this place the whole Yukaghir group lived for
some time. From there two tents moved farther up the Korkodon River.
They had two boats, preceded by four canoes (4). One tent moved back
and ascended the Rassokha (6). There they stopped for a time on the
left shore and moved up the Rassokha with two boats and two canoes. This
means that the people of the tent consisted of two families, although they

From Jochelson, *The Yukaghir and the Yukaghirized Tungus,* The Jesup North
Pacific Expedition, edited by Franz Boas, *Memoirs of the American Museum of
Natural History,* Vol. IX (New York: 1926), pp. 434-436; 444-450.

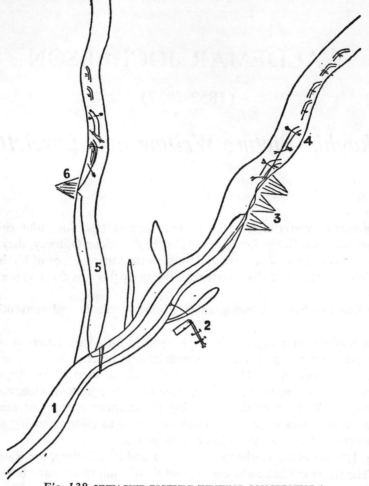

Fig. 138. YUKAGHIR PICTURE WRITING CONCERNING A
FISHING EXPEDITION.

had only one tent. A boat is distinguished by its steering oar and paddles
while the canoe has only a double paddle. This letter was found on a tree
by my Yukaghir travelling companions when we ascended the Korkodon
River in the autumn of 1895, so that my companions learned where their
clansmen had been during the summer and what they had done. They
guessed who had died and told me why two families had one tent on the
Rassokha River. The cover of the other tent was in our boat; one of my
oarsmen belonged to the family that lived in a neighbor's tent. On the
Korkodon River are shown three small tributaries. The information such
a letter gives is not quite accurate, as the exact time of the beginning and
end of the fishing is not given in the picture writing.

Fig. 139 shows, from right to left, four Yukaghir log huts in the form of squares,—a winter village on the Korkodon River (1). In the spring the inhabitants of the village moved on to hunt and put up four temporary conical tents (2) some distance from the winter dwellings. Near the camp are a larch tree, two sledges, and a pair of snowshoes with a staff. Two loaded sledges leave the camp for hunting. The hunters on snowshoes carrying staffs are driving the dogs. On the sledges some boys are sitting who help the hunters while camping at night and hunting. This letter was found by my travelling companions on a tree when we came to the Korkodon from the Yassachnaya River in the spring of 1896.

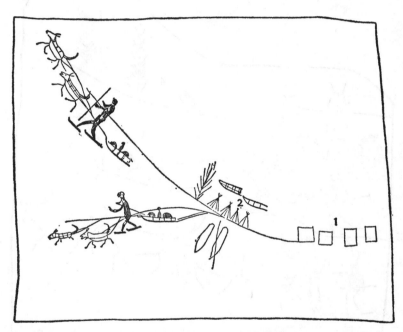

Fig. 139. YUKAGHIR PICTURE WRITING TELLING OF SPRING HUNT.

Fig. 140 shows Yukaghir hunting scenes. Beginning at the bottom, there are three hunters (1) pursuing three wild reindeer. The next line (2) represents two hunters on snowshoes with flintlock guns and staffs. The first hunter, resting his gun on a support, has shot at two reindeer and hit one of them. At the top, in the right hand corner is a hunter (4) on hands and feet stealthily approaching a tree on which two birds are sitting. It is interesting to note that the birds are turned over with their backs resting on the tree. In the left corner (3) are three conical tents, men, a dog and sledges. The small size of the tents might be explained as evidence of a sense of perspective, but two aprons drawn at the top at the left corner argue against this idea. . . .

Fig. 149 represents a sample of a love letter. Each of the figures re-sembling folded umbrellas represents in a conventional way a human being. The inner pair of lines indicates the legs, the outer two lines the arms, and the dots show the joints of the legs and parts of the body. The dotted line extending from the side of the second figure, from right to left, indicates a braid, i. e., the figure is a girl or woman. The contents of the letter are as follows: Above the central figure (a) is an object like

Fig. 140. PICTURE WRITING OF HUNTING SCENES.

a hat which represents a deserted dwelling, i. e., one which figure *a* is leaving. The minds or the desires of the two female figures were directed towards the central figure, *a,* but the latter is too important a person for the Yukaghir girls who composed this letter. Their minds stop on the way, not daring to go to their original destination, turn around for a great while, and go back. The mind of *d* goes to figure *b* and the mind of *e* goes to figure *c.* The figures *c* and *e* and *b* and *d* are united by bands of love, but the bands of *b* and *d* are of a more durable nature than those of *e* and *c.* This is shown by the diagonals uniting the heads of both pairs. In the first case we have two diagonals, and in the other only one.

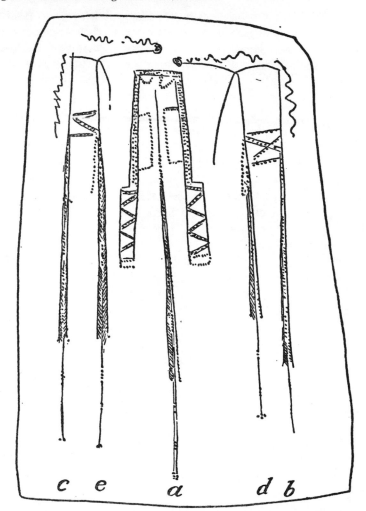

Fig. 149. YUKAGHIR LOVE LETTER ON BIRCHBARK.

I have not been able to find further examples of such letters, neither in my possession nor in the Museum collection. They were probably lost. Copies of the originals may be found in the Museum for Anthropology and Ethnology of the Academy of Sciences in Leningrad.[1]

[1] In order to give here a fuller account on the character of Yukaghir love letters, I reprint the description of those collected on the Yassachnaya River by my friend S. Shargorodsky who lived for some time as a political exile among the Yassachnaya Yukaghir before I arrived there. He published his Yukaghir love letters in the Journal Zemleviedeniye (The Study of the Earth) of the Geographical Division of the Society for the Study of Nature, Anthropology and Ethnography of the University of Moscow, parts 2-3, 1895. Major-General von Krahmer translated Shargorodsky's article into German and published it together with illustrations in "Globus," Vol. LXIX, 1896, pp. 208-211.

In describing his Yukaghir love letters Shargorodsky says: "Only girls occupy themselves with such writings. Married women and men do not. These writings of girls concern exclusively their declarations of love, the expression of sorrow when being abandoned or other utterings of intimate feelings.

"As material for producing such letters, the girl uses birchbark as a substitute for paper and the point of a knife instead of a pen. Of course, girls can indulge themselves in letter writing only in time of leisure, which is very limited. During the work-day they are busy from early morning till late in the evening; even during holidays they have little rest. During the winter an immense quantity of fuel is needed which girls have to bring in from distant places on sledges harnessed with a couple of small badly fed dogs; during the summer they do the hardest work of the fishing season. A real holiday does not arrive until the necessary wood has been brought in and the fishing season is at an end.

"On such a day the neighboring settlements of the Yakut are informed that a dance will take place at a certain place and time. While the young people are slowly assembling the Yukaghir girls use their leisure hours in preparing love-letters. Usually one girl is writing and the bystanders, boys and girls, try to guess the meaning of the drawings. When the guessing fails, there is opportunity for jest and laughter.

"Following are the explanations of Figs. 150–153. In figure 150 the line a, b, c, d, e, f, represents a house. An incompletely drawn house, as in figs. 151 and 152, indicates that the person shown there abandoned it. It

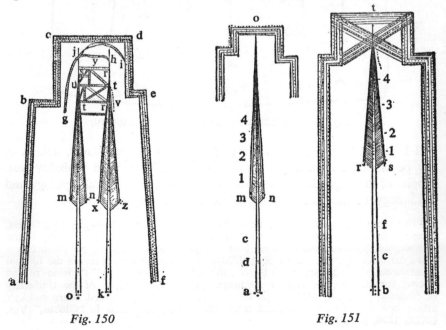

Fig. 150   Fig. 151

may be added that the houses are drawn not with the same care, but this is not significant.

"In the house Fig. 150 there are two figures *oj* and *kh* which bear a likeness to a folded umbrella. The figure *oj* represents a young man, and *kh* a young girl. Although at a first glance looking alike, both figures are nevertheless distinct and characterized by symbols. Of course the men have no beard and wear their hair long, so that they may look like girls; the clothing of a woman is almost the same as that of a man. Both wear leather coats with red and black trimmings, leather trousers and soft leather footwear; the cap for both sexes is also alike. The only difference consists in the long leather tassels of the woman's apron and richer ornamentation of the clothing. The outer appearance of both sexes is so much alike that one can hardly distinguish a man from a woman.

"The dotted line (*vt*) emanating from the side of figure *kh* marks the tresses which girls wear. When this is not indicated then the female figure may still be distinguished from the males by their greater width, *mn xz,* for usually women are more corpulent than men. The Figure *a* in the illustration 152 may be taken as a representation of a Russian woman, as shown by the indication of a skirt.

"The male and female figures are united by many lines crossing each other. Thus the figures *o* and *k* (Fig. 150) are connected by the lines *rs, tu, tr,* which show that the two figures here represented love each other.

"Figure 150 may express in words: 'I love thee with all the might of my soul.'

"Drawing on birchbark is the only means for a young girl to confess her love to a man, as according to Yukaghir custom only the man may declare his love in words.

"In Figure 151 two crossing stripes may be seen over the figure to the right. These consist of many punctured lines. These crossing stripes express the grief, sorrow, and misery of the person concerned. The figure to the left (Figure 151) stands in a house incompletely drawn, which indicates that it is or soon will be abandoned. The meaning of this illustration is: 'Thou goest hence, and I bide alone. For thy sake I still weep and moan.'

"Figure 152 tells us that the young girl *c* is full of sorrow. The lines *lk* and *mn* indicate the person *b* as the source of her affliction. Such lines are necessary, when beside the man on account of whom the girl is in sorrow, there are other man figures represented. The lines *rs, tu, ru, st,* which usually express love, are here intersected by the line *xyz* which proceeds from the point *v,* the head of the Russian woman. This shows that there exists an obstacle between *b* and *c.* By the side of the female figure *a* two small figures are drawn which represent children. The curved line *dc* says that the young girl *c* is thinking of the young man *b.* The young man *d* is thinking of the young girl *c* which is also indicated by a curved line; but these find no response.

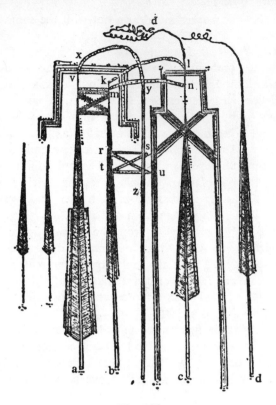

Fig. 152

"The illustration expresses: 'Thou goest forth, lovest a Russian woman, who bars the way to me; there will be children, and in a new home joy wilt thou find, while I must ever grieve, as thee I bear in mind, though another yet there be who loveth me.'

"The Yukaghir, particularly young men, often and for various purposes go to Sredne-Kolymsk. These journeys always arouse the jealousy of the young girls because they think that the Russian women whom the young Yukaghir men meet are much more handsome and attractive than they themselves. They are afraid that the Russian women will alienate their affections. When a young Yukaghir once gets to town, he tries to stay there as long as possible, in order to obtain news, for the more news he can tell on his way back home the more welcome he is. In every dwelling he is gladly met and treated. With this in view, he will rather suffer starvation than leave town prematurely. The Russians in town are not very liberal to their Yukaghir visitors, although the Yukaghir themselves are very hospitable to Russian guests in their homes. The longer a boy is absent, the more jealous his girl becomes; then she cuts a letter on birchbark saying how sad she is. In this way originate compositions like our figure 152.

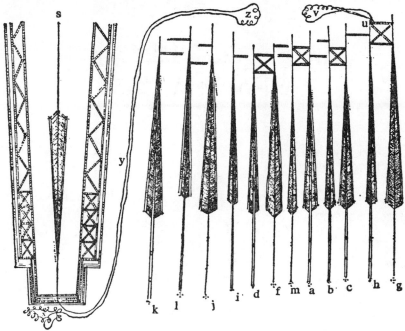

Fig. 153

"The letter fig. 153 shows many figures. Some of them are connected with lines of love, as *d* and *f, m* and *a, b* and *c*; some of them still are single, not having declared their love, but about to do so. In such a position are represented *k, l, j* and *i*. Only one girl stands aside and thinks (line *yz*) of the young man whose thoughts are also occupied with her, as indicated by the line *uv*, but he is already connected with the girl *g*.

"This letter may be expressed as follows: 'Each youth his mate doth find; my fate alone it is of him to dream who to another wedded is, and I must fain contented be, if only he forget me not.' "

Salvaging the Ethnology of
the Northern Plains

CLARK WISSLER
(1870-1947)

ROBERT H. LOWIE
(1883-1957)

J. R. WALKER
(dates unknown)

LESLIE SPIER
(1893-   )

The next great endeavor of the Museum of Natural History after the Jesup Expedition was an immense salvage operation on the Northern Plains. After the disappearance of the buffalo and the end of intertribal warfare and the settlement of the roving, war-like tribes on reservations, Plains Indian culture collapsed and a general cloud of apathy and anomie settled over the prairie. The old men who remembered the days of following the buffalo and the warpath were becoming fewer; they had little will to live. If the details of Plains culture were not to be lost forever they would have to be recorded quickly.

The young anthropologists whom Boas and Livingston Farrand had trained at Columbia in the methods of anthropology and who came to the Museum to work on this problem were not doctors or lawyers or artists who came to study Indian cultures because of some sense of moral responsibility to Indians or some romantic attraction to a more primitive mode of life. They were professional anthropologists, trained in methods of collecting and evaluating data. They were not interested in Indians qua Indians; their interests were much broader. They were concerned with the varieties of man on earth, and Indians were one type of man. They sometimes spoke of the world of primitive men as their "laboratory." However, they were not quite so detached as they pretended to be; each one of them would defend the special excellence of "his" tribe. Empathy is an essential condition of successful field work; it bridges the abyss between two cultures and makes communication possible and it enables one to grasp inner meanings and comprehend the spirit that informs behavior. The young anthropologists did not need to apologize, as they sometimes did, for their emotional bond with their subjects. It was fortunate for them, however, that they were relatively disengaged; the Northern Plains in the 20th century was a depressing place for anyone who wished to absorb and communicate a coherent style of life.

As part of this salvage project the key tribes of the Northern Plains were visited; Kroeber went to the Arapaho and the Gros Ventre; Wissler went to the Blackfoot and the Dakota; Lowie went to the Northern Shoshone, the Assiniboine, the Hidatsa and the Crow; Radin went to the Winnebago. It was no longer possible to sink oneself in a culture, as Cushing did, and emerge after five years; or to return year after year to one's chosen tribe to sit around their campfires and swap yarns, as Grinnell did; or like Fletcher spend twenty-five years learning those things about tribal life that were either too secret or too commonplace to be spoken of. One spent frustrating weeks out of the short summer's field trip trying to find someone who was willing to talk; the informant that one found after weeks of search disappeared after the second interview; one went to his cabin miles away across the prairie to find it deserted; he had gone to visit his daughter. When one found someone who could talk, one listened and wrote; asked questions and wrote down the answers, and checked the answers that one got according to certain rules of evidence. Lowie in his posthumously published autobiography describes what field work was like on the Plains in the early years of this century.[1]

The field researches of this group yielded a large body of comparable ethnographic material which provided the basis for a number of theoretical constructs.

Boas resigned from the Museum in 1905 and was succeeded by Clark Wissler, who carried forward many of Boas' ideas. Wissler first studied psychology; his degree was in psychology and his thesis dealt with individual mental differences. He became interested in anthropology as a graduate student, and shortly after completing his graduate studies accepted Boas' invitation to join the Museum staff. He never went back to psychology; in later years when he lectured at the Institute of Human Relations at Yale University he encouraged interdisciplinary interchange between anthropology and psychology and was hospitable to culture-personality research although he himself was not active in this field.

It was in the analysis of the Plains material that Wissler developed the ideas that are generally associated with his name and which were important guideposts for the ordering and interpretation of data during this period. The culture-area concept grew out of the observation that cultures that were geographically close shared many features, that each of these areas of shared culture traits had a center where the characteristic culture of the area existed in its most highly developed form. The age-area concept assumed that the cultural center is also the place of origin and that traits

[1] *Robert H. Lowie, Ethnologist.* Berkeley University of California Press, 1959.

diffuse outward from the center as ripples from a stone dropped in water, so that the most widely diffused traits may be assumed to be the oldest. Wissler's concept of pattern (not to be confused with the later uses of the word as a synonym for configuration or basic theme) isolated certain basic forms of wide distribution—the form of woman's dress, the medicine-bundle complex, the Sun Dance complex, etc.—of which the individual tribal manifestations are variations.

Leslie Spier's analysis of the Sun Dance complex on the Plains is an application of these ideas to a body of concrete data. The Sun Dance ritual was common to all tribes of the Northern Plains, but in no two tribes is it performed in exactly the same way nor does it always have the same significance. At the time these studies were made the Sun Dance was no longer being performed, having been forbidden by government edict because of the tortures which formed an essential part of it. Lowie, Kroeber and Wissler recorded descriptions of the Sun Dance from old men who had participated in them. J. R. Walker, a physician who lived for years on the Teton reservation, witnessed the last Sun Dance; he was initiated into Teton medicine cults, and his description of the Oglala form of the Sun Dance, recorded from various participants, is the fullest and the most philosophical account. Spier analyzed all recorded accounts of the ritual, breaking it down into its component parts; he plotted the geographical distribution of the various elements, and from this concluded which elements were the most constant, and hence presumably the oldest, and suggested on the basis of these distributions the probable center from which the ritual was diffused. He then went on to show how the Sun Dance was integrated with the different ceremonial patterns of each tribe. This study provided a model for similar studies of other religious and mythological complexes.

Of Wissler's formulations, the age-area concept is the least acceptable, and his own researches on the history of the horse on the Plains and the spread of the use of tobacco around the world contravene any such simple formula. The culture-area concept has been of very great use not only in arranging museum collections but in ordering the vast mass of ethnographic data which now exist and in setting the stage for future field work. Wissler developed and extended his culture-area ideas, relating them to natural conditions of climate and vegetation, and Kroeber (whose work is dealt with in Parts V and VI) integrated the more complex ideas from the field of ecology.

Kroeber left the Museum in 1901 to organize the department of anthropology at the University of California. Lowie remained until 1921. Each summer he went into the field, to the Shoshone, the Paiute, the Assiniboine, the Crow—above all to the Crow who "delighted" him at his first visit and to whom he returned again and again. The proud, lecherous, quarrelsome Crow became "his" tribe. In 1921 Lowie left to join Kroeber's department in California, and Spier followed soon after. Radin went to England. Wissler remained at the Museum until his retirement in 1942. There were no more such concentrated programs as the Jesup Expedition or the work on the Plains, but a far more diversified program. For a while the Southwest was a center of interest: Nelson and Spier worked with archaeological problems; Lowie worked briefly with the Hopi in kinship structure while Kroeber worked on kinship and social structure in Zuñi. Pliny Earle Goddard came from California and joined the Museum staff and worked in linguistics—Navaho and Apache—and published a series of Apache texts. But the Museum never had a systematic integrated program in the Southwest comparable to its Northwest Coast and Plains programs.—R.L.B.

CLARK WISSLER

(1870-1947)

The Social Life of the Blackfoot Indians

HERALDRY AND PICTURE WRITING

THE TERM DEED AS USED BY US HAS THE SAME SOCIAL SIGNIFICANCE AS coup, a full discussion of which has been given by Grinnell. Without going into details, it seems that among the Blackfoot, the capture of a weapon was the coup, or deed, rather than the formal striking of the enemy, though such was also taken into account. Our impression is, from what we have heard in the field, that there was no such formal development of the coup practice as among many other tribes. An old man relating his deeds seldom mentions scalps but dwells upon the number of guns, horses, etc. captured; whereas, according to our observation, a Dakota boasts of his wounds, enemies slain and coups. However, heraldry was a prominent feature in Blackfoot life. By this term, we mean those conventions by which deeds are recorded and accredited, with their social privileges and responsibilities. Anyone with such recognized deeds is likely to be called upon to name a child, to perform special services in social functions as well as specific parts of ritualistic ceremonies. In all cases of this kind the warrior comes forward and in a loud voice states what deed or deeds he has performed and immediately renders the required service. For this, he may receive presents unless the occasion is one of special honor. In theory, at least, the formal announcement is a kind of challenge for contradiction by any of the assembly in so far that it implies the eligibility of him who makes it. Women do not ordinarily perform such deeds but often recount the embroidering of robes, their resistance of temptation, etc., when about to perform some ceremonial function, a truly analogous practice.

As elsewhere, the graphic recording of deeds was chiefly by picture

From Wissler, "The social life of the Blackfoot Indians," *Anthropological Papers, American Museum of Natural History*, Vol. 7 (New York, 1911-1912), pp. 36-41, 43, 107, 100-104, 136-140, 147, 152-155.

writing, upon robes, back-walls and the outsides of tipis. A few might be indicated upon leggings, but in general, garments were not considered the place for such records. The outside and inside of the tipi were the conventional places. Good examples of this are still to be seen. An unusual tipi was collected by the writer in 1903, bearing several hundred figures, representing sixty-six distinct deeds most of which were performed by seven Piegan then living. The tipi was in reality one of the "painted lodges" to be discussed under another head, but may be considered here merely as a good example of picture writing and heraldry.

In the sketches, Fig. 1 is a small vertical section of the tipi cover. Its entire circumference to about half the height is one continuous array of sketches. From this series a number of typical groups were reassembled in Fig. 2. Beginning at the top in Fig. 1, we have Bear Chief (a) on foot

Fig. 1. SECTION OF A DECORATED TIPI.

Fig. 2. SELECTED FIGURES FROM A DECORATED TIPI.

surprised by Assiniboine Indians but he escaped; (b) Double Runner cut
loose four horses; (c) Double Runner captures a Gros Ventre boy; (d)
Double Runner and a companion encounter and kill two Gros Ventre, he
taking a lance from one; (e) even while a boy Double Runner picked up a
war-bonnet dropped by a fleeing Gros Ventre which in the system counts
as a deed; (f) as a man he has two adventures with Crow Indians, taking a
gun from one; (g) he, as leader, met five Flathead in a pit and killed them;
(h) a Cree took shelter in some cherry brush in a hole, but Big Nose went
in for him; (i) not completely shown, but representing a Cree Indian killed
while running off Piegan horses; (j) Double Runner, carrying a medicine
pipe, took a bow from a Gros Ventre and then killed him; (k) Double
Runner took a shield and a horse from a Crow tipi, a dog barked and he
was hotly pursued; (m) he killed two Gros Ventre and took two guns;

(n) he captured a Gros Ventre woman and a boy; (o) he took four mules. From this sample, it will be noted that a great deal is left for the memory, though a little practice will enable one to determine the character of the exploit suggesting each drawing. Fig. 2 needs less comment as the technical aspect of the work speaks for itself. The large man with a pipe is symbolic of the vision in which this type of tipi had its inception and, hence, belongs in a different category. The drawing was done by a number of individuals; in some cases, by the hero of the exploits, but often by a young man under his immediate direction. This is obvious in the varying degree in execution and conventionality, the range of which is adequately shown in the sketches. When considered as a system of recording deeds, it appears that much is left to the whim of the artist, but that certain general modes of suggesting common types of adventure are recognized and allowed to control the composition to such an extent that even a stranger may interpret the sketches with confidence. Of course, the function of such writing is to objectify the formal recounting of deeds, only such performances as are so recognized and carry with them social and ceremonial values being considered worthy of a place in the series.

From the many examples collected, we selected the following more or less conventionalized symbols:

Wounds received or given are indicated by a black spot with a dash of red for bleeding. Enemies killed, when not fully pictured, are represented by a row of skeleton figures as in Fig. 3a, a form always used in heraldic horse decorations. In the pictured form, death is often indicated by three wounds—in the head, heart and thigh, Fig. 3b. A scalp taken is symbolized by human hair and white weasel skin, except in painting when the symbol is as in Fig. 3c.

The capture of the enemies' property, or a deed, is indicated by pictures of the objects recognized as worth considering. While naturally, there is difference of opinion, the following may be taken as the approximate list of captures conferring ceremonial rights:—horses, guns, shields, lances,

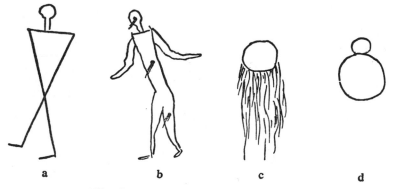

a   b   c   d

Fig. 3. SYMBOLS USED IN WAR RECORDS.

bows and quivers, shot-pouches and powder horns, daggers, war-bonnets, and all medicine objects. The following order or rank, was given by an informant recognized by the Piegan as an authority in heraldry:—gun, lance, bow, the enemy's life, cutting a horse loose from a tipi, leading a war party, acting as a scout, shields, war-bonnets, a medicine pipe, and driving off loose horses. The most significant point is that while the life of an enemy is fourth, the capture of his gun is first. When a man was seen to fall with a gun, it was not unusual for one or more young men to rush boldly out to snatch the prize. To ride up, jerk a gun from an enemy's hand and get away without injury to either party was the greatest deed possible. While in picturing such deeds realistic forms are used, as the symbol for a shield (Fig. 3d), they are often greatly conventionalized. Blankets, if counted, are shown as rectangles with one or two cross lines for the stripes on most trade blankets. Horses taken in open fight, when not pictured, are represented by track symbols [as] under the sketch of a mule in Fig. 1. The rectangular variant as found among many other tribes is not used as an equivalent.

Stealing a horse tied up in the enemies' camp is a deed of special importance and naturally has a definite symbolism. This case is of some interest here because we find among our collection practically all the steps between the full pictured form and the bare symbol. Thus, we find drawings showing the adventurer cutting loose horses picketed near the tipis, Fig. 4; again, the cutting represented by a knife and a hand, the pickets alone representing the horses so taken, and finally, a series of crossed lines. The last is the simplest form but may be said to be an alternate with the preceding one, some persons representing the picket stake one way, some the other. The Hidatsa are reported to use the crossed lines for a coup and the Teton use it as a rescue symbol (a coup saved from the enemy); hence, its substitution in Blackfoot records for the more realistic form of picket stake may have been due to suggestion. . . .

In this connection, it may be well to note that by a system of signs, a

Fig. 4. METHODS OF RECORDING THE CAPTURE OF HORSES.

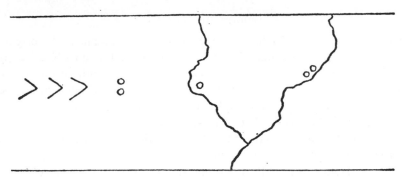

Fig. 6. A SAND MAP SHOWING THE COURSE OF A WAR PARTY.

war party left definite information for the guidance of stragglers or other parties of their tribe on similar errands. On leaving a camp site, a willow bent V-like was stuck in the ground, the apex in the direction taken; if the distance to the next camping place was small, the angle was quite acute, etc. Another sign, used chiefly on the trail, was the mark of a travois, or two converging lines, the apex toward the direction taken. Indeed, the twig is spoken of as a travois sign. Exploit directions were often left for a second party by a kind of map marked in the sand or in bare earth. A sketch by the writer from such a map made at his request is shown in Fig. 6. Two branches of a river are represented easily recognized by one having a knowledge of the country. The travois marks indicate the direction of movement. Pebbles painted black or pieces of charcoal mark the proposed camping places, the number in each case indicating the length of stop. Thus, the sketch would imply that the next camp would be one day's journey from the nearest river; whence, after a stay of two nights, they camped one night on the nearest fork and two nights on the second. To indicate that they were joined by a second party, the travois signs are used to denote two paths converging on a camp site.

MEDICINE BUNDLES

By medicine bundle we mean any object or objects, kept in wrappings when not in use, guarded by the owner according to definite rules and associated with a ritual containing one or more songs. To the Blackfoot this is a definite term denoting an array of such associations, ranging from the simplest war charm to the huge complex beaver bundle. Single or individual ownership is the rule and though the tribe may in a sense have an interest in any large bundle, and relatives may have a property, or investment, relation to it, the fact remains that all the associations treated in this paper are considered by the Blackfoot as examples of rituals of individual ownership. . . .

ORIGINS OF RITUALS

By this time the reader has become aware that a dream is the origin of all these medicines and that the object is after all but an objective part of a ritual. Hence, it seems best to discuss at some length certain aspects of this phase of culture together with certain beliefs and conceptions pertaining thereto, because the complex rituals in the succeeding sections of this paper will thereby be better understood. The great importance still attached to dreams seems to be but a surviving remnant of what once absorbed almost the entire attention of the leading men, for we read in the journal of Henry that, "If a Piegan dreams something particular, on awakening, he instantly rouses his wife, makes a speech about his dream, and begins to sing, accompanied by this woman, and sometimes all his wives join in chorus. If he dreams of having drunk liquor, he gets up, relates the circumstances, sings for a long time with his women, and then, if not too far from the fort, comes in to have his dream accomplished. During my short stay here I have frequently been awakened by such speeches and songs in the dead of the night."

We have not been able to determine whether these experiences are limited to real dreams or include vivid day-dreams and sudden emotional bursts of thought and imagination. We are inclined to believe that anything short of a dream or vision (normal workings of the mind of a person awake) would be rejected by a body of intelligent Blackfoot as of no medicine value. The delirium and hysterical accompaniment of some kinds of sickness are generally regarded as supernatural, but more as glimpses into the future life than as the occasions in which powers are conferred. We do, however, recall a few cases in which sick men claim to have received such powers; but none of the more important rituals are assigned to such origins. The attitude toward alcoholic intoxication is uncertain because there seems to have been a gradual moral awakening to its evil effects, which may account for the present tendency to consider experiences so induced as of no particular consequence. Thus, while it is not at all clear just what psychological phenomena may enter into the origin of a ritual, we shall, for convenience, speak of them as dreams.

A point of special interest in our further discussion of the more complex rituals is the manner of interpreting dreams, for it is apparent that among a people where there are at least as many rituals as there are adult males, the actual dream experiences could scarcely present such uniformity as we observed and certainly not contain so many well composed songs without a system of some kind. It seems to us obvious that in the objective aspects at least, there is a conventional mode of formulating what we choose to call the ritual; this ritual consisting of a narrative, one or more songs, an object and accessories, and in many cases, certain requirements of the person concerned. Owing to difficulties already stated, we have little more than inferential knowledge on this point. We were usually told with every mark of sincerity that the ritual and narrative were precisely as experienced in the origin. On the other hand, it was stated that unless the dreamer was a man of medicine experience or one possessing great confidence in himself, he would call upon one possessing these qualifications for advice. From what we have learned, we feel reasonably certain that the advice is in most cases an interpretation, a deliberate composition of a ritual. For illustration, we offer an incident in which unfortunately the writer did not take full advantage of the situation. Once when crossing the reservation a threatened thunderstorm caused us to make camp quickly. While hurriedly pitching our tent, a bird was observed hopping about within a few feet of the writer, following his movements. During the constant peals of thunder no more than passing attention was given to it, but when the tent was finally pitched, the bird had disappeared and the threatened storm was passing just to our left, leaving us unharmed and dry. On mentioning this to a man of reputed medicine experience we were informed that this was an incident of unusual importance, for the bird had not only protected us from the thunder but had sought to convey some kind of power. He asked if singing had not been heard and a voice speaking, finally suggesting that an experienced man be called upon to "fix it up." All further discussion of the incident he declined as unsafe. Doubtless, if the writer had accepted the veiled offer, a typical ritual would have been produced. Of course, there is no doubt on our part but that rituals are deliberately composed from suggestions received in dreams; the only information we sought was as to the methods and conditions under which this was done. There are reasons for believing that the fundamental conventionality is the tendency to assign a dream origin to everything of importance on the theory that everything is to be truly explained by such phenomena. For example, the writer once remarked that the inventor of the phonograph was a remarkable man. The immediate reply was that he was in no wise different from others but that in a dream he was told to take certain materials and place them in certain relations, with the promise of certain results. The carrying away of the voice was regarded as a great medicine power and the inventor in question as merely a lucky individual, who must have experienced great prosperity and happiness in consequence. While this statement was unusually abstract, it was not otherwise at variance with many others observed in the course of our work. To return to the main point, we believe that the evidence at hand warrants the assumption that the sincerity of many Blackfoot men in their contention that rituals however personal, are literal dream experiences, is due to an unwavering faith in the theory of dream origin and, hence, the feeling that if the thing comes into mind at all, it must in consequence be a dream.

Another important Blackfoot idea is the conception of the transfer of power that takes place in such a dream experience. Allowing for variations, the Blackfoot theory is that there functions in the universe a force (natoji = sun power) most manifest in the sun but pervading the entire world, a power that may communicate with individuals making itself manifest in and through any object, usually animate. Such manifestation is by speech rather than deed and in every narrative based upon it, it is stated or implied that at the moment of speaking the object becomes for the time being "as a person." We found no clear distinction as to whether the power masked as the object or whether the object itself masked as a person. Such logical analysis seems not to have been necessary to the Blackfoot belief and practice. To them it seems sufficient also that power is given, without further speculation as to its ultimate source, simply natoji. The being appearing in the dream offers or consents upon request to give power for some specific purpose. This is done with more or less ceremony; usually the face and hands of the recipient are painted, songs sung, directions given for invoking the power and certain obligations, or taboos, laid upon the recipient. The being conferring power is not content with saying that it shall be, but formally transfers it to the recipient with appropriate ceremonies. This is regarded as a compact between the recipient and the being then manifest, and each is expected to fulfill faithfully his own obligations. The compact is a continuous relation and no matter how complex the ritual may be or how important to the tribe, it is in every case still a matter solely between one individual and the being who gave it. The ritual, to the Blackfoot, is in reality an assumed faithful reproduction of the original transfer. . . . It is important to know that the initial recipient has the right to transfer the compact to another but in doing so relinquishes all right to any benefits to be derived from it. It will then be useless for him to appeal to it in the hour of need for it has, in theory, completely passed out of his life. When such a transfer takes place, the original transfer is reproduced as faithfully as possible. Theoretically, the recipient of a ritual is in the precise relation he would be if experiencing the dream himself; hence, it is impossible to tell from the form of the narrative whether the narrator himself had the initial experience or not. He feels justified in speaking in the first person. Thus, many of the accounts, even some for the men of medicine experience, are probably many times removed from the initial recipient.

It will be observed that the song is in most respects the vital part of the ritual and that the initial transfer of the power usually reaches its climax in the presentation of the song. Thus, we found men often willing to sell the charm or medicine objects but very reluctant even to sing the songs for fear they might thus be transferred to the writer. The objects they said could be readily replaced without a grave breach with the power concerned, but, if the songs went, that was the end of it. We are convinced that the deliberate composing of new songs is going on at the present time. One individual asked the writer to let him hear songs from distant tribes. Having at hand such a phonographic record, his request was complied with. After several repetitions he was able to follow accurately and went away humming it over and over. Some time afterward he reluctantly admitted that he had now arranged words for this song and "expected to dream something."

There are many reasons why dream experiences are desirable to every Blackfoot man, and for that matter, women also, though the women take a far less active part in such activities. Consequently, such dreams are sought. Several individuals have told us in apparent good faith that they never had a dream that could be considered as in any way belonging to this class; one or two of them had sought the experience without success. The usual procedure where such experiences are sought is to go out to some lonely place and fast night and day until the dream comes. A youth is likely to be directed by a man of medicine experience and to be made the object of preliminary ceremonies to propitiate the dream, but he makes the journey alone. While at the chosen place the seeker of dreams or visions is expected to beseech all the things of the sky, earth, and water, to take pity on him. This call is a mournful wail almost like a song, the words being composed at will. The only object used is a filled pipe offered to all the beings addressed and kept in readiness for the manifestation of the dream person previously discussed. It is said that the majority of young men fail in this ordeal as an unreasonable fear usually comes down upon them the first night, causing them to abandon their post. Even old experienced men often find the trial more than they can bear. Men of medicine experience seldom resort to these tortures, as dreams of a satisfactory character are said to come to them in normal sleep. At present, the majority of men seem content to secure their charms and other medicines from those who do have dreams or from the large stock of such available for transfer. On the other hand, every man of consequence is supposed to have one experience in which he acquired a supernatural helper and received a song. Of this, he never speaks definitely, except to an intimate friend to whom he will say, "When I am about to die, you are to paint me and sing this song. Then I may recover." This song is thus secret and never used except in the face of death. We were told by one man that in such an experience as gave a man one of these songs or rituals, the being manifest in the vision announces that he will give his body to the recipient and cause a small object to pass into the body of the recipient, which passes out again at death.

Having now given some general aspects of the beliefs associated with rituals and their accessories we may take up the discussion of more elaborate rituals with their bundles. . . . While each is the exclusive property of its owner until transferred to another, there are what may be considered duplicates in the hands of other individuals; hence, we have given a definite section to each of the known types of bundles. We sought detailed information concerning at least one definite bundle of each type, but owing to the great difficulty in securing the songs and the great amount of time required for the satisfactory mastery of even one ritual, our data are far from complete. We believe, however, that it is sufficient to give a fair idea of the nature of each type.

THE MEDICINE-PIPE

Among the more important medicines of the Blackfoot are the sacred pipe bundles. Something more than seventeen of these are distributed among the several reservations and while there are some differences, as will be noted later, the greater number are of one type and may be assumed to have had a common origin. We refer to what may be considered the thunder's pipe, or the ritual handed down by the thunder, a Blood version of which may be found in our collection of myths. So far as we know, the first clear account of the Blackfoot pipe ceremony is by Kane as observed June, 1846. He has given us a sketch of the dance with the pipes, one of the bundles showing in proper position over the door of a tipi.

Fig. 20. A MEDICINE-PIPE BUNDLE.
Length, 132 cm.

A pipe bundle is shown in Fig. 20. The outer wrapping for these bundles should be the hairy skin of a black bear and next to this a scraped elk hide. Around the middle of the bundle is a broad strip of elkskin. The contents are made up into two bundles which we shall designate as primary and secondary. The former is a long slender poke made of red flannel, both ends open. It contains the decorated stem, or the pipe proper, and a head band of white buffalo skin, with the hair, and an eagle feather to tie on the owner's head. The bundle should always hang so that the mouthpiece of the stem points to the north (in the ceremony, toward the east) and as a guide to this the ends of the poke are tied with different colored cords.

The secondary bundle contains a smaller pipestem,[1] an owl, two loons, two white swans, two cranes, a muskrat skin, an otterskin, a rattle, a skin of a fawn, a whistle, and sometimes the skin of a prairie dog. These are wrapped in pieces of gaily colored calico. Tobacco is put into the bird skins. The rattle is kept in a poke of prairie dog skin. Naturally, the contents of this secondary bundle differ somewhat for the various pipes.

In a square fringed bag are kept paints and smudge materials; also beads for the owner and his wife, a necklace and other accessories. There is also a wooden bowl for the owner, a whip, and a rope. No one must use any of these objects handled by a pipe owner. He must also have a horse for his own use. Should he loan it, something ill would befall the horse or the rider. Special forked sticks are required for the smudge. All these objects are kept coated with red earth paint.[2] The owner's robe was often painted though since the extinction of the buffalo this has almost passed out of mind. A special fan, an eagle's wing, is in the outfit; also a pipe-stoker, and a tobacco board.

The primary bundle is a true bundle and was sometimes carried to war. Around its middle is often a binding, similar to the elkskin wrapping, and a cord for suspension. Though we have no direct evidence, the inference is that the secondary bundle has been added to an original bundle containing the pipestem only. The stem in our collection is shown in Fig. 22. It is about thirty inches long. In two places it is wrapped with wire, in another with red flannel. The intervening spaces are fringed with strips of white weasel skins. From the lower end hangs a fan of eagle tail-feathers. A few bells are also attached.

The headdress is a simple band of white buffalo calfskin (often sheep or goat skin) about two inches wide. The longest feather from an eagle's wing is tied across the head above this band.

The medicine-pipe bundle in the Museum collection contains the following:—

50–5448   a.   The wrappings for the bundle: a tanned elk hide, a bear-skin (in this case an imitation of dog skin), a number of thongs and pieces of gaily colored calico.

          b.   The carrying strap: a woman's belt because it falls to her to carry the bundle.

          c.   A woman's shawl. It is customary to cover all pipe bundles with such a shawl.

[1] The pipe bowls are not kept in the bundle and the medicine stem is rarely smoked. About the only time it is so used is when the bundle is open at the Sun Dance and brought into the enclosure. There it must be lighted with flint and steel by a person who has captured a medicine-pipe from the enemy.

[2] It is said that formerly every pipe owner kept his garment fully coated with red paint so that he could be known at sight.

50–5449 a.   The decorated pipestem, the chief object in the bundle.
         b.   A headdress of mountain goat wool in imitation of white buffalo calf.
         c.   Eagle wing-feather, worn crosswise on the leader's head.
         d.   Small pipestem for smoking in the ceremonies.
         e.   Rattle used by the owner in connection with certain songs.
         f.   Bag of muskrat skin for the rattle.
         g.   A flageolette.
         h.   Head of a crane.
         i.   Skin of a loon in the form of a tobacco pouch.
         j.   Foetus of a deer, tobacco pouch.
         k.   A pipe rack of three sticks.
         l.   Skin of a prairie dog.
         m.   Skin of a squirrel.
         n.   Skin of a squirrel.
         o.   Bowl for pipestem *d*.
         p.   Skin of a muskrat.
         q.   Skin of a mink.
         r.   An owl skin.
50–5716 An owl skin.
50–5717 a–c. Skins of birds.
50–5450   Stick for fastening the bundle over the door on the outside, where it is sometimes placed in the morning.
50–5451 Tripod on which the bundle hangs when out-of-doors.
50–5452 a.   Rawhide bag with accessories.
         b.   Small bag of roots used in the smudge.
         c–h. Bags containing red paints.
         i.   A paint bag.
         j.   Muskrat skin for wiping sweat from the face of the owner.
         k.   Bag of pine needles for the smudge.
         l–m. Necklaces for the owner and his wife.
         n–o. Paint sticks for penciling designs on the face.
50–5453   Tongs used for placing fire on the smudge place.
50–5454 a.   Tobacco cutting board.
         b–c. Pipe-stokers.
50–5455   Wooden bowl for the owner's food.
50–5456   Fan of eagle wing for the owner.
50–5457   Whip for owner's horse.
50–5458   Thong lariat for owner's horse.
50–5459   Painted buffalo robe for owner.

Function. When considering the function of the pipe bundle it may be noted that there are but four occasions on which it can be opened: the sound of the first thunder in the spring; when it is transferred to a new

Fig. 22. A MEDICINE-PIPE.

owner; when the tobacco within is renewed; and in accordance with a vow.

As indicated in the origin myth these bundles are believed to have been handed down by the thunder and are in consequence often spoken of as the thunder's pipe. Curiously enough, it is a belief that the thunder is afraid of an ordinary pipe, or, according to some informants, has an aversion to them and smoking; hence, in the ceremonies the pipe-man is careful to open the prayers with "Thunder, this is your own pipe," etc. Some few years ago (1904) a number of Piegan were gathered in a tipi during a thunderstorm. A man called out in bravado inviting the thunder to come in and smoke. Almost at the same instant, it is said, the bolt struck the tipi, killing some and injuring others. This was cited as recent confirmation of the old belief that the thunder disliked smoking except in case of his own pipe. The opening of the pipe bundle at the return of the thunder is imperative. At the first sound reaching his ears, the owner of a bundle must make immediate preparations for the opening. He goes outside and announces the event, extending an invitation to everybody, old and young. It is said, that everyone is made glad by the sound of the first thunder because they will be prayed for and receive consecrated tobacco.[3] They do not wait for the invitation but at the first thunder hurry to the tipi of the nearest pipe owner. The ceremony does not differ materially from the full ritual given above, except that it may be closed at the end of the twenty-first song at the will of the owner. The pipe is carried out-of-doors, and prayers are made to the thunder while the mouthpiece is held up towards the sky, the home of the thunder. In the prayers at this time the thunder is besought for the welfare of all present and especially that no one be killed by him during the year. Tobacco is taken out of the bundle and distributed among all present. The possession and smoking of this is believed to bring one under the influence of the all pervading good will of the thunder. Also, at this time, soup made of dried berries kept in store for the occasion, is distributed: even small portions of berry food (usually service berries) may be given out.

It has been said that this ceremony is to make berries increase during the summer, but we find no evidence to support such a view as in the prayers plenty of all things are asked, tobacco, meat, vegetables, berries, clothing, horses, children, long life, success in all undertakings, etc. About the only distinctive feature we have observed, is the specific prayer for protection against death by lightning.

The Owner. The owner of a pipe bundle is spoken of as a medicine-pipe man. The name also applies after the ritual has been transferred, though in speaking, the phrase construction when possible is in the past tense, thus distinguishing between the real and the ex-owner. The ex-pipe-man may be called in to officiate at the opening of the bundle and may also receive a bundle into his tipi for temporary care during the incapacity of the owner; but no other person can lead the ceremony no matter how familiar he may be with the ritual. A pipe-man receives great social, religious, and even political recognition, being regarded as of the first rank and entitled to the first seat in a tipi: i.e., opposite the man of the household. As this is disputed by the owners of beaver bundles, a question to be considered later, we may safely assert that he is among the highest ranks in respect to the ownership of rituals. The wife of a pipe-man should be honored and given a seat not lower than that of the head-wife of her host. If possible, everyone is expected to pass behind a pipe-man whether in a tipi or on the road. In theory at least, the same rules should be observed toward his wife. All loud and boisterous conversation should be restrained in their presence. If in the chase one should kill game in front of a pipe-man, the best of the meat goes to him. The pipe-men were also entitled to the best cuts from the buffalo drive. While he is running buffalo no one should cross his tracks lest the horse stumble and fall. Naturally, pipe-men are called

[3] At the sound of the first thunder in the spring everyone is expected to stop in his tracks and pray. He opens with, "I am glad to hear you again," and prays for happiness, health, plenty, etc.

upon to perform certain important functions, as selecting the camp sites for the sun dance, leading the band when moving camp, sitting in councils, offering prayers, etc. Some observers have considered these men as constituting a society but this is scarcely admissible for they are not so regarded by their people and while they have certain bonds of sympathy, they neither meet in a body nor have ceremonies of any kind in common. On the other hand, some of the societies to be discussed later had medicine-pipes, in which case the owners were members, a circumstance no doubt contributing to the confusion.[4]

The owner of a bundle must observe certain prohibitions more or less troublesome in his daily routine. Among these, he must never point at a person with the fingers but with the thumb: to use the finger would endanger the life of the one so designated. He must not loan any of his personal property. If a person asks such a favor, he makes no reply whatever. In such cases, it is usual for the borrower to take what he wants if he can find it. As the owner cannot ask for the return nor send for objects so taken, he is entirely dependent upon the good will and honesty of his neighbors. If he finds an object when walking or riding, he must not pick it up or allow it to be appropriated to his own use. He may call another and allow him to take it. If, however, he has four coups to his record, he may take the object after recounting them to the sun and singing certain songs. In smoking, he must take the pipe in the same hand and hold it in the same way as the person passing it to him. The pipe-men themselves have a special way of holding the pipe at all times when passing it. In formal smoking, the pipe is passed down the circle once and then returned to the leader, but a pipe-man may smoke it every time it passes. If he does not smoke he must hold the end of the stem to his breast at his turn instead of passing it on as others may do. No one must sit on his bed or bedding as misfortune will come to him. The horse that carries the pipe bundle when camp is moved has his face painted like the owner and a stripe over the shoulders and rump. After having borne the pipe bundle once, meat must never be placed in his load, lest he meet with an accident. On the march, the owner must permit no one to pass in front of him. No weapons can be carried on the horse or other conveyance with the pipe bundle. All pipe-men have a fear of dogs. There are other restrictions but these are probably sufficient for our purpose. It will be observed that many of these apply to others as well as the owner, it being the duty of all, old and young,

---

[4] McClintock speaks of the bundle owners as a society (251), but we find no traces of an organization. In his account of the forced transfer, McClintock speaks of the party as composed of pipe-men, or members of the society. Our informants have incidentally stated that in this procession and its ceremonies, the chief parts were assigned to certain men because of requisite war deeds, regardless of their having owned a pipe bundle. The name medicine-pipe men, applies only to those who now own or have owned pipe bundles. Thus the owners, in a sense, constitute a class, but are not organized.

to inform themselves of the requirements of the various rituals and to respect them accordingly.

The home of the pipe bundle is its owner's tipi and its constant care brings no small responsibility to himself and his wife, but especially to the latter. During the day, the bundle is kept outside. It may be hung just above the door of the tipi, a special attachment being provided for that purpose. In most cases, however, it is hung from a tripod set up in the rear of the tipi. Each morning the woman makes a smudge of sweet pine and carries the bundle and tripod out turning to the south and passing around to the rear of the tipi where the tripod is put into position.[5] In all movements and placings, the end of the bundle containing the mouthpiece of the stem must point toward the north. The woman returns to the tipi by the south side. At sunset, she again makes the smudge in which she holds her hands as before, then passes around by the north side and retraces her steps with the bundle. Thus the bundle has made the entire circuit, the usual ceremonial sun-wise movement, and theoretically, should be outside from the moment the sun rises until it sets. During rain or continued cloudiness it is kept within doors. A few bundles are placed on the door in the forenoon and then in the rear during the afternoon. In the tipi, the tripod with the bundle is leaned against the back of the tipi between the backrests. It is always kept well above the ground at all times. We may note, also, that for some bundles the tripods are not set up outside, but leaned against the back of the tipi. Hung up with the true bundle are the other accessories previously described and over all is thrown a robe, formerly a buffalo robe, but now a costly shawl or steamer rug.

In no case must the bundle touch the ground. The name for bear must never be uttered in the tipi nor in the immediate presence of the bundle. He may be spoken of as the "unmentionable one," "that big hairy one," or any other designation. Should one make a mistake, a smudge of sweet pine must be made immediately and in most cases prayers offered for pardon. Even children are expected to know and observe this prohibition. The occupants of the tipi must be very slow to answer or respond to a shout from the outside as it is proper for the caller to enter before speaking.

When the tipi is moved to another place, as formerly in the making and breaking of camp, consideration must be given the pipe bundle. The signal for breaking camp and the selection of a new site are theoretically functions

[5] The smudge places, or altars, while varying somewhat are either rectangular or square. The surface is removed to a depth of about four inches and loose earth deposited outside at the rear along the base of the tipi. The smudge is made at the center. On the left side are placed long tongs made from a forked branch of cherry, used in lifting coals of fire to the smudge place; on the right is a pouch containing needles of the sweet pine. For some pipes the surface of the smudge place is sprinkled with colored earths, but usually it is plain, with a smaller rectangle traced around the center.

of the leader of the band or division, as the case may be; but, if he is not a pipe-man, he leaves it to the owner of such a bundle to act for him, or at least to promulgate his decisions. Thus, when it has been decided that the camp is to break, the bundle is taken some distance from the tipi and the tripod so adjusted that the forward leg extends in the direction to be taken. Thus everyone may know what to expect. For a short period at the start, the owner and his wife sit on a robe in front of the tripod, facing the direction to be taken. Formerly, a special travois, saddle, and other trappings were kept painted red and reserved for the exclusive transportation of the bundle. The horse was painted as previously stated, and ridden by the owner's wife. The bundle was carried on the travois, the tripod tied up against the poles. Sometimes songs were sung and prayers offered at starting and while on the journey, but these can scarcely be considered peculiar to this bundle. On the march the owner, or owners, rode in the lead, usually immediately followed by their wives with the bundles. Likewise, the new camp site was usually designated by setting up the tripods with their bundles. The native partisans of the pipe bundle argue that it is the oldest and most important ritual because it is closely associated with the making of camp and some observers have considered this as one of its important functions. This we believe to be an error, for the data we have indicate that in so far as these moving ceremonies are peculiar to this ritual, they come under the head of the care of the bundle rather than otherwise.

ROBERT H. LOWIE

(1883-1957)

The Crow Indians

CROW INDIAN WARFARE

SOCIAL STANDING AND CHIEFTAINSHIP, WE HAVE SEEN, WERE DEPEND-
ent on military prowess; and that was the only road to distinction. Value
was set on other qualities, such as liberality, aptness at story-telling, success as a doctor. But the property a man distributed was largely the booty
he had gained in raids; and any accomplishments, prized as they might be,
were merely decorative frills, not substitutes for the substance of a reputa-
tion, a man's record as a warrior. I know of at least one Crow of the old
school whose intelligence would have made him a shining light wherever
store was set by sheer capacity of the legal type, but who enjoyed no
prestige whatsoever among his people. In fact, I was repeatedly warned
against his mendacity, though his accounts of tribal life tallied perfectly
with those of generally accredited informants. The point was simply that
he had gained no honors in war and had tried to doctor this deficiency
when publicly reciting his achievements.

War was not the concern of a class nor even of the male sex, but of the
whole population, from cradle to grave. Girls as well as boys derived their
names from a famous man's exploit. Women danced wearing scalps, derived
honor from their husbands' deeds, publicly exhibited the men's shields or
weapons; and a woman's lamentations over a slain son were the most effective goad to a punitive expedition. There are memories of a woman who
went to war; indeed, Muskrat, one of my women informants, claimed to
have struck a coup and scalped a Piegan, thus earning songs of praise.

Most characteristic was the intertwining of war and religion. The Sun
Dance, being a prayer for revenge, was naturally saturated with military
episodes; but these were almost as prominent in the Tobacco ritual, whose

From Lowie, *The Crow Indians* (New York: Farrar and Rinehart, 1935), pp.
215-229, 329-334.

avowed purpose was merely the general welfare. More significant still, every single military undertaking was theoretically inspired by a revelation in dream or vision; and since success in life was so largely a matter of martial glory, war exploits became the chief content of prayer.

Glory, however, was rigorously defined. There were the four standard deeds of valor grouped under the head of the probably synonymous terms ackya'pe or araxtsi', a man with claims to any one of them being an araxtsi'wice, honor-owner. The touching of an enemy—whether he was hurt or not—counted as the "coup" proper, dä'kce. Four men might count coup on the same enemy, but the honor diminished with each successive blow. Also, in any one engagement only one man ranked as the striker of a first-coup; in other words, the first striking of other foemen was not so rated. Snatching away a bow or gun in a hand-to-hand encounter was a second honor; and the theft of a horse picketed in a hostile camp so that it had to be cut loose, was still another. Being the pipe-owner or raid-planner was the fourth deed that counted toward the chieftainship; and a "chief" was simply a man who had achieved at least one of each of these four feats.

In 1910 only two residents of Lodge Grass were regarded as such,— Medicine-crow and Gray-bull; in Pryor there were several, including Bell-rock and Plenty-coups. Though the latter doubtless had an enviable record and was recognized as *the* Crow chief by the U. S. Government, most informants considered Bell-rock supreme among then living men. In Gray-bull's words, Bell-rock was the very first, excelling all others on every count; he had captured five guns, cut loose at least two tethered horses, struck six undisputed coups, and led more than eleven war parties. Gray-bull himself, universally esteemed for bravery, claimed no more than three feats of each category. Hillside fell short of chieftainship only because the enemy retrieved a horse he had cut loose; and Flat-head-woman lacked merely a coup.

Whether all four exploits were on a par remains an open question. Blue-bead gave precedence to captaincy and the coup proper, Gray-bull, speaking in general terms, considered all honors approximately on one plane; yet he put Plenty-coups below Bell-rock notwithstanding Plenty-coups' having seven coups (against six) and four horses (against a possible three). Unconsciously, then, he gave special weight to Bell-rock's two extra war parties.

Irrespective of titular recognition, each new feat added to one's kudos. Even if a man fell short of being a chief, leadership of a successful raid or scalp hunt qualified him as herald and put him next to the chiefs.

Each exploit was symbolically represented on the performer's dress, but the devices varied somewhat. A coup-striker, said Yellow-brow, wore wolf tails at the heels of his moccasins; a gun-snatcher decorated his shirt with ermine skins; and the leader of a party that brought spoils fringed his leggings with ermine or scalps. According to Gray-bull, a captain had the right to put hair on his moccasins as well as his shirt, while a gun-taker or coup-striker might decorate only his shirt in this way.

In the thick of battle disagreement might arise as to which of two combatants had dealt the first blow. This sometimes led to an ordeal or oath-taking called ackya′p-bats-ā′pasū‘a (war-honor-mutually-disputing). Each contestant took a knife, put it into his mouth, pointed it toward the Sun, and uttered such a formula as, "It was I that struck the enemy. Sun, as you looked down, you saw me strike him. Hereafter when I meet an enemy, may I again overcome him without difficulty." Another wording would be: "I struck the coup, you [Sun] saw me. May the one who lies die before winter." In one form of the procedure the people impaled some lean meat on an arrow which they placed on an old dry buffalo skull with its tips painted red. Each rival in turn raised the arrow, pointed his right index-finger at its head, touched the meat with his lips, and pronounced the oath. If both took the test, the people could not at once determine the merits of the case. But if some misfortune befell one of them after the ordeal, he was considered the perjurer and his opponent then justly claimed the contested honor.

Other deeds than the "big four" ranked as meritorious, hence were recited on public occasions and pictured on a man's robe, on the draft screen in his lodge and, rarely, on his tipi cover. In 1910 Shows-a-fish had such decorations on the canvas lining inside his log cabin. On a robe I bought from Charges-strong, pipes near the top symbolize the wearer's captaincy; outlines of heads with upturned lock represent Shoshone, simple outlines standing for Dakota; and horse tracks suggest the capture of horses. In another section of this robe a scout is shown going to the hostile camp and returning to a pile of buffalo chips. Still other parts of the robe depict such details as coups counted on two enemies by the mounted hero, his overtaking and striking a foeman, his driving off Shoshone horses.

At large gatherings the men always formally enumerated their deeds. In 1907 No-shinbone gave me the following list of his own, drawing a line on the ground for each item:

> I captured a gun.
> I captured a bow.
> I led a war party that killed an enemy.
> I was shot.
> I killed a horse.
> I shot a man.
> I brought home ten horses.
> I went to war about fifty times.
> The Dakota were harrying me, I shot one of them.

After each item at a public recital of this type the musicians present would beat the drum once.

The taking of a scalp was evidence of a killing, but did not rank as a deed deserving special notice. "You will never hear a Crow boast of his scalps when he recites his deeds," an informant told me. Some men stretched the trophy in a hoop, scraping off the flesh with a knife and blackening the dried scalp with charcoal. It was subsequently held aloft at the end of a long stick.

Training for war began in childhood. Apart from athletic games, boys counted coups on game animals, made the girls dance with the hair of a wolf or coyote in lieu of a scalp; and in the Hammer Society specifically imitated the adults' military societies.

An ambitious lad, however, would not be content with sham activities, but cast about for a chance to go with a raiding party. On the subject of warfare the older generation, otherwise little inclined to interfere with youth, turned didactic. "Old age is a thing of evil, it is well for a young man to die in battle," summed up the burden of their pedagogy. The prompting of young men by precept and example to gain renown recurs again and again in native tradition. In one story a handsome youth idles at home while his contemporaries go out against the enemy. At length his father, incensed beyond endurance by his son's inactivity, flings himself into the fire, injuring himself, and thus goads the laggard into setting out on a raid. When a youngster did come back from such an experience, he lorded it over his mates, twitting the stay-at-homes with being like a woman. "You are not a boy," Gray-bull used to say to Bird-tail-rattles, "your vulva is blue."

On his maiden trip a boy did not have an easy time of it, for he became the butt of practical jokes. The men were likely to send him to one of their number for shavings from a buffalo hide; on hearing the message, the man told him he had eaten them up and made him go to another member of the party, and so the novice was sent from pillar to post. Moreover, youngsters had to do menial tasks; they were sent for water without instructions where to find it and had to carry the meat. In order to lighten their load, it is said they would encourage their elders to gorge themselves.

Sometimes, of course, a whole band found itself facing a large hostile force, but by far the most typical form of military enterprise was the raid organized by the leader of a small party, the so-called raid-planner or pipe-owner. His venture was a purely personal one, in no way directed by the chief or council; in fact, when the chief considered raids impolitic, he ordered the police to prevent any parties from leaving the camp. Sanction was necessary for a party, but was strictly supernatural. The organizer had dreamt about his enterprise or seen in a vision full particulars about the place to go to, the tribe to be raided, even the kind of loot—to the color of a horse's skin—or the manner of man to be killed, say a thumbless Cheyenne. Failing such inspiration, a would-be leader would apply to a man of note owning a war-medicine and follow this mentor's directions,— likewise based on dreams. An untried captain might not succeed in mustering a large company, for there were always skeptics doubting the potency of his revelation. Even if his medicines were strong, strict rules went with them. In some cases, for instance, no one might pass on his right (or left) side the bearer of the captain's sacred bundle; and however inadvertently the law was broken, dire mishap would befall the entire party.

Lust for fame was axiomatically an end in all warfare. In addition there were two dominant motives,—the desire for booty, which in the main meant horses; and the craving for revenge. Though these drives, varying with individual temperaments and situations, could be combined, we may distinguish horse raids from expeditions for coups and slaughter,—a classification suggested by Flat-back. He set off the former as typically directed against the Piegan from the latter, having the Dakota as an objective.

Raiders characteristically started afoot, hence the need for plenty of footgear. "I had moccasins made for myself" is a formula that denotes preparation for a war party. Often each participant led a dog to carry his moccasins and a small bucket, and afterwards the rope used served to secure the horses purloined. Next to the captain the scouts (ak'tsĭ'te), varying in number with the size of the party, were the most important members; each carried a wolf skin as an emblem and imitated the howling of that animal, so that they were sometimes referred to as "wolves." At a preliminary gathering they sang scout songs, such as these: "I am going to bring horses, I'll bring some back." After the singing a shout went up. A party frequently set out after sunset or even in the dark. For shelter they put up simple windbreaks of sticks, bark, and foliage. At the proper time the captain sent out his scouts to sight the enemy. While the others were still asleep they were up climbing hill after hill, fasting all the time till they saw the camp. Then they returned, giving the wolf howl, to make their report, a sort of homecoming. When close to their party, they brandished their guns to signal that they had really seen something. Now followed a characteristic rite. Their associates had prepared a pile of buffalo chips and sang, forming a semicircle around it. Then the leader of the scouts approached and kicked over the heap of chips. The captain asked for the report, and the scout answered, "The enemy is yonder." Now at last they were allowed to eat meat.

The time having come for final preparations, each brave tied sacred objects to his body and painted his face according to the rules associated with them. The captain spread something to rest *his* medicine on and whistled or sang towards the enemy's camp, possibly saying, "So many horses have been given to me." One man was chosen to lead, and they approached the camp. The captain told his men to gather, went round them, and thus prayed to the Sun: "If all my party get home safe with plenty of horses, I'll make you a sweat-lodge." Then he sent one or two men to camp to drive off all the horses possible. If satisfied with the spoils, he decided to start homeward. The length of their journey naturally varied. Typically, they would run at top-speed all night, the next day, and the second night. On the following day they relaxed, tried to kill a buffalo, and feasted on it. When near their own camp they shot off their guns and rode the captured horses round camp.

In strict theory the captain could claim all the booty; in practice he liberally shared it with his men to avoid the charge of avarice. During the parade the scouts carried wolf hides on their backs and sang tsū'ra songs. At night all the party assembled in the captain's lodge, where the young women came to sit behind them. They sang scout songs, and after that the women got some of the pudding prepared for the occasion and took it home.

No-shinbone thus described one of his raids, atypical only in that it started on horseback. "Where the fortifications were, there we camped. There I ordered moccasins to be made for me. The morning after they were ready I brought my good sorrel horse and saddled him. I went out and took my medicine,—that over there [pointing] is it. I rode away and reached my comrade, the two of us went. Young men kept catching up with us till there were twelve of us. We went and lay down in a little wooded river bed and slept in the night. The next morning we ate; the young men brought the horses, we tied on the saddles and went. It must have been this season of the year. . . . We climbed a hill, there were a great many buffalo. The young men chased them and killed three fat ones. We got there, dismounted, took out our knives, and butchered. When done butchering, we packed the horses and rode away. In a coulée we stopped, young men went as scouts, they reported a sighting. They came, they reached us. 'How is it?' I asked. 'Yonder is the Head-cutters' [Dakota] camp,' they said. 'All right, we'll start against them,' I said. Then I climbed a hill and looked. The camp had killed buffalo, they were carrying huge loads home on their backs. I saw, I came, I reached my party. I lighted buffalo chips and took out my medicine. Then I sang toward the camp. At night we rode, we galloped all the way and approached the camp. At the edge of the camp we sat down. I sent two young men to camp; they brought many horses. Afterwards I again sent two, again they brought many horses. I took a good buckskin, then I said, 'Let us flee.' With many horses we took to flight. At night we continued running, until daylight. We got to a river, mightily we swam it. We were so cold we almost died. We crossed, then it was daylight. That day we ran till night, at night we kept on. Many horses we had brought when we swam the river, plenty of them turned back, but with thirty head I reached camp. The camp was by a creek. There was plenty of meat. Thus I returned."

However,—usually when tribesmen had been slain,—parties were specially organized for the gaining of honors and the killing of enemies.

Gray-bull's report of one of these expeditions is characteristic. He got his war medicine from a medicine-man who had also instructed Hillside and Flat-head-woman. However, unlike these others, who obtained arrows from their adviser, Gray-bull received a tooth extracted from the corpse of a famous Crow warrior killed by the enemy; all three men got similar accessories. Because the original purchaser of the tooth had been notably successful, Gray-bull bought it for ten horses. He, too, enjoyed good luck and got together a herd of from 70 to 90 horses.

One day Gray-bull was seated by his mentor, when a woman mourning her son put a pipe in front of him. The medicine-man told him to light and smoke it. "I obeyed and then handed the pipe to him. There was a crowd of people in the lodge and the pipe was passed round the circle. I did not yet know that the woman had a horse loaded with gifts outside. She unloaded the presents; my 'father' gave me a striped blanket and had his wife distribute the remainder of the property. She gave me the reins of the horse. My 'father' thus spoke to her: 'Well, you have given my son the pipe; I am angry' [at the enemy]. He then spoke to me for a while, and I called out to her, word for word, what he had told me: 'Grandmother, to-morrow I shall make a sweat-lodge, the next night I shall start.' The following day I made a sweat-lodge. Before starting I called on the old woman and again told her I would be on my journey the next morning, that eight days hence she was to pulverize charcoal, mix it with fat, and be on the lookout for me.

"Six days later a body of Piegan saw us and stole our unpicketed horses. We followed in pursuit, found four Piegan, killed them and recovered all but two horses. We then turned homeward. Starting out we had traveled very slowly, but coming home we went as fast as possible. The eighth night was drawing near and I left my party so as to be home in time. The old woman was waiting for me on the outskirts of the camp. She began to cry and asked whether I was coming back with spoils. I told her I had killed four of the enemy, that she should stop crying and prepare charcoal because the rest of the party were coming. She continued to cry and wished to get further details, but I loped away to report to my 'father,' who was with the expedition.

"In the center of the camp they formed a circle and the Long Dance was begun by the men on the expedition. Then each warrior individually invited the people to his lodge to tell them the story of the war party. On this occasion it was a coup-striker's a'sa'ke, i.e. a clansman of his father's, who sang his praises and as compensation received presents, largely contributed by the brave's own clan.

"They waited for a favorable day, then a herald proclaimed a big tsū'ra celebration. The best singers were reassembled for this occasion. Each coup-striker put his medicine on his wife's head and had her carry his weapons. The captain would tie his medicine to his wife's back or to a long stick which she was to raise. All the camp turned out to watch. If a man had duplicate medicines, he and his wife took one apiece. The wives of the captain and the coup-strikers stood in the center and danced till evening, then stopped; but the mourners, with blackened faces, kept on till the next morning. Old men again led the coup-strikers around.

"The next morning, before sunrise, people sneaked into the lodges of the warriors and threw off their blankets, even though they might be lying with their wives. Then the men dressed up and danced with the mourners. The captain called to the coup-strikers to prepare food for these men jostled out of bed. There was bustle in camp and people went to watch the performance. The coup-strikers were again praised in song; and the mourners danced until noon."

Warriors always blackened their faces to symbolize the killing of an enemy, so that "with black face" is a stereotyped phrase for a victorious return. This is the meaning of the charcoal paint on Gray-bull's companions when he got back to them. They had evidently also conformed to another usage, that is, had killed a buffalo and put its blood into a paunch as the material for decorating their garments. The blood was mixed and stirred in warm water with two kinds of charcoal. First the men rubbed their robes with wetted clay, then several eminent men, having enumerated their own deeds, painted each robe with the symbol of the first coup struck. Though four men counted coup on one enemy, the honor decreased in ordinal succession and the painting of the robes varied accordingly. The first man to capture a gun and the first coup-striker had their robe or shirt blackened all over, the second and third men had only half of their garment so decorated, and the fourth men had only the arms of their shirts painted. The distinguished men also instructed the members as to other decorations; thus, there would be horse-tracks, parallel stripes, and, irrespective of the number of enemies struck, from four to six roughly sketched human figures. Thus attired, the party approached the camp, spending the last night very close to it. The following morning, as soon as within shooting distance, they fired off their guns and made a characteristic noise. When at the edge of the camp, they sent the coup-strikers to fetch one drum for every warrior. In the meantime the women, who carried the scalp sticks, got ready and danced into camp ahead of the warriors.

A victorious homecoming was called ara'tsiwe,—apparently whether the Crow had struck coups or stolen horses; however, a successful raid was probably not considered sufficient to "make the women dance." Supposing the warriors had killed an enemy, they painted their faces one or two nights after their return and marched through camp, with the captain in the rear and a herald behind him. The herald cried out, "You women, all of you put on your finery and go to the Pipe-owner's lodge, we shall feast there tonight." So all the people went there after the parade, the women streaming in and sitting down behind the warriors of their choice. They sang scout and scalp songs; each took her favorite's robe and tomahawk, stood up in a conspicuous place by the door, and began to dance. The herald, seated by the door, named the first coup-striker, and after his response told him to fill a pail with cherry dessert brought by the women and give it to his wife. The first scout to sight the enemy was allowed to choose whatever food he preferred, turned it over to his wife, and then waited on the other women present. Both scouts helped themselves first, then waited on the other men. After every one had feasted on stewed berries and other food, the older men ordered the women to take the residue home and return for the performance of "lodge-striking."

For this act the boys cut willow poles and leaned them against the tipi, then lined up to wait for the women's return. A herald shouted, "Untie your horses and take them further away, these young men are going to strike the lodge!" Those of the party who were singers beat drums, the rest took willow sticks, as did the young women, for each man had a girl with him. Amidst victory songs and beating of drums, all rushed towards the captain's tipi and struck it, some men shooting off their guns. The noise was such that horses got frightened and ran away. Hitherto the songs had been without words, but after the striking of the tipi they sang this sentence, "Recently I went away, I have returned, kiss me." Then they proceeded to the center of the camp, where they danced, the men with blankets wrapped about their women partners, and all circling about with a step of the Owl dance type, moving both right and left. Usually five or six tents were struck. The celebration after a killing would last a day and a night.

Praise songs in honor of the returning braves were a distinctive feature of the celebration. It was above all a man's a′sa‘kua and isbāxi′u, i.e., his father's clansmen and clanswomen, who led him about camp as his public panegyrists, calling out his name and singing these chants, which originated in dreams. The words bear no obvious relation to any meritorious deed, Gray-bull and Medicine-crow independently furnishing the following sample: "I'll adopt you as my grandmother." In return the singer received presents. Such songs were sometimes sung on the expedition itself by the leader or old members of the party. In 1910 aged Crow men still sang praise songs in honor of younger people who had presented them with other valuable gifts. Gray-bull sold his praise songs for a horse.

But not all war parties had an auspicious ending. There is a tradition in which the best sorts of captains are mentioned, and "those who never signaled a loss" take precedence of "those who regularly bring horses" and "those who regularly kill." If a member of the party was killed, his associates did not at once enter camp, but dispatched a messenger, who fired off a gun from some high eminence. When people looked thither, he waved his blanket to show from what direction he had come. Every one then knew what had happened and who was the unlucky captain. For each man killed, the messenger lowered the blanket or threw it to one side. He did not approach the camp but sat down, and men were sent to interview him about the details of the disaster. The camp went into mourning while the party stayed in the hills, mourning for ten days; during this period they did not drink from a cup, being served with drink by others. They then set off again without having entered the camp. If they lifted horses on this second trip, their grieving was over; but the bereaved family kept up their mourning until the death of an enemy.

The notion was deep-rooted among Plains Indians that no tribesman's life should be lost if by any possibility it could be avoided, hence the sacrifice of men on behalf of strategic gains was utterly foreign to Crow conceptions. Of course, there were daredevils who risked their necks for sheer bravado, and others who ignored danger from a sublime faith in their supernaturally guaranteed invulnerability. But though long life was theoretically contemptible and a glorious death in battle was held up as ideal in practice more prosaic counsels prevailed with the average man. Hence the amazing phenomenon that recurs in Plains Indian traditions of a single desperado holding back and even routing a dozen foemen; hence the oft-repeated Crow prayer that the supplicant may kill his enemy easily, safely, without injury to himself.

Why did the Crow fight? Certainly not from an uncontrollable instinct of pugnacity. It was disgraceful to fall to fisticuffs within the tribe, and I have heard unfavorable comments on the brawls of white men. Enemies, of course, were fair game, but in spite of high-flown phrases about "wiping them out," I know of no concerted effort to oust the Dakota or Cheyenne from their territory, and tradition tells of relatively few ancient enterprises on a really large scale. Minor operations, sufficing to gratify both the sportive urge and even the craving for revenge, could be more readily harmonized with the repugnance to any loss of tribesmen.

Doubtless the stimuli for military enterprise were not uniform, varying with different men and different situations. Utilitarian urges appear but were certainly not dominant. The desire for horses was the most "economical" motive of Plains Indian warfare, yet a Crow rated higher for cutting loose one picketed horse than for lifting a dozen freely roaming about. And what was the use of horses after one got them? Gray-bull acquired 70 to 90 head, but a few fleet animals for the buffalo chase, several mounts, and a few pack-horses would have been more than ample for his needs. The Crow, unlike the Central Asiatic Turks, never dreamt of milking mares or eating horse flesh. A large herd had sheer ostentation value; the owner could offer twenty horses for a wife instead of five; and he could give frequent presents to his father's clansfolk if he liked to hear himself eulogized.

Again, it was meritorious to kill an enemy, but the lightest tap with a coup-stick was reckoned higher. Obviously the idea was not primarily to reduce a hostile force but to execute a "stunt," to play a game according to whimsical rules. Intrepidity was, it is true, cordially admired,—as when a Crow turned back to save a disabled tribesman. But, like chastity, such daring was praised rather than emulated. Here, too, concessions were made to original sin: in the clubs even the officers "doomed to die" were held to their pledge only for a single season. What is more, the very Crazy Dogs who volunteered deliberately to court death were scot-free of their obligation if they happened to escape by the close of the season.

Counting the capture of a picketed horse toward the chieftaincy was assuredly to reward boldness; yet Hillside who achieved the deed failed to score because the enemy recovered his prize. On the other hand, when the first man to *touch* a foe ranked above the one who had laid him low, it was fleetness, not skill or valor, that carried the day. Similarly, the Crow who struck the first enemy in an engagement need not have been a whit braver than another who struck the fifth or tenth; yet it was the former who gained preeminence. In a possibly historical tale, Plays-with-his-face, a picked champion, together with an inexperienced boy, surprises a Cheyenne easing himself at the edge of the hostile camp. They pursue him, the ingenuous youth boldly dashing into the midst of the camp, where he thinks he is counting coup. But his wily companion has already struck a conveniently close enemy and tauntingly establishes his claim to the highest honor.

The coup was indeed interpreted in so conventional a way that often it bore no relation to true bravery whatsoever. When Bull-tongue was once sent to a Dakota camp as scout, he found a woman urinating and killed her,—which was sufficient. On another occasion a Crow party were patiently but vainly lying in ambush for some one to leave the Dakota camp. At length one of them possessed of power sang his chant, made a motion with his pipe, drew the picture of a man on the ground, and put his pipe on it. Soon an unarmed Dakota sallied forth, riding toward the mountains. "We chased the man toward camp and killed him"—the first one to touch the body naturally claiming first honors. It was enough to warrant a big celebration: "We danced mightily," Grandmother's-knife told me. Again, Flat-back piqued himself not a little on having killed four squaws near a hostile camp. "Medicine-crow is a chief," he said, "yet he does not equal me." This was mere pleasantry, for Medicine-crow was a "brother-in-law," hence fair butt for raillery about war though never about sexual matters; but the jocularity did not disguise the speaker's conviction that he had achieved a real exploit.

WORLD VIEW OF THE CROW

Battered by natural forces and surrounded by enemies, the Crow managed to wrest from existence his portion of happiness. Ask an Indian of the old school whether he prefers modern security to the days of his youth: he will brush aside all recent advantages for a whiff of the buffalo-hunting days. If there was starvation then, there were buffalo tongues, too,—supreme among earthly dishes; if you were likely to be killed, you had a chance to gain glory. What is a Crow to look forward to nowadays? Shall he enter unequal competition with white farmers? And his sister aspire to wash the laundry of frontier towns? Under the old régime, harassed as he might be, the Crow was owner of his soul. He had somehow hammered out for himself standards that lifted him above the sordid animal-like fray for survival. So with all the grossness of his sex life there evolved awe-inspired reverence for immaculate virtue; the callous egotism of the daily struggle for existence could be transmuted into purest self-sacrifice; above the formalized and sometimes tricky competition for honor emerged the loftiest defiance of relentless destiny.

We have found the Indians a mass of contradictions; and nowhere more so than in the matter of bravery. On the one side, old age is decried and youthful death alone looms as a man's proper lot in life. Yet more often than not discretion seems the better part of valor. More than one character in the tales lives to be "so old that his flesh cracked whenever he moved." The visions that mirror so faithfully the hidden longings of the soul again and again bring out the same urge for longevity. Hillside's protector appears with gray hair in earnest of the visionary's old age; a buffalo opens his toothless mouth to show Humped-wolf that he need not fear death until he has lost his teeth; and so forth. So the commonest form of prayer asks for life to be continued until such and such a season. Again, a warrior *could* scry before setting out on a raid: if he saw his image with wrinkled face in a mixture of buffalo and badger blood, all was well; if he saw himself scalped or bloodstained, evil awaited him. But, Gray-bull admitted, people in his heyday were afraid to use this kind of divination; and his grandfather had become very brave *after* seeing his reflection with white hair and wrinkled face.

But as in every generation there were women who would not yield to the temptations of the flesh and fulfilled the qualifications of a Tree-notcher in the Sun Dance, so there were men to whom the traditional ideals were more than empty words to be sung at a dance to impress the young women. "I do not want to be old . . . I don't want to be afraid of anything . . . I'll do something to die," said one Rides-a-white-horse-down-a-bank. He went on four parties and dug himself a hole. When the enemy surrounded it, he leapt out and drove them back. Once there was a Lumpwood dance, and he allowed himself to be led about camp by a man who declared: "If any young women want this man for a sweetheart, let them do it forthwith, he does not want to live long." The young man painted himself white, mounted his white horse, covered its eyes, and made it jump down a steep and rocky bank, so that both of them were crushed.

Such aversion from life was sufficiently common to be pressed into a fixed pattern. A man no longer interested in living became a "Crazy-Dog-wishing-to-die" (micgye-warā'axeakcēwī'a); he wore sashes and other trappings for regalia, carried a rattle, danced and sang distinctive songs as he rode about camp. He "talked crosswise" (irī'-watbakarā'), i.e., he said the opposite of what he meant and expected to be addressed correspondingly. Above all, he was pledged to foolhardiness. In this as in other features he conformed to the pattern of the military clubs. But while the officers in these societies were in the main obliged merely to hold their ground, a Crazy Dog deliberately courted death, recklessly dashing up to the enemy so as to be killed within the space of one season. Whenever one of them rode through camp, the old women cheered him lustily and younger ones came to comfort him at night. But his own kin naturally tried to dissuade him and grieved over his resolve to die. "Why have you done that?" Spotted-rabbit's mother asked: "you are one of the best-situated young men . . . you are one of the most fortunate men who ever lived . . . and were always happy." But Spotted-rabbit was bored with life because he could not get over his father's death. Similarly, Cottontail's sister tried to dissuade him: "This is a bad thing for you to do. Even if you want to die without good cause, there are plenty of enemies and if you are not afraid you can get killed without special effort. If men become Crazy Dogs and are not killed, they become a laughingstock, . . . they are said to be worthless." The account continues: "He did not say 'Yes,' he said nothing at all, but one night some time after this when the people had gone to bed he came out, shouting, and sang the Crazy Dog songs. His sisters fell a-crying, but there was nothing they could do." Cottontail, too, had a motive: he had never wholly recovered from the injury to his knee. "Whenever young men went afoot on a raid or hunting, whenever they undertook anything, he was handicapped and felt envious."

Such men grew restive if the days passed and their longing remained unfulfilled. When Spotted-rabbit received a gift of plums, he said, "I began to be a Crazy Dog early in the spring and did not think I should live so long; yet here am I today eating plums." And Cottontail would complain, "Methinks, we'll *never* meet the enemy." But he, like Spotted-rabbit before him, had his wish. Once the Crow made the enemy fortify himself in a trench. Cottontail said, "Already I was thinking I was not to see the enemy . . . ; yonder I see some. This is what I am looking for." He advanced, shot down at the Dakota, and was instantly killed. That night it rained violently, and the corpse lay in the water until daybreak. Then the Crow hung it over Cottontail's horse. "Then they brought him home, grieving they took him to the camp, all the Crow, the entire camp cried. They laid him on a scaffold, they stuck a tipi pole into the ground and tied his sashes to it, his drum and rattle they tied to it. Above they were blowing in the breeze. Then without him they moved."

The respect paid to a Crazy Dog was probably not altogether due to admiration for egotistical recklessness. It was a foregone conclusion that a man who had renounced life would do the utmost damage possible to the enemy. More than a mere paragon of valor, he was thus at least potentially a source of power to the tribe. But the altruistic value of intrepidity appears in more explicit fashion. There were men willing to make a stand to rescue a fleeing fellow-Crow and honored accordingly. A bereaved mother would go about wailing and implore brave men to avenge her wrongs: "The Dakota have killed my . . . child, who is going to kill one of them for me?" And the warrior's mentor would encourage him with such words as: "A child has been killed, a woman has asked you for help, that is why I want you to help." In the herald's speeches already quoted the appeal is constantly to human sympathy with the pitiable captives subjected to humiliation by a cruel chief and casting wistful glances toward their possible liberators.

The same narrative contains an extraordinary human document exposing at once human frailty and grandeur in the same individual and culminating in a magnificent blending of patriotic fervor on behalf of the oppressed tribesfolk and the spirit of the Crazy Dog who has faced reality and turns his back upon this vale of tears. Double-face has been one of the young braves publicly presented to the tribe by the herald as their champions in the impending battle. But when the crowd has dispersed, Double-face is racked with doubts. To quote Yellow-brow:

"Then this day Double-face was lying around; he stripped, he was nervous, he was uncomfortable. Whatever he undertook turned out ill. The reason he was upset was that there was to be a battle and he was nervous: whether because of eagerness or fear, whatever the cause, that is why he was upset. He would smoke, he would sit up, he lay down, he got up and bathed, he would return and stroll about, then he sat down. Now he had an elder brother, Deer-necklace, and him he sent for. He came and entered. 'Sit there.' This man who had just entered said, 'Well, why are you calling me?' 'Well, I am upset now, that is why I am calling you. There are three things I am now eager to do: I want to sing a sacred song; I want to sing a Big Dog song; I want to cry. Why is it thus?' Double-faced asked. This man answered: 'You are about to go to battle, your medicines are anxious, that is why. Wait!' He boiled wild-carrot root . . . and mixed it with a little white clay. He [Double-face] took it . . . and swallowed it. 'That is all, I'll go now.' This man went out and away.

"Double-face got very hot, he began to perspire. His horse had been standing. 'I have been upset, but I shall accomplish my purpose,' he said and went out. He took his horse, marked it, fitted on his medicines, painted himself, and went out mounted to wail within the camp-circle:

" 'I used to think that since my birth I had had many sorrows. It turns out that there was something in store for me. I was grieving, but I did not know that today all manner of sorrow would be coming to a head. The women at my home are miserable, I daresay. 'How are the captive Crow faring?' they are ever thinking to themselves. My poor dear housemates, my distressed kin, the enemy makes them sit under the dripping water, he is ever abusing them, he thinks his men are the only ones to be brave. What can I do to distress him, I wonder?

" 'You Above, if there be one who knows what is going on, repay me today for the distress I have suffered. Inside the Earth, if there be any one there who knows what is going on, repay me for the distress I have suffered. The One Who causes things, Whoever he be, I have now had my fill of life. Grant me death, my sorrows are overabundant. Though children are timid, they die harsh deaths, it is said. Though women are timid, You make them die harsh deaths. *I* do not want to live long; were I to live long, my sorrows would be overabundant, I do not want it!'

"He went crying," the tale continues, "and those who heard him all cried."

We have here reached the peak of the Crow spirit. With a splendid gesture the hero turns away from the earthly goods that figure so largely in Crow prayer; he has no thought even of glory, he thinks only of his suffering kin in a hostile camp. Bruised by the problem of evil that in retrospect seems to have dogged him from infancy, he asks only for release from his torture. Why linger? Earth and sky are everlasting, but men must die; old age is a scourge and death in battle a blessing.

J. R. WALKER

(dates unknown)

The Sun Dance of the Oglala

ONE DESIRING TO DANCE THE SUN DANCE ACCORDING TO THE CUSTOMS OF the Oglala as they were practised before contact with white people should choose an instructor to prepare him for the ceremony, who should teach him, in substance, as follows:—

The Sun Dance of the Oglala is a sacred ceremony which may be undertaken by any one of mankind, provided he or she:—

1. Undertakes it for a proper purpose.
2. Complies with the essentials for the ceremony.
3. Conforms to the customs of the Oglala.
4. Accepts the mythology of the Lakota.

The proper purposes for undertaking the Sun Dance are:—

1. To fulfill a vow.
2. To secure supernatural aid for another.
3. To secure supernatural aid for self.
4. To secure supernatural powers for self.

The time is:—

1. When the buffalo are fat.
2. When new sprouts of sage are a span long.
3. When chokecherries are ripening.
4. When the Moon is rising as the Sun is going down.

Before beginning to dance the Sun Dance during the ceremony the Candidate must make an acceptable offering to the Sun and have a wound that will cause his blood to flow while he dances. If he dances the Sun Dance to its completion, he may expect a vision in which he may receive a communication from the Sun.

All the requirements and rites pertaining to this ceremony are based upon the Mythology of the Lakota and they must be supervised by a

From Walker, "The Sun Dance and other ceremonies of the Oglala Division of the Teton Dakota," *Anthropological Papers, American Museum of Natural History,* Vol. 16, Pt. 2 (New York, 1917), pp. 60-63, 102, 105-119.

Shaman. A Shaman must control the ceremonial camp and conduct all the ceremonies pertaining to the Sun Dance that take place there, except the dance, which should be conducted by the leader of the dance. This dance may take either of the four forms, which are:—

1. Gaze-at-Sun.
2. Gaze-at-Sun Buffalo.
3. Gaze-at-Sun Staked.
4. Gaze-at-Sun Suspended.

The first is the simplest form and may be undertaken for either of the first three purposes enumerated above and performed with a scant compliance with the essentials, though the Candidate must comply with them to the best of his ability. It should be danced only when one or more of the other forms are danced. It must begin with the first song of the Sun Dance and continue during four songs, though it may continue during as many more songs as the dancer pleases. For this form, any offering may be made to the Sun, but it should be of as much value as the Candidate can afford. The wound to cause the blood to flow must not be smaller than that made by cutting away a bit of skin as large as a louse and it may be as large and deep as the Candidate wills to have it made. Women and children may dance the first form, because there are no tortures inflicted during the dance. Those who have danced the Sun Dance on a former occasion may again dance this form, provided they first make an offering to the Sun and cause the blood to flow from wounds on their persons. Such dancers may begin the dance at any time during the dance by others and may dance for as many songs as they choose.

The second, third, and fourth forms each differ from the others only in the manner of the wounds to cause the flow of blood and the torture inflicted during the dance; but the wounds and tortures for each form should be made alike for each dancer of that form. One may undertake either of these three forms for either of the first three purposes; but one who undertakes to dance for the fourth purpose must dance the fourth form. The torture inflicted in the fourth form, may be, either figuratively or actually, suspending the dancer while he dances. If the dancer is dancing for the purpose of securing the supernatural powers that Shamans should have, he must dance the fourth form actually suspended. A dance thus performed is the Sun Dance in its fullest form which includes most of the Mythology and much of the customs of the Oglala. One who dances the Sun Dance in its fullest form establishes before the Sun, and in the presence of the people, his possession of the four great virtues, which are:—

1. Bravery.
2. Generosity.
3. Fortitude.
4. Integrity.

One who possesses these four virtues should be respected and honored by all the people. Thus, the scars made by the wounds and tortures inflicted during the Sun Dance are honorable insignia.

One who contemplates dancing the Sun Dance should know these things and carefully consider the compliance with the essentials for the performance of the ceremony, for it is done for the benefit of both the dancer and the people. He should endeavor to know whether the people deem his virtues sufficient to enable him to dance the Sun Dance to its completion or not; for, if they think he lacks in one or all of the great virtues, they probably will not become constituents, and he cannot have the ceremony performed.

The Sun Dance is a festal ceremony and provision must be made for feasts that are rites and are to be given by the Candidate, his kindred, and his band, for all these are honored by the performance of the ceremony. Therefore, while it is expected that a Candidate will give all his possessions in making provision for the feasts, his kindred and his friends should also give liberally; indeed, the entire band should contribute for both feasts and presents. A Candidate must give presents to his Mentor and attendant and should give to all the assistants and those who take an active part in the rites of the ceremony. He must provide the equipment necessary for the occasion, and make acceptable offerings to the Sun. If he cannot comply with these conditions in an abundant manner, he should undertake only the first form of the dance, and then little will be expected of him or his people. If he thinks he can make suitable provision, he may proceed.

CHOOSING THE MENTOR

He should choose some one to be his Mentor to prepare him for the ceremony. He should make this choice according to the purpose for which he will undertake the dance, for his Mentor should be one who can fit him for that purpose. He may choose anyone, except that if he is to dance to become a Shaman he must choose a Shaman as his Mentor. This too, should be borne in mind, that to become the leader of the dance the Candidate's Mentor must be a Shaman.

When he has made his choice he should take a present, a pipe, and smoking material, and go to the tipi of the one chosen, enter it, and lay the present at the right side of the *catku,* which is the place at the rear inside the tipi, and opposite the door, the place of honor. By thus placing a present, one indicates that he has a request of importance to make. When he has placed the present, he should fill the pipe, light it, and offer it to the one chosen. In ordinary visits, the one who dwells in the tipi is first to fill the pipe and light it and then offers it to the visitor as a courtesy indicating friendship. If a visitor fills the pipe first and offers it to the host, this indicates that he esteems his host very highly and is willing to be subordinate to him. If the host refuses the pipe this indicates that he does not desire intimate relations with the one offering it. If the pipe thus offered by one who has made a choice for his Mentor is refused, he may choose another, but it would be better for him to proceed no farther in the matter because such a refusal would indicate that all his people are not willing to become constituents in a ceremony performed for him. But if the pipe is accepted, the one offering and the one accepting it, should smoke it in communion until its contents are consumed. Why they two alone should smoke this pipeful and why they should smoke until the contents of the pipe are consumed, will appear in the course of this paper.

Having smoked in communion, which is done by passing the pipe from one to the other and alternately smoking four whiffs from it, the host should ask the visitor regarding his request and the visitor should tell his desires and make his request. In case the request is for the host to become a Mentor, he should take the present and place it with his possessions and appoint a day when he will come to the tipi of the one who has chosen him, and then and there, give his answer to the request. The one who is to receive this answer should make a feast on the appointed day and invite two of his friends to the feast. On that day, the one chosen and the invited friends should go to the tipi where the feast is made and feast with the one who gives it. . . .

SACRED LODGE ERECTED

When the location is established the Sacred Lodge should be erected in the following manner. It should be the new tipi and poles provided with the equipment. The women who are to chop the Sacred Tree should erect these poles and then the Superior should paint a dab of red on the inner side of each pole and paint red on the ears and door flap of the covering. When this is done the women should place and pin the covering.

When this lodge is thus erected the Mentors should prepare it for occupation by the Candidates by each making a bed of sage in it for his Candidate and the Superior should prepare in it an altar between the fireplace and the place of honor. Then he should place beside the altar the ornamented buffalo head, so that it will face toward the place of honor.

When the Sacred Lodge is thus prepared the Candidates should enter it. They should be conducted through the door and to their beds by their Mentors. The first to enter the lodge should be the one who first announced his candidacy, but if he has declined this honor the Candidates should choose another to take it. The first who enters should be conducted to the place of honor and seated there. He is thereby made the leader of the Sun Dance. When all the Candidates have entered the Sacred Lodge, the Superior should fill and light a pipe, and pass it so that all in the lodge may smoke in communion. When all have been thus harmonized, the

Mentors should give such instructions as they deem necessary, and then depart. After this, the attendants may come and go into the Sacred Lodge as the wants of the Candidates may demand; but only the Mentors and the attendants should come near the Sacred Lodge or attempt to talk with its occupants. Soon after the Candidates occupy the lodge the attendants should bring them the robes that have been provided. . . .

CAPTURE OF THE TREE

On the second holy day, after the escort has driven evil beings from the camp and the Superior has formally greeted the Sun, the red herald should proclaim that the people form for the procession of the Bear God. Then a procession should form and march as on the previous day, but it should be done without levity. When the procession disperses, the Superior should command the red herald to proclaim that the hunter has reported that an enemy is near the camp. He then should command the escort to go in search of the enemy and if found take him captive. The escort, and those who wish to join them, should search all about in the vicinity of the camp, as if looking for signs of an enemy. Soon they should return and report to the Superior that no signs of an enemy have been found. The Superior should command them to go and search again, and they should do as before. This is repeated until the fourth time, when the escort finds the Sacred Tree. They should surround it, jeering and taunting it, and then rush upon it, strike it, and bind a thong about it.

When they have done this they should return to the camp singing a victory song and shouting like victorious returning warriors. The people should greet their return with songs and shouts of joy and the women should ululate shrilly. The escort should report to the Superior that the enemy has been found and made captive and the herald should proclaim this to the people who should rejoice and shout and sing warrior songs. The Superior should then command the red herald to proclaim the formation of the procession that is to bring the enemy into the camp. The procession should be formed with the Superior and Mentors leading, followed by the escort, the mothers bearing babes whose ears are to be pierced, the children whose parents wish thus to honor them, the women who are to chop the Sacred Tree, and finally, the people. The procession should go, if practicable, so as to cross running water at its second pause. At about one fourth the distance to the Sacred Tree, the Superior should halt and light a pipe and all should wait until he has smoked a few whiffs. Then the procession should move on until one half the distance is covered; there again the Superior should halt as before, and if there is running water there he should strike it four times with his Fetish, to drive from it the *Mini Watu,* or evil water creatures that can infect the people. Again, at three fourths the distance all should halt as before. Then the procession should go to the tree and surround it. Now the Superior may harangue the people and should proclaim aloud four times the name of some reputable man, preferably one who is renowned for war deeds. The one so named should come forward and take the chopper and may recite the deeds that make him eligible to strike the Sacred Tree. When he has done so, he should strike the Sacred Tree on the west side four times with the chopper, and if he can do so, leave the chopper sticking in the tree. This should be repeated until four men have struck the tree, each four times, first on the west, then the north, then the east, and then on the south. The *nagila* of the tree is thus subdued and made subservient to the people.

When this is done, the children who are to be honored are placed in line, and the herald, beginning at one end of the line should call the names of the children successively as they stand, and when a name is so called those wishing to honor the child should come forward and give it presents. When this is done, the Superior should command that the Sacred Tree be felled. Then the women appointed to chop the Sacred Tree should do so, relieving each other so that all may have a chance. When the tree is about to fall the woman chosen to fell it should strike the last blows that cut it down. As the tree falls, the people should sing and shout and ululate for joy because it is now their servant. To ululate one should utter a prolonged sound in high or falsetto key, patting the lips with the fingers while doing so. This is an expression of intensity of emotion.

When the tree is down it should be trimmed and the bark peeled from it to its smaller end. The bark should be left on the fork at the smaller end. This is the Sacred Pole. Pregnant women, and women who have young babes will eagerly gather the twigs that are trimmed from the tree, for they are powerfully effective against *Anog Ite*.

After the Superior pronounces the pole Sacred, it should not be touched by hands that are not painted red. Then it should be carried to the camp in the following manner:—A sufficient number of carrying sticks should be placed under it and the carriers should lift it on these without touching it with their hands and carry it, butt forward, toward the camp. When about one fourth the distance to be carried, the carriers should halt and lay the Sacred Pole on the ground. Then they should howl like wolves, for this is the cry of returning warriors who come bringing a captive. Then another relay of carriers should lift and carry the pole in the same manner to half the distance, where they should lay it down and howl as did the first relay. Then another relay should carry it in the same manner as before, to three fourths the distance, where they should lay it down and howl.

Then the messenger race should be run in this manner:—The young men who desire to run this race should stand side by side in a line at the Sacred Pole, and starting at a signal should race for the Sacred Spot. The first to place his hand on the Sacred Spot; or in the hole for the erection of the Sacred Pole is thereby entitled to carry a red coup stick, or a banner of feathers. A runner in this race should obstruct his competitors in any manner he can. Thus a runner in this race may be seriously injured by a blow or a fall.

After the race of the messengers the fourth relay of carriers should lift and carry the pole as before, taking it through the entrance to the camp circle and into the Dance Lodge, where they should lay it down with the forked end toward the east and the butt at the hole prepared for its erection. It should be so placed that when it is erected it will follow the course of the Sun. When the Sacred Pole is laid in the Dance Lodge the people may disperse, but the Superior and Mentors should then mix the paints and fats supplied with the equipment, and they, or others, whose hands are painted red, should paint the Sacred Pole, so that its west side will be red, its north blue, its east green, and its south side yellow.

The fork of the pole should not be painted and the paint should be so applied to the body of the pole that when erect the opening of the fork will be toward the west and east. While others are painting the Sacred Pole one of the Mentors should cut from the dried buffalo skins without hair, provided with the equipment, the figures of a bull buffalo and of a man, each with exaggerated genitals, and painted black. When the Sacred Pole is painted, all but the Superior, Mentors, and Shamans should be excluded from the Dance Lodge. Those remaining should sit in a circle around the black images, and by incantation, impart to the image of a man the potency of *Iya,* the patron God of libertinism, and to the image of the buffalo the potency of *Gnaski,* the Crazy Buffalo, the patron God of licentiousness. When thus prepared, these images should be carefully wrapped and bound so as to restrain them until they are elevated.

When the people disperse from the Dance Lodge the societies may give feasts, one or more at the same time, but all should unite in feasting. During this feast, each society should be grouped, and each served by its women folks before the people are served. After feasting, each society may dance its dances and such others as the regulations of the society will permit, may dance with them. These festivities may continue far into the night, but they should cease while the Superior greets the Sun as He disappears from sight.

When it is dark that night the Superior and Mentors should again go in procession about the camp for the same purposes as on the previous night, and then visit the Candidates in the Sacred Lodge. This completes the formalities of the second holy day.

THE PROCESSION OF SEX

From dawn on the third holy day until the Sun shows His face, the same rites should be performed as on the preceding day. Then the herald should call the people to form the procession of sex in which children take no part. It should form near the council lodge, the women in front and the men behind, with an interval between the sexes. This procession should march around inside the camp circle four times, the women with song and speech lauding the Earth and the Feminine, while the men in the same manner laud the Sky and the Wind. When this procession returns to the starting place the fourth time, it should disperse, and then the Superior and Mentors should go to the Sacred Lodge, and remind the Candidates that they may drink, but take no food on that day.

RAISING THE SUN POLE

They should then go in procession on the Sun Trail to the Dance Lodge and enter it. There the Superior should prepare the Fetish of the Sun Dance, making it of four times four wands of chokecherry wood and enclosing in it a wisp of sage, one of sweetgrass, and a tuft of shed buffalo hair. He may also enclose in it such trinkets or ornaments as the people give for that purpose. When this bundle is securely bound, the Superior, assisted by such Shamans as he may select, should, with the aid of his Fetish and by proper ceremony, impart to it the potency of the Buffalo God so that when it is elevated the Buffalo God will prevail in the camp.

Then he should securely bind this Fetish to one fork of the Sacred Pole. When he has done this, he should prepare the banner of the Shamans, making it of some red material that will wave. It should be four arms' length long and four hands' breadth wide, with a wand at one end to keep it spread. This end of the banner should be securely fastened to the fork of the Sacred Pole other than that to which the Fetish is bound. The Fetish and banner should be so securely fastened that they will not be loosened by blows or shooting with arrows.

While the Superior is preparing the Fetish and banner, men whose hands are painted red should prepare the Sacred Pole for erection by tying to it thongs with which to pull it erect. Then a *heyoka* to whom the Winged God has granted a communication should loosely tie to each fork of the Sacred Pole the black images of a man and a buffalo, so that when the pole is erect they will be above the Fetish and the banner, and so that they can be brought down by blows or shooting with arrows.

Then at the command of the Superior the men with red hands should lift the Sacred Pole to about one fourth the distance to the perpendicular and pause, holding it there while the herald proclaims that the Sacred Pole is going up. The people should assemble about the Dance Lodge, men and women grouped apart. At the command of the Superior the men with red hands should lift the pole half way to the perpendicular and pause. During this pause those who wish to do so should make offerings to the Earth by placing the articles offered in the hole at the Sacred Spot. When these offerings are made the Superior should again command the red-handed men to lift the pole and they should raise it to about three-fourths of perpendicular and there pause. Then the herald should proclaim that the Gods elevated on the Sacred Pole must prevail in the camp. Then the Superior should command the men to raise the Sacred Pole erect and they should lift and pull it so with its butt in the hole at the Sacred Spot. When the pole is erect the digger should replace the dirt taken from the hole and tamp it about the pole so that it will stand firmly when bearing the weight of a struggling man.

Then the people may shout the names of *Iya* and *Gnaski* and protest that these Gods prevail in the camp. Immediately, men and women commingle and then follows a period of license when they banter each other and jest of sexual things. At that time a man or a woman may be familiar with one of the opposite sex in a manner that would be an indignity at other times, and the ribald merriment may become boisterous.

When the Superior sees fit, he should command the herald to proclaim that the escort and the warriors come and dance the war dance and drive the obscene Gods from the camp. Those thus called should equip themselves as if for battle and come into the Dance Lodge. There they should dance the war dance on the uncovered space, hooting the obscene Gods hung on the Sacred Pole and shooting and throwing and striking at them until they fall. When these obscene Gods fall, the warriors should strike and trample them as they dance the victory dance and the women should shout their approval and ululate for joy. The Superior should quickly make an incense of buffalo chips on the altar, to appease the elevated Fetish and when the chips have burned to coals he should scorch the fallen images on these coals and thereby destroy their potency for evil. Then he should lean the dried buffalo penis against the Sacred Pole with a pipe beside it, thus making effective the potency of the Fetish to maintain decency in the camp. He should then sprinkle a covering of cedar leaves and twigs over the altar, for these are potent to ward against the anti-natural conduct of the Winged God and of the *heyoka*. The warriors should continue to dance the victory dance, stamping and striking uneven places on the uncovered space until it is made sufficiently level to dance upon easily.

In the meantime, the Mentors and attendants should prepare the Dance Lodge for the forms of the Sun Dance that their Candidates are to dance. For those who are to dance the second form, the buffalo heads should be placed beside the Sacred Pole; for those to dance the third form, the stakes should be fixed upright firmly in the ground of the uncovered space; for those to dance the fourth form, the thongs should be fixed to the Sacred Pole, and for those to dance the fourth form actually suspended, the thongs should be passed through the fork of the Sacred Pole.

When the warriors stop dancing they should leave the Dance Lodge. Then the musicians should bring a dance drum and fix it on its supports not far from the entrance on the covered space at the left of the Dance

Lodge, and they should place four or eight rattles beside the drum. The attendants should bring the dried buffalo hide with the hair on and the buffalo tails attached to handles, and place them next to the drum toward the honor place in the lodge. The mothers who intend to have their babes' ears pierced should make a bed of sage for each babe, placing them at the inner edge of the covered space, between the articles already placed and the uncovered space. . . .

GREETING THE SUN ON THE FOURTH, OR MID-YEAR DAY

The Oglala regard the fourth holy day above all other days, for it is the mid-year day. They anticipate a joyful time on that day, whether on their part it is devoted to ceremonies or spent as a mere holiday. Therefore, they are apt to be astir before dawn. Just before dawn, the herald should make a proclamation that the people prepare themselves to appear before the face of the Sun and all should bedeck themselves with their best attire and ornaments and wear or carry such insignia as they are entitled to have. As the Sun appears, the Shamans, Superior, and Mentors should be at the top of a nearby hill and greet Him as on previous mornings. Then a Shaman should invoke the Sky to give strength and endurance to the Candidates so that they all may dance the Sun Dance to its completion. Another Shaman should invoke the Bear God to give wisdom to the Superior and the Mentors, so that the ceremony held that day may be acceptable to the Gods.

They should then return to the camp and the Superior and Mentors should assemble in the council lodge to deliberate relative to the proceedings on that day. While they are deliberating, the vows of the young braves should be made in the following manner:— Young men who take part in this charge thereby obligate themselves in the presence of the Sun, each to do his duty as a warrior against an enemy of the people. The braves should form in line near the chief place of the camp and at a signal run to, and four times around, the Dance Lodge. They should repeat this from the north, east, and south sides of the areas. Then the people should assemble on both sides of the Sun Trail and the Superior and Mentors should go in procession from the council lodge to the Sacred Lodge, each intoning prayers to his Fetish as he marches. . . .

THE BUFFALO DANCE

The remaining rites are the dances, of which there must be two, though there may be others. These two are the Buffalo Dance and the Sun-Gazing Dance. These dances are divided into periods. The Buffalo Dance has four periods and the Sun-Gazing Dance must have four and may have an indefinite number of periods. A period consists of the dance proper and the intermission. The dancing must take place while the music is sounded; an intermission is the interval between the dancing. The leader should give the signal for the musicians to begin sounding the music for each period and the musicians should repeat the song for each period four times.

The Buffalo Dance should be danced only by those who are to dance the second, third, or the fourth form of the Sun Dance and by those who have danced this dance on some former occasion. It is danced as follows:— The leader should go to the altar and feign three times to lift the ornamented buffalo head; the fourth time he should lift it and place it on the uncovered space so that the dancers can surround it. The dancers should form in a circle about this head when the leader should signal for the music to begin and when it does, the dancers should dance the step of the Buffalo Dance. This step should be synchronous with the beat of the drum, each second beat being emphatic; at the emphatic beat the feet are alternately brought to the ground with a scraping motion. This is done to imitate the pawing of a buffalo bull in rage or defiance and to manifest a defiant bravery of the dancers equal to that of the buffalo bull. During this dance those who are to dance the Sun Dance must keep the whistles in their mouths, but should not sound them. While dancing they must gaze continually at the ornamented buffalo head. The red marshals should watch them, and if one of them ceases to gaze at this head they should admonish him; and if he persists in looking away from it they should conduct him to his robe. One thus removed from this dance loses the privilege of becoming a buffalo man. Those who dance the four periods of this dance become buffalo men. The red herald should proclaim that they are buffalo men and the people should shout and sing, lauding them with such praises as these:— "You now belong to the people of the Sun; you now will not have to pay the price when you take a woman for your wife; you now will have many children who will honor you; you now may receive a communication from the Sun."

The attendants should then each give to his dancer one of the buffalo tails attached to a handle and the buffalo men should sit about the dried buffalo skin and when they sing should drum on it with the tails.

PIERCING CHILDREN'S EARS

During the next rite the musicians should remain silent and the buffalo men should sing and drum as often and when the leader deems fit. When the Buffalo men are seated about the buffalo skin the mothers should place the babes whose ears are to be pierced on the beds of sage they have prepared, and standing, should announce the names of those they have chosen to pierce the ears. Those thus named should come and stand beside the women who have chosen them. They should each have a piercing implement and a suitable block of wood. First each should harangue, reciting the deeds he has done that make him eligible to perform this rite. During this harangue the father of the babe should come and stand beside its mother and when the speech is finished the piercer should exhort the parents, telling them that this rite obligates the parents to rear the babe so that it will conform to the laws and customs of the Oglala and that the ears thus pierced signify a loyalty to these laws and customs. He should then kneel at the head of the babe and place the block under the lobe of one ear and quickly pierce it with his sharp-pointed implement. Then he should pierce the other ear in a like manner. The parents should not heed the cries of the babe until its ears have been pierced and then the mother should take it and comfort it. The mothers should announce the names of the piercers in rapid succession and they should come forward and begin their duties at once. Thus, this rite may be performed by a number simultaneously and the harangues, cries of the babes, and songs of the buffalo men, may make an exciting hubbub to which the people may add in their enthusiasm.

THE SUN-GAZE DANCE

When this rite is over, the fourth intermission of the Buffalo Dance is completed and the buffalo men should return to their robes. The Sun-Gaze Dance should immediately follow. There are four acts in this dance: the capture, the torture, the captivity, and the escape, which should be performed in the order named. The leader should give the signal for the beginning of the first act, when the buffalo men should stand, and in rapid succession announce the name of those chosen to be captors. When practicable, the one so chosen should be a buffalo man and be notified in advance so that he may be prepared to do his part. When his name is announced he should stand beside the one who chose him and relate the deeds that make him eligible. Thus, at one time there may be several captors haranguing, creating or augmenting the enthusiasm of the people. When the harangues are over the captors should come together a short distance from the dancers and feign discovery of the dancers as enemies. They should shout the war cry and rush upon the dancers, each grasp his dancer about the waist, wrestle with him, throw him prone, and loudly announce that he has captured an enemy. When all the dancers are thus made captive, their captors should feign to consult together, and determine to torture the captives. This ends the first act.

In the second act, the captors should each pierce the flesh of his captive and make wounds sufficient to accomplish the form of the Sun-Gaze Dance he is to dance. If he is to dance the second form, the captor should turn his captive's body face down and then grasp the skin and flesh of his back at one side of the spine, draw them out as far as possible, and pierce crosswise through the flesh with a sharp-pointed implement, so as to make a wound that the sharp-pointed stick provided may pass through; then the captor should make a like wound on the other side of the spine. If the captive is to dance the third form, his captor should grasp the skin and flesh of the captive's breast, draw them out as far as possible, and pierce through the flesh, making a wound that will permit the sharp-pointed stick to pass through it; then he should make a like wound through the flesh of the captive's other breast; then he should turn the captive so that he will be face down and make like wounds on the back over each shoulder blade. If he is to dance the fourth form, the Captor should in like manner make wounds through each of the captive's breasts. When the wounds have been made, the captors should thrust through each wound one of the pointed sticks provided with the equipment and this concludes the second act. During this act, the maidens should stand beside the captives and encourage them to bear the torture without flinching and to smile and sing a song of defiance.

The maidens may wipe the blood that flows from the wounds with wisps of sweetgrass, for the incense made of sweetgrass with such blood on it is potent to insure constancy and reciprocity in love. While the tortures are inflicted, the musicians drum, rattle, and sing a war song. The female relatives of the captives should wail as in bereavement. The captors should sing victory songs and the people may shout or sing or ululate, so that the emotions may be wrought to a high pitch when the third act begins.

The act of captivity opens the Sun-Gaze Dance which begins with the binding of the captives, each according to the form he is to dance. If for the first form, the captor should bind to the sticks through the wounds with strong thongs as many of the buffalo heads provided as the captives chooses; if for the third form, the captor should bind to the sticks thrust through the wounds four strong thongs securely fastened to four posts, so that the dancer will be in the midst of the posts; if for the fourth form, the captor should bind the sticks through the wounds with strong thongs that are securely fastened to the Sacred Pole; or if the dancer is to dance actually suspended, the thongs bound to the sticks should pass through the fork of the Sacred Pole so that the dancer can be drawn from the ground or lowered to it. The thongs should be those provided with the equipment and should be so securely fastened that the most violent movement of the dancers will not loosen them, for if they become loosened while the dancers are dancing it is a sign that *Iktomi* has played his tricks to make the ceremony ridiculous.

There are twenty-four songs for the Sun-Gazing Dance, each of which, except the first and last, may be repeated as often as necessary to supply music for the periods. The first is the song of the captive and should be sung in slow measure, and low plaintive tones, the drum and rattles sounding gently. The last is a song of victory that should be sung only when the dance is completed and then in loud and joyous tones, the drum and rattles sounding vigorously.

When the captives are all bound, the leader should give the signal for the dance to begin and then the dancers who are to dance the first form should come upon the uncovered space and those who are to dance the fourth form actually suspended should be hoisted by the thongs until they cannot touch the ground with their feet. Then the leader should signal the musicians and they should sing the first song. The dancers should dance during the first period with a slow and gentle step, the captives, except those suspended, feigning to try their bonds. The female relatives may wail and ululate and the people may shout and encourage them to attempt an escape.

Each period, when the intermission begins, the dancers should sit or recline to rest, the suspended ones being lowered to the ground for this purpose. Then the attendants, the maidens, and the female attendants should give the dancers such refreshment as the rite will permit. If the dancers perspire, the attendants should wipe the perspiration away with wisps of sage. If one dances far into the night, a woman who loves him may chew a little bark of the cottonwood, and mingle it with water, and in a surreptitious manner give him of this to drink and this will be connived at by the Superior.

At the signal of the leader to begin the second period, the attendants should place the buffalo tails in the hands of the captives, and the captors should feign to discover that the captives are buffalo men whom they should befriend. Then they should rush to the captives and protest that they are friends who will help them to escape from captivity. After this they are called the friends and each should remain by his dancer while he dances and should give him such aid to free him from his bonds as the rite will permit. At the signal of the leader the musicians should begin the second song and the dancers should dance as they did during the first period, but more vigorously. But they should not attempt to free themselves from their bonds until during, or after, the fourth period. The music and dancing should increase in vigor with each period and the enthusiasm of the people will probably increase in proportion until it becomes tumultuous.

The third period should be similar to the second, and the fourth similar to the third, except that while dancing during the fourth period the dancers should pull and jerk violently against their bonds and try to tear themselves free. During each of the following periods, the dancing should be similar to that during the fourth period. During each intermission, the attendants, the maidens, and the female attendants should minister to the comfort of the dancers. A dancer should dance during each period until he escapes captivity which is accomplished by being freed from his bonds. If he escapes by tearing the sticks from the wounds, he has danced the Sun Dance to its completion in the most effective manner. But a dancer may swoon before he escapes, and if he does so his friend should unfasten his bonds and take the sticks from his wounds, and then it is considered that he has danced the Sun Dance to its completion in the least effective manner. Or, a dancer may become so exhausted that he cannot make a strong effort to free himself; if so, his female relatives may throw weighty things on the thongs that bind him to tear them loose. If this does not do so, they may offer the friend a valuable present if he will aid the dancer to escape.

Then the friend may grasp the dancer about the waist and add his strength to the effort to tear the sticks from the wounds. If they succeed, it is considered that the dancer has danced the Sun Dance to its completion in a less effective manner than if the sticks had been torn from the wounds by the dancer unaided. It is most meritorious to dance until the sticks are torn from the wounds or until the leader announces that the Sun Dance is finished.

Each dancer escapes from captivity when he is freed from his bonds and his freedom should be celebrated by the people of his band accompanying him from the Dance Lodge to his tipi, his attendant, and a maiden supporting him as he goes there.

LESLIE SPIER

(1893-   )

The Sun Dance of the Plains Indians: Comparison with the Tribal Ceremonial System

THE [VARIOUS] SUN DANCES ARE NOT MERELY AGGREGATES OF DIFFUSED elements: the ideas locally injected to integrate the whole and the rituals originated have transformed them into something unique. How each tribe has made the ceremony peculiarly its own cannot be determined for want of precise historical data. But an approach is possible by recasting the question: in how far does the sun dance conform to pre-existing ceremonial patterns?

The fundamental Blackfoot concept is based on the medicine bundle; in this the rituals for personal medicines, the organized bundles (otter, etc.), and even the societies, whose regalia correspond to the more orthodox form of bundles, conform to type. None of these ceremonies involve the whole tribe. Bundles are individual property and, except for doctor's medicines, can be transferred or sold with their rituals. Such a transfer is directed by a former owner, with the principals' wives offering ancillary aid. Sometimes the ceremonies are held within a roughly constructed dance enclosure, but they are never elaborate. Invariably the ritual is sung and the participants dance with the articles comprising the bundle. In the group ceremonies, the transfer within a tipi is often immediately followed by a public dance.

By way of contrast the sun dance is a tribal ceremony, that is, the entire group acts in concert on this occasion, with functionaries drawn from the public at large. Objectively it is quite at variance with other

From Spier, "The Sun Dance of the Plains Indians, its development and diffusion," *Anthropological Papers, American Museum of Natural History,* Vol. 16, Pt. 7 (New York, 1921), pp. 505-511.

ceremonies: the dance structure, the elaborate altar, and the torture dance have no parallels. On the other hand it is emphatically a bundle ceremony, and Wissler has clearly shown that both the natoas bundle and the weather dancer's functions conform closely to type. The only important difference is that the natoas is a woman's bundle. Together with the woman's society, it forms the sole exception to an otherwise solid array of man-owned rites. Like other group ceremonies, the rites of the preliminary tipi precede the dance. But here is an important difference: in the sun dance the same set of individuals does not take part in the two performances, the bundle transfer and the dance of the weather shamans. . . .

The general aspect of the relation of the sun dance to their [Blackfoot's] other rites is quite clear. Objectively it is quite unlike any other ceremony: structure, dance, and dual organization have no equivalents. Where it is a question of who shall participate, however, the condition is otherwise: only the owner of the natoas bundle and the owner of the right to dance (the weather dancer) can perform the ritual—in other words, it is orthodox Blackfoot in being an individually owned ceremony. Its mythological background is far from coherent, since several distinct myths have been drawn on to provide an etiological setting, but as Wissler points out such growth of native theory by accretion of folkloristic elements is a characteristic Blackfoot trait. As a result, the particular combination they have concocted is unique.

The Crow sun dance differs from all others in having a specific motive, namely, the desire of a mourner to obtain a vision which guarantees revenge on the enemy for the death of a relative. He obtains this vision through the agency of a sacred doll under the tutelage of its owner. While the motive and the mode of acquiring this vision conform to the characteristic Crow practice, as Lowie has pointed out, it occupies an anomalous position in Crow life by reason of a ritual far more elaborate than that connected with any other war medicine. This appears more forcibly when we consider the general tenor of their other ceremonies.[1]

The personal medicines, among which the war medicines are to be numbered, are characteristically devoid of ceremonial: in particular, by contrast to the Blackfoot, they lack the systematic uniformity of the transfer and manipulation dances. As a personal medicine, then, the sun dance is noteworthy for its exuberance of objective detail.

Its position among other elaborate ceremonies is equally clear. It occupies first rank with the sacred Tobacco performance as a tribal ceremony. In passing it may be noted that while the Tobacco planting is conducted by a small group, it is for the tribal good, but the sun dance, in which the tribe as a whole functions, is for distinctly individual ends. It has been noted that the religious factor in the military societies is

---

[1] I have drawn at length on Dr. Lowie's unpublished data on Crow religion.

weak,[2] and it may be said that, in contrast to equivalent societies of other tribes, there is little ceremonialism. On the whole, the lengthy public performance of the sun dance is not only unusual in association with a personal medicine but is also somewhat more elaborate than the usual Crow ceremony.

Specifically, the vow is not the normal mode of inaugurating cere-monies, although it is sometimes the cause for the performance of the Cooked Meat Singing, adoption into the Tobacco Society, and acquisi-tion of the Medicine Pipe. Preparation in a preliminary tipi with a formal procession to the dance ground also occurs in the Tobacco adoption and the Bear Song dance. Special dance structures, other than a temporarily enlarged tipi, are uncommon: the Hot dance and Tobacco adoption lodges being the only other examples noted. The sun dance lodge is identical, except in size, with the Tobacco lodge on which it must have been pat-terned. Tongues are also distributed to qualified warriors in a peculiar manner in the Tobacco ceremony. Self-torture is practised by would-be visionaries acting individually, but not in any other ceremony. For the rest, while many generalized details re-occur commonly on ceremonious occasions, there is no single ceremony that parallels the particular com-bination of them which the sun dance embodies.

The situation essentially duplicates that of the Blackfoot, but it is somewhat more clear cut. The motivation of the dance is characteris-tically Crow, but the organization does not conform so strictly to current practice, as it is the applicant for assistance who seeks the vision, not the medicine owner. The ritual, however, is again the divergent phase, not only because it is far in excess of any other personal medicine manipu-lation, but because it has no specific parallel among their other cere-monies.

There is less information on the Arapaho. Nevertheless, the place of the sun dance is fairly clear. From a behavioristic viewpoint it stands apart from their more sacred performance, i. e., those connected with the tribal flat-pipe, the sacred wheels, the woman's bags, and the seven sacred bundles, for with these there is no singing and, except for the last, no dancing. Yet it occupies an equally high position in tribal esteem since the pipe and wheels are incorporated in it.

The Arapaho equate the sun dance to their age-societies, although participation in it bears no relation to progressive membership in that series. The native estimate is correct, for the parallelism between the two is far more systematic than that in any other tribe. The typical age-society ceremony is divided into a three-day preliminary period, followed by one of four days. The secret preliminaries are for prepara-tion: on the first two evenings a practice dance without regalia is held

---

[2] Lowie, *Crow Military Societies*, 149–151.

in the dance lodge. The third evening a public dance is given there: it is repeated on the three following nights. They dance each day before sunrise, concluding with a race to a pole outside the lodge. The first night there is a begging procession. The dance lodge is a low circular enclosure, with a screen blocking its wide entrance. The dance is performed or new grades are acquired in fulfilment of one man's vow. Instruction and regalia are bought from ceremonial grandfathers, selected from among those who once held the grade. These in turn are under the direction of the seven sacred bundle owners. The initiates are assisted in their purchase by members of the second higher age-grade (elder brothers), who in turn select the leaders of the society. The grandfathers dance with the members. The latter may provide substitutes if they are unable to participate. The initiate surrenders his wife to the grandfather in two of the dances, Crazy-lodge and Dog-lodge.[3]

Now all these essential characteristics are repeated in the sun dance: in fact the close coördination which exists can only be due to a continued interchange of features from one to the other. For example, the vow to acquire a new grade is peculiar to the Arapaho alone among all the tribes with military societies, but the vow has an identical function in the sun dance. Hence it is probable that the Arapaho have carried this idea from their sun dance over to their societies. As Lowie has pointed out, this is one indication of the unusual sacred character the Arapaho societies have acquired.[4] On the other hand, it seems that the three day preliminary period and the four day dance period of the sun dance has been patterned on their society procedure. To be sure, other tribes have a somewhat similar division of preparation and performance, but this is not characteristic of their society dances. Since this division recurs systematically in the Arapaho age-grades, it would seem that the transfer has proceeded from societies to sun dance and not in the reverse direction. If then the corresponding division of other sun dances is really comparable—which I am not sure is the case—we must regard this feature as one of the original components of the complex diffused from the Arapaho. There is also a begging procession in the sun dance: this seems to be copied from the society ceremonies. Whereas the societies beg for presents for a service already performed, i. e., the dance proper and special performances for the donors, the pledger of the sun dance simply begs for aid in meeting the expense of the ceremony. The fact that he makes his unusual request just before the evening dance is not contrary evidence to my mind, for he is unable to leave the lodge after this dance, that is, at the time corresponding to the society petitions.

The practice dances do not occur in the sun dance, but the sunrise

[3] Lowie, *loc. cit.,* 982.

[4] Kroeber, *The Arapaho,* 151–168, 182, 193, 200, 211; Lowie, *Plains Indian Age-Societies,* 931–932.

dance does. Inasmuch as it does not take place systematically in other sun dances where it occurs at all, we may assume that the Arapaho transferred this rite from societies to sun dance, and that other tribes then copied it. The race to a pole, closing each morning dance, has no sun dance analogues. Both sun dance and society dances are held in circular enclosures, but there is no specific resemblance.

Lowie has pointed out the Arapaho anomaly of buying a new grade in a rigidly ordered series from a heterogeneous group of grandfathers, instead of from members of the next higher grade as is customary in other tribes.[5] The sun dance grandfathers are similarly those who once bought the right to dance. Like them too, they dance with the initiates. The "elder brother" group does not occur in the sun dance. As the evidence stands it might be assumed that a relation which was rational in the sun dance was duplicated in the age grades. Still the relation is so essential in the latter that it is difficult to believe that it displaced an equally fundamental idea. Perhaps we are only justified in assuming that the Arapaho norm is always the purchase of ceremonial prerogatives from anyone who has ever held them.

The sun dance, like the society ceremonies, is under the direction of the custodians of the tribal flat-pipe and the seven men's bundles, but with more reason, since the flat-pipe is directly involved in the dance. If the flat-pipe rites were not an original part of the Arapaho sun dance complex, as I have suggested, then we may assume that the society pattern, direction by a bundle owner, has been applied to the sun dance. There is also a minor similarity in the substitute dancers who are permitted in the sun dance as well as the society series.

Wife surrender, occurring in the sun dance and in two of the age-societies, has only a scanty representation in Arapaho ceremonials, whereas it is more common among the Gros Ventre.[6] Both tribes share a specific trait, the transfer of a medicine root through the wife. The trait has undoubtedly been derived from the Village tribes, where it is a customary adjunct of purchase; but it does not follow, as Lowie intimates, that it has partly disappeared among the Arapaho.[7] At any rate, there is no evidence that these people transferred the custom from societies to sun dance or vice versa.

The one woman's dance (buffalo imitators) has points of resemblance to the sun dance: a lodge with a center pole crossed by a digging-stick, painted ridge poles, and the pledger's dance station. The Gros Ventre and Wind River Shoshoni women's dances lack these traits: in that of the Blackfoot and in the Kiowa sun dance the association is palpably

---

[5] Lowie, *Plains Indian Age-Societies*, 932.
[6] Kroeber, *Ethnology of the Gros Ventre*, 228, 244–245.
[7] In fact his conception of the Blackfoot-Village tribe relations might be adjusted in this way too (*loc. cit.*, 934, 948–949).

secondary. But it does not follow that the Arapaho women adopted these features from their own sun dance.

Such a close coördination of sun dance and age-societies implies a long period of common growth: a view that lends justification to the position taken on the basis of distribution, that the Arapaho were largely responsible for the development of the sun dance.

The question was asked how the sun dance agrees with other ceremonies. It seems that in all three cases the agreement is greatest in organization and motivation, less in behavior, and least in material objects, regalia, etc. That is, the peculiar element injected into the mass of borrowed traits appears to have been largely determined by the ceremonial pattern. In the complexes under discussion the pattern takes its familiar form, that is, standards of organization and mythologic sanctions have most effectively operated. But there is not a priori reason for expecting individuality in regalia and behavior, for it will be recalled that Boas found that the Kwakiutl pattern applied to these as well.[8] The operation of patterns is certainly not a mechanical process; borrowed traits are not forced in a mould. The new is explained in terms of the familiar, and, as I believe the Arapaho data in particular show, the currently approved mode changes as the chances of history dictate.

---

[8] Boas, *Social Organization and Secret Societies of the Kwakiutl Indians,* 43, et seq.

PART V

BUILDING A SCIENCE
OF MAN
IN AMERICA:

The Classical Period in American Anthropology, 1900-1920

Introduction

by Ruth L. Bunzel

THE FIRST TWO DECADES OF THE 20TH CENTURY IN AMERICAN ANTHRO-
pology might be called the Age of Boas, so completely did that giant
dominate the field. Boas came to New York in 1895 from the Field
Museum in Chicago as Curator of Ethnology at the American Museum
of Natural History and Lecturer in Physical Anthropology at Columbia
University. The connection between these two great institutions proved
most advantageous. Columbia had no research funds at that time, but the
Museum had. Through the Museum, Boas was able to send his students
into the field establishing the American model for anthropological education. Several students later found employment at the Museum at a time
when anthropology was just emerging as a profession and still was not
recognized in most of the country's colleges and universities.

Boas soon attracted able scholars. The roster of his students reads like a
Who's Who of American anthropology. For a generation, almost every
young anthropologist who went out into teaching or research in the fields
of linguistics, ethnology and physical anthropology was trained at Columbia. Harvard and Yale Universities, which also gave graduate degrees in
anthropology at this time, concentrated on archaeology and European
prehistory, fields in which Boas was only peripherally interested.

Among Boas' first students were Alfred L. Kroeber and Clark Wissler.
Neither one started out to become an anthropologist; Kroeber's first inter-
est was English literature, Wissler's, as we have seen, was psychology.
A little later Robert Lowie, Edward Sapir, Alexander Goldenweiser, Paul
Radin and Leslie Spier all studied with Boas at around the same time.

Having been educated in Europe, Boas brought into anthropology the
atmosphere of international scholarship. Although his methods were empirical, his knowledge was not limited to the American scene, but ranged
the whole field of anthropology. Many of the students whom he attracted
were foreign-born and all read at least two languages, and the influence of
European thought began to be felt in American anthropology.

New York was now the center of anthropological study, as Washington
had been earlier. The old Ethnological Society was revived and met at the
Museum of Natural History. Boas was winding up the Jesup Expedition,
directing the mammoth work of publication of the results; he continued
his own research on the Kwakiutl and other tribes of the North Pacific

Coast; for the U. S. Immigration Department he had begun the anthropometric investigation of the children of immigrants which was to rock physical anthropology with its evidence of the instability of human types.

This was the period when the Museum was engaged in its gigantic salvage operation among the Plains Indians, and it was there that Boas' fledglings first tried their wings. Kroeber, Lowie, Wissler, Radin, Spier all served their term of apprenticeship in the tattered tipis with the old men who remembered. Sapir specialized in linguistics, and Goldenweiser was excused after his one field trip produced nothing but trouble.

All of Boas' students read German and did not consider it unreasonable to expect that a scholar should have read the major theoretical contributions in his subject, no matter what the language. No student of Boas' seminars would have dared to justify his ignorance of the distribution of spirals or safety pins, or the characteristics of Melanesian art, by the plea that it was "not his field." Their area of research was concentrated—in this they shared a "common culture," and communication was easy; they could talk about parfleches and medicine bundles, joking relations and age societies with no problems of semantics—but their "field" was Man. In the dusty corridors between the storerooms of the Museum, in the fly-specked coffee shops around Columbia, but above all in Boas' seminars to which graduates returned year after year, were thrashed out the main ideas that dominated anthropology for years to come.

These were the idea of the culture area as a reality and as a heuristic device; the age-area concept in the interpretation of distribution of cultural phenomena and historical reconstruction; the techniques for dealing with discontinuous distributions; the particularism of cultural development—"Now in that time at that place," to quote the Osage ritualist. Related to this approach were the ideas that anthropology, except for physical anthropology, was an historical and not a natural science, that the data with which it dealt were events unique and unrepeatable and that, therefore, the concepts and methods developed in the natural sciences were inappropriate; that historical formulations should begin with things whose relationships were known—the tribes within a geographical area, the different dialects of a single linguistic stock—and proceed from there to more problematical comparisons. These were the ideas especially associated with the so-called Boas school.

But Boas himself had always been concerned also with another theoretical orientation—with the nature of culture and the nature of man. He recognized that the units of observation were people, that cultures served human needs, and however diverse in origin the constituent elements of a culture might be they fitted together into a system of interrelated parts. These concepts were first worked out in a series of papers on folklore— their golden nuggets of theory buried and almost unrecognizable in the plethora of examples. Studies of ritual (e.g.: the "Sun Dance") and "totemism" followed. These studies did not appear to deal with culture wholes, but actually they did. When Spier said that the "Sun Dance" was a medicine bundle ceremony among the Blackfoot and the sanction for a revenge party among the Crow, he was making a statement about Blackfoot and Crow culture wholes. But one who had not gone through the mill of Boas' seminars would not have recognized it as such.

When Radcliffe-Brown and Malinowski arrived in America in the 20's, bearing the gospel of functionalism, American anthropologists caught in their own provincialism could look at them in surprise and say, "But, of course. We knew it all the time. Don't these people read?"

FRANZ BOAS

(1858-1942)

Franz Boas belonged to the same tradition of liberal romanticism that produced Carl Schurz and the philosophical anarchists of the 19th century. He was the essential protestant; he valued autonomy more than comfort, perhaps more even than affection; he believed that man was a rational animal and could, with persistent effort, emancipate himself from superstition and irrationality and lead a sane and rational life in a good society—although he admitted that humanity had a long way to go. This, perhaps, was the basis of his unalterable opposition to Freud and psychoanalysis with its fundamentally tragic view of life and its acceptance of irrationality as an essential part of the human condition. In the last years of his life (he died during World War II) a deep depression overwhelmed him as he saw how man had retrogressed from the goals he envisioned. But his depression sprang from his own age and helplessness. "If I were young, I would do something about it," he said to a colleague who had remarked how difficult life must be for their students growing up in the depression and under the threat of war. An activist to the end!

Boas' passionate temperament was held in bounds by the rigorous discipline of his mind. He was trained in physics and only switched to anthropology when his trip to the Arctic brought him into contact with the Eskimo and confronted him with the intriguing problem of cultural differences and common humanity. What he carried over to his anthropological studies from his training in the physical sciences was not a specific method, for he realized early in his career that the methods of one discipline could not be applied to another and that the formulations of a social science must be of a different order from those of a laboratory science. He brought to anthropology rigorous standards of proof, a critical scepticism toward all generalization, and the physicist's unwillingness to accept any generalization or explanation as anything more than a useful hypothesis until it has been clearly demonstrated that no other explanation is possible. This aspect of Boas' theoretic framework especially irked those of his students who would have liked more facile generalization and who regarded Boas' standards of proof as a "methodological strait jacket."

Boas made voluminous and important contributions in three of the four fields of anthropology—physical anthropology, linguistics, and ethnology— and his one contribution in the fourth field, archaeology, served to define new procedures and goals in the study of Mexican prehistory.

Despite the great diversity of his activities his work had a certain mono- lithic quality. So consistent was his theoretical position that it is frequently hard to tell whether a paper was written in 1888 or 1932. His mind was not closed to new ideas. He created no closed system; he saw research as a progression through constantly emerging problems to ever widening horizons.

Boas was not an easy man to work with. Prickly, unbending, often in- tolerant, he was scornful of disagreement or stupidity. He valued auton- omy but was often highhanded. He was deeply concerned about his students' lives and careers, but in terms of what he thought was best for them. He arranged field trips for them without consulting them; he schemed and maneuvered to get them positions and was deeply hurt when they refused to accept his arrangements. But he never wavered in his loyalty to them, even when he disapproved of them.

Boas wrote one popular book, The Mind of Primitive Man, *which is a rather curious title. It does not deal, as might be supposed, with the peculiar- ities of primitive mentality—a conception which Boas did not harbor— but with the psychic unity of man, the evidence for the equality of races and the proper approach to the study of the differences between groups. These were the ideas for which he fought as an anthropologist and as a citizen throughout his long career.*

In the field of physical anthropology he was interested only in the study of living people. In this area he was an extraordinary innovator. His demonstration of the instability of physical types dealt a body blow to generally held racial theories. His discussion of the relationship of family lines in a population, disposed of theories of "racial" heredity. His studies of growth established the concept of physiological as opposed to chron- ological age with far-reaching effects in the fields of pediatrics and edu- cation. In this field alone he achieved more than most specialists do in a lifetime.—R.L.B.

The Mental Traits of Primitive Man

APPARENTLY THE THOUGHTS AND ACTIONS OF CIVILIZED MAN, AND THOSE found in more primitive forms of society, prove, that, in various groups of mankind, the mind responds quite differently when exposed to the same

From Boas, *The Mind of Primitive Man* (New York: The Macmillan Company, 1911), pp. 98-114, 287.

conditions. Lack of logical connection in its conclusions, lack of control of will, are apparently two of its fundamental characteristics in primitive society. In the formation of opinions, belief takes the place of logical demonstration. The emotional value of opinions is great, and consequently they quickly lead to action. The will appears unbalanced, there being a readiness to yield to strong emotions and a stubborn resistance in trifling matters.

Unfortunately the descriptions of the state of mind of primitive people, such as are given by most travellers, are too superficial to be used for psychological investigation. Very few travellers understand the language of the people they visit; and how is it possible to judge a tribe solely by the descriptions of interpreters, or by observations of disconnected actions the incentive of which remains unknown? But even when the language of the people is known to the visitor, he is generally an unappreciative listener to their tales. The missionary has his strong bias against the religious ideas and customs of primitive people, and the trader has no interest in their beliefs and in their barbarous arts. The observers who seriously tried to enter into the inner life of a people, the Cushings, Callaways, and Greys, are few in number, and may be counted on one's fingers. Nevertheless the bulk of the argument is always based on the statements of hasty and superficial observers.

Numerous attempts have been made to describe the peculiar psychological characteristics of primitive man. Among these I would mention those of Klemm,[1] Carus,[2] De Gobineau,[3] Nott and Gliddon,[4] Waitz,[5] Spencer,[6] and Tylor.[7] Their investigations are of merit as descriptions of the characteristics of primitive people, but we cannot claim for any of them that they describe the psychological characters of races independent of their social surroundings. Klemm and Wuttke designate the civilized races as active, all others as passive, and assume that all elements and beginnings of civilization found among primitive people—in America or on the islands of the Pacific Ocean—were due to an early contact with civilization. Carus divides mankind into "peoples of the day, night and dawn." De Gobineau calls the yellow race the male element, the black

[1] Gustav Klemm, Allgemeine Kultur-Geschichte (Leipzig, 1843), vol. i, pp. 196 *et seq.* His opinions are accepted by A. Wuttke, Geschichte des Heidentums (Breslau, 1852-53), vol. i, p. 36.

[2] Carl Gustav Carus, "Ueber die ungleiche Befahigung der verschiedenen Menschheitsstämme für höhere geistige Entwicklung" (*Denkschrift zum hundertjährigen Geburtsfeste Goethe's,* Leipzig, 1840).

[3] J. A. de Gobineau, Essai sur l'inégalité des races humaines (Paris, 1853-55).

[4] Nott and Gliddon, Types of Mankind (Philadelphia, 1854), i, Indigenous Races of the Earth (Philadelphia, 1857).

[5] Theodor Waitz, Anthropologie der Naturvölker, (2d ed., Leipzig, 1877).

[6] Herbert Spencer, Principles of Sociology.

[7] Edward B. Tylor, Researches into the Early History of Mankind; Primitive Culture.

race the female element, and calls only the whites the noble and gifted race. Nott and Gliddon ascribe animal instincts only to the lower races, while they declare that the white race has a higher instinct which incites and directs its development.

The belief in the higher hereditary powers of the white race has gained a new life with the modern doctrine of the prerogatives of the master-mind, which have found their boldest expression in Nietzsche's writings.

All such views are generalizations which either do not sufficiently take into account the social conditions of races, and thus confound cause and effect, or were dictated by scientific or humanitarian bias, by the desire to justify the institution of slavery, or to give the greatest freedom to the most highly gifted.

Tylor and Spencer, who give an ingenious analysis of the mental life of primitive man, do not assume that these are racial characteristics, although the evolutionary standpoint of Spencer's work often seems to convey this impression.

Quite distinct from these is Waitz's point of view.[8] He says, "According to the current opinion the stage of culture of a people or of an individual is largely or exclusively a product of his faculty. We maintain that the reverse is at least just as true. The faculty of man does not designate anything but how much and what he is able to achieve in the immediate future and depends upon the stages of culture through which he has passed and the one he has reached."

The views of these investigators show that in the domain of psychology a confusion prevails still greater than in anatomy, as to the characteristics of primitive races, and that no clear distinction is drawn between the racial and the social problem. In other words, the evidence is based partly on the supposed mental characteristics of races, no matter what their stage of culture; partly on those of tribes and peoples on different levels of civilization, no matter whether they belong to the same race or to distinct races. Still these two problems are entirely distinct. The former is a problem of heredity; the latter, a problem of environment.

Thus we recognize that there are two possible explanations of the different manifestations of the mind of man. It may be that the minds of different races show differences of organization; that is to say, the laws of mental activity may not be the same for all minds. But it may also be that the organization of mind is practically identical among all races of man; that mental activity follows the same laws everywhere, but that its manifestations depend upon the character of individual experience that is subjected to the action of these laws.

It is quite evident that the activities of the human mind depend upon these two elements. The organization of the mind may be defined as the

8 Theodor Waitz, Anthropologie der Naturvölker (2d ed.) vol. i, p. 387.

group of laws which determine the modes of thought and of action, irrespective of the subject-matter of mental activity. Subject to such laws are the manner of discrimination between perceptions, the manner in which perceptions associate themselves with previous perceptions, the manner in which a stimulus leads to action, and the emotions produced by stimuli. These laws determine to a great extent the manifestations of the mind. In these we recognize hereditary causes.

But, on the other hand, the influence of individual experience can easily be shown to be very great. The bulk of the experience of man is gained from oft-repeated impressions. It is one of the fundamental laws of psychology that the repetition of mental processes increases the facility with which these processes are performed, and decreases the degree of consciousness that accompanies them. This law expresses the well-known phenomena of habit. When a certain perception is frequently associated with another previous perception, the one will habitually call forth the other. When a certain stimulus frequently results in a certain action, it will tend to call forth habitually the same action. If a stimulus has often produced a certain emotion, it will tend to reproduce it every time. These belong to the group of environmental causes.

The explanation of the activity of the mind of man, therefore, requires the discussion of two distinct problems. The first bears upon the question of unity or diversity of organization of the mind, while the second bears upon the diversity produced by the variety of contents of the mind as found in the various social and geographical environments. The task of the investigator consists largely in separating these two causes, and in attributing to each its proper share in the development of the peculiarities of the mind.

We will first devote our attention to the question, Do differences exist in the organization of the human mind? Since Waitz's thorough discussion of the question of the unity of the human species, there can be no doubt that in the main the mental characteristics of man are the same all over the world; but the question remains open, whether there is a sufficient difference in grade to allow us to assume that the present races of man may be considered as standing on different stages of the evolutionary series, whether we are justified in ascribing to civilized man a higher place in organization than to primitive man.

The chief difficulty encountered in the solution of this problem has been pointed out before. It is the uncertainty as to which of the characteristics of primitive man are causes of the low stage of culture, and which are caused by it; or which of the psychological characteristics are hereditary, and would not be wiped out by the effects of civilization. The fundamental difficulty of collecting satisfactory observations lies in the fact that no large groups of primitive man are brought nowadays into conditions of real equality with whites. The gap between our society and theirs always remains open, and for this reason their minds cannot be expected to work in the same manner as ours. The same phenomenon which led us to the conclusion that primitive races of our times are not given an opportunity to develop their abilities, prevents us from judging their innate faculty.

It seems advantageous to direct our attention first of all to this difficulty. If it can be shown that certain mental traits are common to all members of mankind that are on a primitive stage of civilization, no matter what their racial affinities may be, the conclusion will gain much in strength, that these traits are primarily social, or based on physical characteristics due to social environment.

I will select a few only among the mental characteristics of primitive man which will illustrate our point,—inhibition of impulses, power of attention, power of original thought.

We will first discuss the question, in how far primitive man is capable of inhibiting impulses (Spencer).[9]

It is an impression obtained by many travellers, and also based upon experiences gained in our own country, that primitive man of all races, and the less educated of our own race, have in common a lack of control of emotions, that they give way more readily to an impulse than civilized man and the highly educated. I believe that this conception is based largely upon the neglect to consider the occasions on which a strong control of impulses is demanded in various forms of society.

Most of the proofs for this alleged peculiarity are based on the fickleness and uncertainty of the disposition of primitive man, and on the strength of his passions aroused by seemingly trifling causes. I will say right here that the traveller or student measures the fickleness of the people by the importance which he attributes to the actions or purposes in which they do not persevere, and he weighs the impulse for outbursts of passion by his standard. Let me give an example. A traveller desirous of reaching his goal as soon as possible engages men to start on a journey at a certain time. To him time is exceedingly valuable. But what is time to primitive man, who does not feel the compulsion of completing a definite work at a definite time? While the traveller is fuming and raging over the delay, his men keep up their merry chatter and laughter, and cannot be induced to exert themselves except to please their master. Would not they be right in stigmatizing many a traveller for his impulsiveness and lack of control when irritated by a trifling cause like loss of time? Instead of this, the traveller complains of the fickleness of the natives, who quickly lose interest in the objects which the traveller has at heart.

The proper way to compare the fickleness of the savage and that of the white is to compare their behavior in undertakings which are equally important to each. More generally speaking, when we want to give a true

[9] Herbert Spencer, The Principles of Sociology (New York, 1893), vol. I, pp. 55, et seq., 59-61.

estimate of the power of primitive man to control impulses, we must not compare the control required on certain occasions among ourselves with the control exerted by primitive man on the same occasions. If, for instance, our social etiquette forbids the expression of feelings of personal discomfort and of anxiety, we must remember that personal etiquette among primitive men may not require any inhibition of the same kind. We must rather look for those occasions on which inhibition is required by the customs of primitive man. Such are, for instance, the numerous cases of taboo,—that is, of prohibitions of the use of certain foods, or of the performance of certain kinds of work,—which sometimes require a considerable amount of self-control. When an Eskimo community is on the point of starvation, and their religious proscriptions forbid them to make use of the seals that are basking on the ice, the amount of self-control of the whole community which restrains them from killing these seals is certainly very great. Other examples that suggest themselves are the perseverance of primitive man in the manufacture of his utensils and weapons; his readiness to undergo privations and hardships which promise to fulfil his desires,—as the Indian youth's willingness to fast in the mountains, awaiting the appearance of his guardian spirit; or his bravery and endurance exhibited in order to gain admittance to the ranks of the men of his tribe; or, again, the often-described power of endurance exhibited by Indian captives who undergo torture at the hands of their enemies.

It has also been claimed that lack of control is exhibited by primitive man in his outbursts of passion occasioned by slight provocations. I think that in this case also the difference in attitude of civilized man and of primitive man disappears if we give due weight to the social conditions in which the individual lives.

What would a primitive man say to the noble passion which preceded and accompanied the war of the Rebellion? Would not the rights of slaves seem to him a most irrelevant question? On the other hand, we have ample proof that his passions are just as much controlled as ours, only in different directions. The numerous customs and restrictions regulating the relations of the sexes may serve as an example. The difference in impulsiveness may be fully explained by the different weight of motives in both cases. In short, perseverance and control of impulses are demanded of primitive man as well as of civilized man, but on different occasions. If they are not demanded as often, the cause must be looked for, not in the inherent inability to produce them, but in the social status which does not demand them to the same extent.

Spencer[10] mentions as a particular case of this lack of control the improvidence of primitive man. I believe it would be more proper to say, instead of improvidence, optimism. "Why should I not be as successful

[10] Spencer, *loc. cit.*

to-morrow as I was to-day?" is the underlying feeling of primitive man. This feeling is, I think, no less powerful in civilized man. What builds up business activity but the belief in the stability of existing conditions? Why do the poor not hesitate to found families without being able to lay in store beforehand? We must not forget that starvation among most primitive people is an exceptional case, the same as financial crises among civilized people; and that for times of need, such as occur regularly, provision is always made. Our social status is more stable, so far as the acquiring of the barest necessities of life is concerned, so that exceptional conditions do not prevail often; but nobody would maintain that the majority of civilized men are always prepared to meet emergencies. We may recognize a difference in the degree of improvidence caused by the difference of social status, but not a specific difference between lower and higher types of man.

Related to the lack of power of inhibition is another trait which has been ascribed to primitive man of all races,—his inability of concentration when any demand is made upon the more complex faculties of the intellect. I will mention an example which seems to make clear the error committed in this assumption. In his description of the natives of the west coast of Vancouver Island, Sproat says, "The native mind, to an educated man, seems generally to be asleep. . . . On his attention being fully aroused, he often shows much quickness in reply and ingenuity in argument. But a short conversation wearies him, particularly if questions are asked that require efforts of thought or memory on his part. The mind of the savage then appears to rock to and fro out of mere weakness." Spencer, who quotes this passage, adds a number of others corroborating this point. I happen to know through personal contact the tribes mentioned by Sproat.[11] The questions put by the traveller seem mostly trifling to the Indian, and he naturally soon tires of a conversation carried on in a foreign language, and one in which he finds nothing to interest him. As a matter of fact, the interest of those natives can easily be raised to a high pitch, and I have often been the one who was wearied out first. Neither does the management of their intricate system of exchange prove mental inertness in matters which concern the natives. Without mnemonic aids, they plan the systematic distribution of their property in such a manner as to increase their wealth and social position. These plans require great foresight and constant application.

Finally I wish to refer to a trait of the mental life of primitive man of all races which has often been adduced as the primary reason why certain races cannot rise to higher levels of culture; namely, their lack of originality. It is said that the conservatism of primitive man is so strong, that the individual never deviates from the traditional customs and beliefs (Spencer).[12] While there is certainly truth in this statement in so far as

[11] G. M. Sproat, Scenes and Studies of Savage Life (1886), p. 120.
[12] Herbert Spencer, *loc. cit.*, p. 70.

more customs are binding than in civilized society, at least in its most highly developed types, originality is a trait which is by no means lacking in the life of primitive people. I will call to mind the great frequency of the appearance of prophets among newly converted tribes as well as among pagan tribes. Among the latter we learn quite frequently of new dogmas which have been introduced by such individuals. It is true that these may often be traced to the influence of the ideas of neighboring tribes, but they are modified by the individuality of the person, and grafted upon the current beliefs of the people. It is a well-known fact that myths and beliefs have been disseminated, and undergo changes in the process of dissemination (Boas).[13] Undoubtedly this has often been accomplished by the independent thought of individuals, as may be observed in the increasing complexity of esoteric doctrines intrusted to the care of the priesthood. I believe one of the best examples of such independent thought is furnished by the history of the ghost-dance ceremonies in North America (Mooney).[14] The doctrines of the ghost-dance prophets were new, but based on the ideas of their own people, their neighbors, and the teachings of missionaries. The notion of future life of an Indian tribe of Vancouver Island has undergone a change in this manner, in so far as the idea of the return of the dead in children of their own family has arisen. The same independent attitude may be observed in the replies of the Nicaraguan Indians to the questions regarding their religion as were put to them by Bobadilla, and which were reported by Oviedo.[15]

It seems to my mind that the mental attitude of individuals who thus develop the beliefs of a tribe is exactly that of the civilized philosopher. The student of the history of philosophy is well aware how strongly the mind of even the greatest genius is influenced by the current thought of his time. This has been well expressed by a German writer (Lehmann),[16] who says, "The character of a system of philosophy is, just like that of any other literary work, determined first of all by the personality of its originator. Every true philosophy reflects the life of the philosopher, as well as every true poem that of the poet. Secondly, it bears the general marks of the period to which it belongs; and the more powerful the ideas which it proclaims, the more strongly it will be permeated by the currents of thought which fluctuate in the life of the period. Thirdly, it is influenced by the particular bent of philosophical thought of the period."

If such is the case among the greatest minds of all times, why should

---

[13] Franz Boas, "The Growth of Indian Mythologies" (*Journal of American Folk-Lore*, vol. ix [1896], pp. 1-11.

[14] J. Mooney, "The Ghost-Dance Religion" (*Fourteenth Annual Report of the Bureau of American Ethnology*, pp. 641, *et seq.*).

[15] Oviedo y Valdés, Historia General y Natural de las Indias [1535-57] (Madrid, 1851-55), Bk. xlii, Chaps. 2, 3 (quoted from Spencer, Descriptive Sociology, No. II, pp. 42-43).

[16] Rudolf Lehmann, Schopenhauer.

we wonder that the thinker in primitive society is strongly influenced by the current thought of his time? Unconscious and conscious imitation are factors influencing civilized society, not less than primitive society, as has been shown by G. Tarde,[17] who has proved that primitive man, and civilized man as well, imitates not such actions only as are useful, and for the imitation of which logical causes may be given, but also others for the adoption or preservation of which no logical reason can be assigned.

I think these considerations illustrate that the differences between civilized man and primitive man are in many cases more apparent than real; that the social conditions, on account of their peculiar characteristics, easily convey the impression that the mind of primitive man acts in a way quite different from ours, while in reality the fundamental traits of the mind are the same.

Report on an Anthropometric Investigation of the Population of the United States (1922)

CHARACTERISTICS OF THE POPULATION OF THE UNITED STATES

The White population of the United States differs from that of Europe not so much in character as in the mode of assemblage of its component elements. The important theoretical and practical problems that arise in a study of the biological characteristics of our population relate largely to the effects of the recent rapid migrations of the diverse type of Europeans. The problem is further complicated by the presence of a large Negro population, of small remnants of Indian aborigines, and by a slight influx of Asiatics.

It would be an error to assume that the intermingling of different European types is a unique historical phenomenon which has never occurred before. On the contrary, all European nationalities are highly complex in origin. Even those most secluded and receiving the least amount of foreign blood at the present time have in past times been under entirely different conditions.

Intermixture in Europe was largely confined to antiquity, although in

[17] G. Tarde, Les Lois de l'Imitation.

From Boas, "Report on an Anthropometric Investigation of the United States," first published in *The Journal of the American Statistical Association,* Vol. 18 (1922), pp. 181-209. Reprinted in *Race, Language and Culture* (New York: The Macmillan Company, 1940), pp. 28-59.

some parts it continued into the Middle Ages, whereas the intermingling of different local types in the United States is recent. Owing to the social conditions in ancient Europe amalgamation of distinct elements may have been rather slow. Notwithstanding the relatively small numbers of migrating individuals, it may have taken several generations for the intrusive and native populations to become merged. In the United States, owing to the absence of hereditary social classes, the amalgamation is on the whole more rapid and involves larger numbers of individuals than the intermixture which took place in earlier periods in the Old World.

The impression that the population of European countries is comparatively speaking "pure" in descent is founded on its stability. In northern and central Europe this condition developed after individual hereditary landholding was substituted for the earlier forms of agricultural life, and with the attachment of the serf to the soil which he inhabited. These conditions prevailed in the Mediterranean area even in antiquity, but in the northern parts of Europe they did not develop until the Middle Ages, when the more or less tribal organization of the people gave way to feudal states. During the period when the Keltic and Teutonic tribes moved readily from place to place a vast amount of mixture occurred in all parts of Europe. Later on, when families became settled, those parts of the populations which were proprietors of the soil, or otherwise attached to the soil, became stationary, and consequently intermixture between distant parts of the continent became much less frequent than in previous times. On the other hand, the mutual permeation of neighboring communities probably became much more thorough.

These conditions of stability continued until by the development of cities diverse elements were brought together in the same community. This process became important with the growth of modern industrialism and with the concomitant growth of urban populations that were drawn together from large areas. Investigations made in different parts of Europe, particularly in Italy[1] and in Baden,[2] show differences in type between city populations and those of the open country. These may in part be explained by the strong intermixture of types drawn from a wide area which assemble and intermarry in the city. Observations of the population of Paris[3] indicate the same kind of intermixture of north European and central European types.

The settlement of the unoccupied districts of the United States has brought about an intermixture of types similar to that occurring in modern city populations, because settlers from different parts of Europe may dwell in close proximity in newly opened countries. Although in many

[1] Ridolfo Livi, *Antropometria Militare* (Rome, 1896), p. 87 *et seq.*
[2] Otto Ammon, *Zur Anthropologie der Badener* (Jena, 1899), p. 641.
[3] Franz Boas, "The Cephalic Index," *American Anthropologist*, N. S., vol. I (1899), p. 453.

cases we find a strong cohesion of farmers who come from the same European country, there is also a great deal of scattering.

It should, therefore, be understood that the problems presented by the population of the United States do not differ materially from the analogous European problems. The differences are due to the larger numbers of individuals involved in the whole process, in its rapidity, in its extension over rural communities, and in the forms of cohesion between members of the same group which are dependent upon the mode of settlement of the country. The process resembles earlier European mixtures in so far as many diverse European types are involved. In modern Europe only European types enter into the mixture, but a number of races morphologically removed from the White race enter into certain phases of the problem in America. Even this aspect of the problem was probably present in antiquity when slaves of foreign races formed a considerable part of the population.

The long continued stability of European populations which set in with the beginning of the Middle Ages and continued, at least in rural districts, until very recent times, has brought about a large amount of inbreeding in every limited district. In default of detailed statistical information in relation to the development of populations it is impossible to give exact data, but a cursory investigation shows that inbreeding of this type must have occurred for a very long time. The theoretical number of ancestors of every living individual proceeds by multiplication by two from generation to generation back, so that ten generations (or approximately 300 or 350 years) ago every single individual would have had 1,024 ancestors. Therefore, about 600 or 700 years ago there would be more than 1,000,000 ancestors for each individual. Considering the stability of population, and the fact that brothers and sisters have the same ancestors, such an increase in the number is, of course, entirely impossible, and it necessarily follows that a very large number of individuals in the ancestral series must be identical, which means that there must have been a large amount of inbreeding.

The "loss of ancestors" becomes the greater the further back we go in the ancestry and the more stable the population. It is obvious that particularly in the landholding group of families which remains from generation to generation in the same place, there must have been much inbreeding. Statistical information is available only for a few village communities and for the high nobility of Europe. The genealogies of all these families demonstrate that the decrease in the number of ancestors is very considerable. The calculations for the high nobility of Europe[4] show that in the sixth ancestral generation there are only 41 ancestors instead of 64; in the twelfth generation, only 533 instead of 4,096. These numbers seem

[4] Ottokar Lorenz, *Lehrbuch der gesammten wissenschaftlichen Genealogie* (Berlin (1898), p. 289 *et seq.*, pp. 308, 310, 311.

to be quite similar to those found in the stable village communities of Europe. Owing to this intermixture and to the similarity of descent of the families constituting the population, each family represents fairly adequately the whole population, or as we might express it, the whole population is homogeneous, in so far as all the families have the same kind of descent. On the other hand, in a population that results from recent migration and in which individuals from the most diverse parts of the world come together, a single family will not be representative of the whole population, because entirely different ancestral lines will be present in the various families. Therefore the population will be heterogeneous in so far as the different families belong to different lines of descent. To illustrate this point we might assume a community consisting of Whites and Negroes in which the Whites always intermarry among themselves, and the Negroes among themselves. Obviously in such a population, a single family would not be representative of the whole community, but only of its own fraction. On the other hand, if we had a community in which Whites and Negroes had intermarried for a long time, as is the case among the so-called Bastards of South Africa—a people very largely descended from Dutch and Hottentots and in which this intermingling has continued for a long time—we have a homogeneous population in so far as every family represents practically the same line of descent.[5] It will therefore be seen that homogeneity is not by any means identical with purity of race. In the case of a homogeneous population of mixed descent we may expect, on the whole, a high degree of variability in the family, while all the families will be more or less alike. On the other hand, in a heterogeneous population in which each part is, comparatively speaking, "pure," we may expect a low variability of each family with a high variability of the families constituting the whole population. On account of its migratory habits the American city population must be heterogeneous. Heterogeneous are also the immigrants and their immediate descendants, whereas in the stationary populations of New England villages and of the Kentucky mountains we have presumably homogeneous groups.

HEREDITY

For determining the characteristics of a population knowledge of the laws of heredity is indispensable. Ordinarily the term heredity in relation to racial[6] characteristics is used in a somewhat loose manner, and we should distinguish clearly between the hereditary stability of a population and the hereditary characteristics which determine the bodily form and

[5] Eugen Fischer, *Die Rehobother Bastards* (Jena, 1913); Franz Boas, "On the Variety of Lines of Descent Represented in a Population," *American Anthropologist* N. S., vol. 18 (1916), p. 1 *et seq.*

[6] The terms "race" and "racial" are here used in the sense that they mean the assembly of genetic lines represented in a population.

416   FRANZ BOAS

functions of an individual. The concept of hereditary stability in a population can mean only that the distribution of forms which occur in one generation will be repeated in exactly the same way in the following generation. This is clearest in the case of a homogeneous population as defined before. In every population varying bodily forms of individuals will occur with characteristic frequencies. In an undisturbed homogeneous population we must necessarily assume that each generation will show the same characteristic distribution of individual forms. If it did not do so there would be a disturbance of the hereditary stability.

Conditions are quite different in a heterogeneous population like that of the United States. Owing to intermarriages between the various constituent types there must be a tendency toward greater homogeneity, setting aside, of course, the influx of new immigrants. Experience shows that no matter how rigid may be the social objection to intermarriages between different groups, or how strong the pressure to bring about marriages between members of the same group, they will not prevent the gradual assimilation of the population. An instance of this kind is presented by the castes of India in Bengal. Notwithstanding the rigid endogamy of castes it has been observed that the highest castes are similar in type to the peoples of Western Asia, while the lower down in the scale of castes we go the more this type becomes mixed with the older substratum of the native population.[7] This can be explained only by intermarriage between the different castes which must have occurred notwithstanding the rigid laws forbidding it. The less the tendency toward segregation of different groups, the more rapid will be the approach toward homogeneity. Therefore notwithstanding the laws of hereditary stability in individual strains, there cannot be a hereditary stability of a heterogeneous population until homogeneity has been attained. It may even be considered doubtful whether a disturbance of the distribution of bodily forms may not occur as an effect of the intermingling of two populations similar or even identical in type, but of different ancestry, in which, therefore, a heterogeneity of ancestry exists.[8]

Thus it will be seen that the physiological laws of heredity are quite different from the statistical expression of the effects of heredity upon a large population. The latter depends upon both the biological laws of heredity and the peculiar social structure of the population which is being considered. These two aspects of heredity must be kept clearly apart.

Unfortunately, the laws of heredity in man are not clearly known, and it is not yet possible without overstepping the bounds of sound, critical, scientific method to apply them to the study of the characteristics of a

[7] H. H. Risley and E. A. Gait, *Census of India, 1901* (Calcutta, 1903), vol. 1, pp. 489 *et seq.*
[8] M. D. and Raymond Pearl, "On the Relation of Race Crossing to the Sex Ratio," *Biological Bulletin*, vol. 15 (1908), pp. 194 *et seq.*

population. A considerable amount of preliminary fundamental work must be done before we can proceed to the explanation of special complex phenomena. One fundamental point of view may be considered as established, namely, that when a definite couple of parents is given, the probability of occurrence of a given form among the descendants of this couple is fixed. In man it is not easy to demonstrate this fact because the number of children for each couple is small. If we assume, however, an organism in which each parental couple has an infinitely large number of offspring, the laws of heredity may be so expressed that each form that occurs among the offspring has a definite probability. In man these laws can be investigated only by combining many families in which both parents, or at least one of the parents, has the same characteristic form, although in this case the phenomenon is obscured by the fact that the same form in the parent does not necessarily mean the same ancestry. Observation of various features of the body of man shows that the simple forms of Mendelian heredity are not often applicable. It is true that in a number of cases of pathological modifications, the validity of the simple Mendelian formulas has been established. Even in these cases the number of observations is not sufficient to determine whether we are dealing with exact Mendelian ratios or with approximations. Practically all other cases are still open to doubt. Even in the case of eye color, which has been claimed to be subject to a simple Mendelian ratio with dominance of brown over blue, the available figures are not quite convincing.[9] For the more complex variable measurements of the body simple Mendelian ratios are certainly not applicable. Up to the present time the complex laws governing the frequencies of occurrence of bodily forms among descendants of an ancestral line are not known.

The investigation of any population must, therefore, take into consideration the detailed study of the laws of heredity.

THE INFLUENCE OF ENVIRONMENT

In settling in the United States the immigrants have been brought into a new environment, geographically as well as socially, and the question arises whether the new environment exerts an influence upon bodily form and functions. It has been customary to consider certain features of bodily development as absolutely stable, and anthropologists have characterized modern human types as "permanent forms" which have lasted without variation from the beginning of our modern geological period up to the present time. It is fairly easy to show that in this view exaggerated importance is ascribed to the phenomena of observed hereditary stability.

We know that the bulk of the body of an adult depends to a certain extent upon the more or less favorable conditions under which the child

[9] Helene M. Boas, "Inheritance of Eye Color in Man," *American Journal of Physical Anthropology,* vol. 2 (1919), pp. 15 *et seq.*

grows up. It has been shown that malnutrition or pathological conditions of various kinds may retard growth, and that the retardation may be so considerable that it cannot be made up by long continued growth. As a matter of fact, the bulk of the body at the time of birth is so small as compared to the bulk of the body of the adult that it is easy to understand that environmental conditions must exert a considerable influence upon its development. Proof of this is the gradual increase of stature during the past fifty years, until 1914, which has been demonstrated by investigations in a number of countries in Europe, and the difference in stature which is found in the same nationality for people living under different economic conditions.[10]

Since many proportions of the body are related to stature and bulk, these will also undergo modifications due to environmental conditions. The influence of environment is not so obvious in those cases in which the bodily form is practically determined at the time of birth, or in those in which the total growth from the time of birth until the adult stage is very slight. It might be assumed that in all cases of this type heredity alone determines the characteristic form of the body.

From a wider point of view the assumption that environment has no influence upon the form of the body does not seem justified. It must be understood that the question of stability or instability of the body in relation to environmental influences has no relation to the question of the inheritance of acquired characteristics. Even if we should adhere most rigidly to the dogma of the impossibility of the transmission of acquired characteristics, we must admit that a modification of the bodily form of the individual is easily conceivable without the necessity of assuming any modification of the germ plasm owing to individually acquired variation. We should rather have to say that adaptability of a definite type is one of the hereditary characteristics of the germ plasm. The problem involved is readily understood in the case of plants which appear in strongly modified form according to the environment in which they grow. In many cases the amount of hairiness, the form of the leaves, etc., are subject to the degree of moisture of the soil, and an accurate description of the species would therefore involve a statement that the plant has a certain degree of hairiness, dependent as a definite function upon the moisture of the soil, or that the leaves have a certain form dependent upon outer circumstances. In other words, the plant has a definite form only under a definite environment, and with changing environment, the form changes.

We may include under the group of environmental effects also all those variants of form and function that are dependent upon social habits which influence the organism. An influence upon bodily form is exerted by the habitual uses to which groups of muscles are put. Thus the rest position

[10] Rudolf Martin, *Lehrbuch der Anthropologie* (Jena, 1914), p. 225. Second edition (Jena, 1928), vol. 1, p. 297.

of the lower jaw is different in different areas. The English seem to hold the lower jaw a little farther forward than the Americans. The people of the western states relax the soft palate more than those of the North Atlantic area. The facial expression is determined by the development of the groups of facial muscles; the variations of certain aspects of the form of the hand and the foot are of this kind. The functioning of organs is even more markedly dependent upon habits, particularly upon habits firmly established during childhood. This is illustrated by the characteristic gait of individuals and of whole groups of people; by the involuntary movements in response to certain stimuli; by many of the expressive movements of the body; by habits of articulation; and by the dexterity and accuracy of movements obtained by early training.

Since we recognize the influence of environment upon the form of body including such features as bulk of body, or muscular forms and the functioning of organs, it seems justifiable to define racial characteristics as we do those of a variable plant, namely, by stating that under definite environmental conditions the bodily form of a race and its functioning are such as we observe, without prejudging the question in how far modifications in form and function may result from changing environment. The actual problem, then, would be to determine whether and how far the traits of the body may be so influenced. We should also bear in mind that it is perfectly conceivable that there may be congenital modifications in forms which are nevertheless not hereditary. Constitutional changes in the body of the mother may bring about modifications in prenatal growth which to the superficial observer might give the impression of hereditary changes. These considerations demonstrate that it is necessary to consider this problem in any thorough investigation of the characteristics of the American population.

SELECTION

The question must be asked in how far selective agencies may determine the movements of the population, including immigration and emigration, the settlement of the western parts of the United States by the inhabitants of the eastern states, and the migration from country to city. Besides migration, the selective influences of mating, of mortality, and of fertility have to be taken into account. Of late years much stress has been laid upon the effect of selection upon the constitution of a population.

The effect of selection as determined by bodily form can be investigated to advantage only in a homogeneous population. When every family may be considered as representative of the whole population, and when all strata of society present the same physical characteristics, selective forces that are based on social stratification will not influence the selective results, because all social strata will be alike. If it should be found that groups representing different bodily forms have different tendencies to migrate, or different rates of mortality or fertility, we might have an expression of the direct dependence of selection upon bodily form.

As a matter of fact, however, homogeneous populations do not exist anywhere in the world. A greater or less amount of heterogeneity has always been observed, and heterogeneity in our modern civilization, at least, is always connected with social stratification. In a heterogeneous population like that of the United States the difficulties in the way of determining a direct relation between selective influences and bodily form are almost insurmountable. If, for instance, descendants of a certain nationality are attracted to a particular area, as the Scandinavians to the northwest, the Hungarians to the mines of Pennsylvania, the Mexicans to the southern borderland of the United States, or the French Canadians to the New England states and northern New York, we must remember that each one of these social groups represents a certain physical type and that there will be, therefore, an apparent relation between selection and physical type which in reality is based on social factors.

Similar observations may be made with regard to selective mating. Since mating depends upon social contact, marriages will occur among the groups that associate together. Wherever nationalities cluster together, where denominational or racial considerations act as endogamic restrictions, there will be selective mating of similar types due to social heterogeneity. Besides this there may be a certain amount of selection that unites tall with tall or expresses the sexual attractiveness of other bodily features.

Social heterogeneity exerts an influence also upon the mortality and the fertility of different groups. The more recent immigrants are on the whole less well-to-do than the earlier immigrants and their descendants. We know that there is a relation between fertility and economic well-being and we find, therefore, that the number of children of the more recent immigrants is greater than that of the descendants of earlier immigrants, so that, setting aside the question of mortality, there would be a shifting in the distribution of the population in favor of later immigrants. Since the earlier immigrants represent the northwestern European type and the later immigrants the south and east European types, there will appear in this case also a selection according to bodily form, which is due not to the direct relation between physical characteristics and fertility, but rather to the fact that the one economic group is composed of one type, and the other economic group of another type. In many cases the relation between descent and social stratification is so complex that it easily escapes our notice, and for this reason we may observe phenomena of selection apparently related to bodily form but actually due to obscure social causes that are discovered with great difficulty only.

On the other hand it cannot be denied that in some cases at least there must be a direct relation between bodily form and physiological function on the one side and selective processes on the other. It is, for instance, quite obvious that in the settlement of the new western countries a certain bodily and mental vigor was necessary to enable a person to undertake the venture. It has often been pointed out, although it has never been proven empirically, that in this way there must have been a selection from the inhabitants of the New England villages who migrated westward and that the emigrants represented a physically superior type. Even though this conclusion is not based on observation it seems highly probable. To the same group of phenomena would belong the supposed greater susceptibility to certain forms of disease of slightly pigmented individuals, as compared with the greater power of resistance of brunet individuals. I am not by any means convinced that incontrovertible proof of this assumption has been given; but if it were true that the constitution of the blond is weakened by exposure to intense sunlight, there might be a selective influence of this kind when a people move from the cloudy temperate zones to the brilliant sunlight of more southern and more arid climes.

In considering the selective influences of environment it should be borne in mind that the human body is so constituted that all its organs can operate adequately under widely varying circumstances. Our lungs are able to supply the needs of our body under the air pressure that prevails at the level of the sea, and they operate adequately at an elevation of 20,000 feet where the air is highly rarefied. The heart can adjust itself to the variation in demands made upon it, either in sedentary life at the level of the sea, or in active life in high altitudes. Our digestive organs may adapt themselves to a purely vegetable diet or again to a purely meat diet. Our central nervous system is also capable of adjusting itself to the most varied conditions of life. As long, therefore, as the conditions of environment do not exceed very elastic limits, it is not probable that selective influences would become operative to any very great extent, at least not in so far as they are determined solely by the form and functioning of the organs of the body.

RACIAL AND INDIVIDUAL DIFFERENCES

An investigation of the bodily forms of the individuals constituting a race, homogeneous or heterogeneous, shows that they differ considerably among themselves in every single feature, such as pigmentation, form of hair, size and proportions of the body, physiological reactions. These differences are measurable and express the degree of variability of the race. A complete presentation of the characteristics of a race would contain a statement of the relative frequency of each particular bodily form which occurs among the individuals constituting the race. When comparing, from the point of view of anatomical or physiological characteristics, the racial types of Europe which constitute the bulk of the American population, it appears that the range of variation for the different types is of such a character that a great many individuals belonging to one type correspond to other individuals belonging to another type. In other words, there are certain forms common to all populations of Europe. To give an example: We find strongly contrasting head forms in northern Italy and in Sardinia. Nevertheless an investigation of the distribution of head forms in each one of these districts shows that 27 per cent of the population may belong either to Sardinia or to northern Italy. In other words, there is a very considerable amount of overlapping of bodily form between neighboring types, and it is only when we consider races that are fundamentally different that we find certain characteristics that do not overlap. Comparing, for instance, the blond north European White and the dark Sudanese Negro, there is no overlapping with regard to pigmentation, form of hair, form of nose, form of lips, etc. If, on the other hand, we proceed by steps from northern Europe to the Sudan, a great many intermediate and overlapping steps between these extreme forms will be found, so that only the extremes would really be entirely separate. While it may be that two races are quite distinct with regard to certain features, there are always other features with regard to which the differences are so slight that the assignment of any one individual to either one race or the other would be beset with doubt.

It has been customary to express the differences between racial types by the difference between the averages of each type or between the modes (the most frequent values) that are characteristic for each type. It is easily shown that such a description is misleading. If we wish to express the difference between two individuals, each of whom has constant characteristics, we may proceed in this manner. If one individual measures 170 cm. and another 165 cm., the difference between them is 5 cm. If, however, a certain population has an average stature of 170 cm., and another population an average stature of 165 cm., we cannot say that the difference between the two is 5 cm., because if there is a wide range of variability there will be a large number of individuals among the taller population who have exactly the same statures as individuals of the shorter population. To give arbitrarily selected figures, the one may range perhaps from 150 to 190 cm., the other from 145 to 185 cm. In this case an individual that measures anywhere between 150 and 185 cm. might belong to either class. It must, therefore, be clear that if we speak of differences between two races we do not necessarily mean differences between individuals, and these two concepts must be kept clearly apart. The bulk of our modern literature concerning racial differences is open to misinterpretation owing to a lack of a clear understanding of the significance of the term "difference" as applied on the one hand to individuals and on the other hand to races. The generalization, which is often made (to use our previous instance), that the one population is 5 cm. shorter than the other is often interpreted as meaning that this implies a characteristic of all the individuals of a race, while actually a single selected individual of the shorter race may be much taller than a single selected individual of the taller race. This is equally true of all those anatomical, physiological, and psychological characteristics which exhibit overlapping of individuals. It is also true of those that show no overlapping, because the difference between two selected representative individuals may vary within wide limits. If it is stated that the Whites have larger brains than the Negroes, this does not mean that every White person has a larger brain than any Negro, but merely that the average of the Negro brains is lower than the average of the brains of the Whites. With regard to many characteristics of this kind, we find that the difference between the averages of different races is insignificant as compared to the range of variability that occurs within each race.

An additional point should be considered in connection with this phenomenon. Most of the anatomical characteristics of the body are stable throughout adult life, until senile degeneration begins. On the other hand, physiological and psychological functions are not the same in the same individual at all times. They vary strongly with environmental conditions and particularly with different demands made upon the organism. The variability of physiological and psychological responses is therefore much greater than the variability of anatomical form, because the two former combine the variability due to the difference in the functioning in various individuals with the variations of response under varying conditions. When comparing racial types we must therefore avoid expressing a difference of types simply as a difference of averages.

Another point must be considered which may be illustrated by an example. Let us assume that in one area the color of the hair varies from black to dark brown with an average value on a certain definite shade, and that in another population the color of the hair varies from dark blond to very light blond with an average on a certain shade of blond. In this case the two distributions will not overlap at all. On the other hand, let us assume that we have two populations with the same average shades of brown and of blond as before, but in the one a variation which begins with black and extends into blond shades, and in the other a pigmentation which begins with a very dark brown and extends into very light blond, so that the two overlap. Obviously the two differences will not impress us as the same, notwithstanding the fact that the two averages remain the same. It is therefore indispensable that in an investigation of this kind the significance of the difference between two populations should be clearly expressed, and that the impression should be avoided that the difference between racial types is identical with the difference between individuals.

Still another point deserves attention. Many writers assume that an individual of a certain type represents the same biological type regardless of the racial group to which he belongs. To give an example: a round-headed person of the Tyrols is equated with a round-headed person of southern

Italy, at least in so far as the form of the head is concerned. Even if we assume that the round-headedness of the two individuals is of the same kind, this inference is not tenable. It is true that by chance the two individuals may belong to the same lines of descent, but a study of a series of homologous individuals shows that genetically, and therefore physiologically, they are not the same notwithstanding the sameness of the particular trait that is made the subject of study. When we select, for instance, individuals with the same head index of 82 in a population that has the average head index of 85, the children of the selected group will be found to have an average head index of 84; when we select individuals with the same head index of 82 in a population that has the average head index of about 79, the children of the selected group will be found to have an average head index of about 80, for the reason that there will be in each case reversions to the average type of the population to which the selected group belongs. In other words, the individuals which are selected from any population must always be considered as part of this population and cannot be studied as though they were an independent group.

EUGENICS

One of the reasons for the special stress that is laid upon race investigations is the fear of race degeneration. It is assumed that the intermixture between different racial types and the rapid increase of the poorest part of the population have a deteriorating effect upon the nation. In the introductory remarks I have tried to show that there is little reason to believe that racial intermixture of the kind occurring in the United States at the present time should have a deteriorating effect. I do not believe that it has been adequately proved that there is a clearly marked tendency toward general degeneration among all civilized nations. In modern society the conditions of life have become more varied than those of former periods. While some groups live under most favorable conditions that require active use of body and mind, others live in abject poverty and their activities have more than ever before been degraded to those of machines. At the same time the variety of human activities is much greater than it used to be. It is therefore quite intelligible that the functional activities of each nation must show an increased degree of differentiation, a higher degree of variability. Even if the general average of the mental and physical types should remain the same, there must be a larger number now than formerly who fall below a certain given low standard, and also a larger number who can exceed a given high standard. The number of defectives can be counted by statistics of poor relief, delinquency, and insanity, but there is no way of determining the increase of those individuals who are raised above the norm of a higher standard, and they escape our notice. It may therefore very well be that the number of defectives increases without influencing the value of a population as a whole, because it is merely an expression of an increased degree of variability.

Furthermore, arbitrarily selected absolute standards of value do not retain their significance. Even if no change in the absolute standard should be made, the degree of physical and mental energy required under modern conditions to keep oneself above a certain minimum of achievement is greater than it used to be. This is due to the greater complexity of our life and to the increasing number of competing individuals. Greater capacity is required to attain a high degree of prominence than was needed in other periods of our history. The claim that we have to contend against national degeneracy must, therefore, be better substantiated than it is now.

The problem is further complicated by the advance in public hygiene which has resulted in lowering infant mortality and has thus brought about a change in the composition of the population, in so far as many who would have succumbed to deleterious conditions in early years enter into the adult population and must have an influence upon the general distribution of vitality.

Notwithstanding the doubtful basis of many of the assertions relating to degeneracy, the problem of eugenics is clearly before the public, and the investigation of racial and social types cannot be separated from the practical aims involved in the eugenic movement.

The fundamental thought underlying eugenic theory is that no environmental influences can modify those characteristics which are determined by hereditary nature. *Nurture,* it is said, cannot overcome *nature.*

We should recall here what has been said before regarding the difference between the characteristics of hereditary strains and those of races, and that while it is true that strains differ greatly in physical and mental vigor and in specific characteristics, it is not equally true of races as a whole, because strains which are very much alike in all these characteristics are found in every single race. Even if it is not possible to prove with absolute certainty the complete identity in mental traits of selected strains belonging to races as diverse as Europeans and Negroes, there is not the slightest doubt that such identity prevails among the various European types. Eugenics, therefore, cannot have any possible meaning with regard to whole races. It can have a meaning only with regard to strains. If the task of the eugenist were the selection of that third of humanity representing the best strains, he would find his material among all European and Asiatic types, and very probably among all races of man; and all would contribute to the less valuable two-thirds.

As an objection to this point of view it is sometimes claimed that closely allied animal types are so different in their physical make-up and mental characteristics that members of one race can be clearly differentiated from those of another race. It is, for instance, said that the race horse and the heavy dray horse are so different in character that no matter what may be done to the dray horse its descendants can never be transformed into race horses. This is undoubtedly true, but the parallelism between the races of dray horses and race horses on the one hand and human races on the other is incorrect. The races of horses are developed by careful selection, by means of which physical and mental characteristics are fixed in each separate strain, while in human races no such selection occurs. We have rather a racial panmixture, which brings it about that the racial character- istics are distributed irregularly among all the different families. As a matter of fact, dray horses and race horses correspond to family strains, not to human races, and the comparison is valid only in so far as race horses and dray horses are compared to the characteristics of certain family lines, not to human races as a whole. In Johannsen's terminology the human races are to a much greater extent phenotypes than races of domesticated animals.

For this reason the task of eugenics cannot be to devise means to sup- press some races and to favor the development of others. It must rather be directed to the discovery of methods which favor the development of the desirable strains in every race.

This problem can be attacked only after the solution of two questions. First of all, we have to decide what are the desirable characteristics; and secondly, we must determine what characteristics are hereditary. With regard to the former question, we shall all agree that physical health is one of the fundamental qualities to be desired; but there will always be funda- mental disagreement as to what mental qualities are considered desirable —whether an intense intellectualism and a repression of emotionalism or a healthy development of emotional life is preferable. Obviously, it is quite impossible to lay down a standard that will fit every person, every place, and every time, and for this reason the application of eugenic measures should be restricted to the development of physical and mental health. Even if it were possible to control human mating in such a way that strains with certain mental characteristics could be developed, it would seem entirely unjustifiable for our generation to impose upon future times ideals that some of us may consider desirable. It might furthermore be ques- tioned whether the interests of humanity will be better served by eliminat- ing all abnormal strains which, as history shows, have produced a number of great men who have contributed to the best that mankind has done, or by carrying the burden of the unfit for the sake of the few valuable indi- viduals that may spring from them. These, of course, are not scientific questions, but social and ethical problems.

For the practical development of eugenics it is indispensable to deter- mine what is hereditary and what is not. The ordinary method of deter- mining heredity is to investigate the recurrence of the same phenomenon among a number of successive generations. If, for instance, it can be shown that color-blindness occurs in successive generations, or that certain malformations like polydactylism are found repeatedly in the same family, or that multiple births are characteristic of certain strains, we conclude that these are due to hereditary causes; and if parents and children have the same head form or the same or similar statures, we decide that these similarities also are due to heredity. It must be recognized that in many of these cases alternative explanations are conceivable. If, for instance, a family lives under certain economic conditions which are repeated among parents and children, and if these economic conditions have a direct influence upon the size of the body, the similarity of stature of parents and children would be due to environment and not to heredity. If a disease is endemic in a certain locality and occurs among parents and children, this is not due to heredity but to the locality which they inhabit. In other words, wherever the environmental conditions have a marked influence upon bodily characteristics, and wherever these environmental conditions continue for a number of generations, they have an effect that is apparently identical with that of heredity. In many cases the causes are so obvious that it is easy to exclude persistence of characteristics due to environment. Under other conditions the determination of the causes is not so easy.

It is still more difficult to differentiate between heredity and congenital features. For example, if a child before birth should be infected by its mother, there might be the impression of a hereditary disease, which, however, is actually only congenital in the sense that it is not inherent in the structure of the germ plasm. Although the distinction between environmental causes as previously defined and hereditary causes is generally fairly easy, the distinction between congenital causes and true hereditary causes is exceedingly difficult, in many cases impossible. The long continued discussions relating to hereditary transmission of disease are a case in point. Most of these questions cannot be solved by statistical inquiries, but require the most careful biological investigation. The conditions, however, are such that we must demand in every case a clear differentiation among these three causes.

There is little doubt that in the modern eugenic movement the assumption of hereditary transmission as a cause of defects has been exaggerated. Although certain mental defects that occur among well-to-do families seem to be determined by heredity, the mental defects generally included in eugenic studies are of such a character that many of them may readily be recognized as due to social conditions rather than as expressing specific hereditary traits. A weakling who is economically well situated is protected from many of the dangers that beset an individual of similar characteristics whose economic condition is not so favorable, and it must be admitted that criminality in families that may be mentally weak and which are at the same time struggling for the barest subsistence is at least as much determined by social conditions as by heredity. Investigators of criminal families have succeeded in showing frequencies of occurrence of criminality which are analogous to frequencies which may be due to heredity, but they have failed to show that these frequencies may not as well be explained either wholly or in part by environmental conditions. We should be willing to admit that among the poor undernourished population, which is at the same time badly housed and suffers from other unfavorable conditions of life, congenital weakness may develop which lowers the resistance of the individual against all forms of delinquency. Whether this weakness is hereditary or congenital is, however, an entirely different question. Experiments made with generations of underfed rats[11] suggest that a strain of rats which has deteriorated by underfeeding can be fed up by a careful amelioration of conditions of life, and it may well be questioned whether delinquent strains in man may not be improved in a similar way. Certainly the history of the criminals deported to Australia and of their descendants is very much in favor of such a theory. In other words, it seems very likely that the condition of our subnormal population is not by any means solely determined by heredity, but that careful investigations are required to discriminate between environmental, congenital, and hereditary causes.

FORMULATION OF PROBLEM

From the preceding discussion, we may formulate the principal problems that must be taken up in a study of the population of the United States. We have to investigate first the degree of homogeneity of the population; second, the hereditary characteristics of the existing lines; third, the influence of environment; fourth, the influences of selection. On the basis of the data thus collected, we have to interpret the significance of the differences between various types, and investigate the bearing that our results may have upon public policies.

The study of the adult population alone would not give us adequate data to enable us to clear up the causes which determine the final development of the body—the events which take place during the period of growth must also be taken into consideration.

Familiarity with the bodily forms of children is necessary also from a morphological point of view. On the whole, the development of individuals is divergent, so that the most characteristic forms of each type are found in the adult male. The adult female forms are not quite so divergent, perhaps in part for the reason that the period of development of the female is shorter than that of the male, although it must be remembered that secondary sexual characteristics are present in childhood. The younger the human form that we investigate, the less clearly are racial characteristics expressed. We may, therefore, say that the most generalized forms of a racial type will be found in the infant or, even still more clearly, in pre-

[11] Helen Dean King, *Studies on Inbreeding* (Wistar Institute, 1919).

natal stages, while the most highly specialized local forms will be found in the male adult. A knowledge of the specialized forms ought to include, therefore, a study of progressive differentiation. Particularly for the study of the influences of environment it is indispensable that the development of the body in childhood should be studied while the influences are still at work. We have to know the conditions which bring about retardation or acceleration in the development of various parts of the body, and their ultimate effects upon the human form. We must study other minute changes that may perhaps not be related to retardation or acceleration, but that may be due to a direct effect of environmental causes. In the adult these changes have been completed and can no longer be subjected to analysis, while in the growing child, their gradual development and unfolding may be observed.

The same is true with regard to selection. If selection is related to bodily form, it will probably act with particular intensity during the early years of childhood. It might be revealed by a comparison of the surviving and dying parts of the population of various ages.

These considerations make it quite necessary to include in the study of the population, not only adults, but also children.

One method of approach should consist, therefore, in the study of the growth and development of children, classified according to descent and geographical and social environment. If it were feasible to include records of the longevity of the individuals measured in childhood, the problem of selection could also be attacked. In the study of adults a careful classification according to descent and social position will be necessary.

The phenomena of homogeneity and of heredity make it necessary that the investigation should not be confined to studies of individuals, but that the anatomical characteristics of families should be made the subject of inquiry.

For the study of the influence of environment the investigation of growing children is, if anything, more important than for the investigation of racial characteristics. After the adult stage has been reached environment will not exert any further influence. The earlier in life the investigation can begin, the more likely we are to obtain adequate results.

In this investigation the generalizing method of comparing local types or types presented in social strata is of little use, because in order to establish definitely an influence of environmental causes, we must be certain that the hereditary composition of the populations which we study is the same. For instance, when we compare a rural and an urban community, there is nothing that will guarantee to us that both populations are derived from the same ancestry. On the contrary, we may assume that the urban population is drawn from a wider group than the rural population. In the same way, when we compare the inhabitants of a long secluded valley and find differences in bodily form between the people living in the lower part and those living in the upper part, the question would arise whether the ancestry of the two groups is the same and whether the people in the upper regions have not been more isolated than those farther down. It is on the whole easier to exclude obvious environmental influences in an investigation of racial types than to exclude differences of racial descent in studies of the influence of environment. The only way to escape from these complications is by confining the studies strictly to a comparison between parents and children.

It has been explained before that in a number of cases we may find apparent hereditary traits which may be deduced from the similarity of parents and their own children, and which nevertheless are primarily due to environmental causes. If we should find, for instance, a low stature among individuals who have been undernourished as children, and if the next generation will also be undernourished, we may have an apparent similarity in stature which is not due primarily to heredity, but rather to the fact that the same environmental causes act upon the parental group and upon the group of children. In most cases these elements cannot be eliminated unless we have the opportunity to study the same racial type in different forms of environment.

It has been stated before that a modification of bodily form due to environment which is observed by comparing parents and their children does not contradict the phenomena of heredity. If we find, for instance, that the stature of Jewish immigrants into the United States is lower than that of their children, the hereditary stability of stature will nevertheless manifest itself. The children of an exceptionally tall couple who exceed the average stature of the immigrant Jew by a certain amount may be expected to show an excess of stature which is correlated to the excess of stature of the parents, which, however, has to be added to the increased average stature of the children of immigrants. In short, a change in type due to environmental influences simply means that the correlated deviations in the group of parents and of children must be reckoned from the point which is typical for the generation in question.

In some cases in which the environmental influences are very strong, a generalizing method may give adequate results. Bowditch, in his investigation of Boston children, was able to show that Irish children differ in their development according to the economic condition of the parents, and there is little reason to doubt the uniformity of the genetic composition of his various Irish groups. But whenever the differences involved are slight, and when they may be equally well explained on the basis of difference in genetic composition, the comparison between parents and children is indispensable. . . .

At the present time it is unknown to what extent the influences of environment may determine bodily form. Notwithstanding the numerous claims of the fundamental effect of climate upon the body of man, we have

no evidence whatever that will show that pigmentation undergoes fundamental changes under climatic conditions; that the White race would become darker in the tropics; or that the Negroes would become lighter in
the north. Whatever statistics we have on this subject show rather a remarkable stability of pigmentation. We have not even any definite indication that the pigmentation of the hair undergoes changes under different
climatic conditions, although in this case the change in color from the
period of childhood until middle life is so great that we might very well
expect environmental influences to express themselves. On the other hand,
we know that the bulk of the body is very susceptible to environmental influences, and it is but natural that retardation or acceleration during the
period of growth will also leave its effect upon those proportions of the
body which depend upon bulk. Other changes which occur very early in
life are not so easily explained. I think the evidence showing that the form
of the head is susceptible to environmental influences is incontrovertible. I
also believe that adequate proof has been given for modifications in the
width of the face under changed conditions of life. The causes of these
changes are still entirely obscure. It may well be, as suggested by Harvey
Cushing, that chemical changes occur under new environmental conditions
and unequally influence growth in different directions. This would agree
with the changes in chemical constitution found in lower animals living in
different types of environment. If it is true that changes of this kind do
occur and modify the form of body so fundamentally that according to
the ordinary schemes of classification a people might be removed from one
group and placed in another one, then we have to consider the investigation
of the instability of the body under varying environmental conditions as
one of the most fundamental subjects to be considered in an anthropometric study of our population.

ALEŠ HRDLIČKA

(1869-1943)

Aleš Hrdlička was a physical anthropologist who liked bones. He was associated with the National Museum from 1903 until his death. It was through his efforts that the Museum's collections of physical anthropology, which are regarded as the most complete of their kind, were built up. This was only one of the varied activities of his long career devoted to building the science of physical anthropology in America.

Hrdlička was born in Czechoslovakia (then Bohemia), received his elementary education in public schools of his native city, and came with his family to New York at the age of thirteen. He was working in a tobacco factory when a physician who attended him in a serious illness persuaded him to study medicine and made it possible for him to do so. After graduating from the Eclectic Medical College and the New York Homeopathic Medical College, he accepted a research position in a state hospital for the insane, where he began to accumulate anthropometric data. He accompanied Lumholz (an anthropologist working on problems of northern Mexican ethnology for the American Museum of Natural History) on his last trip to Mexico, an experience which decided the course of his life. He resigned from the hospital and thenceforth devoted himself to the problems of physical anthropology.

Hrdlička made a number of trips to the Southwest for the American Museum of Natural History, and became interested in the problem of the antiquity of man in America. His views, considered unorthodox at the time, were supported by later discoveries.

The problem of the evolution of man attracted him next. He examined all the existing skeletal remains of early man and published a comprehensive monograph on the subject. He was an indefatigable worker; his bibliography contains over three hundred titles. He founded the American Association of Physical Anthropologists, and the American Journal of Physical Anthropology, *which he edited for a quarter of a century. A physical anthropologist of the old school, he deplored the application of modern statistical methods to anthropological problems, and therefore was out of step with one important line of development.*

In other ways, too, he belonged to another age. He had a strong antipathy to women in science and avoided any contact with them. He is

known to have walked out of a scientific meeting in which the sexual be-
havior of monkeys was being discussed. For all of his propagandizing for
physical anthropology, he was probably happiest when he was studying
bones.—R.L.B.

Origin of the American Aborigines

WHEN COLUMBUS DISCOVERED THE NEW WORLD HE AND HIS COMPANIONS imagined, as is well known, that they had reached India, and the people met were naturally taken for natives of India. Later, as the true nature of the new land became better known, speculations concerning the newly dis- covered race took other directions, and some of the notions developed proved disastrous to the Indians. History tells us that many of the early Spaniards, up to Las Casas' time, reached the conclusion that, as no men- tion was made concerning the American people in Hebrew traditions, they could not strictly be regarded as men, equivalent to those named in biblical accounts, and this view, which eventually had to be counteracted by a special papal bull, led directly or indirectly to wholesale enslavement and destruction of the Americans.

One of the effects of this papal edict was that thenceforth the origin of the Indians was sought in other parts of the world, and the seeming neces- sity of harmonizing this origin with biblical knowledge led eventually to several curious opinions. One of these, held by Gomara, Lerius, and Les- carbot, was to the effect that the American aborigines were the descendants of the Canaanites who were expelled from their original abode by Joshua; another, held especially by McIntosh,[1] was that they were descended from Asiatics who themselves originated from Magog, the second son of Japhet; but the most widespread theory, and one with the remnants of which we meet to this day, was that the American Indians represented the so-called Lost Tribes of Israel.[2]

During the course of the 19th century, with Levêque, Humboldt,[3] McCullogh,[4] Morton,[5] and especially Quatrefages,[6] we begin to encounter

From Hrdlička, "Origin of the American Aborigines," *American Anthropologist*, XIV, N. S., (1912), pp. 5-12.

[1] McIntosh, J., *Origin of the North American Indians*, New York, 1843.
[2] Adair, J., *History of the North American Indians*, London, 1775.
[3] Humboldt, *Political Essay*, I, 115; Humboldt and Bonpland, *Voyage, Vue des Cordilleras*, Paris, 1810.
[4] McCullogh, *Researches, Philosophical and Antiquarian, Concerning the Aboriginal History of America*, Baltimore, 1829.
[5] Morton, S. G., *Distinctive Characteristics of the Aboriginal Race of America*, 2d ed., pp. 35-36, Philadelphia, 1844. (Also his *Crania Americana*, and *Origin of the Human Species*.)
[6] Quatrefages, *Histoire générale des races humaines*, Paris, 1887.

more rational hypotheses concerning the Indians, although by no means a single opinion. Lord Kaimes, Morton, and Nott and Gliddon[7] professed the belief that the American natives originated in the New World and hence were truly autochthonous; Grotius believed that Yucatan had been peopled by early Christian Ethiopians; according to Mitchell the ancestors of the Indians came to this country partly from the Pacific ocean and partly from northeastern Asia; the erudite Dr. McCullough believed that the Indians originated from parts of different peoples who reached America over lost land from the west "when the surface of the earth allowed a free transit for quadrupeds"; Quatrefages viewed the Americans as a conglomerate people, resulting from the fossil race of Lagoa Santa, the race of Paraná, and probably others, in addition to which he believed there had been settlements of Polynesians; and according to Pickering the Indians originated partly from the Mongolian and partly from the Malay.

The majority of the authors of the last century, however, including Humboldt, Brerewood, Bell, Swinton, Jefferson, Latham, Quatrefages, and Peschel,[8] inclined to the belief that all the American natives, excepting the Eskimo, were of one and the same race and that they were the descendants of immigrants from northeastern Asia, particularly from the "Tartars" or Mongolians.

The most recent writers, with one marked exception, agree entirely that this country was peopled through immigration and local multiplication of people; but the locality, nature, and time of the immigration are still much mooted questions. Some authors incline to the exclusively northeastern Asiatic origin; others, such as ten Kate and Rivet, show a tendency to follow Quatrefages in attributing at least some parts of the native American population to the Polynesians; Brinton[9] held that they came in ancient times over a land connection from Europe; and Kollmann,[10] basing his belief on some small crania, believes that a dwarf race preceded the Indian in America.

A remarkable hypothesis concerning the origin of the American native population, deserving a few words apart, has within the last thirty years, and especially since the beginning of this century, been built up by Ameghino,[11] the South American paleontologist. This hypothesis is, in brief, that man, not merely the American race, but mankind, originated in South America; that man became differentiated in the southern continent into a number of species, most of which are now extinct; that from South America he migrated over ancient land connections to Africa, and from there

[7] Nott and Gliddon, *Types of Mankind,* and *Indigenous Races.* (The latter includes statements by Leidy and Morton.)

[8] Peschel, O., *The Races of Man,* p. 418, 1876.

[9] Brinton, D. G., *The American Race,* New York, 1891.

[10] Kollmann, J., *Die Pygmäen* (Verh. d. Naturforsch. Ges. Basel, XVI, Basel, 1902).

[11] Ameghino, F., *El Tetraprothomo Argentinus* (Anal. Mus. Nac., XVI, Buenos Aires, 1907); also *Le Diprothomo platensis* (ibid., XIX, 1909).

peopled all the Old World; that a strain from the remaining portion multiplied and spread over South America; and that eventually, somewhere in relatively recent times, a portion of that branch which peopled Africa and then Asia, migrated, by the northern route, into North America. In part this theory is also favored by Sergi.

In addition there have been some suggestions that the Americans may have arrived from the "lost Atlantis"; and the theory has even been expressed that man, instead of migrating from northeastern Asia into America, may have moved in the opposite direction, and especially that, after peopling this continent, a part of the Americans reached Siberia.

The Eskimo have been generally considered as apart from the Indian, some holding that they preceded and others that they followed him. They have been connected generally with the northeastern Asiatics, but there are also those who see a close original relation between the Eskimo and the Lapps, and even between the Eskimo and the paleolithic Europeans.

These are, in brief, the various more or less speculative opinions that so far have been advanced in an effort to explain the ethnic identity and the place of origin of the American Indian; and it is only logical that the next word on these problems be given to physical anthropology, which deals with what are, on the whole, the least mutable parts of man, namely, his body and skeleton.

THE BEARING OF PHYSICAL ANTHROPOLOGY ON THE PROBLEMS UNDER CONSIDERATION

The somatology of the Indians, which barely saw its beginnings in the time of Humboldt and Morton, has now advanced to such a degree that at least some important generalizations concerning the American aborigines are possible. We have now at our disposal for comparison, in American museums alone, upward of twenty thousand Indian crania and skeletons from all parts of the continent, while several thousand similar specimens are contained in European collections. A considerable advance, particularly in North America, has also been made in studying the living natives. Unfortunately we are much less advantageously situated in regard to comparative skeletal material as well as with respect to data on the living from other parts of the world, particularly from those parts where other indications lead us to look for the origin of the Indian.

What can be stated in the light of present knowledge concerning the American native with a fair degree of positiveness is that, first, there is no acceptable evidence, or any probability, that man originated on this continent; second, that man did not reach America until after attaining a development superior to that of even the latest Pleistocene man in Europe, and after having undergone advanced and thorough stem and even racial and tribal differentiation; and third, that while man, since the peopling of this continent was commenced, has developed numerous secondary, sub-racial, localized structural modifications, these modifications can not yet be regarded as fixed, and in no important feature have they obliterated the old type or types of the people.

We are further in a position to state that, notwithstanding the various secondary physical modifications referred to, the American natives, barring the most distantly related Eskimo, present throughout the Western Hemisphere numerous important features in common, which mark them plainly as parts of one stem of humanity. These features are:

1. The color of the skin. The color of the Indian differs, according to localities, from dusky yellowish-white to that of solid chocolate, but the prevailing color is brown.

2. The hair of the Indian, as a rule, is black and straight; the beard is scanty, especially on the sides of the face, and it is never long. There is no hair on the body except in the axillæ and on the pubis, and even there it is sparse.

3. The Indian is generally free from characteristic odor. His heart-beat is slow. His mental characteristics are much alike. The size of the head and of the brain cavity is comparable throughout, averaging somewhat less than that of white men and women of similar stature.

4. The eyes as a rule are more or less dark brown in color, with dirty yellowish conjunctiva, and the eye-slits show a prevailing tendency, more or less noticeable in different tribes, to a slight upward slant, that is, the external canthi are frequently more or less higher than the internal.

5. The nasal bridge, at least in men, is throughout well developed, and the nose in the living, as well as the nasal aperture in the skull (barring individual and a few localized exceptions), show medium or mesorhinic relative proportions. The malar regions are as a rule rather large or prominent.

6. The mouth is generally fairly large, the lips average from medium to slightly fuller than in whites, and the lower facial region shows throughout a medium degree of prognathism, standing, like the relative proportions of the nose, about midway between those found in whites and negroes. The chin is well developed. The teeth are of medium size, when compared with those of mankind in general, but perceptibly larger when contrasted with those of the white American; and the upper incisors are characteristically shovel-shaped, that is, deeply and peculiarly concave on the buccal side. The ears are large.

7. The neck, as a rule, is of only moderate length, and is never very thin; the chest is somewhat deeper than in average whites; the breasts of the women are of medium size and generally more or less conical in form. There is a complete absence of steatopygy; the lower limbs are less shapely and especially less full than in whites; the calf is small.

8. The hands and feet, as a rule, are of relatively moderate or even of small dimensions, and what is among the most important of all the charac-

teristics, the relative proportions of the forearms to arms and those of the distal parts of the lower limbs to the proximal (or, in the skeleton, the radio-humeral and tibio-femoral indices), are in general, throughout the two parts of the continent, of much the same average value, which differs from that of both the whites and the negroes, standing again in an intermediary position.

This list of characteristics which are, generally speaking, shared by all American natives, could readily be extended, but the common features mentioned ought to be sufficient to make clear the fundamental unity of the Indians.

The question that necessarily follows is, "Which, among the different peoples of the globe, does the Indian, as here characterized, most resemble?" The answer, notwithstanding our imperfect knowledge, can be given conclusively. There is a great stem of humanity which embraces people ranging from yellowish white to dark brown in color, with straight black hair, scanty beard, hairless body, brown and often more or less slanting eye, mesorhinic nose, medium prognathism, and in every other essential feature much like the American native; and this stem, embracing several races or types and many nationalities and tribes, occupies the eastern half of the Asiatic continent and a large part of Polynesia.

From the physical anthropologist's point of view everything indicates that the origin of the American Indian is to be sought among the yellowish-brown peoples mentioned. There are no two large branches of humanity on the globe that show closer fundamental physical relations.

But difficulties arise when we endeavor to assign the origin of the Indian to some particular branch of the yellowish-brown population. We find that he stands quite as closely related to some of the Malaysian peoples as to the Tibetans, the Upper Yenisei natives, and some of the northeastern Asiatics. It is doubtless this fact that accounts for some of the hypotheses concerning the origin of the Indian that attribute his derivation partly to the "Tartars" and partly to the Polynesians.

All that may be said on this occasion is that the circumstances point strongly to a coming, not strictly a migration, over land, ice, water, or by all these media combined, from northeastern Asia, of relatively small parties, and to comings repeated probably nearly to the beginning of the historic period.

As to Polynesian migrations within the Pacific, such were, so far as can be determined, all relatively recent, having taken place when America doubtless had already a large population and had developed several native cultures. It is, however, probable that after spreading over the islands, small parties of Polynesians may have accidentally reached America; if so, they may have modified in some respects the native culture, but physically, being radically like the people who received them (barring their probably more recent negro mixture), they would readily blend with the Indian and their progeny could not be distinguished.

The conclusions, therefore, are that the American natives represent in the main a single stem or strain of people, one *homotype;* that this stem is the same as that of the yellow-brown races of Asia and Polynesia; and that the main immigration of the Americans has taken place gradually by the northwestern route, in the Holocene period, and after man had reached a relatively high stage of development and multiple racial differentiation. The immigration, in all probability, was a dribbling and prolonged over-flow, likely due to pressure from behind and a search for better hunting and fishing grounds. This was followed by rapid multiplication, spread, and numerous minor differentiations of the people on the new, vast, and environmentally highly varied continent. It is also probable that the western coast of America, within the last two thousand years, was on more than one occasion reached by small parties of Polynesians, and that the eastern coast was similarly reached by small groups of whites; but these accretions have not modified greatly, if at all, the mass of the native population.

EDWARD SAPIR

(1884-1939)

Of the students whom Boas attracted, none was more brilliant than Edward Sapir. He was born in Lauenberg, Germany, and came to this country with his parents when he was five years old. He grew up as a poor boy on New York's Lower East Side, in the ghetto that produced so many distinguished scholars. All doors opened to the brilliant child; private schools and Columbia University welcomed him. After a year of graduate work in Germanics and linguistics, he began the study of primitive languages and this held him. From his Indo-European studies he learned a method which was to serve him well later when he embarked seriously on comparative work. But at the beginning, it was the phenomenon of language itself that intrigued him—the function of language in organizing thought, its perfection as a closed system, and the excitement of bringing logical order out of the chaos of sounds of unrecorded language. He worked by flashes of intuition, which he then worried like a dog with a bone until things fell into place.

Sapir had little taste for the kind of ethnological research that was current in the pre-war years. He disliked field work and found monographs boring. He was dissatisfied with the answers ethnologists found to their problems; however insightful, they lacked the completeness and self-proving perfection of good linguistic analysis. He had an impish humor; he once announced to a seminar in Chicago that he proposed to conduct a seminar in sloppy ethnology. This was at a time when he was especially irritated with Boas for not accepting, without proof, his wildest suggestions of linguistic relationships, such as Athabascan with Thibetan.

As he became more and more deeply involved with problems of psychology and personality, he grew increasingly impatient with classical ethnology with its normative statements: "The Navaho do thus and so." No two individuals have precisely the same life experience, how then can they share the same culture? He was fond of saying, "There are as many cultures as there are individuals." He proclaimed the study of the individual as the proper study of anthropologists. He welcomed to his circle the younger students of Boas as well as those whom he had trained in Chicago. This worried Boas not a little; he felt that his most promising students were

being lured from the straight and narrow path of methodological purity.
Sapir heralded a new kind of ethnology. But he himself never entered
into the new land he marked out for others. He remained caught in a
dilemma: Where does individual behavior end and culture take over? His
position was analogous to that of the generation of anthropologists who had
first discovered the infinite variety of human cultures, and had not yet real-
ized, as did Bastian, the "appalling monotony" underlying the variety of
manifestations.—R.L.B.

The Grammarian and His Language

THE NORMAL MAN OF INTELLIGENCE HAS SOMETHING OF A CONTEMPT FOR
linguistic studies, convinced as he is that nothing can well be more
useless. Such minor usefulness as he concedes to them is of a purely
instrumental nature. French is worth studying because there are French
books which are worth reading. Greek is worth studying—if it is—
because a few plays and a few passages of verse, written in that curious
and extinct vernacular, have still the power to disturb our hearts—if
indeed they have. For the rest, there are excellent translations.

Now it is a notorious fact that the linguist is not necessarily deeply
interested in the abiding things that language has done for us. He
handles languages very much as the zoölogist handles dogs. The zoologist examines the dog carefully, then he dissects him in order to examine him still more carefully, and finally, noting resemblances between
him and his cousins, the wolf and the fox, and differences between
him and his more distant relations like the cat and the bear, he assigns
him his place in the evolutionary scheme of animated nature, and has
done. Only as a polite visitor, not as a zoölogist, is he even mildly interested
in Towzer's sweet parlor tricks, however fully he may recognize the fact
that these tricks could never have evolved unless the dog had evolved
first. To return to the philologist and the layman by whom he is judged,
it is a precisely parallel indifference to the beauty wrought by the instrument which nettles the judge. And yet the cases are not altogether parallel.
When Towzer has performed his tricks and when Porto has saved the
drowning man's life, they relapse, it is true, into the status of mere dog—
but even the zoölogist's dog is of interest to all of us. But when Achilles
has bewailed the death of his beloved Patroclus and Clytaemnestra has
done her worst, what are we to do with the Greek aorists that are left on
our hands? There is a traditional mode of procedure which arranges them

From Sapir, "The Grammarian and his Language," *American Mercury* (1924),
pp. 150-159.

into patterns. It is called grammar. The man who is in charge of grammar and is called a grammarian is regarded by all plain men as a frigid and dehumanized pedant.

It is not difficult to understand the very pallid status of linguistics in America. The purely instrumental usefulness of language study is recognized, of course, but there is not and cannot be in this country that daily concern with foreign modes of expression so natural on the continent of Europe, where a number of languages jostle each other in everyday life. In the absence of a strong practical motive for linguistic pursuits the remoter, more theoretical, motives are hardly given the opportunity to flower. But it would be a profound mistake to ascribe our current indifference to philological matters entirely to the fact that English alone does well enough for all practical purposes. There is something about language itself, or rather about linguistic differences, that offends the American spirit. That spirit is rationalistic to the very marrow of its bone. Consciously, if not unconsciously, we are inclined to impatience with any object or idea or system of things which cannot give a four square reckoning of itself in terms of reason and purpose. We can see this spirit pervading our whole scientific outlook. If psychology and sociology are popular sciences in America today, that is mainly due to the prevailing feeling that they are convertible into the cash value of effective education, effective advertising, and social betterment. Even here, there is, to an American, something immoral about a psychological truth which will not do pedagogical duty, something wasteful about a sociological item which can be neither applied nor condemned. If we apply the rationalistic test to language, it is found singularly wanting. After all, language is merely a level to get thoughts "across." Our business instinct tells us that the multiplication of levers, all busy on the same job, is poor economy. Thus one way of "spitting it out" is as good as another. If other nationalities find themselves using other levers, that is their affair. The fact of language, in other words, is an unavoidable irrelevance, not a problem to intrigue the inquiring mind.

There are two ways, it seems, to give linguistics its requisite dignity as a science. It may be treated as history or it may be studied descriptively and comparatively as form. Neither point of view augurs well for the arousing of American interest. History has always to be something else before it is taken seriously. Otherwise it is "mere" history. If we could show that certain general linguistic changes are correlated with stages of cultural evolution, we would come appreciably nearer securing linguistics a hearing, but the slow modifications that eat into the substance and the form of speech and that gradually remold it entirely do not seem to run parallel to any scheme of cultural evolution yet proposed. Since "biological" or evolutionary history is the only kind of history for which we have a genuine respect, the history of language is left out in the cold as another one of those unnecessary sequences of events which German erudition is in the habit of worrying about.

But before pinning our faith to linguistics as an exploration into form, we might cast an appealing glance at the psychologist, for he is likely to prove a useful ally. He has himself looked into the subject of language, which he finds to be a kind of "behavior," a rather specialized type of functional adaptation, yet not so specialized but that it may be declared to be a series of laryngeal habits. We may go even further, if we select the right kind of psychologist to help us, and have thought put in its place as a merely "subvocal laryngeating." If these psychological contributions to the nature of speech do not altogether explain the Greek aorists bequeathed to us by classical poets, they are at any rate very flattering to philology. Unfortunately the philologist cannot linger long with the psychologist's rough and ready mechanisms. These may make shift for an introduction to his science, but his real problems are such as few psychologists have clearly envisaged, though it is not unlikely that psychology may have much to say about them when it has gained strength and delicacy. The psychological problem which most interests the linguist is the inner structure of language, in terms of unconscious psychic processes, not that of the individual's adaptation to this traditionally conserved structure. It goes without saying, however, that the two problems are not independent of each other.

To say in so many words that the noblest task of linguistics is to understand languages as form rather than as function or as historical process is not to say that it can be understood as form alone. The formal configuration of speech at any particular time and place is the result of a long and complex historical development, which, in turn, is unintelligible without constant reference to functional factors. Form is even more liable to be stigmatized as "mere" than the historical process which shapes it. For our characteristically pragmatic American attitude forms in themselves seem to have little or no reality, and it is for this reason that we so often fail to divine them or to realize into what new patterns ideas and institutions are balancing themselves or tending to do so. Now it is very probable that the poise which goes with culture is largely due to the habitual appreciation of the formal outlines and the formal intricacies of experience. Where life is tentative and experimental, where ideas and sentiments are constantly protruding gaunt elbows out of an inherited stock of meagre, inflexible patterns instead of graciously bending them to their own uses, form is necessarily felt as a burden and a tyranny instead of the gentle embrace it should be. Perhaps it is not too much to say that the lack of culture in America is in some way responsible for the unpopularity of linguistic studies, for these demand at one and the same time an intense appreciation of a given form of expression and a readiness to accept a great variety of possible forms.

The outstanding fact about any language is its formal completeness. This is as true of a primitive language, like Eskimo or Hottentot, as of the carefully recorded and standardized language of our great cultures. By "formal completeness" I mean a profoundly significant peculiarity which is easily overlooked. Each language has a well defined and exclusive phonetic system with which it carries on its work and, more than that, all of its expressions, from the most habitual to the merely potential, are fitted into a deft tracery of prepared forms from which there is no escape. These forms establish a definite relational feeling or attitude towards all possible contents of expression and, through them, towards all possible contents of experience, in so far, of course, as experience is capable of expression in linguistic terms. To put this matter of the formal completeness of speech in somewhat different words, we may say that a language is so constructed that no matter what any speaker of it may desire to communicate, no matter how original or bizarre his idea or his fancy, the language is prepared to do his work. He will never need to create new forms or to force upon his language a new formal orientation—unless, poor man, he is haunted by the form-feeling of another language and is subtly driven to the unconscious distortion of the one speech-system on the analogy of the other. The world of linguistic forms, held within the framework of a given language, is a complete system of reference, very much as a number system is a complete system of quantitative reference or as a set of geometrical axes of coördinates is a complete system of reference to all points of a given space. The mathematical analogy is by no means as fanciful as it appears to be. To pass from one language to another is psychologically parallel to passing from one geometrical system of reference to another. The environing world which is referred to is the same for either language; the world of points is the same in either frame of reference. But the formal method of approach to the expressed item of experience, as to the given point of space, is so different that the resulting feeling of orientation can be the same neither in the two languages nor in the two frames of reference. Entirely distinct, or at least measurably distinct, formal adjustments have to be made and these differences have their psychological correlates.

Formal completeness has nothing to do with the richness or the poverty of the vocabulary. It is sometimes convenient or, for practical reasons, necessary for the speakers of a language to borrow words from foreign sources as the range of their experience widens. They may extend the meanings of words which they already possess, create new words out of native resources on the analogy of existing terms, or take over from another people terms to apply to the new conceptions which they are introducing. None of these processes affects the form of the language, any more than the enriching of a certain portion of space by the introduction of new objects affects the geometrical form of that region as defined by an accepted mode of reference. It would be absurd to say that Kant's "Critique of Pure Reason" could be rendered forthwith into the unfamiliar accents of Eskimo or Hottentot, and yet it would be absurd in but a secondary degree. What is really meant is that the culture of these primitive folk has not advanced to the point where it is of interest to them to form abstract conceptions of a philosophical order. But it is not absurd to say that there is nothing in the formal peculiarities of Hottentot or of Eskimo which would obscure the clarity or hide the depth of Kant's thought—indeed, it may be suspected that the highly synthetic and periodic structure of Eskimo would more easily bear the weight of Kant's terminology than his native German. Further, to move to a more positive vantage point, it is not absurd to say that both Hottentot and Eskimo possess all the formal apparatus that is required to serve as matrix for the expression of Kant's thought. If these languages have not the requisite Kantian vocabulary, it is not the languages that are to be blamed but the Eskimo and the Hottentots themselves. The languages as such are quite hospitable to the addition of a philosophic load to their lexical stock-in-trade.

The unsophisticated natives, having no occasion to speculate on the nature of causation, have probably no word that adequately translates our philosophic term "causation," but this shortcoming is purely and simply a matter of vocabulary and of no interest whatever from the standpoint of linguistic form. From this standpoint the term "causation" is merely one out of an indefinite number of examples illustrating a certain pattern of expression. Linguistically—in other words, as regards form-feeling—"causation" is merely a particular way of expressing the notion of "act of causing," the idea of a certain type of action conceived of as a thing, an entity. Now the form-feeling of such a word as "causation" is perfectly familiar to Eskimo and to hundreds of other primitive languages. They have no difficulty in expressing the idea of a certain activity, say "laugh" or "speak" or "run," in terms of an entity, say "laughter" or "speech" or "running." If the particular language under consideration cannot readily adapt itself to this type of expression, what it can do is to resolve all contexts in which such forms are used in other languages into other formal patterns that eventually do the same work. Hence, "laughter is pleasurable," "it is pleasant to laugh," "one laughs with pleasure," and so on *ad infinitum,* are functionally equivalent expressions, but they canalize into entirely distinct form-feelings. All languages are set to do all the symbolic and expressive work that language is good for, either actually or potentially. The formal technique of this work is the secret of each language.

It is very important to get some notion of the nature of this form-feeling, which is implicit in all language, however bewilderingly at variance its actual manifestations may be in different types of speech. There are many knotty problems here—and curiously elusive ones— that it will require the combined resources of the linguist, the logician, the psychologist, and the critical philosopher to clear up for us. There is one important matter that we must now dispose of. If the Eskimo and the Hottentot have no adequate notion of what we mean by causation, does it follow that their languages are incapable of expressing the causative relation? Certainly not. In English, in German, and in Greek we have certain formal linguistic devices for passing from the primary act or state to its causative correspondent, e.g., English *to fall, to fell,* "to cause to fall"; *wide, to widen;* German *hangen,* "to hang, be suspended"; *hängen,* "to hang, cause to be suspended"; Greek *pherō,* "to carry"; *phoreō,* "to cause to carry." Now this ability to feel and express the causative relation is by no manner of means dependent on an ability to conceive of causality as such. The latter ability is conscious and intellectual in character; it is laborious, like most conscious processes, and it is late in developing. The former ability is unconscious and nonintellectual in character, exercises itself with great rapidity and with the utmost ease, and develops early in the life of the race and of the individual. We have therefore no theoretical difficulty in finding that conceptions and relations which primitive folk are quite unable to master on the conscious plane are being unconsciously expressed in their languages —and, frequently, with the utmost nicety. As a matter of fact, the causative relation, which is expressed only fragmentarily in our modern European languages, is in many primitive languages rendered with an absolutely philosophic relentlessness. In Nootka, an Indian language of Vancouver Island, there is no verb or verb form which has not its precise causative counterpart.

Needless to say, I have chosen the concept of causality solely for the sake of illustration, not because I attach an especial linguistic importance to it. Every language, we may conclude, possesses a complete and psychologically satisfying formal orientation, but this orientation is only felt in the unconscious of its speakers—is not actually, that is, consciously, know by them.

Our current psychology does not seem altogether adequate to explain the formation and transmission of such submerged formal systems as are disclosed to us in the languages of the world. It is usual to say that isolated linguistic responses are learned early in life and that, as these harden into fixed habits, formally analogous responses are made, when the need arises, in a purely mechanical manner, specific precedents pointing the way to new responses. We are sometimes told that these analogous responses are largely the result of reflection on the utility of the earlier ones, directly learned from the social environment. Such methods of approach see nothing in the problem of linguistic form beyond what is involved in the more and more accurate control of a certain set of muscles towards a desired end, say the hammering of a nail. I can only believe that explanations of this type are seriously incomplete and that they fail to do justice to a certain innate striving for formal elaboration and expression and to an unconscious patterning of sets of related elements of experience.

The kind of mental processes that I am now referring to are, of course, of that compelling and little understood sort for which the name "intuition" has been suggested. Here is a field which psychology has barely touched but which it cannot ignore indefinitely. It is precisely because psychologists have not greatly ventured into these difficult reaches that they have so little of interest to offer in explanation of all those types of mental activity which lead to the problem of form, such as language, music, and mathematics. We have every reason to surmise that languages are the cultural deposits, as it were, of a vast and self-completing network of psychic processes which still remain to be clearly defined for us. Probably most linguists are convinced that the language-learning process, particularly the acquisition of a feeling for the formal set of the language, is very largely unconscious and involves mechanisms that are quite distinct in character from either sensation or reflection. There is doubtless something deeper about our feeling for form than even the majority of art theorists have divined, and it is not unreasonable to suppose that, as psychological analysis becomes more refined, one of the greatest values of linguistic study will be in the unexpected light it may throw on the psychology of intuition, this "intuition" being perhaps nothing more nor less than the "feeling" for relations.

There is no doubt that the critical study of language may also be of the most curious and unexpected helpfulness to philosophy. Few philosophers have deigned to look into the morphologies of primitive languages nor have they given the structural peculiarities of their own speech more than a passing and perfunctory attention. When one has the riddle of the universe on his hands, such pursuits seem trivial enough, yet when it begins to be suspected that at least some solutions of the great riddle are elaborately roundabout applications of the rules of Latin or German or English grammar, the triviality of linguistic analysis becomes less certain. To a far greater extent than the philosopher has realized, he is likely to become the dupe of his speech-forms, which is equivalent to saying that the mould of his thought, which is typically a linguistic mould, is apt to be projected into his conception of the world. Thus innocent linguistic categories may take on the formidable appearance of cosmic absolutes. If only, therefore, to save himself from philosophic verbalism, it would be well for the philosopher to look critically to the linguistic foundations and limitations of his thought. He would then be spared the humiliating discovery that many new ideas, many apparently brilliant philosophic conceptions, are little more than rearrangements of familiar words in formally satisfying patterns. In their recently published work on "The Meaning of Meaning" Messrs. Ogden and Richards have done philosophy a signal service in indicating how readily the most hardheaded thinkers have allowed themselves to be cajoled by the formal slant of their habitual mode of expression. Perhaps the best way to get behind our thought processes and to eliminate from them all the accidents or irrelevances due to their linguistic garb is to plunge into the study of exotic modes of expression. At any rate, I know of no better way to kill spurious "entities."

This brings us to the nature of language as a symbolic system, a method of referring to all possible types of experience. The natural or, at any rate, the naïve thing is to assume that when we wish to communicate a certain idea or impression, we make something like a rough and rapid inventory of the objective elements and relations involved in it, that such an inventory or analysis is quite inevitable, and that our linguistic task consists merely of the finding of the particular words and groupings of words that correspond to the terms of the objective analysis. Thus, when we observe an object of the type that we call a "stone" moving through space towards the earth, we involuntarily analyze the phenomenon into two concrete notions, that of a stone and that of an act of falling, and, relating these two notions to each other by certain formal methods proper to English, we declare that "the stone falls." We assume, naïvely enough, that this is about the only analysis that can properly be made. And yet, if we look into the way that other languages take to express this very simple kind of impression, we soon realize how much may be added to, subtracted from, or rearranged in our own form of expression without materially altering our report of the physical fact.

In German and in French we are compelled to assign "stone" to a gender category—perhaps the Freudians can tell us why this object is masculine in the one language, feminine in the other; in Chippewa we cannot express ourselves without bringing in the apparently irrelevant fact that a stone is an inanimate object. If we find gender beside the point, the Russians may wonder why we consider it necessary to specify in every case whether a stone, or any other object for that matter, is conceived in a definite or an indefinite manner, why the difference between "the stone" and "a stone" matters. "Stone falls" is good enough for Lenin, as it was good enough for Cicero. And if we find barbarous the neglect of the distinction as to definiteness, the Kwakiutl Indian of British Columbia may sympathize with us but wonder why we do not go to a step further and indicate in some way whether the stone is visible or invisible to the speaker at the moment of speaking and whether it is nearest to the speaker, the person addressed, or some third party. "That would no doubt sound fine in Kwakiutl, but we are too busy!" And yet we insist on expressing the singularity of the falling object, where the Kwakiutl Indian, differing from the Chippewa, can generalize and make a statement which would apply equally well to one or several stones. Moreover, he need not specify the time of the fall. The Chinese get on with a minimum of explicit formal statement and content themselves with a frugal "stone fall."

These differences of analysis, one may object, are merely formal; they do not invalidate the necessity of the fundamental concrete analysis of the situation into "stone" and what the stone does, which in this case is "fall." But this necessity, which we feel so strongly, is an illusion. In the Nootka language the combined impression of a stone falling is quite differently analyzed. The stone need not be specifically referred to, but a single word, a verb form, may be used which is in practice not essentially more ambiguous than our English sentence. This verb form consists of two main elements, the first indicating general movement or position of a stone or stonelike object, while the second refers to downward direction. We can get some hint of the feeling of the Nootka word if we assume the existence of an intransitive verb "to stone," referring to the position or movement of a stonelike object. Then our sentence, "The stone falls," may be reassembled into something like "It stones down." In this type of expression the thing-quality of the stone is implied in the generalized verbal element "to stone," while the specific kind of motion which is given us in experience when a stone falls is conceived as separable into a generalized notion of the movement of a class of objects and a more specific one of direction. In other words, while Nootka has no difficulty whatever in describing the fall of a stone, it has no verb that truly corresponds to our "fall."

It would be possible to go on indefinitely with such examples of incommensurable analyses of experience in different languages. The upshot of it all would be to make very real to us a kind of relativity that is generally hidden from us by our naïve acceptance of fixed habits of speech as guides to an objective understanding of the nature of experience. This is the relativity of concepts, or as it might be called, the relativity of the form of thought. It is not so difficult to grasp as the physical relativity of Einstein nor is it as disturbing to our sense of security as the psychological relativity of Jung, which is barely beginning to be understood, but it is perhaps more readily evaded than these. For its understanding the comparative data of linguistics are a *sine qua non*. It is the appreciation of the relativity of the form of thought which results from linguistic study that is perhaps the most liberalizing thing about it. What fetters the mind and benumbs the spirit is ever the dogged acceptance of absolutes.

To a certain type of mind linguistics has also that profoundly serene and satisfying quality which inheres in mathematics and in music and which may be described as the creation out of simple elements of a self-contained universe of forms. Linguistics has neither the sweep nor the instrumental power of mathematics, nor has it the universal aesthetic appeal of music. But under its crabbed, technical, appearance there lies hidden the same classical spirit, the same freedom in restraint, which animates mathematics and music at their purest. This spirit is antagonistic to the romanticism which is rampant in America today and which debauches so much of our science with its frenetic desire.

LEONARD BLOOMFIELD

(1887-1949)

Leonard Bloomfield is credited by contemporary linguists with having established the science of linguistics. His interest in the general character-istics of language rather than the specific features of particular languages or groups of languages brought him closer to anthropologists than to the specialists in linguistics of a generation ago. It is this interest, rather than the fact that he devoted time to the study of a primitive language, Algon-kian, that entitles him to a place in a book on anthropology.

Bloomfield's life was uneventful—an academic life. He was born in Chicago, and there is a story that instruction in the Chicago school he attended so bored him that he failed. Harvard, however, did not bore him, and he was graduated in 1906, having majored in Germanic and Semitic languages. At the University of Wisconsin where he went as an assistant in the German department he met Eduard Prokosch who, he claimed, was a major influence in turning his attention to problems of general linguistics. After receiving a Ph.D. from the University of Chicago he held a number of teaching posts in Midwestern colleges. He joined the faculty at Yale University in 1940 and remained there until his death.

While he was at Yale during World War II he became involved in the intensive language program of the United States Government. He had always been interested in the teaching of languages and early in his career had written a German grammar. Now he helped to set up the intensive language training courses which were to prove such a spectacular success, and he contributed four manuals for use in the program.

His book on Language *which outlined his system of structural linguistics was published in 1933.*—R.L.B.

The Structure of Language

PHONEMIC STRUCTURE

IN LANGUAGE WE ORDER AND CLASSIFY THE FLOWING PHENOMENA OF OUR universe; our habit of doing this is so pervasive that we cannot describe things as they may appear to an infant or a speechless animal. The price we pay is a sensible inadequacy of our speech, offset by the privilege of any degree of approximation such as may be seen in some microscopic investigation of science or in the work of the poet. It is the entire task of the linguist to study the ordering and formalization which is language; he thus obtains the privilege of imagining it removed and catching a distant glimpse of the kind of universe which then remains.

The ordering and formalizing effect of language appears, first of all, in the fact that its meaningful forms are all composed of a small number of meaningless elements. We should obtain, in this respect, a parallel to language if, with a dozen or so of different flags, we devised a code in which the exhibition of several flags (in the limiting case, of one flag) in a fixed position and arrangement would constitute a meaningful sign.

The forms of every language are made up out of a small number—ranging perhaps between fifteen and seventy-five—of typical unit sounds which have no meaning but, in certain fixed arrangements, make up the meaningful forms that are uttered. These signals are the *phonemes* of the language. The speakers have the habit of responding to the characteristic features of sound which in their language mark off the various phonemes and of ignoring all other acoustic features of a speech. Thus, a German who has not been specially trained will hear no difference between such English forms as 'bag' and 'back,' because the difference in his language is not phonemic; it is one of the acoustic differences which he has been trained to ignore. In the same way, a speaker of English will hear no difference, until he is trained to do so, between two Chinese words which sound to him, say, like 'man,' and differ as to their scheme of pitch; we fail to hear the difference because in our language such a difference is not connected with a difference of meaning and is consistently ignored whenever it chances to occur. The acoustic features which set off a phoneme from all other phonemes in its language, and from "inarticulate" sound, exhibit some range of variation. It is not required that this range be continuous: acoustically diverse features may be united, by the habit of the speakers, in one phoneme.

From Bloomfield, "The Structure of Language," *International Encyclopedia of Unified Science,* Vol. I, No. 4 (Chicago: The University of Chicago Press, 1939), pp. 21-33.

The number of phonemes which will be stated as existing in any one language depends in part upon the method of counting. For instance, we shall recognize an English phoneme [j] which appears initially in forms like 'yes,' 'year,' 'young,' and another phoneme [e] in the vowel sound of words like 'egg,' 'ebb,' 'bet.' The longer vowel sound in words like 'aim,' 'say,' and 'bait' may then be counted as another phoneme, or else one may describe it as a combination of the phonemes [e] and [j]. This option would not exist if our language contained a succession of [e] plus [j] which differed in sound, and as to significant forms in which it occurred, from the vowel sound of 'aim,' 'say,' 'bait.' Thus, the English sound [č], which appears in words like 'chin,' 'rich,' 'church,' must be counted as a single phoneme and not as a combination of [t] as in 'ten' and [š] as in 'she,' because in forms like 'it shall' or 'courtship' we have a combination of [t] plus [š] which differs in sound and as to significant forms from [č] in 'itch Al' or 'core-chip.' The fact that these last two forms are unusual or nonsensical does not affect the distinction. The count of phonemes in Standard English will vary, according to economy, from forty-odd to around sixty.

For the most part, the phonemes appear in utterance in a linear order. Where this is not the case, the arrangement is so simple that we can easily put our description into linear order. For instance, the noun 'convict' has a phoneme of stress (loudness) which starts with the beginning of the word and covers the first vowel phoneme; the verb 'convict' differs in that the same stress phoneme is similarly placed upon the beginning of the partial form '-vict.' If we wish to put our description of these forms into linear order, we need only agree upon a convention of aligning a symbol for the stress phonemes, e.g., *'convict* and *con'vict*.

Thus, every speech in a given dialect can be represented by a linear arrangement of a few dozen symbols. The traditional system of writing English, with its twenty-six letters and half-dozen marks of punctuation, does this very imperfectly but sufficiently well for most practical needs.

This rigid simplicity of language contrasts with the continuous variability of non-linguistic stimulation and response. For this reason linguists employ the word '*form*' for any meaningful segment of speech, in contrast with their use of 'meaning' for stimulus and response.

The sound produced in a speech is to all ordinary purposes a continuum. To determine which features are phonemic, we must have some indication of meaning. A German observer, say, who, studying English as a totally unknown language, noticed in a few utterances the acoustic difference between 'bag' and 'back,' could decide that this is a phonemic difference only when he learned that it goes steadily hand in hand with a difference of meaning.

Two utterances, say of the form 'Give me an apple,' no matter how much they may differ in non-phonemic features of sound, are said to consist of the *same* speech-form; utterances which are not same are *different*. The decision of the speakers is practically always absolute and unanimous. This fact is of primary concern to us, since by virtue of it the speakers are able to adhere to strict agreements about speech-forms and to establish all manner of correspondences, orderings, and operations in this realm. To take an everyday instance: anyone can look up a word in a dictionary or a name in a directory.

It would not do to overlook the fact that the phonemes of a language are identifiable only by differences of meaning. For this, however, a relatively small number of gross differences will suffice: once the phonemes are established, any form of the language is completely and rigidly definable (apart from its meaning) as a linear or quasi-linear sequence of phonemes. We do not possess a workable classification of everything in the universe, and, apart from language, we cannot even envisage anything of the sort; the forms of language, on the other hand, thanks to their phonemic structure, can be classified and ordered in all manner of ways and can be subjected to strict agreements of correspondence and operation. For this reason, linguistics classifies speech-forms by form and not by meaning. When a speech-form has been identified, we state, as well as may be, its meaning: our success depends upon the perfection of sciences other than linguistics. The reverse of this would be impossible. For instance, we shall usually seek a given word in a thesaurus of synonyms by looking it up in the alphabetical index. We could not use a telephone directory which arranged the names of the subscribers not in their alphabetical order, but according to some non-verbal characteristic, such as weight, height, or generosity.

GRAMMATICAL STRUCTURE

Some utterances are partly alike in form and meaning; for instance:

> Poor John ran away.
> Our horses ran away.
> Poor John got tired.
> Our horses got tired.

This forces us to recognize meaningful constituent parts, such as 'poor John,' 'our horses,' 'ran away,' 'got tired.'

A form which can be uttered alone with meaning is a *free* form; all our examples so far are free forms. A form ('form' always means 'meaningful form') which cannot be uttered alone with meaning is a *bound* form. Examples of bound forms are the suffix '-ish' in 'boyish,' 'girlish,' 'childish,' or the suffix '-s' in 'hats,' 'caps,' 'books.'

A free form which does not consist entirely of lesser free forms is a *word*. Thus, 'boy,' which admits of no further analysis into meaningful parts, is a word; 'boyish,' although capable of such analysis, is a word, because one of the constituents, the suffix '-ish,' is a bound form; other words, such as 'receive,' 'perceive,' 'remit,' 'permit,' consists entirely of bound forms.

A free form which consists entirely of lesser free forms is a *phrase;* examples are 'poor John' or 'poor John ran away.'

Sets of words, such as 'perceive: receive: remit' or 'perceive: permit, remit,' establish a parallelism between the extremes, 'perceive' and 'remit.' The habit which is thus revealed is a *morphologic construction.* In the same way, sets of phrases, such as 'John ran: John fell: Bill fell' or 'John ran: Bill ran: Bill fell,' establish a parallelism between the extremes 'John ran' and 'Bill fell,' and illustrate a *syntactic construction.* The parts of a form which exhibits a construction are the *constituents* of the form: the form itself is a *resultant* form.

In the study of an unknown language we proceed as above: partial similarities between forms reveal their complexity, and we progressively recognize constituents and determine, often with some difficulty, whether they are free or bound. In presenting the description of a language, however, we begin with the constituents and describe the constructions in which they appear.

A construction, morphologic or syntactic, consists in the arrangement of the constituents. In addition to the meaning of the constituents, the resultant form bears a constructional meaning, which is common to all forms that exhibit the same construction. Even more than other elements of meaning, constructional meanings are likely to present difficulties of definition, for they are often remote from simple non-linguistic events.

The features of arrangement differ in different languages. *Modulation* is the use of certain special phonemes, *secondary* phonemes, which mark certain forms in construction. In English, features of stress play a large part as secondary phonemes. We have seen this in the contrast between the verb 'convict' and the noun 'convict.' In syntax it appears in the absence of word-stress on certain forms. Thus, in a phrase like 'the house,' the word 'the' is unstressed; on the other hand, it may receive a sentence stress when it is an important feature of the utterance.

Phonetic modification is the substitution of phonemes in a constituent. For instance, 'duke,' when combined with the suffix '-ess' or '-y' is replaced by 'duch-'; in syntax the words 'do not' are optionally replaced, with a slight difference of meaning, by 'don't.' Neither modulation nor phonetic modification plays any part in the specialized scientific uses of language; it is otherwise with the features of arrangement which we now have to consider.

The *selection* of the constituent forms plays a part apparently in all languages. If we combine the word 'milk' with words like 'fresh,' 'cold,' 'good,' we get designations of special kinds of milk: 'fresh milk,' 'cold milk,' 'good milk'; if we combine it with words like 'drink,' 'fetch,' 'use,' we get designations of acts: 'drink milk,' 'fetch milk,' 'use milk.' The difference in constructional meaning goes hand in hand with the selection of the forms. We describe these habits by saying that the construction has two (or more) *positions* which are *filled* by the constituents. A *function* of a form is its privilege of appearing in a certain position of a certain construction. *The function,* collectively, of a form is the sum total of its functions. Forms which have a function in common constitute a *form-class.* Thus, the forms 'milk,' 'fresh milk,' 'cold water,' 'some fine sand,' etc., are in a common form-class, since all of them combine with forms of the form-class 'drink,' 'don't drink,' 'carefully sift,' etc., in the construction of action-on-object. In syntax, as these examples indicate, words and phrases appear in common form-classes. If words alone are considered, their largest inclusive form-classes are known as *parts of speech.* In many languages, and very strikingly in English, the form-classes of syntax overlap in so complex a fashion that various part-of-speech classifications are possible, according to the functions which one chooses primarily to take into account.

The forms of a form-class contain a common feature of meaning, the *class meaning.* The traditional grammar of our schools gets into hopeless difficulties because it tries to define form-classes by their class meaning and not by the formal features which constitute their function.

The use of *order* as a feature of arrangement is by no means as widespread as the use of selection, but, on account of its simplicity and economy, it plays a great part in the scientific specializations of language. In English the order of the constituents is a feature of nearly all constructions; thus, in 'fresh milk' or 'drink milk' the constituents appear only in this order. In some instances, features of order alone distinguish the positions: contrast, for example, 'John hit Bill' with 'Bill hit John.'

THE SENTENCE

In any one utterance a form which, in this utterance, is not a constituent of any larger form is a *sentence.* By definition, any free form and no bound form can occur as a sentence. Various supplementary features are used in different languages to mark the sentence, especially its end. In English, secondary phonemes of pitch are used in this way. In much the same manner as constructions, *sentence types* are distinguished by features of arrangement. The meanings of these types have to do largely with the relation of speaker and hearer ("pragmatic" features of meaning.) Thus, pitch and, in part, selection and order determine in English such types as statement ('at four o'clock'), yes-or-no question ('at four o'clock?') and supplement question ('at what time?').

In many languages, perhaps in all, certain free forms are marked off as especially suited to sentence use. A sentence which consists of such a form is a *full* sentence. In English the favorite sentence forms are phrases which exhibit certain constructions. The most important is the actor-action construction in which a nominative substantive expression is joined with a finite-verb expression: 'Poor John ran away.' 'John ran.' 'I'm coming at four o'clock.' 'Can you hear me?' A sentence which does not consist of a favorite sentence form is a *minor* sentence: 'Yes,' 'Fire!' 'At four o'clock.' 'If you can hear me.'

English and many other languages distinguish clearly a type of sentence whose type-meaning can perhaps be described by the term 'report.' In English the report sentences are full-sentence statements exhibiting the actor-action construction or a co-ordination of several actor-action phrases. A great deal of labor has been spent upon attempts at giving a precise definition of this type-meaning in disregard of the likelihood of its differing in different languages and in oblivion of the danger that our sociology may not be far enough advanced to yield such a definition. For our purpose, at least a rough outline of this meaning will be needed. In the normal response to a report the hearer behaves henceforth as if his sense organs had been stimulated by the impingement of the reported situation upon the sense organs of the speaker. Since the meaningful speech-forms of the report, however, constitute at bottom a discrete arrangement, the hearer's responses can correspond to the speaker's situation to the extent only that is made possible by the approximative character of the report. Thus, when a speaker has said, 'There are some apples in the pantry.' the hearer behaves as though his sense organs had been stimulated by the impingement of the apples upon the speaker's sense organs—as though the speaker's adventure with the apples, to the extent that it is represented by the meanings of the speech-forms, had been witnessed by the hearer, not visually, but through some sense organ capable of a certain discontinuous range of stimulation.

Irony, jest, mendacity, and the like represent derived types of speech and response; they need not here concern us.

CONSTRUCTIONAL LEVEL AND SCOPE

Constructions are classified, first of all, by the form-class of the resultant form.

If the resultant form differs, as to the big distinctions of form-class, from the constituents, the construction is said to be *exocentric*. For instance, actor-action phrases like 'John ran away' or 'He ran away' differ in form-class from nominative substantive expressions like 'John' or 'he' and from finite-verb expressions like 'ran away.' Similarly, the functions of prepositional phrases, such as 'in the house' or 'with him,' differ from those of a preposition ('in,' 'with') and from those of an objective substantive expression ('the house,' 'him').

If the resultant form agrees as to the major distinctions of form-class with one or more of the constituents, then the construction is said to be *endocentric*. For instance, the phrase 'bread and butter' has much the same function as the words 'bread,' 'butter.'

If, as in this example, two or more of the constituents have the same function as the resultant form, the construction is *coordinative* and these constituents are the *members* of the coordination. If only one constituent agrees in form-class with the resultant form, the construction is *subordinative;* this constituent is the *head* of the subordination, and any other constituent is an *attribute* of this head. Thus, in 'fresh milk,' the head is 'milk' and the attribute is 'fresh'; in 'this fresh milk,' the head is 'fresh milk' and the attribute 'this'; in 'very fresh' the head is 'fresh' and the attribute 'very'; in 'very fresh milk,' the head is 'milk' and the attribute is 'very fresh.'

The difference of analysis in these two cases is worth observing:

> this / fresh milk
> very fresh / milk

Although we are unable to give precise definitions of meaning, especially of such ethnically created ranges as constructional meanings and class meanings, yet the mere subsistence of like and unlike sets determines schemes of construction. Only in rare cases does the structure of a language leave us a choice between different orders of description. At each step of analysis we must discover the *immediate* constituents of the form; if we fail in this, our scheme will be contradicted by the constructional meanings of the language.

If a form contains repeated levels of endocentric construction there will be a word or co-ordinated set of words which serves as the *center* of the entire phrase. Thus, in the phrase 'this very fresh milk,' the word 'milk' is the center.

The formal features of construction—selection of constituent forms, order, phonetic modification, and modulation by means of secondary phonemes—differ greatly in various languages and sometimes lead to very complex structures of word or phrase, but they seem nowhere to permit of an unlimited box-within-box cumulation. Even simple formations may lead to ambiguity because the *scope*—that is, the accompanying constituents on the proper level—of a form may not be marked. For instance, 'an apple and a pear or a peach' may mean exactly two pieces of fruit: then the immediate constituents are 'an apple / and / a pear or a peach,' and the phrase 'a pear or a peach' and the phrase 'an apple' constitute the scope of the form 'and.' On the other hand, the phrase may mean either two pieces of fruit or one piece: then the immediate constituents are 'an apple and a pear / or / a peach,' and the scope of 'and' now consists, on its level, of the phrases 'an apple,' 'a pear.' Similarly, 'three times five less two times two' may mean 26, 18, 11, or 3. These uncertainties are not tolerable in the scientific use of language; it is a striking peculiarity of this use that they are removed only in written notation—as especially by the parentheses and brackets that are used in algebra. The result is a system of writing which cannot be paralleled in actual speech.

VARIETIES OF REFERENCE

A thoroughgoing comparison of speech-forms, say in some one language, with features of the non-linguistic world is impossible at the present state of our knowledge. Our system of responses, with its neat discrimination of objects, classes, positions, qualities, movements, etc., results very largely from our use of language. We cannot return to the animal's or the infant's state of speechless response.

In order to find out how much of our world is independent of any one language, we might try to compare the grammars and lexicons of different languages. At present we have reasonably complete data for a few languages only; at some future time, when this task can be undertaken, the results will be of great interest. The forms of any one language could scarcely serve as a frame of reference: we should need, instead, a non-linguistic scale by which to measure.

It is the task of science to provide a system of responses which are independent of the habits of any person or community. These responses are twofold, in accordance with the universal scheme of human behavior: science provides relevant handling responses and clarified speech-forms. In the nature of the case, however, the entire result is transmitted and preserved in a verbal record. If science had completed its task, we could accurately define the meanings of speech-forms.

Even the most favorable type of meaning will show the difficulty of definition. Clusters of stimuli which produce roughly the same elementary responses in all people and, in accordance with this, are not necessarily tied up with communal habits, have been successfully studied: this is the domain of so-called external phenomena, the domain of physical and biological science. Here some of the simpler lexical classifications of language correspond in the main to the classifications of science, as, for instance, in the names of familiar species of plants and animals. However, there is often some gross divergence, as when several species are called by the same name, or one species by several names, and there is a great deal of less manageable vagueness at the borders—species which sometimes are and sometimes are not included in a designation. Even in this simplest sphere, the meaning of many speech-forms involves ethnological features. Here, too, we encounter, on the simplest level, speech-forms which have no extra-linguistic validity, unless it be in the designation of secondarily created artifacts: dragons, griffins, unicorns, etc.

Where science reveals a continuous scale of phenomena, such as color, the segments included under linguistic terms vary greatly in different languages; they overlap and grow vague at the edges; and they are subject to extraneous limitations ('bay,' 'roan').

When we come to meanings which are involved in the habit of communities and individuals, we fall even farther short of accurate definition, since the branches of science which deal with these things are quite undeveloped. In practice we resort here to artistic, practical and ethical, or religious terminologies of definition, and these, however valuable for our subsequent conduct, fail to satisfy the peculiar requirements of science.

In all spheres the structure of languages reveals elements of meaning which are quite remote from the shape of any one situation and are attached rather to constellations which include, often enough, personal or ethnical features. Relatively simple instances are words like 'if,' 'concerning,' 'because,' or the subtle difference, so important in English, between the types 'he ran' : 'he was running' : 'he has run' : 'he has been running.' The difficulty is even greater in the case of bound forms, which cannot be isolated in their language; consider, for instance, the depreciative feature in some of the uses of '-ish' ('mannish').

Constructional meanings and class meanings pervade a language, in part as universally present *categories;* they generally defy our powers of definition. The singular and plural categories of nouns in English are relatively manageable, but include some troublesome features, such as 'wheat' versus 'oats.' Gender-classes, as in French or German, are almost entirely ethnological in character. The normal speaker, without special training, is incapable of talking about these features; they are not reflected in any habits beyond their mere presence in the structure of the language. The major form-classes are remote from any extra-linguistic phenomena. If we assign to the English class of substantives some such meaning as "object," then words like 'fire,' 'wind,' and 'stream' require an ethnologic commentary. The mechanics of a language often require that otherwise similar designations occur in more than one grammatical class. Thus, in English, as a center for the actor in the actor-action construction, we require a noun: hence we have forms like 'height' beside 'high' or 'movement' beside '(it) moves.' Duplications of this kind are not symptoms of any special level of culture but result merely from a rather common grammatical condition.

SUBSTITUTION AND DETERMINATION

Apparently, all languages save labor by providing *substitute* forms whose meaning rests wholly upon the situation of speaker and hearer, especially upon earlier speech. Since these occur more frequently than specific forms, they are easily uttered and understood; moreover, they are nearly always short and, often enough, bound forms. Thus 'I' and 'you' replace names, and 'this' and 'that' the naming of a thing which may be identified by gesture. The most important type of substitution, for our subject, is *anaphora:* the substitute replaces repetition of a speech-form which has just been uttered or is soon to be uttered. Thus, the set 'he, she, it, they' replaces noun expressions, and the set 'do, does, did' replaces finite-verb expressions ('I'll go by train if John does'). A form competent to fill one position of a construction may suffice for anaphora of a phrase embodying the whole construction: 'Mary dances better than Jane'; here 'Jane' serves as the anaphoric substitute for 'Jane dances.'

Akin to the substitute forms, and very often identical with them are *determiners,* which indicate a range within the class of phenomena that is designated by an ordinary speech-form: 'this apple,' 'the apple' (anaphora), 'every apple,' 'all apples,' etc. We shall be interested in determiners which leave the specimen entirely unrestricted: 'an apple,' 'some apple,' 'any apple.' If only one specimen is involved, anaphora is easily made ('it,' 'the apple,' 'this apple'); but, where several specimens are involved, English, like other languages, provides very poor means for distinguishing them. To provide for the identification of more than one variable, we must look to other phases of language which contain the germs of a more accurate system of speech.

FRANZ BOAS

(1858-1942)

Throughout his life Boas maintained a constant interest in linguistics. Wherever he went he collected hundreds of pages of native texts— Kwakiutl, Bella Coola, Tsimshian, Dakota, Keres, to name but a few. He analyzed these masses of texts and copied them in his own hand for the printer. The introduction he wrote for the Handbook of American Indian Languages *was a masterly discussion of the variety in human speech and of the problem of linguistic relations in America. He founded and edited the* International Journal of American Linguistics.

Boas always said that linguistics was one thing he did for his own pleasure; it was the work he turned to in times of great personal suffering —after the death of his wife, or when he was ill. He made a game out of the course in linguistics which he taught at Columbia. After a few introductory lectures on the nature of language he would announce that he was a Kwakiutl or a Dakota and permit himself to be interviewed, making it clear that he spoke no English. He was very proud of his performance.—R.L.B.

Introduction: International Journal
of American Linguistics

THE INTERNATIONAL JOURNAL OF AMERICAN LINGUISTICS WILL BE DEVOTED to the study of American aboriginal languages. It seems fitting to state briefly a few of the problems that confront us in this field of research.

It is not necessary to set forth the fragmentary character of our knowledge of the languages spoken by the American aborigines. This has been well done for North America by Dr. Pliny Earle Goddard, and it is not

From Boas, "Introduction" to the *International Journal of American Linguistics,* reprinted in *Race, Language, and Culture* (New York: The Macmillan Company, 1940), pp. 199, 201-210.

461

saying too much if we claim that for most of the native languages of Central and South America the field is practically *terra incognita*. We have vocabularies; but, excepting the old missionary grammars, there is very little systematic work. Even where we have grammars, we have no bodies of aboriginal texts.

The methods of collection have been considerably improved of late years, but nevertheless much remains to be done. While until about 1880 investigators confined themselves to the collection of vocabularies and brief grammatical notes, it has become more and more evident that large masses of texts are needed in order to elucidate the structure of the languages.

Notwithstanding the progress that during the last few decades has been made in the character of the material recorded, both as regards the accuracy of phonetic transcription and the character of the matter recorded, there is ample room for improvements of method.

With the extent of our knowledge of native languages, the problems of our inquiry have also assumed wider and greater interest. It is quite natural that the first task of the investigator was the registering and the rough classification of languages. It appeared very soon that languages are more or less closely related, and that comparison of brief vocabularies was sufficient to bring out the most striking relationships. The classification of North American languages, that we owe to Major J. W. Powell, which will form the basis of all future work, was made by this method. Further progress on these lines is beset with great difficulties that are common to America and to those continents in which we cannot trace the development of languages by means of historical documents. The results of the historical and comparative studies of Indo-European languages show very clearly that languages that have sprung from the same source may become so distinct that, without documents illustrating their historical development, relationships are difficult to discover; so much so, that in some cases this task might even be impossible. We are therefore permitted to assume that similar divergences have developed in American languages, and that quite a number of languages that appear distinct may in a remote period have had a common origin.

Here lies one of the most difficult problems of research, and one in which the greatest critical caution is necessary, if we wish to avoid the pitfalls that are besetting the path of scientific inquiry. The method of investigation has to take into account possibilities of linguistic growth, in regard to which generalized data are not available. Modern languages have developed by differentiation. In so far as this is true, the establishment of a genealogical series must be the aim of inquiry. On the other hand, languages may influence one another to such an extent that, beyond a certain point, the genealogical question has no meaning, because it would lead back to several sources and to an arbitrary selection of one or another as the single ancestral type. Our knowledge of linguistic processes is sufficiently wide to show that lexicographic borrowing may proceed to such an extent that the substance of a language may be materially changed. As long, however, as the inner form remains unchanged, our judgment is determined, not by the provenience of the vocabulary, but by that of the form. In most Indian languages etymological processes are so transparent that borrowing of whole words will be easily detected; and, on the whole, the diffusion of words over diverse groups does not present serious difficulties, provided the borrowed material does not undergo radical phonetic changes.

The matter is different when we ask ourselves in how far phonetics and morphological features may have been borrowed. In these cases our experience does not permit us to give a definite answer. The system of sounds of a language is certainly unstable; but in how far inner forces and in how far foreign influence mould its forms is a question not always easy to answer. In America we can discern various areas that have common phonetic characteristics; like the areas of prevalence of nasalization of vowels, of glottalization, of superabundant development of laterals, of absence of bi-labials or of labio-dental spirants, or of trills. These areas do not coincide with any morphological groupings, and are apparently geographically well defined. If we are dealing here with phenomena of late assimilation, a disturbing element is introduced that will make it more difficult to assign a language to a definite genealogical line, much more so than is the case in the borrowing of words. The conditions favoring such phonetic influence must have been much more frequent in primitive America than they were in the later development of European languages. The number of individuals speaking any given American dialect is small. Many women of foreign parentage lived in each tribe, and their speech influenced the pronunciation of the young; so that phonetic changes may have come about easily.

Still more difficult is the problem presented by the distribution of morphological traits. Even with our imperfect knowledge of American languages, it may be recognized that certain morphological types have a wide continuous distribution. This is true of morphological processes as well as of particular psychological aspects of American languages. Thus the incorporation of the nominal object, which in former times was considered one of the most characteristic features of American languages, is confined to certain areas, while it is foreign to others. The tendency to qualify generalized verbal terms by means of elements which express instrumentality is characteristic of some areas. The occurrence of various specific elements that define locality of an action, as affecting objects like "hand," "house," "water," "fire," or other special nominal concepts, is characteristic of other regions. Classification of actions or of nouns according to the form of the actor or of the object also belong to several groups of languages. Nominal cases are present in some languages, absent in others. In a similar way we find present in some regions, absent in others, processes like that of reduplication or of vocalic or consonantic modification of stems.

Attempts to classify languages from these distinct points of view do not lead to very satisfactory results. Not only would the purely morphological classifications be contradictory, but in many cases where a close morphological agreement exists, it remains highly unsatisfactory to co-ordinate vocabularies and the phonetic equivalent of similar morphological ideas. On the basis of Indo-European experience, we should be inclined to seek for a common origin for all those languages that have a far-reaching morphological similarity; but it must be acknowledged that, when the results of classifications based on different linguistic phenomena conflict, we must recognize the possibility of the occurrence of morphological assimilation. The problem is analogous to that of the relation between Finnish and Indo-European languages, which Sweet assumed as established, while the observed relations may also be due to other causes.

Owing to the fundamental importance of these questions for the solution of the problem of the historical relationship between American languages, it seems particularly important to attempt to carry through these classifications without prejudging the question as to the genealogical position of the various groups. It is quite inconceivable that similarities such as exist between Quileute, Kwakiutl, and Salish, should be due to a mere accident, or that the morphological similarities of California languages, which Kroeber and Dixon have pointed out, should not be due to a definite cause. The experience of Aryan studies might induce us to agree that these must be members of single linguistic stocks; but this assumption leaves fundamental differences unaccounted for, and neglects the possibility of morphological assimilation, so that at the present time the conclusion does not seem convincing. We ought to inquire, first of all, into the possibility of mutual influences, which will be revealed, in part at least, by lack of correspondence between lexicographic, phonetic, and detailed morphological classifications.

We do not mean to say that the investigation may not satisfactorily prove certain genealogical relationships; but what should be emphasized is that, in the present state of our knowledge of primitive languages, it is not safe to disregard the possibility of a complex origin of linguistic groups, which would limit the applicability of the term "linguistic family" in the sense in which we are accustomed to use it. It is certainly desirable, and necessary, to investigate minutely and carefully all suggestive analogies. The proof of genetic relationship, however, can be considered as given, only when the number of unexplained distinct elements is not over-large, and when the contradictory classifications, to which reference has been made before, have been satisfactorily accounted for.

It is quite evident that, owing to the lack of knowledge of the historical development of American languages, convincing proof of genealogical relationship may be impossible to obtain, even where such relation exists; so that, from both a practical and a theoretical point of view, the solution of the problems of genetic relationship presents a large number of attractive problems.

Considering the complexity of this question, and the doubts that we entertain in regard to some of the principles to be followed in our inquiry, it seems probable that a safer basis will be reached by following out dialectic studies. Very little work of this kind has been done on our continent. James Owen Dorsey was able to point out a few phenomena pertaining to the interrelation of Siouan dialects. Similar points have been made in regard to the Salish languages and in a few other cases, but no penetrating systematic attempt has been made to clear up the processes of differentiation by which modern American dialects have developed. It is fortunate for the prosecution of this study that quite a number of linguistic families in America are broken up into numerous strongly divergent dialects, the study of which will help us the more in the investigation of the relations between distinct languages, the more markedly they are differentiated. Siouan, Algonquian, Muskhogean, Salishan, Shoshonean, Wakashan, Caddoan, are languages of this type. They present examples of divergence of phonetic character, of differences in structure and vocabulary, that will bring us face to face with the problem of the origin of these divergent elements.

The more detailed study of American languages promises rich returns in the fields of the mechanical processes of linguistic development and of the psychological problems presented by languages of different types. In many American languages the etymological processes are so transparent that the mechanism of phonetic adaptation stands out with great clearness. Contact-phenomena, and types of sound-harmony that affect more remote parts of words, occur with great frequency. Phonetic shifts between related dialects are easily observed, so that we can accumulate a large mass of material which will help to solve the question in how far certain phonetic processes may be of more or less universal occurrence.

Remotely related to this problem is the question that was touched upon by Gatschet, in how far the frequent occurrence of similar sounds for expressing related ideas (like the personal pronouns) may be due to obscure psychological causes rather than to genetic relationship. Undoubtedly, many hitherto unexpected types of processes will reveal themselves in the pursuit of these studies.

The variety of American languages is so great that they will be of high value for the solution of many fundamental psychological problems.

The unconsciously formed categories found in human speech have not been sufficiently exploited for the investigation of the categories into which the whole range of human experience is forced. Here, again, the clearness of etymological processes in many American languages is a great help to our investigation.

The isolation of formal elements and of stems, or of co-ordinate stems —whichever the case may be—is easily performed, and the meaning of every part of an expression is determined much more readily than in the innumerable fossilized forms of Indo-European languages.

Lexicographic differentiation corresponds to the morphological differentiation of languages. Where ideas are expressed by means of separate stems or by subordinate elements, generalized stems will be found that express a certain action regardless of the instrument with which it has been performed; while, in languages that are not provided with these formal elements, a number of separate words will take the place of the modified general stem. In languages that possess a full equipment of adverbial and locative formative elements, generalized words of motion may be qualified by their use; while, wherever these elements are absent, new stems must take their place. The same is true of grammatical elements that designate form or substance. Where these occur, the languages may lack words expressing predicative ideas relating to objects of different form and consisting of different substances (like our words "to lie," "to sit," "to stand," "to tear," "to break").

A lexicographic analysis based on these principles of classification promises important results, but requires a much more accurate knowledge of the meaning of stems than is available in most cases.

No less interesting are the categories of thought that find expression in grammatical form. The older grammars, although many of them contain excellent material, do not clearly present these points of difference, because they are modelled strictly on the Latin scheme, which obscures the characteristic psychological categories of Indian languages. Thus the idea of plurality is not often developed in the same sense as in Latin, but expresses rather the idea of distribution or of collectivity. The category of gender is rare, and nominal cases are not common. In the pronoun we find often a much more rigid adherence to the series of three persons than the one that we apply, in so far as the distinction is carried through in the pronominal plural and in the demonstrative. Furthermore, new ideas—such as visibility, or position in regard to the speaker in the six principal directions (up, down, right, left, front, back), or tense—are added to the concept of the demonstrative pronouns. In the numeral the varied bases of numeral systems find expression. In the verb the category of tense may be almost suppressed or may be exuberantly developed. Modes may include many ideas that we express by means of adverbs, or they may be absent. The distinction between verb and noun may be different from ours. In short, an enormous variety of forms illustrates the multifarious ways in which language seizes upon one or another feature as an essential of expression of thought.

Besides the greater or lesser development of categories that are parallel to our own, many new ones appear. The groups of ideas selected for expression by formative elements are quite distinctive, and they belong to the most important features in the characterization of each language. In some cases they are poorly developed, but most American languages possess an astonishing number of formative elements of this type.

In some cases their number is so great that the very idea of subordination of one element of a word under another one loses its significance; and we are in doubt whether we shall designate one group as subordinate elements, or whether we shall speak of the composition of co-ordinate elements. While in some languages, as in Algonquian or Kutenai, this may be a matter of arbitrary definition, it involves a problem of great theoretical interest; namely, the question whether formative elements have developed from independent words, as has been proved to be the case with many formal suffixes of European languages.

The objectivating tendency of our mind makes the thought congenial, that part of a word the significance of which we can determine by analysis must also have objectively an independent existence; but there is certainly no *a priori* reason that compels us to make this assumption. It must be proved to be true by empirical evidence. Although the history of American languages is not known, and therefore cannot furnish any direct evidence for or against this theory, the study of the etymological processes will throw light upon this problem, because in many cases the very phonetic weakness of the constituent elements, their internal changes, and the transparency of the method of composition, make it clear that we are performing here an analytical process that does not need to have as its counterpart the synthesis of independent elements. The same question may also be raised in regard to phonetic modifications of the stem, which may be secondary, and due to the influence of changing accents in composition or to vanished component elements, while they may also be primary phenomena.

This problem is in a way identical with the whole question of the relation between word and sentence. Here also American languages may furnish us with much important material that emphasizes the view that the unit of human speech as we know it is the sentence, not the word.

The problems treated in a linguistic journal must include also the literary forms of native production. Indian oratory has long been famous, but the number of recorded speeches from which we can judge their oratorical devices is exceedingly small. There is no doubt whatever that definite stylistic forms exist that are utilized to impress the hearer; but we do not know what they are. As yet, nobody has attempted a careful analysis of the style of narrative art as practiced by the various tribes. The crudeness of most records presents a serious obstacle for this study, which, however, should be taken up seriously. We can study the general structure of the narrative, the style of composition, of motives, their character and sequence; but the formal stylistic devices for obtaining effects are not so easily determined.

Notwithstanding the unsatisfactory character of the available material, we do find cases in which we may at least obtain a glimpse of the intent of the narrator. In many cases metaphorical expressions occur that indicate a vigorous imagination. Not much material of this character is available, but what little we have demonstrates that the type of metaphor used in different parts of the continent shows characteristic differences. It would be interesting to know in how far these expressions have become purely formal without actual meaning, and in how far they reflect an active imagination.

Evidence is not missing which shows that the sentence is built up with a view of stressing certain ideas or words by means of position, repetition, or other devices for securing emphasis. There are curious differences in the tendency to fill the discourse with brief allusions to current ideas difficult to understand for anyone who is not versed in the whole culture of the people, and the enjoyment of diffuse, detailed description. Collectors of texts are fully aware that in the art of narrative there are artists and bunglers in every primitive tribe, as well as among ourselves. At present there is hardly any material available that will allow us to characterize the tribal characteristics of the art of narrative.

The most promising material for the study of certain aspects of artistic expression are the formal elements that appear with great frequency in the tales of all tribes. Most of these are stereotyped to such an extent that little individual variation is found. Even in poorly recorded tales, written down in translation only, and obtained with the help of inadequate interpreters, the sameness of stereotyped formulas may sometimes be recognized. Conversation in animal tales and in other types of narrative, prayers and incantations, are probably the most important material of this character.

Attention should also be paid to the existing forms of literature. The narrative is of universal occurrence, but other forms show a much more irregular distribution. The psychological basis of the trivial American anecdote is not easily understood. The connotation of meaningless syllables that occur in songs, the frequent use of distorted words in poetry, and the fondness for a secret language, including obsolete, symbolic, or arbitrary terms, deserve the most careful attention. Here belong also the peculiar modes of speech of various personages, that are recorded in many tales, and which Dr. Sapir has found so fully developed among the Nootka, and Dr. Frachtenberg among the Quileute. The fixity of form of the recitative used by certain animals, to which Dr. Sapir has called attention in his studies of the Paiute, also suggests an interesting line of inquiry.

Equally important is the absence of certain literary forms with which we are familiar. The great dearth of proverbs, of popular snatches, and of riddles, among American aborigines, in contrast to their strong development in Africa and other parts of the Old World, requires attentive study. The general lack of epic poetry, the germs of which are found in a very few regions only, is another feature that promises to clear up certain problems of the early development of literary art. We are able to observe lyric poetry in its simplest forms among all tribes. Indeed, we may say that, even where the slightest vestiges of epic poetry are missing, lyric poetry of one form or another is always present. It may consist of the musical use of meaningless syllables that sustain the song; or it may consist largely of such syllables, with a few interspersed words suggesting certain ideas and certain feelings; or it may rise to the expression of emotions connected with warlike deeds, with religious feeling, love, or even to the praise of the beauties of nature. The records which have been accumulated during the last few years, particularly by students of primitive music, contain a mass of material that can be utilized from this point of view.

Undoubtedly the problems of native poetry have to be taken up in connection with the study of native music, because there is practically no poetry that is not at the same time song. The literary aspects of this subject, however, fall entirely within the scope of a linguistic journal.

Let us hope that the new journal may be able to contribute its share to the solution of all these problems!

EDWARD SAPIR

(1884-1939)

Language and Literature

LANGUAGES ARE MORE TO US THAN SYSTEMS OF THOUGHT-TRANSFERENCE. They are invisible garments that drape themselves about our spirit and give a predetermined form to all its symbolic expression. When the expression is of unusual significance, we call it literature.[1] Art is so personal an expression that we do not like to feel that it is bound to predetermined form of any sort. The possibilities of individual expression are infinite, language in particular is the most fluid of mediums. Yet some limitation there must be to this freedom, some resistance of the medium. In great art there is the illusion of absolute freedom. The formal restraints imposed by the material—paint, black and white, marble, piano tones, or whatever it may be—are not perceived; it is as though there were a limitless margin of elbow-room between the artist's fullest utilization of form and the most that the material is innately capable of. The artist has intuitively surrendered to the inescapable tyranny of the material, made its brute nature fuse easily with his conception.[2] The material "disappears" precisely because there is nothing in the artist's conception to indicate that any other material exists. For the time being, he, and we with him, move in the artistic medium as a fish moves in the water, oblivious of the existence of an alien atmosphere. No sooner, however, does the artist transgress

From Sapir, *Language: An Introduction to the Study of Speech* (Harcourt, Brace, 1921), pp. 236-247.

[1] I can hardly stop to define just what kind of expression is "significant" enough to be called art or literature. Besides, I do not exactly know. We shall have to take literature for granted.

[2] This "intuitive surrender" has nothing to do with subservience to artistic convention. More than one revolt in modern art has been dominated by the desire to get out of the material just what it is really capable of. The impressionist wants light and color because paint can give him just these; "literature" in painting, the sentimental suggestion of a "story," is offensive to him because he does not want the virtue of his particular form to be dimmed by shadows from another medium. Similarly, the poet, as never before, insists that words mean just what they really mean.

the law of his medium than we realize with a start that there is a medium to obey.

Language is the medium of literature as marble or bronze or clay are the materials of the sculptor. Since every language has its distinctive peculiarities, the innate formal limitations—and possibilites—of one literature are never quite the same as those of another. The literature fashioned out of the form and substance of a language has the color and the texture of its matrix. The literary artist may never be conscious of just how he is hindered or helped or otherwise guided by the matrix, but when it is a question of translating his work into another language, the nature of the original matrix manifests itself at once. All his effects have been calculated, or intuitively felt, with reference to the formal "genius" of his own language; they cannot be carried over without loss or modification. Croce[3] is therefore perfectly right in saying that a work of literary art can never be translated. Nevertheless literature does get itself translated, sometimes with astonishing adequacy. This brings up the question whether in the art of literature there are not intertwined two distinct kinds or levels of art—a generalized, non-linguistic art, which can be transferred without loss into an alien linguistic medium, and a specifically linguistic art that is not transferable.[4] I believe the distinction is entirely valid, though we never get the two levels pure in practice. Literature moves in language as a medium, but that medium comprises two layers, the latent content of language— our intuitive record of experience—and the particular conformation of a given language—the specific how of our record of experience. Literature that draws its sustenance mainly—never entirely—from the lower level, say a play of Shakespeare's, is translatable without too great a loss of character. If it moves in the upper rather than in the lower level—a fair example is a lyric of Swinburne's—it is as good as untranslatable. Both types of literary expression may be great or mediocre.

There is really no mystery in the distinction. It can be clarified a little by comparing literature with science. A scientific truth is impersonal, in its essence it is untinctured by the particular linguistic medium in which it finds expression. It can as readily deliver its message in Chinese[5] as in

[3] See Benedetto Croce, "Æsthetic."

[4] The question of the transferability of art productions seems to me to be of genuine theoretic interest. For all that we speak of the sacrosanct uniqueness of a given art work, we know very well, though we do not always admit it, that not all productions are equally intractable to transference. A Chopin étude is inviolate; it moves altogether in the world of piano tone. A Bach fugue is transferable into another set of musical timbres without serious loss of esthetic significance. Chopin plays with the language of the piano as though no other language existed (the medium "disappears"); Bach speaks the language of the piano as a handy means of giving outward expression to a conception wrought in the generalized language of tone.

[5] Provided, of course, Chinese is careful to provide itself with the necessary scientific vocabulary. Like any other language it can do so without serious difficulty if the need arises.

English. Nevertheless it must have some expression, and that expression must needs be a linguistic one. Indeed the apprehension of the scientific truth is itself a linguistic process, for thought is nothing but language denuded of its outward garb. The proper medium of scientific expression is therefore a generalized language that may be defined as a symbolic algebra of which all known languages are translations. One can adequately translate scientific literature because the original scientific expression is itself a translation. Literary expression is personal and concrete, but this does not mean that its significance is altogether bound up with the accidental qualities of the medium. A truly deep symbolism, for instance, does not depend on the verbal associations of a particular language but rests securely on an intuitive basis that underlies all linguistic expression. The artist's "intuition," to use Croce's term, is immediately fashioned out of a generalized human experience—thought and feeling—of which his own individual experience is a highly personalized selection. The thought relations in this deeper level have no specific linguistic vesture; the rhythms are free, not bound, in the first instance, to the traditional rhythms of the artist's language. Certain artists whose spirit moves largely in the non-linguistic (better, in the generalized linguistic) layer even find a certain difficulty in getting themselves expressed in the rigidly set terms of their accepted idiom. One feels that they are unconsciously striving for a generalized art language, a literary algebra, that is related to the sum of all known languages as a perfect mathematical symbolism is related to all the roundabout reports of mathematical relations that normal speech is capable of conveying. Their art expression is frequently strained, it sounds at times like a translation from an unknown original—which, indeed, is precisely what it is. These artists—Whitmans and Brownings—impress us rather by the greatness of their spirit than the felicity of their art. Their relative failure is of the greatest diagnostic value as an index of the pervasive presence in literature of a larger, more intuitive linguistic medium than any particular language.

Nevertheless, human expression being what it is, the greatest—or shall we say the most satisfying—literary artists, the Shakespeares and Heines, are those who have known subconsciously to fit or trim the deeper intuition to the provincial accents of their daily speech. In them there is no effect of strain. Their personal "intuition" appears as a completed synthesis of the absolute art of intuition and the innate, specialized art of the linguistic medium. With Heine, for instance, one is under the illusion that the universe speaks German. The material "disappears."

Every language is itself a collective art of expression. There is concealed in it a particular set of esthetic factors—phonetic, rhythmic, symbolic, morphological—which it does not completely share with any other language. These factors may either merge their potencies with those of that unknown, absolute language to which I have referred—this is the

method of Shakespeare and Heine—or they may weave a private, technical art fabric of their own, the innate art of the language intensified or
sublimated. The latter type, the more technically "literary" art of Swinburne and of hosts of delicate "minor" poets, is too fragile for endurance.
It is built out of spiritualized material, not out of spirit. The successes of
the Swinburnes are as valuable for diagnostic purposes as the semi-failures
of the Brownings. They show to what extent literary art may lean on the
collective art of the language itself. The more extreme technical practitioners may so over-individualize this collective art as to make it almost
unendurable. One is not always thankful to have one's flesh and blood
frozen to ivory.

An artist must utilize the native esthetic resources of his speech. He may
be thankful if the given palette of colors is rich, if the springboard is
light. But he deserves no special credit for felicities that are the language's
own. We must take for granted this language with all its qualities of flexibility or rigidity and see the artist's work in relation to it. A cathedral on
the lowlands is higher than a stick on Mont Blanc. In other words, we
must not commit the folly of admiring a French sonnet because the vowels
are more sonorous than our own or of condemning Nietzsche's prose because it harbors in its texture combinations of consonants that would
affright on English soil. To so judge literature would be tantamount to
loving "Tristan und Isolde" because one is fond of the timbre of horns.
There are certain things that one language can do supremely well which
it would be almost vain for another to attempt. Generally there are compensations. The vocalism of English is an inherently drabber thing than
the vowel scale of French, yet English compensates for this drawback by
its greater rhythmical alertness. It is even doubtful if the innate sonority
of a phonetic system counts for as much, as esthetic determinant, as the
relations between the sounds, the total gamut of their similarities and
contrasts. As long as the artist has the wherewithal to lay out his sequences
and rhythms, it matters little what are the sensuous qualities of the elements of his material.

The phonetic groundwork of a language, however, is only one of the
features that give its literature a certain direction. Far more important
are its morphological peculiarities. It makes a great deal of difference for
the development of style if the language can or cannot create compound
words, if its structure is synthetic or analytic, if the words of its sentences have considerable freedom of position or are compelled to fall into
a rigidly determined sequence. The major characteristics of style, in so
far as style is a technical matter of the building and placing of words, are
given by the language itself, quite as inescapably, indeed, as the general
acoustic effect of verse is given by the sounds and natural accents of the
language. These necessary fundamentals of style are hardly felt by the
artist to constrain his individuality of expression. They rather point the

way to those stylistic developments that most suit the natural bent of the language. It is not in the least likely that a truly great style can seriously oppose itself to the basic form patterns of the language. It not only incorporates them, it builds on them. The merit of such a style as W. H. Hudson's or George Moore's[6] is that it does with ease and economy what the language is always trying to do. Carlylese, though individual and vigorous, is yet not style; it is a Teutonic mannerism. Nor is the prose of Milton and his contemporaries strictly English; it is semi-Latin done into magnificent English words.

It is strange how long it has taken the European literatures to learn that style is not an absolute, a something that is to be imposed on the language from Greek or Latin models, but merely the language itself, running in its natural grooves, and with enough of an individual accent to allow the artist's personality to be felt as a presence, not as an acrobat. We understand more clearly now that what is effective and beautiful in one language is a vice in another. Latin and Eskimo, with their highly inflected forms, lend themselves to an elaborately periodic structure that would be boring in English. English allows, even demands, a looseness that would be insipid in Chinese. And Chinese, with its unmodified words and rigid sequences, has a compactness of phrase, a terse parallelism, and a silent suggestiveness that would be too tart, too mathematical, for the English genius. While we cannot assimilate the luxurious periods of Latin nor the pointilliste style of the Chinese classics, we can enter sympathetically into the spirit of these alien techniques.

I believe that any English poet of to-day would be thankful for the concision that a Chinese poetaster attains without effort. Here is an example:[7]

> Wu-river[8] stream mouth evening sun sink,
> North look Liao-Tung,[9] not see home.
> Steam whistle several noise, sky-earth boundless,
> Float float one reed out Middle-Kingdom.

These twenty-eight syllables may be clumsily interpreted: "At the mouth of the Yangtsze River, as the sun is about to sink, I look north toward Liao-Tung but do not see my home. The steam-whistle shrills several times on the boundless expanse where meet sky and earth. The steamer, floating gently like a hollow reed, sails out of the Middle Kingdom."[10] But we must not envy Chinese its terseness unduly. Our more sprawling

[6] Aside from individual peculiarities of diction, the selection and evaluation of particular words as such.

[7] Not by any means a great poem, merely a bit of occasional verse written by a young Chinese friend of mine when he left Shanghai for Canada.

[8] The old name of the country about the mouth of the Yangtsze.

[9] A province of Manchuria.

[10] I.e., China.

mode of expression is capable of its own beauties, and the more compact luxuriance of Latin style has its loveliness too. There are almost as many natural ideals of literary style as there are languages. Most of these are merely potential, awaiting the hand of artists who will never come. And yet in the recorded texts of primitive tradition and song there are many passages of unique vigor and beauty. The structure of the language often forces an assemblage of concepts that impresses us as a stylistic discovery. Single Algonkin words are like tiny imagist poems. We must be careful not to exaggerate a freshness of content that is at least half due to our freshness of approach, but the possibility is indicated none the less of utterly alien literary styles, each distinctive with its disclosure of the search of the human spirit for beautiful form.

Probably nothing better illustrates the formal dependence of literature on language than the prosodic aspect of poetry. Quantitative verse was entirely natural to the Greeks, not merely because poetry grew up in connection with the chant and the dance,[11] but because alternations of long and short syllables were keenly live facts in the daily economy of the language. The tonal accents, which were only secondarily stress phenomena, helped to give the syllable its quantitative individuality. When the Greek meters were carried over into Latin verse, there was comparatively little strain, for Latin too was characterized by an acute awareness of quantitative distinctions. However, the Latin accent was more markedly stressed than that of Greek. Probably, therefore, the purely quantitative meters modeled after the Greek were felt as a shade more artificial than in the language of their origin. The attempt to cast English verse into Latin and Greek molds has never been successful. The dynamic basis of English is not quantity,[12] but stress, the alternation of accented and unaccented syllables. This fact gives English verse an entirely different slant and has determined the development of its poetic forms, is still responsible for the evolution of new forms. Neither stress nor syllabic weight is a very keen psychologic factor in the dynamics of French. The syllable has great inherent sonority and does not fluctuate significantly as to quantity and stress. Quantitative or accentual metrics would be as artificial in French as stress metrics in classical Greek or quantitative or purely syllabic metrics in English. French prosody was compelled to develop on the basis of unit syllable-groups. Assonance, later rhyme, could not but prove a welcome, an all but necessary, means of articulating or sectioning the somewhat spineless flow of sonorous syllables. English was hospitable to the French suggestion of rhyme, but did not seriously need it in its rhyth-

[11] Poetry everywhere is inseparable in its origins from the singing voice and the measure of the dance. Yet accentual and syllabic types of verse, rather than quantitative verse, seem to be the prevailing norms.

[12] Quantitative distinctions exist as an objective fact. They have not the same inner, psychological value that they had in Greek.

mic economy. Hence rhyme has always been strictly subordinated to stress
as a somewhat decorative feature and has been frequently dispensed with.
It is no psychologic accident that rhyme came later into English than in
French and is leaving it sooner.[13] Chinese verse has developed along very
much the same lines as French verse. The syllable is an even more integral and sonorous unit than in French, while quantity and stress are
too uncertain to form the basis of a metric system. Syllable-groups—so and
so many syllables per rhythmic unit—and rhyme are therefore two of the
controlling factors in Chinese prosody. The third factor, the alternation
of syllables with level tone and syllables with inflected (rising or falling)
tone, is peculiar to Chinese.

To summarize, Latin and Greek verse depends on the principle of contrasting weights; English verse, on the principle of contrasting stresses;
French verse, on the principles of number and echo; Chinese verse, on the
principles of number, echo, and contrasting pitches. Each of these rhythmic
systems proceeds from the unconscious dynamic habit of the language,
falling from the lips of the folk. Study carefully the phonetic system of a
language, above all its dynamic features, and you can tell what kind of
a verse it has developed—or, if history has played pranks with its psychology, what kind of verse it should have developed and some day will.

Whatever be the sounds, accents, and forms of a language, however
these lay hands on the shape of its literature, there is a subtle law of compensations that gives the artist space. If he is squeezed a bit here, he can
swing a free arm there. And generally he has rope enough to hang himself with, if he must. It is not strange that this should be so. Language is
itself the collective art of expression, a summary of thousands upon thousands of individual intuitions. The individual goes lost in the collective
creation, but his personal expression has left some trace in a certain give
and flexibility that are inherent in all collective works of the human spirit.
The language is ready, or can be quickly made ready, to define the artist's
individuality. If no literary artist appears, it is not essentially because the
language is too weak an instrument, it is because the culture of the people
is not favorable to the growth of such personality as seeks a truly individual verbal expression.

[13] Verhaeren was no slave to the Alexandrine, yet he remarked to Symons, *à
propos* of the translation of *Les Aubes,* that while he approved of the use of
rhymeless verse in the English version, he found it "meaningless" in French.

ALFRED L. KROEBER

(1876-1960)

Of all the anthropologists who came to maturity in the early years of the 20th century, Kroeber ranged farthest. For this reason, if for no other, he is perhaps the best representative of the Golden Age. In the present age of dreary specialization, when the Sinologist cannot communicate with the Americanist, and when the study of the types of Middle Congo masks is considered a "field of study," it is especially pleasant to contemplate Kroeber. Like Boas, he made important contributions in three of the four fields of anthropology, although his work was not in the identical fields. Kroeber's accomplishments in archaeology are substantial; it is quite possible that his studies in Peruvian prehistory will prove, in time, to be his most significant contribution to knowledge.

Anthropology is a wide street with many houses, but other streets are inviting. Kroeber is no respecter of disciplinary labels. He borrows with equal ease from history, geography, ecology, psychology, and he feels no hesitation in dropping ideas or methods if they prove unrewarding. One great continuity in Kroeber's scientific life has been the building of California anthropology. He first went to California in 1901 and combined teaching with research. Since then he and his students have been adding regularly and systematically to our knowledge of the languages and cultures of that area.

There are also certain recurrent themes in Kroeber's writings, ideas that reappear over the years in fresh interpretations. One of these is the concept of the superorganic—the idea that culture is a reality of a different order from the particular habits of the individuals composing a society. Another is that culture areas are realities, not merely abstract classification devices and where considered in relation to geographical areas can be analyzed in terms of concepts borrowed from ecology. Another is the idea of periodicity in cultural development, the small swings in fashion, and the large swings in the rise and fall of cultures.

As this book was going to press, Kroeber died in Paris in October, 1960, on his way home from an international conference.—R.L.B.

The Nature of Culture

WHAT CULTURE IS

WHAT CULTURE IS CAN BE BETTER UNDERSTOOD FROM KNOWLEDGE OF what forms it takes and how it works than by a definition. Culture is in this respect like life or matter: it is the total of their varied phenomena that is more significant than a concentrated phrase about them. And again as with life and with matter, it is true that when we are dealing with the actual manifestations we are less often in doubt as to whether a phenomenon is or is not cultural than we are in deciding on what is includable in the concept of culture when we reason abstractly about it. Nevertheless, it will be worth while to consider some definitions briefly.

Tylor says that "culture or civilization is that complex whole which includes knowledge, belief, art, morals, law, customs, and any other capabilities and habits acquired by man as a member of society." Linton equates culture with "social heredity." Lowie calls it "the whole of social tradition." All three statements use the term "social" or "society," but in an attributive or qualifying sense. We can accept this: society and culture, social and cultural, are closely related concepts. There can obviously be no culture without a society—much as there can be no society without individuals. The converse—no society without culture—holds for man: no cultureless human society is known; it would even be hard to imagine. But it does not hold on the subhuman level. As we have seen, ants and bees do have genuine societies without culture, as well as without speech. Less integrated and simpler associations are frequent among animals. Even a pair of nesting birds rearing their young constitute a society, though a small and temporary one. Accordingly, so far as man is concerned, culture always has society as a counterpart; it rests on, and is carried by, society. Beyond the range of man there are societies, but no cultures. Cultural phenomena thus characterize man more specifically than his social manifestations characterize him, for these latter he shares with vertebrate and invertebrate animals.

Roughly, then, we can approximate what culture is by saying it is that which the human species has and other social species lack. This would include speech, knowledge, beliefs, customs, arts and technologies, ideals and rules. That, in short, is what we learn from other men, from our elders or the past, plus what we may add to it. That is why Tylor speaks of "capabilities and habits acquired by man," and what Lowie means when

From Kroeber, *Anthropology: Race—Language—Culture—Psychology—Prehistory* (New York: Harcourt, Brace and Company, 1948), pp. 252-256, 288-290.

he says "the whole of social tradition," or Linton by "social heredity." The last term is unfortunate because heredity now denotes in biology precisely what is received organically or genetically to the exclusion of what is acquired socially or culturally. But if we substitute for "heredity" the more noncommittal near-synonym "inheritance," the phrase then conveys much the same meaning as Lowie's "social tradition."

The terms "social inheritance" or "tradition" put the emphasis on how culture is acquired rather than on what it consists of. Yet a naming of all the kinds of things that we receive by tradition—speech, knowledges, activities, rules, and the rest—runs into quite an enumeration. . . . Things so diverse as hoeing corn, singing the blues, wearing a shirt, speaking English, and being a Baptist are involved. Perhaps a shorter way of designating the content of culture is the negative way of telling what is excluded from it. Put this way around, culture might be defined as all the activities and non-physiological products of human personalities that are not automatically reflex or instinctive. That in turn means, in biological and psychological parlance, that culture consists of conditioned or learned activities (plus the manufactured results of these); and the idea of learning brings us back again to what is socially transmitted, what is received from tradition, what "is acquired by man as a member of societies." So perhaps *how it comes to be* is really more distinctive of culture than what it *is*. It certainly is more easily expressed specifically.

In one sense culture is both superindividual and superorganic. But it is necessary to know what is meant by these terms so as not to misunderstand their implications. "Superorganic" does not mean nonorganic, or free of organic influence and causation; nor does it mean that culture is an entity independent of organic life in the sense that some theologians might assert that there is a soul which is or can become independent of the living body. "Superorganic" means simply that when we consider culture we are dealing with something that is organic but which must also be viewed as something more than organic if it is to be fully intelligible to us. In the same way when we say that plants and animals are "organic" we do not thereby try to place them outside the laws of matter and energy in general. We only affirm that fully to understand organic beings and how they behave, we have to recognize certain kinds of phenomena or properties—such as the powers of reproduction, assimilation, irritability—as added to those which we encounter in inorganic substances. Just so, there are certain properties of culture—such as transmissibility, high variability, cumulativeness, value standards, influence on individuals—which it is difficult to explain, or to see much significance in, strictly in terms of the organic composition of personalities or individuals. These properties or qualities of culture evidently attach not to the organic individual man as such, but to the actions and the behavior products of societies of men—that is, to culture.

In short, culture is superorganic and superindividual in that, although carried, participated in, and produced by organic individuals, it is acquired; and it is acquired by learning. What is learned is the existent culture. The content of this is transmitted between individuals without becoming a part of their inherent endowment. The mass or body of culture, the institutions and practices and ideas constituting it, have a persistence and can be conceived as going on their slowly changing way "above" or outside the societies that support them. They are "above" them in that a particular culture, a particular set of institutions, can pass to other societies; also in that the culture continuously influences or conditions the members of the underlying society or societies—indeed, largely determines the content of their lives. Further, particular manifestations of cultures find their primary significance in other cultural manifestations, and can be most fully understood in terms of these manifestations; whereas they cannot be specifically explained from the generic organic endowment of the human personality, even though cultural phenomena must always conform to the frame of this endowment.

An illustration may make this superorganic quality more vivid. A religion, say Roman Catholicism or Mohammedanism, is of course a piece of culture, and a typical piece or sample. Obviously Catholicism exists only in so far as there are Catholics; that is, when and where there are human individuals who have acquired the faith. Once established, however, the Catholic hierarchy, beliefs, rituals, habits, and attitudes can also be viewed as going on century after century. Popes, bishops, communicants succeed one another; the church persists. It certainly possesses a continuity and an influence of its own: it affects not only its adherents but the course of history. On a smaller scale, or for shorter periods, the same thing holds for smaller segments of culture—institutions, beliefs, or customs down to short-lived trivialities of fashion and etiquette. On a larger and more general scale, the same holds for the totality of human culture since it first began to develop. Big or little, then, culture affects human action. It is the accident of what culture happens to be in Occidental countries toward the middle of the twentieth century which determines that when I get up in the morning I put on a shirt and pants and not a chlamys or a toga or just a breech-clout. Can we call this contemporary Western culture the cause of my shirt-wearing? In ordinary parlance, we might; the specific custom can certainly not be derived from anything in human hereditary constitution. Dialectically, the cultural causation might be challenged; it depends on logical definitions. But everyone will agree at least that the concrete cultural fact of habitual shirt-wearing is specifically related to or conditioned by other cultural facts, such as antecedent dress styles, manners, laws, or religion.

Again, the English language is a piece of culture. The faculty of speaking and understanding some or any language is organic: it is a faculty of the human species. The sounds of words are of course made by individual men and women, and are understood and reacted to by individuals, not by the species. But the total aggregation of words, forms, grammar, and meanings which constitute the English language are the cumulative and joint product of millions of individuals for many centuries past. No one of us creates or invents for himself the English he speaks. He talks it as it comes to him, ready-made, from his millions of predecessors and from his elders and age mates. English is obviously superindividual in the sense that it is something enormously bigger and more significant than the speech of any individual man, and in that it influences his speaking infinitely more than his speaking can hope to contribute to or influence the English language. And English is superorganic in that its words and meanings are not direct outflows or consequences of men's being human organisms— else all men would spontaneously talk as much alike as they walk alike. Instead, how they talk depends overwhelmingly on how the societies in which they were raised talked before.

A piece of culture such as the English language is therefore a historical phenomenon. This means that its specific features cannot be adequately explained by the organic features of our species—nor of a race—but are most intelligible in the light of the long, complex, and locally varied history of the institution we call English speech. In short, a cultural fact is always a historical fact; and its most immediate understanding, and usually the fullest understanding of it to which we can attain, is a historical one. To a large degree calling culture superorganic or superindividual means that it yields more readily to historical interpretation than to organic or psychosomatic explanations.

A simile that may further help the realization of what culture is and how it works is that of a coral reef. Such a reef may be miles long and inhabited by billions of tiny polyp animals. The firm, solid part of the reef consists of calcium carbonate produced by the secretions of these animals over thousands of years—a product at once cumulative and communal and therefore social. What is alive and organic in the reef is these innumerable little animals on its ocean-fronting surface. Without their ancestors, there would have been no reef. But the reef now exists independently of the living polyps, and would long continue to endure even if every polyp were killed by, say, a change in ocean temperature or salinity. It would still break the surf, would now and then wreck ships, and would bar off quiet water behind. While a coral reef is the accumulated precipitate of dead polyps, it is also a phenomenon affording to millions of living polyps a base and a foothold, and a place to thrive.

This parallel is incomplete. It breaks down in that a reef is actual physical matter, whereas only the artifacts and the manufactures of culture are material or physical, most of culture consisting of ideas and behaviors. Also, a reef determines that and where new polyps are to live, but not how they will live, not the specific way of many possible ways in which they will function, which on the contrary is just what culture does largely determine for men. Yet the simile is valid and suggestive on one point: the minute role played by the individual polyp or human being in proportion, respectively, to the mass of reef or of culture. Each of us undoubtedly contributes something to the slowly but ever changing culture in which we live, as each coral contributes his gram or two of lime to the Great Barrier Reef. In the main, though, it is our culture that directs and outlines the kind of life we can lead. There is left to our individual gifts and temperaments the relative success and happiness we attain in life; and to our own volition, the alternative choices provided by our culture—the choice, perhaps, between being doctor, lawyer, or merchant chief; or whether our next drink shall be water, beer, tea, or milk. Even this last set of choices would not be wholly free to the individual if he were a participant in strict Methodist or Mohammedan culture; and in old China the beer would not be available and the milk considered too nasty to want.

At any rate, the comparison may be of aid toward seeing things in perspective; with a consequence, perhaps, of somewhat deepened personal humility in the face of the larger world and human history.

MOLDING THE INDIVIDUAL

Through being born into a society, every individual is also born into a culture. This culture molds him, and he participates in it.

The degree to which every individual is molded by his culture is enormous. We do not ordinarily recognize the full strength of this shaping process, because it happens to everyone, it happens gradually, it is satisfying at least as often as it is painful, and usually there is no obvious alternative open anyway. Hence the molding is taken for granted and is accepted, like the culture itself—perhaps not quite unconsciously, but uncritically. The formal or deliberate part of the process we call education: education through schools, in religion, and in manners and morals primarily at home. These agencies convey the mores and some of the folkways. But perhaps a larger fraction of the cultural tradition is acquired by each individual at his own initiative. He is left to "pick it up," to grow into it. In this class are his speech, bodily postures and gestures, mental and social attitudes, which he imitates from his elders or from near-age mates, and a thousand and one activities, such as putting on shoes, splitting firewood, or driving a car, which a child "learns," often without any formal instruction, because he has seen others do these things and wants to do them too.

How much of all that a person knows how to do, and does do, comes to him from outside, from the cultural environment that surrounds him, and how much from within, from his independent personality? The former is surely much the larger mass. That he speaks, say, English and not

Chinese is the result of "where he is born" or raised; that is, of which language forms part of the culture in which he grows up. Similarly with his being a Christian instead of a Buddhist, casting his vote in November, observing Sunday, celebrating New Year on January 1 instead of in February, eating with a fork and not with chopsticks, and bread and butter in place of rice, tucking his shirt in and not out (in Kipling's day at least), saying hello to his parents instead of using honorifics, steering a tractor and not a lightly shod wooden plow, writing with letters instead of a thousand logograms, and so on endlessly. In fact, the mass of what any person receives from his culture is so great as to make it look at first glance as if he were nothing but an individual exemplar of his culture, a reduction of it abbreviated to the scope of what one personality can contain. All there remains of him that is not induced by his culture consists of two sets of things. First are his innate general human capacities, and second, his individual peculiarities.

The capacities merely ensure, just because they are generic, that our normal person has the faculty of learning to speak, to read, to operate tools, to practice a religion of some kind or other. What the kind of speech, tools, religion is depends absolutely on the culture, not on him. In other words, his birth as a normal man gives him certain potentialities, but his birth in a culture determines how these potentialities will be expressed and realized.

Individual peculiarities comprise such traits as speaking with a lisp or a drawl, having a bass or a tenor voice, worshiping piously or perfunctorily, being naturally tidy or hasty or bright or the opposite. These are individual variations from the average intelligence, energy, or temperament. They range all the way from genius to imbecility, from superexcitability to ultrasluggishness; but of course the great majority of individuals depart only slightly from the mean in any one trait. These "individualisms" or idiosyncrasies do have a physiological and hereditary basis, in the main. Yet in part their qualities too can be culturally induced, as when a drawl is a Southerner's or a cowboy's, or the tidiness and phlegm are those of Hollanders. In such instances it is the occasional Southerner who doesn't drawl, or drawls infernally, the Dutchman who is precipitate and disorderly, who represents the individual variation from the norm that is characteristic of the culture or the subculture of his society.

This brings us to a second class of features in which individuals differ: roughly, those areas which are alternatives within one's culture. Shall I be a farmer or a storekeeper or a dentist, go in for tennis or baseball or golf, join the Army or the Navy, be a Methodist or a Presbyterian or a Quaker? Here the culture leaves several choices more or less open to the individual members, though it is well to remember that each culture has a different array of choices. In unwesternized China, for instance, there would be no choice of dentistry or baseball or Navy, and the religious denominations available would be altered to Confucian, Buddhist, and Taoist. Even among ourselves, not all choices would be open to everyone everywhere: golf might be only a theoretical possibility to a farm laborer or a sheep-shearer on the Great Plains. In fact in rigidly segregated India only a few of all occupations, worships, amusements, and foods known to Hindu civilization would be open to the members of any one caste.

In summary, heredity gives us at birth certain generic human faculties. How we shall use these, and therefore how we shall mainly live, the culture in which we are launched thereupon decides. But it leaves us, theoretically at least, certain choices between alternatives in its total scheme; and it leaves us also a degree of freedom of departure from its norms in personal mannerisms, innovations, and successes.

This enormous influence of culture in molding the individual has a bearing on psychology. This science is set up to study particular individuals in order to reach understanding of human beings in general; that is, of what might be called the abstracted human person. But since all individuals as they actually occur in life are patterned by culture, and their behavior is full of culture, the task of psychology is made difficult. This was not clear at first. But then psychologists began to realize how great was the effect on individuals of their happening to be exposed to different influences, as these exist within our civilization; how the children of articulate parents generally come to be above-average in verbal facility; how the children of unhappy or broken marriages are more likely than the average to be emotionally unstable in their adjustments to other persons; and so on. So "conditioning" came to be one of the slogans of modern psychology where innateness of behavior had been assumed before. Then, as psychologists gradually came to be culture-conscious also, the variety of cultures was seen to increase enormously the range of the conditioning people are subject to. The abstract man, or what the psychologist felt he could properly say about him, shrank in proportion. This is why there is such great difficulty, as we have seen, in deciding how alike or different the heredity equipment of races or descent groups is. It is not that psychological tests are unsound. The tests are valid enough, within limits, within the culture for which they were constructed. They show at any rate how much culture an individual has absorbed in comparison with other individuals. They are less good at showing, per se, whether greater absorption is due to greater exposure or to greater inborn capacity. And the tests break down, or become dubious, when they are applied interculturally. Hence it is that we do not yet know how different the races are in their endowment, while we do know that cultures differ enormously in content and orientation. And of course individuals differ both in their heredity and in what their conditioning has made them.

ROBERT H. LOWIE

(1883-1957)

Lowie wrote in his autobiography that when Kroeber invited him to come to California he was reluctant to give up museum work for teaching. He had no desire to teach and felt that he would not be good at it. He was wrong on both counts. He liked teaching and he was a successful teacher. He brought to California his urbane scholarship, and he found the emergence from the gathering dust of the Museum into the fresh air of the California department both stimulating and mellowing.

Lowie was born in Vienna, although he came to the United States as a child and had all of his higher education here. Yet he retained a certain cosmopolitanism in his habits of mind. This showed especially in the range of his reading and in his mastery of European sociological literature. He was hospitable to many points of view but skeptical and cautious in building theory. His spirit was not controversial and he derived neither pleasure nor profit from setting up straw men.

He published many articles and reviews and several volumes on anthropological theory. His books were short, and he was economical with words. Even his monograph on the Crow Indians is not overloaded with repetitious details. He is best known for his sympathetic study of the Crow and his lucid discussions of kinship and social organization.

The events of World War II brought many anthropologists out from their ivory tipis to apply their minds to the problems of contemporary culture. Lowie, who used German in preference to English, and kept a copy of Faust *by his bed, lectured on German and Balkan cultures in specialized training programs for Army personnel. After the war he did his last stint of field work—this time in Germany, traveling around the country, picking up hitch-hikers, talking to everyone. The results of this trip were embodied in his book,* Toward Understanding Germany, *published in 1954. It eschewed clichés and exhibited Lowie's urbane and detached commitment to an understanding of culture.—R.L.B.*

Social Organization

EVERY HUMAN GROUP IS ORGANIZED; ITS INDIVIDUAL COMPONENTS DO NOT behave independently of one another but are linked by bonds, the nature of which determines the types of social unit. Kinship, sex, age, coresidence, matrimonial status, community of religious or social interests, are among the unifying agencies; and in stratified societies members of the same level form a definite class.

Maine, who introduced the valid distinction between kinship and territorial ties, incorrectly denied the existence of the latter in ruder societies; this position was popularized by Lewis H. Morgan. Both ignored phenomena anticipating the state of civilized countries, a deficiency partly supplied by Schurtz' theory of associations. Primitive communities do not conform to the simple pattern conceived by earlier writers but are often segmented according to several coexisting principles. To determine the comparative influence of the several resulting loyalties is one of the most important problems of social organization.

The societies of the ruder hunting peoples, as exemplified by the Bushmen of South Africa, the Andamanese or the Washo of Nevada and California, lack centralized authority and hereditary class distinctions. This does not preclude the dominance of powerful personalities or the control of the community by leaders for a definite purpose, as when a Washo of recognized competence superintends a rabbit hunt. As a rule, however, the headman of these tribes exercises no special authority, since authority is vested in the totality of adult males. In parts of Australia this situation involves a gerontocracy, the fully initiated elders assuming the reins of government and even reserving to themselves the choicest food; thus age status determines government relations. Other hunting communities, such as the northwest Californians, define influence in terms of wealth, a factor likewise prominent among the pastoral nomads of the Old World. Inasmuch, however, as the size of herds and flocks is subject to great vicissitudes, these peoples rarely develop hereditary castes. Such castes evolved in Polynesia and Micronesia, where loftiness of rank depended theoretically on directness of descent from the gods. These differences in rank may or may not be coupled with distinctions as to political power; in Hawaii the supreme ruler was likewise the highest in rank, while in Tonga the *tuitonga,* although regarded as spiritually and socially superior, was overshadowed in the affairs of state by a secular chief.

From Lowie, "Social Organization," *Encyclopedia of the Social Sciences,* Vol. 14 (New York: The Macmillan Company, 1934), pp. 141-148.

The Polynesian states were miniature kingdoms even where, as in New Zealand, geographical conditions did not hinder expansion. On the other hand, enormous African Negro populations have repeatedly been united under a single despot. Although this development was fostered by Mohammedanism, it long antedated Islam and occurred independently of its range, as in the case of Chaka, who made the Zulu, once a petty tribe, into the dominant people of south Africa. Among the Bakuba of the southwestern Congo the king became a slave to court etiquette and a puppet in the hands of his ministers. On the west coast of Africa the ruler may either encounter a check from an independent secret society or enhance his prerogatives by gaining control of that organization. In some of the African kingdoms autocracy precludes aristocracy; the king was the only blue blood of Uganda and even the most powerful officials acted only by delegated authority. A different condition is found in Ruanda, where the subjugation of peasant tribes by cattle breeders has resulted in the dominance of a privileged pastoral aristocracy over the agricultural commoners, who in turn despise the roving pygmoid hunters of the area. On a higher level the Bedouins have subjugated the Arabian peasantry as their nomadic ancestors subjected the agricultural civilizations of the Near Orient.

African kingdoms refute the view that primitive groups are built on the exclusive basis of kinship, that the territorial tie is an extremely recent peculiarity of literate societies. In Uganda the kinship grouping by clans remained, yet government rested on the supremacy of the king and the realm was divided into minor regional units. Wherever a gifted primitive despot ruled by divine right, whether in Polynesia or in Africa, in theory he approached closely the modern ideal of a totalitarian state. In the New World authentic instances of such processes are rare. At the time of the Spanish conquest the Incas of Peru, claiming descent from the sun god, had achieved a state socialism which regulated economic organization in all its details.

Even in ruder societies the concept of a territorial unit is dimly foreshadowed. The Ifugao of Luzon have been described an anarchists who regulate all social relations in terms of kindred. Were this so, two bodies of kinsmen would treat one another as do two autonomous civilized states; but there is no such independence. Fellow residents recognize definite obligations not to embroil one another in feuds with outsiders; while the thief from another settlement is killed outright, larceny within the village is merely punished by a fixed fine. Among Plains Indians also a nascent clan feud was not a matter of indifference to the rest of the community. The neutrals realized that the result of such dissension would be the inevitable weakening of the tribe and made every effort to restrain the warring kindreds. There is here no lack of local ties but rather an absence of coercive authority within the local unit; persuasion takes the place of authority. In Luzon a go-between unofficially attempts to mediate. In case

of a Plains Indian murder the police society merely urged a peace pipe on
the victim's kin and conveyed the indemnity offered by the culprit's
family.

Although local contiguity creates union among preliterate peoples, the
tie of kinship unquestionably eclipses it. It precipitates two group forms,
the family and several types of unilateral segment. The family consists of a
father, a mother and their children, the latter not being always biological
offspring but sometimes merely reckoned as such by legal fiction. In such
a group the children's relations are bilateral; that is, they are linked to
both parents. This is not true in the series represented by the lineage, clan
and phratry, in which the children, for certain purposes, are related to only
one parent, the rule of descent varying in different tribes and areas.
Theoretically a clan (sib) embraces the descendants of a single ancestor
or ancestress, the sense of common descent leading to the rule of exogamy.
Actually it is often impossible to prove common derivation; at times the
clans folk are demonstrably constituted of several distinct bodies of kin.
It is also certain, as Parsons has shown among the Pueblos and Goldenweiser among the Iroquois Indians, that succession to office, loosely
described by earlier writers as following clan lines, really follows in a
line of blood relatives. It has thus become necessary to distinguish with
Gifford the lineage, that is, the body of persons unilaterally related by
blood, from the clan composed of two or more lineages. The Hopi of
Arizona present the case of a tribe subdivided into roughly equivalent
matrilineal units, some of which are mere lineages while others, not necessarily larger, comprise more than one lineage. In the Pueblo area groups
of diminished membership attach themselves to those in a more flourishing
condition, thus furnishing historical instances of how originally distinct
unilateral groups may fuse.

Clans often become associated through common social or ceremonial
interests into major units, called phratries, or brotherhoods of clans. The
bond within the phratry may be relatively loose; that is, the association
may not imply more than an informal feeling of preferential friendship.
On the other hand, the phratry may be charged with the most important
functions. The phratry becomes a moiety (French *moitié*) when each clan
is recognized as part of one of two major units; but moieties also occur
without any subdivision, that is, the entire tribe may consist of two clans.

The moiety, or dual organization, appears typically in Australia, Melanesia and North America and is strangely lacking in Africa. In its typical
form the moiety is a clan of major extent, whence follows the rule of
exogamy. The moieties are complementary halves charged with reciprocal
duties and privileges, a phenomenon which is important in conjunction
with kinship rules. Given two exogamous halves, an individual's father is
in one and his mother in the other; hence he connects with one moiety the
rules regulating his behavior to maternal kin and with the complementary

moiety the conduct he owes to his paternal relatives. Since etymologically moiety means merely a half, it may properly be used whenever a tribe is correspondingly divided into groups other than clans. Thus the Pawnee and eastern Pueblos have ceremonial moieties not connected with exogamy; and the Todas of India have endogamous moieties.

The looser form of phratry is clearly but a secondary combination of clans. But when the phratry or the exogamous moiety has definite functions, the problem arises whether it may not be the primary unit from which clans arose by segmentation. The alternative is to postulate a later association of clans into a few major units. Both processes have occurred at different times. In some parts of the world overgrown clans split into seceding bodies; yet so long as a sense of kinship persists, the parent group and its off-shoots continue to form a larger functional unit. On the other hand, distinct clans have merged into a larger body, as in the fusion of two or more lineages among the Hopi.

Lewis H. Morgan was so much impressed with the intrinsic oddity of a unilateral alignment of kin that he postulated a single origin for the idea —in striking contravention of his general evolutionistic philosophy, which favored the multiplication of similar phenomena in diverse regions through some immanent social law. Morgan's theory as to the clan, which he called gens, implied several ideas. The family, he believed, was a recent development from a primeval state of promiscuity progressively tempered by reformatory steps. One of the major reforms was the institution of the exogamous clan, which barred marriage of siblings and also of more remote kindred within the clan. Finally, Morgan accepted the popular belief in the biological harmfulness of consanguine marriages; he contended that a tribe which eliminated this possibility by a clan system ipso facto would have a better chance of survival than its rivals, and that the advantages accruing from it would lead to its rapid dissemination. He and his followers assumed the priority of the clan over the family, although they did not put the clan at the beginning of social evolution. Among the arguments adduced were the kinship terminologies of various peoples, which were said to be explicable solely on the basis of the supposed sequence.

The distribution of unilateral systems does not bear out these hypotheses. The clan is a widespread but far from universal phenomenon and is absent from some of the rudest marginal peoples, such as the Andamanese pygmies, the Ona and Yahgan of southernmost America, the unequivocally simple peoples of the Mackenzie area, of Washington, Oregon, Nevada and Utah. On the other hand, the family is of virtually universal significance: whether the father is the putative or actual progenitor, socially there is always a male provider for the household, a differential tie between this functional father, his spouse or spouses, and her or their offspring. A possible exception is found in some Oceanian islands, where the hypertrophied practise of adoption sometimes leads to doubt as to whether a child belongs socially to one or the other set of parents; whatever the ultimate interpretation of these facts may be, they are extremely rare and appear in communities far too complex to be regarded as samples of primeval mankind. In the large and culturally diversified area, such as America north of Mexico, the rudest peoples lack clans; unilateral systems are generally associated with farming tribes and exceptionally complex societies of hunters, such as the Tlingit of northern British Columbia. In Siberia equivalent findings appear; the simple Chukchi and Koryak are clanless and have kinship terminologies which in no way suggest a pristine unilateralism; but the Yakut and other Turkic peoples, the felt making, iron smelting pastoral nomads of the area, are organized into rigid patrilineal clans and phratries. On both continents unilateral systems appear as later grafts on an earlier family organization.

In Australia, where clans generally coexist with the family, the same conclusion emerges from another line of argument. All individuals are here ranged in classes whose social behavior toward one another is fixed. A man treats the entire group of his real and potential fathers-in-law according to the same pattern determined by the kinship term he applies to all of them indiscriminately. Apparently such classificatory usage militates against the family principle. But social conduct maintains distinctions ignored in nomenclature. A man owes duties of the same kind to all his fathers-in-law, but the husband of his wife's own mother may claim differential treatment; the man is potential mate to a bevy of mothers' brothers' daughters, but if possible he espouses the daughter of his own mother's own brother. A distinction is thus systematically drawn between the next of kin and those more remotely related, and the true family is segregated from the rest of the camp. The most important unit in daily life is that composed of a woman, her husband and the offspring he has fathered: it is the primary economic group and is likewise the one with the strongest sentimental bonds (Malinowski, Radcliffe-Brown, Warner).

The question of how the clan came to supplement the earlier family system may be answered conjecturally from a survey of clanless tribes, with attention directed toward potential germs of unilateral alignment. Such factors may be detected in the rules of residence, as described by Tylor, and of inheritance. Newly married couples reside either with the husband's or with the wife's parents or wherever they please. Simple clanless tribes like the Yurok of northwestern California practise local exogamy from a sense that all fellow villagers are likely ultimately to be blood kindred, and the residence is theoretically patrilocal. The men therefore bring wives from other villages, thus creating the core of what under favorable conditions might blossom into a full fledged paternal lineage; and two or more such unilateral groups would form a typical clan. The Yurok never attained that condition because of two contradictory features. Residence was not absolutely patrilocal; if a man failed to pay an adequate bride price, he had to serve for his wife in her village and was thus lost to his own potential lineage. Equally significant was the lack of a unifying designation for the nascent lineage. The family is an intrinsically loose unit, because as the children grow up they inevitably found new families; and although in the agricultural communities of the Old World there are extended families formed of blood brothers with their wives and descendants, the girls are inevitably lost to their family on marriage. The lineage or clan, however, operates on the principle of once a member always a member, usually by affixing to each member an unmistakable and permanent badge in the form of a name. Hence these unilateral groups never lose their constituents, ticketed as they are by their group name. Even in China persons with similar surnames do not marry, a phenomenon plausibly interpreted as a survival of clan exogamy.

Matrilocal residence would correspondingly create a core of a maternal kin. Where, as among the Hopi, all women bring their husbands to the bride's mother's home, a woman is united with her sisters, her and their daughters and the off-spring of these daughters. If such coresidents affix a common label to all the children born in such a household, irrespective of sex, a maternal lineage is at once set off from the rest of the community.

Not merely coresidence but common property interests may be invoked in this connection. As soon as property of a certain type is highly valued, its transmission tends to become regulated in a definite way. Even simple hunting populations recognize such exclusive claims; for example, Washo families own clumps of pine nut trees and Veddas reserve to themselves special tracts of land. Here the auxiliary principle of the sexual division of labor helps to segregate the core of a lineage. Since women are responsible for the garnering of wild vegetable food, a woman claiming a patch for exclusive use will exploit it with her daughters, who automatically become her heiresses. Correspondingly the male core of a paternal lineage is segregated by the phenomenon observed by Speck among the northeastern Algonquin, the prerogative of hunting in a delimited tract. A common name for the children, male and female, who are associated with such a territory would define a true lineage.

This question leads directly to the problem of the relationship between matrilineal and patrilineal descent. Lowie and Schmidt, who derives the maternal clans from the horicultural activities of women, treat paternal and maternal clans as having a distinct origin. Kroeber and Olson, on the other hand, do not postulate any necessary sequence of the two but see no difficulty in the change from one form of descent to the other. To earlier anthropologists the priority of "mother right" was a foregone conclusion; in the irregular conditions imputed to early cultures paternity would be unknowable, while the bond between mother and child could never be ignored. But primitives are often not at all interested in knowing who is the begetter of a child. Thus in south Africa the purchaser of a bride ipso facto becomes the social father of her future children, whether these are conceived out of wedlock or not, and among the Todas of India legal paternity is determined by a purely conventional ritualistic act.

Likewise among patrilineal peoples the avunculate, that is, the assignment of significant functions to the maternal uncle, who may exercise parental authority, is interpreted by the earlier anthropologists as a survival from an earlier matrilineal condition. But such avuncular privileges can be interpreted in several ways involving no such assumption. The specific powers of a maternal uncle are often balanced by those of the paternal aunt; and when paternal kin are charged with special functions in a matrilineal people, as, for example, among the Crows or Hopi, an earlier patrilineal reckoning could just as plausibly be invoked to explain the facts. Moreover the avunculate may often be the effect not of maternal descent but of matrilocal residence which has never ripened into a full fledged maternal clan organization.

The clan, although sometimes a wholly secular institution, may be strongly charged with religious values. Thus according to Laufer the older form of Chinese ancestor worship probably consisted in the adoration of the heroic founder of a clan, who was supposed to watch over his descendants. Primitive peoples frequently have totemic names for their clans, and while emotional associations with the plant or animal eponym may be tenuous, they often assume deeper significance; in Australia some of the most serious rituals are linked with the clan.

The unilateral system rarely occurs on the lowest levels but makes its first appearance in somewhat more complex cultures, persisting in pre-Columbian Peru with a definite political organization and in the backward portions of Europe, such as the Balkans, in the most recent period. Founded on kinship, like the family, but capable of marshaling far greater forces, it made or enhanced cohesiveness until it came into opposition with the potentially still wider principle of local contiguity.

Associations in a measure paved the way for recognition of the principle of local contiguity. In simpler cultures individuals are not ranged solely according to either kinship or local ties; as Schurtz first pointed out, they unite in associations according to sex, age and religious and social interests. An Australian boy is not merely a member of his family and totemic clan; he joins, possibly at about seven years of age, the group of bachelors, who dwell apart from the rest of the camp and whose example exerts henceforth a deep influence on his behavior. As he grows older he advances to higher status by a series of initiation rites, in some tribes automatically becoming with age a member of the gerontocracy. The importance most primitive tribes attach to the notion of seniority appears in the widespread distinction drawn between elder and younger brother and sister, which is not a purely terminological difference but reflects differences in attitude and conduct. Thus the levirate is a common custom, but often it is only the younger brother who is allowed to wed his elder's widow. Among the Yakut of Siberia a woman is forbidden to show herself before her father-in-law and all her husband's elder kinsmen. Relative age, in other words, determines status and so does sex. In a Yakut hut definite spaces are apportioned to the male and to the female inmates. Among the Andaman Islanders a double form of segregation appears; married couples live apart from the unmarried camp mates, who are divided into a bachelors' and a spinsters' group at opposite ends of the settlement.

The Masai of east Africa demonstrate in the most striking fashion the inadequacy of the older view that primitive communities are made up solely of clans. At least as important as their clan system, even in the regulation of sex life, is associational alignment. Every male individual is either an uncircumcised boy, an unmarried warrior or a married man, and equivalent grades divide the women. The bachelors occupy a separate kraal with the single girls. What is more, the individuals jointly initiated by circumcision form lifelong groups with fixed mutual obligations and rights. North American tribes outside the Mackenzie, plateau and basin areas exhibit an almost infinite variety of organization. There are societies of rain makers and doctors in the southwest; the Plains have military organizations, which in some tribes are divided into age companies as well as all sorts of ceremonial fraternities; in the northwest common hereditary guardian spirits lead to a regrouping of individuals during the season of the winter festival. Melanesia has ghost societies and men's clubs, and Africa, especially in the west, is honeycombed with age classes, men's and women's societies and secret fraternities dispensing justice and sometimes controlling all public life. Among more advanced peoples the Chinese are conspicuous for the inordinate number of their organizations; there are religious and political societies, trade unions, merchant guilds which have perfected the code of business life, mutual benefit associations for policing the crops of a village or from organizing a hare hunt.

Although associations, territorial aggregates, families and clans have been treated largely as separate entities, they are often intricately and intimately interlocked. Hopi fraternities are in a sense religious associations; yet the higher offices in them descend preferentially in a maternal lineage, which thus constitutes the core of the group. Similarly, although Crow military clubs barred no one on principle, men tended to affiliate themselves with a society previously joined by some kinsmen. The Masai blacksmiths form a spatially and socially segregated pariah caste into which no Masai of ordinary standing will marry; they thus represent an inferior occupational subdivision, but affiliation may not be escaped by giving up the trade—the group is a hereditary class of outcasts over and above its association with a despised calling. Such occupational castes are relatively common in east Africa, blacksmiths and tanners usually ranking as the lowest. Considering the absolute dependence of the natives on their metallurgists for tools and weapons, this position of the smiths, who in Siberia are treated with the utmost esteem, is puzzling. It may be explained by the fact that useful arts are often practised by peaceful folk who readily fall prey to more warlike tribes and are then degraded to a lower level. For example, when the cattle breeding aristocracy of Ruanda, interested in no useful occupation except animal husbandry, looks with contempt on the older farming populations, which perform all the other necessary labors, it links occupational classes with fixed hereditary differences in rank. Among the Masai the warriors form simultaneously a standing army and a status class.

There are infinitely varied ways in which a society may combine units of different types. The coordination or subordination is achieved with varying degrees of elegance, which can be appraised, however, only by the assumption of an arbitrary subjective standard. An individual who belongs simultaneously to two units may be confronted with a conflict of loyalties. In primitive matrilineal societies lineage and family affiliation are likely to clash. A Trobriander or a Tsimshian is legally bound to transmit his most valued possessions to a uterine nephew, yet attachment to his own sons, in a social if not in a physiological sense, impels him to favor them to the detriment of his matrilineal kinsmen. As Malinowski has shown, such conflicts between love and duty may precipitate tragedy among simpler peoples. On higher levels the possibilities for antagonism do not disappear. Attachment to a religious body, an economic class, an idealistic fraternity, may even evoke revolt against the state itself, as is illustrated by the attitude of a patriotic German Catholic during Bismarck's Kulturkampf, of the I. W. W. in the United States and of conscientious objectors to war in any militaristic country.

As Vinogradoff has pointed out, the claim of the modern state to absolute sovereignty within its territorial limits is comparatively recent in Europe. A new Scandinavian king traveled from province to province in order to gain the support of local groups. The Althing, the assembly of Iceland, passed laws but was impotent to enforce them. On the continent compulsory arbitration, self-help and outlawry preceded coercive measures. Under Charlemagne the crown executed its own decrees only in specific cases. In recent times the absolute supremacy of the state has become a favorite dogma, but practise often fails to tally with ideology. The constitutional rights of Negroes do not become realities in Mississippi any more than the Eighteenth Amendment achieved automatic recognition through the sovereign federal government. The contrast appeared more glaringly in imperial China. The emperor was in theory the vice regent of Heaven, hence the source of all power and the rightful claimant to implicit obedience. Actually the viceroys of provinces were virtually independent monarchs; the emperor was hedged in by the codified law, and his official acts were subject to criticism by a board of censors, so that imposition of new taxes was likely to meet with determined opposition.

There are many parallel forms of social structure but few instances of far reaching duplication through stage after stage in diverse areas; there is little evidence of complex laws of sequence. Economic conditions limit the character of developments; highly organized states, for example, are hardly consistent with the life of hunters, and modern individualism tends to destroy the traditional bonds of the clan or the family, but beyond this it is difficult to generalize. . . .

That societies should dichotomize on the basis of sex or split up into lesser bodies of uninitiated and initiated bachelors and married elders seems a priori plausible, and abstract psychological arguments have been adduced to show how natural it is to form secret societies. Siberian tribes seem to have been predisposed to such developments. There women were generally rated as inferior, had disabilities as to property rights and were even spatially set off in the household; notwithstanding their lower legal status, however, they were not excluded from public and ceremonial festivities, like their Australian and Melanesian sisters, but took an active part in them. Among the Yakuts, for example, female shamans ranked higher than male shamans; and in the great kumiss festivals women participated freely. Siberia is preeminently the land of shamanism, which has elsewhere led to the formation of secret societies; yet no such developments occur throughout this vast area. The only safe inference is that social phenomena pursue no fixed sequences, or at least that their sequences are so intricate as to elude perception.

The Family as a Social Unit

A FAMILY IS "THE GROUP OF PERSONS CONSISTING OF THE PARENTS AND their children, whether actually living together or not" (Murray's dictionary). The concept may be enlarged to embrace "those who are nearly connected by blood or affinity," but such expansion makes for greater vagueness. Adhering to the narrower definition, let us ask whether human society must a priori be constituted of family units. The answer is negative. There are sexually reproducing species without a semblance of family life, hence the segregation of husband, wife, and child into a distinct group remains to be empirically demonstrated. As a matter of fact, the existence of such a unit in early man has been categorically denied by

From Lowie, "The Family as a Social Unit," *Papers of the Michigan Academy of Science, Arts and Letters,* Vol. XVIII (Ann Arbor: University of Michigan Press, 1933), pp. 53-69.

many writers. In the beginning, we are told, was promiscuity—sexual license unchecked by any restraint. The earliest inhibitions prevented interbreeding of parent and child; they were followed by interdicts against the union of siblings (brother and sister); and so by a series of reformatory movements humanity finally attained the giddy heights of Victorian monogamy, at least in theory.

Unfortunately, we can know nothing directly about the sex life of man's immediate precursor, and a comparison of primate behavior, though definitely ruling out certain assumptions, offers a minimum of positive fact for the reconstruction of ancestral habits. A zoölogist, Mr. Gerrit S. Miller, Jr., has recently brought together what is known. He has proved that, contrary to a widespread misconception, virtually all the primates observed lack a rutting season. Accordingly, it is in the highest degree improbable that man's immediate forerunner mated seasonally. Like his fellow-primates, he was presumably ready to indulge in amours whenever an occasion arose. Furthermore, it seems that recent human aberrations have their counterparts among primates, and their potentiality may thus well be a heritage from a fairly remote past.[1]

From available information, however, we can gather nothing to test the theory of early human promiscuity. Indeed, the field observations on the nearest anthropoids, chimpanzees and gorillas, are indecisive and at times contradictory as to the traits of the same species. Reichenow, for example, credits the gorilla with monogamous habits, while Akeley cautiously suggests the possibility of polygamy. "The truth is," he wisely adds, "that people know little about the habits of the gorilla."[2]

Yerkes, with exemplary restraint, makes the following statement: "Our tentative inference is that both monogamy and polygamy exist in one or another or all of the anthropoid types and that in all probability both relationships are discoverable in each of the manlike apes. With many misgivings we propose as order of increasing probability of monogamic relation: gibbon and siamang, gorilla, orang-outan, chimpanzee. Much more systematic, thorough, and critical investigation than has heretofore been conducted will be essential to discover the truth. Indicated as points of contrast among the three types of great ape are temporary monogamous or polygamous relations in the orang-outan, relatively permanent monogamous and possibly also polygamous relations in the chimpanzee, and in

[1] Miller, G. S., "Some Elements of Sexual Behavior in Primates and Their Possible Influence on the Beginnings of Human Social Development," *Journal of Mammalogy*, 9 (1928):273-292; *idem*, "The Primate Basis of Human Sexual Behavior," *The Quarterly Review of Biology*, 6 (1931):379-410. After writing this paper, I find that Miller's inferences are challenged by Dr. S. Zuckerman in *Social Life of Monkeys and Apes* (New York, 1932). The matter is one for zoölogists to decide.

[2] Akeley, Carl E., *In Brightest Africa* (Garden City, 1925), p. 247.

the gorilla a patriarchal family, with polygamy presumably in the mountain species and monogamy, possibly, in the lowland species."[3]

If we know nothing more positive about existing species, any dogmatic conclusion as to the behavior of a hypothetical, extinct ancestral type seems rash indeed.

On one point, however, we can be certain. Whatever may have been the mating habits of this or that precursor of *Homo sapiens,* no believer in evolution can deny a stage of promiscuity somewhere along the line, that is, of promiscuity in the technical sense of socially unrestrained lust. Anthropologically, there is no "index of promiscuity," calculated by dividing the number of actual mates, regardless of kinship, by the number of physically possible ones. From this angle, it is a question of "all or nothing." Is carnal desire checked in some of its manifestations by the disapproval of the group? If it is, there is no promiscuity; otherwise, there is. Take the case of a male gorilla which Akeley found with three females. The point is not whether the male cohabited with all three females. It is rather this: Assuming two of them to be his daughters, would the attitude of other gorillas be one of indifference or not? The situation is not inconceivable even on the human level. A widespread tale of Great Basin and Western Plains Indians revolves about this very theme. The trickster by his wiles gains access to his own daughters. In the story, however, such behavior arouses intense moral condemnation. Now, I, for one, fail to find evidence for such a social consciousness in either Koehler's[4] or other data from the infrahuman plane. If this interpretation holds, the anthropoids are promiscuous. On the other hand, no known group of *Homo sapiens* is indifferent to the sex behavior of its constituent members. Wherever evidence is adequate, matings are judged—outlawed, reprobated, condoned, accepted, or definitely sanctioned. The definitely sanctioned forms of mating may be termed "marriage," and from them evolves the family. Nowhere are fornication and marriage submerged in an undifferentiated category of animal-like "copulation."

A chasm thus yawns between *Homo sapiens* and the chimpanzee or gorilla. At what stage of evolution, then, was the leap taken from unjudged to judged sex behavior? I do not know. I venture a guess that Neanderthal man showed some discrimination. I so conjecture because he demonstrably had a social tradition as to craftsmanship, and it thus seems probable to me that he had likewise evolved norms of social conduct. I refuse even to guess whether Heidelberg man, Eoanthropus, Peking man, and Pithecanthropus displayed equal fastidiousness. I am content to believe that, somewhere between the more remote anthropoid ancestor and the

[3] Yerkes, Robert M. and Ada W., *The Great Apes, a Study of Anthropoid Life* (New Haven and London, 1929), p. 542 f.
[4] *The Mentality of Apes* (New York, 1925).

more immediate hominid ancestor whose descendants constitute geologically recent humanity, there was a stage of uncontrolled sexual license.

I am not sure whether I agree or disagree with Mr. Miller as to the distance of this stage. He offers the argument that living samples of men are specialized survivors and that many races have become extinct. Hence, he infers, "the search among these specialized existing peoples for a race or tribe living under social conditions that represent anything closely resembling an unmodified reflection of man's primitive mentality can have little chance of success."[5] Here everything hinges on the meaning of the terms "man," "closely," "primitive mentality." I not merely admit but contend that Andamanese, Fuegians, Australians, and Chukchi tell us nothing definite about the mentality of Piltdown or Peking man. I emphatically insist that no one primitive group represents the first hominid's mentality in unmodified form. But if such highly specialized groups as Andamanese, Australians, and others, without exception exercise social control of sex life, then such control does not date back to yesterday nor, say, to 4000 B.C., but, presumably, to a period embracing the earliest samples of *Homo sapiens,* even though some of the races of this species are irrecoverably removed from direct observation.

Time does not permit detailed consideration of more than one recent human society. I shall select the Australians, whose anatomical inferiority and crudeness in the arts of life have made them a favorite starting point for speculative historians on the origins of the family, religion, and what not. Moreover, they have been credited with a form of sex life that might be viewed as intermediate between promiscuity and obligatory monogamy, viz., "group marriage." This institution has been defined as the non-preferential mating of a group of men with a group of women. It would not represent promiscuity, inasmuch as Australians would never tolerate unions of brothers and sisters. But anyone who favors the theory of promiscuity in Aurignacian or Mousterian times would naturally regard that mixture of polyandry and polygyny involved in group marriage as a step toward increasing control of mating. On the other hand, so long as a whole group of men mated indiscriminately with a group of women, the family would remain non-existent as a social unit.

In the interests of concreteness I shall base my statement on what Professor Radcliffe-Brown describes as the clearest available account of Australian conditions, Warner's report on the Murngin living west of the Gulf of Carpentaria.[6] This picture I shall eke out with supplementary data on the Australians and shall then proceed to cull relevant data from the literature on other groups. The questions asked will include the following:

[5] Miller, G. S., "The Primate Basis of Human Sexual Behavior," *The Quarterly Review of Biology,* 6 (1931):400.

[6] Warner, Wm. Lloyd, "Morphology and Functions of the Australian Murngin Type of Kinship," *American Anthropologist,* 32 (1930):207-256.

Is there a form of marriage as distinguished from cohabitation? If so, what are the social relations of husband and wife? Of siblings? Of parent and child?

To begin with the Australians, no Murngin is free to mate with whom he pleases, and in marriage he is always expected to obtain the daughter of his maternal uncle. Failing such a one, a substitute of equivalent kinship status would be sought, for example, the daughter of a mother's male cousin. Potential spouses may be betrothed prenatally. To be sure, a man wants the maximum number of wives safely procurable, but they are never chosen at random. In order to make social intercourse possible for them at all, Australians always range individuals into kinship classes. So, even when the Murngin raid a hostile camp the kidnaped women are allotted to men standing to them in the socially approved relationship. Similarly, adultery is almost always with a cousin of the prescribed category. By a natural extension of these ideas, which rest on the social equivalence of siblings of the same sex, a brother inherits his elder brother's widow, and often the several wives of a polygynous husband are sisters or quasi-sisters.

Unquestionably there are "wrong" marriages among the Murngin, as among ourselves. Yet within certain degrees prohibitions are absolute and, apparently, never flouted. In other cases strong disapproval is voiced: a man who would carry on an intrigue with his "sister's daughter"—actually perhaps his third cousin's daughter—would be compared to a dog, and the woman would be liable to a severe drubbing.

Moreover, within the range of licensed unions a distinct ideal may be noted. A husband may have several wives, but he ought not to seek amours with other women; and a wife is normally expected to content herself with a single mate, her husband. The social relations of spouses, furthermore, assume definite rights and duties. A wife gathers wild fruits and small game; the man supplies fish, turtle, porpoise, dugong. Sentimentally, common devotion to the children constitutes a bond; and even apart from that factor indications are not lacking of an attachment reminiscent of romantic love.

In all this there is not the faintest suggestion of either promiscuity or group marriage. The parental relationship is extended so that a woman's sister may help her suckle two babies; and, in general, a child looks to a maternal aunt for food and care. This, however, develops quite naturally from the practice of sororal polygyny. But, though the principle of sibling equivalence holds, the immediate family group is distinguished. Thus, a childless husband observes food taboos, which are lifted with paternity, "but the child must be his own, not that of a brother." (The term "own" in this context will be discussed later.) It is the father who determines the type of initiation for his son, passes on the right to certain dances, and teaches the ceremonial routine. In short, a man takes a differential interest in "his" children.

The Murngin thus recognize a family unit, but that does not mean that it is *our* family pattern. A contrast at once appears with regard to siblings. Brother and sister can never be on terms of easy familiarity. A brother never sleeps in the same camp with her, and neither may address the other. Associated with such taboos we find the attitude of mutual helpfulness that to us seems altogether intelligible. A brother will give presents to his sister for her son and husband. Two brothers coöperate in economic pursuits and have a sense of joint ownership of property. This naturally in a measure embraces wives, but with such qualifications as to exclude unchecked communism even between true brothers. No younger brother appropriates a sister-in-law without permission. The elder brother preëmptively claims his maternal uncle's daughters. When he has thus acquired two wives, the younger man has a strong *moral* claim on the next oldest sister of the household, and her father may urge the husband to waive his legal prerogative. Even here there is thus definite customary law, not license. But a brother's attitude cannot be the same as ours in a society which makes him look to his older brother as the provider of a mate, either after or during his lifetime.

The family picture would be further modified by the taboo, universal in Australia, forbidding all social intercourse between a man and his mother-in-law. Yet, notwithstanding the lavish use of such kinship terms as "father," "brother," etc., to embrace fairly remote kinsfolk, the immediate family group is clearly separated from the rest of the community. A prospective husband tries, first of all, to marry his "own" mother's "own" brother's "own" daughter; and the uncle provokes resentment if he marries off a daughter to a remote nephew.

We have seen that a married man's social status depends on his having "own" children. This distinction between near and remote kin of the same category holds throughout. Remote "brothers" ambush and slay one another, or at least suspect one another as potential adulterers; but between true brothers there is implicit trust and unfailing devotion. So in periods of ceremonial license distant, not "own," brothers participate in the temporary exchange of wives. Thus, at every step we stumble on clear-cut evidence for the aboriginal feeling that relationship to the next of kin is a thing *sui generis*. The resulting family is a bilateral unit since, from the child's angle, relations are maintained with both parental sides.

The condition described by Warner is not unique, but typical for the island continent. Malinowski's synthetic review[7] of the earlier literature and Radcliffe-Brown's more recent summary[8] leave no doubt on that point. Throughout Australia the nearest equivalent of our polical unit, the state,

[7] Malinowski, Bronislaw, *The Family among the Australian Aborigines; a Sociological Study* (London, 1913).

[8] Radcliffe-Brown, A. R., "The Social Organization of Australian Tribes" (Oceania Monographs, No. 1, 1931), esp. pp. 4, 6, 11 ff., 103, 107.

is a localized "paternal lineage" or "horde" owning and exploiting in common a definite territory. Such a group embraces as a permanent core a number of brothers with their sons, sons' sons, and so forth. The women of the group normally come from another similarly constituted horde. Of the children the boys remain, acquiring from early childhood that intimate economic knowledge of the hereditary land which is a prerequisite to survival. The girls marry outside their horde, so that female children are only temporary constituents of the group into which they are born. Within this clearly defined horde, however, the aborigines recognize a lesser social unit, to wit, the individual family of parents and children. "The important function of the family," says Radcliffe-Brown, "is that it provides for the feeding and bringing up of the children. It is based on the coöperation of man and wife, the former providing the flesh food and the latter the vegetable food, so that quite apart from the question of children a man without a wife is in an unsatisfactory position since he has no one to supply him regularly with vegetable food, to provide his firewood, and so on. This economic aspect of the family is a most important one and it is partly this that explains Australian polygyny. I believe that in the minds of the natives themselves this aspect of marriage, i.e. its relation to subsistence, is of greatly more importance than the fact that man and wife are sexual partners. . . . sexual relations between a man and a woman do not constitute marriage in Australia any more than they do in our own society."

I believe that the picture our foremost authorities give of Australian conditions may be generalized for recent races of man. Twelve years ago I wrote: "The bilateral family is . . . an absolutely universal unit of human society."[9] These are strong words, but I still regard them as essentially correct. In only one area of the world am I able to detect phenomena tending to qualify this view. In parts of Oceania, where adoption plays an extraordinary rôle, children are reported to divide their time more or less evenly between two homes, thus participating simultaneously in two family groups. I have recently taken cognizance of such facts, writing: "In this extreme form the custom [of adoption] inevitably modifies the principle of the universality of the individual family."[10] Let us note in passing that the exceptions occur in highly sophisticated horticultural societies which cannot possibly be regarded as illustrating primeval usage; and that the exceptions rest on a custom which by definition is derivative.

The general prominence of the family cannot, of course, be demonstrated without passing in review one primitive society after another, which space does not permit. I should like, however, to point out one rather significant North American phenomenon. If we examine the kinship systems of the

[9] Lowie, R. H., *Primitive Society* (New York, 1920), p. 78.
[10] Lowie, R. H., "Adoption, Primitive," in *Encyclopædia of the Social Sciences,* 1 (1930):459-460.

rudest peoples in North America, the purely hunting tribes devoid of complex political, social, and ceremonial organization, we find that almost uniformly they distinguish in speech the immediate members of the family from the more remote kin. That is to say, while the Australians recognize the distinction in behavior, the simpler North American aborigines go so far as to express the sense of the difference in their vocabularies: a father is not only treated differently from an uncle, but is designated by a separate term; similarly, a brother is not included in the same term as a cousin; and so forth. The fact that the majority of non-horticultural tribes from the Arctic to northern California and Nevada fail to merge these relatives strongly suggests that the family unit is clearly recognized precisely on the lowest cultural level north of Mexico. It appears as though the family enjoyed undisputed ascendancy at a very early period, its significance being subsequently modified, though never abrogated, by other forms of organization. Thus, in Australia the partial equivalence of siblings of the same sex readily qualifies the character of the individual family, though its persistence is now demonstrated beyond cavil.

Terms for social units, such as "family," have misleading suggestiveness; therefore I shall try to indicate the empirical range of the data properly coming under this head. Let me first explain that the biological family is not necessarily identical with its social equivalent. A clever writer has recently credited me with a belief in the social omnipresence of the *biological* family. She contrasts with this the saner view of Radcliffe-Brown, who, while taking the biological group as the chief point of reference in a treatment of social organization, "gives due weight to more complex developments characteristic of many primitive societies."[11] Actually, there is no conflict; what is particularly important, both Radcliffe-Brown and I emphatically warn against attaching too much weight to the biological aspect of the unit. "Bilateral" and "biological" are not synonymous terms. When an Australian speaks of his "own" father, he does not necessarily mean his begetter at all, but the adult male whom he preëminently associated from infancy with a certain emotional behavior, economic activities on behalf of the household, and so forth. Elsewhere I have pointed out, on Rivers' authority, that among the Toda of southern India polyandry often makes the determination of paternity very difficult. But the natives do not care at all about biological paternity: that husband who performs a certain rite during his wife's pregnancy becomes *legal* father of all children borne by the woman until another husband goes through the same ceremony. "Biological paternity is completely disregarded, for a man long dead is considered the father of a child provided no other man has perfomed the essential rite."[12] So, in some South African tribes a man claims as his own legal issue the offspring of a duly purchased wife, even if she has for years

[11] Mead, Margaret, "Family, Primitive," *ibid.*, 6 (1931):65-67.
[12] Lowie, R. H., *Primitive Society*, p. 48.

been living in adulterous union with a lover. What counts, then, is not the biological but the legal kinship. The omnipresence of the bilateral family, then, means this: Virtually everywhere a male, who is not necessarily the procreator, and a female, who is not necessarily the bearer, maintain preferential relations to a given child or number of children, thus forming a distinct unit within any major social group.

The fact that substitutions for biological parental relations are possible and even relatively frequent is precisely one of the most outstanding revelations which ethnography has to offer to her sister science, psychology. For it sweeps away once and for all the assumption of a paternal *instinct*. In its place we must recognize a much vaguer tendency of adult males to form an attachment to infants of their species.

Toda and Bantu indifference to the identity of the procreator suffices to mark off their conception of the family from that traditional in Western civilization. To these natives the insistence on recognizing as one's children only those duly begotten by oneself must appear as ludicrously irrelevant physiological pedantry. Appraisal of the children's status may rest on quite different considerations. Among Northwest Californian Indians the equivalent of the Occidental bastard is the boy whose father failed to pay the customary bride-price, for with that blot on his escutcheon he is never permitted to enter the men's club house.

Socially, however, the family pattern is only moderately altered by the lack of interest in physiological bonds. For, in the examples cited, one male simply supersedes another as the embodiment of the paternal principle. In other words, a social tie of our own parent-child relationship category remains. That category may be more definitely affected by a maternal clan organization. Where such an institution occurs, the bond with the father and his kin is still recognized, but all children are, *for certain purposes,* reckoned as of kin only with the mother and, specifically, bear the name of *her* clan, not their father's. In this way may be set up a series of sentiments, of legal rights and duties, that come to compete with the parental ties and even enter into open conflict with them. By so doing they also inevitably clash with the family as an autonomous social unit. This appears most clearly where the avunculate holds sway. There the maternal uncle usurps, according to our notions, many paternal functions, and, correlatively, it is his uterine nephews and nieces that often stand to him in a relationship *we* regard as filial. Thus, he, and not the father, may dispose of a girl's hand; he, and not the father, will give certain kinds of instruction to boys; and, though in some patrilineal African tribes, a man's son inherits his *father's* wives, barring only his own mother, certain matrilineal American and Melanesian groups permit a nephew to marry the widow of his mother's brother. To take a concrete case, a Dobu in Melanesia cannot bequeath his name, land, status, or fruit trees to his son; all of them are automatically inherited by a sister's son. A man may indeed teach his son what he knows of magical formulae; but to his uterine nephew he *must* convey such knowledge.[13]

Nevertheless, the sociological father is not abolished by avuncular customs. In the very region from which my last example is taken Professor Malinowski has demonstrated the depth of attachment linking father and son. The lurid and tragic conflict between paternal sentiment and avuncular duty has never been more vividly set forth.[14]

Another condition modifying the pattern of family life may be generalized under the head of "sex dichotomy," which manifests itself in many ways. Among the Australian Murngin we found the rather widespread custom of brother-sister avoidance, which at once precludes one of the most typical forms of family intimacy in our civilization. But we also saw that such usage does *not* snap the bond which links siblings together: brother and sister may not chat together, but they do aid each other, and the brother is keenly sensible of certain duties toward his sisters. Another type of dichotomy separates husband and wife. In many communities, for example, in South America and Oceania, spouses never eat together—an arrangement almost inconceivable to us. Yet the Banks Islanders of Melanesia go further. Among them virtually every adult male has bought his way into the men's club house, which is strictly tabooed to women, while the men not only lounge and work, but eat and sleep there, paying intermittent visits to their wives. Notwithstanding this institution, the family still holds together, so far as a husband exercises definite rights over his wife and is bound to her and the children by fixed duties.[15] Generally, we may say that the universal sex dichotomy as to occupation is precisely a factor that fosters the family unit, for such division of labor, with its frequently correlated part-time separation as to companionship, obviously accrues to the advantage of the common household.

One other significant feature must be mentioned as modifying family relations. There may be segregation by age or status as well as by sex, or both forms of cleavage may be combined. Among the Masai of East Africa the bachelors occupy a separate hut, where they are joined by the young girls of the village with whom they consort apparently *ad libitum*. This is promiscuity in the popular but not in the scientific sense. For with meticulous care the Masai abstain from sex relations both with kinswomen and with their prospective wives, i.e. girls betrothed to them in infancy. And this once more accentuates the persistence of the family concept. For notwithstanding the license of the celibates' corral, it is definitely

[13] Fortune, Reo, *Sorcerers of Dobu; the Social Anthropology of the Dobu Islanders of the Western Pacific* (Routledge, 1931), p. 15.

[14] Malinowski, Bronislaw, *Crime and Custom in Savage Society* (London and New York, 1926).

[15] Rivers, W. H. R., *The History of Melanesian Society* (Cambridge, 1914), 1:60-143; Codrington, R. H., *The Melanesians: Studies in Their Anthropology and Folk-lore* (Oxford, 1891), p. 101 f.

expected that every youth and maiden settle down in marriage after they have had their fling. Premarital freedom is followed by regular family life.[16]

In other areas, for example, in parts of Australia, only the boys are separated from the married couples. Usually this takes place after an initiation ceremony, sometimes at the age of seven. Relatively young boys are thus to some extent liberated from parental influence and subjected to the precept and example of somewhat older members of their own generation. In Samoa the unmarried are segregated from married folk in distinct male and female groups. The bachelors cultivate the soil, cook for the masters of the several households, and perform necessary communal tasks. The female counterpart embraces widows and wives of commoners as well as spinsters, and seems to have grown out of the custom of having companions of the same age groups and older chaperons sleep with a chief's favorite daughter.[17] Again, among the Banks Islanders the men's club was divided into degrees, membership into each being acquired by purchase. Thus, there was a separation not merely of spouses, but of fathers and sons: normally a man would eat neither with his wife nor with his children, and a mother would be dissociated from her sons as soon as they had entered the club house, an act which was rarely deferred until adolescence.

I have thus not merely admitted but stressed the diversity of family patterns in recent human societies. This differentiation, however, virtually never militates against the principle that husband, wife, and child constitute a definite social unit set off from other like and unlike units in their community.

Lest the oddity of some savage arrangements make us lose our sense of perspective, it is well to recall historic changes in the concept of the "family" as held by civilized peoples. Certainly the Chinese are not lacking in a family sense, but it is coupled with notions foreign to us of wifely duty, of polygyny, and of concubinage. Scriptural patriarchs, too, were polygynous and concupiscent, but no one challenges the prominence of the family in Biblical times. Much nonsense is lavished nowadays on the destruction of the family by industrial civilization. Yet the legal ties between parent and child, husband and wife, are clearly recognized. What has happened is an alteration of the family ideals among large portions of our population. For better or worse, the change from rural to urban residence, the stress of economic conditions, an individualistic ideology, the partial abandonment of traditional religious doctrines have jointly affected the relationships involved in the family concept. In the latter half of the

[16] Merker, M., *Die Masai. Ethnographische Monographie eines ostafrikanischen Semitenvolkes* (Berlin, 1910), pp. 44, 84.

[17] Mead, Margaret, "Social Organization of Manua," *Bernice Pauahi Bishop Museum of Polynesian Ethnology and Natural History, Memoirs,* Bulletin 76 (1930): 14, 92 f.

eighteenth century Dr. Samuel Johnson, that paragon of Christian piety, laid it down as a principle that "wise married women don't trouble themselves about infidelity in their husbands." He considered a woman who should turn the tables on an erring husband as "very fit for a brothel." These ideas, I believe, are no longer universally held with equal fervor. What I should like to point out is that between the upholders of a double standard and the modern sex egalitarians the difference is roughly like the difference between either and the Murngin or Banks Islanders. Only those iconoclasts would fall outside the common practice who should consign infants to communal baby farming and who would not tolerate any but quite temporary sexual attachments. Such societies have indeed been reported with much extravagance of vituperation, but with great frugality of proof.

A few conclusions of general interest may be summarized:

1. We know nothing whatsoever about the sex behavior of the immediate forerunner of modern hominids except that it very probably conformed to the generalized primate norm. Specifically, if Mr. Miller's summary is trustworthy, this implies the lack of a rutting season.

2. Though we cannot picture the sexual life of the protohominid, we may be sure that there was a stage of promiscuity, i.e. of socially unchecked sex activity. For, by definition, social checks are a characteristic of culture; hence before there was a culture there was, in the scientific sense, promiscuity.

3. All the unequivocally rude tribes of the world—Andamanese, Bushmen, Australians, Fuegians, Paiute—have a violent reaction against incest with the closest kindred. It is, therefore, extremely probable that this sentiment is of great antiquity.

4. Nevertheless, I no longer believe, as I once did, that incest is *instinctively* objectionable to man. On the one hand, I am assured on good legal authority that the criminal calendar of Western nations shows relatively many instances of paternal lust directed against daughters; and if only one tenth of psychoanalytic evidence is rated valid, the Oedipus complex remains as a factor to be reckoned with. As regards siblings, we have at least three historic cases in which the supposed instinct was deliberately set aside—ancient Egypt, Peru, Hawaii. In each of these aristocratic societies no mate was considered more appropriate for a ruler than his own sister, the only one, evidently, who fully shared his illustrious pedigree.

The aversion to incest is, therefore, best regarded as a primeval cultural adaptation which certain individuals potentially or actually override in all societies and which certain sophisticated societies have expressly disregarded in the interests of an inflated sense of aristocratic lineage.

5. There is no parental instinct. No man can know instinctively that he is the begetter of an infant presented by his wife. Demonstrably, savage

men in many and diverse societies utterly and deliberately ignore the question of physiological relationship while emphasizing that of sociological kinship. The maternal sentiment seems to rest on a firmer basis. Actually, economic pressure or the desire to avoid the shame of an illegitimate birth may be stronger. Among the Murngin, "Sometimes a mother kills her newborn babe because it has followed too closely to her others and she has not enough milk to feed it." Here, as well as in many other savage communities, the superstitious objection to twins invariably leads to the immediate killing of at least one of them.

What is of course universal in the interests of group survival is a generic interest of adults in children. This sentiment, however, as we have just seen, is not manifested by all members of the species uniformly, but may be ignored by the superior force of utilitarian rationalism or ideological irrationalism.

6. Every known society distinguishes between mere cohabitation and that socially approved form of relatively permanent cohabitation known as marriage. It may not be superfluous to point out that, as there is social fatherhood without the notion of procreation, so there is frequently social wifehood without physiological relations. A man may inherit a woman so old that she is unfit or undesirable from a sexual point of view; nevertheless, she would engage in the feminine occupations with the other women of the household and would be entitled to protection and care on the part of its master. To cite a concrete case, among the Manyika of East Africa a woman becomes the property of her elder sister's eldest son. "He does not cohabit with her, but otherwise has complete control over her. He may keep her at his kraal, where she does the usual woman's work for him. She has no recognized husband, but is encouraged to have a lover or even several." The children from such unions, it is interesting to add, are in no way under the tutelage of their biological father, but are wards of the man who inherited their mother; he, and he alone, receives the girls' bride-price and provides the boys with the wherewithal for acquiring a wife.[18]

7. Apart from minor modifications or rare and highly localized deviations, the family based on marriage is a quite general phenomenon in known samples of *Homo sapiens*. A man socially functioning as a father and husband practically everywhere combines with a woman functioning as mother and wife to provide for their common household and the children begotten by them or by legal fiction reckoned as their offspring. Since this pattern is common precisely to the unequivocally rudest known tribes, it is presumably one of great antiquity in *Homo sapiens*. How far back it goes in his history and to what extent it even antedates him, no one knows.

University of California

[18] Bullock, Charles, *The Mashona; the Indigenous Natives of S. Rhodesia* (London, 1928), p. 65.

ALEXANDER GOLDENWEISER

(1880-1940)

Goldenweiser was described by one of his contemporaries as "the most philosophical of American anthropologists." He was born in Kiev, Russia. His father was a Jewish scholar, active in promoting Jewish cultural movements. His early education was European, and he was widely traveled and widely read in many languages. The European flavor to his thought and habits was never completely obliterated. He was distinctly uninterested in salvaging the remnants of Indian cultures; the inconveniences and restrictions of life in the field were not for him, the recording of texts bored him to distraction. The library, the lecture platform, the coffee house—these were his milieux. There was something of the perpetual European student in him—the student who would go without dinner to buy a book, and go without sleep in order to talk.

Goldenweiser was preoccupied with theory. To him it had no national limits; he knew and used French, German, Russian and Dutch theoretical writings. His papers are models of logical presentation. The argument proceeds in perfect progression, the evidence carefully marshaled at each step and documented in illuminating footnotes that spread out before the reader the world of international scholarship.

However, his theoretical writing was somewhat arid; it opened no new avenues of investigation. Boas, against whom the accusation of negativism has so frequently been leveled by a later generation, constantly opened doors on new problems. Goldenweiser, on the other hand, was less interested in exploring new problems than in ordering systematically and coherently the vast body of ethnographic data.

In 1922, Goldenweiser wrote Early Civilization, *the first real textbook on anthropology. It began by introducing Man. The first part of the book is taken up with brief accounts of five contrasting cultures. This arrangement suggests the growing concern with culture wholes, a return to the basic problem of man's inner world, and the variety of ways in which he orders his life on this planet. Goldenweiser, unfortunately, was never able to order his own life satisfactorily, and his problems of living interfered with his productivity. He never reached the full development which his unquestioned brilliance and learning promised.—R.L.B.*

The Principle of Limited Possibilities
in the Development of Culture

THE CONCEPT OF CONVERGENCE, LONG FAMILIAR TO BIOLOGISTS, HAS recently been applied to ethnological phenomena. . . .

In the following pages I shall designate as "convergence" or "genuine convergence" the independent development of psychologically similar cultural traits from dissimilar or less similar sources, in two or more cultural complexes.

When the similarities between the cultural traits are not psychological, but merely objective or classificatory, I shall speak of "false convergence."

"Dependent convergence," finally, will be used of those similarities that develop from different sources, but under the influence of a common cultural medium.

No attempt will be made in what follows to deal with the problem of convergence in an exhaustive way, nor to assign even speculatively the limits of applicability of the principle of convergence; nor do I propose to present historically verifiable instances of convergence.

The following remarks are strictly theoretical, and were born of the desire to formulate a theoretical justification of the principle of convergence.

Some may doubt the wisdom, nay the propriety, of such a discussion, in the absence of concrete demonstrations, of convergence. But does not this lack of historical evidence rather suggest the need of a theoretical vindication of convergence? When that is achieved, many will doubtless still refuse to accept the principle, unless demonstrated historically; but there will no longer be any justification in rejecting its use as a methodological principle on a par with the principles of parallelism and diffusion.

THE LIMITATION OF POSSIBILITIES AND CONVERGENCE[1]

A superficial acquaintance with the culture of a group usually leads to the impression of great complexity. One is confronted with a maze

From Goldenweiser, "The Principle of Limited Possibilities in the Development of Culture," *Journal of American Folk-lore*, Vol. XXVI, 1913, pp. 259, 270-280.

[1] The central thought of this section was first expounded in a paper read before The Pearson Circle of New York, in 1910. Since then, the "principle of limited possibilities" has been made a frequent subject for discussion with a number of friends, of whom I shall name Professor Boas, Dr. Robert H. Lowie, and Dr. Paul Radin. Although I am not able to discern any specific contribution to the subject made by these gentlemen, I here express my thanks to them for their assistance in the clarification of my own ideas.

of heterogeneous facts,—beliefs, customs, ceremonies, industrial activities, peculiarities of dress. But a relatively brief familiarization with the same culture suffices to radically modify that first impression. The chaos of cultural traits, so bewildering at first, easily yields to certain obvious forms of classification; the multiplicity of customs and beliefs is found to follow certain patterns, usually few in number and well defined; industrial and artistic activities resolve themselves into a number of characteristic processes, deviations from which are found to be exceedingly rare. No sooner are these traits of a culture discovered than the task of describing it, apparently hopeless at first, becomes feasible. It is indeed obvious that, unless the fundamental traits of a culture were well defined and limited in number, a description of the culture would be well-nigh impossible, for it would have to consist in an endless enumeration of happenings, customs, beliefs.[2]

---

[2] This limitation of the objective, and, as will presently appear, of the psychic, manifestations of a culture, must not be regarded as without parallel in other groups of facts. Language is a case in point, with reference to two of its aspects, phonetics and grammar. The number of sounds that can be articulated is practically unlimited; but in a language, only a definite and relatively small number of sounds is used. Obviously, this is not an incidental but a necessary condition of language; for, if the sounds articulated by the members of a group tended to vary all the time, no associations between clusters of sound and definite meanings could be formed, and there would be no language. Language as a means of communication of thought requires an automatic co-ordination between "ideas" and "words," which cannot exist unless the sounds used are fixed, and limited in number. The same applies to grammar. Of the unlimited possibilities of classification of experience that find expression in grammatical categories, a fixed and limited set is utilized in a language; and, if this were not the case, there could be no grammar. (Compare Boas, in *Handbook of American Indian Languages,* part i, Introduction, pp. 15–16 and 24.)

Now, the same limitation in fundamental classifications and in the number and character of cultural features was shown above to apply to a culture. To point out a situation is, of course, not to solve it, but merely to direct attention to a problem,—a problem which in this case has scarcely been broached. I shall here merely refer to two factors which furnish a partial explanation. A culture does not merely comprise certain of the outer activities and psychic states of a people: it also involves a co-ordination between the outward activities and accompanying inner states. This co-ordination is to a large extent automatic. Indeed, unless this were so, every individual of the group would find himself in the position of a globe-trotter who visits a totally strange country, or of an ethnologist who for the first time comes in contact with an aboriginal culture. In fact, his position would be more precarious than either that of the globe-trotter or that of the ethnologist. He could not comprehend the activities of his surroundings: the motives of action, the standards of judgment and of values applied by others, would to him appear as a maze of tantalizing puzzles.

This consideration, however, cannot properly be regarded as an explanation of the automatism of culture. It merely tends to indicate that this character of culture is not incidental, but, as in the case of grammatical structure and phonetics, essential to the existence itself of culture.

A principle of greater explanatory value is the importance of precedent in determining the course of culture. When a special form of social organization, style of art or mythology, develops in an area, not only does it tend to perpetuate itself, but it also becomes operative in checking other developments in the same sphere of culture. While the bearing of this factor ought not to be overestimated, in view of the un-

When several cultures thus resolved into their component units are compared, a further fact comes to light. The classification of cultural traits which proved so helpful in the first instance is found to apply in other instances also, although not without certain variations. One discovers that any of the cultures under discussion can be described in a treatise containing sections with similar headings, more or less. All comprise a social and ceremonial organization, a religious system, a mythology, an art, etc. The fact that a description of all human cultures according to a uniform plan is possible, the fact that we can have ethnographic monographs the general table of contents of which can be foreseen before the book is opened,—this fact alone suffices to establish the fundamental and far-reaching psychic unity of man.

Several further facts presently appear. The observation made on the culture first noted, that each phase of the culture is characterized by a few well-defined traits, is supported by the evidence from other cultures. Not only do we find in each instance a social organization, a ritualistic system, an art, a body of myths, but we also find that the social organization resolves itself into a set of social or local units with definite functions, and standing to one another in definite relations; that the ceremonial system consists of a number of rituals which all follow the same pattern, or at most of a number of such sets of rituals with similar patterns; that the art has a definite style, that is, consists of a certain technique, represents a certain more or less restricted class of objects, or, without representing any objects, consists of certain motives, quite definite in character and definitely correlated; and so on.[3]

---

doubted tendency toward the differentiation of culture, it remains of the highest importance as a partial explanatory principle of the fixity and numerical limitation of the characteristic forms belonging to the various aspects of a culture. I made use of this principle in *the pattern theory* of the origin of totemism (*American Anthropologist*, 1912, pp. 600–607); Lowie applied it in an interpretation of the development of societies among the Plains Indians ("Some Problems in the Ethnology of the Crow and Village Indians," *American Anthropologist*, vol. xiv [1912], pp. 68–71); Wissler expounded the principle in a chapter on the "Origins of Rituals" among the Blackfoot ("Ceremonial Bundles of the Blackfoot Indians," *Anthropological Papers of the American Museum of Natural History*, vol. vii, part 2 [1912], pp. 100–106).

[3] A word of warning is due here. The representation of cultures as given above may easily produce an exaggerated impression of the simplicity of culture. While it is doubtless true that in every culture the characteristic and essential framework of the culture consists of a set of well-defined and numerically limited features; while it is no less true that the vast majority of cultural re-actions proceed and must proceed unconsciously and automatically,—it must nevertheless not be forgotten that culture changes, and that certain at least of the cultural elements constantly tend to rise into consciousness. If a culture consisted only of a set of perfectly fixed features, and if, within that culture, all associations and responses were thoroughly automatic, there could, of course, be no change, no advancement. The fact that the reverse is true indicates the presence of a cultural fringe, which, like the perceptional fringe, is less clearly defined than the essential nucleus of the culture, but which, unlike the perceptional fringe, lies more within the domain of conscious deliberation than the cultural nucleus itself. The presence of such a fringe, moreover, need not be merely

Thus the impression of uniformity derived from the fact that all cultures are resolvable into a number of factors or phases which are practically fixed, begins to waver. As soon as we go beyond the formal classification, the similarities between the cultures seem to cease: each phase of culture in a group shows certain definite characteristics which are readily recognizable. The sum of such characteristics constitutes the individuality of the culture which thus becomes distinguishable from other cultures.

With further analysis, however, this observation also is found to represent but part of the truth; for, as culture after culture passes in review, one fails to discover that multiplicity of elementary styles and patterns of social organization, myths, ceremonies, etc., which one might expect if the elementary factors into which the phases of a culture are resolvable differed for each culture. Instead, one soon observes that certain fundamental cultural forms occur again and again; and, if the number of cultures under observation is large, one presently becomes aware that the recurrences of such fundamental forms are exceedingly frequent, that the forms lend themselves to a classification into a fairly small number of types, which constantly recur as one passes from culture to culture. Thus one

---

postulated on theoretical grounds, for its presence is well attested by our experience.

These remarks apply even to the most primitive cultures. In the case of higher and more complex cultures, the application of the argument propounded in the text becomes increasingly difficult. In a primitive group consisting, as it always does, of a relatively small number of individuals, every individual represents almost the whole of the culture of the group, and the best individuals represent the whole of it. But with increasing complexity, with division of labor, specialization of classes, religious, ceremonial, industrial, etc., it becomes more and more difficult for an individual, or small set of individuals, to be thoroughly representative of the culture of the group. The man, even in most primitive conditions, cannot do all the woman does, and *vice versa;* nor does he know all she knows, and *vice versa.* The priest, the medicine-man, the basket-maker, the potter, tend to monopolize certain phases of culture with their concomitant knowledge, ability, emotional associations, which, to that extent, cease to be common possessions of the group. What we find in these still relatively primitive stages is more emphatically true of the higher civilizations. The gulf between what is called the "culture of a group" and the amount of it carried by any individual, or set of individuals, has grown to enormous proportions. Each one of us is thoroughly saturated with, and automatically responds to, but a very small fraction of the totality of our culture. Certain ideas and emotions—as, for instance, the moral ones—are shared by a relatively large number of people; although even here the variations from class to class, from group to group, are often considerable, sometimes radical. As to knowledge, even the most "cultured" among us would have to confess to a total ignorance of many intellectual and material acquisitions of what they call "their" culture. A culture, psychically considered, may thus be visualized as a large series of partly overlapping circles, which stand for the actual cultural participation of individuals and sets of individuals, and which, together with their objective correlates, constitute the totality of the culture.

These reflections do not invalidate the argument in the text referring to the definiteness and fixity of a culture and the numerical limitation of its features; but, to use again the analogy of the psychology of perception, while we may well choose as the object of our study the image which lies in the main line of vision and in the focus of attention, it may be of importance to consider the perceptional fringe, and it is always dangerous to ignore it.

finds that a social organization consists of social units (in the limited sense), or of families, or of local groups, or of various combinations of these units; that an art consists of carving, or drawing, or painting, or of a combination of these; that the form of it is realistic, or semi-conventionalized, or purely geometrical; that, if it is geometrical, either curves or straight lines predominate or are used one to the exclusion of the other; that a mythology comprises epics, or animal stories with explanatory features, or nature myths, or traditional accounts of historical happenings, or creation legends, or several of these types together; and so on, through the entire series of cultural forms.[4]

Still deeper study would not fail to reveal a much larger set of similarities, —similarities more detailed, but scarcely more significant, than those discussed above. I refer to the countless, often most striking, similarities in custom, ritual, belief, myth, which fill the scholarly volumes of a Tylor, a Lang, a Hartland, a Frazer, a Farnell.

We have now established the following facts that have a bearing on the problem of convergence. The objective manifestations of a culture are limited in number, and are readily amenable to classification into a set of types. The different phases of a culture are characterized by certain definite features, the sum of which constitute the individuality of the culture. Practically the same classification of cultural traits applies to all cultures. The characteristic features which distinguish the different phases of a culture are not specific in each culture, but show marked similarities, and can be classified into a number of fundamental cultural traits which are found again and again in different cultures.

Of the above generalizations, the two of greatest importance for our immediate problem are, the one, that which refers to the limitation in number, and definiteness in type, of the concrete manifestations of a culture; the other, that which speaks of the similarities obtaining between such concrete manifestations of different cultures.

If, now, we leave the descriptive aspects of culture; if we turn from a consideration of cultural features as ascertainable by modern experience, or by cross-sections of cultural developments by means of historical reconstructions of certain definite periods or stages, and fix our attention upon

---

[4] A plausible objection to the argument must be met here. Are not the classifications referred to in the text artificial? Are they not altogether determined by the point of view from which we analyze culture? Is not, therefore, the limitation of features in a culture, resulting from such classification, illusory, and the entire argument purely formal? These remarks are justified in so far as our classification of cultural features is certainly determined by a definite point of view. It is also true that other conceivable view-points would lead to different forms of classification. The argument in the text, however, is not invalidated by these considerations; for, whatever the point of view, whatever the resulting classification of cultural features, the characterization of a culture as outlined above would hold true. A culture would always embrace a limited set of features definite in type. If so much is granted, we may safely pursue our argument.

the historical antecedents of culture,—the aspect of the observed phenomena changes. It becomes at once apparent that the historical and
psychological sources of cultural traits—some that are objectively verifiable, and some that are merely probable or possible—are much more
multiple and multiform than the cultural features that face us in an individual culture. This multiplicity and multiformity of sources of development is, of course, nothing but the cumulative result of the multiple
possibilities of origin and development of any individual cultural feature.

As this observation is of crucial importance for the subject at hand,
we must dwell on it for some time. The oft-quoted instance of taboos
may again serve as an example. The prohibition to eat or kill certain
animals, a cultural feature almost universal in its distribution, may develop
from, for instance, the following sources:[5] the animal, as such, is sacred,
as, for instance, snakes in India, and cats in Egypt; the animals are believed
to be incarnations of ancestors, as again in Egypt, or among the South
African Bantu; the animal is a totem, as in innumerable instances; the
animal is a guardian spirit, as commonly among North American Indians,
in the Banks Islands, etc.; the animal is associated with evil spirits, as
among the Aranda in the case of some few animals that are not totems;
certain animals must not be killed or eaten during a particular season,
as among the Eskimo, where caribou must not be killed, eaten, handled,
during the season when sea-animals are hunted, and *vice versa*;[6] the animal
is regarded as an ancestor, as in many totemic communities where the
taboo applies to a clan or a family, as well as in some non-totemic groups
where the idea of descent refers to the entire tribe; the animal is unclean,
as the pig among the Jews; the animal is too closely akin to man, as in
modern ethical vegetarianism;[7] the animal is too closely associated with
man, as the dog or other pets; pregnant women, boys before initiation,
women after first child-birth, etc., must not eat certain animals for various
reasons; the animal is a sacred symbol, as the dove in Christianity; and
so on.

The possible origins of a clan system or of individual clans may
furnish another illustration. A clan may arise as a subdivision of a
tribe through migration due to excess of numbers in the tribe, or internal
strife, or the quest of new hunting-grounds, etc. Evidence of such origins
of new clans is plentiful,—on the Northwest coast, among the Iroquois

[5] In the absence of data as to historical origins of animal taboos, the above
examples are adduced to suggest the wide range of psychological settings of such
taboos. It is highly probable, however, that most of the psychological connotations
of taboos here given have at different times and places figured as the psychological
sources of taboos.

[6] The source of these taboos, as Professor Boas suggests, was probably the habitual
separation of the two forms of activity, which became standardized, and assumed the
form of a taboo.

[7] This and similar instances do not, of course, have the character of absolute
taboos; but the instances may be cited here as psychologically cognate phenomena.

tribes, and elsewhere. Or a phratry organization, comprising two or more major subdivisions of a tribe, may already be in existence, and the clans may arise as subdivisions of the phratries. That such was the origin of clans in more than one tribe in Australia seems, at least, highly probable. Or a clan may be formed by the fusion of fragments of depleted clans, of which process, again, the Northwest coast people, the Iroquois, the Siouan tribes, offer abundant evidence. Or a clan system may spring up on the basis of a group of villages, which, by assuming various social and ceremonial functions and becoming closely associated with one another, become socialized, and assume the rôle of clans in a clan system. That such was the history of the clan systems of the Coast Salish and Bella Coola can scarcely be doubted, unless, indeed, among the latter the formation of a clan system out of an original tribal association of villages antedated their migration to Bentinck Arm. The same type of development must be assumed also for the Lillooet, Shuswap, perhaps also the Athapascan Tahltan, among all of whom the first impetus and continued stimulation in the direction of such development were given by the suggestive influence of the coast culture. An alternative possibility of the development of a clan system out of a group of villages must also be mentioned. As I have referred to this process on another occasion, the passage may be reproduced here: "In the course of social evolution the transformation of such loose local groups into a clan system must have occurred innumerable times. With increasing solidarity the local groups would gradually assume the character of at first vague social units. Through intercourse and intermarriage between the groups, with or without exogamy, the individuals would become distributed in the different localities. Thus a foundation would be laid for a clan system, which in time would become fixed and rigid."[8] We need not repeat here the arguments for the multiple origin of exogamy.[9]

The field of art supplies plentiful illustrations of similar nature. One will suffice. A realistic design may originate as an attempt to represent an animal in life-like form; or it may be part of a pictograph designed to convey the content of a myth or an occurrence; or it may result from a process of reading a realistic significance into a geometric design, which process, in its turn, leads to a modification of the design in a realistic sense. In groups, on the other hand, where realistic designs are already in vogue, the execution of realistic figures in each generation is due to a reproduction of the precedents of the preceding generation.[10]

[8] *American Anthropologist,* vol. xiv (1912), p. 605, footnote 1.

[9] Compare *Journal of American Folk-Lore,* vol. xxiii (1910), pp. 245–247.

[10] It is, of course, apparent that very few of the "origins" here suggested are historically verifiable. The procedure adopted in the text may thus be objected to as altogether hypothetical. Now, it must at once be granted that, in individual instances, the possible or plausible development is no criterion of the historic event. This, however, does not apply when the possibilities of origin and development of ethnic

Examples like the above could be multiplied *ad infinitum,* but it will probably be admitted without further specification of the argument, that the historical and psychological sources of cultural traits are much more multiform than the traits themselves, objectively considered, in any one culture, or in several cultures that are being compared. Taboos, clans, realistic designs, are found among many peoples; but the origins, both historical and psychological, of all these features, are multiform. It thus appears that *the cultural features, as they occur in concrete cultural complexes, constitute, when compared to the multiplicity of their sources, a limitation in the possibilities of development.* In other words, there is convergence, for convergence is the development of cultural similarities which arise from different sources. Considering the relatively small number of aspects that the different phases of culture assume, the number of such convergences must be exceedingly great. But so far, we have only referred to phenomena of a generalized character, such as clans, taboos, realistic designs. If, now, we turn to cultural features as actually found in existing cultures, we observe that they are always more complex than the generalized features referred to above. The complexity consists in the elaboration of the feature itself through various functions, specifications, etc., as well as in the co-ordination between separate features. Now, a survey of cultures shows notable similarities also between such complex features and combinations of features. The more complex a feature, either in itself or through association with other features, the greater the number of its possible historical and psychological sources; for every definite aspect, every function of a feature, may itself have multiple origins; and, similarly, the association of several features may proceed along quite different lines,—different in origin, in mechanism, in the chronological succession of individual events. Any attempt to correlate the similarities between different cultures in such complex features imposes the principle of convergence with even greater force than in the case of the more simple and general cultural traits.

It will be observed that so far the objective manifestations of cultures

---

features are considered from a more general standpoint. The study of sociological phenomena and historic experience have revealed, with varying degrees of clearness and certainty, a large number of tendencies and developments resulting in certain cultural features. With these fairly well understood processes as guidance, a much larger number of possible processes of development may be constructed. We must, of course, allow for the fact that some of the processes regarded as possible on theoretical grounds may never have occurred; but, on the general theory of probability, a large majority of the processes suggested as possible or probable by theoretical study or concrete experience, must actually have occurred in the course of cultural development. Moreover, the origins and processes that have occurred must, in number and variety, vastly exceed our hypothetical reconstructions; for, whereas some of the latter may never have been realized, many developments must have taken place in the course of the historic process, which never occur to us as possible, on account of the limitation of our knowledge and experience. I trust that these considerations fully vindicate the methodology of the foregoing pages.

alone have been considered: in other words, the convergences invoked to account for the similarities may, after all, prove to be false convergences. We may have clans that have sprung from different sources and also remain different in their functions; one clan may regulate marriage and the election of chiefs, the other may be associated with ceremonial and religious or mythological ideas and practices. The resemblance, then, would be of that superficial, formal kind characteristic of false convergences. Similarly with taboos: animal taboos of heterogeneous origin and development may also differ in their psychological connotations; the one may emanate at a given time from the conscious prescription of a chief, the other may be based on the totemic character of the animal. Again the convergence would be purely objective. But if, in these or similar instances, the cultural features, while of different derivation, acquire a similar psychological content, or, in case of social divisions, similar functions, the case is one of genuine convergence.

Another circumstance must here be invoked to show that convergences of this latter type, genuine convergences, are more likely to arise than would at first sight appear.

We have so far spoken of the objective manifestations of cultures; that is, of cultural manifestations as viewed by the investigator who is satisfied to describe what he sees without following up the precise cultural setting or psychological content of the observed phenomenon. Now, when these latter aspects of culture engage one's attention, he finds what we have already established for the objective cultural manifestations: the psychic settings of cultural traits are also limited in number in each culture, and to a considerable extent similar in different cultures. We find that social divisions (whether clans, phratries, families, villages) regulate marriage, figure as ceremonial, religious, political units, exercise reciprocal functions at burial, games, feasts, contests, etc. These functions, either in isolation or in different combinations, occur everywhere in connection with social divisions; and often in quite different cultures the same individual functions, or even combinations of functions, occur in connection with the same kind of social divisions. These facts are too well known to require specification. But the same also applies to other customs, activities, functions, ideas. The functions of religious and military societies, clubs, age classes, are limited in number, and recur in different groups. The varieties of interpretations of designs, realistic and geometrical, are strictly limited in each cultural area, and similar interpretations occur in distinct areas. The forms and psychic contents of initiation ceremonies, of all *rites de passage,* are no less similar within separate cultures, and, to a high degree, between cultures. The ceremonial cycles attending birth, marriage, death, burial, are quite as characteristic of cultural areas; and many of the ceremonial details, with their concomitant interpretations, are facts of wide distribution. Mechanisms of trade and barter, legal procedure and magical rite, behave in no different manner. Thus *the psychic aspects of culture, when compared to the multiplicity of their possible psychological and historical origins, constitute a further limitation in the possibilites of development.*

The set of facts just referred to, when correlated with the limitation of forms in the objective manifestations of culture, constitute irrefutable evidence of genuine convergence. The evidence, in fact, points not merely toward the reality of genuine convergence, but toward its inevitableness and frequency.[11] But the case of convergence does not rest there.

Of the more involved manifestations of convergence, I propose to deal briefly with one,—the totemic complex. It has been shown that the separate features entering into the composition of a totemic organization are cultural traits which in no sense may be regarded as derived from totemism. Clan exogamy, animal names of social groups, beliefs in descent from an animal, are features of complex historical and psychological derivation, which, under certain psychosociological conditions, enter into intimate association with one another, thus constituting a totemic complex.[12] Now, when totemic complexes in different cultural areas are compared, one finds certain rather marked similarities in the component features of the complexes, as well as a much more striking similarity in certain forms of socialization, by means of which the totemic features become consolidated into a morphologically integral system.[13] But over and above these resemblances there occurs in totemic complexes a psychic re-interpretation and assimilation of cultural features which transforms

[11] In his "On the Principle of Convergence in Ethnology" (*Journal of American Folk-Lore,* vol. xxv, pp. 37–38), Dr. Lowie refers to the principle of limited possibilities, and illustrates it by a number of examples. An analysis of these examples will show that a physical or logical limitation of possibilities is involved in each instance. Descent can be either maternal or paternal; there must be either evolution or permanence of species; the number of ways in which a skin membrane can be fastened to a drum is limited; etc. The same idea is expressed by A. Haberlandt in his "Prähistorisch-ethnographische Parallelen" (*Archiv für Anthropologie,* vol. xii [1913] pp. 1–25), where he speaks, for example, of the limited possibilities in the development of arrow-points, most of which have been realized at some time or other (*Ibid.,* p. 10), or of the conditions that must be satisfied by every sword-handle (*Ibid.,* pp. 7–8). How wide an application can be made of this principle may be gathered from its use by Dilthey, who believes in a logical limitation of possible systems of philosophy (cf. also Boas, "Anthropology," *Columbia University Press,* 1908, p. 24).

The principle of limited possibilities as formulated by these authors must, from the point of view of convergence, be regarded as a special instance of the principle expounded in the text. Wherever the sources of development are many, and the possibilities of the results are limited through the operation of logical, objective, or cultural factors, there must be convergence; and the greater the possible number of sources of development, and the smaller the possible number of results, the stronger is the case for convergence.

[12] See "Totemism, an Analytical Study," *Journal of American Folk-Lore,* vol. xxiii (1910), pp. 264 *et seq.*

[13] See "The Origin of Totemism," *American Anthropologist,* vol. xiv (1912), p. 603; and "Andrew Lang on Method in the Study of Totemism," *Ibid.,* p. 384.

these totemic organizations into strictly comparable cultural complexes lying, as it were, on the same psychic plane. This re-interpretation of features through their assimilation by the totemic medium, finds expression in the fact that the features are conceived and felt as totemic features by the totemites. Whatever the derivation of British Columbia carvings, whatever the sources of their clan myths and ceremonies, these traits are for them expressions of their totemism. The magical ceremonies of the Central Australian are for him indissolubly fused in his totemic circle of participation. And so with other features and other totemic complexes. The real comparability of totemic organizations is thus seen to be based on these two facts: on the one hand, the consolidation of totemic features through the merging with a definite form of social organization,—*the totemic association;* on the other, the re-interpretation of the features in the spirit of the totemic medium,—*the totemic assimilation.*

Totemic complexes must, then, be conceived as products of convergent developments in three distinct respects: the separate features in the different complexes involve convergence; the typical totemic social structures with their features, which in different complexes develop in different ways, involve convergence;[14] the totemic atmosphere, finally, with its psychically transformed features, involves convergence.

Similar psychic transformations, of a more or less temporary character, and leading to convergence, could be studied in feudal systems, revolutionary periods, wars, financial panics. . . .

---

[14] The socio-psychological factor responsible for this association of the social system with totemic features has been referred to before as the tendency for specific socialization ("Exogamy and Totemism defined: A Rejoinder," *American Anthropologist,* vol. xiii [1911], pp. 596–597). The tendency itself, then, is not the product of convergence.

CLARK WISSLER

(1870-1947)

New World Origins

THE ULTIMATE GOAL OF [ANTHROPOLOGICAL INVESTIGATION] . . . IN THE NEW
World is the discovery of the origin of the Indian and the causes and conditions leading to the development of his culture. Though thus simply
stated, the problem is truly complex. . . . A great array of facts must be considered and one must draw upon the resources of zoology, geography, and
geology, before the various parts of the problem can be formulated for
critical consideration. As to the origin of the New World man himself, we
have achieved one point: *viz.,* that he migrated hither from Asia where
his nearest relatives still reside. Yet, we are far from the truth as to the
exact relationship between the Indian and the Asiatic, and have still much
to learn as to his own subdivisions.

Now, with the main facts before us and recognizing that the differentiation of cultures is a historical phenomenon, we should be able to project
the general outlines of man's career in the New World. Recalling our conclusion that the Indian came here from Asia at a relatively recent period,
we find ourselves confronted with the question as to what elements of
culture man brought with him when he crossed over to America. Even the
casual reader will be impressed by the close general parallelism between
the two halves of the world, and, it is this obvious fact more than anything
else, that has stimulated speculative writings upon the subject. Repeated
efforts have been made to show that all the higher culture complexes of the
New World were brought over from the Old, particularly from China or
the Pacific Islands. Most of these writings are merely speculative and may
be ignored, but some of the facts we have cited for correspondences to
Pacific Island culture have not been satisfactorily explained. Dixon has
carefully reviewed this subject, asserting in general that among such traits
as blowguns, plank canoes, hammocks, betel chewing, head-hunting cults,

From Wissler, *The American Indian, an Introduction to the Anthropology of the
New World* (New York and London: Oxford University Press, 1938), pp. 378-388.

the men's house and certain masked dances common to the New World and the Pacific Islands, there appears the tendency to mass upon the Pacific side of the New World. This gives these traits a semblance of continuous distribution with the Island culture. Yet it should be noted that these traits, as enumerated above, have in reality a sporadic distribution in the New World and that there are exceptions. On the other hand, there is no great *a priori* improbability that some of these traits did reach the New World from the Pacific Islands. Satisfactory proof of such may yet be attained, but such discoveries would not account for New World culture as a whole. Then there are abundant data to show that the Polynesians are recent arrivals in the Pacific; in fact, Maya culture must have been in its prime when they were within striking distance of the American coast.

In the preceding discussions, we found evidences of a certain unity in the fundamentals of culture for all parts of the New World, and unless we find among these some fundamentals that are also conspicuous in the Old World, we need look no farther than the New for their place of origin. The Old World also has its fundamental traits, particularly the ancient cultures of Asia, but so far, few close parallels between these and those of the New have come to light. Again, the originality of many New World traits is apparent when our subject is viewed from the cultural horizon of the Old World. It has been very aptly said that the fundamentals of Old World culture are expressed by the terms "cereals, cattle, plough, and wheel." Yet, what have we found in the New World that can be set down as specifically similar to these? We are left, therefore, little choice but to recognize that the cultures of the New World peoples were developed independently of the ancient centers of higher culture in the Old.

The old argument against such a conclusion was that the barbarous Indian was incompetent to develop the cultures of Yucatan and Peru. This view is now somewhat antiquated, but still lingers as a kind of intellectual reaction in the minds of modern Europeans. Perhaps back of it is a habit of thought, since in Old World culture, in which we ourselves live and think, fundamental traits are often found to have a single origin. For example, the horse, ox, wheat, glass, printing, gunpowder, etc., seem to have had each a single place of origin from which they were diffused. Yet, in contemplating New World culture we must not forget that the comparisons between the two hemispheres should be specific. It will not do, for instance, to say that because agriculture is found in both the Old and New Worlds one must have been derived from the other, for we are here dealing with a mere abstraction, like eating, writing, fishing, etc. The proper method is to examine the agricultural traits found in each hemisphere. Thus, one basic factor in agriculture is the development of specific food plants. Let us, therefore, compare the plants cultivated by the Indian with those grown in the Old World.

De Candolle has listed more than forty plants grown by the Indians whose wild ancestors were, without reasonable doubt, peculiar to the New World. On the other hand, the ancestors of the leading food plants of the Old World have been found peculiar to it. Thus, we find that each hemisphere developed agriculture by drawing upon its own peculiar flora and that in consequence their seed lists had nothing in common before 1492. Now, when we consider the rapidity with which maize, tobacco, and other New World plants were taken up in the Old World after the commemorable voyage of Columbus, it is scarcely conceivable that the peoples of the two hemispheres could ever have been in contact without exchanging some of their seeds, and certainly impossible to assume that the agriculture of the New World was directly derived from the Old.

But our case does not rest upon this one observation, for there are others of almost equal weight. The wheel is a fundamental concept in the Old World and clearly of great antiquity, but is singularly absent from the New World, even its spinners and potters failing to grasp the principle. The use of iron is another, though perhaps later, invention of the Old World that remained peculiar to it. However, the facts of cultivated plants and the wheel, which must be very ancient in origin, make a strong case for the peopling of the New World either at a very remote period or by wild tribes only, such as might arise from contact between the historic tribes of Alaska and Siberia.

On the other hand, the New World peoples did achieve some of the specific inventions of the Old; for instance, the making of bronze and casting gold, silver, copper, etc.; again, in certain methods of weaving and dyeing. It is sometimes objected that the knowledge of these traits could have been handed over or relayed from southern Asia to Mexico by the intervening wild tribes; but this seems fanciful, for while we do find certain traits spread over adjacent parts of the two continents, as the sinew-backed bow, the bow-drill, the magic flight myth, the opium type of smoking, all of which are considered as of Asiatic origin, their distribution is continuous from Alaska downward, and fades out before we reach the southern continent. Further, it has been assumed that the ideas underlying a trait could be carried along as part of a myth and so pass from one of the higher cultures of Asia to Mexico by way of Siberia and Alaska. There is no *a priori* improbability in this notion that specific ideas can be carried from tribe to tribe as constituent parts of mythical tales. The difficulty is that notwithstanding our very complete knowledge of typical tribal mythologies, we are so far unable to find examples of such extensive transmissions of the process concepts underlying specific culture traits. As we have noted under Mythology, myths do seem to have carried a few mythical conceptions from the Old World to the New, but these have remained as mere parts of tales and do not function in practical life.

Hence, the general condition for any interpretation of Old and New World relations is the full recognition that their great culture centers were well isolated by a complex chain of wilder hunting peoples and that direct contact between the two was impossible without modern means of transportation. Only such traits could, therefore, filter through from one to the other as were assimilated by these more primitive tribes. When we consider their great number and the diversity of their speech, we realize that Mexico was completely isolated from China in agriculture, metal work, and similar arts, but not necessarily so in simpler traits like the sinew-backed bow. The proof of independent development thus rests largely in chronological and environmental relations.

We must not overlook one difficulty in dealing with culture similarities between the New World and the Old; viz., the proof that these similarities are real. In 1915 certain well known elephant-like figures found in Maya sculptures were heralded as proof of direct connection between India and Mexico. Special students in this field doubt the reality of the similarity between these figures and southern Asiatic drawings of elephants, because those who have studied the actual Maya sculptures instead of the sketches made by earlier observers, find proof that another creature was in the artist's mind. When we are dealing with the conventionalized drawings from the New World and the Old, it can scarcely be expected that the mere objective similarity between a few of them is proof of their identity in origin. Other check data must be appealed to before even a useful working hypothesis can be formulated. Yet, if it should ultimately turn out that a stray vessel did drift ashore in Mexico and land a sculptor who created a new art motif, this would be a mere incident in the culture history of the New World. Further research into the chronology of archæological remains ought to show just how abruptly this fancied elephant motif appeared and at what relative period. The basis for the real solution of the problem may be expected in such chronological data. . . .

We have found the highest centers of culture in Mexico and Peru to be not really unique growths, but to possess many of the fundamental traits common to the wilder folk in the marginal areas of both continents. New World culture is thus a kind of pyramid whose base is as broad as the two Americas and whose apex rests over Middle America. We have found no just ground for assuming that the culture of the Maya was projected into the New World from the Old, where it rested as an isolated replica of cultures beyond the Pacific. That influences of various kinds did reach the New World from the Old is apparent, but each of these must, upon its own merits, particularly as to its chronology, be subjected to the most exacting investigation.

However, the discovery of New World origins is not merely a problem in culture. Language also is regarded as a reliable index to origin. Some similarities between Tibetan and Athapascan, Melanesian and Hokan, Australian and Fuegian, etc., have been suggested. Long ago Duponceau saw certain resemblances between the languages of east Siberia and

American Indian languages in general. So far, none of these resemblances have been regarded as sufficient to indicate more than vague relationships. As we have seen, the New World itself presents such a mystifying array of languages that it would seem reasonable to expect that when colonies were planted here by Old World cultures, such colonization would have introduced Old World tongues. Yet, so far, there is not a trace of direct intrusion. New research may clear up this confusion, but as the case now stands, language data suggest a reasonable antiquity for the peopling of North America.

Finally, there is the question of blood. Our review of New World somatic characters revealed the essential unity of the Indian population. It is also clear that there are affinities with the mongoloid peoples of Asia. Hence, we are justified in assuming a common ancestral group for the whole mongoloid-red stream of humanity. We have already outlined the reasons for assuming the pristine home of this group to be in Asia, but when it comes to locating the precise cradleland of this parent group, we must proceed with caution. This is, however, not of prime importance, for if we start with the known facts, the present distribution of the mongoloid-red stem, we note that it concentrates in the colder northern halves of both hemispheres, where the cultures of its units are primitive, but that in each case its southern outposts developed complex cultures. The New World branch can claim originality for its high center and while it is clear that the ancient Chinese center was stimulated by non-monogoloid centers, the pioneer students of Chinese origins have already presented a strong brief for their priority in many Old World inventions. Thus, the future may lead to the opinion that inherent in this mongoloid stem was a germ of originality which blossomed forth wherever the environment permitted, and we may be able, by contrasting these two independent cultures—the ancient Chinese and the Maya—with those of southern Asia and Europe, to arrive at last at the knowledge of elements peculiar to both. What these may be, we can but guess, but there seems to be a similarity between the Indians and the Asiatics in the weakness for loosely coordinated social groups, failure to develop nationalism, and relatively greater regard for tradition. Returning to our subject, we may note that the geographical position of these two centers of higher cultures on the frontiers of the extended swarming ground of the mongoloid-red stem, one of which could not have been borrowed from the other, necessitates the assumption of a northern cradleland and an expansion into more favorable environments. It also presupposes a main horde of the mongoloid-red peoples with a culture not materially different from that of the great mass of wilder North Asiatic and American tribes known to history. Like a great crescent this horde stretched from Cape Horn, through Alaska, across Asia and beyond to the shores of the Baltic and the Mediterranean. It appears, in the main, as a virile horde of hunting and fisher folk most at home in cold, elevated or semi-arid lands.

Among other traits, we find the main body characterized by tailored skin clothing, the sinew-backed bow, the snowshoe, the sled, etc. These are all fairly primitive characters; yet, wherever the outposts of this great horde met with favorable uplands they developed agriculture and other complex traits. It seems, therefore, that the solution of our New World problem lies as much in the heart of Asia as in Mexico or Peru. But, reverting once more to this great mongoloid-red horde, we may ask from what sources in its primitive cultures sprang the impulses that produced the two great cultures of ancient China and Yucatan? In the New World, the fundamentals of Maya culture are found among the wilder folk; in Asia there are also evidences that Chinese culture sprang from the primitive heritage of the original mongoloid group settling in the valley of the Yellow River. And while it is true that the most fundamental traits in Old World culture can not be ascribed to these same early Chinese, they did, nevertheless, achieve great originality in the invention of new traits, many of which are now elements of modern culture. Hence, unless we return once more to the old theory of the fall of man, we must look upon these two great cultural achievements as the special contributions of the mongoloid-red peoples to the culture of mankind.

Now, as a final conclusion to this volume on the man of the New World and his culture, we beg the reader's indulgence in the formulation of an hypothetical statement. The New World received a detachment of early mongoloid peoples at a time when the main body had barely developed stone polishing. That this was contemporaneous with the appearance of stone polishing in Europe does not necessarily follow, for future research in Asia may show it to have been much earlier. The hunters who killed bison at Folsom and those who hurled spears at the mammoth floundering in a pit at Clovis may not have been the first immigrants from the northwest, but they belonged to the primitive nomadic stratum which seems to underlie the aboriginal cultures of the New World. Their mongoloid kin, remaining in Central Asia, received culture stimuli from the south and east, urging them to greater achievements, but in the New World these primitive hunters had only themselves. Yet, in the course of time, increase in numbers and the development of sub-social groups led to considerable varieties of culture. Some of the traits probably brought from the motherland, are the firedrill, stone chipping, twisting of string, the bow, throwing stick, the harpoon, simple basketry and nets, hunting complexes, cooking with stones in vessels of wood, bark, or skin, body painting, and perhaps tattooing, and the domestication of the dog. Not all of these came in at the beginning, for there are archæological evidences suggesting that the bow and the dog came relatively late. Independently, the New World developed agriculture, pottery, the higher types of basketry and cloth weaving, the working of the softer metals, and the manufacture of bronze. The progress in astronomical knowledge and the fine arts compares favorably with that achieved by the early Asiatics. Yet, in all, we see the marks of originality which are alone sufficient evidence of their independent origin.

The centers of civilization in the New World were the highlands of Mexico and western South America which, as they developed, reacted to the stimulus of their more backward brothers in other parts of the land in much the same fashion as did the different groups of mongoloid peoples in Asia. One of the significant points in our discussion has been the identification of the fundamental widely diffused complexes in the cultures of the New World, many of which seem to center in the Mexican and Andean regions of higher civilization and from which their respective radiations are often apparent. The more recent studies of ancient Chinese culture show that a somewhat parallel condition existed in Asia. Apparently then, in the New World, we did have an isolated people who did not travel the road to higher cultures as rapidly as their relatives in Asia, the connection between whose centers of development has long been broken by climatic changes and later almost completely blocked by hordes of primitive hunter and fisher folk. We can only speculate as to what a few more thousand years of this freedom would have done for the New World, for in the sixteenth century a calamity, which has no exact parallel in history, befell the New World. A militant foreign civilization, fired by a zeal not only to plunder the material treasures of mankind, but to seize the very souls of men in the name of its God, fell upon the two great centers of aboriginal culture like a thunderbolt from a clear sky. The blow was mortal. But the man of the New World went down fighting. Though his feeble survivors still continue the struggle in a few distant outposts, the first great onslaught that annihilated the Aztec and the Inca marks the end of our story. In this volume we have been concerned only with the history of a race and a culture of which the aboriginal city-states of Mexico and Peru were the culmination. As we look back upon the long and tortuous career of man in the New World, comprehend his crude equipment as he first set foot upon the land, and pass in review his later achievements, we cannot but regret that the end came so suddenly.

ALFRED L. KROEBER

(1876-1960)

Patterns

PATTERNS ARE THOSE ARRANGEMENTS OR SYSTEMS OF INTERNAL RELATION-
ship which give to any culture its coherence or plan, and keep it from being
a mere accumulation of random bits. They are therefore of primary importance. However, the concepts embraced under the term "pattern" are
still a bit fluid; the ideas involved have not yet crystallized into sharp meanings. It will therefore be necessary to consider in order several kinds of
patterns. We may call these provisionally the universal, the systemic, the
societal or whole-culture, and the style type of patterns.

THE UNIVERSAL PATTERN

The *universal pattern* was proposed by Wissler, with the alternative designation of "the culture scheme." It is a general outline that will more or less
fit all cultures. It is therefore fundamentally different from the other kinds of
pattern, since these all apply either to particular cultures or only to parts of
cultures. The universal pattern consists of a series of nine heads under
which all the facts of any culture may be comprehended. The nine heads
are: Speech, Material Traits, Art, Knowledge ("mythological" as well as
"scientific"), Religion, Society, Property, Government, and War. These
subdivide further, as desirable. Thus under Society, Wissler suggests marriage, kinship, inheritance, control, and games; under Material Traits,
food, shelter, transport, dress, utensils, weapons, and industries; Government is divided into political forms and legal procedures.

It is apparent at once that this universal pattern with its heads and sub-
heads is like a table of contents in a book. It guides us around within the
volume rather than giving us the essence or quality of it. Except for minor
variations, the universal pattern is in fact identical with the table of

From Kroeber, *Anthropology: Race—Language—Culture—Psychology—Prehistory* (New York: Harcourt, Brace and Company, 1948), pp. 311-318, 331-336.

contents of most books descriptive of a culture, such as a standard ethnographic report on a tribe. The main heads are conventional captions for those classes of facts which common sense and common experience lead us to expect to be represented in every culture. We know of no people without speech, food habits, artifacts, property, religion, society, and so on. We can say therefore that these captions represent a sort of common denominators found in all cultures, and that the universal pattern consists merely of the series of these common denominators expectably represented in any culture—represented perhaps very variably but represented somehow.

It is evident that the greater the range of cultures considered, and the more diverse these are, the more will the universal elements or common denominators shrink or become vague. The proportion of universal or common traits in the total range becomes less and less as this total grows more diverse, while at the same time the concepts corresponding to the captions have to be increasingly stretched to accommodate the facts or traits. Thereby the most characteristic features of each culture get blurred out. The Yurok, and again the Ifugao, have a highly intricate legal system, but a minimum of political institutions—in fact it might be argued whether they properly have any. This is certainly an interesting situation in that it differs so radically from our own culture, where not only both law and government are highly developed but law is made to depend on government or to derive from it. This characterizing distinction, which is obviously significant for the understanding of Yurok or Ifugao culture, and almost certainly significant also for understanding our own culture better —this and similar distinctions are lost in the degree that one does one's describing in terms of the common denominators of the universal pattern.

This universal pattern thus boils down to a rough plan of convenience for a preliminary ordering of facts awaiting description or interpretation. No one seems to have developed the idea since it was set forth in 1923, or to have made serious use of it toward deeper understanding. We will therefore pass on to other kinds of patterns.

SYSTEMIC PATTERNS

A second kind of pattern consists of a system or complex of cultural material that has proved its utility as a system and therefore tends to cohere and persist as a unit; it is modifiable superficially, but modifiable only with difficulty as to its underlying plan. Any one such systemic pattern is limited primarily to one aspect of culture, such as subsistence, religion, or economics; but it is not limited areally, or to one particular culture; it can be diffused cross-culturally, from one people to another. Examples are plow agriculture, monotheism, the alphabet, and, on a smaller scale, the *kula* ring of economic exchange among the Massim Melanesians. What distinguishes these systemic patterns of culture—or well-patterned systems, as they might also be called—is a specific interrelation of their component parts, a nexus that holds them together strongly, and tends to preserve the basic plan. This is in distinction to the great "loose" mass of material in every culture that is not bound together by any strong tie but adheres and again dissociates relatively freely. As a result of the persistence of these systemic patterns, their significance becomes most evident on a historical view.

As we mentally roam over the world or down the centuries, what is impressive about these systemic patterns is the point-for-point correspondence of their parts, plus the fact that all variants of the pattern can be traced back to a single original form.

The alphabet is an example. Its history and variations are set forth [later in this work]. But we may anticipate here by pointing out that the alphabet was invented only once, by a Semitic people in southwestern Asia previous to 1000 B.C.; that it operates on the principle of a letter symbol for each minimal acoustic element of speech; that the letters for most sounds in any form of alphabet, no matter how specialized, always resemble the letters in some other alphabet, and through that, or still others, they resemble and are derived from the letters of the original alphabet; and that for the most part the order and often the names of the letters are the same, or where different, it is evident where and why they were altered. Thus Hebrew aleph, beth, gimel, daleth, correspond in sound, order, and name to Greek alpha, beta, gamma, delta, and to Roman and our A, B, C, D.

The pattern of plow agriculture comprises the plow itself; animals to draw it; domestication of these beasts; grains of the barley or wheat type sown by broadcast scattering, without attention to the individual seed, seedling, or plant; fields larger than gardens and of some length; and fertilization with dung, primarily from the draft animals. This system originated in the Neolithic period, probably in western Asia or near it, and by A.D. 1500 had spread from Morocco to North China—since then to the Americas and Australia as well. There are two other and parallel systems, both without plows originally: the rice and maize types of agriculture. The former involves small fields flooded by nature or irrigation, hand planting of seedlings and hand weeding; the associated animals, pigs and buffalo, were not formerly utilized in the rice-growing, though the buffalo is now put before the plow in some areas. This rice pattern began as a hoe-and-garden culture and still largely is such. Native American agriculture, centering around maize, also did not attempt to use the available domestic animals—llamas in the Andes—and therefore was also hoe farming, or even digging-stick farming. The planting was done in hillocks. Irrigation and fertilizing were practiced locally and seem to have been secondary additions. The plants grown in addition to maize were, with the exception of cotton, wholly unrepresented in the plow or rice patterns. The histories of the three systems have remained essentially as separate as their origins, except for some relatively recent transfers of draft animals and plows from the plow pattern into the two others where these began to be drawn into modern international, metropolitan civilization.

The exclusive-monotheistic pattern is Hebrew-Christian-Mohammedan. The three religions are outgrowths of one another and originated in a small area of southwestern Asia. The pattern comprises a single deity, of illimitable power, and exclusive of all others; so far as there are other spiritual beings, such as angels or saints, they are derivative from him; the deity is proclaimed by a particular human vessel inspired by the deity; and worship according to this revelation excludes and forbids any other worship. Cults and philosophies outside these three organized monotheisms have repeatedly attained to monotheism, or to a pantheism or a henotheism that would be hard to distinguish logically from monotheism. And many religions, even of backward peoples, recognize a supreme deity. But all these others regularly lack some of the features of the exclusive-mono-theistic pattern, and their resemblances are thus only partial convergences of an analogical type. This merely analogical similarity of these "high-god" and miscellaneously monotheistic religions goes hand in hand with their diversity of origin: they are not connected with the exclusive mono-theisms, nor for the most part with one another. By contrast, the three exclusive monotheisms are homologous—structurally or part-for-part similar —and they are connected in origin: Jesus was a Jew, and Mohammed took his ideas from Jews and Christians.

The systemic type of pattern accordingly not only partakes of the quality of a system, but is a specific growth. It originates in one culture, is capable of spread and transplantation to others, and tends strongly to persist once it is established. It recalls the basic patterns of structure common to groups of related animals developed from a common origin, with the original pattern persisting through all superficial modifications as they occur under evolution. For instance, the basic vertebrate pattern includes a skull with lower jaw, vertebrate column, and, above the level of the fishes, two pairs of limbs each ending in five digits. Within the range of this pattern, there is endless variation. A snake has no legs, whales and some reptiles and amphibians possess only one pair. Birds have converted the front pair into wings; seals, into flippers; and moles, into "shovels." The digits carry claws in carnivores, hoofs in running mammals, nails in ourselves. They number five in man as in the salamander, never more than four in birds and in pigs, three in the emu, two in the ostrich and the cow, one only in the horse—not counting nonfunctioning vestiges. Not one of the thousands of species of amphibians, reptiles, birds, or mammals ever possesses more than two pairs of limbs or more than five digits; any six-fingered vertebrate is an individual malformation.

By contrast there are the arthropods, among whom the higher crustaceans have five pairs of legs (modifiable to claws or paddles), the spiders four, and the insects three pairs of legs and two pairs of wings; but none of the hundreds of thousands of species of arthropods ever show a five-digited limb. Such are the basic arthropod plans, which are endlessly modified according to order, family, and species. Thus many butterflies have only two pairs of legs; bees have two pairs of wings, but the related ants break theirs off after mating; flies have only one pair; beetles have two pairs but fly mainly with one, the other having become converted into a protective shell; worker ants, fleas, lice, and many others have long since become wingless. We might add that all arthropods have definitely segmented bodies, a skeleton on the outside, antennae, and pale bluish blood containing copper-protein, haemocyanin, as compared with the non-segmentation, inner skeleton, lack of antennae, and blood reddened by the iron-protein haemoglobin of all vertebrates.

It is true that these fundamental plans of structure of the subkingdoms of life such as the arthropods and the vertebrates, or of their classes like insects and mammals, constitute something very much bigger than the system patterns of culture. They are hundreds of millions of years old, expressed in thousands to hundreds of thousands of species and in trillions upon trillions of individuals. The culture patterns muster an age of only a few thousand years. Once established, the great biological patterns predetermine, as it were, the main frames within which evolution will operate. No arthropod can give rise to a vertebrate, or vice versa; their patterns are separated by profound, unbridgeable clefts. Evolutionary change takes place in the domains between these chasms—stricly speaking, between their subchasms. By contrast, cultural system patterns, such as exclusive monotheism, plow agriculture, the alphabet, pass from one race or society, from one major culture, to another, and rather freely. Each year men who otherwise remain in their ancestral culture are for the first time learning to plow, to read letters, to fixate on a single God. Such a transfer of pattern to new kinds of carriers is of course impossible in subhuman organisms, whose forms are dominated by irreversible heredity. But the transfer is characteristic of the very nature of culture, which is plastic, reversible, and capable of unlimited absorptions, anastomosings, and fusions. Hence the patterns within cultures impress us as shifting and often transient. They are so, in comparison with the grand patterns of organic life, just as everything cultural, being an epiphenomenon, something super-added to life, is relatively unstable, modifiable, and adaptable. What the present type of cultural pattern system shares with the fundamental organic patterns is that they both embody a definable system, in the repeated expressions of which, no matter how varied, there nevertheless is traceable a part-for-part correspondence, which allows each form or expression to be recognized as related to the others and derived from the plan as it originally took shape.

In fact, the peculiar interest of these systemic patterns is that, within the endless kaleidoscope of human culture, they allow us to recognize things that are actually related in origin as against things that appear similar but are not connected in origin. The patterns differentiate homologies from analogies, the biologist would say. Thus, the several examples of exclusive monotheism are both homologous and historically interconnected through derivation of one from the other. But the Chinese Heaven, the Indian Brahma, the Egyptian Aten, "god" in the abstract of the Greek philosophers, the supreme deities of many primitive religions, represent analogies or convergences. They are distinct, separate developments which led to results that seem similar. And so, Egyptian hieroglyphs, Mesopotamian cuneiform, Indus Valley, Mayan, and other ancient ideographic or mixed systems of writing, and the surviving Chinese system are like alphabets in that they function as more or less effective methods of visible-speech communication. But they are like them only in that functioning. All alphabets are genetically one—derived from a single source; the other methods of writing have separate sources, operate on different principles, are built on different plans. They resemble alphabets as a whale does a fish—both communicate or swim—but without genuine similarity of structure or meaningful relationship. But alphabet resembles alphabet as whale and porpoise and dolphin resemble one another.

It is in the working-out of these real relationships, structural and genetic relationships as against mere functional similarities, that the recognition of culture patterns of the systemic type finds one of its chief uses.

TOTAL-CULTURE PATTERNS

Next, there are patterns that relate to whole cultures. There is an Italian, a French, a British pattern or form of European civilization. There is an Iroquoian, Algonkin, and Siouan aspect or facies of North American Indian Woodland culture. This Woodland culture in turn has its own larger total pattern, which, together with the Southeastern, Southwestern, North Pacific Coast, Mexican, and other patterns make up the still larger native North American pattern. It is evident that we are here dealing with culture wholes, not, as in the last section, with specific complexes or systems that form only part of any one culture but can be grafted onto others.

East is East and West is West, Kipling said in vivid allusiveness to the different physiognomies or qualities of Occidental and Asiatic civilizations. When he added that never the twain shall meet, he was technically overstating things, in that civilizations do borrow and learn from each other, do assimilate or "acculturate"—which fact he was perfectly aware of when he went on: "But there is neither East nor West, Border, nor Breed, nor Birth, when two strong men stand face to face." But the "never-meeting" is also a poetical way of saying that civilizations are vast things like great ocean currents flowing past each other, and perhaps of implying that the sets or trends of civilizations as wholes vary profoundly, quite apart from the sum total of the items which make up their content. Civilizations differ in "configuration," in modern scientific jargon; "spirit" would have been an earlier word, "genius" before that.

There is of course nothing new in the fact that civilizations are distinct. Innumerable items can always be cited, either of differential or of likeness. To engage a button, we cut a slit in the cloth; the Chinese sew on a loop; and so on. But what do a hundred or a thousand or ten thousand such items mean? What do they add up to that is of wider import or deeper significance? If the items just scatter with equal randomness in two or more cultures, their effect will be equivalent, in spite of the endless variation of detail. Obviously, the specific items must concentrate in some peculiar way in each civilization, must gather or weight themselves along certain lines, if they are to have a larger meaning. And therewith we have a pattern or configuration.

There remains a difficulty, however. Items like buttonholes are definite and are readily ascertained or established, but their significance is limited. The pattern or physiognomy or trend of a great civilization is certainly an important thing to know, but it is difficult to formulate accurately and reliably. Such a pattern has in it breadth and complexity, depth and subtlety, universal features but also uniqueness. In proportion as the expression of such a large pattern tends to the abstract, it becomes arid and lifeless; in proportion as it remains attached to concrete facts, it lacks generalization. Perhaps the most vivid and impressive characterizations have been made by frank intuition deployed on a rich body of knowledge and put into skillful words. Yet this does not constitute proof and is at best at the fringe of the approved methods of science and scholarship. These difficulties will explain why the formulation of whole-culture patterns has not progressed farther, though it is surely one of the most important problems that anthropology and related researches face.

A spirited depiction of the total pattern of any culture possesses much the same appeal and interest as a portrait by a good painter. Some cultures, like some faces, are more interesting than others, but all can be given an interest and meaning by the hand of the skilled master. This gift of "seizing" character, with its suffusion by insight, admittedly partakes as much of the faculties of the artist as of those of the scientist. Excellent delineations of culture patterns have in fact been presented by nonanthropologists, by historians and travelers. More than eighteen hundred years ago Tacitus gave to posterity one of the masterpieces of this genre in his analysis of German custom and character. So keen was his penetration that many qualities of his subjects are still recognizable in the Germans of today.

Other notable examples are the mediaeval Persian Al-Biruni writing in Arabic on Indian civilization; and in the nineteenth century, Burckhardt's *Renaissance,* Doughty's *Arabia Deserta,* Codrington's *Melanesians.* The first was a historian, the second a crotchety Semitist, the third a missionary bishop. At the risk of making invidious distinctions, Malinowski, Benedict, Mead, Evans-Pritchard, might be cited among recent avowed anthropologists. Through the medium of fiction, Pierre Loti, Freuchen's *Eskimo,* Maran's *Batouala,* and Mofolo's *Chaka* have done something similar with exceeding vividness.

A requisite for the recognition of the whole-culture type of pattern, besides of course insight and articulateness, is willingness to see a culture in terms of itself, of its own structure, values, and style. There must be an interest in the culture for its own sake. Without this, the depiction tends to degenerate into a recital of oddments, or of those features in which the culture's standards differ from our own—to its own worsening, of course. The disengagement from the biases and values of the describer's own culture should be complete, at least for the time being. Such preconceptions should never block his sympathies for the culture he is describing, where its qualities call for sympathy. Of course the account must not be a laudation, but an appraisal of what the culture's own standards and valuations are, and how far they are adhered to.

This process is akin to recognition of style in art; to "appreciation" in the stricter sense of that word, before it acquired its popular meaning of mere liking. There too we do not judge Michelangelo by the standard of Rodin, or Mozart by that of Shostakovich; nor, for that matter, Shostakovich by the values of Mozart, though unconsciously that is what conservatives may tend to do. What is in question in such endeavors is the recognition of the art of a certain region and period as expressed by its best exponents, the evaluation of how far it achieved its aims, and the definition of what these aims and values were. Attempts to recognize and define whole-culture patterns are of the same kind, but are larger in that they try to grasp the totality of styles—the nexus of social, ethical, intellectual, and economic as well as aesthetic styles or manners which together constitute the master pattern of a culture.

BASIC PATTERN AND STYLE VARIABILITY

Dress obviously is heavily involved in the matters under discussion. The first association of many women to "pattern" is likely to be the paper model from which dresses are cut and shaped. Vulgarly, the word "style" refers to dress first of all; and it is certainly plain that dress in general is heavily conditioned by style. But beyond all this, dress excellently exemplifies even basic pattern and its influence.

For instance, Occidental civilization, Ancient Mediterranean, and East

Asiatic are each characterized by a distinctive, long-term basic pattern of clothing. In comparison with our fitted clothing, Greek and Roman clothing was draped on the body. While this statement is not wholly exact, it is true comparatively. Sleeves were little developed, trousers lacking, the waist of clothing was not fitted in to follow the body, the general effect accentuated the fall of drapery and the flowing line. The Roman toga was a wraparound blanket. One did not slip into it like a coat, one adjusted it to hang in proper folds.

After prevailing for many centuries, this basic pattern of dress began to crumble and become transformed toward the end of the Roman Empire, when the old Hellenic-Latin religion had yielded to Christianity and the total Mediterranean civilization was disintegrating and at the point of gradually being replaced by the beginnings of our Occidental one. Trousers, in spite of protests and counterlegislation, were adopted from the barbarians. Sleeves came into general use. During the Dark Ages, the transition was gradually accomplished. The fitted clothes might be pretty well concealed under a long coat or cloak, as in the sixth-century mosaics of the Eastern Emperor Justinian and the Empress Theodora; but they were there. By the Middle Ages, they were in the open; and their pattern is still the fundamental pattern of own own clothing. The characteristic of this, in contrast with ancient clothing, is that it is cut and tailored, fitted to the figure. Our word "tailored" is from French *tailleur,* one who cuts, carves, or trims; and *taille* still denotes both the figure as a whole and the waist. The plan of Western clothing for men is that its parts follow the limbs as well as the figure. For women, on the contrary, the legs are withdrawn from sight in a skirt that during most centuries has been ample. From the hips up, however, the pattern of Western women's wear makes up for the loose skirt and has a bodice or an equivalent that follows waist, bosom, shoulders, and arms fairly closely.

How thoroughly this is our basic type of dress even today, underneath all local or national variations and fluctuations of period and fashion, is evident when we compare Western dress as a whole for the past thousand years with the East Asiatic in the same millennium. Chinese and Japanese dress is also cut and tailored, but it is not fitted. It is cut loose, with ample sleeves, or kimono style, to suggest a broad figure. Trousers are ample, so as to have almost a skirt effect. The use of clothing to model or suggest women's bust, waist, and hip contour is wholly outside the Far Eastern pattern. Witness the Japanase *obi* sash and bow intended to conceal these features, while European women for four centuries or more have worn corsets and girdles to accentuate them.

Of course dress is notoriously subject to fashion change. But it is remarkable how virtually all changes of fashion, alike in Classical, Western, and East Asiatic costume, have consistently operated each within the basic dress pattern of its own civilization. Fashion creates a thousand bizarre forms and extravagances; but it never has produced, among Occidentals, a man's type of dress based on toga instead of trousers, nor a woman's with a Japanese silhouette. The matter of fashion changes, which represent a minor sort of restless and anonymous innovation or invention, is discussed elsewhere, with emphasis on a concealed rhythm or regularity much greater than the participants in a fashion are ordinarily aware of. But there is another aspect of fashion change—what may be called the intensity of its alteration, its momentary degree of variability—that both defines the basic pattern and helps to explain variation from it. Variability is high when the fashion of one year differs considerably from that of the year before; it is still more so when a series of particular dresses, all of the same year, differ considerably from one another. Low variability of course is marked by small differences of this sort. Such variabilities are easily expressed statistically.[1]

The underlying fashion swings or trends change what might be called the total silhouette of dress rather than its details. These minor features may come and go quite rapidly, and are what give the impression nearly everyone has that dress fashions are highly unstable. On the contrary, the total silhouette shifts rather steadily for perhaps fifty years toward one extreme of proportion, such as a narrow skirt for women, and then for about fifty years toward the opposite, giving a wavelength of close to a century for the periodicity, which seems to be adhered to with fair consistency in case after case.

It might be thought that the basic pattern (for Occidental women's dress during the last hundred and fifty years) would lie somewhere between these proportion extremes. Occasionally it does. But mostly the basic pattern proves to coincide with one of the extremes. The other extreme then represents a sort of opposition or aberration from the pattern. One might describe these aberrant extremes as the proportions still just inside the pattern but as far away as possible from its center of gravity. Or one might say the aberrant extreme is antithetical—almost perversely antithetical—to the ideal or saturation point of the pattern, though still barely remaining within its range. Thus, as the permanent Western pattern aims at amplitude from the hips down but slenderness above, the silhouette-extremes conformable to the pattern would be: full or wide skirt, long or low skirt, narrow waist, and therefore waistline just at the waist proper. The antithetical extremes would be: narrow skirt, short skirt, wide or full waist, and waistline moved from the anatomically narrowest part up toward the broader breast or down toward the broader hips. In this last proportion—position of the waistline—pattern saturation evidently falls at the midpoint between extremes. In the three other proportions, pattern saturation coincides with one of the extremes.

[1] By the standard deviation or sigma, converted into a percentage of the mean as the coefficient of variability.

Fig. 19. BASIC STYLE PATTERN IN WOMEN'S CLOTHES.

Transient fashions conforming to basic pattern in upper stagger contrast with intrinsic departures from pattern in the lower. Also, upper figures are accompanied by low variability of fashion, and date from the calm Victorian era; lower figures show high variability and date from Revolution, Napoleonic, and World War periods.

A glance at the silhouettes in the upper row of Figure 19, showing characteristic dress at twenty-year intervals during the latter and larger part of the nineteenth century, reveals what characterizes the pattern—its constant stable features underneath temporary fluctuations. The lower row gives two silhouettes from the period of the French Revolution and Napolcon, and two from the period of the World Wars—two eras of socio-political restlessness enclosing the relative calm of Victorian times. Here skirts are in evidence that are narrow or high or both, and waists that are thick or ultrahigh or ultralow—the aberrant extremes.

VARIABILITY IN EUROPEAN WOMEN'S DRESS SILHOUETTE DURING
FOUR YEARS OF PATTERN CONFORMITY AND STABILITY
COMPARED WITH
FOUR YEARS OF PATTERN STRAIN AND INSTABILITY

Stable Pattern Years: Low Variability*

	1839	1859	1879	1899	Mean of 4 years
Skirt length	27	0	55	0	21
Skirt width	61	22	73	61	54
Waist height	53	40	53	53	50
Waist width	170	107	43	138	115

Unstable Pattern Years: High Variability*

	1789	1813	1916	1935	Mean of 4 years
Skirt length	164	492	219	109	246
Skirt width	61	235	151	162	152
Waist height	93	253	106	186	160
Waist width	277	107	128	256	192

* Figures express 100(V for year)/(mean V for 150 years).—$V = 100\sigma/M$

When we look at the statistical expression of fashion variability in the same selected eight years as given in corresponding position on the preceding page, it is at once clear that the years and decades of pattern saturation or concordance are marked by definitely low variability, indicative of stability; and the years and eras of pattern antithesis or stretch are marked by a surprisingly great variability, indicative of instability. Stability and instability here refer to the dress style pattern and its behavior. Since the periods of dress-pattern instability were also periods of marked sociopolitical instability and churning, there is presumably a connection.

The connection or relation seems functional rather than causal. There is nothing to indicate that the mere presence of wars and revolutions will make designers deliberately plan consecutive dresses as different as is possible within the mode, whereas in times of calm they design them as alike as they can make them and will keep them from being identical. What evidently happens is merely that in periods of general stress, when the foundations of society and civilization seem rocked, the pattern of dress is also infected and subject to strain. It expresses this strain by moving from stable saturation to aberration, antithesis, restlessness, and instability.

This example may make more concrete the role of patterns—both style patterns and total-culture patterns—in cultural change and stability. Not that patterns are the beginning and end of everything about civilization. But practically everything in culture occurs as part of one or more patterns.

Hence whatever happens in the way of accomplishment, alteration, succession, or persistence in any culture is likely to happen through the mechanism of patterns. We do not yet know too much about them, because awareness of patterns is relatively recent in anthropology. But it is already clear that understanding of culture as something more than an endless series of haphazard items is going to be achieved largely through recognition of patterns and our ability to analyze them.

Cultural Intensity and Climax

THE EIGHTY-FOUR AREAS INTO WHICH NORTH AMERICA HAS BEEN DIVIDED are cultural in the sense that, within each, culture is relatively uniform. Many of them also approximate natural areas; that is, they often possess one or more features, such as drainage, elevation, land form, climate, or plant cover, which also are relatively uniform over the tract, or alter at its borders. They are, further, historical areas, in that their relations with one another reflect currents or growths of culture, as soon as the areas are viewed not as equivalents but as differing in intensity or level. The ten or so larger culture areas hitherto customarily recognized differ from one another essentially in culture material or content; consideration of differences in level has usually been avoided as subjective or unscientific. The more numerous areas of native North America dealt with in the present work are in part based avowedly on culture intensity as well as content.

In practice, these two aspects of intensity and content cannot be rigorously separated. A precise calendar system, a complex interrelation of rituals or social units, invariably embodies special culture material as well as intensity of its development and organization. Simple culture material cannot well be highly systematized; refined and specialized material seems to demand organization if it is to survive. What we call intensity of culture therefore means both special content and special system. A more intensive as compared with a less intensive culture normally contains not only more material—more elements or traits—but also more material peculiar to itself, as well as more precisely and articulately established interrelations between the materials. An accurate time reckoning, a religious hierarchy, a set of social classes, a detailed property law, are illustrations of this.

Granted this interdependence of richness of content and richness of systematization, it should be possible to determine an approximately objective measure of cultural intensity by measuring culture content—by count-

From Kroeber, *Cultural and Natural Areas of North America* (Berkeley: University of California Press, 1939). Reprinted in *The Nature of Culture* (Chicago: University of Chicago Press, 1952), pp. 337, 339-343.

ing distinguishable elements, for instance. This is a task which no one is yet ready to perform for the continent; but theoretically it is feasible; and it might be worth while. Wider historical conclusions can hardly be formulated without consideration of intensity factors. Permanent neglect of these will tend to limit investigations to narrowly circumscribed regions and periods, or to abstract consideration of processes as such.

Each of the six major areas here dealt with, except that of the Eskimo, shows at least one climax or focus of cultural intensity—even the Intermediate tract possesses a low-grade one in California. . . .

In general, a culture climax or culmination may be regarded as the point from which the greatest radiation of culture material has taken place in the area. But it is always necessary to remember that as a culture becomes richer, it also tends to become more highly organized, and in proportion as its organization grows, so does its capacity to assimilate and place new material, whether this be produced within or imported from without. In the long run, accordingly, high-intensity cultures are the most absorptive as well as the most productive. It is by the interaction of both processes that culture culminations seem to be built up. Consequently, an unusually successful degree of absorption tends to lead to further "inventive" productiveness and outward influencing, and so on, until the process fails somewhere and a condition of stability is reached or a decline sets in; or a newer center begins to dominate the old.

On the whole, accordingly, it can be assumed that culture climaxes are not mushroom growths; though their finest flowerings are evidently brief, and the introduction of a radically new subsistence mechanism, such as agriculture or the horse, may occasionally cause a rapid growth. Where there is no evidence of such fundamental economic introduction, it may be taken for granted with a reasonable degree of assurance that a climax in the historic period was also a climax, or at least a subclimax, in the later prehistoric period, and probably at least of fairly high level of intensity before that. Maya, Aztec-Toltec, Southwestern archaeology—in general that of the continent as a whole—confirms this assumption.

Archaeology does indicate some minor shifts of climax area: of the Maya from the base to the tip of the Yucatan Peninsula, of the Pueblo center from San Juan to Little Colorado and upper Rio Grande drainage. Analogous to these is the hypothetical northward movement of the Northwest Coast culmination. On the whole, however, these shifts are of small range. The only region of the continent in which there is evidence of a large-scale culture recession is the Ohio Valley. Even here the lowering of culture intensity from the prehistoric to the historic period seems not very great; and the whole eastern major area of which the Ohio Valley forms part is the one whose historic climax is the least.

Of all the greater currents in American prehistory, that which brought stimuli of Mexican origin to the region of the Mississippi and Ohio is the most obscure, on account of the unusually low-level cultures intervening in Tamaulipas and Texas. The Southwest is more evenly linked to central Mexico by tribes like the Opata, Tarahumara and Cáhita, Sinaloans and Cora. At any rate, agriculture is continuous from the Southwest to central Mexico; discontinuous from the Southeast. The Northwest Coast seems so free, relatively, of specific Mexican influences that its culture, beyond many general American elements, is readily construable as a re-working primarily of Asiatic and possibly Oceanic stimuli. It therefore presents quite different problems. The most satisfactory hypothesis to explain the more intensive eastern culture is that this was due to the same influences which introduced maize agriculture, presumably from Mexico; and that with the introduction of this fundamental subsistence factor all cultural values shifted, and there ensued a period of unsettlement and activity, during which now this and now that local center forged ahead. Gradually, however, cultural productivity or "creativeness" diminished in these minor climaxes and became more evenly diffused, owing presumably to the fact that Mexican relations never became established as something direct and continuous. Since no region in the area thus had a first monopoly of culture import nor continued to have its intensity reinforced by maintenance of contacts with the high center, the result was a gradual leveling, along with sporadic retention here and there of this or that introduced element. Some slight precedence still remained, until early Caucasian times, in the region where it seems inherently most likely that the introduction of maize first occurred—about the lower Mississippi; but even this was waning.

The opinion of the early French observers that the Natchez represented but the remnant of something greater is, then, perhaps not wholly unfounded. With reference to what has just been said about culture content and organization, the Natchez make the impression of having possessed a type of organization more developed than the simple content of their culture as a whole called for. The material of this culture—its arts, war customs, ritual elements—was only barely distinguishable from that of Muskogi culture; the conscious emphasis put on the system of social values appears to have been perceptibly greater. It has always seemed a problem how such a system could develop from the inside, spontaneously as it were, among a small ethnic group. It is much easier to see it as a survival from a time when the content of the culture was also richer.

In a measure, the same type of situation appears to be true of the Pueblo climax. Pueblo culture material of the historic and late prehistoric period, to be sure, remained relatively rich as compared with earlier prehistoric times—perhaps even continued to increase; but one has an impression that its organization was still more preponderant.

On the Northwest Coast the reverse seems to hold. The patterns of the culture are definite enough, and the impulses toward organization obvious. But no single consistent scheme appears to have been evolved. Everything is elaborated and rated, and yet there is no real system. Active production of culture material was evidently going on, but the attempts toward its organization were still vigorous rather than successful.

Northwestern climax culture then was in the ascendant phase and nearing its culmination; Southwestern and Southeastern were declining—the former slowly, owing to long intrenchment of its system and perhaps partial maintenance of exposure to Mexico; the latter, never firmly established nor well connected with its fountainhead, already almost at the bottom of the descent. Reference is to culminations: the general level of the culture of an area may well rise while that of its climax sinks.

In Mexico, Aztec and Maya civilizations in A.D. 1500 evidently contrasted in a parallel manner: the one probably in the ascendant, the other surely declining.

If it ever proves possible to find some objective measure of culture intensity other than indicators chosen from among its contents as suggested above, the relative strength of the two factors of cultural evolution and devolution would be computable, and the history of nonhistoric peoples and cultures could be better projected than now when feeling or intuition is our chief guidance.

Parallels with historic civilizations suggest themselves. Wherever one of these attained a clearly recognizable culmination, this seems to have corresponded essentially with a period of successful organization of culture content—organization in part into a conscious system of ideas, but especially into an integrated nexus of styles, standards, and values. Before the culmination, the absorption or development of culture material was apparently outstripping its organization into new values, as in Greece from 800 to 500 B.C. At the culmination, organization overtook and mastered content: the value-system of the culture was set. After the culmination, there followed a period at first usually of continued production or assimilation of material, but this soon slackened, while organization, though more and more limited to revision or perpetuation of the value-system, continued to be maintained: as in Greece after 200 B.C.

Ancient Egypt is now well enough known to show the same cycle in outline. The specific developmental process must have been under way by 4000 B.C. The culmination was reached soon after 3000, perhaps around 2600. After that, consolidation prevailed. This brought its benefits, and the greatest realm extension, wealth, and perhaps population were not attained until 1500. New culture material also continued to be taken in and assimilated: bronze, iron, the horse, and so on. But the standards and values had been essentially settled on by about 2600, and altered relatively little after that. Art, writing, architecture, religion, remained cast in the familiar molds. These molds largely survived the political breakup after 1100, and the first foreign conquests. Even Greek domination did not more than partly obliterate the old patterns, and it required several additional centuries of strong Roman and Christian influence, in part even the Arab shock, to reduce the obsolescent survivals to extinction.

Flinders Petrie has gone so far with the concept of cultural cycle as to try to determine the respective moments of culmination of the several aspects of a number of civilizations, and to derive from these a recurrent pattern. Climax attainment in sculpture precedes that in painting, for instance; literature also comes early; science and wealth reach their peaks late in each cycle, he argues, specifying both achievements and dates for each civilization. He is at times so peremptorily immediate in his judgments, and so individualistic in his chronology, that his essay has won little following. Even in those who might be interested in his idea, distrust has probably been aroused by the drastic handling of facts. Nevertheless, art or literature or both do seem to culminate earlier than mechanical science, wealth, and population in the Egyptian, classic Mediterranean, and Occidental civilizations, probably in Chinese, Indian, and Mesopotamian also, and there is no clear example of a reversal of order. The indication thus is that Petrie may have got some hold on a general principle of culture growth.

In native America both literature and science were relatively undeveloped and are imperfectly known. Art, however, attained to some high developments, and its recovered specimens have generally been sedulously preserved. It is possible, therefore, to take this part of Petrie's scheme—that the culmination of art tends to come early in the history of a culture—and to test it against the inferences on developmental phases reached on other grounds in the foregoing pages. In short, the hypothesis, based on precedent in the Old World, is that a culture with a flourishing art would still be in the ascendant phase; one with a decaying or dead art, at its peak or in the descendant.

The Maya culture fits perfectly. All the known great sculpture of highest fine-art value comes in the Old Period, before A.D. 900 by the usual reckoning. The semigeometric architectural decoration, the Toltec-influenced reliefs and frescoes of Chichen, and the codex illustrations of the Late period cannot begin to compare in quality with the Old Maya art. And yet calendar, script, religion, architecture, kept their essential forms more than half a thousand years longer.

In the valley of Mexico and environs, decision upon what is earlier and later among many pieces of art is more difficult. There may have been successive and more or less discrete pulses of Toltecan and of Aztecan period. Still, one would be inclined to doubt the essential separateness of these on the same spot: Old World precedent is too uniformly to the contrary. With the two periods reckoned as parts of one culture growth, we have left, in sculpture, a number of specimens that can be pretty positively assigned to each. Among these, precedence in aesthetic merit almost certainly goes to the "Aztec" examples. This culture, then, by hypothesis, would still have been in or near the ascending phase at its discovery.

The lesser Mexican cultures like the Zapotec and Totonac are too little known, so far as time development is concerned, to make their discussion in this connection profitable. To pass to South America, however, we have in Peru a partial fit to theory. The Late or Inca culture was evidently the richest attained there, in totality of content as expressed by number of inventions or known devices. Quipu, balance, roads, suspension bridges, bronze, for instance, are either Late only or not known to be Early. Easily the best sculpture, however, is that of Tiahuanaco, the finer and still earlier sculpture of Chavin, and, if clay modeling be included, the pre-Tiahuanaco Early Chimú pottery. All these date long before the Incas. This is not a wholly comparable illustration, because the Early cultures in which the arts culminated were markedly local or provincial, Inca culture essentially pan-Peruvian. It is conceivable that this Late civilization marked the beginning of a new era on a wider areal basis, and that this was still so new that its pure art had not begun to develop. This suggestion, however, leads to a number of counterconsiderations, which are too complicated to follow up here. It does remain a fact that Inca sculpture is inferior to the best Early Peruvian sculpture, and that where a local art, like that of Chimú pottery, can be traced consecutively, the summit of aesthetic quality is Early (Mochica), whereas variety, elegance, and geographical spread culminate in Late Chimú times.

In the Southwest, plastic and pictorial art never reached even moderate achievements, but the history of pottery is well known. The finest types are generally considered to be the Mimbres and the Sikyatki wares, with which some would rank certain of the San Juan black-on-white styles. These all fall in Pueblo period 3 or early 4. Post-Spanish wares are generally deteriorated, except for very recent Caucasian-stimulated renaissances. This accords with the general recognition of period 3 as the Great Pueblo period—great with reference to its values. In quantitative richness of total culture content, periods 4 and 5 perhaps equal or surpass it: for instance, there are no positive indications of masks in the prehistoric periods; and it is hard to believe that any ancient town maintained rituals so elaborately organized as those of modern Zuñi. The content and system of the culture have been well maintained; its best art has been dead several centuries. Here, then, is another illustration of fit to hypothesis.

In eastern North America art was at a low level at the time of discovery. The finest specimens all seem prehistoric; pottery trophy heads in Arkansas, incised shell gorgets from about Tennessee, Hopewell culture ornaments of copper, mica, and bone in Ohio. None of these productions rises to the level of a great art; but a number evince both skill and feeling in a definite, rather unique style. This agrees with the interpretation, advanced above, of Mississippi Valley culture—as a growth that reached its modest peak some centuries before Caucasian advent, and had then spread and shallowed, with fragmentary persistences like those among the Natchez.

These, however, were essentially organizational and unaccompanied by aesthetic productivity. The somewhat scattered and diverse art achievements point to provincial and transient flowerings.

Northwest Coast art, on the other hand, was fairly flourishing when discovered, and was evidently stimulated to higher quality by its first Caucasian contacts. The archaeological remains in the area are cruder, and none of them shows the full style of the historic period. To be sure, they are rather scant; but in view of the unanimously simple quality of such specimens as there are, their fewness itself argues a lack of aesthetic vigor. Here, then, an active and successful art exists in a culture which on other grounds has been construed as still in its growth phase.

The tantalizing and fundamental subject of cultural phase can hardly be pursued farther here, for a variety of reasons, among them the outstanding one that the exactest determinations of period can obviously be made best on datable and therefore documentary materials. What I have tried to show is that both in art and in degree of systematization the more outstanding American cultures seem to conform to a general pattern of culture growth, the outlines of which gleam through the known historic civilizations. Further, the very concept of climax, or, if one will, culture center, involves not only the focus of an area but also a culmination in time. Through the climax, accordingly, geography and history are brought into relation; or, at any rate, the areal and temporal aspects of culture cannot be really related unless consideration is accorded to climax. This view has guided me in the present work—which in turn, I trust, validates the view by its concrete exemplifications.

ELSIE CLEWS PARSONS

(1875-1941)

Externally, Elsie Clews Parsons' scientific life seems to fall into two distinct phases which might be called pre-Boas and post-Boas. Actually, the distinction is more apparent than real. Toward the end of her life she achieved a synthesis of the two parts. Throughout her life she consistently sought an answer to the problem of the nature of social pressures on the individual. It was only the techniques of her search that changed.

Elsie Parsons was born in New York, of a wealthy and socially prominent family. Furthermore she was beautiful and was predestined for a brilliant career in fashionable society. Her rebellion against it set the pattern of her life. She attended Barnard College, then newly organized, and went on to obtain a Ph.D. in sociology in 1899.

During the next fifteen years she wrote a number of books, The Old-Fashioned Woman *(under the pseudonym of John Main),* Fear and Conventionality, Social Rule, *all dealing in one way or another with the problem that obsessed her: the pressure of society on the individual, especially as it affected the role of woman. She saw that no answers were to be found by multiplying examples. It was at this point that she met Boas and realized the possibilities in the study of anthropology for gaining insight into social process. Wherever she went in her wide travels, she collected folk tales. Her interest in folklore, although it absorbed a great deal of her time, seems, in retrospect, a detour from the true path of her interest. It was her work in the pueblos that brought her back to the main track.*

Here was a culture which demanded even greater conformity than our own. She began collecting the material which eventually went into her book, Pueblo Indian Religion. *Her short papers describing ceremonies or fragments of ceremonies seem to follow the pattern of Fewkes or Voth. But the real substance is in the footnotes where she recorded her observations and impressions, comments on the participating personnel, deviations from official versions, and village gossip. Her two volumes on pueblo religion are encyclopedic, her analysis of ceremonial patterns is definitive. She paid her debt to anthropology. Her next book,* Mitla, Town of Souls, *is her one complete study of a primitive community. (Her book on the pueblo of Jemez is fragmentary and much of it done of necessity away from the*

*village.) Here she put to use what she learned in the pueblos, and has pre-
sented a study of the unformalized techniques of social control in another
society, written from the woman's point of view.*

*No discussion of Elsie Clews Parsons is complete without mention of
her support of anthropology. She gave generously to anthropological causes,
but always somewhat awkwardly, because the role of Lady Bountiful embarrassed her. No one knows the number of students whom she helped,
the field work she made possible, the books she had published, or the
financial difficulties which she smoothed over.—R.L.B.*

Holding Back in Crisis Ceremonialism

BY CRISIS CEREMONIAL I MEAN CEREMONIAL TO SIGNALIZE OR ALLOW OF
the passing from one stage of life to another, what Van Gennep calls *"rites
de passage,"* what the Greeks called *têlêtē,* the putting off of the old, the
putting on of the new—adolescence or initiation rites, marriage rites,
funeral rites or mourning.

In the interpretation of crisis ceremonialism I am suggesting, there are
two main features, related features, for both refer to what I take to be the
characteristic attitude of primitive culture towards change, the attitude
that change can be ignored—up to a certain point—and controlled—within a certain degree. Through ceremonialism change is ignored, *i.e.,* it is
not met as it occurs and it is controlled, *i.e.,* it is made dependent on the
ceremony, established and disposed of ceremonially. . . .

At any rate the particular feature of crisis ceremonial I wish to discuss,
its features of reluctance, of holding back, may be taken as an outcome of
the pull of habit, actual or conventionalized, an outcome too, which is
tolerated or encouraged because it increases through resistance natural or
simulated the group's sense of power.

What display of resistance or of reluctance is there at initiation? I will
give a few instances:

In Central Australia preparations for the initiation are made unknown
to the lad to be initiated.[1] Then frightened when hands are laid upon him,
he struggles to get free. Similarly in Queensland a girl is decoyed away
from camp, ambushed and then operated upon despite all her shrieks and
entreaties.[2] Indeed in every Blackfellow tribe the initiate or adolescent, boy
or girl, is regularly taken by surprise and subjected to force. In the New

[1] Spencer, B. and Gillen, F. J. *The Native Tribes of Central Australia,* p. 219.
London and New York, 1899.
[2] Roth, W. E. *Ethnological Studies among the North-West Central Queensland
Aborigines,* p. 174. Brisbane and London, 1897.

From Parsons, "Holding Back in Crisis Ceremonialism," *American Anthropologist,* N.S., Vol. XVIII (1916), pp. 41-47, 49-51.

Britain ceremonial, a coil of shell-money is thrown over the initiate's head, to placate him it is said. If he succeeds in breaking away from his captors before the coil is thrown, he is allowed to escape. The next time he is caught and breaks away it is etiquette for him to try to kill his pursuers.[3]. . .

On the part of an initiate's kindred, particularly his kinswomen,[4] resistance and reluctance are also displayed. Narrinyeri initiates are seized upon at night by the men. The women resist or pretend to resist, pulling back the captives and throwing firebrands at the captors.[5] In the Port Lincoln district after the initiate is seized the women are forced out of their shelters to shout and lament as if in deep grief. Their fears, it is said, are ceremonial.[6] In the Mita-Koodi tribe throughout the first night of the initiation the women are supposed to wail.[6a] . . . When a Banks island initiate leaves his kinswomen they cry as if he were leaving them for a long time.[7] A Tikopia boy is incised when he is about twelve years old. During the operation his relatives weep, the men cutting themselves on the forehead, the women tearing their cheeks with their nails.[8]

The initiation of offspring marks among several peoples the entrance of parents into another age-class. Ceremonial expressions of reluctance to be promoted among the elders appear to be scant, perhaps because the privileges of seniority in early culture are so great. To our formulas for the occasion—"I hear your boy is entering college. What an old fellow you must feel," or, "My daughter is coming out, it makes me feel like an old woman," to such formulas of regret I find but one analogue. A Masai may not be circumcised and qualified for the warrier class until his father has observed a ceremonial called "the passing of the fence." After four days of isolation, as the father is passing the fence, he is addressed by an elder: "Go, become an old man." He replies: "Ho, I shall not!" Four times the order is given and four times objected to. The fifth time, the father answers: "Ho! I have gone then."[9]

---

[3] Danks, B., in *Journal Anthropological Institute,* XVIII (1888-9), p. 286-7.

[4] Part of the feelings of the women is no doubt grief over the more or less permanent separation of the boys. The lifelong separation of the sexes is begun at initiation and no doubt ceremonially accentuated.

By one engaged in proving that women are more sentimental than men, more reluctant to face the facts of change, their attitude at initiations and in other crisis ceremonials merits attention.

[5] Smyth, R. Brough. *The Aborigines of Victoria,* I, 166. Melbourne and London, 1878.

[6] *Ib.,* I, 67.

[6a] Roth, p. 173.

[7] Rivers, I, 101. Confined in the *salagoro* in old days it not infrequently happened that they never did see him again. Dr. Rivers believes, however, that the wailing is part of the conception of initiation as a ceremonial death. (*Ib.,* I, 127). Belief thus explicit may be held, but it is not necessary, to explain the mourning. The wailing is quite adequately accounted for by the diffuse feeling that the boy is setting forth in life.

[8] Rivers, *Ib.,* I, 312.

[9] Hollis, A. C. *The Masai,* p. 295. Oxford, 1905.

In marriage ceremonial the observation of resistance and reluctance has been closer and fuller. Much of it has been compiled too—to illustrate or prove the existence of marriage by capture and its survival in the so-called rape symbols. It is not good proof for the most part for that historic speculation just because it does illustrate the theory of marriage as crisis ceremonialism. The resistance or holding back is generally an individual display of the bride, often against her own people, and when her kindred do resist or hang back it is the women rather than the men of the family who are most assertive. Other circumstances also suggest that the "capture" is merely of the girl herself, and not of the girl away from her people. The capture may be connived at by her family or even planned for. After it she may be taken back to her home for the subsequent part of the ceremonial, or even to live there for a period. Again in widow marriage the "rape symbol" may be dropped out—just as one might expect in the case of a rite to express reluctance against a novel relationship, but not to be expected if the loss of a woman to her family were the idea in mind.

Bridegroom as well as bride may show reluctance and in ways too that are a droll commentary on the much discussed theory of the "rape symbol."

Among the Roro-speaking tribes of New Guinea when the bridegroom sees the bridal procession coming, he hides in the *marea* or clubhouse. The village youths drag him forth, and disregarding his protests, having painted and decorated him, bring him to his father's house. Here he is made to sit down near the bride. Neither pays any attention to the other.[10] From his place among the bachelors the Andamanese bridegroom has also to be dragged away. When the chief or elder approaches him he at once assumes a modest demeanor and simulates the greatest reluctance to join his *fiancée*.[11] For five days a New Britain bride stays alone in the bridegroom's house, while he hides away in the forest or in some place in the high grass known only to the men.[12] Among the Abschasses of the Caucasus the bridegroom runs away and hides on his wedding night, to be brought back by force the following day.[13]

The analogous behavior of the bride is far too well known to need particularization. But to one of the methods in use to overcome her reluctance I would draw attention, the method of bribery. Almost as misleading to the ethnographer as the tag of "rape symbol" has been the tag of "brideprice." Any present on the occasion of a marriage he puts down as part of

[10] Seligmann, C. G. *The Melanesians of British New Guinea,* p. 269. Cambridge, 1910.

[11] Man, E. H., in *Journal Anthropological Institute,* XII (1882-3), p. 137.

[12] Danks, pp. 286-7. Cf. Parkinson, R., *Dreissig Jahre in der Südsee,* pp. 65-6, Stuttgart, 1907. After two or three days the bridegroom begins to pay a daily visit to the bride, she giving him a meal. Then he may go with her to her field work. After some weeks he builds a house and the first night the couple spends in it the marriage is considered to be finally contracted. See p. 51.

[13] Seidlitz, N. V. "Die Abchasen." *Globus,* LXVI (1894), 40.

the purchase sum signalizing a marriage by purchase. Whether the presents are made before the wedding, during its celebration or afterwards, whatever their nature, from a lock of hair or a bunch of flowers to a pig or a diamond tiara, whether they are made by the bridegroom or his family or friends or by the bride or her family or friends it makes no difference, they are all likely to be accounted for as a bride-price or derivatives at least of a bride-price. In this welter of wedding-presents may be distinguished, I think, presents that appear to be, far more than a compensation, a bribe, a short-cut to overcome the reluctances, sometimes of the bride, sometimes of kindred, to enter into or envisage the new relationship or the new stage of life.

Among the Zambales Negritoes during the *leput* or ceremonial homecoming of the bridegroom with his bride, the lady squats down on the ground from time to time and refuses to budge until she receives a present.[14] A bride's conduct in Uganda is similarly contrary. Carried by the bridegroom's retainers she is set down at his threshold. There she balks until the bridegroom comes out to give her cowries. Indoors she declines to sit down and make herself at home until she gets another present of cowries. Later still another present has to be forthcoming to induce her to eat.[15] In Fiji the presents the weeping[16] bride receives from the bridegroom's party are actually called "drying-up-of-the-tears," *vakamamaca*.[17] In the account George Sand[18] gives us of the wedding practices of Berry, a district in the heart of France, the French bride is quite as unmistakably bribed as the Fijian. Barred out, the bridegroom's party sing to her:

> "Ouvrez la porte, ouvrez,
> Marie, ma mignonne,
> *J'ous* de beaux cadeaux a vous présenter
> Hélas! ma mie, laissez-nous entrer."

And then the song goes on to specify all the charming things they have for[19] her—ribbons and lace, a fine apron, a hundred pins, a cross of gold[20] Among the Bashkirs although a girl may have been visited by her be-

---

[14] Reed, W. A. *Negritoes of Zambales*, pp. 59-60. Manila, 1904.

[15] Roscoe, J., in *Journal Anthropological Institute*. XXXII (1902), 37.

[16] She weeps although her marriage has been the outcome of a mutual attachment, not, as in other types of Fijian marriages, of betrothal in infancy, or of purely parental determination.

[17] Williams, T. *Fiji and the Fijians*, I, 169. London, 1858.

[18] *La Mare au Diable.*

[19] None of them appears to materialize; but in the church the bridegroom gives the bride *le treizain,* thirteen pieces of silver.

[20] It is this account which is cited by McLennan as evidence for the survival of a rape symbol in France. "Primitive Marriage," App. in *Studies in Ancient History*. But the bride's refrain, sung for her by the matrons, suggests an explanation other than that of the rape symbol for all that follows.

"Mon père est en chagrin, ma mère en grand' tristesse"—a father angry and a mother sorrowing over the disturbance of their family life.

trothed most intimately for a long time when on the final payment on the bride-price he takes her home, she refuses to embrace him until he gives her a piece of money.[21] . . . Unmistakable bribes, all these, but even more dubious instances, even the *morgen gab* for example, and its many variations I prefer to think of as originally a prospective bribe rather than as compensation money, its orthodox explanation. . . .

Another ceremonial display of reluctance at marriage is the separation of bride and groom until the close of the ceremonial, sometimes very protracted, and even for some time afterwards. The avoidance practised in the so-called Tobias nights is a taboo not limited to the early Christian Church. In Australia the Mukjarawaint bride sleeps the first night of her marriage on the ground outside her bridegroom's camp.[22] The Euahlayi bride is expected to sleep with a fire between herself and her bridegroom.[23] In Queensland, Frazer island, bride and bridegroom live alone for two months in huts about six yards apart.[24] The Roro-speaking bridegroom is just as "shy" after his wedding as before. On his wedding night he goes back to his clubhouse leaving his bride to sleep alone in the house of his father. He is brought back to her the following day, but he does not spend the night. The third day the couple is supposed to be "reconciled," but the bridegroom continues to sleep at the clubhouse for several weeks.[25] Among the Andamanese "it often happens that a young couple will pass several days after their nuptials without exchanging a single word, and to such an extent do they carry their bashfulness that they even avoid looking at each other."[26] That formality may enter into this attitude one may at least surmise. . . . Among the Massim no trace of ceremonial deferment has been observed and yet a man at Mukana, a bridegroom of at least two months, volunteered to Dr. Seligmann the information that he had not yet had connection with his wife for if a child were born within a year of marriage people would sneer, saying, "What sort of children are these?"[27] Among the Roro-speaking tribes where deferment, we remember, is customary a woman in former times did not expect to bear a child until her garden was bearing well, *i. e.*, until she had been married one to two years.[28] In the New Britain islands children were not born for a period from two to four years after marriage. "Women did not like to speedily become mothers."[29]

Of the conventionalized expression of reluctance to meet change that

[21] Van Gennep, A. *Les Rites de Passage*, p. 173. Paris, 1909.
[22] Howitt, A. W. *The Native Tribes of South-East Australia*, p. 245. London and New York, 1904.
[23] Parker, K. L., *The Euahlayi Tribe*, p. 58. London, 1905.
[24] Smyth, I, 84 ft.
[25] Seligmann, pp. 269-70.
[26] Man, X, p. 138.
[27] Seligmann, p. 745.
[28] *Ib.*, pp. 269-70.
[29] Danks, p. 287.

occurs in marriage and initiation ceremonial I have given illustrations, some of the facts having been otherwise interpreted; but I need not particularize with illustrations about the unwillingness to meet the change made by death. I have only to refer to various well-known beliefs or practices— the belief that the spirit of the deceased lingers for a period—hours or days or longer—about his home; the set appeals to the dead to return or— to be off; the provision for the wants of the lingering ghost, for both his material and his emotional wants; the preservation of his remains or relics or of his memory or influence; early theories of the life after death, the continuation theory, the theory of reincarnation. . . .

Nativity Myth at Laguna and Zuñi

DURING A VISIT TO LAGUNA IN FEBRUARY, 1918, I HAD NOTICED IN THE church a model in miniature of the Nativity group. Jesus, Mary and Joseph, the ox and the mule, were represented, and there was a large flock of sheep. José or Tsiwema or Tsipehus,[1] the "sextana," was one of my Laguna informants, and, on asking him the meaning of the crib, he narrated as follows:—

The baby José Crito, god's child (hus[2] ka iach, "god his child") was brought from a far country by his father José and his mother Mari.[3] They took the journey about the time he was going to be born. He was born in a stable. A big fire, a big star, came down from the sky. There was an ox in the stable. When he was born, the ox came there. He blew[4] on the baby. A little after a shepherd came. That is the reason the priest put the sheep there. That was the way he was born. He went from there to another town,

From Parsons, "Nativity Myth at Laguna and Zuñi," *Journal of American Folk-Lore,* Vol. XXXI (1918), pp. 256-263.

[1] Meaning "God's Ear." Since José has been sexton, according to his own account, for more than half a century, since he is also the *shiwanna* (thunder) *cheani,* one of the two surviving medicine-men of Laguna, the nickname appears singularly appropriate, and yet it was given him for quite another than the obvious reason. When he was courting the girl who was to be his second wife, his prospective mother-in-law, a Zuñi, referred to him as a very rich man, boasting that he had come to the house wearing a silver belt and *tsipe hus,* here meaning "godlike ear-rings."

[2] *Hus* (*yus*) is associated with the sun. "*Osach* [Sun] was sent by naishdya [father] *yus*. That is the reason all look up to him as one with authority [*ityetsa*]." In Keresan mythology the sun is a secondary creation.

[3] From another informant I got the terms *Maria Santichuma* and *Esu Christu*.

[4] *Gisach* (*chishatsa*). It is the same term as that used for blowing on the feather-sticks or other sacred objects. It corresponds to the Zuñi rite of *yechu;* although at Zuñi the breath is ordinarily drawn in, whereas at Laguna, according to one informant, it is expelled.

to the king's house, his mother and father and himself, on a horse. He grew up at the king's house. After he had grown up, the others, the Jews, were not satisfied with him. They were going to kill him. There were three brothers, three children of god; but this one born in the stable was the leader. They were hunting everywhere for him to kill him. One of the Jews asked the middle brother which was Jesus. The Jew said, "Which one is it?" He said, "I am not going to tell you." They said, "Yes, you must tell us." So they bribed him. So another party of Jews came into his house. They were all sitting at the table, and still they kept asking which one was it. He was sitting in the north direction. "That's he." So they took him. "Wait a little," he said. "Wait a little, my brothers! Which one of you has been given some money?"—"None of us." The one sitting at the east end of the table was the one that had been bribed. "You are the one, you have been paid some money. Now I am going away. I am going up to Konamats ['place of being thankful'].''[5] So they took him out of the room. They stood up a cross. He was a spirit. So it took some time for them to get ready. When god's child made everything ready, they nailed him to the cross through the middle of his hands. There was one who could not see. There was another who was lame, so his brother carried him on his back. They pierced him through the heart. "Now all is ready," said the Jews. They made the blind man and the lame man pierce his heart. When they pierced him, the blood spurted everywhere. In this way (that is the reason why) from the spattered blood all living beings came, horses and mules and all creatures. The man that was lame got up and walked, and the blind man could see, because they had been spattered with the blood. So at last they dug a hole and stood up the cross. They dug the hole so deep, that the cross could never be taken up. They buried him in this deep hole; they threw dirt and rocks on him, some of the rocks so big that they could hardly lift them; still they threw them in. They buried him. The first day, the second day, he was still buried; the third day he was to leave his grave. He went up to Konamats, back to his father, God. The Jews kept shooting upwards. His father was glad he came back up, so they would live there together in Konamats. The season when he was treated so mean is coming back again. Tomorrow is the first day of mass. For seven weeks I have to ring the bell. On the sixth (seventh?) Sunday it will be *kuitishi*. On the seventh Sunday it is coming back to the same time he went up to heaven. On the Wednesday before *kuitishi* will be the covering.[6] All the people come in to take a turn watching. It is covered Wednesday, Thursday,

---

[5] *Konama,* "thanks." Wenimats, a place said at Laguna to be west of Zuñi (the Hopi identify it with St. John's), is the "heaven" of native theory. On being questioned, the *sextana* opined that *konamats* and *wenimats* were the same, meaning perhaps equivalents.

[6] The bell and all the figures in the church are covered with cloth.

Friday. On Saturday it is uncovered. He goes back to his father. It will be *kucheachsi*.[7] That is all.

At Zuñi I had frequently asked for a tale (*telapnane*) about the *santu;* but until I asked Kłippelanna,[8] none was forthcoming.[9] Kłippelanna narrated as follows:—

In the West there lived a Mexican girl who never went out. She staid all the time in her own house. She would sit where the sun shone in. The sun impregnated her ("gave her a child"). At this time soldiers were guarding her.[10] One of the soldiers saw her, and said to the others, "The one we are guarding is pregnant. If she does such things, what is the use of guarding her? Let us kill her!" The next day in the morning she was to die. That evening the Sun by his [power] came into her room, and said, "To-morrow you are to die."—"Well, if it is to be, I must die," she said. He said, "No, I won't let you die, I will get you out." The next morning early by his [power] he lifted her up out of the window.[11] "Now go to where you are to live." So she went on till she came to a *sipaloa* planting. She said, "What are you planting?" He said, "Round stones." Because he did not answer right, she did something to the seed, and his corn did

[7] End or breaking of taboo. Were a masked dancer to break a restriction (e.g., were he to have sexual intercourse during the ceremonial), it would be *cheachsi*. After a birth, continence is required for twelve days. In case of *cheachsi* a medicineman will be called in to give a purge; otherwise the woman will dry up (*tsipanito*). Compare E. C. Parsons, "Zuñi Death Beliefs and Practices" (AA 18:246).

[8] A very garrulous and unusually naïve old man, who is sometimes reputed a witch. He is the fraternity director (*tikya mosi*) of the Little Fire fraternity (*matke tsannakwe*).

[9] Sometimes the *santu* was admitted to be Mexican, sometimes it was stated that she had been with them "from the beginning," she came up with them. One of the paramount priests (*ashiwanni*) who asserted the latter origin added that the *santu* had never staid [sic] in the church except during her lying-in at the winter-solstice ceremony.

[10] Men volunteer as soldiers (*sontaluk*) to guard the *santu* during her ceremonial. Analogously, among the Keresans the "war captains" guard the mother (*iyebik, uretseta*).

[11] At this point our usually amenable interpreter refused to go on translating. He said that he had heard the story otherwise; that Kłippelanna was not telling it right; and that if I told the story wrong, he himself would be held responsible. Asked to particularize, he said that as Kłippelanna was telling the story, the domestic animals came to Kołuwela. That was not right; there were no such animals in Kołuwela ("god town," where the gods [*koko*] live, and the dead). I argued that it was "ours not to reason why," that all he and I had to do was to take down the story as it was given to us; but I suggested and pleaded in vain. He refused to translate. "No, let us have another story!" he firmly concluded. The story was retold another time, and translated by Margaret Lewis, a non-Zuñi. Leslie's refusal to translate seemed to me a striking illustration of Zuñi tenacity to pattern; and it calls to mind an opinion of Dr. Kroeber, our most authoritative student of Zuñi, namely, that, although fifty per cent of Zuñi culture may be borrowed from White culture, the Zuñi have so cast what they have taken over into their own patterns, that ninety-nine per cent of their culture may be called indigenous.

not come up. She went on a little ways, and she came to another one planting. She asked him what he was planting. He said, "I am planting corn and wheat." Because he answered her right, she did nothing to his seed, and they all came up. Then the soldiers found she was gone, and they came on after her. They asked the first man if he had seen a girl coming. He said, "Yes, she has just gone over the hill." They said, "Well, we must be nearly up with her, we will hurry on." So they went on over the hill, and they saw no one. They came to another little hill, and they could not see her. They came to a river, and it was very deep. They cut some poles, and they said, "We'll see how deep it is." They stuck the poles down, and they said, "It is too deep. There is no use in hunting any more for her." So they turned back. But the girl had crossed the river, and went on until she came to Kołuwela, and there she lay in. She had twins. The pigs and the dogs kissed her. That is why the pigs and the dogs have children. The mules would not kiss her. That is why the mules have no children. They came on to Itiwonna (middle, i.e., Zuñi). At Kołuwela they all (the mother and twins) became another sort of person, they became stone.[12] When they had the dances (at Zuñi), she did not care to see them. She did not like their dances. They had the *hematatsi*. She liked that dance. So she went on to Acoma, because *hematatsi*[13] was a dance of Acoma. She lives there to-day. The elder sister, i.e., of the twins, is here. The younger went south to where the other Zuñi live. That is all.

The elder sister, I learned from one of the paramount rain priests, had been kept by Naiuchi, famous half a century ago as priest of the north, and bow-priests' director. From his house the *santu* had been taken to the house where she now lives, a house on the south side.[14] Naiuchi was of the Eagle clan, and the present abode of the *santu* belongs to a child of the Eagle; i.e., the paternal clan was Eagle. (It is a house of the Frog clan.) For some time a certain Eagle clan family has been trying to get possession of the *santu*. It is assumed that she belongs to the Eagle clan.

In other words, the *santu* has been put into the pattern of the Zuñi fetiches, which are clan property. Unlike them, she is not kept secreted; but, like them, she is a source of light in the sense of life. "All want life from her." And she is also a specific for rain. After a dry season, she will be carried around the fields, as she was two years ago, in the course of her ceremonial. "The *santu* is a rain-priest."

The *santu* is likewise a direct agent of fertility or reproduction. Four

[12] *Variant:* The *santu* had been a real baby belonging to a Mexican lady; then the *santu* turned into stone. The *santu* was one of the raw people (*kyapenahoi*); i.e., supernaturals.

[13] Said to be the *upikaiupona*.

[14] In a house on the west side there is said to be another *santu,* one bought from Mexicans. It belongs to the Tansy-mustard clansman who figures in the *molawia* ceremonial.

days after the winter solstice she lies in for four days; and small clay images of the domestic animals, of bracelets, rings, etc., are placed around her; and to them all she is supposed to give increase during the year.[15] A similar practice has been noted at Acoma.[16] At Laguna there is a practice of making small dough images of animals, but these representations are merely baked and eaten. The existence of any ceremonial point of view in connection with them was in general[17] denied; and the practice of making clay images in connection with the saint appears, according to my Laguna informants, not to occur. The saint is connected with reproduction, however, according to a Zuñi informant[18] who had grown up in Acoma, and had visited Laguna only last year. The night before the *santu* childbirth[19]

[15] See E. C. Parsons, "Notes on Zuñi," pt. I (Memoir of the American Anthropological Association 4:170-171).

[16] C. F. Lummis, *The Land of Poco Tiempo* (New York, 1897), 276.

[17] According to one informant, *ushumini* were offered to "animals" before hunting. If the images disappeared, it meant that deer would be killed.

[18] He also asserted that clay animals were placed around the saint, both at Acoma and Laguna. At both places, we may note, the saint is male.

[19] Kuashe was referring to Christmas Eve, for he also used the Mexican term *nochowena* (*nochebuena*). From this the Zuñi *santu chalia* would appear to be a Christmas rite, *santu chalia* being merely a translation of *la navidad*. It is at *nochowena* that the Zuñi will visit Laguna. At Laguna as well as at Acoma (see E. C. Parsons, "Notes on Acoma and Laguna" [AA 20:162-186]) there is a prolonged Christmas celebration. Beginning Dec. 16, the church-bell is rung each morning about nine o'clock, and mass is said by the *sextana*. Every one counts the days. On Dec. 22, rehearsal of the dances (*Kutanigwia*, "trying") is held at night, — held, it happens, in Jefferson's house, a large house, an *osach* (sun) clan house. Dec. 24, the ninth day, the "great day," after mass at 11 A. M., by the priest, there are Comanche, Eagle and Corn (*yakohanna* or *talawaie*) dances (*katsetia*). Everybody is on hand, eager to see or take part. After midnight mass the dances continue in the church until 2 or 3 A. M. Dec. 25, Comanche, *talawaie*, etc., dances first in church about 11 A. M., and then in the plaza, the Christmas Eve dancers being called upon to dance till sunset. — Dancers from outlying villages, as in 1918 the Eagle dancers, may quit earlier. Private presents of food are made, and there is an interchange of presents — bread, chile, fruit, china, cloth — between *comadres;* i.e., the godmother gives a present to her godchild, and the child's mother, a present to the godmother. Mexicans go singing from house to house, and receive presents of food. *Talawaie* (*danawaiye*) is danced in the plaza from Dec. 26 through Dec. 29. During these four days children may take part. The last day in particular is made much of. Jan. 1, king day (*lei shashte*), election of governor and officers (*tenientes*). Jan. 6, dances, Comanche, Navaho, etc., at night in different houses in honor of newly-elected officers. Jan. 7, 8, 9, dances (mostly *talawaie*) in the plaza in all the villages for *tenientes*. (Jan. 9, 1918, was stormy, and in consequence the dance was in the church.) Jan. 10 great *fiesta* by Mexicans at Seboyeta. — The dance-place in the church is below the altar, the different sets of dancers taking turns until towards the end all the sets dance at the same time. In 1917-18 there were about twenty dancers in the *talawaie,* men and women dancing in two lines, the sexes alternating. There were six men in the Comanche dance, and two men in the Eagle dance. The delight-makers (*kachale*) are said to appoint the Christmas-time dancers, and none may refuse. Unlike the *katsena* dances, for which new songs are composed, only old songs are sung in the Christmas-time dances. The Comanche and Eagle dancers have a choir. — All the dances are without masks, but formerly in the *talawaie* the women wore squared wooden turkey-befeathered headpieces or tablets (*uteduish,* "on the top"). The older men wear white cotton trousers and shirts; the younger men, their ordinary American

said this man, men were free "to plant seeds" in any woman they met. The practice was "to make more children." Resulting offspring were accounted the saint's children. "That is why the saint has so many children."[20]

One more function of the Zuñi *santu*. She is a source of omen,[21] telling "what will happen." She does "tricks." If the ground looks "dry" around her house,[22] as her bower in the *satechia* (*santu* ceremony) may be called, there will be a drought; if the ground is grassy, there will be rain. To a girl to whom something is going to happen the saint's clothes in the *satechia* would look ugly. One year, during the *satechia,* there appeared on her person spots of blood, and in the dance two men were shot. "Last year," narrated my informant, "the first day of the *satechia* when I looked at the *santu,* her eyes were all right; but the second day they were rolling, like the dead. They told me it was an omen. That winter my cousin died of pneumonia, alone in a sheep-camp, and for three days the sheep were by themselves."[23]

Nothing corresponding to the story of Jesus as heard at Laguna have I been able to find at Zuñi. Stevenson frequently refers to Poshaiyanki as the Zuñi "culture-hero." The myth she gives appears somewhat reminiscent of the Christ myth,[24] and her statement that on the feather-sticks offered to Poshaiyanki a cross figures, appears significant. I learned but little about Poshaiyanki feather-sticks except that all fraternity members do plant feather-sticks to him at the winter-solstice ceremonial. The very existence of Poshaiyanki was unknown to my non-fraternity informants,[25] and denied

---

clothes, plus high buckskin leggings tied with the woman's hair belt. Comanche dancers wear a head-dress of eagle-feathers and ribbons. The eagle-feather head-dress of the Eagle dancers reaches to the feet. The faces of the Eagle dancers are painted.

[20] This practice was described to a company of Zuñi, and the description amused them just about as it would have amused a company of sophisticated whites. The practice was plainly not Zuñi. Nevertheless at the "big dances" (i.e., the dances in which the people take part), — formerly the scalp-dance and the *owinahaiye,* and to-day the saint's dance (*satechia,* — it lasts two days or more, according to whether any one asks for a repetition), there is always a certain amount of license among the girls. — A Zuñi informant told me he had seen a bereaved Mexican woman praying to the Zuñi *santu* for a child that would live.

[21] Compare E. C. Parsons, "Notes on Zuñi," pt. I (MAAA 4:189).

[22] Similarly at Laguna the bower in the plaza (*kakati*) to which the *santu* is carried is called *santu gama.* In the anti-sunwise circuit from the church the padre leads, followed in order by the governor (*tapup*), the *sextana,* the *santu* carried by the women, and all the people.

[23] Compare beliefs about *achiyelotopa* (M. C. Stevenson, "The Zuñi Indians," (Annual Report, Bureau of American Ethnology 23:462).

[24] The Sia Poshaiyänne myth is in part indubitably Christian (M. C. Stevenson, "The Sia," RBAE 11:65-67).

[25] A priest excepted, who stated that non-fraternity persons would not know about Poshaiyanki. This priest also stated that there was no cross on the feather-sticks to Poshaiyanki, and that the fraternity feather-stick on which a face is painted is that which is offered to Poshaiyanki. Note J. W. Fewkes, "Hopi Shrines near the East Mesa, Arizona" (AA 8:367, 368); also Fewkes, "Winter Solstice Ceremony at Walpi" (AA 11:75). Prayer-sticks in the form of a cross for the increase of domestic animals

by one fraternity informant, who never hesitated to lie when he wished to conceal a fact. On the other hand, Klippełanna, when questioned about Poshaiyanki, narrated as follows:—

Poshaiyanki was a "raw person" (a supernatural). He was a man of magic. All the fraternities belong to him. Some time in the beginning he came out with all the fraternities. He went all over the country to different towns, and he made all the things for them to do in their fraternities. He went all over the world. He got to Lea.[26] When he got to Lea, Lea said to him, "Now you are a great man, you are powerful, a raw person, and do things nobody else can do. Now, to-morrow you and I will do tricks to each other." Lea was tall, and Poshaiyanki was short. "To-morrow, when the sun comes out, the sun will shine on one of us first; that is the one who will win." Lea said to him, "All right!" He had parrot tail-feathers.[27] In the morning they both stood together, looking to where the sun would rise. When the sun came out, it did not shine on Lea. It shone first on Poshaiyanki. Then he won.[28] "Now, with all the animals we are going to do tricks," he said to him. "All right!" he said. So Lea asked him to be the first. He said he would not be the first. "You will be the first," he said to him, "because it was you who wanted to try it." So Lea began. And he called all the animals that belonged to him,—sheep, horses, mules, pigs, chickens. So all gathered together. He told Poshaiyanki to try it. "Now, you try it,"—"All right! I am but an Indian,"[29] he said. So he called all the birds, eagles, hawks, wild turkeys, all kinds of birds, and all flew to them. He called deer, bear, cougar, wolf, and all the other animals. At last all the animals gathered together where they were, and Poshaiyanki had four time more than Lea. So Poshaiyanki beat him again.[30]

From my priest informant I learned that Poshaiyanki was the father of the fraternities, and that he had lived at Shipap, which famous starting-

are mentioned, likewise (pp. 72, 75) to the same end the use of clay or wooden images of animals.

[26] "King," Leslie translated, quite properly, but much to my surprise. *Lea,* usually pronounced *lei,* is from *rei,* and the word has become at Zuñi a proper name. Leslie had learned its generic meaning, I suspect, from non-Zuñi sources.

[27] Such as are worn by the dancers, more particularly the *kokokshi,* in their hair. There is a suggestion here of magical quality in the feathers.

[28] Compare "The Sia" (RBAE 11:33-34).

[29] *Ho'ite. Ho'ite* appears to be a generic term for any Indian.

[30] Compare "The Sia" (RBAE 11:59-65); Father Dumarest, MS. on Cochiti in the Brooklyn Institute Museum. Poshaiyanki becomes Montezuma, and included in the myth is the following unmistakably Christian incident: "Montezuma made a house where none could find him, because he had enemies, and where he could deliberate on what he had to do. He had to reform the unmarried mothers. He made a serpent like a fish with wings. It would go into a house and throw itself upon the mother and child as if to devour them. It lived in a lake, where it became very large. Instead of merely frightening the mothers and children, it ended by devouring them. Montezuma had to confine the serpent to the lake forever."

point was on this occasion placed at Las Vegas. Poshaiyanki discovered the fraternities. Through him they had their animals and birds and medicines.[31] When he talked to the people, those in front heard more plainly than those sitting behind. That is why some fraternity members know more than others. After he had told them everything, he was lost. He did not die. He went through the earth.[32]

[31] On another occasion the same informant stated that Poshaiyanki also brought sheep, burro, and horses. Having first asserted that nothing at all had come to the Zuñi through the Spaniards, he admitted that the *sipaloa* or *kishdyan* (an old word for "Mexican") had brought wheat and watermelons. Peach-trees were already there when the Zuñi came up, and they brought with them corn and squash.

[32] We recall that Kołuwela is underground.

JOHN MONTGOMERY COOPER

(1881-1949)

It is a strange coincidence—if it is a coincidence—that when Father Cooper turned to anthropology, the place he chose for field work was the area where, in the 17th century, the Jesuit missionaries had labored.

Anthropology was not Father Cooper's first choice as his life work. He was called to the priesthood as a young man. After graduating from college in Maryland, he went to Rome where he spent six years in advanced studies. He was ordained in Rome and appointed as priest to a Washington, D.C. parish. It was during his summer vacations in the North Woods that he first became interested in primitive people, and decided to pursue this interest in Washington, specifically in the Smithsonian Institution. During this time he was teaching in the Department of Religious Education at Catholic University. After a while he added some courses in anthropology to the curriculum. Eventually the long road to anthropology was completed; he was relieved of his parish duties in 1928 in order to establish a new Department of Anthropology at Catholic University.

Father Cooper's second specialization was South America, although he never had an opportunity to do field work on that continent. He used his exhaustive command of the old and new materials to organize a coherent picture of culture areas and culture sequences in South America.—R.L.B.

The Relations Between Religion and Morality in Primitive Culture

THE PROBLEM

THE PRESENT PROBLEM, THAT OF THE RELATIONSHIP BETWEEN RELIGION and morality among primitive peoples, is one of the most difficult and elusive in the whole field of culture history. The question itself is complex, as there are so many angles to it. Our field evidence is none too abundant,

From Cooper, *Primitive Man,* Vol. IV (Washington: Catholic University, 1931), pp. 33-48.

and is often vague, inconclusive, and open to criticism. The interpretation of such evidence as we possess calls for the exercise of the utmost caution and reserve.

In the present paper, we shall endeavor, first, to define our problem as clearly as limited space permits; secondly, to summarize the available factual evidence; thirdly, to reconstruct, from the anthropological evidence, the probable early prehistorical relations of religion with morality. We shall not deal with the ultimate origins of morality or of religion.

By religion we here mean a belief in plus emotional and persuasive attitudes toward supernatural personal beings. Religion, so described, is distinguished from magic, that is, a belief in plus emotional and coercive attitudes toward supernatural impersonal forces.

By morality we here mean codes or types of behavior, viewed as prescribed or obligatory, toward supernatural beings or, in matters of justice or charity, toward fellow men. Morality, so described, is distinguished from purely non-obligatory customs, from rules of etiquette, and from 'non-moral' taboos.

Primitive peoples, as a rule, draw some distinction between these three types of behavior. We may illustrate from the people best known personally to the writer, the Tête de Boule of Quebec province. A young woman who would stroll through camp with head uncovered would be acting contrary to a purely non-obligatory custom. So likewise would a man who killed a moose and refused to share it freely with his friends and fellow-tribesmen. The Tête de Boule all agree that he has a perfect right to keep all of the meat for his own use, and no one would think of charging him with dishonesty if he refused to share it, but he would be regarded as stingy and niggardly. He would be breaking a customary, but non-obligatory, observance. If you should unwittingly ask a native the name of his deceased father, you would be guilty of a gross breach of etiquette. If one Indian should trap beaver on another Indian's hunting ground, or should steal food or raiment or ammunition from another's cache, he would be looked upon as guilty of infringement of strict right, as guilty of moral misconduct. If he wantonly slaughtered more food than he could use, and so deliberately wasted meat, he would subject himself to a religious sanction. For Our Grandfather, the benevolent being who was from the beginning of the world and who will live "so long as the earth is the earth," who sends the snow and the North wind, and who brings the Indian the hare and the ptarmigan as winter food, would be angry, and next year would not send the deep snow in which the large game flounder and become easy victims for the hunter. Nor would he send the North wind in the late winter to put a hard crust on the snow and so to make traveling and the pursuit of game less arduous. Not only the culprit, but the rest of the tribe would suffer. The lines that separate non-obligatory custom, etiquette, and moral precept are not as sharply defined perhaps among primitive peoples as they are among us, although even among us the lines are often blurred. But the difference is in the main recognized by them, even though in concrete cases it may, as among us, be difficult to say definitely whether custom, etiquette, or morality proper is being offended.

Primitive peoples also have a number of what may be called 'non-moral' taboos. The act is avoided or prohibited, but there seems to be neither social nor religious sanction attached to the taboo, and its breach does not infringe on the rights of neighbor. Thus, for example, among some of the Ojibwa, if you swallow the kneecap bone of a hare, you will have no more luck in hunting that animal, unless or until you take an expiatory plunge in lake or river. In the evidence, at least as gathered by the present writer, there is no indication of offence taken by the rabbit-spirit or other supernatural being. Bad luck just automatically follows. The sanction, if we call the penalty such, is a non-religious, non-social, perhaps a 'magical' one.

In the following pages we are excluding, as not germane to our subject, such observances as pure customs, rules of etiquette, and 'non-moral' (magical or non-magical) taboos. We shall confine attention to precepts or prohibitions that come more clearly within the circle of morality proper as described on a preceding page.

THE FACTS AND THEIR DISTRIBUTION

The 'lawless' savage given over to sheer impulse is a creature of fable. Anthropology knows of no such animal. Not only are primitive peoples everywhere under numerous restrictions imposed by custom, etiquette, and non-moral taboo, but everywhere are they bound by codes of morality proper. In fact, all things considered, the uncivilized man lives his life under probably as many non-moral and moral restrictions as does his civilized brother. He does not consider himself bound by some of the restrictions which hem in our western liberty. On the other hand, where we are untrammeled, he is cribbed, cabined and confined by a host of precepts, prohibitions, and taboos.

Furthermore, running through the myriad moral codes of the peoples of the earth, there is a certain uniformity, a certain common pattern. One's first impression on reading through a collection of the moral precepts and codes of the primitive world is one of bewilderment. These seems to be neither rhyme nor reason, neither system nor order. Confusion and contradiction appear to reign supreme. What one code commands, the next prohibits. What one people calls good, the other calls bad. Man's moral codes look at first·glance like a chaotic pathless jungle. For a long time this impression widely prevailed, and one still finds it set down as fact in popular or other works. But in the last two or three decades we have been seeing more and more clearly that underlying this superficial confusion and contradiction are a certain fundamental order and uniformity.

The peoples of the world, however much they differ as to details of morality, hold universally, or with practical universality, to at least the following basic precepts. Respect the Supreme Being or the benevolent being or beings who take his place. Do not 'blaspheme'. Care for your children. Malicious murder or maiming, stealing, deliberate slander or "black" lying, when committed against friend or unoffending fellow clansman or tribesman, are reprehensible. Adultery proper is wrong, even though there be exceptional circumstances that permit or enjoin it and even though sexual relations among the unmarried may be viewed leniently. Incest is a heinous offence. This universal moral code agrees rather closely with our own Decalogue understood in a strictly literal sense. It inculcates worship of and reverence to the Supreme Being or to other superhuman beings. It protects the fundamental human rights of life, limb, family, property, and good name.[1]

Two broad generalizations, therefore, emerge from the vast multitude of facts at our disposal. First, all peoples have a moral code. We know of no exception to this rule. Second, beneath the bewildering variety of local and tribal differences, there is a perceptible underlying uniformity in the moral codes of humanity the world over.

But the further questions arise: What sanctions enforce these codes or this code? Purely social or secular sanctions? Magical sanctions? Or religious sanctions as well? In other words, are these 'moral' codes in reality 'magical' or 'social' codes, deriving their driving and controlling force from magical beliefs, or, from society, from purely social, natural, or secular motives and incentives? Or are they looked upon as emanating from, expressing the will of, and, through rewards or punishments here or hereafter, sanctioned by the Supreme Being or by inferior but superhuman personal beings? As our evidence stands today, no simple 'yes' or 'no' answer can be given to these questions. The facts we possess demand that we follow good scholastic precedent. We must distinguish. Before attempting to do so systematically, we may do well to present some concrete illustrations of actual conditions existing among peoples for whom we have sufficient information on the point. These illustrations, together with those given in the three preceding papers of the present symposium,[2] should give us a better basis for discussion.

We are indebted to Hose for our most thorough-going account of the Kayans, an agricultural people of Borneo. He sums up their relations between religion and morality as follows: "As regards the influence of their

[1] For details, see E. Westermarck, *The origin and development of the moral ideas,* 2 vols., 2d ed., London, 1912; L. T. Hobhouse, *Morals in evolution,* 2 vols., 2d ed., London, 1908, esp. i, 32.

[2] See PRIMITIVE MAN, Jan.-Apr., 1931, iv, nos. 1-2; an excellent detailed study by W. Matthews, of religio-moral relations among the Navaho may be found in *Jour. of Amer. Folk-Lore,* 1899, xii, 1-9; ditto for Winnebago morality in P. Radin, *Primitive man as philosopher,* New York, 1927, chs. vi-vii.

religious beliefs on the moral conduct of the Kayans, we have seen that
the fear of the *toh* [minor spirits or powers] serves as a constant check on
the breach of customs, which customs are in the main salutary and essential for the maintenance of social order. . . . The part which the major
spirits or gods are supposed to play in bringing or fending off the major
calamities remains extremely vague and incapable of definition; in the
main, faithful observance of the omens, of rites, and of custom generally,
seems to secure the favour of the gods, and in some way their protection;
and thus the gods make for morality. Except in that part of conduct which
is accurately prescribed by custom and tradition, their influence seems to
be negligible, and the high standard of the Kayans in neighborliness, in
mutal help and consideration, in honesty and forbearance, seems to be
maintained without the direct support of their religious beliefs".[3]

Among the Ifugao, one of the rice-planting hill tribes of the Mountain
Province of Northern Luzon, in the Philippine Islands, irreverence to the
Kabunyan, the deities, such as laughing at or insulting a man when he is
sacrificing to them, would be punished by them. But, if a man be insulted
when not so worshiping, the deities would not be concerned about the
offence. It would be up to the man himself to punish the offender. It is
forbidden to leave the village on an obligatory rest day, for then the deities
would not protect the crops and the harvest would be bad. It is likewise
forbidden to eat vegetables and shellfish when the rice is planted, for the
bagol-deities would be angry and you would become ill or perhaps die.

The Ifugao believe in a future life, but have a very vague idea of its
nature, and as regards happiness or unhappiness therein there seems to
be no difference between the fate of the good and of the wicked. In the
moral education of the young, religious motives appear quite absent, and
purely secular motives are proposed. Parents or elders will say to a boy:
"Be truthful, do not lie. If you lie, you will disgrace your family, nobody
will believe you, and you will lose your standing. Be honest, do not steal.
By honesty you protect the good name of your family. If you steal, you
will be found out and thus disgraced. When you go to war, fight to revenge
the life of your relative, or to show your bravery. When the fight is over,
come back home, and do not take your enemies' land from them, else they
will have no rice." And so for the whole moral code, as regards the relations of man to man.[4]

The nearest aproach we get to a relation between religion and man-to-
man morality among the Ifugao is in the ordeals. In some of these the
ancestral spirits of the litigants are invoked to see that the party who is

[3] C. Hose and W. McDougall, *The pagan tribes of Borneo,* 2 vols., London, 1912,
ii, 204-5.
[4] Information obtained by present writer from Adriano Kimayong, an Ifugao and
former student at Catholic University, and checked up and amplified by Rev. Francis
Lambrecht, I.C.M., Kiangan, Mt. Prov., P. I., our ablest authority on Ifugao religion.

right wins, or the gods of war and justice intervene on the side of the innocent.[5]

Melanesian ordeals, as recorded by Codrington, have a connection with magic. But only in the following case does there seem to be any relation with religion. "In Lepers' Island a man to prove his innocence will submit to be shot at with arrows; if he be hit he is of course guilty; if he be innocent, Tagaro [a superior being] will protect him, just as he protects in fighting any young man whom he preserves that he may be prosperous and great. The favour of Tagaro in either case is sought for with the appropriate charm".

Codrington's Melanesians believe or believed in a place called Panoi to which the dead go. Thither go those who have led good lives and there they live in harmony. Those of bad character,—those who have killed without due cause, or have caused death by charms, or have stolen, or have lied, or have been guilty of adultery,—are not allowed to enter. Instead they must live in the bad place where there is quarreling and misery, and where they eat excrement. These penalties are seemingly not imposed upon the wicked by Tagaro or other gods. The penalties, so far as they are inflicted at all by beings, are inflicted by the wronged ghosts who bar the way of the offender to the happy land of Panoi.[6]

Among the Tête de Boule, a Cree-speaking non-agricultural tribe of northwestern Quebec, small children are trained not to wander off into the woods, where they might get lost or suffer harm. They are warned that if they should stray away, *Kokodje'o,* the cannibal giant, will catch them and eat them.[7]

The Thonga, a group of Bantu peoples of the eastern coast of South Africa, are best known to us through the exceptionally able studies of Junod. Their religion is partly ancestral, partly theistic. The ancestral spirits are jealous and avenge themselves when forgotten. They condemn certain serious ritual transgressions and kill a man who loses all restraint in sexual relations. To other sins they are quite indifferent. Ancestral worship among the Thonga has no connection, or at least very little, with the moral conduct of the individual, and it neither promises reward nor threatens punishment, for the future life.

To the Thongas' vaguely conceived Supreme Being (or Heaven), *Tilo,* men's moral relations with one another are of little or any greater concern than they are to the ancestral spirits. *Tilo* detects and exposes theft in the interest of his devotees who have been the victims thereof and in so far he is a moralizing influence. But in general, theft, blows, insults, murder, and witchcraft are condemned and punished by the Thonga merely because

[5] R. F. Barton, *Ifugao law,* U. of Cal. publ. in Amer. arch. and ethn., 1919, xv, 96-99.
[6] R. H. Codrington, *The Melanesians,* Oxford, 1891, 212-13, 273-75.
[7] Field notes, J. M. Cooper.

these actions endanger society and its recognized modes of life. The moral law is not regarded as having been proclaimed by a personal transcendental God. No direct relation is established between duty and divinity. Religion is non-moral. The ancestor-gods themselves are non-moral. No supreme legislator has ordained Bantu morality.[8]

Among at least some of the southeastern Australian aborigines, the Supreme Being or 'All-Father' is conceived as emphatically the guardian of the moral order.[9]

Thus among the Kurnai, a coastal tribe of Gippsland, in the adolescent initiation rites, instituted by the Supreme Being, *Mungan-ngaua,* the boys are instructed carefully in the ways of the tribe, including the duties of listening to and obeying the old men, sharing everything they have with their friends and living peaceably with them, not interfering with girls or married women, and obeying the food restrictions until released therefrom by the old men.[10]

Among the Euahlayi, an Australian tribe of northwestern New South Wales, there are three unpardonable sins: unprovoked murder, lying to the elders of the tribe, and stealing a woman within the forbidden degrees. Those guilty of these sins go at death to the lower world, where, but for the big fires kept up, there would be darkness, and where the culprits must hold their right hands motionless at their sides while they themselves must keep in perpetual movement. Kindliness toward the old and sick is strictly inculcated as the will and command of *Byamee,* the Supreme Being. All breaches of his laws are reported to him by the all-seeing spirit at the man's death, and he is judged accordingly.[11]

Illustrations such as the several we have given could be easily multiplied, but these will probably suffice to exemplify the various types of association and dissociation between belief and practice, between religion and morality, among primitive peoples of modern times. For the sake of order, we may divide these types as follows, without however insisting too much on the division or upon the names by which we are here designating the various types of association.

Relationship between Religion and Morality
    I. Indirect
        a. Impersonal
        b. Personal
            1. Permeative
            2. Judicative

[8] H. A. Junod, *The life of a South African tribe,* 2 vols., 2d rev. and enl. ed., London, 1927, ii, 426-28, 442-44, 582-83.
[9] Cf. W. Schmidt, *Der Ursprung der Gottesidee,* 2nd ed., 1931, iii, 567-1114 *passim*; Westermarck, *loc. cit.,* ii, 670-73.
[10] A. W. Howitt, *Native tribes of south-east Australia,* London, 1904, 630, 632-33, 638-39.
[11] K. L. Parker, *The Euahlayi tribe,* London, 1905, 78-79.

3. Protective
4. Educative
II. Direct
    a. Duties to deity (deities)
    b. Duties to fellowman

It is doubtful if there be any people living among whom there is no trace whatsoever of either direct or indirect relationship of one kind or another between religion and morality. We may run over each of the above headings rapidly before endeavoring to draw our very tentative conclusions as to the origin and early development of the relations between religion and morality.

I. *Indirect Relationship.* a. *Impersonal.* Among a great many primitive peoples, happiness, or unhappiness in the future life depends upon moral conduct in this life.[12] But, while the belief in survival after death is seemingly universal among the uncivilized peoples of the world, the concept of future reward and punishment for moral conduct is absent from many, perhaps the majority of such peoples. Even where it is present, the reward or punishment very commonly, perhaps again in the majority of cases, is conceived as following automatically upon earthly conduct, not as being bestowed or inflicted by Deity or deities. Whether such automatic future retribution should be called a religious sanction or not will depend upon our definition of religion. Under the definition we have adopted in this paper, the sanction would be a non-religious one, since no intervention upon the part of any supernatural personal being is involved. It is for this reason that we have called this relationship, if it can be called such a relationship at all, an 'impersonal' one.

b. *Personal.* 1. *Permeative.* Among a number of peoples, perhaps most of them, the whole social order, including practical ways of life, political and social institutions, customs, rules of etiquette, taboos, ritual, morality, and so forth, constitutes a unitary system looked upon more or less clearly or vaguely as instituted by or in conformity with the will of the supernatural world. The whole social order is thus *permeated* in greater or lesser measure with the supernatural. Gods and spirits may not be appealed to as guardians of morality, nor do explicitly religious motives function in the moral training of the young or in the daily conduct of their elders. Yet a distant, diffused relationship may be said to exist between moral conduct and religious concepts. The Kayans' beliefs, cited above, exemplify this permeative relationship.

Exactly how widespread this 'permeative' relationship between religion and morality may be, and exactly how deeply the moral behavior of peoples is influenced thereby, we cannot with confidence say. The facts

---

[12] A partial list of such peoples, from the older sources, may be found in Westermarck, *loc. cit.,* ii, 691.

are elusive, and not easily discovered, isolated, and evaluated. But we have some reason to believe that such a causal relationship is very common. This, however, is about all that can be said, in the present state of our field evidence.

2. *Judicative.* By judicative relations between religion and morality we here mean the intervention of supernatural beings on the part of the innocent or of their devotees in matters like oaths and ordeals. For the sake of brevity, we shall confine our attention chiefly to ordeals. In many, perhaps the majority of, ordeals, automatic non-supernatural forces, or magical but non-religious forces, or purely non-moral personal intervention by supernatural beings are really what bring about the exculpation of the innocent or the triumph of justice or truth. Where truth or justice or innocence prevails through the working of automatic secular forces or of magical non-religious forces, it would be incorrect to call this a religious relation to morality. Even where personal deities intervene, frequently they do so, not as protectors of truth and justice, but as protectors of their favorites and devotees. They do so, not because they are interested in morality,—they themselves may be far from paragons of virtue,—but because they wish to defend their special votaries or to requite them for sacrifices offered or for other services rendered.

In some cases, the deities intervene in ordeals on the side of right out of a more disinterested concern for truth or justice as such. But even in such cases, the same deities, as among the Ifugao cited above, may have no moral concern for or interest in morality. Outside this limited circle of the ordeal (or oath), the deities are non-moral, the moral code is not looked upon as their will, reward or punishment in this life or in the next does not come from them, religious considerations and motives do not function in the individual life as incentives toward better social and personal morality. We may further recall that ordeals are far from being universal. The custom is absent or else present only in traces among, for instance, the American Indians and the lower nomad hunting peoples.

3. *Protective.* In some cases, deities do indeed protect their devotees and favorites from thieves and murderers, just as they protect them from sickness, famine, and death. But, as noted in the two preceding paragraphs, the same deities may show little or no concern for the moral order as such. The dominant or exclusive concept in such cases appears to be non-moral protection or beneficence. The same devotee who asks and receives protection against thief and killer, may himself steal and kill, and yet feel himself in no way morally accountable to his supernatural patron or to any other supernatural being. We do not seem justified, therefore, in looking upon such intervention of the supernatural being as constituting a true relationship between religion and morality. Fear of such intervention may serve as a check upon thievery and murder. But this is about all. The relationship, such as it is, is at best a very indirect one.

4. *Educative.* Threatening young children with visits from bugaboos or with similar bogey-man punishments to train them in obedience and in other desired behavior, as among the Tête de Boule cited above, is quite common among primitive peoples of all levels of culture, as it still is among ourselves.[13] This custom certainly constitutes a relation of morality and moral training to supernatural or superhuman beings and makes for conformity to current moral codes. But whether it can be said to constitute a relationship with religion in the sense we are here using the term is another matter. It would not seem so. The bugaboos may or may not be conceived by elders as real beings. But in either case, these 'supernatural' beings are, generally speaking, essentially non-moral, uninterested in the moral order as such, and, more frequently, as is the case of the Tête de Boule *Kokodje'o* or *Wi'tago,* malevolent, immoral, or totally unmoral beings. Outside the very limited field of training the very young, they are not at all associated in the native mind with morality or with the maintenance of the social order.

II. *Direct Relationship.* a. *Duties to Deity or deities.* What Archbishop Le Roy writes of his Bantu is in the main true of the primitive world in general, at least as regards the Supreme Deity or lesser benevolent deities and spirits. "Nowhere in Bantu Africa is God, properly speaking, blasphemed. At times they find fault with him, they think him indifferent or severe, they call him bad, as on the occasion of a drought, a misfortune, a public calamity, or a death. But they have no idea of addressing God with words of contempt or insult".[14] As a rule our American Indians have no expressions in their languages corresponding to our English 'theological' profanity. An old Ojibwa medicine man, a pagan, recently expressed to the writer his wonderment and bewilderment at the blasphemy he had so often heard from the lips of Christian whites. He could not understand how they could speak so of the great Good Being.

All or practically all peoples consider it a matter of obligation, or of custom closely akin to obligation, to manifest in some form or another,— through prayer, or sacrifice, or ceremonial, or taboo,—their reverence, fear, regard, dependence, or other feeling or attitude to the Deity or deities.

So far as morality is concerned with duties of worship and respect to higher personal beings, a direct relation between morality and religion appears universal or well-nigh so on all levels of primitive culture. The more controversial issue is that of the relation of religion to morality as concerned with man's duties to his fellow men.

[13] E. C. Parsons, *Links between religion and morality in early culture,* in Amer. anthropologist, 1915, n. s. xvii, 41-46; see good short treatment in W. D. Wallis, *Introduction to anthropology,* New York, 1926, 316-23.
[14] A. Le Roy, *The religion of the primitives,* tr., New York, 1922, 122.

b. *Duties to fellow man.* We have evidence from a great number of primitive peoples that moral duties of man to man are looked upon as the express will of the Deity or deities, and that observance or neglect of such duties entails reward or punishment from the Deity or deities, either in this life, or in the next, or both here and hereafter.[15]

Among what percentage of the primitive peoples of the world this belief prevails, it is not easy to say. It is not exactly rare, but is very far from being widespread or even common. It is not so common as is the belief in a Supreme Being.

Nor, so far as the present writer can see, does the conception of social and personal morality as the express will of the Deity or deities appear as proportionally more prevalent among the marginal or lower nomad hunting peoples than among the intramarginal or higher hunter, horticultural, and pastoral peoples. The belief stands out sharply and clearly defined among some of the marginals, such as the Southeastern Australians and Fuegians.[16] Among some of the other marginals, such as the Andamanese pygmies, our evidence is contradictory, and the contradiction has not been satisfactorily cleared up.[17] Among still other marginal tribes, our available sources are silent or else affirm or imply the absence of the belief. Further field investigation may bring to light many things now hidden from our eyes, but, as our evidence stands, we can only say that the belief is found in its fullness among a few of the marginals, with bare traces or no traces at all among the others. At any rate, the fact that the belief *is* present, sharply and clearly defined, among some at least of the lower nomad marginal peoples is a point of capital importance, a point that cannot be neglected in any attempt at reconstructing the early history of the relationship between religion and morality. To this point we shall return later on.

We may summarize the facts of distribution as follows. It would not be easy to find a primitive people having all the forms of direct and indirect relationship between religion and morality which have been enumerated. But it would be equally difficult to find one with no trace whatsoever of any type of either direct or indirect relationship. A direct relationship as regards duties to Deity or deities is probably universal or nearly so. A direct relationship as regards duties to fellow man is found among at least a minority of the intramarginal and marginal peoples but among the remainder is so

[15] For partial list of such tribes, see Westermarck, *loc. cit.,* ii, 669-85.
[16] For Fuegian data, see W. Schmidt, *Der Ursprung der Gottesidee,* 2d ed., Muenster i. W., 1929, ii, 905, 950-51, 978, 991.
[17] Affirming relationship: E. H. Man, *On the aboriginal inhabitants of the Andaman Islands,* London [1883], 85-86, 89-90, 94; denying relationship: M. V. Portman, *A history of our relations with the Andamanese,* 2 vols., Calcutta, 1899, i, 44; A. R. Brown, *The Andaman Islands,* Cambridge, 1922, 152-60, 174; endeavoring to clear up contradiction: W. Schmidt, *loc. cit.,* iii, 85-104, 140-44. For extensive review and discussion of evidence on relations between Supreme Being and morality among the various lower nomad hunting peoples, see Schmidt, *loc. cit.,* 3 vols., 1926-1931, *passim; cf.* also files of Anthropos.

tenuous or distant, where it may be said to exist at all, that it is for all practical purposes non-operative.

INTERPRETATION OF FACTS

Two theories of origin and early development have or have had their respective champions and advocates. One, the classical theory, holds that morality in the sense of duties to fellow men arose quite independently of religion, remained so dissociated for a long time, and only later came to be looked upon as the expression of the will of supernatural beings. The other theory holds that in earlier times both duties to God and duties to neighbor were looked upon as the will of God and that only later did religion tend among certain peoples to drift apart from morality.[18]

On both sides it would be generally agreed that morality in so far as it implies duties to God or gods goes back to very early times, probably to the very origin of religion itself. The facts we have outlined would certainly seem to point in this direction. Everywhere, and on all, even the lowest and most primitive, cultural levels, we find a recognition of certain vaguely or clearly conceived duties to God or gods, fidelity to or neglect of which duties entails divine pleasure or displeasure, present or future reward or punishment.

As regards the impersonal and personal indirect relationships between religion and morality which we have enumerated and illustrated, these too, with perhaps the exception of the ordeal and oath, seem to occur among peoples of all levels of culture, and to occur rather commonly. We have therefore reasonable ground for inferring that such relationships may well go back to very early prehistoric times.

But the real crux of the problem, the real issue that is controverted, is the question of the early prehistoric association or dissociation of religion and of *man-to-man* morality. What light do our facts throw upon the issue?

Actually, among some of the most primitive nomad marginals, duties of man to man are conceived as the will of a Supreme Being or of superior beings. There is no valid ground for ascribing this conception to white influence. The evidence points convincingly toward aboriginal origin of the conception. The highly significanct fact of the occurrence of this conception on such very primitive cultural levels, even though the conception cannot be shown to exist among all the marginal peoples, takes most, if not all, the wind out of the sails of the classical theory. Until the theory of

---

[18] A typical formulation of the classical theory may be found in E. B. Tylor, *Primitive culture,* 2 vols., London, 1871, i, 386, ii, 68-98, 326-27. The most outstanding living exponent of the theory of the early association of morality with the Supreme Being is Father W. Schmidt: see his Ursprung d. Gottesidee, previously cited, and his more popular work, *The origin and growth of religion,* tr., New York, 1931, esp. 271-72, 274-77.

the original dissociation of religion and man-to-man morality finds some objective way of explaining away this solid fact, it hangs in the air as an hypothesis based on surmise rather than on hard facts, and as an hypothesis in seeming contradiction with many of the facts we have.

On the other hand, we do not, the present writer feels, seem to be scientifically justified, as our evidence stands today, in asserting confidently, from the data of anthropology, that religion and man-to-man morality were in their origin and everywhere in earliest or earlier prehistoric times associated. If we actually found them so associated among all or most of the marginal nomads, the conclusion that, at least in earlier prehistoric times and probably in the very beginning, religion and man-to-man morality were associated would rest on a reasonably firm basis. But actually we do not find them so associated among all or most of the marginals. Such an association is clearly demonstrated for some only of the marginal peoples.

Field investigations of the last decade or two suggest that some important facts may have escaped us. Future field research may reveal instances of association which are now hidden from us. Facts of this kind are not easily dug out, even by sympathetic, interested, experienced and trained investigators. Moreover, there are many indications in our source literature that this particular question of the relation between religion and social and personal morality has not received at the hands of field workers, professional and other, the attention its importance deserves. But when all is said, as our evidence stands, while the classical theory of early dissociation has gotten a body blow from which it has not yet begun to recover, its rival theory has not definitely won the belt.

References

We have no thorough critical study of the whole problem of religious-moral relations. One is badly needed. Even the problem itself has never been systematically defined, divided, and formulated in all its many ramifications and intricacies.

A considerable number of the pertinent facts have been assembled from the firsthand sources in the following: E. Westermarck, *The origin and development of the moral ideas,* 2 vols., 2nd ed., London, 1912, especially ii, ch. 48-52; L. T. Hobhouse, *Morals in evolution,* 2 vols., 2nd ed., London, 1908, esp. ii, ch. 2; E. C. Parsons, *Links between religion and morality in early cultures,* in American anthropologist, 1915, n. s. xvii, 41-57. These three older studies, while useful, leave much to be desired on the score of completeness, or of interpretation, or of both. A critical and pretty thorough combing of sources on the special question of the relations of the Supreme Being to the moral codes of the lower nomads has been made more recently by W. Schmidt, *Der Ursprung der Gottesidee,* 3 vols., 2d rev. and enl. ed., Muenster i. W., 1926-31; but most anthropologists would challenge his assumption of the validity of the Kulturkreis theory and would seriously question whether some of the peoples he selects are as primitive as he maintains. Any reader, who desires to consult for himself the best firsthand sources will find an excellent selected list thereof in R. H. Lowie, *Primitive religion,* New York, 1924, 331-41.

PART VI

NEW HORIZONS

Introduction

by Ruth L. Bunzel

AROUND 1920 ANTHROPOLOGY BEGAN TO CHANGE. THERE WAS A COMPLE-
tion and a new beginning—or perhaps several new beginnings, for a crossroads had been reached.

In the first place the ethnographic fever and sense of urgency that had
driven anthropologists for fifty years, the need to "get it down before it's
gone," had passed. Partly because by 1920 "it" was gone—"it" being the
culture of tipis and buffaloes, salmon fishing and potlatches, naïvely assumed to be the "pure" cultures of the Indians before they had been "con-
taminated" by white contact. Although in a few spots, such as the pueblos,
distinctive Indian cultures lingered on, in most parts of the United States
Indians were living in frame houses, wore store clothing, ate store bread,
raised some miserable crops or worked in canning factories, and sometimes came together on July 4 for a "Sun Dance"—a Sun Dance without
ritual and without torture. They no longer had much appeal as subjects
of study.

But there was another side to the picture. Not only was "it" gone but
"it" had been gotten down on paper. The eager students of the early 20th
century had done their work well; there was a sense of completion. The
main culture areas of the United States and their characteristic cultures
had been recorded. We knew the distribution of tipis and earth lodges
and when one had replaced the other and how the Plains Indians had gotten
their horses. There was nothing very new or startling to be learned about
the formal aspects of aboriginal American Indian culture. Archaeologists
continued to discover new and interesting facts, pushing back the date of
man's first appearance on this continent. Those with a taste for the traditional "classic" style of ethnography had to look for new fields to conquer—
Africa or Australia or the South Seas. Others thought that anthropology
had come to the end of the road. We had exhausted the field; there were
no more primitives to study.

Moreover, the problems which had generated so much heat in the age
of Boas no longer seemed very exciting. Parallelism vs. diffusion (even
Boas, who rarely thought anything was finished, said "Diffusion is finished."), the priority of maternal or paternal descent, arguments against
theories of unilinear evolution, the limitations of theories of geographic
or economic determinism, all seemed pretty dead issues by the 20's—

although one might still argue about the interpretation of some specific sets of facts. Had all the problems been solved and could we now all go home?

Not quite. The same 20's saw the emergence of a whole new set of problems. They were, in order of first appearance:

Culture Change. Many studies had been made of diffusion, tracing "traits" of culture around the world, the earliest ones being in folklore and mythology, or the spread of tobacco, but very little thought had been given to the process of change. Wissler's paper on the influence of the horse on Plains culture suggested that "borrowed" traits are not simply just *there* as evidence of intertribal contact, but that some sort of process is involved in their entrance, and that this process and its consequences are matters worthy of study. A whole field of study—culture change or "acculturation" as it came to be called—opened up. And as every new problem involves new methods the methods of field work changed. The preferred place of study was no longer the tribe where no ethnologist had ever been before, but rather one which had been well studied and on which there already was good material. More and different use was made of documentary material. And observation, which went out of fashion when field work meant sitting down with an old man and recording what he remembered, came back as an important field technique. One went into houses to see whether native pottery or gasoline tins were used. One went to church socials and noted who came and who stayed away, and how people behaved. One noted who bought the first automobile and how many women from which families had their babies in a hospital.

Another area that beckoned at this time was the study of *the individual in culture*. In what ways did individual behavior conform to the expressed norms? How did individuals view their own culture patterns, and their own behavior? To what extent is the individual so molded by his culture (the question was phrased thus in early culture-personality studies) that he *must* act in certain ways? What does it feel like to be a Zuñi Indian or a Winnebago? Here, even more than in culture change studies, new problems required new methods. Now one had to know who lived in every house and how they were related; no statement was complete unless one knew who said it to whom and when. One had to look as well as listen. The personality of the field worker and a clear understanding of his relations with his informants became important. One tool that became important in the new kind of field work was the life history. Paul Radin, who was trained by Boas in the traditional techniques of field work and recorded thousands of pages of texts and descriptions of rituals, collected what is probably the first full life history of an American Indian, the *Autobiography of a Winnebago Indian.*

It was written for him by a Winnebago, a reformed character who looked back on his former life with a mixture of disgust and pride. Radin

RUTH L. BUNZEL

does not analyze his life history, he presents it as ethnographic data, another document, another piece of description not very different from the Crow reminiscences of participation in war parties as reported by Lowie. The use of the life history for extracting consistent patterns of behavior and thought and analyzing systematic distortions and other manifestations of the unconscious—all this came later.

Psychoanalysis and Anthropology. Freud's *Totem and Taboo* was published in 1919 and was read by anthropologists, for the most part with shocked nonacceptance. The evolutionary bias and above all the equating of the primitive with the child and the neurotic—ideas which anthropologists had been trying for twenty years to eliminate from popular thought— were unacceptable. But more and more the influence of Freud was becoming evident in the application of such concepts as the unconscious, ambivalence, and the latent symbolic content of myth and ritual. Sapir was one of the first anthropologists to realize how much both anthropology and psychiatry had to gain from a mutual exchange of ideas. Anthropologists had not yet looked seriously at learning theory. They spoke about "culture" molding the individual as if culture were some kind of mechanical press into which most individuals were poured to be molded, and not the sum of patterned experience channeled by the universal tendency towards imitation.

Value as a subject of inquiry began to be taken seriously once again. In one sense this concern with value was a logical outgrowth of the interest in culture wholes and patterns. The problem of value and value systems had often occupied Kroeber. (He sometimes called them styles of culture.) In the postwar period which no longer provided ivory towers for scientists the question of value could not be evaded.

When Boas rewrote *The Mind of Primitive Man* in 1928, incorporating new material, he called it *Anthropology and Modern Life,* thus presaging the role that anthropology was to play in the years ahead. Primitive man is no longer the center of our thoughts or the end of our endeavors; essential as is the study of all varieties of man, research among primitive cultures is still a means to an end. There are many golden ages; one can think of the golden age as that bright morning of the world when one could walk freely in the garden of delights with no responsibilities and no care for the morrow. In that sense the golden age of anthropology came to an end in 1930 when the shadows in the world began to lengthen. Anthropology in America had never been entirely free of its involvement with man's practical and ethical problems; today more than ever before anthropologists are so involved.

FRANZ BOAS

(1858-1942)

The Aims of Anthropological Research

THE SCIENCE OF ANTHROPOLOGY HAS GROWN UP FROM MANY DISTINCT beginnings. At an early time men were interested in foreign countries and in the lives of their inhabitants. Herodotus reported to the Greeks what he had seen in many lands. Caesar and Tacitus wrote on the customs of the Gauls and Germans. In the Middle Ages Marco Polo, the Venetian, and Ibn Batuta, the Arab, told of the strange peoples of the Far East and of Africa. Later on, Cook's journeys excited the interest of the world. From these reports arose gradually a desire to find a general significance in the multifarious ways of living of strange peoples. In the eighteenth century Rousseau, Schiller and Herder tried to form, out of the reports of travelers, a picture of the history of mankind. More solid attempts were made about the middle of the nineteenth century, when the comprehensive works of Klemm and Waitz were written.

Biologists directed their studies towards an understanding of the varieties of human forms. Linnaeus, Blumenbach, Camper are a few of the names that stand out as early investigators of these problems, which received an entirely new stimulus when Darwin's views of the instability of species were accepted by the scientific world. The problem of man's origin and his place in the animal kingdom became the prime subject of interest. Darwin, Huxley and Haeckel are outstanding names representing this period. Still more recently the intensive study of heredity and mutation has given a new aspect to inquiries into the origin and meaning of race.

The development of psychology led to new problems presented by the diversity of the racial and social groups of mankind. The question of mental characteristics of races, which at an earlier period had become a

From Boas, "The Aims of Anthropological Research," Presidential address, American Association for the Advancement of Science, *Science* N.S., Vol. 76 (1932). Reprinted in *Race, Language and Culture* (New York: The Macmillan Company, 1940), pp. 243-259.

subject of discussion with entirely inadequate methods—largely stimulated by the desire to justify slavery—was taken up again with the more refined technique of experimental psychology, and particular attention is now being paid to the mental status of primitive man and of mental life under pathological conditions. The methods of comparative psychology are not confined to man alone, and much light may be thrown on human behavior by the study of animals. The attempt is being made to develop a genetic psychology.

Finally sociology, economics, political science, history and philosophy have found it worth while to study conditions found among alien peoples in order to throw light upon our modern social processes.

With this bewildering variety of approaches, all dealing with racial and cultural forms, it seems necessary to formulate clearly what the objects are that we try to attain by the study of mankind.

We may perhaps best define our objective as the attempt to understand the steps by which man has come to be what he is, biologically, psychologically and culturally. Thus it appears at once that our material must necessarily be historical material, historical in the widest sense of the term. It must include the history of the development of the bodily form of man, his physiological functions, mind and culture. We need a knowledge of the chronological succession of forms and an insight into the conditions under which changes occur. Without such data progress seems impossible and the fundamental question arises as to how such data can be obtained.

Ever since Lamarck's and Darwin's time the biologist has been struggling with this problem. The complete paleontological record of the development of plant and animal forms is not available. Even in favorable cases gaps remain that cannot be filled on account of the lack of intermediate forms. For this reason indirect proofs must be resorted to: These are based partly on similarities revealed by morphology and interpreted as proof of genetic relationship, partly on morphological traits observed in prenatal life, which suggest relationship between forms that as adults appear quite distinct.

Caution in the use of morphological similarities is required, because there are cases in which similar forms develop in genetically unrelated groups, as in the marsupials of Australia, which show remarkable parallelism with higher mammal forms, or in the white-haired forms of the Arctic and of high altitudes, which occur independently in many genera and species, or in the blondness and other abnormal hair forms of domesticated mammals which develop regardless of their genetic relations.

As long as the paleontological record is incomplete we have no way of reconstructing the history of animals and plants except through morphology and embryology.

This is equally true of man, and for this reason the eager search for early human and prehuman forms is justified. The finds of the remains of the

Pithecanthropus in Java, the Sinanthropus in China, of the Heidelberg jaw and of the later types of the glacial period are so many steps advancing our knowledge. It requires the labors of the enthusiastic explorer to furnish us with the material that must be interpreted by careful morphological study. The material available at the present time is sadly fragmentary. It is encouraging to see that it is richest in all those countries in which the interest in the paleontology of man has been keenest, so that we may hope that with the increase of interest in new fields the material on which to build the evolutionary history of man will be considerably increased.

It is natural that with our more extended knowledge of the evolutionary history of the higher mammals certain points stand out that will direct the labors of the explorer. Thus on the basis of our knowledge of the distribution of ape forms, nobody would search for the ancestors of humanity in the New World, although the question when the earliest migration of man into America took place is still one of the problems that is prominent in researches on the paleontology of the glacial period of America.

The skeletal material of later periods is more abundant. Still it is difficult to establish definitely the relation of early skeletal remains and of modern races, because many of their most characteristic traits are found in the soft parts of the body that have not been preserved. Furthermore, the transitions from one race to another are so gradual that only extreme forms can be determined with any degree of definiteness.

On account of the absence of material elucidating the history of modern races, it is not surprising that for many years anthropologists have endeavored to classify races, basing their attempts on a variety of traits, and that only too often the results of these classifications have been assumed as expressions of genetic relationship, while actually they have no more than a descriptive value, unless their genetic significance can be established. If the same metric proportions of the head recur in all races they cannot be a significant criterion of fundamental racial types, although they may be valuable indications of the development of local strains within a racial group. If, on the other hand, a particular hair form is a trait well-nigh universal in extensive groups of mankind, and one that does not recur in other groups, it will in all probability represent an ancient hereditary racial trait, the more so, if it occurs in a geographically continuous area. It is the task of the anthropologist to search out these outstanding traits and to remember that the exact measurement of features which are not exclusive racial characteristics will not answer the problems of the evolution of fundamental types, but can be taken only as an indication of independent, special modifications of late origin within the large racial groups.

From this point of view the general question of the occurrence of parallel development in genetically unrelated lines assumes particular importance. We have sufficient evidence to show that morphological form is subject to environmental influences that in some cases will have similar effects upon unrelated forms. Even the most skeptical would admit this for size of the body.

Changes due to environment that occur under our eyes, such as minute changes in size and proportion of the body, are probably not hereditary, but merely expressions of the reaction of the body to external conditions and subject to new adjustments under new conditions.

However, one series of changes, brought about by external conditions, are undoubtedly hereditary. I mean those developing in domestication. No matter whether they are due to survival of aberrant forms or directly conditioned by domestication, they are found in similar ways in all domesticated animals, and because man possesses all these characteristics he proves to be a domesticated form. Eduard Hahn was probably the first to point out that man lives like a domesticated animal; the morphological points were emphasized by Eugen Fischer, B. Klatt and myself.

The solution of the problem of the origin of races must rest not only on classificatory studies and on those of the development of parallel forms, but also on the consideration of the distribution of races, of early migrations and consequent intermingling or isolation.

On account of the occurrence of independent development of parallel forms it seems important to know the range of variant local forms that originate in each race, and it might seem plausible that races producing local variants of similar types are closely related. Thus Mongoloids and Europeans occasionally produce similar forms in regions so wide apart that it would be difficult to interpret them as effects of intermingling.

The biological foundations of conclusions based on this type of evidence are, to a great extent, necessarily speculative. Scientific proof would require a knowledge of the earliest movements of mankind, an intimate acquaintance with the conditions under which racial types may throw off variants and the character and extent of variations that may develop as mutants.

The solution of these problems must extend beyond morphological description of the race as a whole. Since we are dealing to a great extent with forms determined by heredity, it seems indispensable to found the study of the race as a whole on that of the component genetic lines and of their variants, and on inquiries into the influence of environment and selection upon bodily form and function. The race must be studied not as a whole but in its genotypical lines as developing under varying conditions.

In the study of racial forms we are too much inclined to consider the importance of races according to the number of their representatives. This is obviously an error, for the important phenomenon is the occurrence of stable morphological types, not the number of individuals representing each. The numerical strength of races has changed enormously in historic times, and it would be quite erroneous to attribute an undue importance to the White race or to the East Asiatics, merely because they have outgrown in numbers all other racial types. Still, in descriptive classifications the local types of a large race are given undue prominence over the less striking subdivisions of lesser groups. As an example, I might mention Huxley's divisions of the White race as against his divisions of other races.

We are interested not only in the bodily form of races but equally in the functioning of the body, physiologically as well as mentally. The problems presented by this class of phenomena present particular difficulties on account of the adjustability of function to external demands, so that it is an exceedingly precarious task to distinguish between what is determined by the biological make-up of the body and what depends upon external conditions. Observations made on masses of individuals in different localities may be explained equally well by the assumption of hereditary racial characteristics and by that of changes due to environmental influences. A mere description of these phenomena will never lead to a result. Different types, areas, social strata and cultures exhibit marked differences in physiological and mental function. A dogmatic assertion that racial type alone is responsible for these differences is a pseudo-science. An adequate treatment requires a weighing of the diverse factors.

Investigators are easily misled by the fact that the hereditary, biologically determined endowment of an individual is intimately associated with the functioning of his body. This appears most clearly in cases of bodily deficiency or of unusually favorable bodily development. It is quite a different matter to extend this observation over whole populations or racial groups in which are represented a great variety of hereditary lines and individuals, for the many forms of bodily make-up found in each group allow a great variety of functioning. Hereditary characteristics are pronounced in genetic lines, but a population—or to use the technical term, a phenotype—is not a genetic line and the great variety of genotypes within a race forbids the application of results obtained from a single hereditary line to a whole population in which the diversity of the constituent lines is bound to equalize the distribution of diverse genetic types in the populations considered. I have spoken so often on this subject that you will permit me to pass on to other questions.

While paleontological evidence may give us a clue to the evolution of human forms, only the most superficial evidence can be obtained for the development of function. A little may be inferred from size and form of the brain cavity and that of the jaw, in so far as it indicates the possibility of articulate speech. We may obtain some information on the development of erect posture, but the physiological processes that occurred in past generations are not accessible to observation. All the conclusions that we may arrive at are based on very indirect evidence.

The mental life of man also can be studied experimentally only among living races. It is, however, possible to infer some of its aspects by what past generations have done. Historical data permit us to study the culture of past times, in a few localities, as in the eastern Mediterranean area, India, China as far back as a few thousand years—and a limited amount of information on the mental life of man may be obtained from these data. We may even go farther back and extend our studies over the early remains of human activities. Objects of varied character, made by man and belonging to periods as early as the Quaternary, have been found in great quantities, and their study reveals at least certain aspects of what man has been able to do during these times.

The data of prehistoric archeology reveal with progress of time a decided branching out of human activities. While from earliest periods nothing remains but a few simple stone implements, we see an increasing differentiation of form of implements used by man. During the Quaternary the use of fire had been discovered, artistic work of high esthetic value had been achieved, and painted records of human activities had been made. Soon after the beginning of the recent geological period the beginnings of agriculture appear and the products of human labor take on new forms at a rapidly accelerating rate. While in early Quaternary times we do not observe any change for thousands of years, so that the observer might imagine that the products of human hands were made according to an innate instinct, like the cells of a beehive, the rapidity of change becomes the greater the nearer we approach our time, and at an early period we recognize that the arts of man cannot be instinctively determined, but are the cumulative result of experience.

It has often been claimed that the very primitiveness of human handiwork of early times proves organic mental inferiority. This argument is certainly not tenable, for we find in modern times isolated tribes living in a way that may very well be paralleled with early conditions. A comparison of the psychic life of these groups does not justify the belief that their industrial backwardness is due to a difference in the types of organism, for we find numbers of closely related races on the most diverse levels of cultural status. This is perhaps clearest in the Mongoloid race, where by the side of the civilized Chinese are found the most primitive Siberian tribes, or in the American group, where the highly developed Maya of Yucatan and the Aztecs of Mexico may be compared with the primitive tribes of our western plateaus. Evidently historic and prehistoric data give us little or no information on the biological development of the human mind.

How little the biological, organic determinants of culture can be inferred from the state of culture appears clearly if we try to realize how different the judgment of racial ability would have been at various periods of history. When Egypt flourished, northern Europe was in primitive conditions, comparable to those of American Indians or African Negroes, and yet northern Europe of our day has far outdistanced those people, who at an earlier time were the leaders of mankind. An attempt to find biological reasons for these changes would necessitate innumerable unprovable hypotheses regarding changes of the biological make-up of these peoples, hypotheses that could be invented only for the purpose of sustaining an unproved assumption.

A safer mode of approaching the problems at issue would seem to lie in the application of experimental psychology which might enable us to determine the psychophysical and also some of the mental characteristics of various races. As in the case of biological inquiry it would be equally necessary in this study to examine genotypical lines rather than populations, because so many different lines are contained in the mass.

A serious difficulty is presented by the dependence of the results of all psychophysical or mental tests upon the experiences of the individual who is the subject of the tests. His experiences are largely determined by the culture in which he lives. I am of the opinion that no method can be devised by which this all-important element is eliminated, but that we always obtain a result which is a mixed impression of culturally determined influences and of bodily build. For this reason I quite agree with those critical psychologists who acknowledge that for most mental phenomena we know only European psychology and no other.

In the few cases in which the influence of culture upon mental reaction of populations has been investigated it can be shown that culture is a much more important determinant than bodily build. I repeat that in individuals a somewhat close relation between mental reaction and bodily build may be found, which is all but absent in populations. Under these circumstances it is necessary to base the investigation of the mental life of man upon a study of the history of cultural forms and of the interrelations between individual mental life and culture.

This is the subject-matter of cultural anthropology. It is safe to say that the results of the extensive materials amassed during the last fifty years do not justify the assumption of any close relation between biological types and form of culture.

As in the realm of biology our inferences must be based on historical data, so it is in the investigation of cultures. Unless we know how the culture of each group of man came to be what it is, we cannot expect to reach any conclusions in regard to the conditions controlling the general history of culture.

The material needed for the reconstruction of the biological history of mankind is insufficient on account of the paucity of remains and the disappearance of all soft, perishable parts. The material for the reconstruction of culture is ever so much more fragmentary because the largest and most important aspects of culture leave no trace in the soil; language, social organization, religion—in short, everything that is not material—vanishes with the life of each generation. Historical information is available only for the most recent phases of cultural life and is confined to those peoples who had the art of writing and whose records we can read. Even this information is insufficient because many aspects of culture find no expression in literature. Is it then necessary to resign ourselves and to consider the problem as insoluble?

In biology we supplement the fragmentary paleontological record with data obtained from comparative anatomy and embryology. Perhaps an analogous procedure may enable us to unravel some of the threads of cultural history.

There is one fundamental difference between biological and cultural data which makes it impossible to transfer the methods of the one science to the other. Animal forms develop in divergent directions, and an intermingling of species that have once become distinct is negligible in the whole developmental history. It is otherwise in the domain of culture. Human thoughts, institutions, activities may spread from one social unit to another. As soon as two groups come into close contact their cultural traits will be disseminated from the one to the other.

Undoubtedly there are dynamic conditions that mould in similar forms certain aspects of the morphology of social units. Still we may expect that these will be overlaid by extraneous elements that have no organic relation to the dynamics of inner change.

This makes the reconstruction of cultural history easier than that of biological history, but it puts the most serious obstacles in the way of discovering the inner dynamic conditions of change. Before morphological comparison can be attempted the extraneous elements due to cultural diffusion must be eliminated.

When certain traits are diffused over a limited area and absent outside of it, it seems safe to assume that their distribution is due to diffusion. In some rare cases even the direction of diffusion may be determined. If Indian corn is derived from a Mexican wild form and is cultivated over the larger part of the two Americas we must conclude that its cultivation spread from Mexico north and south; if the ancestors of African cattle are not found in Africa, they must have been introduced into that continent. In the majority of cases it is impossible to determine with certainty the direction of diffusion. It would be an error to assume that a cultural trait had its original home in the area in which it is now most strongly developed. Christianity did not originate in Europe or America. The manufacture of iron did not originate in America or northern Europe. It was the same in early times. We may be certain that the use of milk did not originate in Africa, nor the cultivation of wheat in Europe.

For these reasons it is well-nigh impossible to base a chronology of the development of specific cultures on the observed phenomena of diffusion. In a few cases it seems justifiable to infer from the worldwide diffusion of a particular cultural achievement its great antiquity. This is true when we can prove by archeological evidence its early occurrence. Thus, fire was used by man in early Quaternary times. At that period man was already widely scattered over the world and we may infer that either the use of fire was carried along by him when he migrated to new regions or that it spread rapidly from tribe to tribe and soon became the property of mankind. This method cannot be generalized, for we know of other inventions and ideas that spread with incredible rapidity over vast areas. An example is the spread of tobacco over Africa, as soon as it was introduced on the coast.

In smaller areas attempts at chronological reconstruction are much more uncertain. From a cultural center in which complex forms have developed, elements may radiate and impress themselves upon neighboring tribes, or the more complex forms may develop on an old, less differentiated basis. It is seldom possible to decide which one of these alternatives offers the correct interpretation.

Notwithstanding all these difficulties, the study of geographical distribution of cultural phenomena offers a means of determining their diffusion. The outstanding result of these studies has been the proof of the intricate interrelation of people of all parts of the world. Africa, Europe and the greater part of Asia appear to us as a cultural unit in which one area cannot be entirely separated from the rest. America appears as another unit, but even the New World and the Old are not entirely independent of each other, for lines of contact have been discovered that connect northeastern Asia and America.

As in biological investigations the problem of parallel independent development of homologous forms obscures that of genetic relationship, so it is in cultural inquiry. If it is possible that analogous anatomical forms develop independently in genetically distinct lines, it is ever so much more probable that analogous cultural forms develop independently. It may be admitted that it is exceedingly difficult to give absolutely indisputable proof of the independent origin of analogous cultural data. Nevertheless, the distribution of isolated customs in regions far apart hardly admits of the argument that they were transmitted from tribe to tribe and lost in intervening territory. It is well known that in our civilization current scientific ideas give rise to independent and synchronous inventions. In an analogous way primitive social life contains elements that lead to somewhat similar forms in many parts of the world. Thus the dependence of the infant upon the mother necessitates at least a temporary difference in the mode of life of the sexes and makes woman less movable than man. The long dependence of children on their elders leaves also an inevitable impress upon social form. Just

what these effects will be depends upon circumstances. Their fundamental cause will be the same in every case.

The number of individuals in a social unit, the necessity or undesir-
ability of communal action for obtaining the necessary food supply constitute dynamic conditions that are active everywhere and that are
germs from which analogous cultural behavior may spring.

Besides these, there are individual cases of inventions or ideas in
lands far apart that cannot be proved to be historically connected. The
fork was used in Fiji and invented comparatively recently in Europe;
the spear, projected by a thong wound spirally about the shaft, was used
on the Admiralty Islands and in ancient Rome. In some cases the difference in time makes the theory of a transfer all but unthinkable. This
is the case, for instance, with the domestication of mammals in Peru,
the invention of bronze in Peru and Yucatan and that of the zero in
Yucatan.

Some anthropologists assume that, if a number of cultural phenomena
agree in regions far apart, these must be due to the presence of an
exceedingly ancient substratum that has been preserved notwithstanding all the cultural changes that have occurred. This view is not admissible without proof that the phenomena in question remain stable not
only for thousands of years, but even so far back that they have been
carried by wandering hordes from Asia to the extreme southern end of
South America. Notwithstanding the great tenacity of cultural traits,
there is no proof that such extreme conservatism ever existed. The apparent stability of primitive types of culture is due to our lack of historical perspective. They change much more slowly than our modern
civilization, but wherever archeological evidence is available we do find
changes in time and space. A careful investigation shows that those
features that are assumed as almost absolutely stable are constantly
undergoing changes. Some details may remain for a long time, but the
general complex of culture cannot be assumed to retain its character
for a very long span of time. We see people who were agricultural become hunters, others change their mode of life in the opposite direction.
People who had totemic organization give it up, while others take it
over from their neighbors.

It is not a safe method to assume that all analogous cultural phenomena must be historically related. It is necessary to demand in every
case proof of historical relation, which should be the more rigid the less
evidence there is of actual recent or early contact.

In the attempt to reconstruct the history of modern races we are
trying to discover the earlier forms preceding modern forms. An analogous attempt has been demanded of cultural history. To a limited
extent it has succeeded. The history of inventions and the history of
science show to us in course of time constant additions to the range of

inventions, and a gradual increase of empirical knowledge. On this basis we might be inclined to look for a single line of development of culture, a thought that was pre-eminent in anthropological work of the end of the past century.

The fuller knowledge of to-day makes such a view untenable. Cultures differ like so many species, perhaps genera, of animals, and their common basis is lost forever. It seems impossible, if we disregard invention and knowledge, the two elements just referred to, to bring cultures into any kind of continuous series. Sometimes we find simple, sometimes complex, social organizations associated with crude inventions and knowledge. Moral behavior, except in so far as it is checked by increased understanding of social needs, does not seem to fall into any order.

It is evident that certain social conditions are incompatible. A hunting people, in which every family requires an extended territory to insure the needed food supply, cannot form large communities, although it may have intricate rules governing marriage. Life that requires constant moving about on foot is incompatible with the development of a large amount of personal property. Seasonal food supply requires a mode of life different from a regular, uninterrupted food supply.

The interdependence of cultural phenomena must be one of the objects of anthropological inquiry, for which material may be obtained through the study of existing societies.

Here we are compelled to consider culture as a whole, in all its manifestations, while in the study of diffusion and of parallel development the character and distribution of single traits are more commonly the objects of inquiry. Inventions, economic life, social structure, art, religion, morals are all interrelated. We ask in how far are they determined by environment, by the biological character of the people, by psychological conditions, by historical events or by general laws of interrelation.

It is obvious that we are dealing here with a different problem. This is most clearly seen in our use of language. Even the fullest knowledge of the history of language does not help us to understand how we use language and what influence language has upon our thought. It is the same in other phases of life. The dynamic reactions to cultural environment are not determined by its history, although they are a result of historical development. Historical data do give us certain clues that may not be found in the experience of a single generation. Still, the psychological problem must be studied in living societies.

It would be an error to claim, as some anthropologists do, that for this reason historical study is irrelevant. The two sides of our problem require equal attention, for we desire to know not only the dynamics of existing societies, but also how they came to be what they are. For an intelligent understanding of historical processes a knowledge of living processes is as necessary as the knowledge of life processes for the under-standing of the evolution of life forms.

The dynamics of existing societies are one of the most hotly contested fields of anthropological theory. They may be looked at from two points of view, the one, the interrelations between various aspects of cultural form and between culture and natural environment; the other the inter-relation between individual and society.

Biologists are liable to insist on a relation between bodily build and culture. We have seen that evidence for such an interrelation has never been established by proofs that will stand serious criticism. It may not be amiss to dwell here again on the difference between races and indi-viduals. The hereditary make-up of an individual has a certain influ-ence upon his mental behavior. Pathological cases are the clearest proof of this. On the other hand, every race contains so many individuals of different hereditary make-up that the average differences between races freed of elements determined by history cannot readily be ascertained, but appear as insignificant. It is more than doubtful whether differences free of these historic elements can ever be established.

Geographers try to derive all forms of human culture from the geo-graphical environment in which man lives. Important though this may be, we have no evidence of a creative force of environment. All we know is that every culture is strongly influenced by its environment, that some elements of culture cannot develop in an unfavorable geographical setting, while others may be advanced. It is sufficient to see the funda-mental differences of culture that thrive one after another in the same environment, to make us understand the limitations of environmental influences. The aborigines of Australia live in the same environment in which the White invaders live. The nature and location of Australia have remained the same during human history, but they have influenced different cultures. Environment can affect only an existing culture, and it is worth while to study its influence in detail. This has been clearly recognized by critical geographers, such as Hettner.

Economists believe that economic conditions control cultural forms. Economic determinism is proposed as against geographic determinism. Undoubtedly the interrelation between economics and other aspects of culture is much more immediate than that between geographical en-vironment and culture. Still it is not possible to explain every feature of cultural life as determined by economic status. We do not see how art styles, the form of ritual or the special form of religious belief could possibly be derived from economic forces. On the contrary, we see that economics and the rest of culture interact as cause and effect, as effect and cause.

Every attempt to deduce cultural forms from a single cause is doomed to failure, for the various expressions of culture are closely interrelated and one cannot be altered without having an effect upon all the others. Culture is integrated. It is true that the degree of integration is not always the same. There are cultures which we might describe by a single term, that of modern democracies as individualistic-mechanical; or that of a Melanesian island as individualization by mutual distrust; or that of our Plains Indians as overvaluation of intertribal warfare. Such terms may be misleading, because they overemphasize certain features, still they indicate certain dominating attitudes.

Integration is not often so complete that all contradictory elements are eliminated. We rather find in the same culture curious breaks in the attitudes of different individuals, and, in the case of varying situations, even in the behavior of the same individual.

The lack of necessary correlations between various aspects of culture may be illustrated by the cultural significance of a truly scientific study of the heavenly bodies by the Babylonians, Maya and by Europeans during the Middle Ages. For us the necessary correlation of astronomical observations is with physical and chemical phenomena; for them the essential point was their astrological significance, i.e., their relation to the fate of man, an attitude based on the general historically conditioned culture of their times.

These brief remarks may be sufficient to indicate the complexity of the phenomena we are studying, and it seems justifiable to question whether any generalized conclusions may be expected that will be applicable everywhere and that will reduce the data of anthropology to a formula which may be applied to every case, explaining its past and predicting its future.

I believe that it would be idle to entertain such hopes. The phenomena of our science are so individualized, so exposed to outer accident that no set of laws could explain them. It is as in any other science dealing with the actual world surrounding us. For each individual case we can arrive at an understanding of its determination by inner and outer forces, but we cannot explain its individuality in the form of laws. The astronomer reduces the movement of stars to laws, but unless given an unexplainable original arrangement in space, he cannot account for their present location. The biologist may know all the laws of ontogenesis, but he cannot explain by their means the accidental forms they have taken in an individual species, much less those found in an individual.

Physical and biological laws differ in character on account of the complexity of the objects of their study. Biological laws can refer only to biological forms, as geological laws can refer only to the forms of geological formations. The more complex the phenomena, the more special will be the laws expressed by them.

Cultural phenomena are of such complexity that it seems to me doubtful whether valid cultural laws can be found. The causal conditions of cultural happenings lie always in the interaction between individual and society, and no classificatory study of societies will solve this problem. The morphological classification of societies may call to our attention many problems. It will not solve them. In every case it is reducible to the same source, namely, the interaction between individual and society.

It is true that some valid interrelations between general aspects of cultural life may be found, such as between density and size of the population constituting a community and industrial occupations; or solidarity and isolation of a small population and their conservatism. These are interesting as static descriptions of cultural facts. Dynamic processes also may be recognized, such as the tendency of customs to change their significance according to changes in culture. Their meaning can be understood only by a penetrating analysis of the human elements that enter into each case.

In short, the material of anthropology is such that it needs must be a historical science, one of the sciences the interest of which centers in the attempt to understand the individual phenomena rather than in the establishment of general laws which, on account of the complexity of the material, will be necessarily vague and, we might almost say, so self-evident that they are of little help to a real understanding.

The attempt has been made too often to formulate a genetic problem as defined by a term taken from our own civilization, either based on analogy with forms known to us or contrasted to those with which we are familiar. Thus concepts, like war, the idea of immortality, marriage regulations, have been considered as units and general conclusions have been derived from their forms and distributions. It should be recognized that the subordination of all such forms, under a category with which we are familiar on account of our own cultural experience, does not prove the historical or sociological unity of the phenomenon. The ideas of immortality differ so fundamentally in content and significance that they can hardly be treated as a unit and valid conclusions based on their occurrence cannot be drawn without detailed analysis.

A critical investigation rather shows that forms of thought and action which we are inclined to consider as based on human nature are not generally valid, but characteristic of our specific culture. If this were not so, we could not understand why certain aspects of mental life that are characteristic of the Old World should be entirely or almost entirely absent in aboriginal America. An example is the contrast between the fundamental idea of judicial procedure in Africa and America; the emphasis on oath and ordeal as parts of judicial procedure in the Old World, their absence in the New World.

The problems of the relation of the individual to his culture, to the society in which he lives have received too little attention. The standardized anthropological data that inform us of customary behavior, give no clue to the reaction of the individual to his culture, nor to an understanding of his influence upon it. Still, here lie the sources of a true interpretation of human behavior. It seems a vain effort to search for sociological laws disregarding what should be called social psychology, namely, the reaction of the individual to culture. They can be no more than empty formulas that can be imbued with life only by taking account of individual behavior in cultural settings.

Society embraces many individuals varying in mental character, partly on account of their biological make-up, partly due to the special social conditions under which they have grown up. Nevertheless, many of them react in similar ways, and there are numerous cases in which we can find a definite impress of culture upon the behavior of the great mass of individuals, expressed by the same mentality. Deviations from such a type result in abnormal social behavior and, although throwing light upon the iron hold of culture upon the average individual, are rather subject-matter for the study of individual psychology than of social psychology.

If we once grasp the meaning of foreign cultures in this manner, we shall also be able to see how many of our lines of behavior that we believe to be founded deep in human nature are actually expressions of our culture and subject to modification with changing culture. Not all our standards are categorically determined by our quality as human beings, but may change with changing circumstances. It is our task to discover among all the varieties of human behavior those that are common to all humanity. By a study of the universality and variety of cultures anthropology may help us to shape the future course of mankind.

CLARK WISSLER

(1870-1947)

The Conflict and Survival of Cultures

GROUP DOMINANCE AND LEADERSHIP

THE RIVALRY OF CULTURE GROUPS CAN BE STUDIED BY THE USE OF anthropological data. The culture areas to which we referred at the outset are best explained as the fringes to centers of culture influence. The situation here is, however, not essentially different from that of a modern nation leading economically, intellectually, or artistically, as the case may be; all the surrounding nations do their best to follow. In this case the effort may be largely socially directed and in so far a conscious process. On the other hand, the efforts of primitive tribes to acquire the culture of the dominant tribe is often conscious. We have the example of the Nez Perce Indians sending a committee to the frontier settlements along the Mississippi to invite a white missionary and teacher to give them the elements of the superior culture. Other instances of such initiative are on record, and the traditions of primitive folk recount how one or more of their number went abroad to learn new traits of culture.

Looking at groups in general, we see that they not only recognize differences between themselves and other groups but are conscious of their own position. If they are the dominant group, they are aware of that; if not, they recognize the superiority of their neighbor and attempt to emulate him. In other words, they are conscious of their relative position whether they admit it or not.

CONFLICT OF CULTURES

. . . When two contrasting cultures come into contact, single traits may compete with each other. Examples of this are seen in the displacement of the bow by the gun, the fire-drill by the match, the earthen pot by the

From Wissler, "The Conflict and Survival of Cultures," *The Foundations of Experimental Psychology,* edited by Carl Murchison (Worcester: Clark University Press, 1929), pp. 798-807.

iron kettle, etc. There is a minimum of resistance in such cases, but indirectly the displacement may jar the whole tribal system of procedure. It is easy to throw down the bow and take up the gun and to learn to kindle fires with matches; but this new equipment cannot be produced within the tribe, as heretofore. The tribe is now dependent upon the trader. Further, in order to secure these objects, other goods must be produced in sufficient quantity, perhaps furs. This seems simple enough, but standards of individual property are involved, social obligations must be adjusted to the trapping calender, etc. Success in trapping becomes more important, so the magical beliefs of the tribe must be adjusted. Nevertheless, such conflicts as arise are rarely serious unless some strong taboo is violated. Thus it is said that some Hindu troops once mutinied because the paper cartridges, whose ends they were required to bite off, were greased with an animal fat, against which there was a taboo. But the obvious ease of adjustment in this case may be taken as typical and indicating that, on the whole, no serious conflict need be anticipated from the introduction of single traits.

Before leaving this subject, it is well to be reminded that not all introduced traits are dependent upon foreign trade. Thus the horse was introduced to the American Indian, who propagated and equipped the horse by their own labor; the tribe was thus in no wise dependent upon a foreign source of supply. Economically, the tribe was enriched, but no important adjustments to other culture traits were necessary. That there was a psychological reaction is probable, since this new mode of transportation gave a feeling of power, increased geographical knowledge, and gave more leisure. The tribe receiving horses might be expected to feel superior to neighboring tribes and the reverse. Finally, new information may be acquired as to distant lands, as to the properties of natural resources, etc., thus increasing the store of knowledge. A new tale or myth may be acquired, a new song learned, a new game adopted, all without disturbing existing traits. So in general the introduction of a useful domestic animal, a plant, a new industrial art, or a new fact will enrich a culture with a minimum of conflict.

On the other hand, trait complexes displacing other complexes seem to present serious situations. Yet these seem to vary according to the relative values attached to the complexes involved. An example of conflicts of this kind are those which arise respecting individual property and thrift. Most primitive peoples feel that every individual is entitled to food and other necessities, whether he is a producer or not. They do possess the idea of individual property, but entertain an ideal of hospitality which requires frequent sacrifice to others. Lewis H. Morgan[1] first sensed the significance of this aspect of primitive cultures, designating it as the

---

[1] Morgan, L. H., *Ancient Society* (Chicago: Kerr).

law of hospitality. When nations are subject to European control, this tendency conflicts with the system of individual economic independence. For example, the younger members of the tribe may be educated and induced to undertake farming, but when the crop is harvested, the old law of hospitality requires that the producer give it away. To refuse to do so would be grossly immoral from the point of view of his tribe. Such a conflict of culture complexes may be very distressing but of a less emotional character than some others.

Among all primitive peoples the distinctions between the work of men and women are sharply drawn. To disregard these distinctions is to stigmatize oneself. Among some tribes all preparation of food is not only the work of women but they also own the food; under such circumstances, for a man to claim ownership in food would be disgraceful. In most languages, the strongest terms of contempt are those describing the individual in characterization of the opposite sex. Yet while there are everywhere distinctions between the work of men and women in the tribe, these distinctions may vary as to the kind of work. Among certain hunting tribes of Indians, it was woman's place to tend the fields, man's place to hunt. The customs of white culture, more dependent upon agriculture, reversed the distinction. So when Indian and white culture came in contact, the Indian resisted assuming responsibility for work in the fields as shameful and humiliating. When hunting was no more possible, the white man insisted that the Indian turn to agriculture; the conflict resulting and its emotional intensity are obvious. Humiliation and degradation were the price the Indian must pay.

Still other examples may be cited. Among many tribes, the place in which a person dies is taboo; thus, if a person dies in a house, the place will be deserted, to fall into ruins. With the simple shelter of primitive peoples, this custom was easily maintained, but when the European custom of more substantial and expensive buildings is brought in, the difficulties increase. Fear of spirits, bad luck, the whole background of beliefs concerning the dead, all combined to make life in such a house unbearable. Their feelings would be about the same as those of a European asked to live in a cemetery. But on some of our Indian reservations there is still further conflict. To provide the Indians with adequate medical care, hospitals have been built; the difficulties in their use by the Indians are obvious. Once a patient dies in the hospital, it is no place for a sick person. The violation of the taboo, the emotional effect upon the patient, if forcibly taken to the hospital, all tend to unite the tribe in opposition. Suspicion may follow as to the motives of the white race in inducing them to use the hospital, and this crystallize into a belief that the whites desire their lands and so seek to kill them off. In general, fear and dread of the possible consequences are bred in conflicts of culture complexes; the trait complexes favoring such responses may be wholly objective, but conflicts arise because of the beliefs and customs associated with the traits to be displaced.

The missionary is usually charged with being the arch-instigator of conflicts. Yet many of his teachings need not make great disturbances. Such general concepts as theft, lying, murder, slander, adultery, etc., will be taken by the natives as a matter of course; the differences will lie in the application of these concepts. Thus, adultery may be defined differently by the tribe and the missionary; but usually the missionary comes to teach a new belief, to recount a revelation which exacts new taboos, violates old ones, and so sets up a conflict of beliefs. We usually think of these conflicts as between pagan and Christian, but they occur in respect to any kind of religious propaganda. In our earlier discussion of cults we noted how they might spread from one tribe to another and how they needed a leader and a number of devotees to maintain themselves. Their introduction into a tribal culture will produce more or less conflict according to circumstances. We cite this merely to call attention to the obvious: i.e., Christian missionaries are no different from other missionaries, a gathering host whose origin is as old as culture itself.

The economic school frequently asserts that many conflicts arise from economic situations. What is meant is that the storm centers lie in the traits having to do with food and comfort. It is not for us to evaluate this theory, but to consider economic change resulting from culture contact as provocative of conflict. In 1893 there culminated a religious, militant movement among the Indian tribes west of the Mississippi known in literature as the Ghost Dance religion. A few years before, the herds of bison, upon which these Indians depended for food, were swept from the plains by white hunters. At the same time the tribes were gathered into reservations and refused permission to leave them. Privation was the common experience, and starvation a possibility, though scanty rations were issued by government orders; from the Indian point of view the situation was desperate. At this psychological moment a new religion was launched, a belief in an Indian Messiah, who was to return, sweep away the white race and its culture, and restore former economic conditions. The new belief spread rapidly and revived the hopes of the Indians. By a prompt and energetic concentration of troops, the militant aspect of the movement was repressed, but as a cult or a religion this new trait complex functioned for a long time. The religious movement, the attempt to revolt, may be said to represent a response to a specific economic change. In this case the economic change affected all members of the tribe so that a group conflict was initiated.

THE SUBJECT GROUP

When the group is made subject by conquest, there may be for a time the smart of defeat, but an adjustment will evolve. If, however, the culture differences between the groups are extreme, the dominating group may seem so superior that a feeling of helplessness and despair may prevail. This is perhaps due to a failure to understand the culture to which adjustment must be made. One such group, once visited by the writer, found it incomprehensible why the white official dispensing justice dealt harshly with the native who beat his wife, but turned a deaf ear when a husband complained that his wife beat him. The natives could see nothing consistent in such procedure; they were, of course, wholly ignorant of the historic background to white culture, with its idealization of women. How could the natives understand such a situation, unless familiar with a large sector of white belief? On the other hand, the white practice of demanding virginity of the woman and a lower standard for the male was wholly intelligible to this primitive group, because they followed similar practices. Economic adjustments are also often beyond the comprehension of such a primitive group. For example, an American Indian community was advised that one way to earn some money would be to make hay of the grasses growing in their locality; accordingly they labored successfully during the season, harvesting a large crop. Yet, when it came to finding a market, they failed. White men, they observed, did make a living by producing hay, but not being able to do it, they regarded themselves as inferior, entirely unable to live according to the standards of the new culture. It is this feeling of helplessness in the face of a crisis in culture adjustment that is a significant factor in the conflict problem.

The transition from a conquered group to a dependent one is easy and perhaps natural. When confronted with a crisis for which there is no ready solution, the individual appeals to his fellows; this is true of all, whether civilized or savage. In an analogous manner, a group feeling itself helpless will hope for succor from a stronger group. But under primitive conditions, each small tribe is a law unto itself, must stand upon its own feet; hence, in the face of a culture crisis, they have no group to which to turn for support. Their status is in striking contrast to that of a white colony among primitive tribes, for such a settlement can tap the reserves of a nation in case of need. The natives easily recognize the confidence and security of the white man, and therefore spontaneously lean toward him. Moreover, natives living in harsh environments cannot escape uneasiness as to the future, as instanced by Rasmussen[2] in his studies of the Eskimo. A wise old Eskimo, after pointing out the hungry families in camp waiting for the return of the hunter, the sick and the aged, asked, "Why should this be so?" He said further, "We fear! We fear the elements with which we have to fight in their fury to wrest our food from land and sea. We fear cold and famine in our snow huts. We fear the sickness that is daily to be seen amongst us. Not death,

2 Rasmussen, K., *Across Arctic America* (New York: Putnam's, 1927).

but the suffering. We fear the souls of the dead, of human and animal alike. We fear the spirits of earth and air . . . And for all our angakoqs and their knowledge of hidden things, we yet know so little that we fear everything else."

In his natural state, primitive man usually looks to the supernatural for aid. In more technical terms, he resorts to magic. He feels that somewhere must reside a power able to cope with the danger that confronts him, and that, if he knew how to adjust himself to this power, his problem would be solved. The superior group would be one having such knowledge and skill as would enable it to cope with its environment. To such a group a native tends to turn, as we have stated, but fear may inhibit the impulse. The superiority of the white man is taken to mean superiority in magic as well, a power for evil as well as good. Further, the white man has no understanding or sympathy with the magic of the native, and by ridicule deepens the inferiority feeling of the native. The difficulty, of course, lies in a conflict of culture traits, not in differences in human nature. The native is thus in a conflict of responses on his part, his inclination being to seek the protection and leadership of the more powerful white man, but he hesitates because he fears the white man as hostile, intending to destroy rather than protect. Such states may be attributed to culture conflicts; they are the response complexes of the native group. In most cases of white vs. native, the conflict is wholly one-sided; the culture of the white group is not disturbed by the presence of the native culture.

It may be profitable to examine a few more examples of conflict. The culture patterns for primitive groups seem less individualistic than our own. Their groups are small, but possess great solidarity. The individual is accustomed to act in unison with his fellows; if food is to be gathered, they proceed in a party, etc. Spontaneous response to suggested procedures marks all activities. One phase of the conflict with white culture arises in these differences respecting such a group and individual activities. The outstanding examples of successful native adjustment to economic conditions are cases of adapting the native pattern of group procedure to individualistic conditions. In New Zealand, for example, a few native groups have become self-supporting and prosperous by operating as communities in production and marketing. The point seems to be that whereas a culture may be a conglomeration of traits, it is carried on by a closely knit series of response patterns. It is these patterns that conflict in case of culture contact. The white man expects the natives to take plots of land and scatter in the population as individuals, finding their place in the culture at large. This is asking too much; the social habits of the native follow another pattern; so he tries to operate as a community in phases of culture where the white man operates as an individual. A quotation from Pitt-Rivers[3] is appropriate here. "In all his activity the primitive savage merges his self-regarding sentiments in— or, rather, projects them on to—his social group, either his clan or his tribe. He feels himself an inseparable part of that group, and identifies his passions with those of the other members of the group. There is no sense of sacrificing himself for the good of the whole group. There is merely a spontaneous and unrationalized feeling of identity with the group; just as he regards any member of a social unit outside his own as identified with that outside group."

Finally, another conflict factor may be here commented upon—the tendency of cultures to change. In particular, this is characteristic of white cultures. The adjustment of the native to white cultures must be slow; but the disconcerting aspect of the case is that as the white culture changes, this renders such adjustments as he may have made inadequate. It is difficult enough to bridge the gap between two contrasting cultures, but to see the gap widening as fast as he can build is wholly depressing. In conclusion, then, we see how, on every hand, culture contact between a primitive group and a white presents a maze of conflict that cross-sections the life of the former, resulting in a variety of responses.

REACTION ON THE INDIVIDUAL

It is a prevailing opinion that when a primitive people come into contact with white culture, they rapidly die off. On the whole, observation does seem to show that during the conflict period the death rate is abnormally high. Various causes have been assigned for this, for one, the introduction of new diseases against which the native lacks resistance or the necessary knowledge to mitigate. This argument has some validity, but on the other hand white settlements in a new country suffer also. The survival of the white settlers is, however, insured by the reserve populations of the home community. The native is further handicapped by the depression resulting from the situations we have just discussed. Usually, the first step in the subjugation of a native group is to remove it to a strange habitat. This habitat may not vary greatly from the former home, but it is strange, and nostalgia results. The suggestion is that anything that seriously disturbs the peace in a native group tends to increase the death rate. Thus in 1838 a large part of the Cherokee Indian nation was forcibly moved from Georgia to Oklahoma; contemporary accounts tell us that about one-half of the cavalcade died on the way and shortly after arrival. The Pawnee were moved from their traditional home in Nebraska in 1874 and settled in their present home in Oklahoma; many died the first year. Further, many young men are reported to have committed suicide, because there were no bison to hunt and wars were forbidden; the future offered nothing

[3] Pitt-Rivers, G. H. L. F., *The Clash of Cultures and the contact of races* (London: Routledge, 1927).

to them but to till the soil, to take up women's work. New diseases and malnutrition are certainly to be set down as causes for the high death rate observed, but there is good reason to believe that emotional factors were also operative.

Yet, in the Pawnee example of suicide, we see another aspect of conflict. The new situation created by culture contact leaves the individual no outlet for his aspirations. Where the pattern of individual expression placed social value upon deeds of war and the zest of the hunt, walking behind the plow of the farmer to be rewarded by a few coins made no appeal. The white social values of industry, achievement, and economic independence belonged to a conflicting pattern. A recent study[4] of the Maori in New Zealand shows how the suppression of inter-tribal wars and the elimination of personal combat left the native no outlet for self-expression. His only course was to eke out an existence and live in the mental imagery of the past. However, the New Zealand native seems to have been quite above the average in ability to understand the new culture and to adapt himself. His conflicts were grievous and are still, but on the whole he seems to be conserving much of his old group life and at the same time adjusting to new economic condition.

In general, then, it appears that culture conflict bears hard upon the individual. It produces a condition bordering upon the psychopathic, analogous to institutional cases in contemporary society. Emotional disturbances are evident. Not only does the group break down in its functioning, but individuals fail. It appears that the severity of conflict is somewhat proportioned to the degree of contrast between the cultures involved.

INTER-GROUP CONFLICTS

So far we have dealt with cultures as wholes; that is, we have sought to observe what takes place when two cultures come into collision. On the other hand, we find that the adaptation of one culture to another is often attended by conflicts within the group. The ethical values of white culture are perhaps best presented in the culture complex which we call Christianity. One of the great organized drives against a primitive group is seen in the process of Christianization. This proceeds by seeking individual converts. One prominent characteristic of new converts to any cause is their hostility to the beliefs they have thrown over, and as soon as a reasonable minority of the native group takes up the new teaching, they form a bloc in opposition. Such a conflict may become a serious menace, particularly if the minority has the backing of the white group. We meet with this in the United States, when the Christian Indians on a reservation seek the aid of the government in suppressing social gather-

4 Keesing, F. M., *The Changing Maori* (New Plymouth, New Zealand: Board of Ethnological Research, 1928).

ings and ceremonies among the opposition. In objective terms, the phenomenon may be stated as an inter-tribal conflict of social values. One
observed result in such situations is for the conservative wing to draw
more into isolation, to reduce contact with outsiders to the minimum, to
resist suggestions from without, in short to induce a state of mental and
social stagnation. . . .

<h2 style="text-align:center">SURVIVAL</h2>

To complete this review of the subject, it may be well to consider the
factors that make for the survival of cultures. The group feels uneasy
if anything threatens to take its culture away. The emotional and other
responses we have noted in specific cases of culture conflict are most intense when the culture breaks down. So the normal functioning of the
community depends largely upon the smooth operation of its culture,
and the survival of mankind indicates the presence of protective responses.
In sociology, comment is made upon tradition and resistance to change as
a detriment in so far as progress may be inhibited, but as an advantage in
stabilizing culture or in controlling innovations. The reactionary response,
when viewed philosophically, is one of the protective factors in guaran-
teeing the survival of cultures. We have noted that cultures change spontaneously without jarring the group and so without invoking any of the
protective responses. On the other hand, an abrupt change, an innovation,
will invoke these responses.

One aspect of culture not adequately explained by social science is
the balance that seems to exist among the many traits composing it. It
appears as a finely balanced whole; if the economic basis drops out, the
whole structure threatens to go down. Yet, in much the same way, the
breaking-down of a taboo system may topple over the whole structure.
The destruction of established values, as head-hunting, scalp-taking, etc.,
has also been observed to disarrange the whole culture. At first this
may seem inconsistent with our previous discussion in which cases were
cited of the taking-over of new traits successfully, but cultures grow in
large part by reacting to each other in this way. It is only under certain
conditions that the balance holding cultures in function is disrupted. Since
such disruption follows white domination, it behooves us to learn to avoid
the conditions that favor such upsets. One set of problems in economics
and politics deals with the maintenance of balances between cultures.

Pitt-Rivers[5] has attempted to explain declining birth rate and vitality
as due to emotional states resulting from culture conflict. He thinks there
is a delicate balance between the biological functioning of the organism
and culture; that, if there is a real conflict, the resulting emotions act
upon sex and nutritive functions to such a degree as to disturb organic
life. The inference from this is that there is a fine adjustment between

5 Pitt-Rivers, *op. cit.*

culture and the human organism. If this is true, we may expect culture conflict to be accompanied by emotional disturbances.

The question is often discussed as to whether isolation favors the survival of cultures over long periods with little change. We have noted that culture contact under normal conditions favors progressive change, but have not considered the behavior of the group in isolation. It is usually assumed that the cause for the backward state of such peoples as the Tasmanians, Andamans, and Fuegians was their lack of contact with other cultures, but we can best approach the question through examples of adjustment in partial isolation. In the course of immigration into the United States, numerous communities of foreign folk have been established, some of which have survived over long periods. A study of a few such shows that they have survived by making the minimum economic adjustment, but otherwise avoiding all the culture contacts possible. The core of organization is religious and social. The peculiarity, however, is that in such communities many aspects of the culture are about what they were in the home land when the group emigrated, so revealing themselves the more conservative of the two. In these cases, the community sought by isolation to resist change and so approach a stabilized level. Such survival may be said to be largely self-determined, in contrast to the primitive groups cited above. Parallel cases can be found in subject peoples, as among some village Indians in southwestern United States. These Indians were agricultural when discovered and have continued self-supporting to this day; thus their economic adjustment is satisfactory. On the other hand, they have drawn aloof from white contact; fearing ridicule, they have carried on in secret, putting forth every effort to conserve things as they were centuries ago. In this they have succeeded to a large degree. However, these examples of survival by withdrawing from culture contact rather strengthen the case for the growth of culture through the interaction of culture groups.

In conclusion, we have reviewed a phase of psychological inquiry in the making. No great leads to research in this field have been discovered, but . . . while humanitarian ideals may make direct experiment impossible, governments are setting experiments for us. The statements made in the preceding pages are based upon observation on the behavior of groups under specific conditions. Such studies can be carried out systematically, are in fact now being initiated. On the other hand, some group experiments are possible, among children, communities, etc., and may be expected when the observation studies of selected culture groups have progressed far enough to make the formulation of test experiments desirable.

PAUL RADIN

(1883-1959)

The Autobiography of a Winnebago Indian

IN THOSE DAYS THERE WERE NOT MANY WHITE PEOPLE LIVING NEAR US AS to-day. My father went out hunting continually. The lodge in which we lived was covered with rush mattings, with reed mattings spread over the floor. After hunting for some time in one place we would move to another. My father, mother, older sisters, and older brothers, all carried the packs. Thus we would spend our time until the spring of the year and then in the spring we would again move in order to live near some stream where father could hunt muskrats, mink, otter, and beaver. . . .

In the fall of the year we would pick cranberries. When the hunting season was open, I would begin to fast again.

This was my life for a number of years.

After a while we bought a pony on which we used to pack all our belongings whenever we moved our camp. In addition three of us would ride on top of the pack. Sometimes my mother and sometimes my father drove the pony.

After I had grown a little older and taller all of us brothers would fast together. My father would indeed repeatedly urge us to fast. "Do not be afraid of the burnt remains of the lodge center-pole," he would say to us.[1] "Whatever are the true possessions of men, the apparel of men and the gift of doctoring—all these things that are spread out before you—do try and obtain one of them."[2] Thus he would speak to us.

I would then take a piece of charcoal, crush it and blacken my face and he would be very grateful to me.

From Radin, *Crashing Thunder: the Autobiography of a Winnebago Indian* (New York: Appleton & Co., 1926), pp. 56-59, 26-29, 148-151.

[1] Symbolical manner of describing the crushed charcoal with which fasters must blacken their faces.

[2] By "possessions of men" he means mainly that knowledge which will make a man honored and respected in his community; and by "apparel of men," he means power and ability.

I would at first break my fast at noon but then gradually I began to fast all night. From the fall of the year until spring I would fast until nightfall and then eat. After a while I trained myself to pass the night without eating and after that I was able to go two nights and days without taking any food. Then my mother went to the woods at some distance from the village and there she built me a small lodge in which I and my elder brother were to remain whenever we had to fast through the whole night. At this fasting-place we used to play and before we were really able to spend a night at this particular place we moved away.

After a time I passed from this stage of childhood to another. I now began to use a bow and arrow and I spent my day at play, shooting arrows.

It was at about this time also that I found out that my mother had been told just before I was born that she was about to give birth to a child who would not be an ordinary being, and from then on I felt that I must be an uncommon person.

My father used to keep up the old habit of teaching us the customs of the Winnebago. He would wake us up early in the morning and, seated around the fireplace, speak to us. The girls would be taught separately. Now this is what my father told me:

My son, when you grow up, see to it that you are of some benefit to your fellowmen. There is only one way in which you can aid them and that is by fasting. Our grandfather, the Fire, he who stands at all times in the center of our dwelling, sends forth all kinds of blessings. Be sure that you make an attempt to obtain his.

My son, do you remember to have our grandfathers, the war chiefs,[3] bless you. See to it that they have compassion upon you. Then some day as you travel along the road of life, you will know what to do and encounter no obstacles. Without any effort will you then be able to gain the prize you desire. The honor will be yours to glory in, yours without exertion. All the disposable war-blessings belong to our grandfathers, the war-controllers, and if reverently you fast and thirst yourself to death, then these will be bestowed upon you. Yet if you do not wear out your feet in frequent journeyings to and fro, if you do not blacken your face with charcoal, it will be all for naught that you inflict this suffering upon yourself. Not without constant effort are these blessings procurable. Try to have one of the spirits created by Earthmaker take pity on you. Whatever he says will come about. If you do not possess one of the spirits from whom to obtain strength and power, you will be of no consequence socially and those around you will show you little respect. Indeed they will jeer at you.

My son, it is not good to die in the village; in your homes. Above all, do not let women journey to the spirit land ahead of you. It is not done.

[3] Symbolical name for all those spirits who were supposed to be in control of war powers.

To prevent this from happening do we speak to our sons and encourage them to fast. Some day in life you will find yourself traveling along a road filled with obstacles and then you will wish you had fasted. When such an event confronts you, that you may not find it necessary to reproach yourself, I counsel you to fast. It you have not obtained any knowledge from the spirits, why it may happen that some day, in later life, warriors will be returning from the warpath and as they distribute the war prizes to their sisters,[4] your own sisters will stand there empty-handed envying the rest. But if you obtain blessings from the war-controllers, your sisters will be happy. How proud they will be to receive the prizes, to wear them, and to dance the victory dance! Your sisters too will be strengthened thereby and you will be content and happy. . . .

My son, if you cast off your dress for many people, that is, if you give to the needy, your people will be benefited by your deeds. It is good thus to be honored by many people. And even more will they honor you if you return victorious from the warpath with one of the four limbs, that is, one of the four war honors. But if you obtain two, or three, or perhaps even four limbs, then all the greater will be the honor. Then whenever a war feast is given you will receive part of the deer that is boiled, either part of its body or part of the head.[5] When on some other occasion, such as the Four Nights' Wake, you are called upon to recount your war exploits in behalf of the departed souls, be careful, however, not to claim more than you actually accomplished. If you do, you will cause the soul of the man in whose behalf you are telling it, to stumble[6] in his journey to spirit land. If you tell a falsehood then and exaggerate, you will die before your time, for the spirits, the war-controllers, will hear you. It is indeed a sacred duty to tell the truth on such an occasion. Tell less than you did. The old men say it is wiser.

My son, it is good to die on the warpath. If you die on the warpath, you will not lose consciousness at death. You will be able to do what you please with your soul and it will always remain in a happy condition. If afterwards you wish to become reincarnated as human being, you may do so, or you may take the form of those-who-walk-upon-the-light, the

[4] Among the Winnebago a man's sisters, especially his elder sisters, were very highly respected and all war prizes, such as wampum-belts, wampum necklaces, etc., were always given to them whenever a man returned from a successful war-party in which he had secured some honor. These war honors were of various kinds. The greatest was considered to be the feat of having struck the body of a dead enemy first.

[5] The meat of a deer at such a feast is given only to great warriors. The head is regarded as the choicest piece.

[6] According to Winnebago belief the soul of a deceased individual in his journey to spirit land must cross a very slippery, swinging bridge and it is thought that if, during the wake following the man's burial, any of the invited warriors exaggerate their achievements the unfortunate soul will not be able to cross this bridge and will stumble and fall into the abyss of fire over which it is thrown.

birds, or the form of any animal you please, in short. All these benefits will you obtain if you die on the warpath. . . .

At this stage of life I secretly got the desire to make myself pleasing to the opposite sex.

The Indians then lived in their old-fashioned lodges. Women, however, whenever they had their menses, were placed in special huts. There the young men would go to court them at night when their parents were asleep. I used to go along with the men on such occasions, for even although I did not enter any lodges but merely accompanied the older men, I enjoyed it.

My parents were greatly in fear of my coming into contact with menstruating women so therefore I went with these men secretly. My parents were even afraid of having me cross the path over which a menstruating woman had passed. They worried so much about it at that time, because I was to fast as soon as autumn came. They did not wish me to be near menstruating women, for were I to grow up in their midst I would assuredly be weak and of little account. Such was their reason.

Before long I started to fast again together with an older brother of mine, both day and night. It was during the fall moving, and several lodges of people were living near us. There it was that my elder brother and I fasted. Among the people of the other lodges were four girls whose duty it was to carry wood. Whenever these girls went out to get wood my older brother and I would play around with them a great deal. We did this even although we were fasting at the time. Of course we had to do it in secret. Whenever our parents found out we got a scolding and so did the girls. At home we were warned to keep away from menstruating women, but we ourselves always sought them.

After a while some of the people living in the lodges moved away and we were left alone. They moved far ahead of us. We ourselves were to move only a short distance at a time. My father and my brother-in-law went out hunting and killed seventy deer between them, so that we had plenty of meat.

When the girls with whom I used to play moved away I became very lonesome. In the evenings I used to cry. I longed for them greatly and they had moved far away!

Soon we got fairly well started on our way back. We moved to a place where all the leaders used to give their feasts. Near the place where we lived there were three lakes and a black-hawk's nest. Right near the tree where the nest was located, they built a lodge and our war-bundle was placed in it. There my elder brother and myself were to pass the night. It was said that if any one fasted at such a place for four nights, he would be blessed with victory and the power to cure the sick. All the spirits would bless him. . . .

So there I fasted at the black-hawk's nest where a lodge had been built for me. The first night I stayed there I wondered when something would happen. But nothing took place. The second night, rather late in the night, my father came and opened the war-bundle and then taking out a gourd, began to sing. I stood beside him without any clothing except my breech-clout and, holding tobacco in each hand, I uttered my cry to the spirits:

"O spirits, here humble in heart I stand beseeching you."

My father sang war-bundle songs and wept as he sang. I also wept as I uttered my cry to the spirits. When he was finished he told me some sacred stories; he told me about my ancestor Weshgishega.

In the morning, just before sunrise, I uttered my cry to the spirits:

"O spirits, here humble in heart I stand beseeching you."

The fourth night found me still there. Again my father came and we did the same thing, but in spite of it all I experienced nothing unusual. Soon another day dawned upon us. That morning I told my elder brother that I had been blessed by the spirits and that I was going home to eat. I was not speaking the truth. I was hungry and I also knew that on the following night we were going to have a feast, and that we would have to utter our cry to the spirits again. I dreaded that. So I went home. When I got there I told my people the story I had told my brother; that I had been blessed and that the spirits had told me to eat. I was not speaking the truth, yet I was given the food that is carefully prepared for those who have been blessed. Just then my older brother came home and they objected to his return for he had not been blessed. However, he took some food and ate it.

My brother J., however, obtained a blessing. When he reached the age of puberty my father called him aside and told him to fast. He told him that it was his fervent wish that he should begin to fast in order to become holy, to become invincible and invulnerable in war. He wished him to become like one of those Winnebago of whom stories are told. He assured him that if he fasted he would really be holy and that nothing that exists on this earth would be able to molest him; that he would live a very long life and that he would be able to cure the sick. He told him that if he were blessed no one would dare to make fun of him and that they would be very careful how they addressed him; first, because they really respected him and secondly, because they were afraid of getting him angry. He was to fast until spring and then he was to stop, for there are many bad spirits about in the spring who are likely to deceive a faster.

Near our village there was a hill called *Place-where-they-keep-weapons*. This hill was very high, steep and rocky. It was a very holy place. There it was that my father wished my brother to fast for it was the place where he himself had fasted. Within this hill lived the spirits whom we call *Those-who-cry-like-babies*. These spirits are supposed to possess arrows and bows.

Twenty of them were supposed to be in this hill. My father had control of them and when he wished to bless a man he would take his bow and arrows and, holding them in his hands, lead the man around the hill and into the lodge (*i.e.,* into the hill). There he would look for a stone pillar, and upon it, at about arm's length, he drew the pictures of a number of different animals. My father possessed only one arrow, but that one was a holy one. Then dancing around the stone pillar and singing some songs, he finished by breathing upon the pillar. Finally he walked around and shot at it and when he looked at the stone, it had turned into a deer with large horns which fell dead at his feet. He repeated this a number of times. The little spirits living in the hill breathed with him and said, "Winnebago, whenever you wish to kill a deer with one horn, do as you have done, and offer us tobacco and you will be able to obtain whatever you wish."

This was the power my father wished my brother to obtain. My father was a very famous hunter and my brother wished to be like him.

Now of all these things my brother dreamed; with all these powers he was blessed. He also had a vision of visiting the village of the ghosts. There he was able to steal a costly shawl and escape with it. He dreamed that all the inhabitants of the ghost village chased him but that they were unable to overtake him and were compelled to return back when my brother reached the earth.

The night after we had stopped fasting we gave our feast. There, however, our pride received a fall, for although the feast was supposedly given in our honor, we were placed on one side of the main participants. After the kettles containing the food had been put on twice, it became daylight and the feast was over.

The following spring we moved to the Mississippi in order to trap. I was still fasting and ate only at night. My brothers used to flatter me, telling me that I was the cleverest of them all and, in consequence, I used to continue fasting although I was often very hungry. In spite of my desire to fast, however, I could not resist the temptation of being around the girls. I wanted always to be near them. They were generally in their menstrual lodges[7] when I looked for them. My parents did not wish me to go near the girls then but I went nevertheless.

My parents told me that only those boys who had no connection with women would be blessed by the spirits. Throughout this time my sole wish was to appear great in the sight of the people. To be praised by my fellow-men was all I desired. And I certainly received what I sought. I stood high in their estimation. That the women might like me was another of the reasons why I wanted to fast. But as to being blessed, I learned nothing

[7] Any contact with menstruating women, or even with objects in any way connected with them, will, it is the firm belief of the Winnebago, destroy the power of sacred objects or individuals temporarily sacred. Fasting youths were regarded as such.

about it, although I went around with the air of one who had received many blessings and talked as such a one would talk.

I never married any woman permanently. I would live with one for awhile, and then with another. Sometimes upon my return after an absence I would find my temporary wife living with another man. This is the way in which I acted. . . .

At that time I had a comrade, and one day he said to me, "We have been thinking of something, have we not, friend? We ought to try and obtain some external emblem of our bravery. Do we not always try to wear feathers at a Warrior Dance? Well, then, let us try to obtain war honors, so that we can wear head ornaments." So did we both speak to each other. We both liked the idea, and so we decided to go in search of war honors. We decided to kill a man of another tribe; we meant to perform an act of bravery. We started out finally. There were four of us, and we went to a place where other tribesmen congregated. We took the train and carried some baggage with us. We took ropes along, for we intended to steal some horses, and if we found the opportunity, kill a man. Horse stealing was regarded as a praiseworthy feat, and I had always admired the people who recounted the number of times they had stolen horses, at one of the Warrior Dances. That was why I wished to do these things.

We proceeded to a place where horses of other tribes used to pasture. Just as we got there we saw the owner of some of these horses and killed him. My friend killed him. Then we went home, and secretly I told my father all about it. I said to him, "Father, you said it was good to be a warrior and you encouraged me to fast and I did so. You encouraged me to give feasts and I did so. Now we have just returned from a trip. We were looking for war honors and the young people who were accompanying me decided that I should lead them. I told them that it was a difficult thing to lead warriors, my father had always told me, and that I had always been given to understand that a person could lead a war-party only in consequence of a specific blessing received from the spirits. I was not conscious of having received any such, I told him. Thus I spoke. However, they made me an offering of tobacco as they asked me, and I accepted the tobacco saying that I would at least make an offering of tobacco for them. Then I offered tobacco to the Thunderbirds and asked them for rain, that we might walk in the protection and power of rain. This offering we made in the morning and it rained all that day. Then we went to the place where we knew that we could find horses. When we got there we met the owner of the horses and spoke to him. We accompanied him to a carpenter shop nearby, and there killed him. I struck his dead body, counted coup first, and announced my new name, as I gave a war-whoop. I shouted '*Big-Winnebago* has counted coup on his man.' Then the others counted coup also. We searched his pockets and found medicine and money in them. The money we divided among ourselves. After that we cut out his heart, for we had heard that hearts were used for medicine. That is why we cut out his heart. He had a gun and that we took away from him and hid."

Then my father said to me, "My son, it is good. Your life is no longer an effeminate one. This is the manner in which our ancestors encouraged us to live. It is the will of the spirits in control of war that has led you to do this. Of your own initiative you could not possibly have done it. However, we had better not have a Victory Dance as yet. We have the honor anyhow. We must be careful about the Whites. In the old days we were at liberty to live in our own way, and when such a deed as yours became known, your sisters would rejoice and dance, we are told. Now, however, the law of the Whites is to be feared. In due time you will get a chance to announce your feat and then you can wear a head ornament for you have earned that right for yourself."

EDWARD SAPIR

(1884-1939)

The Contributions of Psychiatry to an Understanding of Behavior in Society

IT IS WITH GREAT PLEASURE THAT I ACCEDE TO THE REQUEST TO COMMENT in a general way on the present symposium on psychiatry and the social sciences. The relation between the two suggests many interesting and complicated problems, both of definition and interpretation. It is a bold man who would venture to speak with assurance about such abstruse entities as "individual" and "society," but where it is difficult for any intelligent person to withhold a theory or an opinion, I may be pardoned for not doing so either. I have read the seven psychiatric papers with great interest. Unless I am greatly mistaken, the language used in these contributions as a whole is measurably nearer the terminology used by social scientists than was formerly the case in psychiatric literature. I doubt if this is entirely due to the fact that the psychiatrists have felt under a compulsion to be courteous to the sociologists responsible for the journal to which they now find themselves a collective contributor. I find no "pussyfooting" here; rather a sincere recognition of the importance, perhaps even the reality, of the things connoted by the words "society" and "culture." Even if these words still remain largely unanalyzed in terms that ought to be completely satisfying to a psychiatrist, it is a great gain to have them given a hearing. The extreme individualism of earlier psychiatry is evidently passing. Even the pages of Freud, with their haunting imagery of society as censor and of culture as a beautiful extortion from the sinister depths of desire, are beginning to take on a certain character of quaintness; in other words, it looks as though psychiatry and the sciences devoted to man as constitutive of society were actually beginning to talk about the same events—to wit, the facts of human experience.

In the social sciences, too, there has been a complementary movement toward the concerns of the psychiatrist. At long last the actual human being, always set in a significant situation, never a mere biological illustration or a long-suffering carrier of cultural items, has been caught prowling about the premises of society, of culture, of history. It is true that long and anonymous confinements within the narrow columns of statistics

From Sapir, "The Contributions of Psychiatry to an Understanding of Behavior in Society," *The American Journal of Sociology,* Vol. 42 (1937), pp. 862-870.

have made him a timid subject for inquiry. He seems always to be slink-
ing off into anxiety-driven flesh and bone or else, at the oddest moments,
unexpectedly swelling himself up into an institution. But it is easy to see
that the firm hand of the psychiatric sociologist will some day nab him in
one of his less rapid moments of transition.

Of these seven papers, it is chiefly Dr. Sullivan's and Dr. Alexander's
that give me the most comfortable housing. They seem to be camped somewhere about the crossroads leading to pure psychiatry and pure sociology
and I confess that I find the uncertainty of their location very agreeable
indeed. In an atmosphere of mollified contrasts one may hope to escape
the policemen of rival conceptual headquarters. Not being bothered by
too strict a loyalty to aristocratic conventions, one may hope to learn
something new. I am particularly fond of Dr. Sullivan's pet phrase of
"interpersonal relations." The phrase is not as innocent as it seems, for,
while such entities as societies, individuals, cultural patterns, and institutions logically imply interpersonal relations, they do little to isolate and
define them. Too great agility has been gained over the years in jumping
from the individual to the collectivity and from the collectivity via romantic anthropological paths back again to the culture-saturated individual.
Reflection suggests that the lone individual was never alone, that he never
marched in line with a collectivity, except on literal state occasions, and
that he never signed up for a culture. There was always someone around
to bother him; there were always a great many people whom his friends
talked about and whom he never met; and there was always much that
some people did that he never heard about. He was never formed out of
the interaction of individual and society but started out being as comfortable as he could in a world in which other people existed, and continued this way as long as physical conditions allowed. It is out of his
manifold experiences that different kinds of scientists derived their tips
for the invention of two or three realms of being.

For a long time psychiatry operated with a conception of the individual
that was merely biological in nature. This is easy to understand if we
remember that psychiatry was not, to begin with, a study of human nature
in actual situations, nor even a theoretical exploration into the structure of personality, but simply and solely an attempt to interpret "dis-
eased" modes of behavior in terms familiar to a tradition that was operating with the concepts of normal and abnormal physiological functioning.
It is the great and lasting merit of Freud that he freed psychiatry from its
too strictly medical presuppositions and introduced an interpretative psychology which, in spite of all its conceptual weaknesses, its disturbingly
figurative modes of expression, and its blindness to numerous and important aspects of the field of behavior as a whole, remains a substantial
contribution to psychology in general and, by implication, to social psychology in particular. His use of social data was neither more nor less

inadequate than the use made of them by psychology as a whole. It is hardly fair to accuse Freud of a naïveté which is still the rule among the vast majority of professional psychologists. It is not surprising that his view of social phenomena betrays at many points a readiness to confuse various specific patterns of behavior, which the culturalists can show to be derivative of specific historical backgrounds, with those more fundamental and necessary patterns of behavior which proceed from the nature of man and of his slowly maturing organism. Nor is it surprising that he shared, not only with the majority of psychologists but even with the very founders of anthropological science, an interest in primitive man that did not address itself to a realistic understanding of human relations in the less sophisticated societies but rather to the schematic task of finding in the patterns of behavior reported by the anthropologist such confirmation as he could of his theories of individually "archaic" attitudes and mechanisms. If the contemporary anthropologist is scandalized by the violence with which Freud and his followers have torn many of the facts of primitive behavior out of their natural cultural setting, he should recall that just such violence was the hallmark of the most approved kinds of thinking about ethnological data not so long ago. When all is said and done, and in spite of the enormous documentation of the cultures of primitive groups, how easy is it to get even an inkling, in strictly psychological terms, of the tempo, the relative flexibility, the individual variability, the relative openness or hiddenness of individual expression, the characteristic emotional qualities, which are implied or "carried" by even the most penetrating cultural analyses that we possess of primitive communities? It seems unexpectedly difficult to conjure up the image of live people in intelligibly live relationships located within areas defined as primitive. The personalities that inhabit our ethnological monographs seem almost schizoid in their unemotional acceptance of the heavy colors, tapestries, and furniture of their ethnological stage. Is it any wonder that actors so vaguely conceived, so absent-mindedly typical of something or other, can be bludgeoned by a more persistent intelligence than theirs into sawing wood for still remoter stages, say that dread drama of the slain father and the birth of totemism?

At the present time the advance guard of psychiatric thinking is rapidly discovering the fruitfulness of the concepts of society and culture for a richer and a more realistic analysis of personality. The close relation of personal habit systems to the general patterning of culture—that very insight which has for so long been the special pride of anthropology—comes to psychiatry as something essentially new. Supposedly universal feelings and attitudes, sentiments about parents and children and sex mates, are found to be almost as relative to a culture's set patterns of behavior as fashions in clothes or types of artifacts. At any rate, this formula of the relativity of custom has long been a commonplace in an-

thropology on purely descriptive grounds and is invading psychiatry as a
new basis for the philosophy of behavior.

An age-old blindness tends to be corrected by opened eyes that are
too confident and undiscriminating, and one wonders whether the special
viewpoint of psychiatry is not tending to yield too readily to the enlightened prejudices of anthropology and sociology. The presumptive or "as
if" psychological character of a culture is highly determinative, no doubt,
of much in the externalized system of attitudes and habits which forms the
visible "personality" of a given individual, and, until his special social
frame of reference is clearly established, analyzed, and applied to his
behavior, we are necessarily at a loss to assign him a place in a more
general scheme of human behavior. It does not follow, however, that
strictly social determinants, tending, as they do, to give visible form and
meaning, in a cultural sense, to each of the thousands of modalities of
experience which sum up the personality, can define the fundamental structure of such a personality. If culture and its presumptive psychology were
all that is needed to explain what we dimly reach out for and call "individual personality," we should be put in the position of a man who
claimed, for instance, that the feeling called love could not have started
its history until the vocabulary of a specific language suggested realities,
values, and problems hitherto unknown. All of which would be true in
a sense which matters more to the culturalist than to the closer student
of behavior. A culture which is constantly being invoked to explain the
necessities and the intimacies of individual relations is like an *ex post facto*
legalization of damage done. The biological and implied psychological
needs of individuals are continuous and primary. If we think, not of culture in the abstract nor of society as a hypothetically integrating concept
in human relations, but rather of the actual day-to-day relations of specific
individuals in a network of highly personalized needs, we must see that
culture is the inevitable coin of the realm of behavior but that it is far
from synonymous with those actual systems of meaning, conscious and unconscious, which we call personalities, and that the presumptive psychology of a culture as a whole is not equatable with any actual personalized psychology. Cultural analysis is hardly more than a preliminary
bow to the human scene, giving us to know that here are people, presumably real, and that it is here rather than there that we must observe
them.

It is the privilege of psychiatry to be always looking at individuals and
to think of society as merely a convenient term to cover the manifold
possibilities of actual human relationships. It is these actual relationships
that matter, not society. This simple and intuitively necessary viewpoint
of the psychiatrist is shared, of course, by the man in the street. He cannot be dislodged from it by any amount of social scientific sophistication.
It is to be hoped that no psychiatrist will ever surrender this naïve and

powerful view of the reality of personality to a system of secondary concepts about people and their relations to each other which flow from an analysis of social forms. The danger of a too ready acquiescence in the social formulations of the anthropologist and the sociologist is by no means an imaginary one. Certain recent attempts, in part brilliant and stimulating, to impose upon the actual psychologies of actual people, in continuous and tangible relations to each other, a generalized psychology based on the real or supposed psychological implications of cultural forms, show clearly what confusions in our thinking are likely to result when social science turns psychiatric without, in the process, allowing its own historically determined concepts to dissolve into those larger ones which have meaning for psychology and psychiatry. We then discover that whole cultures or societies are paranoid or hysterical or obsessive! Such characterizations, however brilliantly presented, have the value of literary suggestiveness, not of close personality analysis. At best they help us to see a new facet of the problem of personality.[1] If they do not help us to see the individual, in however exotic a society, with that quiet sharpness of gaze which makes the true student of personality something other than a discourser on "interesting" facts about people, the psychiatrist will have essentially little to learn from them beyond the fact, which he might, of course, have suspected all along, that human motivation has expressed itself in far more varied forms and through far more complex channels of transformation than he had believed possible on the basis of his limited ethnic experiences. This in itself is a far from unimportant insight, but it does not constitute the true basis of a science of psychology, or of a science of psychiatry, which may be defined as that science of man which undertakes to grasp the fundamental, and relatively invariable, structure of the individual personality with as great a conceptual economy as our still inadequate psychologies allow.

It is the obvious duty of psychiatry, once it has enriched its interpretative techniques with the help of the social sciences, to be always returning to its original task of the close scrutiny of the individual personality. Not what the culture consists of or what are the values it seems to point to will be the psychiatrist's concern, but rather how this culture lends itself to the ceaseless need of the individual personality for symbols of expression and communication which can be intelligently read by one's fellowmen on the social plane, but whose relative depth or shallowness of meaning in the individual's total economy of symbols need never be adequately divined either by himself or by his neighbor. It should be the aim of the psychiatrist to uncover just such meanings as these. He must be too little satisfied with a purely social view of behavior to accept such statements as that A's reason for joining the orchestra is the same as B's, or that the

[1] The necessity of disentangling it from problems of personality value in a given society.

motive of either can ever be strictly defined in terms of a generalized pleasure which socialized human beings derive from listening to music or participating in the production of it. Such blanket explanations as these are useful in that they enable people to join hands and give each other an effective hearing. To the culturalist joining an orchestra is a valuable illustration of an important social pattern. To the psychiatrist it is as irrelevant as the interesting biographical fact that this "lover of music" first met his future wife at the corner of Fifth Avenue and Forty-second Street. What the psychiatrist can get out of the orchestra-joining pattern depends altogether on what symbolic work he can discover this behavior to accomplish in the integrated personality systems of A and B. To the culturist A's joining the orchestra is "like" B's joining the orchestra. To the psychiatrist the chances of these two events being in the least similar are quite small. He will rather find that A's joining the orchestra is "like" his earlier tendency to waste an enormous amount of time on trashy novels, while B's apparently similar behavior is more nearly "like" his slavish adherence to needlessly exacting table manners. The psychiatrist cares little about descriptive similarities and differences, for, in his view of things, all manner of flotsam and jetsam of behavior rush into an individual vortex of few and necessary meanings. He does well to leave the study of the scheme of society to those who care for unallocated blueprints of behavior.

I have, perhaps, overstressed the fundamental divergence of spirit between the psychiatric and the strictly cultural modes of observation. I have done so because it is highly important that we do not delude ourselves into believing that a lovingly complete analysis of a given culture is *ipso facto* a contribution to the science of human behavior. It is, of course, an invaluable guide to the potentialities of choice and rejection in the lives of individuals, and such knowledge should arm one against foolish expectancies. No psychiatrist can afford to think that love is made in exactly the same way in all the corners of the globe, yet he would be too docile a convert to anthropology if he allowed himself to be persuaded that that fact made any special difference for the primary differentiation of personality. With every individual of whom the psychiatrist essays an understanding he must of necessity reanalyze the supposedly objective culture in which this individual is said to play his part. When he does this he invariably finds that cultural agreement is hardly more than terminological, and that, if culture is to be saddled with psychological meanings that are more than superficial, we shall have to recognize as many effective cultures as there are individuals to be "adjusted" to the one culture which is said to exist "out there" and to which we are supposed to be able to direct the telescope of our intelligent observation.

It would appear from all this that the psychiatrist who has become sufficiently aware of social patterning to be granted a hearing by the social scientist has at least as much to give as to receive. It is true that he cannot be given the privilege of making a psychological analysis of society and culture as such. He cannot tell us what any cultural pattern is "all about" in psychological terms, for we cannot allow him to indulge in the time-honored pursuit of identifying society with a personality, or culture with actual behavior. He can, of course, make these identifications in a metaphorical sense, and it would be harmful to his freedom of expression if he were denied the use of metaphor. In his particular case, however, metaphor is more than normally dangerous. An economist or historian can talk of the soul of a people or the structure of a society with very little danger of turning anybody's head. It is generally understood that such phraseology means something but that the speed of verbal communication is generally too great to make it seem worth while to try to convert the convenient metaphor into its realistically relevant terms. But the psychiatrist deals with actual people, not with illustrations of culture or with the functioning of society. It is our duty, therefore, to hold him to the very strictest account in his use of social terms. If he, too, is the victim of slipshod metaphor, we have no protection against our own credulity. We cannot be blamed if we tend to read out of the society and culture which the necessities of verbal communication have conjured into a ghostly reality of their own an impersonal mandate to behavior and its interpretation.

So far the psychiatrist has had too many superstitions of his own to help us materially with the task of translating social and cultural terms into that intricate network of personalistic meanings which is the only conceivable stuff of human experience. In the future, however, we must be constantly turning to him for reminders of what is the true nature of the social process. The conceptual reconciliation of the life of society with the life of the individual can never come from an indulgence in metaphor. It will come from the ultimate implications of Dr. Sullivan's "interpersonal relations." Interpersonal relations are not finger exercises in the art of society. They are real things, deserving of the most careful and anxious study. We know very little about them as yet. If we could only get a reasonably clear conception of how the lives of A and B intertwine into a mutually interpretable complex of experiences, we should see far more clearly than is at present the case the extreme importance and the irrevocable necessity of the concept of personality. We should also be moving forward to a realistic instead of a metaphorical definition of what is meant by culture and society. One suspects that the symbolic role of words has an importance for the solution of our problems that is far greater than we might be willing to admit. After all, if A calls B a "liar," he creates a reverberating cosmos of potential action and judgment. And if the fatal word can be passed on to C, the triangulation of society and culture is complete.

ALFRED L. KROEBER

(1876-1960)

Values as a Subject of
Natural Science Inquiry (1949)

THIS ESSAY MAINTAINS THE PROPOSITION THAT THE STUDY OF VALUES IS A proper and necessary part of the study of culture, viewed as an existing part of nature. This is said not merely as proposal or program, but as a descriptive fact holding for much of actually existing practice in anthropology and the study of culture.

Whenever a cultural fact has significance or historical reference, it also contains a value. Significance must be distinguished from cause—from that which made a cultural phenomenon happen or come to be. Significance must also be distinguished from the end or purpose served; and from organic needs, which in their turn can be resolved either into causes or into ends of culture phenomena.

That needs—also called drives, press, imperatives, and such—exist, and that they underlie and precondition culture, is indubitable. It is also obvious that culture cannot be explained or derived from needs except very partially. Hunger has to be satisfied; but *how* it is satisfied by human beings can never be derived from their being hungry, nor from their specific bodily construction. Overwhelmingly the *how* can be understood only with reference to the remainder of the culture adhered to, present and past; modified somewhat—or preconditioned—by interaction with the opportunities afforded by natural environment. Moreover, large segments of culture begin to operate, to come into being, only after the primal needs have been satisfied, have had their tensions reduced or alleviated. Such are art, religion, science. Hence these segments cannot be explained at all from physiological needs.

From Kroeber, *The Nature of Culture* (Chicago: University of Chicago Press, 1952), pp. 136-138, 402-408.

The essential characteristic things about a culture are its forms and patterns, the interrelations of these into an organization, and the way these parts, and the whole, work or function as a group of human beings lives under them. A culture is a way of habitual acting, feeling, and thinking channeled by a society out of an infinite number and variety of potential ways of living. The particular channeling adopted is heavily preconditioned by antecedent ways and organizations or systems of culture; though it is not predetermined thereby except within certain limits. Every such system of channeling is accompanied by or contains a system of affects, which vary from place to place of their appearance, and from time to time, but some of which are usually powerful and persistent. Interconnected with these affects is a system of ideas and ideals, explicit and implicit. The combined affect-idea system of a culture at once reflects the habitual ways of action of members of the society, validates these ways to themselves, and to an extent controls and modifies the ways. It is in this affect-laden idea system that, in a certain sense, the core of a culture is usually considered to reside: in it lodge its values, norms, and standards—its ethos and its eidos.

When we speak of the significance of a cultural trait or item or complex of traits, what is meant is the degree to which the trait is meshed, affectively as well as structurally and functionally, into the remainder of the total system or organization that constitutes the culture. Low degree of integration normally indicates that the trait has relatively low significance for the culture as a functional unit—though it may still have considerable significance as an index of historical relationship with other cultures.

It follows that if we refuse to deal with values, we are refusing to deal with what has most meaning in particular cultures as well as in human culture seen as a whole.

What we have left on elimination of values is an arid roster of cultural traits or cultural events which we are constantly tempted to animate by reintroducing the values we have banned, or else by backhandedly introducing values from our own culture. Or it is possible to attempt to explain the value-rid phenomena of the culture and their changes in terms of some causality—or possibly by a teleology.

As a matter of fact, it is and long has been prevailing practice in the description of cultures by anthropologists, or of civilizational phases by historians, to formulate the values of these cultures. Thereby the description becomes a physiognomic characterization of the culture. Such a characterization has internal import as regards both its own coherence and consistency, and its external import through implicit or explicit comparison with other characterized cultures. This type of presentation, with clear-cut value designations, comprises all the most successful characterizations or resynthesized analyses of cultures, both by anthropologists such as

Malinowski, Firth, Evans-Pritchard, and by nonprofessionals like Codrington on the Melanesians, Doughty in Arabia Deserta, Fustel de Coulanges's Ancient City, Albiruni on India a thousand years ago, and as far back as the Germania of Tacitus.

Reference in this matter is to values as they exist in human societies at given times and places; to values as they make their appearance in the history of our species; in short, to values as natural phenomena occurring in nature—much like the characteristic forms, qualities, and abilities of animals as defined in comparative zoölogy. There is no reference to any absolute standard or scale of values, nor to judgments of values as better or worse—which would imply such a standard.

An absolute standard involves two qualities. First, it must be extranatural, or supernatural, to be an a priori absolute. And second, ethnocentricity is implied in the elevation of any one actual standard as absolute. By contrary, standards or value-systems conceived as parts of nature are necessarily temporal and spatial, phenomenal, relative, and comparative. That the first condition to the scientific study of culture is the barring of ethnocentrism has been a basic canon of anthropology for three-quarters of a century.

The forms of any culture must be described—can be appraised, one might say—only in terms of their relation to the total pattern-system of that culture. The pattern-system in its turn needs portrayal in terms of its total functioning and products. And so far as the pattern-system is appraisable, it is in terms of comparison with the functions and results achieved by other total cultures with their respective master-patterns. This is like the comparison of the total functioning and capacities of, say, an earthworm with the functioning and capacities of other organisms.

In a sense, recognition of the functioning and capacities of an organic species is a sort of formulation of the values genetically inherent in that species. At any rate, it *can* be that, even if biologists usually are not aware of the fact and might resent the imputation of any concern with values. Further, the comparison of such values, in order to ascertain their common elements, their particularities, their apparent total range of variability, their effectivenesses and long-range permanences—such a comparison of biological values would still be within the scope of examination of natural phenomena by natural science methods.

It is as something analogous to this kind of biology or potential biology that the study of cultural forms, structures, and values must be conceived. Or rather, we should say that such study has actually been made, time and again, often without explicit awareness of values being involved, and perhaps as often without awareness that the study had natural scientific significance.

It is true that values can also be viewed extra-scientifically or supernaturally. Mostly they have been so construed, with ascription to deity, soul, spirituality, or a self-sufficient system of eternal, unmodifiable values lying outside the domain of science over nature. But the present paper has no concern with such a view. Contrarily, it claims values, along with all other manifestations of culture, as being part of nature and therefore in the field of science.

A few specifications seem desirable.

There is always a gap between values and behavior, between ideals and performance. Even though values always influence the behavior of cultural organisms, that is, of men, they never control it exclusively. Hence the student of culture needs to distinguish, but also to compare, ideal values and achieved behavior, as complementary to each other. The one alone falls short in substantiality, the other in significant motivation and organization of the data.

Next, values being sociocultural, they inevitably also possess psychological aspects. But as a specific quality of culture—as, indeed, a product of culture—their reduction to explanations in psychological terms, and of these to physiological and biochemical explanations, necessarily loses or destroys the essential specific properties of the values. These are retainable in full only as long as the phenomena of value continue to be inspected on the cultural level.

Finally, since cultural phenomena are determined in several ways— inorganically by environment, organically, psychologically, and socially, as well as by existent culture—it is evident that the causality of cultural phenomena is likely to be unusually complex. Moreover, they lend themselves with very great difficulty to the isolation and simplification of experiment. Within culture itself, these considerations seem to apply with even more strength to values than to, say, artifact production or subsistence economy. Other things being equal, a descriptive or historical approach would accordingly seem more readily fruitful, in scientific inquiry into values, than any searching for causes—even immediate causes. This statement is not to be construed as a methodological ban against the study of causality in values, but as an intimation that the causal approach is inherently difficult and that valid, nonspeculative results bid fair to be thin and slow. While a formal approach is thus indicated as more fruitful, this need by no means be limited to enumerative description, nor to enumeration of sequences. Beyond these, the comparison of organization, functioning, and interrelations of cultural values, and value-systems invite methodical scientific research.

Is Western Civilization Disintegrating or Reconstituting? (1951)

IT IS POSSIBLE TO CONCEIVE CIVILIZATIONS AS BEING EACH CONSTITUTED to a considerable extent of an assemblage of styles and as being specifically characterized as to their particularities by these styles. A style, in turn, is a self-consistent way of behaving or of doing things. It is selected out from among alternatively possible ways of doing. And it is selective with reference to values; that is, the things the style does and the way it does them are felt by the doers as intrinsically valuable—they are good, right, beautiful, pleasing, or desirable in themselves.

This most characteristic part of civilizations, which we may call value culture, is not their only component. There is also what may be called reality culture, concerned with finding out, mastering, and directing nature —and sometimes mastering and directing fellow-men as well. Technology, the useful arts, ways of successful practical living, are the avenues by which reality culture is expressed. There is a third component, social struc- ture and relations, which in principle might be thought to be independent of the rest of civilization or culture, because it also occurs well developed among cultureless, nonsymbolizing animals, especially the social insects. But since human societies always operate with symbols and thus possess culture, their social structure and relations are channeled into variable cul- tural forms instead of being constant, autonomous, and mainly hereditary. Social culture is therefore, in man, always interwoven with value culture and reality culture. Anthropologists generally see it as such. Sociologists tend to see the same set of phenomena, namely, social culture, as "society," something abstracted from culture and underlying it—as divorced from the remainder of culture, most anthropologists would say.

Within any one civilization, the various styles constituting its value com- ponent not only coexist in the same society, region, and period; they also tend toward a certain consistency among themselves. If they were not interconsistent at first—as might well be the case, owing to some of them having been introduced from outside in the frequent hybridizing to which cultures are subject—the styles would nevertheless tend to become more consistent as they remained associated. This assumption seems validated by the simple consideration that consistent and coherent civilizations would on the average work out better and get farther, and presumably survive better, than inconsistent ones dragging on under malfunction and strain.

It is in their reality ingredients that civilizations chiefly show the quality of accumulativeness which has been noted as one of the properties that distinguish human cultural development from subhuman organic evolution. Technological activities, while not unmitigatedly accumulative, are more accumulative, on the whole, than other parts of culture. By contrast, a value activity, such as a fine art, a philosophy, or a science, contains a creative ingredient. As long as it retains this, it is prevented from repetitiousness. It tends first to develop and progress, even though it later degenerate and die. An art or a philosophy moves on; it cannot continue to spin on a pivot. Those more trivial styles which we call fashions, as in dress, change with particular rapidity. Not expressing or achieving much of intrinsic value significance, they lack the full rise and fall, the consistent growth curve, of greater styles; but they are even more restless in the profile of their movement.

The more creative activities of civilizations thus are imbued with change in their very nature. To each such activity there corresponds, at any given time, a style, a bundle of manners and qualities all its own. The style successively forms, develops, matures, decays, and either dissolves or atrophies into a dead petrification—unless it has previously budded into a new style. The one thing a style does not do is to stand still. Styles are the very incarnation of the dynamic forms taken by the history of civilization. They are the most sensitive expression extant of cultural change—its most delicate galvanometer.

As to the causes of styles, we know very little. Obviously, the causes of qualities and values are going to be difficult to find. At best, we can do little more than describe the circumstances amid which a style forms. From there on, however, the story of the career of a style has unity. Its history usually possesses an internal self-consistency proportional to the discriminateness of the style itself. A style definite in its themes, its manners, its affects, can be expected to run a definite course. Its successive stages we tend to describe in terms like groping, growth of control, full power, slackening, dissolution; or, again, as formative, developing, climactic, overripe, decadent.

When we possess enough examples of an art, and adequate information as to the time sequence of its individual products, a newly discovered specimen within the style—say, an anonymous or hitherto unassigned example—can normally be dated within a half-century, and often within a decade or two. This is possible on the basis of two things. First, the specific quality of the piece in question, and second, the recognized flow of successive qualities within the style. This ability of experts to agree in assigning its place in the style to any object holds for Mediaeval sculpture, for Renaissance and modern painting, for five or six centuries of European music, for Greek vases and poetry, for Chinese painting. Such dating is in a sense prediction: we predict what the date will turn out to be when all the facts are in. The whole procedure certainly implies that a style has a one-way course.

Equally convincing, as to the compulsive strength of style viewed as a course, is the long-recognized clustering of great men in time-limited constellations within each civilization or national subcivilization. This clustering certainly is as conspicuously true for intellectual as for aesthetic creativeness. Looking for cause, one can here argue indefinitely in a circle. Is it the greatness of geniuses that causes a style to come into being, such as the geniuses need to express themselves? Or does the growth of the style evoke successively greater geniuses until the culmination is reached—after which there is increasingly less left for talented individuals to do within the confines of the style? Yet as soon as we leave off the vain effort of tracking down the original or ultimate cause of the phenomenon of clustering, and concentrate on its recurrent generalized form or pattern, it is an indubitable fact that genius *occurs* preponderantly in conjunction with the developmental courses of outstanding styles within successful civilizations.

As for one-wayness, a true style does not travel so and so far and then retrace its steps; nor does it suddenly go off in a random new direction. The tendency is very strong for its direction not only to persevere up to a culmination, but to be irreversible. At its culmination, a style is utilizing its potentialities to their utmost. A bit of reflection shows that this quality of irreversibility is really implicit in most of our formulations of what style is, provided only that we let ourselves conceive it as flowing in time, as it normally does flow.

It is because of this one-wayness of growth that we often speak of the history of a style as if it were a life-history. It is also why a concrete exemplification taken from one style, such as Greek sculpture, of what is meant by terms like "archaic severity" or "primitive stiffness," or by "increasing freedom of control" or "full liberation"—why such an illustration often suffices for us to recognize a corresponding stage of development in a wholly different art. Qualities such as flamboyant, overornate, Churrigueresque, Rococo, which were first defined as characteristic of particular developmental phases of Gothic and Renaissance architecture, can at times be applied with aptness to analogous phases in literatures, or in decorative and applied arts, or in music. Again and again we find in diverse arts a similar course beginning with restraint, attaining balanced mastery, and ending in luxuriance, conscious emotionality, extremity, and disintegration.

Let us now proceed to examine how far the special stylistic quality of irreversibility attaches also to civilizations, which we are construing as consisting at least partly of more or less coherent associations of styles. Or again, conceivably, whole civilizations, being so much larger phenomena than styles, may possess special properties leaving room if not for outright reversibility, at least for divertibility into new directions.

The idea of "direction" is fundamental in this inquiry because we are examining civilizations not as static objects but as limited processes of flow in time.

Greek civilization probably tends to serve as our archetype when we think generically about civilizations and their direction. The Greek civilization was sharply characterized, high in creative power, brief in duration. To an unusual degree, almost all the activities of Greek civilization culminated nearly simultaneously, and at least overlappingly, within a mere three centuries. The course of this civilization is therefore particularly like that of a style. It unrolls like the consistent plot of a drama. Consequently it suggests strongly the quality of irreversibility. And irreversibility, whether of entropy in physics or of human destiny, carries implications of fate and doom.

It is evident that Spengler's system of declines and extinctions—his *Untergang* means literally a "sinking" or "setting"—was derived basically from a contrastive comparison of Greek civilization with European or Western civilization. And as this latter is still a going concern, his idea of the pessimistic fate and extinction awaiting it was evidently taken over from what had happened to Graeco-Roman civilization.

Spengler assumes as something that does not need to be argued—and so does Toynbee—that Greek culture and Roman culture were only the two halves of a larger Graeco-Roman civilization. Spengler calls this larger unit "Classical Antiquity"; and Toynbee calls it simply "Hellenic civilization." Historians also often group the two together as "Ancient History," as against Mediaeval-Modern History which deals largely with other peoples in another part of Europe in a subsequent period.

A next step brings us to the period often called the Dark Ages, the interval between Ancient and Mediaeval times. This is the period of Goths, Lombards, Saxons, and Franks; of decay of government, arts, letters, and wealth—a time when our Western civilization had not yet begun to crystallize out but the Imperial Roman days and ways were irretrievably over. It was a time definitely of cultural retreat, of sag and decay, both quantitative and qualitative; not a distinctive civilization as such, but a chaotic, amorphous interregnum between civilizations. It was a time of disintegration of the patterns of one civilization that had ceased functioning—a very decomposition of its substance and form. And at the same time there must have been dim stirrings, blind gropings, the germinating seeds from which Western civilization would begin to grow within a few centuries.

In short, our Dark Ages are not really a reversal, a retracing, of a current of flow. They mark the cessation of flow of one civilization, a consequent slack water and hesitation of confused fluctuating drift; and then the gradual and slowly increasing flow of a new Western civilization—new precisely because the set of its current is in a new direction.

Our slump, the Dark Ages, accordingly is the falling-apart and the dissolution of most of an old civilization, because of which dissolution a new civilization was able to rise—and move in a new direction.

With the Graeco-Roman civilization essentially dead in the West around A.D. 500, its still surviving patterns disintegrated still more for some centuries thereafter. Christianity, though established, was still too raw, too nearly illiterate and undisciplined, to have evolved many new patterns of creativity outside its own immediate functioning, in contrast with the way it did evolve them later. The Dark Ages following 500 were dark not only because of ignorance but because people had lost the old patterns and had not yet evolved new ones of any definiteness or moment. This absence of specific Dark Age patterns, due to previous ones having dissolved away and new ones having not yet formed, is the symptom that most marks off Ancient from Western civilization. The nexus of patterns and values in Europe after the Dark Age interregnum was, all in all, more different from the nexus existing before, during Graeco-Roman Antiquity, than it was similar. We have here, incidentally, a tentative, empirical definition of what a particular civilization is, what sets one off from another: it is an excess of distinctive patterns, values, or directions over shared ones.

Some time after Charlemagne, around 900 or 950, the new Western civilization at last emerged. Compared with the vague stirrings of germination in the preceding dark centuries, it now emerged with definite form, however rude and in need of further development. It manifested several patterns that were to continue in its structure thereafter. First of all, the new civilization was unmitigatedly committed to being Christian. There was no room in it for anything else religious; and its Christianity was still unified. Second, the European nationalities had pretty definitely crystallized out by 950, much as they were to endure for a thousand years. There were now Frenchmen, Germans, Italians, Englishmen, Danes, Poles, instead of tribal agglomerations or the loose Frankish empire of Charlemagne. These nationalities found political expression in feudalistic monarchies. Fortified castles were rising, and in their lee, or within their own walls, towns grew up—still puny but a beginning toward urban life. Romanesque-Gothic building got under way, and then the associated sculpture and glass-staining. A revival of learning had commenced—still very modest but to bear fruit within a century in the first pulse of Scholastic philosophy. Much in the same way, the writing of vernacular tongues—French instead of Latin—also emerged in the nine hundreds, proceeded to poetical compositions in the ten hundreds, and culminated in the vernacular Mediaeval literatures—French, Provençal, Castilian, and German—in the eleven and twelve hundreds.

This civilization here arising was Western civilization; but it was Western civilization in its High Mediaeval phase or stage. It came to a conspicuous peak—its Christianity and church, its monarchies, its Christian architecture and sculpture, its Christian philosophy—in the mid-thirteenth century: let us say in the decades around 1250. In fact, the *Summa* of St. Thomas Aquinas in 1265 may be construed as the literal summation, formal and inward, of the High Middle Ages.

This High Mediaeval civilization did not wither away. Instead, its patterns loosened and partly dissolved, during the two centuries or so following 1300. But as they broke down they were also *reconstituting* themselves, and on an ampler scope. This went on until, at some time between 1500 and 1600, the filling-in of these newly enlarged patterns, the actualization of their new and greater potential, had got under way: and therewith "Modern History" began—the history of the second or Modern phase of Western civilization.

What had confronted western Europeans around 1300 or 1325, though they could not of course see it in the perspective of subsequent history, was an alternative. They might either adhere to their cherished patterns of High Mediaeval civilization as they had first begun to rough them out four centuries before, and had since filled them in and realized them so successfully. In that case, the saturation of the patterns having been essentially achieved, life under the continuing culture would have become increasingly repetitive, creativity would have been checked, atrophy ensued, and an irrevocable withering of the Mediaeval civilization would have got under way. The other choice was for the Europeans of 1300 to stretch their cultural patterns to accommodate a civilization of larger scope: to stretch them if necessary until some of them burst; to stretch them by stuffing into them a content of far greater knowledge of fact, more experimentation and curiosity, new undertakings, wider horizons, greater wealth, a higher standard of living.

Unconsciously, they took the risk of this second course. They did stretch their patterns of living a civilized life, they ruptured many of them, they developed more new ones in their place; until, after two to three centuries, the set of patterns, the over-all design for living, had been reconstituted, and a new stage of Western civilization, the Modern stage, was entered upon.

High Mediaeval civilization was like its cathedrals of high-reared arches but narrow base. What it lacked seems almost incredible today; at least it seems incredible that Mediaeval men—our ancestors and the founders of our civilization of today—could have been complacent about it. As against the contented parochialism of High Mediaevalism, the thirteen, fourteen, and fifteen hundreds brought first a wider knowledge of Asia, next of the African peripheries, then of America. Trade followed, industry grew, wealth expanded. A true civilian architecture arose in Italy; painting blossomed beside sculpture. The hold of the Church—that Church from which so many of the High Mediaeval patterns had ramified—this hold was loosened or broken. The papacy was dragged to Avignon, then split in the Great Schism; Councils were held to heal the breach and—

unsuccessfully—to combat the worldliness and profligacy of churchmen, a worldliness that in turn was building up sentiments of anticlericalism, and the dissidency of Wycliffe and Hus. Not long afterward, the Reformation tore away from the hitherto unified Church nearly half of Europe.

All this was certainly a process of disintegration of what had been firmly fitted around the Church in the true Middle Ages. In philosophy, the Scholastic system was similarly disrupted by the skeptical negativism of Occam or dissolved into mysticism by the Germans—after which its field lay fallow. Science, after a thousand years' sleep, was slow in reconstructing itself. It finally got into motion toward the end of our period of readjustment with Copernicus' 1543 revolution of astronomy, and with contemporary Italian discoveries in mathematics and medicine. Printing was invented to meet the demands for more knowledge and ideas on the part of a greatly enlarged civilian and urban clientele of sharpening curiosity.

In many ways this era of Reconstitution and Rebirth between the Mediaeval and Modern periods of Western civilization must have felt to the people of Europe much as the twentieth century feels to us. It was a period of strains and unsettlement. The timorous must often have wondered if the world were not coming wholly out of joint.

True, such sentiment must also have been felt in some degree in the Dark Ages. The difference is that the Dark Ages were an actual recession: more civilization was abandoned than was originated in them.

By contrast, there was more knowledge in 1400 and 1500 than in the High Middle Ages, increased understanding and cultivation, and more urbane living and wealth and graciousness. Growth, not recession, continued through the interval, even while the reconstruction of set and structure was taking place. That, incidentally, is why no one has yet proposed separating the Middle Ages off from the Modern period as being two wholly distinct civilizations. Their respective sets or directions, though altered and enlarged in the period of Reconstitution, were not wholly torn apart, nor was there loss or destruction of most of what existed in Western Civilization I—the Middle Ages—during the Reconstitution into Western Civilization II—Modern Europe.

Our Western period of Reconstitution evidently corresponds fairly to A.D. 200-600 in China, which was also a time of unsettlement and reorientation, after which Chinese civilization resumed its course on a reorganized and broadened base. Therefore the prevalent usage seems justified of recognizing the two phases as China I and II, or as Ancient China and Mediaeval-Modern China, rather than as two disparate civilizations separated even by their names, Sinic and Far Eastern, as Toynbee proposes.

There is one interesting difference from Europe, however: China acquired a new organized religion, Buddhism, in its era of Reconstitution; Europe loosened the hold of Christianity on its non-religious activities.

When now we match the present condition of our civilization comparatively against these two analogues, it seems that the correspondence is greater with the previous European stage of Reconstitution than with the Graeco-Roman final stage of Dissolution. This is because now, as in 1300-1550, population, wealth, curiosity, knowledge, enterprise, and invention are definitely still in an expanding phase. It appears somewhat likely, accordingly, or at any rate possible, that we are now in the throes of a second stage of Reconstitution of our civilization. In that case, Period II of Western Civilization would already be mainly past, whether we in it so recognize or not; and Period III of Western Civilization would lie ahead of us whenever we shall have finished reorganizing our former cultural style patterns into a resultant new over-all pattern or set.

Civilizations are like life-histories in that they are normally marked by a developmental flow, and by the fact that they are not reversible into a series of beats and back-and-forth swings. But cultural processes and organic processes are so distinct in their factors that it would be unwise to expect their manifestations to run parallel, except in occasional features. There does seem to be this difference, that, while a civilization cannot retrace its past course rearward any more than can an organism, a civilization can regather or regroup itself and start off in an altered or partially new direction, with expanded and reconstituted value patterns. After all, the organic parallel or analogy must not be pressed too hard. Birth, maturation, senility, and death characterize the individual organisms whose repetitions constitute a species; and what civilizations in their size and compositeness evidently more nearly resemble than they resemble individual organisms is species—and especially the groupings of species into families or orders of common properties and qualities.

The foregoing has turned out to be an endeavor in applied anthropology —a somewhat new kind of applied anthropology, of a long-range variety. It leans little on economics or sociology or psychology or personality study, but a great deal on history. Only it asks that history be viewed now and then with maximum of elbow room and freedom of perspective; with emphasis, for the time being, not on the mere events of history, which are as unending as the waves of the sea, but on the qualities of its secular trends; and that these trends be construed, so far as possible, in terms of the style-like patterns which so largely characterize civilization, and in terms of the developmental flow, interactions, and integration of these patterns.

Suggestions for Further Reading

Further selections from the authors of
THE GOLDEN AGE OF AMERICAN ANTHROPOLOGY:

Franz Boas: *Primitive Art,* Cambridge, Harvard University Press, 1927 (available in reprint); *Anthropology and Modern Life,* New York, Norton, 1928; *Race, Language, and Culture* (selected papers), New York, Macmillan, 1949.

> *About* Boas: A. L. Kroeber, Ruth Benedict and others: *Franz Boas,* Memoir of the American Anthropological Association, 1943; Melville J. Herskovits: *Franz Boas; the science of man in the making,* New York, Scribner, 1943; Walter Goldschmidt (Ed.), *The anthropology of Franz Boas, American Anthropologist,* N.S. Vol. 61, No. 4, Part 2. 1959.

Alfred L. Kroeber: *The Nature of Culture,* Chicago, University of Chicago Press, 1952; *Configuration of Culture Growth,* Berkeley, University of California Press, 1944.

Robert H. Lowie: *Are We Civilized?* New York, Harcourt, Brace, 1929; *Toward Understanding Germany,* Chicago, University of Chicago Press, 1954; *Robert Lowie, Ethnologist,* Berkeley, University of California Press, 1959.

Elsie Clews Parsons: *Mitla, Town of the Souls,* Chicago, University of Chicago Press, 1936; *Pueblo Indian Religion,* Chicago, University of Chicago Press, 1939.

Elsie Clews Parsons (Ed.): *American Indian Life,* New York, Huebsch, 1922.

Paul Radin: *Primitive Man as Philosopher,* Dover (paperback), 1957.

Edward Sapir: *Selected Writings in Language, Culture and Personality,* Berkeley, University of California Press, 1949.

Clark Wissler: *Man and Culture,* New York, Crowell, 1923.

Selected reading in anthropology since 1920:

General:

> Clyde Kluckhohn, *Mirror for Man,* New York, Whittlesey House, 1949.
>
> Ralph Linton, *The Study of Man,* New York, Appleton-Century, 1936.
>
> Robert Redfield, *The Little Community,* Chicago, University of Chicago Press, 1955.

American Indians in the twentieth century:

> Clyde Kluckhohn and Dorothea Leighton: *The Navaho,* Cambridge, Harvard University Press, 1946.

Ralph Linton (Ed.): *Acculturation in Seven American Indian Tribes.*

Oliver La Farge (Ed.): *The Changing Indian,* Norman, University of Oklahoma Press, 1942.

Ruth Underhill: *Red Man's America,* Chicago, University of Chicago Press, 1953.

American archaeology:

Paul Martin: *Indians before Columbus,* Chicago, University of Chicago Press, 1947.

Eric J. Thompson: *Mexico before Cortez,* New York, Scribners, 1937.

George C. Vaillant: *The Aztecs of Mexico,* Garden City, Doubleday, Doran & Company, 1941.

Culture and personality:

Ruth Benedict: *Patterns of Culture,* Boston, Houghton Mifflin, 1934; *The Chrysanthemum and the Sword,* Boston, Houghton Mifflin, 1946.

A. I. Hallowell: *Culture and Experience,* Philadelphia, University of Pennsylvania Press, 1955.

Abram Kardiner: *The Individual and His Society,* New York, Columbia University Press, 1939.

Margaret Mead: *Coming of Age in Samoa,* New York, Morrow, 1928 (available in reprint); *Male and Female,* New York, Morrow, 1949.

Some modern ethnographies:

Ruth Bunzel: *Chichicastenango, a Guatemalan Village.* Publication of the American Ethnological Society, J. J. Augustin, 1952.

Cora Du Bois: *The People of Alor,* Minneapolis, University of Minnesota Press, 1944.

W. Lloyd Warner: *A Black Civilization,* Harper, 1958.

Anthropologists study American culture:

Robert S. and Helen Merrell Lynd: *Middletown,* New York, Harcourt, Brace, 1929.

James West, *Plainville, U.S.A.,* New York, Columbia University Press.

W. Lloyd Warner and others: *Yankee City series.* Vols. 1-5, New Haven, Yale University Press, 1941-47.